*Oxford Readings in*
# Ancient Literary Criticism

# Oxford Readings in Classical Studies

*All available in paperback*

*Oxford Readings in*

# Ancient Literary Criticism

*Edited by*
ANDREW LAIRD

OXFORD
UNIVERSITY PRESS

*This book has been printed digitally and produced in a standard specification in order to ensure its continuing availability*

OXFORD
UNIVERSITY PRESS

Great Clarendon Street, Oxford OX2 6DP

Oxford University Press is a department of the University of Oxford.
It furthers the University's objective of excellence in research, scholarship,
and education by publishing worldwide in

Oxford  New York

Auckland   Cape Town  Dar es Salaam   Hong Kong   Karachi
Kuala Lumpur  Madrid  Melbourne  Mexico City   Nairobi
New Delhi  Shanghai  Taipei  Toronto
With offices in
Argentina  Austria  Brazil  Chile  Czech Republic  France  Greece
Guatemala  Hungary  Italy  Japan  South Korea  Poland  Portugal
Singapore  Switzerland  Thailand  Turkey  Ukraine  Vietnam

Oxford is a registered trade mark of Oxford University Press
in the UK and in certain other countries

Published in the United States
by Oxford University Press Inc., New York

© Oxford University Press 2006

The moral rights of the author have been asserted

Database right Oxford University Press (maker)

Reprinted 2009

ISBN 978-0-19-925865-9

# PREFACE

The first chapter of this book will attempt to define and defend the field of ancient literary criticism, and to provide a brief introduction to ancient authors and issues that will not be treated directly in the subsequent chapters. It is hoped that such a discussion may prove more useful and stimulating than a conventional *résumé* of the other individual contributions—which were selected partly on the basis that they could stand on their own. The Suggestions for Further Reading are designed to help readers explore for themselves some important areas that, given inevitable constrictions on space, could not be included (or covered in sufficient depth) in the present volume.

Only a foolhardy editor would venture to produce an anthology on a subject of this complexity without seeking advice: I would like to thank Donald Russell for discussing this project with me at an early stage. Kathryn Gutzwiller, Doreen Innes, Hilary O'Shea, and the Press's anonymous readers also made a number of useful recommendations. More recently, David Levene, Penelope Murray, Donald Russell, and Michael Silk were kind enough to comment on my introductory chapter and each provided some vital additions to the Suggestions for Further Reading. However, it should be made clear that my own approach to the subject does not always reflect the views of those whose help I sought.

It remains to thank all the authors who personally allowed their work to be included in this volume. Most of them willingly checked their own contributions, taking pains to transliterate Greek or translate Greek and Latin passages, in order to make their work accessible to a wider readership; or else advised me of corrections or changes that needed to be implemented. I am especially grateful to Jennifer Barnes for providing a new translation of 'Aristotle on the Effect of Tragedy', and to Jonathan Barnes for his introductory comments on this important essay by Jacob Bernays.

A.L.

# CONTENTS

# ABBREVIATIONS

Citations are generally given in full in the Suggestions for Further Reading and in Chapter 1. Elsewhere, classical authors, Greek and Latin works, collections of fragments and inscriptions, titles of modern periodicals, etc. will often be abbreviated according to the system used in the Oxford Classical Dictionary, 3rd edn., ed. Simon Hornblower and Antony Spawforth (Oxford, 1996)—which is itself sometimes abbreviated to *OCD* iii. Common abbreviations of modern works are as follows (sometimes authors used different abbreviations for the same work).

| | |
|---|---|
| *AJP* | *American Journal of Philology* |
| *AJPh* | *American Journal of Philology* |
| *ANRW* | *Aufstieg und Niedergang der römischen Welt* |
| *Ant. u. Abend.* | *Antike und Abendland* |
| *Arch. Delt.* | *Archaiologikon Deltion* |
| *BICS* | *Bulletin of the Institute of Classical Studies* |
| *CP* | *Classical Philology* |
| *CPh* | *Classical Philology* |
| *CQ* | *Classical Quarterly* |
| *CR* | *Classical Review* |
| *FGH* | F. Jacoby (ed.), *Die Fragmente der griechischen Historiker* (Berlin/Leiden, 1923–58; Leiden, 1994– ) |
| *GRBS* | *Greek, Roman, and Byzantine Studies* |
| *HSCP* | *Harvard Studies in Classical Philology* |
| *JHS* | *Journal of Hellenic Studies* |
| *JRS* | *Journal of Roman Studies* |
| *LSJ* | H. G. Liddell, R. Scott, H. S. Jones *et al.* (eds.), *Greek–English Lexicon* (1940; suppl. 1968; repr. 1992). |
| *MD* | *Materiali e Discussione per l'analisi dei testi classici* |
| *Mnem.* | *Mnemosyne* |
| *Mus. Helv.* | *Museum Helveticum* |
| OCT | Oxford Classical Texts |

| | |
|---|---|
| PCG | R. Kassel and C. Austin (eds.), *Poetae comici graeci* (Berlin and New York, 1983–2001). |
| PCPhS | *Proceedings of the Cambridge Philological Society* |
| PLLS | *Papers of the Liverpool* [superseded by: *Leeds International*] *Latin Seminar* |
| RE | G. Wissowa *et al.* (eds.), *Paulys Realencyclopädie der classischen Altertumswissenschaft* (Stuttgart, 1893–1978) |
| REG | *Revue des études grecques* |
| Rh.M | *Rheinisches Museum für Philologie* |
| SIFC | *Studi Italiani di Filologia Classica* |
| Stud. Ital. | *Studi Italiani di Filologia Classica* |
| SVP | *Stoicorum Veterum Fragmenta* (Stuttgart, 1974) |
| TAPA | *Transactions and Proceedings of the American Philological Association* |

# DATES OF MAJOR AUTHORS AND CRITICS

This highly selective list is in chronological order for quick reference. Many of the dates given below can only be estimates. For biographical details and other information about ancient critics and sources, readers are advised to consult the most recent *Oxford Classical Dictionary* and material in the Suggestions for Further Reading at the end of this book.

| | |
|---|---|
| Homer | 8th century BC |
| Hesiod | *c.*700 BC |
| Pindar | *c.*518–*c.*446 BC |
| Protagoras | *c.*490–*c.*420 BC |
| Gorgias | *c.*485–*c.*380 BC |
| Socrates | 469–399 BC |
| Aristophanes | *c.*460–386 BC |
| Isocrates | 436–338 BC |
| Plato | *c.*429–347 BC |
| Aristotle | 384–322 BC |
| Epicurus | 341–270 BC |
| Callimachus | 3rd century BC |
| Neoptolemus | 3rd century BC |
| 'Demetrius' | 2nd century BC |
| Philodemus | *c.*110–*c.*40/35 BC |
| Cicero | 106–43 BC |
| Dionysius of Halicarnassus | Later 1st century BC |
| Virgil | 70–19 BC |
| Horace | 65–8 BC |
| Seneca the Elder | *c.*50 BC–AD *c.*40 |
| Ovid | 43 BC–AD 17 |
| Seneca the Younger | *c.*1 BC–AD 65 |
| Pliny the Elder | AD 23/4–79 |
| Quintilian | AD *c.*35–90s |
| 'Longinus' | 1st century AD |

| | |
|---|---|
| Dio Chrysostom | AD 40/50–110 |
| Plutarch | AD c.50–120(+) |
| Pliny the Younger | AD c.61–c.112 |
| Tacitus | AD c.56–c.120 |
| Lucian | AD 120–180(+) |
| Philostratus | AD 170–244–9 |
| Plotinus | AD 205–69/70 |
| 'Servius' | 4th century AD |
| Augustine | AD 354–430 |

# I

# The Value of Ancient Literary Criticism

## ANDREW LAIRD

Whilst in all likelihood every art and philosophy has repeatedly been explored to the utmost and has then perished again, these opinions have been preserved like relics until the present.

(Aristotle, *Metaphysics* 12. 1074$^{b}$10)

There exists a very strong idea that in order better to understand an alien culture, one must enter into it, forgetting one's own, and view the world through the eyes of this alien culture . . . but if this were the only aspect of this understanding, it would be merely duplication and would not involve anything new or enriching.

(Bakhtin, Response to a Question from the *Novy Mir* Editorial Staff, 1970)

## I

There could be a reason to feel gloomy about the emergence of the subject of this book as a specific field of study. Accepting that *ancient* literary criticism is something distinct from literary criticism in general must amount to conceding that the judgements of classical writers have little to do with contemporary production, evaluation, and theory of literature.

Yet well into the twentieth century, the prescriptions and verdicts of classical authors continued to inform writers from Jean Anouilh to James Joyce, just as they influenced aestheticians and theorists as far apart as Northrop Frye and Jacques Derrida.[1] Even the most

---

[1] Frye's *Anatomy of Criticism* (Princeton, 1957) adopts the Platonic and Aristotelian division of poetry into drama, epic and lyric and employs rhetorical criticism. That generic divisision has been developed more recently in G. Genette, *The Architext* (Oxford, 1992): see also Rosenmeyer in this volume. I. A. Richards's distinction of the

iconoclastic literary figures, like André Breton and Bertolt Brecht, knew the ancient authorities whose canons they sought to oppose.[2] The absorption of poetics and rhetoric, among other influences from antiquity, into modern intellectual life was palpable enough for exponents of ancient literary criticism to appeal habitually to its 'value'. That word 'value' was used several times by J. W. H. Atkins, a Professor of English Literature, in the opening of his study of *Literary Criticism in Antiquity*, first published in 1934:

Ancient criticism has much to offer all students of literature. There is for one thing, a definite historical value attached to the works. Coming first as they did in the order of time, they represent the earliest application of the critical spirit to literary matters; and what is more they constitute the first enquiry into that Graeco-Roman tradition in art upon which most of the modern literatures are ultimately based . . . In addition, these critical works of the ancients possess considerable value of an intrinsic kind. In their pages were first brought to light certain literary principles of enduring value. They were, for instance, the first to to set forth certain profound views as to the nature and art of poetry, as well as some of the laws that govern good writing in prose, while they also led the way in the discussion of literary values, and in the formation of aesthetic judgments.[3]

A scholar writing now would probably be reluctant to promote the study of ancient criticism in quite the same way. Atkins's conception of its historical value seems to presuppose that what he calls the

'emotive' language of poetry from the referential language of prose in his influential *Practical Criticism: A Study of Literary Judgment* (London, 1929) and *Principles of Literary Criticism* (London, 1926) exhibited a debt to ancient rhetoric (compare e.g. Quintilian, *Institutio* 12. 10. 43), already prior to *Philosophy of Rhetoric* (London, 1936). Two of Derrida's most influential works—*Of Grammatology* (Baltimore, 1976) and the essay 'Plato's Pharmacy' in *Dissemination* (Chicago, 1981), 63–171—discuss theories of speech and writing in the *Phaedrus*. J. Ellis, *Against Deconstruction* (Princeton, 1989) considers Derrida's sources. Other twentieth-century theorists have drawn from Aristotle and the rhetoricans as well as from Plato.

  [2] Breton had a hand in a collective declaration in a Surrealist broadsheet of 1931 'Lisez, Ne Lisez pas', which recommends the philosopher Heraclitus in place of Plato and in preference to Virgil (who heads the list of authors *not* to be read): see *Tracts surréalistes et déclarations collectives* (1922/1969), i (Paris, 1980), 202: compare the inverted canon of classical authors in J.-K. Huysmans, *À Rebours* (1884). Brecht's Epic theatre was pointedly anti-Aristotelian, though see M. S. Silk's discussion of Aristotle, Rapin, and Brecht in Ø. Andersen and J. Haarberg (eds.), *Making Sense of Aristotle: Essays in Poetics* (London, 2001). Brecht's verdict on Horace, *Ars Poetica* 99–103 is in J. Willett, *Brecht on Theatre* (London, 1964), 270: 'I must say there is only one word for such an operation: barbaric.'

  [3] J. W. H. Atkins, *Literary Criticism in Antiquity: A Sketch of its Development* (Cambridge, 1934), i. 1.

'critical spirit' has a cohesive and consistent identity—that is not uncontroversial. His assertion of the 'intrinsic' value of ancient critical works appears to rest on the claim that such works contain literary principles of 'enduring value' or that they heralded the discussion of 'literary values', and the seemingly essentialized notion of 'literature', as Atkins implicitly attributes it to the ancients, looks especially vulnerable.[4] Definitions of history, narrative, text, and discourse have been subjected to interrogation in recent years, but no category in the modern humanities has undergone a more sustained and systematic probing and dismantling than the idea of literature.[5]

Indeed, one of the first hurdles confronting a student of ancient literary criticism is the fact that neither the Greeks nor the Romans possessed a word or idea precisely corresponding to 'literature'—a notoriously post-Enlightenment category. The realization then follows that the numerous texts which conventionally constitute 'ancient literary criticism' are drawn from a variety of sources. These sources occupy a very wide chronological range: newcomers to the subject may well end up appraising discussions from periods of antiquity hitherto unfamiliar to them. And these sources could be presented in different genres of discourse—spoken and written—in verse as well as in prose. Poetry, invective, and drama and other forms of expression which were oral in origin, are no less pertinent than the dialogues, essays, epistles, satires, and scholia penned in later times.[6] Most dauntingly perhaps, the three major areas of expertise from which our sources for ancient criticism derive— poetry, rhetoric, and philosophy—represent quite distinct spheres of intellectual activity.

---

[4] The notion of the *intrinsic* qualities of literature itself had a special currency at the time Atkins was writing in the 1930s: see M. H. Abrams, *The Mirror and the Lamp* (Oxford, 1953) on *objective* and 'autotelic' theories of poetry; J. C. Ransom, *The New Criticism* (Norfolk, Conn., 1941); R. Wellek and A. Warren, *A Theory of Literature* (London, 1949).

[5] For current views about the definition of literature, see the beginning of section III below.

[6] Andrew Ford in *The Origins of Criticism* (Princeton, 2002) emphasizes the critic's role in early Greece as a 'performer before a social group'. ' "Praise" and "blame" ', Ford continues (p. 3), 'are the Greeks' own general terms for what one says in response to song; they remind us that interpretation need not be the primary function of criticism and helpfully separate the history of criticism from the history of aesthetic response. What people felt as opposed to what they said about poetry is not only inaccessible to the historian but should not be accorded *a priori* the same importance it may have in modern, privatized notions of aesthetic experience.'

Ancient literary criticism challengingly exposes the weighting of today's classics curricula in favour of poetry and the narrative genres, at the expense of philosophy and oratory. The remarkably enduring role of rhetoricians and philosophers in education and society throughout antiquity can still be underplayed. Moreover, ancient criticism—and its origins in a culture of poetic and oratorical performance have much to do with this—continued to lay emphasis on sound and on the musical capacity of both verse and prose texts.[7] This preoccuppation contrasts sharply with contemporary responses to classical literature: metre itself is all too often regarded as little more than a generic marker, determining the configuration of words on a written or printed page.[8]

In spite of the very different character of ancient literary culture, studies on the lines of Atkins's endeavour and broader accounts of aesthetics and poetic theory tended to stress the continuities and resemblances between ancient positions and modern humanistic conceptions of literature.[9] Such accounts, perhaps through seeking to address historians of criticism in general as well as classicists, conceived of ancient theories as a contribution to more enlightened later thinking—and made less of an attempt to approach those theories in their own right. This has led to some slanted if not condescending characterizations: Grube, for instance, more than once disparaged 'Plato's attitude' and was somewhat reproachful of

---

[7] In addition to Ford (n. 6), see P. Murray and P. Wilson (eds.), *Music and the Muses: Song, Dance and Word in Classical Athenian Culture* (Oxford, 2004). The well-known observation in Plato, *Phaedrus* 267d–e that written words have no speakers to come to their aid is also relevant (Derrida's responses to this are cited in n. 1). In the first century AD, Quintilian (*Institutio* 1. 7. 31) notes 'the use of letters is that they serve as guardians of voices, returning them to readers as something once deposited' (*hic enim usus litterarum, ut custodiant voces et velut depositum reddant legentibus*). J. I. Porter underlines the importance of writing as 'inscribed voice' in 'Philodemus on Material Difference', *Cronache Ercolanesi*, 19 (1989), 149–78 at 171–4. See also Porter, 'Des sons qu'on ne peut pas entendre: Cicéron, les κριτικοί et la tradition du sublime dans la critique littéraire', in C. Auvray-Assayas and D. Delattre (eds.), *Cicéron et Philodème: La Polémique en philosophie* (Paris, 2001), 315–41.

[8] Inevitably, such contemporary responses to ancient texts have been determined, to some extent, by the fact that many modern readers, even if they know Greek and Latin, no longer learn to compose verses in those languages.

[9] M. H. Abrams, *The Mirror and the Lamp: Romantic Theory and the Critical Tradition* (Oxford and New York, 1953); M. Beardsley, *Aesthetics from Classical Greece to the Present: A Short History* (New York, 1966); G. M. A. Grube, *The Greek and Roman Critics* (Toronto, 1965); A. Sheppard, *Aesthetics: An Introduction to the Philosophy of Art* (Oxford, 1987).

Aristotle:[10] 'If Aristotle's philosophical approach enabled him to make a great contribution to literary and stylistic theory, it also has a certain weakness. His interest being theoretical, he naturally expounds his theories, and literature is merely used to provide illustrations . . . Aristotle must bear some responsibility for initiating or continuing this method.' It would be wrong to maintain that nothing fruitful emerges from considering in the round a range of ideas of criticism from different periods of history. On the contrary, it will be maintained here that a major advantage of studying the ancient critics is to acquire a necessary perspective on later controversies, whether they involve specific texts or questions of a more general theoretical nature. But an unselfconscious attempt to trace diachronically, from antiquity onwards, the development of 'literary criticism' always risks turning into a teleological narrative, offering verdicts on the past which are as much informed by a selection of current opinions as they are by current knowledge.

A different outlook was presented by scholars who had a more positive interest in ancient rhetoric—even if one purpose of that interest was to throw light on the writing of periods after antiquity. In the 1920s the North American scholar C. S. Baldwin (who went on to treat medieval and Renaissance rhetoric) showed that an understanding of ancient rhetorical theory is as important for understanding the principles on which poetry was *composed*, as well as criticized, by Greek and Roman writers.[11] For example, Baldwin's account of the determinations of rhetoric for Virgil's techniques of characterization—in the wake of Heinze's *Virgil's Epic Technique*—remains salutary for students today.[12] Whilst a major aim of the compendious *Handbook of Literary Rhetoric* by Heinrich Lausberg was to show how knowledge of rhetoric is essential for appreciation of medieval and early modern literature, that handbook also details the

---

[10] Grube, *Greek and Roman Critics*, 46–65, treats Plato; the excerpt quoted here is from the conclusion to his chapter on Aristotle, at 101–2.

[11] C. S. Baldwin, *Ancient Rhetoric and Poetic, Interpreted from Representative Works* (New York, 1924). Baldwin's other studies include *Medieval Rhetoric and Poetic (to 1400) Interpreted from Representative Works* (New York, 1928); *Renaissance Literary Theory and Practice: Classicism in the Rhetoric and Poetic of Italy, France, and England, 1400–1600* (New York, 1939); and a practical manual—*College Composition* (New York, 1922).

[12] R. Heinze, *Vergils Epische Technik* (Leipzig, 1915); English tr. (H. Harvey, D. Harvey, and F. Robertson): *Virgil's Epic Technique* (Bristol, 1993). Baldwin's discussion of Virgil is in *Ancient Rhetoric and Poetic*, 196–215.

ways in which ancient rhetorical categories, figures, and tropes actually function in Greek and Roman texts.[13] Due recognition of the role of rhetoric has shaped some of the most important scholarship on ancient criticism in recent decades. George Kennedy's substantial studies of rhetoric in both Greece and Rome have highlighed the fundamental importance of this 'art of persuasion' in the histories of both civilizations, as well as demonstrating its part in forming the very nature of poetry and prose writing in antiquity.[14]

This consideration of rhetoric is at least partly responsible for the realization, in authoritative accounts like D. A. Russell's *Criticism in Antiquity* (first published in 1981) and *The Cambridge History of Literary Criticism* (1989), that the texts constituting ancient criticism are by their nature—as well as by their provenance—distinct from whatever may be counted as modern literary criticism.[15] Yet references and appeals continue to be made to the influences, parallels, and resemblances which connect discourses of ancient criticism to their modern equivalents. Although that tension has not been overlooked by scholars like Russell and Kennedy, it clearly arises from the habitual, perhaps inevitable, anachronism of referring to a varied body of Greek and Roman texts and discourses as *literature* in the first place. This has led a prominent Hellenist to propose an extreme solution—the complete eradication of the word 'literature' from (ancient) literary history:

The poverty of the category of 'literature' [is destructive] for the way in which the critical engagement with language production functions in the ancient world. The establishment of the sphere of the literary with its various exclusions does not merely distort the interconnections between the texts of poetry, say, and other textual productions of the ancient world, but also throroughly twists the connections between those texts and the culture in which and for which they were produced. In short the seventeenth and eighteenth centuries may turn out to be better guides for the classical world

[13] H. Lausberg, *Handbuch der Literarischen Rhetorik* (Munich, 1960); tr. M. Bliss, A. Jansen, and D. Orton (1998): *Handbook of Literary Rhetoric* (Leiden, 1998).
[14] Some of Kennedy's works are listed under Suggestions for Further Reading ('Rhetoric and Education in Antiquity') at the end of this book. In addition see *Quintilian* (New York, 1969); 'The Genres of Rhetoric' and 'Historical Survey of Rhetoric', in S. E. Porter (ed.), *Handbook of Classical Rhetoric in the Hellenistic Period, 330 B.C.–A.D. 400* (Leiden and New York, 1997), 3–50; and nn. 23, 29, and 41 below.
[15] See Suggestions for Further Reading ('Ancient Literary Criticism and Poetics: General Treatments').

than the nineteenth and twentieth—and the literary history that I would like to see written may well exclude 'literature' altogether.[16]

There is some sense in that suggestion. Many terms classicists and ancient historians use to classify all kinds of things are not neutral labels (like 'hexameter' and 'aqueduct'); they are actually dynamic characterizations. For example, scholarly formulations like *epyllion* or *paraklausithuron* run the risk of being regarded as prevalent Greek or Roman concepts; constructed trends such as 'Romanization' acquire the status of ancient realities; and periodizations ('Hellenistic', 'Late antique') are salient enough to determine university courses and academic careers. Such terms are helpful tools to think with, and it would be hard to imagine doing classics or any kind of historical investigation without them. The notions of 'Greek literature' and of 'Latin literature' *are* useful—as long as we remain aware of the potential of these categories to become falsely credited with an independent historical existence. Even those who seek to oppose the idea of literature themselves end up using words like 'literary' quite unselfconsciously. Perhaps, then, there is some justification for allowing specialists in ancient poetics and rhetoric to do so too.

However, that entitlement could be jeopardized by a claim made for *The Cambridge History of Literary Criticism* that its writers 'have thought it best to expound the ancient critics in [those critics'] own terms rather than to recast their thought in alien concepts'.[17] That ideal can never be realized. At a very fundamental level, producing a history of criticism, or a history of anything else, requires a kind of translation: primary material *has* to be recast in 'alien' concepts or formats in order to be described at all. But the misconception that the past can be explained solely in its own terms seems to be enjoying a more general currency in classical studies: fashionable 'cultural-historical' approaches to the study of ancient texts often exhibit the sort of positivism which governed the purportedly scientific reconstruction of antiquity advocated by Germanic scholars from the nineteenth century onwards.[18]

[16] S. Goldhill, 'Literary History without Literature: Reading Practices in the Ancient World', *SubStance* (*Review of Theory and Literary Criticism*), 88 (1999), 57–89 at 84.
[17] G. A. Kennedy, Preface to the *Cambridge History of Literary Criticism*, i (1989), p. xii.
[18] The term *Altertumswissenschaft* ('science of antiquity') was coined by Friedrich

The practical consequences of all this for contemporary researches into ancient criticism are significant, and it is worth specifying them. There is an increase of concentration on the (re)construction of Greek and Roman categories for their own sake, and a corresponding diminution of interest in comparisons with, or in the interrogation of, modern and contemporary thought on language and literature—a diminution that has perhaps been more pronounced in the study of ancient criticism than it is in other areas of classical studies. As new evidence, particularly in the form of papyri, becomes available, attention has turned to different sources. A figure like Philodemus, for example, is of considerable importance for an understanding of poetic theory in antiquity, but he had no direct influence on the classical literary tradition in the West (simply because no one could have even read Philodemus' critical works until the early nineteenth century). Among classical specialists, the views of Epicurean and Stoic thinkers on speech and poetry as well as those of the rhetoricians now command as much attention as the canonical prescriptions of Plato and Aristotle. There has also been an increasing inclination to examine Hellenistic and late imperial Greek authors—this is perhaps part of a more general trend in classics.

In some of its recent manifestations the study of Greek and Roman poetics and rhetoric is coming to resemble that of Sanskrit or Chinese theories: connections with later European criticism and theory, though asserted, are less likely to be validated or explored. But as classicists have been narrowing their focus on ancient sources, scholars of modern languages and literature, and practitioners in a range of other fields, including modern history and social anthropology, have become increasingly preoccupied with apsects of classical theory and criticism.[19] In fact an extensive body of work bearing

August Wolf, author of the influential *Prolegomena to Homer*, published in 1795. See R. Pfeiffer, *History of Classical Scholarship from 1300 to 1850* (Oxford, 1976), 176, and J. Sandys, *A History of Classical Scholarship*, iii (Cambridge, 1908), 60: '[Wolf] raised that study to the rank of a single comprehensive and independent science, and thus deserves to be reverently regarded by posterity as the eponymous hero of all the long line of later scholars.'

[19] The appropriation of ancient rhetoric for the influential theory of historiography advanced in H. White, *Metahistory* (London, 1973) has prompted some responses from classicists: A. Momigliano, 'On Hayden White's Tropes', *Settimo Contributo alla storia degli studi classici e del mondo antico* (Rome, 1984), 49–59; and A. J. Woodman, *Rhetoric in Classical Historiography* (London, 1988). J. Clifford and G. Marcus (eds.), *Writing Culture: The Poetics and Politics of Ethnography* (Berkeley, 1986), reviewed by

on a variety of disciplines seeks to customize ideas of ancient thinkers—mostly those of Aristotle and the rhetoricians—and to apply them to a variety of domains. This renaissance—although most conspicuous to English readers in more recent years—had its origins in the earlier work of the Russian Formalists and of the linguist Roman Jakobson.[20] In effect, modern literary and cultural theory, in so far as it bears on poetics, has been cosmopolitanizing and promoting ancient literary criticism while classicists have been more concerned with establishing the context of critical production in antiquity.

## II

This tension in the study of ancient literary criticism— between its position in the classical tradition and its role in the task of reconstructing the culture of antiquity—is a tension currently facing the whole discipline of classics which cannot be fully addressed here. But that tension has played a part in determining the selection of pieces offered in this book: a major criterion for inclusion was the pertinence of certain ancient writers for students and specialists in modern literature and poetics. Those readers will have more interest in authors like Homer, Plato, Aristotle, Longinus, Horace, and Ovid than they will have in pseudo-Heraclitus or even Quintilian. Partly on this basis—perhaps more hazardously—a discussion of Plutarch's

A. Free 'Written or Living Culture?', *Journal of Anthropological Society of Oxford*, 21/1 (1990), 59, and R. Grillo (ed.), *Social Anthropology and the Politics of Language* (Sociological Review Monograph, 36; London, 1990), illustrate the impact of poetics and rhetoric on social anthropology.

[20] See e.g. R. Jakobson, *Language in Literature* (Cambridge, Mass., 1987); L. Lemon and M. Reis (eds.), *Russian Formalist Criticism: Four Essays* (London, 1965); L. Matejka and K. Pomorska (eds.), *Readings in Russian Poetics* (Ann Arbor, 1978); V. Shklovsky, *Theory of Prose* (Elmwood Park, Ill., 1990; Russian orig. 1925). Bakhtin's original formulation of intertextuality as 'dialogism' also emerged from this tradition: see *The Dialogic Imagination* (Austin, Tex., 1981), 259–422. The 'narratological' distinction between 'narrative' (*récit*) and 'story' (*histoire*) usually attributed to Gérard Genette was rooted in the division Shklovsky made in 1926 between *fabula* and *sjuzet*, in an essay on *Tristram Shandy* (tr. in Lemon and Reis, *Russian Formalist Criticism*, 25–57). That in turn has its origins in Plato's opposition between *logoi* and *lexis* in *Republic* 392–5; the political significance Valentin Voloshinov attached in the 1920s to direct and indirect speech in *Marxism and the Philosophy of Language* (Cambridge, Mass., 1973) also has an analogue in the same passage of the *Republic*.

*How to Study Poetry* has been presented in preference to a piece on Demetrius.[21] A second fundamental principle was to include discussions which could introduce and elucidate particular primary texts, given the many available studies that convey the more general tenets and trends of ancient criticism and poetics. But I have not clung stubbornly to either of these criteria: there are some rather more panoramic articles in this collection as well as those covering the Epicurean and Stoic tendencies and authors like Dionysius and Servius, who are less well known outside the field of classical studies.

The ideal for a collection of this kind would be something large enough and coherent enough to serve as a self-contained introduction to the subject. However, commercial constraints on the size of this book, and the fact that the constituent essays were not originally conceived to be read together mean that this ideal cannot be realized. A more realistic aim is to make more widely available some standard scholarship on canonical texts or major themes of ancient theory and criticism. The contributions are meant to be clear, substantial, and wide-ranging, and to engage with the main issues raised by their subjects. These are meant to be mainstream discussions. As most of them are relatively recent, they can alert readers to further important bibliography and offer a retrospective of previous debates. An obvious exception is Jacob Bernays's essay on Aristotle's *Poetics*, first published in Breslau in 1857, which has not been available in English for some time.

But any selection inevitably involves omissions. Given the range and complexity of ancient criticism, compared to other spheres of classical literature, the omissions here will be all too evident to many readers. Nonetheless, it is necessary to indicate at this point— especially for the benefit of students and newcomers to the subject— some major authors and key developments in antiquity that are not given adequate coverage in what follows.

To begin with, there are elements of theory and criticism in early Greek iambic, lyric, and epic poetry, as well as in pre-Socratic philosophical writing, and there is an abundance of material in fifth-century texts—none of which could be specifically addressed in this volume. For example, an account of *logos* (speech) in the *Defence of*

---

[21] A brief account of Demetrius' *On Style* is given later in this section; some bibliography is supplied in the Suggestions for Further Reading ('Prominent Ancient Critics') in this volume.

*Helen* by the rhetorician Gorgias of Leontini is important for, among other things, its relation to modern conceptions of literature: 'I hold all poetry to be speech with metre, and that is how I use the word. Those who hear poetry feel the shudders of fear, the tears of pity, the longings of grief. Through the words, the soul experiences it own reaction to the successes and misfortunes in the affairs and persons of others.'[22] A generation or so later, Isocrates offered reflections on the nature of his own speech-making and Plato subjected the basic principles of rhetoric, poetry, and fictional invention to more radical kinds of scrutiny.[23] It has become traditional for historians of criticism to concentrate on the discussions of imitation and the emotive effects of poetry in the *Republic*, although other dialogues like the *Ion, Phaedrus, Symposium, Menexenus*, and *Laws* give some serious attention to poetry; the *Phaedrus* and *Gorgias* also provide sustained and systematic accounts of rhetoric. Further works including the *Cratylus, Hippias Minor*, and the *Timaeus* involve broader issues of criticism at certain points. And it is important to recognize that the discussion in the third book of the *Republic* does not just apply to poetry. In referring to 'poets and storytellers', Plato's Socrates seems to be casting a wide net—his theory of discourse might equally bear on the productions of historians for example.[24]

Aristophanes' comedies engage with poetry, particularly tragic drama: Euripides figures as a huge and enigmatic force in the *Thesmophoriazusae*; the *Frogs*—in which Dionysus judges a contest between Aeschylus and Euripides for the throne of poetry in Hades—provides some important critical insight as well as parody of the poets concerned. Aristophanes' 'literary criticism', however is very much embedded in the current affairs which inform his comedy. The

---

[22] *Helen* 9, tr. Russell and Winterbottom (1972), 7. Compare also (ibid. 6) Gorgias' definition of tragedy preserved in Plutarch, *Moralia* 348d: '[Tragedy] lent to myth and emotion a deceit wherein, as Gorgias says, the deceiver is more just than the non-deceiver and the deceived is wiser than the undeceived. The deceiver is more just because he has fulfilled his promise; the deceived is wiser because it takes a measure of sensibility to be accessible to the pleasures of literature (*logoi*).' Some bibliography specifically on Gorgias is given in Suggestions for Further Reading ('Homer, Aristophanes, and the Sophists'). Ample discussion can also be found in the reading on Greek rhetoric ('Rhetoric and Education in Antiquity').

[23] On Isocrates and criticism, see G. A. Kennedy, *Cambridge History of Literary Criticism*, i. 185–8 and Kennedy, *Classical Rhetoric and its Christian and Secular Tradition from Ancient to Modern Times* (Chapel Hill, NC, 1999), 38–44.

[24] G. Cerri, *Platone sociologo della comunicazione* (Lecce, 1996).

judgements on poetry (by no means confined to these two plays) are also determined by a consistent concern with the nature and identity of comedy.[25] Thus any proper investigation of Aristophanic criticism would have to involve a broader frame of reference—accommodating (for instance) consideration of the relation of comedy to tragedy and some sense of the cultural context of Aristophanes' plays. As the best discussions concerned with his criticism show, Aristophanes is much more than a critic.[26]

It was noted earlier that ancient poetry is a repository of criticism. Poetry quite frequently serves a conduit for the expression of highly influential poetical theory. This could not be more true of the 'Alexandrian' authors like Callimachus and Theocritus. Their outlook could be deemed 'post-Aristotelian', in that it embraces a wide range of genres, more loosely episodic forms of narration, and the privileging of terse, highly crafted diction. These principles were inherited by the Romans and they illuminate the practice of major Latin poets: Catullus, Virgil, Horace, Propertius, and Ovid all signal a debt to Callimachus. The only justification for excluding a discussion of Alexandrian poets from this collection would rest on an appeal to a very limited notion of what criticism is: texts like Callimachus' *Aitia* should certainly not be ignored merely because they are not *primarily* about poetics.[27]

The absence from the contents of any sustained discussion of Demetrius' *On Style* will be of concern to specialists—but although there are some good and accessible treatments of 'Demetrius', none of them could easily be incorporated.[28] Demetrius of Phalerum, a fourth-century critic who is cited in the treatise itself, is *not* the author of *On Style*: the text is now widely agreed to date from the second century BC. The work's importance partly consists in the fact that it is broadly representative of literary criticism after Aristotle, which sought to distinguish between different 'styles' of

---

[25] See M. S. Silk, *Aristophanes and the Definition of Comedy* (Oxford, 2000), 50 and *passim*.

[26] Perhaps appropriately, there are few discussions of Aristophanic 'criticism': however, see I. Lada, ' "Empathetic Understanding": Emotion and Cognition in Classical Dramatic Audience Response', *Proceedings of the Cambridge Philological Society*, 39 (1993), 94–140; K. Sidwell, 'From Old to Middle to New? Aristotle's *Poetics* and the History of Athenian Comedy', in D. Harvey and J. Wilkins, *The Rivals of Aristophanes: Studies in Athenian Old Comedy* (London, 2000), 247–58.

[27] Suggestions for Further Reading on 'Callimachus and "Alexandrian" Poetics'.

[28] See n. 21.

expression.[29] Although a division into three styles (high, medium, low) came to be standard, 'Demetrius' outlines at length a theory of *four* styles: the 'grand' and 'elegant' are in the higher range; the 'plain' and the 'forceful' in the lower. His account is of interest because it addresses a range of topics including sentence structure, the sound of words and phrases, metaphor, charm, and humour.

Aspects of the relation of Hellenistic philosophy to literary questions will be addressed in essays that follow; but the significance of two figures, Neoptolemus and Philodemus, who wrote at different ends of this period should be underlined here.[30] Neoptolemus of Parium was probably a third-century contemporary of Callimachus who produced poetry of his own as well as treatises on philology and literary criticism, which are accessible to us only through Philodemus. A division between poem (*poiema*: equivalent to diction or style), poetry (*poiesis*: a conception of content, plot, and character), and poet (*poietes*: attention to the role and moral responsibility of the poet) appears to have been a major part of Neoptolemus' theory. This three-part schema thus fuses the Alexandrian emphasis on verbal style with an emphasis on the grander structure which appears more Aristotelian, along with the idea that the poet, like the orator, should provide edification as well as pleasure.

Philodemus of Gadara came to Rome in the 70s BC. He was probably a teacher of Virgil and his patron was L. Calpurnius Piso, consul in 58, and the object of political opposition from Cicero. As well as being a practising poet (some epigrams are in the *Anthologia Palatina*), Philodemus was a prolific author of philosophical prose, much of which was devoted to aesthetics and literary criticism. The *On Poets*, parts of which have been preserved in papyri, attacks Neoptolemus (amongst many others), but its more original theses are of greater significance: for Philodemus poetry need not have a moral or utilitarian function but should exist for pleasure. His dismissals of allegorical interpretation and of the need for poetry to be truthful

---

[29] The chapter on 'Theories of Style', in D. A. Russell, *Criticism in Antiquity* (London, 1981), 129–47, and G. A. Kennedy's chapter 'The Evolution of a Theory of Artistic Prose' in the *Cambridge History of Literary Criticism*, i. 184–99, introduce the central issues. For a specific treatment, see D. C. Innes, 'Theophrastus and the Theory of Style', *Rutgers University Studies*, 2 (1985), 251–67.

[30] See Russell in this volume. A good outline of Neoptolemus is provided by Brink, *Horace on Poetry*, i (Cambridge, 1963), 43–150, and a shorter account by D. C. Innes in *Cambridge History of Literary Criticism*, i. 204. See also Suggestions for Further Reading on 'Philodemus'.

appear consistent with this position. More remarkably perhaps, Philodemus, unlike most ancient theorists, grasps the artificiality of separating literary form and literary content.

There is a far larger number of chapters in this collection on Greek (as opposed to Latin) texts and authors. That is not so much due to a perception of a longer or more varied cultural history in Greece as it is to the nature of Roman writing on the subject. Most of our sources for ancient criticism in Latin are mainly or exclusively concerned with oratory: but, with the exception of Tacitus, the chapters that follow on Roman authors deal with sources on poetry. It was remarked above that the important role of oratory throughout antiquity is not represented in most current curricula. Tempting though it might have been to use this book to redirect or modify the inclinations of teachers and students, the aim here is to meet existing needs and interests. An unfortunate consequence of that pragmatism is that space could not be left for specific discussions of some major Latin prose authors from the Republic to the Empire: Cicero, the Senecas, Quintilian, Pliny the Younger, Fronto, and Gellius.[31] Cicero and Quintilian were not only highly significant in antiquity: Cicero in particular had a massive influence on later literary and cultural traditions—especially in the Renaissance.[32]

Cicero's views on oratory are expressed in a range of works. *On Invention* is concerned with techniques of argument—*inventio*, as Cicero himself defines it, consists of 'working out the true issues or those that are close to the truth that might render one's case plausible'.[33] But the two books of the work, especially in their introductory sections, contextualize the study of rhetoric. According to the first chapter of the treatise, wisdom without rhetoric is of little

---

[31] See E. Fantham's discussions, 'The Growth of Literature and Criticism at Rome' and 'Latin Criticism in the Early Empire', in the *Cambridge History of Literary Criticism*, i. 220–44 and 274–96 on these Roman authors, as well as the material on Cicero and Quintilian in Suggestions for Further Reading.

[32] For Renaissance debates about imitation of Cicero, see J. Binns, 'Ciceronianism in 16th Century England, *Lias*, 7 (1980); *Collected works of Erasmus*, xxviii, ed. A. Levi (Toronto, 1986); A. C. Clarke, 'Ciceronianism', in G. Gordon, *English Literature and the Classics* (Oxford, 1912); R. Sabbadini, *Storia del ciceronianismo e di altre questioni letterarie nell'età della rinascenza* (Turin, 1885); J. M. Nuñez González, *El ciceronianismo en España* (Valladolid, 1993); on reception of Quintilian, see e.g. M. Baxandall, *Giotto and the Orators* (Oxford, 1971); A. Grafton and L. Jardine, *From Humanism to the Humanities* (London, 1986), 66–82.

[33] *On Invention* I. 7: *Inventio est excogitatio rerum verarum aut veri similium quae causam probabilem reddant.*

use, while rhetoric without wisdom can be harmful. Cicero's later writings *On the Orator*, *Brutus*, and *Orator* represent a more original and substantial contribution to the study of rhetoric, but these works also accentuate the importance of wider knowledge (of poetry, philosophy, culture) for success in public speaking. Thus *On the Orator* and *Brutus* are presented as dialogues which themselves have a broad conception, designed to transcend the confines of specialized instruction: the former is devoted to portrayal of the ideal orator; the latter presents a history of Roman oratory in which successful style is discussed with reference to particular individuals who are compared or contrasted. The *Orator*, in the form of a letter, is a more explicit defence by Cicero of his version of 'Attic' oratorical practice and theory: the ongoing debates of the time about the desirable styles are addressed there, as well as in the *Brutus*.

In addition to the *Divisions of Rhetoric* and the *Topics* (the *De optimo genere oratorum* may not be genuinely Ciceronian), Cicero's philosophical works, letters, and speeches contain all kinds of observations which should not be overlooked by historians of literary criticism. For instance, *On Divination* contains a discussion and translation into Latin hexameters of Odysseus' speech to the Greeks in *Iliad* 2. 299–331.[34] Cicero's musings on the omens described in that speech amount to an interpretation of the Homeric verses themselves. Again, Cicero's letter to Lucceius on how to approach the writing of history is an essential text for anyone concerned with ancient historiographical theory.[35] And in his speech *For Archias*, which was made to defend a Greek poet's suit for Roman citizenship, Cicero presents what has long been seen as an idealized picture of the appropriate functions of poetry and of the poet's place in society.

Quintilian's *Education of an Orator* (*Institutio oratoria*) marked a return to Ciceronian values at the end of the first century AD. after what had been perceived as a period of decline in oratory—this decline was also to be a major concern in Tacitus' *Dialogus*.[36] Like

[34] *De divinatione* 2. 63–5. Cicero wrongly attributes the speech he translates to Agamemnon.
[35] See A. J. Woodman, *Rhetoric and Historiography in Classical Literature* (London, 1988).
[36] On Tacitus, see Luce in this volume. The same decline can be identified in the discussion that opens our text of Petronius' *Satyricon*—a work conventionally dated to the reign of Nero: see G. A. Kennedy, 'Encolpius and Agamemnon in Petronius', *American Journal of Philology*, 99 (1978), 171–8, and (for general accounts) H. Caplan,

Cicero, Quintilian laid stress on the importance of a general education for orators: his compendious work traces the process of that education from the earliest stages. The tenth book of the *Institutio* is particularly interesting for the virtually comprehensive survey of Greek and Roman literature it contains. The purpose of that survey is to highlight the authors whom orators should read with profit or imitate. This is why Quintilian says (quoting Livy): 'Read Demosthenes and Cicero, then those who are most like Demosthenes and Cicero.'[37]

Quintilian's judgements on writers from Homer to Seneca display a set of priorities which are not only alien to a modern perspective— they also seem inappropriate to the original purposes of the authors he considers (he remarks for instance that Livy's own style is no good for effecting a prosecution). Quintilian's agenda leads him apparently to play down or ignore the more general achievements of many writers he is obliged to mention: Lucretius is deemed worth reading but 'difficult', and although Catullus' invective is acknowledged, his lyrics and other verses are not mentioned. The survey in the *Institutio* covers a wide range of literature, but it is very cursory.[38] One suspects that the rather legislative tone must have contributed to the extensive influence of this part of the work on taste in later ages, but many of the evaluations are of limited use to later readers because Quintilian saw little need to justify verdicts which he probably regarded as conventional.

The emergence of Latin literature and the rise of Rome as a political power did nothing to diminish the development of literary criticism in Greece. On the contrary, some of the most important and enduring Greek contributions to the subject were produced in the Empire: the accomplishments of Plutarch and 'Longinus'—assuming the latter wrote in this period—will be treated in chapters to come. Dio Chrysostom, like Plutarch, was born in the middle of the first

---

'The Decay of Eloquence at Rome in the First Century', in *Of Eloquence: Studies in Ancient and Medieval Rhetoric* (Ithaca, NY, 1970), 160-95, G. Williams, *Change and Decline: Roman Literature in the Early Empire* (Berkeley, 1978), and K. Heldmann, *Antike Theorien uber Entwicklung und Verfall der Redekunst* (Munich, 1982).

[37] *Institutio Oratoria* 10. 1. 39: *legendos Demosthenem atque Ciceronem, tum ita, ut quisque Demostheni et Ciceroni simillimus.*

[38] The catalogue of authors in *Institutio Oratoria* 10. 1 seems to depend on the Greek Dionysius' *On Mimesis* (Περὶ μιμήσεως): clearly Quintilian was at pains to show that orators could make use of their recreational reading.

century AD.[39] His speeches contain a number of pertinent arguments and observations: one of the orations devoted to Homer defends the poet from Plato's attack; a speech on tragedy usefully compares versions of the same myths by Aeschylus, Euripides, and Sophocles.[40] The Second Sophistic was also to produce rhetoricians such as Hermogenes and authors who set out rules for rhetorical composition in the texts known as the *progymnasmata*.[41] But the second and third centuries AD are perhaps better known for savants and sophists like Lucian, Maximus of Tyre, and later, in the third century, Philostratus. Lucian's essay *On How to Write History* is in a light vein but it makes some serious points: history should be distinguished from poetry and panegyric; it should relate plainly what happened; facts should be organized but related vividly, ideally in the light of autopsy, and with the needs of posterity in mind.[42] Maximus of Tyre makes good use of Homer and Plato in his *Orations*, and three of these speeches defend poetry on ethical grounds.[43] Philostratus gives a brief but important account of the role of imagination in representation (which can be applied to poetry) when he has Apollonius of Tyana explain how sculptors like Pheidias and Praxiteles managed to fashion their beautiful statues of the gods:[44] 'Imagination (*phantasia*) did this work, a more cunning craftsman than your imitation. Imitation (*mimesis*) will fashion what she has seen, imagination also what she has not seen.' This illustration,

[39] D. A. Russell (ed.), *Dio Chrysostom Orations VII, XII, and XXXVI* (Cambridge, 1992) has useful information on Dio's life and cultural background in the introduction. S. Swain (ed.), *Dio Chrysostom: Politics, Letters, and Philosophy* (Oxford, 2000) contains some important studies.

[40] *Oration* 53 'On Homer'; *Oration* 52 on Philoctetes' bow.

[41] See G. A. Kennedy, *Progymnasmata: Greek Textbooks of Prose Composition and Rhetoric Translated with Introductions and Notes* (Leiden and Boston, 2003).

[42] Other works of parody by Lucian are rich in literary critical or theoretical observation: characters in *Philopseudes* debate the nature of fiction and *Dream* 2, in commenting on the anomaly of the talking horse in *Iliad* 19. 407, questions the plausibility of Homeric personages actually speaking in hexameters. See further D. A. Russell's account of Lucian and Philostratus in *Cambridge History of Literary Criticism*, i. 311–14.

[43] *Orations* 4, 17, 37. The speeches are translated with an introduction and notes in M. B. Trapp, *The Philosophical Orations: Maximus of Tyre* (Oxford, 1997). For a text and bibliography, see Trapp's Teubner edn.: *Dissertationes: Maximus Tyrius* (Leipzig, 1994).

[44] *Life of Apollonius* 6. 19. Compare Longinus' account of *phantasia* in *On the Sublime* 15, but also Aristotle *Poetics* 9. 1451[a]37: 'the poet's job is saying not what did happen but the sort of thing that would happen'.

which was extensively prefigured in an oration by Dio Chrysostom
(12. 55–77), was also incorporated by Plotinus to find a way around
Plato's own strictures on the arts—Plotinus argues that those arts
do not just imitate things visible in nature but also the very archetypes (*logoi*) which natural things themselves imitate: 'Pheidias did
not base his statue of Zeus on a model perceived by the senses but
grasped what Zeus would be like if he wanted to appear before one's
eyes.'[45]

This was just one element of a further strain of aesthetic and
literary theory which developed in the traditions of Neoplatonism
from the third century AD onwards. The Neoplatonists were not of
course the first ancient thinkers to discern allegory in the poets,
but they contributed significantly to the development of this current
of literary exegesis.[46] Plotinus' follower and biographer Porphyry
paid particular attention to poetry—his *Homeric Questions* and
other writings on Homer are extant in fragments, but *On the Cave
of the Nymphs* survives in full.[47] This is an attempt to interpret
allegorically the curious description in Homer's *Odysssey* (13. 102–
12) of the cave in Ithaca in which Odysseus hid the gifts he had
received from the Phaeacians. Drawing from a variety of intellectual
traditions, Porphyry's erudite treatise endorses competing readings:
the Cave can stand both for 'sensible nature' and for 'intelligible
essence', depending on the different attributes attached to it by
Homer. Such accommodation of a plurality of meanings or interpretations is rare in ancient criticism.[48] And even as late as the 1300s,
when Dante first applied the term 'polysemy' to an entire work (as
opposed to individual words), only *one* allegorical interpretation

---

[45] Plotinus, *Enneads* 5. 8. 1. On *phantasia* theory, see J. J. Pollitt, *The Ancient View of Greek Art: Criticism, History and Terminology* (New Haven, 1974).

[46] A. Ford, 'Performing Interpretation: Early Allegorical Exegesis of Homer', in M. Beissinger, J. Tylus and S. Wofford (eds.), *Epic Traditions in the Contemporary World: The Poetics of Community* (Berkeley and Los Angeles, 1999), 33–53, treats Homeric allegorization in archaic Greece; A. A. Long's contribution to this volume surveys the extensive tradition of Stoic allegorization of Homer; ps-Heraclitus' *Homeric Questions* are especially important in this regard. See *Cambridge History of Literary Criticism*, i. 320–1 and D. A. Russell, 'The Rhetoric of the Homeric Questions', in G. Boys-Stones (ed.), *Metaphor, Allegory, and the Classical Tradition* (Oxford, 2003).

[47] *The Cave of the Nymphs in the Odyssey: A Revised Text with Translation by Seminar Classics 609* (State University of New York at Buffalo, 1969).

[48] As Russell notes in the *Cambridge History of Literary Criticism*, i. 325. Plato's Socrates in the *Cratylus* prefers to settle on a single 'correct' interpretation in where individual words are concerned.

seems to be admitted in addition to the primary significance of a text.[49]

The authors who provide our testimonia for the fragments of Porphyry give some indication of the extent of Porphyry's legacy.[50] These include Augustine, Eusebius, Eustathius, Macrobius, and Proclus. The commentaries by Proclus on Plato's *Timaeus* and *Republic*, written late in the fifth century, constitute a very thorough defence and exploration of the philosophical value of poetry. In his fifth and sixth essays (which largely constitute the *Republic* commentary), Proclus argues that Homer was excluded from Plato's condemnation of the poets: the various theories offered in support of this position amount to a metaphysical philosophy of poetry.[51] Macrobius, a Latin author who wrote some time before Proclus, produced a commentary on Cicero's *Dream of Scipio*, and the *Saturnalia*— a sequence of dialogues set in the 380s AD. The commentary on Scipio's dream in Cicero's *De republica* is a vehicle of Neoplatonic thought. As well as exhibiting the influence of Plotinus, this work seems to cite a lost commentary on the *Timaeus* by Porphyry. Macrobius' approach certainly resembles that of his predecessor's treatment of the Cave of the Nymphs, in so far as it provides a rich allegorical intepretation of the philosophical, scientific, and mystical elements discerned in the source text. The *Saturnalia* is also of interest for the responses of its various speakers (who include Servius) to the poetry of Virgil.

The importance of Augustine's conceptions of literature deserve a specific mention. Whilst the theories of language offered in the *Confessions* (and in his other writings) have been much debated by modern literary theorists and philosophers, Augustine tends to be

---

[49] Dante, *Epistolae* 10. 7 (ed. E. Moore and P. Toynbee, *Le Opere di Dante Alighieri*, Oxford 1924): 'It must be understood that the meaning of this work [the *Commedia*] is not of one kind only (*non est simplex sensus*); rather the work may be described as *polysemos*, that is, having several meanings (*plurium sensuum*); for the first meaning is that which is conveyed by the letter, and the next is that which is conveyed by what the letter signifies; the former of which is called "literal", while the latter is called allegorical, or moral, or mystical.' Dante's innovation possibly arose from his transference of ideas in Christian biblical hermeneutics to a more secular form of writing.

[50] See the Teubner text of the *Porphyrii philosophi fragmenta*, ed. A. Smith (Leipzig, 1993).

[51] A. J. Festugière, *Commentaire sur la République* (Paris, 1970) is an excellent text and translation of Proclus' commentary; see also A. Sheppard, *Studies on the 5th and 6th essays of Proclus' Commentary on the Republic* (Göttingen, 1980).

given short shrift in most surveys of ancient criticism, doubtless because, as a Christian writer, he tends to be regarded as belonging to a subsequent phase in the history of criticism.[52] However, not only do the *Confessions* and other writings by Augustine offer a number of important insights on classical authors, notably Virgil; they also add much to our understanding of ancient reading practices, enabling us to understand ways in which the criticism of ancient thinkers and rhetoricians can be connected with responses to literary texts in the medieval period and the Renaissance.[53]

A catalogue of omissions from this book need not stop here. Any and every instance of description, illumination, or evaluation in a classical text of another text, group of texts, or of an author can constitute or imply criticism. Cross-referral is an inevitable feature of all kinds of discursive production, but it is especially prevalent in literary discourse. Poets like Catullus and Propertius who mention other poets such as Cinna and Gallus may not be full-time critics but such mentions nonetheless constitute ancient literary criticism. The very conception of some literary works can be taken to offer implicit comment on others: the interaction with Aeschylus' *Choephoroi* in the recognition scene of Euripides' *Electra* (487–698) and the implicit criticism of Homer in the poetic practice of Apollonius of Rhodes' *Argonautica* are just two well-known examples. Classical texts exhibit far more community of reference and general interconnection than the disjointed, confusing, and contested 'corpus' of literary production in English.[54] Works in Greek and Latin are best understood

---

[52] Ludwig Wittgenstein famously attacked Augustine's conception of language in the *Confessions* at the beginning of the *Philosophical Investigations*, tr. G. Anscombe (Oxford, 1953); see also T. Todorov, tr. C. Porter, *Theories of the Symbol* (Ithaca, NY, 1982).

[53] B. Stock, *Augustine the Reader: Meditation, Self-Knowledge and the Ethics of Interpretation* (Cambridge, Mass., 1996) offers a substantial study which compensates for some neglect of this subject among ancient literary historians.

[54] A conspectus of classical authors as diverse as (e.g.) Homer, Aristotle, and Petronius, writing over the duration of roughly 1,400 years yields far more than a conspectus of equivalently diverse authors (Chaucer, Bacon, E. M. Forster) from England between 1300 and 1900. The interconnections of the Graeco-Roman canon perhaps find a better modern counterpart in the literary culture of Russia, where Pushkin has occupied a position somewhat analogous to Homer's in antiquity: even 20th-century writers and film directors routinely alluded to precursors and to each other. This extraordinary literary history might help to account for the strong tradition of poetics and literary theory in Russia (n. 20).

through acquaintance with other works in Greek and Latin: students who are interested in ancient literary criticism will want to keep a record of testimonies they can find for themselves.

However, even though this collection has no claim to be comprehensive, its exclusion from further consideration of many sources treated briefly here is undesirable. Leaving aside appeals to practical constraints, the existing selection can really only be defended on pedagogical grounds. First, given that anything like total coverage of the field was impossible, there has been a preference for contributions that are accessible and stimulating. That is not to say that the pieces are all pitched at an equivalent level: a reader who requires an introduction to Dionysius of Halicarnassus will probably have more experience of classical scholarship and more familiarity with appropriate contexts than will the student who is encountering for the first time Horace's criticism or the application of rhetorical principles to literature.[55]

Secondly, this collection aims to foreground authors like Aristotle, Horace and Longinus, who essentially affected the course of modern and early modern criticism, and who helped to determine the identity of criticism as a distinct form of discourse.[56] This historical consideration has to be acknowledged, however much people may now want to take issue with its consequences. But a good indication of the full range and breadth of the ancient sources that ought to be taken into account is given by the large number of texts translated in Russell and Winterbottom's *Ancient Literary Criticism* (Oxford, 1972). The readings asembled here are partly designed to serve as a companion to the relevant parts of that important anthology. It is also hoped that the 'Suggestions for Further Reading' at the end of this book will compensate to some extent for the omissions by drawing attention to central studies easily available elsewhere which could, or probably should, have been included, either in full or in excerpted form, in the pages that follow.

It remains to address an omission of quite another kind. The clear majority of the ensuing discussions make no reference to modern or

---

[55] For background to Dionysius of Halicarnassus, see Suggestions for Further Reading, 6.

[56] The evidence for this is overwhelming. See Suggestions for Further Reading, 7, 'Literary Theory and Criticism in the Classical Tradition'.

contemporary theories of literature, and that is bound to prompt objections from certain quarters. Those objections could be deemed unfair and unreasonable, however; moreover, they betray an outlook which is actually quite parochial. Some classicists seem only to be capable of accommodating two cultures: the period of antiquity with which they are academically concerned and the period they inhabit now. It is unfortunate that not only do the methodologies of such classicists tend to be overdetermined by contemporary trends—the very objects of their investigations are often overdetermined too.

There is no evident reason, at least where scrutiny of ancient criticism is concerned, why current applications of ethics to literature (e.g. gender, identity, postcolonialism), recent ideas of form (in terms of e.g. intertextuality, narratology), or of historicism and performance should have to blot out the presentation of similar and sometimes identical issues in the compendious traditions of poetics, which stretch from the Middle Ages and the Renaissance, via the Baroque and Enlightenment, to the more discrete phases of romanticism, modernism, and Marxism. It ought to be more widely acknowledged that theorists of poetry, literature, and art from previous generations—Geoffrey of Vinsauf, Politian, Vida, Joseph Scaliger, Gracián, Boileau, Johnson, Pope, Schiller, Coleridge, Taine, Nietzsche, Pound, Leavis, Benjamin, to name some central figures—can enhance the comprehension of ancient literary theory and criticism just as they can profoundly develop our perception of literature in general by drawing attention to issues overlooked by many contemporary theorists.

The point here is *not* that classicists should ignore more recent developments—quite the contrary. Rather it is to suggest that contributions from earlier in our own epoch to debates prompted by ancient authors should be taken into consideration along with the newer—and evidently more popular—views on the same issues. On this basis, engagement with contemporary theory in the contributions in this book was limited, so as not to convey a lopsided perspective on the subject which, by presenting the views of an ancient critic in conjunction with modern theoretical opinion, would ignore everything that has come between. Notions of value, the aesthetic, and the sublime, for instance, which were so important from the seventeenth century onwards, and which had some equivalents in ancient literary criticism, have all but vanished from contemporary literary theory—moreover, they have been discarded without ever having been decisively discredited.[57]

A second reason for privileging descriptive accounts of Greek and Roman sources and for not throwing too many contemporary pre-occupations into the mix was the simple remit of the title: *Ancient Literary Criticism* (not 'Ancient and Modern'). As the discussion up to now has indicated, the literary criticism of antiquity is a large enough subject as it is: the objective of this book is to provide an initial orientation rather than to involve the reader in partisan debates from the outset. There is a good case for another anthology of essays which synthesize ancient and modern poetics—but such an anthology will serve a more specialized purpose.[58] Although there are no introductory accounts offering a survey of Western ideas of literature as whole, introductions to modern and contemporary the-ory abound—some of which are excellent.[59]

However, anyone who has read one of those introductions to modern theory could object to the approach of this collection by wheeling in the now familiar truism that everyone has a theory.[60] It could be held that it is disingenuous, even deceitful, for this book to present itself as an innocent introduction which claims not to involve the reader in partisan debates, when no descriptive account of ancient critical practices can ever be neutral or impartial. Of course that objection is as valid as it is obvious. Admittedly, many of the contributions to follow have a varsity hue; and a good number of them were penned at a time before it had been customary for reflection of an ideological nature to prompt scholars self-consciously to 'situate' themselves and their subjects. For better or worse, the rhetoric of classical scholarship has remained, by and large, a positivist rhetoric. But I would argue that allowances should be made

---

[57] Charles Martindale brings a Neo-Kantian conception of the aesthetic to bear on Roman literature in *Latin Poetry and the Judgement of Taste* (Oxford, 2005) (see also his review of Y. L. Too, *The Idea of Ancient Literary Criticism*, 'Banishing the Poets', in *Arion*, 8/3 (2002), 115–27); on value, see n. 80 below and M. S. Silk 'Pindar Meets Plato: Theory, Language, Value and the Classics', in S. J. Harrison (ed.), *Texts, Ideas and the Classics: Scholarship and Theory in Classical Literature* (Oxford, 2001), 26–45.

[58] Alessandro Barchiesi is currently editing a collection *Classical Literature in Theory: An Anthology of Criticism, 1960–2001* to be published by Blackwell.

[59] Suggestions for Further Reading, 9. 'Modern Theories of Literature'.

[60] See e.g. the Preface to T. Eagleton, *Literary Theory: An Introduction* (Oxford, 1983). The truism was addressed influentially and with considerable sophistication by Karl Marx and Friedrich Engels in *The German Ideology* (1845).

for that: the absence of (contemporary) theoretical self-awareness in
a discussion of the literary criticism of antiquity matters no more
than it matters in a discussion of anything else from antiquity. It is
worth saying again that the need for *accessibility* was a criterion for
the pieces selected for this book. While positivism has endured in
classics, so too has the clarity of expression which accompanies it,
and there is something to be said for that.

There is though a more serious objection to the omission of later
theory in the chapters that follow. A virtually inevitable consequence
of that omission is that many of these chapters end up appearing too
deferential to the ancient 'authorities' whom they treat. That may
not be so commendable for a book which has a pedagogical purpose:
students getting to grips with ancient critics should realize that, from
certain perpectives, much of their writing about literature seems to
be misdirected, inadequate, or simply, wrong.[61] For example, the
interpretations of Virgil in 'Servius' are often regarded as rather
unhelpful for today's readers of the *Aeneid* who see certain tensions—
between nation and individual, between duty and personal loss,
between the claims of imperial power and the suffering it inflicts— as
central to the poem, tensions which the Servian corpus, Quintilian,
and Tiberius Claudius Donatus fail to mention. Again, even
Aristotle's *Poetics*, undoubtedly the most influential document of
poetic theory ever produced, has been regarded as a failure, for
different reasons, by those who reach certain conclusions or hold
certain presuppositions about Greek tragedy or about literature in
general.[62]

---

[61] One straightforward example of misplaced emphasis in ancient criticism is a preoccupation with 'euphony' at the expense of other forms of assonance: see the article
'assonance, Greek' in the *Oxford Classical Dictionary*, 3rd edn. (Oxford, 1996), 193–4.
D. A. Russell *Criticism in Antiquity* (London, 1981), 97, comments generally on
ancient criticism: 'No one in antiquity seems to have had the idea that, instead
of beginning with a message and embodying it in fiction, one might begin with a
story and treat it as a symbol of the happenings or truths which have some formal
resemblance to it. And this is odd.'

[62] M. S. Silk and J. P. Stern, *Nietzsche on Tragedy* (Cambridge, 1981) discuss past
responses to Aristotle's omission of the gods *inter alia*; E. Hall 'Is there a Polis in
Aristotle's *Poetics*?', in M. S. Silk (ed.), *Tragedy and the Tragic: Greek Theatre and Beyond*
(Oxford, 1996), 295–309, is a narrower attack, according to contemporary lights.
M. Bakhtin, *The Dialogic Imagination* (Austin, Tex., 1981) notes that the novel cannot
be comprehended in terms of the *Poetics*—although T. J. Binyon, *Murder Will Out: The
Detective in Fiction* (Oxford, 1989) observes that detective stories can closely follow an

## III

Ultimately, for any of our judgements about the value of criticism in ancient sources to be meaningful, it is necessary for us to have a clear idea of our own presuppositions about the nature and purpose of literature and of literary criticism—whatever those presuppositions may be. This section of the chapter will therefore begin by relaying some contemporary definitions of 'literature'. Then, more importantly, it will outline the various axes along which the coordinates of various theories can be plotted. This form of mapping should help readers to contextualize *conceptually* the views of various ancient critics (along with more general currents of ancient thought). The mapping will also facilitate consideration in *synchronic* terms of the range of critical responses, whether ancient or modern, to literature. The acquisition of such a synchronic vantage point is just as important as an apprehension of the diachronic development of ancient literary criticism, and it should help readers to integrate ancient and modern conceptions for themselves.

The problem of defining literature has perhaps been exaggerated: it can be regarded as a synthetic, evaluative category, the development of which is historically contingent. The upshot of debates in recent years is to reconcile the various senses of 'literature' with each other by appealing to a Wittgensteinian definition, by 'family resemblances'. Words like *literature* or *game* have a variety of overlapping definitions, only some of which can be found in any actual instance.[63]

But there might also be a common marker of *all* texts deemed to be literary: the reusability conferred on them by readers. An oration of Cicero, for example, even if it was once a document or speech act with material causes and effects, can differ from other kinds of texts

---

Aristotelian blueprint; see also G. W. Most and W. Stowe, *The Poetics of Murder: Detective Fiction and Literary Theory* (San Diego, 1983).

[63] L. Wittgenstein, *Philosophical Investigations* (Oxford, 1953), s. 65 following. See e.g. 'Introduction: What is Literature?', in T. Eagleton, *Literary Theory* (Oxford, 1983), 1–15. W. Van Peer, 'But What is Literature? Toward a Descriptive Definition of Literature', in R. D. Sell (ed.), *Literary Pragmatics* (London, 1991), 127–41 criticizes Eagleton's 'verdict of aporia' and attempts to offer a descriptive definition of literature from the vantage point of pragmatics.

and utterances because it is 'reusable'.[64] In common with some other kinds of text (legal, religious, poetic), a speech of Cicero becomes literary because it can be meaningfully reissued and reused, again and again. The idea of literature being reusable is connected with the 'defamiliarized' quality of its language and the aesthetic value attributed to it.

Another way of defining literature has centred precisely on the defamiliarization of its language. Such language is held to be 'connotative' (as opposed to the denotative language of science). However much the presence of literary language may be a consequence of surrounding factors, it can still be scrutinized in isolation, at least in principle.[65] And to avoid begging the question of what is meant by 'literary', literary language can itself be defined in terms of family resemblances: it consists of attributes belonging to other kinds of discourse which, in combination, can serve as markers of literary language: certain kinds of vocabulary and diction (e.g. Homeric epithets), certain rhetorical figures (e.g. metaphor), certain types of acoustically patterned discourse (e.g. identifiable metres), certain accidental forms (e.g. the past historic tense in French or the narrative present in English) and certain forms of syntax (e.g. free indirect discourse).

On these lines, literature itself can be defined broadly and relatively uncontentiously—and such forms of definition can be applied to every epoch, from classical antiquity to the present day. But things become more complex once the issue of *criticism* comes to the fore. Needless to say, critics have never simply confined themselves to judgements about the extent to which texts are defamiliarized or reusable. Simply to classify a text as literature is to confer upon it

---

[64] The issue of 'reusability' is discussed in the chapter entitled 'Poetic Memory: Its Historical and Systematic Features', in G. B. Conte, *The Rhetoric of Imitation* (Ithaca, NY, 1986), 40.

[65] The idea that there are various formal, linguistic features in a text which demonstrate its literary quality has not gone unchallenged: see M. L. Pratt, *Towards a Speech Act Theory of Literary Discourse* (Bloomington, 1977); R. Fowler, *Literature as Social Discourse* (London, 1981). N. Enkvist, 'On the Interpretability of Texts in General and of Literary Texts in Particular', in Sell, *Literary Pragmatics*, 1–25, has considered literary communication in the light of discourse linguistics and makes the obvious suggestion (at 23–4) that it is 'definable only in relative, social terms, not in absolute linguistic or textual ones . . . Literature is what a certain social group at a certain time choose to regard as literature.' The latter proposition has problems—if only because 'Literature' and 'regarding as literature' have been terms of reference since the 18th century.

some kind of value. But what can constitute appropriate evaluation, elaboration, description, or interpretation? It may well seem as if any attempt to systematize criticism is bound to be doomed from the start. However, the totality of theories that can be distilled from the divergent practices of critics ever since antiquity may actually be reduced to four basic conceptions of literature. This schema is very rough of course; it is meant to be practically helpful rather than theoretically watertight:[66]

(i) Representational: Literary productions can be conceived, and evaluated, in terms of the world or reality they presuppose, represent, or construct.

(ii) Expressive: Literary productions can be conceived, and evaluated, in terms of expression of the identity, personality, or state of mind of the author.

(iii) Formal: Literary productions can be conceived and judged in terms of form or style.

(iv) Pragmatic: Literary productions can be conceived and judged in terms of their effects (emotional, educational, social, etc.) on readers or audience.

These four basic conceptions—in terms of represention, expression, form, and pragmatic effects—are the axes on which the presuppositions of various critics or brands of criticism can be plotted, whatever historical situations or personal inclinations may have led to them.

It should be noted that aesthetics, morality, and politics do not in themselves constitute additional conceptions of literary theory: ethical and aesthetic considerations can bear on any of the four conceptions already adumbrated. Although it may look as if any kind of ethically oriented literary criticism would have to entail a pragmatic theory, it is worth remarking that ethical criticism can equally be articulated in terms of representation, expression, and form.[67]

---

[66] The schema is largely modelled on M. H. Abrams's article on 'Poetry, Theories of' in the 1965 edn. of the *Princeton Encyclopedia of Poetry and Poetics*. My version of the taxonomy presupposes more importance for the 'pragmatic' axis than Abrams (who was anyway primarily concerned with poetry) implied. In the overtly ideological forms of criticism that have emerged since Abrams was writing in the early 1960s, didacticism, ethics, and politics are now more prominent than the concern with pleasure and other emotions. W. J. Verdenius, in *The Principles of Greek Literary Criticism* (Leiden, 1983) chooses to organize his important survey of Greek criticism in a comparable way: in terms of 'Form, Skill, Authority, Inspiration, and Contemplation'.

[67] Horace's *Ars Poetica* is well-known for endowing technical excellence in poetry with a positive ethical value.

Conversely, formal theories do not have to be aesthetically oriented (although they often are)—they can just as easily be ethically driven.[68] Few critics in antiquity confined themselves to just one of these four conceptions, although they may have grounded their judgements on some more than others. At the same time, it is rare for any critic to operate with all of them.

For instance the discussion of form and representation in Aristotle's *Poetics* cannot escape recognition of the pragmatic functions of literature, but the part played by the author is barely considered. Longinus, on the other hand, who foregrounds the importance of the author in his pragmatically and formally oriented treatment of sublimity, is less consistently concerned with the representational aspects of the texts he considers.[69] Plato's writings are diverse enough to accommodate all four conceptions: the *Republic* celebratedly treats *mimesis* and the social effects of literature, but it also offers a penetrating account of literary form, and it gives some attention to the role of the poet. The expressive dimension of literature (with regard to inspiration) is elaborated in other Platonic dialogues like the *Phaedrus* and the *Symposium*.

The endeavours of critics after antiquity can be plotted in similar ways. To provide some familiar examples: at the close of the nineteenth century Leo Tolstoy was in part concerned with the pragmatics of literature in terms of its moral efficacy; around the same time the Italian aesthetician Benedetto Croce was evaluating all literary forms (including drama) as expression of emotion through an 'image'.[70] Traditions of criticism which have conceived and judged

---

[68] It is worth pointing out that avowedly 'ahistorical' or 'apolitical' formalisms of Barthes's semiotics, Foucauldian post-structuralism, and deconstruction are not of course without moral consequences: Fredric Jameson, *The Prison House of Language* (Princeton, 1972) considers the hazards for literary interpretation of removing language from historical change and social experience.

[69] *On the Sublime* nonetheless exhibits a clear awareness of the function of representation in its coverage of *phantasia* and *enargeia* (15, 25–7), including (e.g.) the remarks on the vividness of the historic present tense (25. 1).

[70] L. Tolstoy, *What is Art?*, tr. V. Tomas (Indianapolis, 1960); B. Croce, *Aesthetic as Science of Expression and General Linguistic*, tr. D. Ainslie (New York, 1966). The first chapter of S. T. Coleridge, *Biographia Literaria* (1817) is a *locus classicus* for the Romantic view that expression was inseparable from thought. See F. L. Lucas, *Literature and Psychology* (London and Toronto, 1951); G. Orsini, 'Expression, theory of', in the *Princeton Encyclopedia of Poetry and Poetics* (Princeton, 1965), 266–7; and bibliography on 'Author, Authority, and Inspiration' in Suggestions for Further Reading, 10 'Modern Literary Categories and Ancient Theory'.

works in terms of *mimesis* or represention have been consistently prominent in the Western tradition.[71] More recently New Historicist approaches to literature which centre on representation have been very widespread, but in the past fifty years or so there has also been a resurgence of criticism based on form, on pragmatics, or on both. The trends of 'Practical Criticism' and 'New Criticism' in the mid-twentieth century drew attention to structure, arrangement, and diction of texts—and of poetry especially. A revival of rhetorical criticism preceded a growing interest in narrative; both interests have drawn more or less directly from classical sources, with Aristotle's *Poetics* and *Rhetoric* and Plato's *Republic* as major influences.[72] It should be noted, however, that rhetorical criticism is not exclusively formalist—nor are many recent forms of narrative theory which involve consideration of the reader. A specifically rhetorical approach is obviously concerned with the pragmatic effects of literature—so too is the application to criticism of any theory concerned with narrative in relation to ideology.

An increasing perception of the social and ideological significance of language has generated kinds of criticism which can be seen as directly pragmatic: feminist, religious, and political criticism generally present texts as performing certain (non-literary) functions, or as illustrating or endorsing certain perceived historical or cultural tendencies. Audience-oriented criticism is often pragmatic in this way: it is quite routine for today's classicists, for instance, to regard Greek drama as primarily addressing contemporaneous civic ideology or much Roman poetry as political propaganda.[73] The application of critical strategies derived from 'philosophical' positions like

---

[71] The final chapter of S. Halliwell, *The Aesthetics of Mimesis: Ancient Texts and Modern Problems* (Princeton, 2002) considers the decline of *mimesis* in the wake of Romanticism and offers a nuanced argument for its enduring role in contemporaray aesthetics even after postmodernism. See also 'Representation and *Mimesis*' in Suggestions for Further Reading, 10.

[72] The Chicago School, a group of pluralist, formalist American literary critics, is significant: W. C. Booth, *The Rhetoric of Fiction* (Chicago, 1961, 2nd edn. 1983) is a representative work. See also n. 1 on I. A. Richards, and n. 20 on the Russian Formalists.

[73] J. Griffin, 'The Social Function of Attic Tragedy', *Classical Quarterly*, 48/1 (1998), 39-61, is a spirited attack on the narrower historicizing tendencies prevalent in criticism of Greek tragedy, although Griffin's opening hint at the importance of the individual poet is not followed through. For a cautious approach to 'Augustan' readings of Virgil, see the beginning of D. P. Fowler, 'Opening the Gates of War: *Aeneid* 7. 601-640', in *Roman Constructions* (Oxford, 2000), 173-92.

deconstruction and Rortian relativism, no less than structuralism or reader-response theory, also reveal a conception of literature as being instrumental to some other design. Such approaches inevitably highlight the methods of analysis or aporias of these perspectives, as well as—or instead of—the supposed themes of the texts that are subject to scrutiny. This is not always a bad thing, but unimaginative implementations of narratology or muddled customizations of intertextuality have sometimes led to the same story being told time and time again about one text after another.

The formalist and pragmatic tendencies in modern and contemporary criticism are, in many respects, akin to much writing in antiquity. Sometimes the correspondences between ancient and modern criticism exist not by coincidence but because of a direct inheritance. The roots of Nietzsche's exploration of discourse and power which influenced late twentieth-century theory, for instance, are laid bare in his lectures on classical rhetoric; Foucault's critique of the 'author' was derived partly from an examination of ancient and medieval categories.[74] Even more conspicuous is the explicit dependence, already noted, of a divergent body of recent literary theory on ancient poetical and rhetorical concepts and terminology.[75] In classical studies, there have been some explicit attempts made to syncretize aspects of ancient theory of discourse with these more recent developments: the elucidation of narratological categories in ancient theory and the endeavour to identify analogues for intertextuality in antiquity have been among them.[76]

---

[74] The lectures are edited and translated in S. Gilman, C. Blair, and D. Parent, *Friedrich Nietzsche on Rhetoric and Language* (Oxford and New York, 1988); Michel Foucault's essay 'What is an Author?' can be found in D. Preziosi (ed.), *The Art of Art History: A Critical Anthology* (Oxford, 1988), 299–314, and in other collections.

[75] Prominent examples include: R. Barthes, 'The Old Rhetoric: An Aide-Mémoire', in *The Semiotic Challenge* (New York, 1988), 11–94, and *A Lover's Discourse: Fragments*, tr. R. Howard (London, 2002); G. Genette, *Figures I–III* (Paris, 1966–72); J. Kristeva, *Sêmiôtikê: Recherches pour une Sémanalyse* (Paris, 1969); P. Ricoeur, *Time and Narrative I–III*, tr. K. McLaughlin and D. Pellauer (Chicago, 1984–8); T. Todorov, *Theories of the Symbol*, tr. C. Porter (Oxford, 1982).

[76] Attempts by classicists to reconcile modern narrative theory with ancient criticism include: M. Fantuzzi, *Ricerche su Apollonio Rodio: Diacronie della dizione epica* (Rome, 1988); M. Fusillo, '"Mythos" aristotelico e "récit" narratologico', *Strumenti critici*, 52/1/3 (1986), 381–92; A. Laird, *Powers of Expression* (Oxford, 1999); C. Lazzerini, 'Historia/Fabula: Forma della costruzione poetica Virgiliana nel commento di Servio all'Eneide', *Materiali e Discussione*, 12 (1984), 17–44. On an ancient notion of intertextuality, see G. D'Ippolito, 'Il concetto di intertestualità nel

## IV

In academic writing at least, the idea of 'literary criticism' is a good deal less prominent than it was fifty years ago. Contemporary critical discourse appears to share a major characteristic of Greek and Roman criticism: insights on literature *tout court* are often once again a by-product of extraneous fields of enquiry. For instance, a widespread preoccupation with the 'rhetorical strategies' of narrative (including historical narrative) has accompanied a reduction of interest in theorizing about *fiction*, when fiction is now very much bound up with the more everyday conceptions of literature—for many people 'literature' and 'fiction' are effectively synonymous.[77] This reluctance to accommodate theories of fiction may not be unconnected with the diminution of the standing of literature in much current thinking.[78]

Anyway it is clear enough that many academics today, not unlike ancient philosophers and rhetoricians, use literary texts to illuminate more general linguistic, aesthetic, ethical, or political ideas and principles. More commonly still—and especially so in the study of classics—the activity of criticism can itself become a form of historiography. It is not just that information about the cultural context of a text is deemed a necessary foundation for its explication: that was realized by Renaissance commentators long before it became a

pensiero degli antichi' in V. Bécares Botas, P. Pordomingo, and R. Cortés-Tovar (eds.), *Intertextualidad en las literaturas griega y latina* (Classica Salmanticensia, 2; Madrid, 2000), 13–32. R. Meijering, *Literary and Rhetorical Theories in the Greek Scholia* (Groningen, 1987) and M. S. Silk, *Interaction in Poetic Imagery* (Cambridge, 1974) also offer syntheses of ancient and modern ideas. For current presuppositions about ancient views of genre, see Rosenmeyer in this volume.

   [77] The theory of fiction, after all, involves theoretically awkward considerations of reference, truth-status, and content which are currently the considerations of analytic philosophers rather than literary theorists and critics: see my own discussion, 'Fiction, Philosophy, and Logical Closure', in S. Heyworth (ed.), *Classical Constructions* (Oxford, 2005). P. Lamarque and S. Olsen (eds.), *Truth, Fiction and Literature* (Oxford, 1994) and C. New, *Philosophy of Literature* (London and New York, 1999) are accessible introductions to the issues.

   [78] Here it is interesting to compare the practice of ancient criticism, which (operating without any category of literature) mainly addressed historiography, oratory, and poetry, and had only a limited grasp of the idea of fiction. The essays in C. Gill and T. P. Wiseman (eds.), *Lies and Fiction in the Ancient World* (Exeter, 1993) offer a variety of perspectives. See 'Fiction' in Suggestions for Further Reading, 10.

precondition for modern classical scholarship.[79] Rather there is an increasing tendency among scholars of classics and of other literatures to regard—or at least to present—important or canonical literary works as nothing more than discourses of evidence which serve to shed light on the past.

But establishing the historical significance of a text, however important that text might be for its own time or for subsequent times, is not the same as criticism, even though these two activities are often confused. The exposure of this confusion helps to point to a key characteristic of discussion of literature in antiquity: ancient authorities, whether they are concerned with poetics, rhetoric, or philosophy, frequently subject authors, texts, and individual passages to aesthetic or at least stylistic evaluation. Current discourses on literature, on the other hand, tend to avoid aesthetic evaluation altogether.[80]

Evaluation, as well as being prominent in writing on rhetoric and oratory, was part and parcel of the original Hellenistic notion of 'criticism': the judgement (*krisis*) of poems was a fundamental activity for grammarians. The Roman poet Horace, who often appears to have been making prescriptions for practising poets of his day, is probably singlehandedly responsible for transmitting those canons of Hellenistic evaluation to the later literary traditions in Europe and beyond. The importance Horace attaches to elegance, decorum, hard work, innovation, and the imitation of good models (in the *Satires* and in other epistles as well as in the *Ars Poetica*) very much affected the way poetry came to be regarded and judged from the Renaissance onwards. Of course ancient evaluations have their problems and discontents: Quintilian is an example of an authority who frequently makes value judgements about poetry, language, oratory, and the ideal orator—judgements which are not cashed out in terms that satisfy the conventions and demands of contemporary critical discourse.

[79] For a discussion and demonstration of this in the case of La Cerda's magisterial Latin commentary on Virgil (1642) which is still a vital resource for modern scholars, see R. Gibson and C. Kraus (eds.), *The Classical Commentary* (Leiden, 2002), 171–203.

[80] Contrast Gary Day's arguments in the introduction to G. Day and B. Docherty (eds.), *British Poetry from the 1950s to the 1990s: Politics and Art* (London, 1997). B. Herrnstein Smith, 'Value/Evaluation', in F. Lentricchia and T. McLaughlin (eds.), *Critical Terms for Literary Study* (2nd edn. Chicago, 1995), 177–85, probably represents the orthodoxy in contemporary literary studies. See also S. J. Kahn, 'Evaluation', in the *Princeton Encyclopedia of Poetry and Poetics* (Princeton, 1965), 259–64.

But to defend the notion of evaluation is not, as is often believed, to seek to institute an unselfconscious, connoisseurish form of critical appreciation which takes no cognizance of its (far more general) ends or foundations. In his 1935 essay *Religion and Literature*, T. S. Eliot conceded that 'the "greatness" of literature cannot be determined solely by literary standards'. 'Though', he went on to say, 'we must remember that whether it is literature or not can be determined only by literary standards.' It would be satisfying if what was literature could be determined by purely literary standards, but a lot rests here on what those 'literary standards' are supposed to be. Nonetheless it is important to continue bearing in mind that 'literature' itself is a value-laden category as well as a descriptive one. So too is 'poetry', and so too are most prominent genres that have names: tragedy, epic, lyric, novels, and so on. Without evaluation, literature simply would not exist. It is a sobering thought that not just the canonization but the very survival of countless works must have depended on the evaluations that ancient critics were prepared to make.

For any culture, criticism probably has to follow rather than precede actual literary production, but it is remarkable how little time it took for criticism to appear in Greece—especially if conceptions of poetry were articulated in Homer. All the same, in spite of the early prominence of criticism in the European literary tradition, it is obvious that modern evaluations do *not* depend on specific judgements made (on whatever bases) by ancient critics. It is my own view that some of the greatest benefits of classical criticism emerge if we consider the wider aspects of its *legacy*, or its reception. This is not to say that the methods and observations of one or another authority in antiquity lack interest in themselves. And the circumstances and conditions which might have led to those verdicts or observations are of historical significance too. But the potent effects of some ancient insights can be lost if we only engage in the activity of reconstructing them. As is the case with classical literature in general, much more can be gleaned from the discourse of ancient criticism if it becomes the subject of active evaluation (in the light of our own realizations) as well as being the object of more passive methods of description.

This can be shown by some examples. Aristotle's famous remark in the *Poetics* (9. 1451ᵃ) that 'poetry is more like philosophy and more worthwhile than history since poetry tends to make general statements' seems to have few parallels or subsequent endorsements in antiquity. But this has not diminished the perception of the importance of that remark for later readers—even for those commentators on Aristotle who are primarily concerned with the *Poetics* in its original context. On the other hand, few scholars are aware that a theoretical distinction between poetry and visual art made by Servius was the direct source for Lessing's highly influential attack on the *ut pictura poesis* principle in his *Laocoön* (1766).[81] And the comparison made in that Horatian tag ('as for a picture so for poetry')—very possibly provisional or capricious in its conception—really acquired its significance through reception.[82]

Connections and parallels between different sources become more apparent when ancient literary criticism is regarded phenomenologically (as it appears to us) rather than ontologically (in terms of whatever it actually is or was). For instance, the Pheidias commonplace which Philostratus and Plotinus used to explain the nature of artistic imagination (see section II above) is employed to a different, more local end in Cicero's *Orator*—to justify cherishing the ideal of perfect eloquence even if we can never actually hear it.[83] Two different functions of the same commonplace in antiquity—one rhetorical and one philosophical—once they are absorbed in a later tradition can end up fusing to acquire a new momentum. Indeed, the

---

[81] The distinction is made in a comment on *Aeneid* 8. 625: *non enarrabile textum* ('the un-narratable fabric'—from the description of Aeneas' shield). Acccording to Servius, a poet narrating the *process of artistic production* (*singula dum fiunt narrantur*) is bound to preserve the pace of his narrative and this means that there is not enough time to allow the reader to visualize the artwork. But if the poet describes the *finished artwork* (*pro perfecto opere*) in enough detail to render it so that it can be visualized, he can no longer be meeting the demands of narrative time: 'because it does not seem that the pace of narration could have been drawn out and the artwork at the same time so swiftly brought out that it could come to meet the word.' (*quia non videtur simul et narrationis celeritas potuisse conecti et opus tam velociter expediri, ut ad verbum posset occurrere*). For Lessing, 'succession of time is the domain of the poet, space is the domain of the painter': Homer thus sensibly recounts the origin and manufacturing of the shield rather than the completed picture (which is the province of visual art rather than poetry). Lessing, tr. E. McCormick (Indianapolis, 1962), 215-17, acknowledges that his distinction between the shields of Homer and Virgil was first made by Servius, although he does not seem to grasp everything Servius is saying.

[82] See e.g. R. W. Lee, *Ut Pictura Poesis: The Humanistic Theory of Painting* (New York, 1967); N. Schweizer, *The Ut Pictura Poesis Controversy in Eighteenth-Century England and Germany* (Frankfurt am Main, 1972).

[83] Cicero, *Orator* 8-9.

Neoplatonic doctrine that poetry imitates a divine archetype, and not a material model, came to elevate the status of poetry (and, by implication, the status of literature in general). This doctrine was prominent in the Renaissance, and it gained even more currency in the Romantic period because of its relation to Kantian idealism.[84]

Consider, too, the following observation by a Renaissance humanist. It seems routine to us, if only because of its resemblance to the remark in Aristotle's *Poetics* (quoted earlier) about poetry making general statements:

Plautus atque Terencius . . . volentes tamen arte sua diversorum hominum mores et verba describere . . . Et hec si de facto non fuerint, cum communia sint esse potuere vel possent.[85]

Plautus and Terence . . . intend by their art to outline the habits and conversations of different kinds of people . . . Even if these things they portray have not actually happened, since they are common, they could have happened or could still do so.

Yet the *Poetics* was not a text to which this writer had access. Instead Boccaccio was probably prompted to think along these lines by a characterization of comedy in the *Ad Herennium*, the rhetorical treatise attributed to Cicero. Boccaccio endows that textbook characterization with a new and important role: it helps him to justify the reading of pagan literature to a potentially hostile Church.[86]

We might chide the critics of antiquity for failing to comment on the universal objects of literary representation (or to put it another

---

[84] Kant's *Critique of Judgment* (1790) argued that the categories of the understanding are subjective and 'ideal': the freedom to shape impressions of transcendent reality could then be equated with a creative inspiration which revealed harmonies between the processes of nature and processes of art. See J. Hankins, *Plato in the Italian Renaissance* (Leiden, 1990); ch 10 of R. Wellek and A. Warren, *A Theory of Literature* (3rd edn. London, 1963); and Abrams, Behler, and Weinberg in Suggestions for Further Reading, 7, 'Literary Criticism and Theory in the Classical Tradition'.

[85] *Genealogiae Deorum Gentilium* 14. 9. This text is from J. Reedy, *Boccaccio in Defence of Poetry: Genealogiae Deorum Gentilium Liber XIV* (Toronto, 1978).

[86] *Ad Herennium* 1. 13, tr. H. Caplan: 'The kind of narrative based on the exposition of the facts has three forms: legendary (*fabula*), historical (*historia*), and realistic (*argumentum*). The legendary tale comprises events neither true nor probable, like those transmitted by tragedies. The historical narrative is an account of exploits actually performed but removed in time from the recollection of our age. Realistic narrative recounts imaginary events, which yet could have occurred like the plots of comedies. (*argumentum est ficta res quae tamen fieri potuit, velut argumenta comoediorum*).' Compare Cicero, *De inventione* 1. 27, *Pro Sexto Roscio Amerino* 47, and Quintilian, *Institutio* 2. 4. 2.

way, on the general insights afforded by literary texts) without lapsing into crude allegory. But at the same time it is important to recognize that modern ideas of literature would not exist without ancient literary criticism—any more than humanism would have come about if there had been no Ciceronian category of *humanitas*. Few things in literary history, if any, are without precedent.

This chapter has sought to assert the value of ancient criticism for its legacy in later poetics, for its applicability to contemporary theory, and for its capacity to legitimize the notion of value for our own thinking. Most of the chapters to follow are concerned with more specific questions but their presuppositions are mostly in line with the observations made here. It was noted at the beginning of this discussion that the gradual institution of ancient literary criticism as a circumscribed field of enquiry illustrated a change in the nature of the classical tradition as a whole. That tradition, which was once a fundamental part of our own literary culture has now become something more remote, something which has fallen into the hands of the specialist. And the specialist is bound to be preoccupied with the problem of reconstruction, with recovering the ideas and concepts which the ancient writers expressed and with which they worked.

But that very process of reconstruction is always fraught with problems of principle, method, and data—problems which are acute in the fields of Greek and Roman criticism. Key terms of varying orders (*mimesis, ethos, phantasia, apostrophe*) could be defined differently or openly contested in antiquity by authors working in distinct times, places, and traditions. The study of ancient literary criticism will never be an exact science. Those who are involved in such study find themselves working in an area of classical studies which combines the challenge of translation with the intellectual hazards of ethnography—the differences between ancient and modern categories constantly interfere. And like all classical authors, the critics of antiquity elude decisive interpretation: in this respect those ancient critics will always remain some steps ahead of us. Not the least of their contributions to the humanities might yet be to save Literature from being sacrificed on the altar of Utility.

# 2
# Poetic Inspiration in Early Greece

## PENELOPE MURRAY

It is generally agreed that the concept of inspiration is one of the most basic and persistent of Greek notions about poetry. Yet there appears to be a certain confusion on the significance of this observation. For instance, while most scholars consider that the idea is of very great antiquity in Greece, there is a recent tendency to regard the concept as a formulation of the fifth century BC. E. A. Havelock, for example, describes the notion of poetic inspiration as an invention of fifth-century philosophers,[1] and G. S. Kirk states, without discussion, that poetic inspiration was 'probably quite a new conception' at the time Euripides was writing.[2] This type of disagreement clearly relates to the more fundamental question of the meaning of the concept of inspiration itself. For although there is an apparent consensus that ancient notions of poetic inspiration correspond in some way to certain modern ideas about the nature of poetic creativity, little attention has been paid to these modern notions of inspiration. And unless such modern notions are investigated, the mere observation that there is a similarity is of little value.[3]

In this paper I consider the idea of poetic inspiration in early Greek literature from Homer to Pindar. Despite variations in the views of

---

[1] *Preface to Plato* (Oxford, 1963), 156. This and the following works are cited by author's name alone: E. R. Dodds, *The Greeks and the Irrational* (Berkeley, 1951); R. Harriott, *Poetry and Criticism before Plato* (London, 1969); G. Lanata, *Poetica pre-Platonica* (Florence, 1963); H. Maehler, *Die Auffassung des Dichterberufs im frühen Griechentum* (Göttingen, 1963). Translations are my own unless otherwise stated.

[2] *The Bacchae* (New Jersey, 1970), 10.

[3] Those scholars who have discussed the subject of poetic inspiration in general have confused rather than clarified the ancient position. C. M. Bowra, for example, in his Rede Lecture on *Inspiration and Poetry* (London, 1955) discusses the writing habits of many modern poets and makes some interesting observations on poetic inspiration. But elsewhere he uses his knowledge of the creative processes of modern poets to make inferences about ancient poets which are purely speculative. See e.g. *Pindar* (Oxford, 1964), 8-10, 13.

individual poets (related, no doubt, to changes in the function and social status of the poet during this period)[4] the early Greek poets share certain basic assumptions about the nature of poetic creativity, and can therefore be treated together as a group. My aim in what follows is to clarify these basic assumptions, and therefore the early Greek concept of poetic inspiration.

It seems to me that there are in particular two theoretical issues in need of analysis, both fundamental to our understanding of ancient views of poetic creativity. The first is the frequent assumption that inspiration necessarily involves ecstasy or possession, and that the inspired poet takes no conscious part in the process of composition, but is merely the passive instrument of some overwhelming force. An important consequence of this assumption is that inspiration and craft or technique are seen as incompatible. All this is, of course, true of Plato's concept of poetic inspiration as *enthousiasmos* or *mania*: throughout his work Plato describes the inspired poet as a passive instrument who knows nothing of what he is saying and who cannot explain the source or the meaning of his poetry.[5] But there is no evidence to suggest that the early Greek poets thought of inspiration in this way. In fact *this* concept of poetic inspiration as a kind of ecstatic madness—*furor poeticus*—appears to be no older than the fifth century.[6] Nevertheless certain scholars persist in equating early Greek notions of inspiration with the Platonic concept of *furor poeticus*. For example, E. Barmeyer[7] refers to the traditional Greek notion 'according to which the inspired poet loses himself and is overcome by divine enthusiasm' and M. Fuhrmann[8] speaks of the 'typically Greek concept of poetic creativity as madness, transport or

---

[4] See e.g. Maehler, *passim*; J. Svenbro, *La parole et le marbre. Aux origines de la poétique grecque* (Lund, 1976).

[5] The most important texts are: *Ion passim*; *Ap.* 22a-c; *Men.* 99c-e; *Phdr.* 245; *Leg.* 682a, 719c-d.

[6] Archil. *fr.* 120 W can be related to the idea of poetic *mania*, as several scholars have rightly pointed out; but perhaps one should not press Archilochus too far towards a general *furor poeticus*: it is the *dithyramb* he can create when lightning-struck by wine. The old analogy between poetry and prophecy, and in particular the use of verse as a medium for prophecy at Delphi, is also relevant to the origins of the notion of *furor poeticus*. But the first firm evidence that we have for such a notion dates from the fifth century. See Dodds 82; E. N. Tigerstedt, 'Furor Poeticus: Poetic Inspiration in Greek Literature before Democritus and Plato'. *JHI* 31/2 (1970), 163-78

[7] *Die Musen: Ein Beitrag zur Inspirationstheorie* (Munich, 1968), 102.

[8] *Einführung in die antike Dichtungstheorie* (Darmstadt, 1973), 73-4.

intoxication, as the poet being out of his mind (ecstasy) or being filled with the god (enthusiasm)'. A particularly good example of confusion is provided by Havelock.[9] He rightly notes that the notion of possession is absent from early Greek poetry, but consequently concludes that the notion of inspiration is equally absent. Before the fifth century, on his view, poetry was thought of as a craft; the 'contrary conception' of poetic inspiration was invented in the fifth century. In other words Havelock assumes both that inspiration and possession are identical and that inspiration and technique are incompatible. He does not recognise any concept of poetic inspiration other than Plato's,[10] nor does he appear to entertain the possibility that the concept was conceived of in different ways at different periods in antiquity.

In fact modern studies of the creative process show that there are different kinds of inspiration, both in theory and in practice.[11] The experience which gives rise to the concept has been described by many different poets at different periods. Obviously the experience differs from poet to poet, but an essential feature of it is the feeling that poetry comes from some source other than the conscious mind. In its most mild form inspiration is simply the moment when a thought or phrase spontaneously presents itself to the poet as the starting point of a poem.[12] Although the initial inspiration appears to come to the poet as if from some source other than himself, the

[9] 156.

[10] One reason for this concentration on Plato is, I suspect, that modern notions of inspiration (which are largely Romantic) bear more resemblance to the Platonic concept of inspiration than to anything which we find in the early Greek poets. Compare, for example, Socrates' well-known words about the inability of the inspired poet to understand his own creations with the following statement of Thomas Carlyle: 'Manufacture is intelligible, but trivial; Creation is great, but cannot be understood. Thus if the Debater and Demonstrator, whom we may rank as the lowest of true thinkers, knows what he has done, and how he did it, the Artist, whom we may rank as the highest, knows not; he must speak of Inspiration, and in one or other dialect, call his work the gift of a divinity' (*Characteristics* (1831), in R. A. Foakes (ed.), *Romantic Criticism: 1800-1850* (London, 1968), 145).

[11] See e.g. R. E. M. Harding, *An Anatomy of Inspiration*[2] (Cambridge, 1942); B. Ghiselin, *The Creative Process* (Berkeley, 1952); J. Press, *The Fire and the Fountain* (London, 1966); P. E. Vernon (ed.), *Creativity* (London, 1970), 53–88; K. Dick (ed.), *Writers at Work* (Penguin, 1972).

[12] See e.g. C. Day Lewis's account in *The Listener*, 28 April, 1966: 'For me, at any rate, "inspiration" is the moment when some phrase comes to me out of the blue and offers itself as a seed from which a poem may grow. This seed, clue, donnée, whatever, as you call it, swims up into my mind, not usually as an idea, but in a form of words.'

subsequent composition of the poem depends on conscious effort and hard work. At the other extreme inspiration can be a much more shattering experience, involving any one or more of the following features. The poet composes with great ease and fluency, sometimes with extreme speed. No subsequent revision is necessary. Composition may be accompanied by an unusually heightened state, variously described as frenzy, intoxication, enthusiasm or ecstasy. Such a state can only be temporary and does not depend on the will of the poet. When inspiration ceases, the poet is amazed at what he has written, and can only describe himself as the instrument of some higher power.[13]

The basic feature in all these experiences of inspiration seems to be the feeling of dependence on some source other than the conscious mind. We might perhaps distinguish between two types of inspiration, one of which involves ecstasy, the other of which does not,[14] but these two types are merely the opposite ends of a spectrum, and within this spectrum there are many different kinds of inspiration. It is a mistake therefore to assume that inspiration either in theory or in practice necessarily involves total abandonment of responsibility for his creation on the part of the poet. And it is certainly a mistake to impute such notions to the early Greek poets, as I shall show.

The second issue which needs clarification concerns the definition of, and the distinction between, the concepts of poetic inspiration and poetic genius. Inspiration can be broadly defined as the temporary impulse to poetic creation, and relates primarily to the poetic process. Genius is a permanent quality on which poetic creativity depends and relates primarily to the poetic personality. These ideas are similar in that they both account for the element in the poetic process which is felt to be inexplicable, and both can be contrasted with the technical aspects of composition. But they are basically distinct from each other. The one—poetic inspiration—accounts for poetic creativity in

[13] See e.g. Rilke's description of the way in which his *Sonnets to Orpheus* were written (*Briefe* (Wiesbaden, 1950), ii. 412): 'They are perhaps the most secret and mysterious dictation that I have ever experienced in the way that they arose and were laid upon me; the whole first part was written down in a single breathless act of obedience between the 2nd and the 5th February 1922 without any word being changed or in doubt.' Cf. Nietzsche's comments on inspiration in *Ecce Homo* (1888), tr. W. Kaufmann (New York 1969), 300-1. Sceptics may like to note T. S. Eliot's comment in *Selected Essays*[3] (London, 1951), 405.

[14] A distinction between two types of inspiration is also made by Harding (n. 11) 65, and by Stephen Spender in Ghiselin (n. 11), 114-15.

terms of a temporary visitation from some external, or seemingly external, force; the other in terms of permanent qualities inherent in the poet. The beginnings of both of these ideas are, I suggest, discernible as early as Homer, and failure to distinguish between them has clouded our understanding of ancient views of poetic creativity.[15]

## THE MUSES

In early Greek poetry inspiration is, of course, characteristically expressed in terms of the Muses. I shall not discuss here the question of how the idea of the Muses originated,[16] but I take it that whatever else the Muses stand for they symbolise the poet's feeling of dependence on the external: they are the personification of his inspiration. The Muses inspire the bard in two main ways: (a) they give him *permanent* poetic ability; (b) they provide him with *temporary* aid in composition. Homer and the early Greek poets in general do not distinguish between these two ideas, neither do classical scholars. But they are nevertheless distinguishable. In fact they are the forerunners of the two concepts, outlined above, which account for the inexplicable element in poetic creation. The Muses' gift of permanent poetic ability corresponds to the explanation of creativity in terms of the poetic personality; their temporary aid in composition corresponds to the explanation of creativity in terms of the poetic process.

Homer expresses the first idea, permanent poetic ability, by saying that the Muses love bards, teach them and give them the gift of poetry. Typical of this attitude is the description of Demodocus at *Od.* viii. 44–5:

> τῷ γάρ ῥα θεὸς πέρι δῶκεν ἀοιδὴν
> τέρπειν, ὅππῃ ἐποτρύνῃσιν ἀείδειν.

to him above all others has the god given the gift of song, to give pleasure in whatever way his spirit moves him to sing.

Homer does not tell us precisely what the gift of poetry entails, nor does he speculate as to the reasons for its bestowal. But evidently it is

---

[15] See below, n. 17.
[16] The etymology of the word *mousa* is uncertain. See e.g. Maehler's summary of the problem, 16–17, n. 5. For general information on the Muses see e.g. M. Mayer, *RE* 16 (1933), 680–757; W. Otto, *Die Musen* (Darmstadt, 1956); Harriott 10–33.

a permanent gift of poetic ability, rather than a temporary inspiration. Failure to recognise this can be exemplified by Harriott's discussion of the gift idiom: 'the Greeks expressed the belief that poetry is in some mysterious way "given", and that it comes from a source external to the poet and is other than he is. This view of inspiration is still current, although partly replaced by psychological theories in which poetry is held to emanate from the unconscious mind.'[17] There is a difference between lines of poetry being 'given' to a poet and the 'gift' of poetic ability, which are here confused. I shall discuss elsewhere the full implications of the uses of the gift idiom to denote the bestowal of permanent poetic ability, and the relationship of the idea to the concept of poetic genius. For the purposes of this paper I wish merely to point out this difference between the temporary inspiration and the permanent gift of poetry which the Muses grant, and the fact that we can discern here the beginnings of a distinction between the concepts of poetic inspiration and poetic genius.

We gather that the Muse is believed to inspire the bard in a temporary sense from, for example, the description of Demodocus at *Od.* viii 73, where the Muse provides the immediate impulse to song: Μοῦσ' ἄρ' ἀοιδὸν ἀνῆκεν ἀειδέμεναι κλέα ἀνδρῶν (The Muse moved the bard to sing of the glorious deeds of men).[18] The invocations to the Muses—a traditional feature of early Greek poetry—also imply the notion of temporary inspiration. Sometimes the poet simply asks the Muse to help him begin, or to join in his song. But often the poet asks the Muse for something specific, such as knowledge of events, or sweetness in song.[19] We can look at these invocations in two ways: (a) in pragmatic terms, that is, in terms of their significance for an audience, (b) in terms of the poet's need for divine assistance. Undoubtedly ancient poets use invocations to establish their

---

[17] 50-1. For confusion over the concepts of inspiration and genius see e.g. E. E. Sikes, *The Greek View of Poetry* (London, 1931), 20; G. M. A. Grube, *The Greek and Roman Critics* (Toronto, 1965), 9; A. Sperduti, 'The Divine Nature of Poetry in Antiquity', *TAPA* 81 (1950), 233.

[18] The same idea may also be expressed at *Od.* viii 499: ὁ δ' ὁρμηθεὶς θεοῦ ἄρχετο, φαῖνε δ' ἀοιδήν. The problem is whether to take θεοῦ with ὁρμηθεὶς or with ἄρχετο. It could mean either (a) 'he, moved by the goddess, began his song' or (b) 'he, starting, began with the goddess' i.e. started with an invocation. See the discussions of e.g. O. Falter, *Der Dichter und sein gott bei den Griechen and Römern* (Würzburg, 1934), 9; Harriott 42. And cf. Pi. *fr.* 151.

[19] On invocations in early Greek poetry see e.g. Falter (n. 18) 4-7, 12, 18-23, 34-50; Harriott 41-9, 72-7.

authority, to guarantee the truth of their words, and to focus the attention of the audience at strategic points. But the invocations also express the poet's belief in divine inspiration. The point at which the appeal ceases to be genuine is, of course, problematic. But a comparison between the invocations of the early Greek poets and those of their literary successors strongly suggests that the former spring from a real, religious belief in the Muses.[20]

KNOWLEDGE

It has often been pointed out that the invocations in Homer are essentially requests for information, which the Muses, as daughters of Memory, provide. This is clear from the detailed invocation before the catalogue of ships:

Ἔσπετε νῦν μοι, Μοῦσαι Ὀλύμπια δώματ' ἔχουσαι—
ὑμεῖς γὰρ θεαί ἐστε, πάρεστέ τε, ἴστε τε πάντα,
ἡμεῖς δὲ κλέος οἶον ἀκούομεν οὐδέ τι ἴδμεν—
οἵ τινες ἡγεμόνες Δαναῶν καὶ κοίρανοι ἦσαν.
πληθὺν δ' οὐκ ἂν ἐγὼ μυθήσομαι οὐδ' ὀνομήνω,
οὐδ' εἴ μοι δέκα μὲν γλῶσσαι, δέκα δὲ στόματ' εἶεν,
φωνὴ δ' ἄρρηκτος, χάλκεον δέ μοι ἦτορ ἐνείη,
εἰ μὴ Ὀλυμπιάδες Μοῦσαι, Διὸς αἰγιόχοιο
θυγατέρες, μνησαίαθ' ὅσοι ὑπὸ Ἴλιον ἦλθον.    (Il. ii. 484-92)[21]

Tell me now, Muses who dwell on Olympus—for you are goddesses, you are there, you know everything, while we hear only repute and know nothing—tell me who were the leaders and princes of the Danoi. Their number I could not tell or name, no, not if I had ten tongues and ten mouths, a voice that would not tire, a heart of bronze, if the Olympian Muses, daughters of aegis-

[20] On this see e.g. R. Häussler, 'Der Tod der Musen', AuA 19 (1973), 117–45; S. Commager, The Odes of Horace (Indiana, 1967), 2–16.

[21] Harriott (40) appears to miss the point of these lines. The bard does not speak 'as if his physical strength will not be equal to the long task of recounting the participants in the war', but rather stresses that, however great his physical strength, he will not be able to recall the necessary information without the prompting of the Muses. The contrast made here for the first time between divine knowledge and human ignorance is a persistent theme in early Greek literature. See e.g. Ibyc. fr. 1. 23–6; Sol. fr. 17; Xenoph. fr. 34; Pi. N. vii 23–4, Pa. vi 50–8, viib 15–20; B. Snell, The Discovery of the Mind, trans. T. G. Rosenmeyer (New York 1960), 136–52. Invocations in Homeric epic occur elsewhere at Il. i 1, ii 761, xi 218, xiv 508, xvi 112; Od. i 1. Cf. also the quasi-invocations at Il. v. 703, viii 273, xi 299, xvi 692. For scholarship on Homeric invocations see Harriott 44.

bearing Zeus, did not tell me how many there were who went to Troy. (trans. Russell)

Some scholars, however, evidently think that it is misleading to connect information with inspiration. Havelock, for example, says that the invocation quoted above 'shows how true it is that the Muses symbolise the minstrel's need of memory and his power to preserve memory, not a spiritual inspiration, which would certainly be inappropriate to a muster-list'.[22] And W. W. Minton observes that in the Homeric invocations 'the poet does not ask for help or guidance in "how" he shall tell his story; there is no suggestion of a plea for "inspiration"; only for information'.[23] Neither scholar makes it clear what he means by 'inspiration': but whatever it is, they both agree that it is incompatible with factual content in poetry. But why should inspiration not include, or even consist of, information? In fact, as Minton himself points out, the Chadwicks have shown that much early oral poetry associated with the 'poet-seer' is informational in character, and that traces which suggest that such 'seer-poets' once existed in Greece have been found in both Homer and Hesiod. What Minton does not note is the Chadwicks' insistence on the widespread connexion between inspiration and information in such poetry, summarised thus by N. K. Chadwick: 'The association of inspiration and knowledge of whatever kind acquired by supernatural means is ancient and widespread. Inspiration, in fact, relates to revealed knowledge.'[24] It is not therefore a contradiction to say that the invocations in Homer are requests for inspiration—even though the inspiration might consist largely of information.

The association of the Muses with knowledge of one sort or another continued throughout the early period. It was, amongst other things, Demodocus' knowledge of the *facts* of the Achaean expedition which caused Odysseus to wonder at the bard: he must have been taught by the Muse or Apollo[25] since he sang of the fate of the Achaeans as if he himself had been present, or as if he had heard from someone else (*Od.* viii. 487–91). Hesiod depicted the Muses on

---

[22] 177.

[23] 'Invocation and Catalogue in Hesiod and Homer', *TAPA* 93 (1962), 190.

[24] *Poetry and Prophecy* (Cambridge, 1942), 41.

[25] As e.g. W. Marg points out, *Homer über die Dichtung* (Münster, 1957), 10, the precise significance of this alternative is now lost to us. But the overlapping of the domains of Apollo and the Muses clearly stresses the importance of knowledge and truth in the poetry of this period.

Mount Olympus singing of past, present and future (*Th.* 36–40) and clearly the gift of poetry which the Muses bestowed on their chosen bards involved the power of true speech. When the Muses made Hesiod a poet they told him that they could reveal the truth when they wished:

ἴδμεν ψεύδεα πολλὰ λέγειν ἐτύμοισιν ὁμοῖα,
ἴδμεν δ᾽, εὖτ᾽ ἐθέλωμεν, ἀληθέα γηρύσασθαι.    (*Th.* 27–8)

We know how to tell many lies that resemble the truth, but we know also how to tell the truth when we wish. (trans. Russell)

These ambiguous lines have been variously interpreted,[26] but what cannot be disputed is the fact that the Muses are here represented as having the power to tell the truth. The chief difficulty is to determine the precise nature of the distinction drawn between truth (ἀληθέα) and plausible fiction (ψεύδεα . . . ἐτύμοισιν ὁμοῖα). The conventional, and I think the correct, interpretation is that Hesiod is here contrasting the true content of his own poetry with the plausible fiction of Homeric epic. West rejects this interpretation on the grounds that 'no Greek ever regarded the Homeric epics as substantially fiction'. But Homer *was* criticised for misrepresenting the truth.[27] Harriott's suggestion that in these lines Hesiod is faithfully reporting the Muses' warning that if he were to offend he would be punished by being 'misled into recording a lying vision'[28] seems to me to be singularly unlikely: Hesiod would hardly preface his work with a warning that what followed might be untrue; on the contrary, the proem to the *Theogony* is surely to be regarded as a plea for the infallibility of the poem as a whole. There is, of course, an important difference between the kinds of knowledge bestowed by the Muses in Homer and in Hesiod. The knowledge which Homer's Muses grant is primarily knowledge of the past—that is, knowledge as opposed to ignorance. Hesiod's Muses, on the other hand, are responsible for both truth and falsehood: what they give Hesiod is true knowledge as

[26] See e.g. K. Latte, 'Hesiods Dichterweihe', *AuA* 2 (1946), 159–63; Lanata 24–5 and bibliography there; Maehler 41; A. Kambylis, *Die Dichterweihe und ihre Symbolik* (Heidelberg, 1965), 62–3; West *ad loc.*; W. J. Verdenius, 'Notes on the Proem of Hesiod's Theogony', *Mnem.* 25 (1972), 234–5; P. Pucci, *Hesiod and the Language of Poetry* (Baltimore, 1977), 9–16.

[27] See e.g. Pi. *N.* vii 20–4; Heraclit. *fr.* 56, cf. *fr.* 42; Xenoph. *fr.* 11; Pl. *Rep.* 377d, and in general F. Mehmel, 'Homer und die Griechen', *AuA* 4 (1954), 16–40. See also Maehler 41 and Verdenius (n. 26), 234.

[28] 113.

opposed to false. And the poet speaks with the authority of one who
believes that his knowledge comes from divine revelation.[29]
Pindar too, often claims to have special knowledge from the Muses,
as for example at *Pa.* vi 51–8:

> ταῦτα θεοῖσι [μ]έν
> πιθεῖν σοφοὺ[ς] δυνατόν,
> βροτοῖσιν δ᾽ ἀμάχανο[ν εὖ]ρέμεν·
> ἀλλὰ παρθένοι γάρ, ἴσθ᾽ ὅτ[ι], Μο[ῖ]σαι,
> πάντα, κε[λαι]νεφεῖ σὺν
> πατρὶ Μναμος[ύν]ᾳ τε
> τοῦτον ἔσχετ[ε τεθ]μόν,
> κλῦτε νῦν.[30]

The gods can persuade the wise of these things, but it is impossible for
mortals to discover them. But since you, maiden Muses, know everything—
you have had this allotted to you with the cloud-wrapped father and
Mnemosyne—listen now.

Like Hesiod, but more obsessively, Pindar insists on the truth of what
he has to say[31]—an insistence which is all the stronger because he is
acutely aware of the power of poetry to perpetrate falsehood.[32]
Pindar sees it as part of his task to combat such falsehood, and he is
able to do so because he, as prophet of the Muses, has access to
knowledge which is hidden from ordinary mortals. In similar fashion
Empedocles appeals to the Muses to give him knowledge which will
set him apart from other mortals, and he evidently regards the supernatural origin of his poetry as a guarantee of its truth.[33] In a more

---

[29] Cf. *Th.* 104–14; *Op.* 661–2.

[30] Cf. e.g. Pi. *O.* x. 1–6, xiii. 93–100; *Pa.* viib. 15–20; Ibyc. *fr.* 1. 23–6; Bacch. xv.
47.

[31] See e.g. *O.* iv. 17–18, vi. 20–1, vii. 20–1, xiii. 52 and *P.* i 86–7 on the importance of truth in general. Ἀλάθεια is invoked at *O.* x. 3–4 and at *fr.* 205. Pindar's
concern for truth is also evident in his characteristic use of arrow and javelin imagery
as at e.g. *O.* xiii. 93–5, *P.* i. 42–5, *N.* i. 18, vi. 26–7. See further Bowra, *Pindar*, 26–33;
Harriott 69–70; Maehler 96–8.

[32] See e.g. *O.* i. 28–32, *N.* vii. 20–3. In general on this persuasive power of poetry
see e.g. Harriott 117–20; J. de Romilly, 'Gorgias et le pouvoir de la poésie', *JHS* 93
(1973), 155–62.

[33] *Frr.* 3, 4, 23.11, 131. The view expressed by Falter (n. 18), 40 that Empedocles'
invocation to the Muse in *fr.* 3 is nothing but 'poetic decoration, a motif, which has
nothing to do with true belief' is rightly refuted by W. J. Verdenius, 'The Meaning of
Πίστις in Empedocles', *Mnem.*[4] 1 (1948), 10–11. Cf. P. Boyancé, *Le culte des Muses
chez les philosophes grecs* (Paris, 1936), 241. Clearly the goddess in Parmenides' proem
*fr.* 1.22–32 also guarantees the truth of his message, but she is not identified as a
Muse. See e.g. Harriott 65–7.

modest Homeric spirit, Plato trades on the traditional function of the Muses as purveyors of the truth when he remarks (albeit ironically) at *Repub.* 547a that the Hesiodic myth of the four ages of man must be true since it comes from the Muses. A. W. Allen has argued that from the first the Muses were not only the inspirers of poetry, but also the possessors of all knowledge. And he makes the pertinent point that 'as long as the range of poetry included all forms of knowledge, it fully corresponded to the range of the Muses' authority'.[34] The frequent and recurrent association of the Muses with knowledge in early Greek poetry suggests a close connection between poetic inspiration and knowledge during this period.

The ancient tradition which made the Muses the daughters of Μνημοσύνη ('Memory') is further evidence of such a connexion. The goddess Μνημοσύνη first appears as mother of the Muses in Hesiod,[35] but the connexion between memory and the Muses is already apparent in Homer's use of the verb μιμνήσκομαι of the Muses' function at *Il.* ii. 492.[36] For Plato it was a commonplace that one of the tasks of the Muses was to remind the poet, as we can see from Socrates' words at *Euthydemus* 275c: he, like the poets, must invoke Memory and the Muses in order to remember a previous conversation. Several scholars have stressed the importance of this aspect of the Muses, pointing out that at times the Muses seem to be little more than a personification of memory.[37] Havelock goes so far as to say that the Muses in Homer have nothing to do with inspiration because they 'are connected with special feats of memory'.[38] This dissociation of inspiration and memory is misguided: there is no inherent incompatibility between inspiration and information, as I have pointed out, and the fact that we might identify the source of the poet's inspiration as an internal one does not mean that the poet or his audience feels it to be so. Furthermore Havelock's contention that the Muses embody the bard's powers of *memorisation* is highly dubious, as is his

---

[34] 'Solon's Prayer to the Muses', *TAPA* 80 (1949), 65.
[35] *Th.* 53-61 with West *ad loc.* To the references there given add *Th.* 915-17; *PMG fr.* 941; Pi. *Pa.* vi. 54-6, viib. 15-16; Pl. *Theaet.* 191d; Plut. *Mor.* 9d, *frr.* 215h, 217j. See further e.g. B. Snell, 'Mnemosyne in der frühgriechischen Dichtung', *Archiv für Begriffsgeschichte*, 9 (1964), 19-21; A. Setti, 'La Memoria e il canto', *Stud. Ital.* 30 (1958), 129-71.
[36] Cf. e.g. *Certamen* 98; Pi. *N.* i. 12.
[37] See e.g. J. Duchemin, *Pindare poète et prophète* (Paris, 1955), 26.
[38] 163-4.

theory that Mnemosyne chiefly implies the notions of recall, record and memorisation.[39] The precise nature of poetic memory in early Greece has been much discussed. J.-P. Vernant, in an article entitled 'Aspects mythiques de la mémoire et du temps'[40] argued that the psychological function of memory in early Greek poetry is not to reconstruct the past accurately, but to transport the poet into the past, to give him a direct vision of 'l'ancien temps' (the past). Memory of this type, to be distinguished from historical memory, is the privilege of poets and seers, who have in common 'un même don de "voyance"' (the same gift of 'vision') As evidence for this latter statement Vernant cites the phrase τά τ' ἐόντα τά τ' ἐσσόμενα πρό τ' ἐόντα (the present, the future and the past) which is used in connexion with Calchas' prophetic skill at Il. i. 70 and of the Muses' song at Hes. Th. 38 (note that it is used of the Muses, not of Mnemosyne as Vernant states). In fact this phrase suggests that what poets and seers have in common is *knowledge* rather than vision. Of course the connexion between knowledge and sight is very close in early Greek literature—at Il. ii. 485, for example, the Muses know everything because they have seen everything[41]—but the 'don de "voyance"' (gift of 'vision') of which Vernant speaks appears to be something rather different from sight in the sense of knowledge. The poet's knowledge, he says, is the result of 'a direct personal vision. Memory transports the poet to the heart of past events', a contention which is supported by reference to Plato's *Ion* 535b-c, where Socrates asks Ion about his mental state during his rhapsodic performances:

τότε πότερον ἔμφρων εἶ ἢ ἔξω σαυτοῦ γίγνῃ καὶ παρὰ τοῖς πράγμασιν οἴεταί σου εἶναι ἡ ψυχὴ οἷς λέγεις ἐνθουσιάζουσα, ἢ ἐν Ἰθάκῃ οὖσιν ἢ ἐν Τροίᾳ ἢ ὅπως ἂν καὶ τὰ ἔπη ἔχῃ;

are you then in your right mind or are you beside yourself? And does your soul, in its enthusiasm, imagine that it is present at those events which you describe, whether in Ithaca or in Troy or wherever the epic sets the scene?

The experience here described by Socrates seems to me to be something quite different from that described by the bard at Il. ii. 484-92

---

[39] 100.

[40] *Journal de Psychologie* (1959), 1-29 repr. in *Mythe et pensée chez les Grecs* (Paris, 1974), 80-107. See also M. Detienne, *Les maîtres de vérité dans la Grèce archaïque*[2] (Paris, 1973), 15, 24-7, 110.

[41] See further Snell (n. 21).

(and, it may be added, has nothing much to do with memory). The rhapsode—and he is a rhapsode, not a poet—is transported into the scenes he evokes, but in the *Iliad* it is the Muses who see the events of the past, not the bard. Furthermore, the ecstatic state of the rhapsode has no parallel in Homer: we are simply told that the Muses were present and saw the events. The implication of the invocation, and in particular of 492, is that the Muses can communicate their knowledge to the bard, but there is no suggestion that they do so by transporting him into the past and giving him a direct vision of a bygone age. Both here and in the other references cited by Vernant[42] the poet is envisaged as being in contact with the powers of the Muses rather than actually having these powers directly himself.

Odysseus' praise of Demodocus at *Od.* viii 489-91 might appear to provide better evidence for Vernant's theory:

> λίην γὰρ κατὰ κόσμον Ἀχαιῶν οἶτον ἀείδεις,
> ὅσσ᾽ ἔρξαν τ᾽ ἔπαθόν τε καὶ ὅσσ᾽ ἐμόγησαν Ἀχαιοί,
> ὥς τέ που ἢ αὐτὸς παρεὼν ἢ ἄλλου ἀκούσας.

Very beautifully you sing the fate of the Achaeans, their deeds and sufferings and toils, as if you were there yourself or had heard from someone else. (trans. Russell)

But the possibility that the bard might have heard of the sufferings of the Achaeans from someone else is somewhat difficult to reconcile with the notion that he was given a personal vision of them. He sings κατὰ κόσμον (very beautifully), a phrase which refers as much to the form as to the content of his song: it is both true and well structured.[43] What amazes Odysseus is the reality and vividness of Demodocus' account, but this does not imply that he has visionary powers. The first of the two alternative ways in which the bard might have acquired his knowledge would be compatible with vision (although it does not imply it), but the second renders this possibility highly unlikely since information from someone else can create the same vividness as the bard's personal presence at the events. In fact it seems to me that Homer is here offering a formulation of the idea of poetic imagination as a form of visualisation, an idea which is found fully developed in Aristotle's *Poetics* ($1455^a22$) and in Longinus (15.1).[44]

---

[42] 83 n. 9.
[43] See Lanata's excellent discussion of this passage, 12-13.
[44] I hope to discuss the history of this concept in a later article.

One of the basic confusions in Vernant's argument is his failure to
distinguish between ecstatic and non-ecstatic inspiration either in
prophecy or in poetry. For example, the 'gift of vision' of which
Vernant speaks is highly appropriate to Cassandra as she is depicted
in the *Agamemnon*. In her frenzy she does have a direct and personal
vision of various episodes relating to the past, present and future of
the house of Atreus. That she actually *sees* what she describes is clear
from her words at, for example, 1125: ἰδοὺ ἰδού (Look, look!).[45] It has
long been recognised, however, that, with the exception of
Theoclymenus at *Od.* xx. 351–7, prophecy of this visionary nature is
absent from Homer. The mantis in Homer is largely concerned with
the technique of interpreting omens, not with having visionary
experiences of events inaccessible to ordinary human beings.[46]
Vernant's remarks about poetry are similarly misleading. For
example: 'Poetry constitutes one of the typical forms of possession
and divine madness, the state of "enthusiasm" in the etymological
sense of the word'. This statement is certainly true of Plato, but
one cannot use Plato as evidence for pre-Platonic views of poetry.
The notion that memory is a power of poetic or prophetic vision is,
I think, easier to reconcile with an ecstatic theory of inspiration in
which the poet or prophet is literally taken out of himself than with
the more intellectual concept of inspiration which we find in Homer
and the early Greek poets. That is not to say that poetic memory
during this period is simply a process of factual recall.

The substantial implications of the ancient connexion between
Memory and the Muses in *oral* poetry were first recognised by J. A.
Notopoulos.[47] He pointed out that there are at least three different
ways in which memory is important in such poetry. First, memory
serves to perpetuate and hence immortalise κλέα ἀνδρῶν (the glorious
deeds of men). The immortalising power of poetry is recognised
from Homer onwards and is a central theme in Pindar's poetry. The
latter repeatedly emphasises the Muses' function as bestowers of
immortality.[48] Second, memory conserves information—a point too

---

[45] Cf. 1114, 1217.
[46] See e.g. E. Rohde, *Psyche*, tr. W. B. Hillis (London, 1925), 289; Dodds 70.
[47] 'Mnemosyne in Oral Literature', *TAPA* 69 (1938), 465–93.
[48] See e.g. Hom. *Il.* vi. 358; *Od.* viii.73, 580; xxiv. 196–7; *h.Ap.* 298–9; Theog.
237–52; Sapph. *fr.* 55, cf. *fr.* 193; Bacch. iii. 71, 90–8, ix. 81–7, x. 9–18; Pi. O. viii.
70–80, x. 86–96, *P.* i. 93–100, iii. 112–15, iv. 293–9, v. 45–9, vi. 5–17, xi. 55–64,

obvious to need substantiation. Third, and most important, memory is the means by which oral poetry is created. Homeric epic is based on a vast and complex system of formulas and word groups, which the bard must retain in his mind to use as the building blocks of his composition: in oral composition of this type memory is a creative force, since the bard must not only memorise the oral diction out of which his poetry is made, but also create his song from it. Memory is thus at the heart of this type of oral poetry for without it composition is impossible. Memory and inspiration, far from being incompatible, are vitally connected: memory is virtually the source of the poet's inspiration.

PERFORMANCE

The widely held view that there are certain fundamental differences between oral and literary poetry has recently been challenged by R. Finnegan.[49] She demonstrates that no one model will cover all types of oral literature and argues that there is no clear-cut differentiation between oral literature on the one hand and written literature on the other. Nevertheless it would clearly be false to say that oral poetry is exactly the same as written poetry in all respects. The one aspect in which oral poetry obviously does differ from literary poetry is in its performance—a point which Finnegan herself stresses. Indeed she describes performance as the 'heart of the whole concept of oral literature'.[50] In general classical scholarship has not seen that this important difference between oral and literary poetry has a direct bearing on the concept of poetic inspiration.

One of the essential features of the Parry–Lord theory of oral formulaic composition is that oral poetry is composed and performed simultaneously. This is not to say that the bard is merely an illiterate improviser or to imply that hard work and thought may not go into the composition beforehand. But it is at the moment of performance that the poem is fully composed for the first time.[51]

N. vi. 26–35, vii. 11–16, ix. 48–55, *I*. v. 53–7, vii. 11–16, viii. 56–63, *fr*. 121; Pl. *Smp*. 209d–e.

[49] *Oral Poetry* (Cambridge, 1977).

[50] *Oral Poetry*, 28, cf. 133.

[51] See M. Parry, 'Studies in the Epic Technique of Oral Verse-Making', *HSCP* 41 (1930), 77–8 = *The Making of Homeric Verse*, ed. A. Parry (Oxford, 1971), 269–70;

Composition, therefore, does not depend on flashes of inspiration which mysteriously provide ideas or phrases to the poet, but on a steady flow of words. The oral poet is both a composer and a performer: he needs not only memory and a command of technique, but also fluency and confidence or 'presence' as a performer. What must therefore be emphasised is that inspiration in oral epic poetry is inextricably connected with performance.

The Muses in early Greek poetry do more than simply provide information. *Od.* xvii, 518-21, for example, shows that they also inspire the bard with the power to mesmerise his audience. When the Muses made Hesiod a poet, they breathed into him a wondrous voice: ἐνέπνευσαν δέ μοι αὐδὴν | θέσπιν (*Th.* 31-2).[52] The significance of these words is not generally stressed. Fluency of composition is a common characteristic of inspiration in all periods. To take one example from ancient literature, Cratinus describes the inspiring effects of wine in *fr.* 186: 'Lord Apollo, what a flood of words! Streams splash, his mouth has twelve springs, Ilissus is in his throat. What more can I say? If someone doesn't stop him up, he'll swamp the whole place with his poems!'[53] Harriott,[54] amongst others, points out that the comparison of flowing speech to a river goes back to Homer. In the *Iliad* (i. 249) Nestor's eloquence is described in the well-known line: τοῦ καὶ ἀπὸ γλώσσης μέλιτος γλυκίων ῥέεν αὐδή (his voice flowed from his tongue sweeter than honey). Hesiod emphasises the effortless flow of the Muses' voices in similar language (*Th.* 39-40), and those whom the Muses love have this gift of fluency (*Th.* 96-7, cf. 84). Harriott and others draw our attention to these passages, but fail to pin-point their significance. Surely the significance of the comparison of the poet's utterance to a stream is that in oral poetry fluency is vital. Since composition and performance are simultaneous, without fluency composition breaks down.

Even when Greek poetry ceased to be orally composed, there was still the association of inspiration with performance: throughout the classical period, poetry was always composed for some kind of

---

A. B. Lord, *The Singer of Tales* (Cambridge, Mass., 1960), 13-29; M. N. Nagler, *Spontaneity and Oral Tradition* (Berkeley, 1974), xxi, xxiii, 20-1. On the whole topic of prior composition, memorisation and performance see Finnegan (n. 49), 73-87.

[52] Cf. *Th.* 97; Hom. *Od.* i. 371.
[53] Cf. Ar. *Eq.* 526-8; Pl. *Leg.* 719c.
[54] 88-9, 124. Cf. Kambylis (n. 26), 144-6.

audience; it was never simply a private expression. Hence performance was important and the Muses continued to provide inspiration in performance as well as in composition. The frequent invocations to the Muses to give sweetness in song should be interpreted with this in mind. For example, Alcman *fr.* 27: Μῶσ' ἄγε Καλλιόπα θύγατερ Διὸς | ἀρχ' ἐρατῶν ἐπέων, ἐπὶ δ' ἵμερον | ὕμνῳ καὶ χαρίεντα τίθη χορόν, 'Come, Muse Calliope, daughter of Zeus, begin the lovely song; shed sweetness on our hymn and grace on our dance.'[55] Pindar begins *Nem.* iii with an invocation which is clearly a request for help in performance:

> Ὦ πότνια Μοῖσα, μᾶτερ ἁμετέρα, λίσσομαι,
> τὰν πολυξέναν ἐν ἱερομηνίᾳ Νεμεάδι
> ἵκεο Δωρίδα νᾶσον Αἴγιναν· ὕδατι γάρ
> μένοντ' ἐπ' Ἀσωπίῳ μελιγαρύων τέκτονες
> κώμων νεανίαι, σέθεν ὄπα μαιόμενοι.[56]

Lady Muse, our mother, come, I beg you, in the sacred month of the Nemean games, to the hospitable Dorian island of Aegina. For the young men, craftsmen of sweet-voiced triumph songs, are waiting by the Asopian water, desiring your voice.

The Choruses in Aristophanes also frequently invoke the Muse for help in performance, as, for example, at *Peace* 775–80: 'Muse, having driven away the war, join in the chorus with me, your friend, celebrating weddings of the gods, banquets of men and festivities of the blessed.'[57] In the context of both victory celebration and dramatic competition, composition and performance are united, and the Muse relates to both.

THE POET AND HIS MUSE

What is the precise nature of the relationship between the Muse and the poet in early Greek poetry? Whatever it is, the poet is certainly not the unconscious instrument of the divine, as some scholars have suggested. G. M. A. Grube, for example, says of the invocations in Homer: 'When Homer invokes the Muses on his own account, everything is inspiration and he speaks as if the poet were but a passive

---

[55] Cf. e.g. Hes. *Th.* 104; Pi. *fr.* 75; Ar. *Av.* 737–50, *Ra.* 675.
[56] Cf. e.g. *P.* iv. 1–3, *N.* vi. 28–9.
[57] Cf. *Ach.* 665–75.

instrument.'[58] The first three words of the *Iliad* (Μῆνιν ἄειδε, θεά, 'Sing, goddess, the wrath') might indeed be taken to suggest that the poet is nothing but the instrument of the goddess. But the request for specific information at 8 (Who then of the gods brought them together to contend in strife?) suggests that the poet is an active recipient of information from the Muse rather than a passive mouthpiece. The same is true of all the other invocations in the *Iliad*.[59] The proem of the *Odyssey* makes the poet's active role even clearer:

Ἄνδρα μοι ἔννεπε, Μοῦσα . . .
τῶν ἀμόθεν γε, θεά, θύγατερ Διός, εἰπὲ καὶ ἡμῖν.

Tell me, Muse of the man . . . of these things, goddess, daughter of Zeus, tell us also.

The relationship here envisaged between the poet and the Muse is an intellectual one—the Muse is asked to communicate with the bard, not to send him into a state of ecstasy—and it would be a mistake to interpret these invocations as evidence for the view that the bard takes no part in composition.

The early Greek poets in general express their belief in their dependence on the Muse, but they also stress their part in composition. For example, at *Od.* viii. 44–5, Alcinous says of Demodocus:

τῷ γάρ ῥα θεὸς πέρι δῶκεν ἀοιδὴν
τέρπειν, ὅππῃ θυμὸς ἐποτρύνῃσιν ἀείδειν.

To him above all others has the god given the gift of song, to give pleasure in whatever way his spirit moves him to sing.

These words make it clear that poetry is both god-given and the product of the bard's own θυμός.[60] There is a similar combination of human and divine elements in Phemius' claim at *Od.* xxii. 347–8:

αὐτοδίδακτος δ᾽ εἰμί, θεὸς δέ μοι ἐν φρεσὶν οἴμας
παντοίας ἐνέφυσεν·

I taught myself; god put all kinds of ways of song into my mind. (trans. Russell)

It might be argued that the two halves of this statement are contradictory: because the gods have implanted the paths of song in him the bard cannot claim responsibility for his composition. But these lines, like the previous example quoted, must surely be understood in

---

[58] *Greek and Roman Critics*, 2.     [59] See above, n. 21.     [60] Cf. *Od.* i. 346–7.

the context of Homer's language. Dual motivation is, of course, a characteristic of Homeric epic and a god's prompting does not exclude a personal motivation.[61] The two halves of Phemius' statement are therefore complementary rather than contradictory: he is both self-taught and the recipient of divine aid. It has been suggested that αὐτοδίδακτος (self-taught) refers to the technical aspects of composition (form, style etc.), whereas οἴμας (ways) refers to the subject matter of his song,[62] but this seems to me to be too precise a distinction. Whilst the word αὐτοδίδακτος (self-taught) clearly implies a notion of skill or technique, the metaphor of the path or way of song should not be restricted to subject matter.[63] The general point of Phemius' claim is that he does not simply repeat songs he has learnt from other bards, but composes his songs himself.[64] The particular point which is relevant to the present discussion is that although Phemius stresses the divine origin of his poetry he is very much aware of his own part in composition. This attitude is typical of the early period of Greek literature as a whole in the way that poetry is described in both human and divine terms.

One of the conventional ways of describing a poet is to call him a Μουσῶν θεράπων (therapon of the Muses), and θεράπων is a revealing word. It does not imply that the poet is passive or servile but rather suggests a close relationship between the Muse and the poet who attends her.[65] Theognis specifies the nature of this relationship more precisely when he describes the poet as a messenger (ἄγγελος) of the Muses.[66] The relationship between the poet and the Muse is described in a number of different ways by Pindar, as for example in fr. 150: μαντεύεο, Μοῖσα, προφατεύσω δ' ἐγώ (Prophesy, Muse, and I will be your interpreter). This metaphor conveys Pindar's sense of

[61] See e.g. Dodds 1–18; A. Lesky, Göttliche und menschliche Motivation in homerischen Epos (Heidelberg, 1961).

[62] See e.g. Lanata, 13–14.

[63] See e.g. O. Becker, 'Das Bild des Weges', Hermes Einzels. iv (Berlin, 1937); Harriott 64–5.

[64] See e.g. W. Schadewaldt, Von Homers Welt und Werk³ (Stuttgart, 1959), 78–9; Dodds 10; Maehler 22–3; Harriott 92 and bibliography there.

[65] See Pi. P. iv. 286–7 where the free attendant (θεράπων) is contrasted with the slave (δράστας). For θεράπων of the poet see e.g. Hes. Th. 100; h. Hom. xxxii. 20; Choeril. fr. 1; Ar. Av. 909. Cf. Bacch. v. 192 (πρόπολος); Sapph. fr. 150 (μοισοπόλος).

[66] See B. A. van Groningen, Théognis: Le premier livre (Amsterdam, 1966), ad. loc. and M. S. Silk, Interaction in Poetic Imagery (Cambridge, 1974), 89, who notes that 'Μουσῶν θεράπων is an absolutely conventional periphrasis for the poet; Μουσῶν ἄγγελος is live metaphor'.

dependence on the Muse, but also stresses his part as the προφήτης (one who interprets and proclaims) of her message.[67] As Dodds explains:

'The words he uses are the technical terms of Delphi; implicit in them is the old analogy between poetry and divination. But observe that it is the Muse, and not the poet, who plays the part of the Pythia; the poet does not ask to be himself "possessed", but only to act as the interpreter for the entranced Muse. And that seems to be the original relationship. Epic tradition represented the poet as deriving supernormal knowledge from the Muses, but not as falling into ecstasy or being possessed by them.'[68] Dodds is clearly right in saying that 'the Muse, and not the poet . . . plays the part of the Pythia', but to infer from this that the Muse is actually *possessed* seems to me dubious. It is difficult to see who or what might be possessing the Muse, and Pindar nowhere makes any reference to possession. The emphasis in the fragment is on Pindar's position as the intermediary between gods and men, not on the psychological state of the Muse. Pindar also emphasises his active role in poetic creation by his use of the term εὑρίσκω (I 'find' or 'invent'), as at *O*. iii. 4–6:

> Μοῖσα δ' οὕτω ποι παρέ-
> στα μοι νεοσίγαλον εὑρόντι τρόπον
> Δωρίῳ φωνὰν ἐναρμόξαι πεδίλῳ
> ἀγλαόκωμον[69]

The Muse stood by my side as I was inventing a new-shining way of harnessing the bright voice of praise to the Dorian chariot.

And elsewhere he describes his poetry as simultaneously the gift of the Muses (*Μοισᾶν δόσιν*) and the product of his own mind (γλυκὺν καρπὸν φρενός).[70] Poetic creativity depends both on inspiration and on conscious effort.

---

    [67] Cf. Pi. *Pa*. vi. 6; Bacch. ix. 3. On προφήτης see E. Fascher *ΠΡΟΦΗΤΗΣ* (Giessen, 1927); H. W. Parke, *CQ* 34 (1940), 85; Fraenkel on Aesch. *Ag*. 1099.
    [68] 82.
    [69] Cf. *O*. i. 110, *N*. vi. 54, viii. 20, *fr*. 122.14; Bacch. *fr*. 5. Cf. ἐρευνᾶν at *Pa*. vii b 20. And in general see Becker (n. 62), 73; Maehler 96; Harriott 60–1.
    [70] *O*. vii. 7–8. Cf. *N*. iv. 6–8; Bacch. xii. 1–3, xiii. 220–9.

CRAFT

Like Pindar the early Greek poets as a whole seem to have had a very balanced view of poetic creativity, more balanced than some scholars would allow. Havelock,[71] as I have already said, maintains that in the early period poetry was thought of as a craft and that the 'contrary conception' of poetic inspiration was invented in the fifth century. Other scholars take the directly opposite view. Barmeyer,[72] for example, suggests that the early Greek bard is to be regarded as inspired rather than as a craftsman. And Svenbro in his recent book argues that 'for Homer and Hesiod the bard takes his words "from the Muse", nowhere does he appear as the producer (*producteur*) of his discourse',[73] and even that 'the very idea of the bard as author of his song is "systematically" rejected by Homer'.[74] The situation of the choral poet, on the other hand, is completely different: 'always in search of commisions . . . he must *insist* on the fact that he is the pro-ducer (*producteur*) of his poem in order to be remunerated, and he does so by means of numerous craft metaphors based on the analogy between poet and craftsman'.[75] In his zeal to stress the importance of the different social situations of the Homeric bard and the choral poet Svenbro ignores the continuity in attitudes to poetry which exists between them. The notion that the poet receives his words from the Muse is not confined to Homer and Hesiod any more than the notion of the poet as craftsman is confined to Pindar and the choral poets.

In the *Odyssey* the bard is included in a list of *demioergoi*

τίς γὰρ δὴ ξεῖνον καλεῖ ἄλλοθεν αὐτὸς ἐπελθὼν
ἄλλον γ᾽, εἰ μὴ τῶν οἳ δημιοεργοὶ ἔασι,
μάντιν ἢ ἰητῆρα κακῶν ἢ τέκτονα δούρων
ἢ καὶ θέσπιν ἀοιδόν, ὅ κεν τέρπῃσιν ἀείδων;    (*Od.* xvii. 382–5)

who seeks out a stranger and calls him from abroad, unless he is one of the *demioergoi*, a seer, or a healer of ills, or a carpenter, or a divine bard, who gives pleasure through his singing?

Svenbro argues that this passage cannot be taken as evidence for the idea of the poet as craftsman, referring to Vernant's observation that

[71] 156.        [72] *Die Musen.* 70.
[73] *La parole*, 5.   [74] Ibid. 193. Cf. 195.
[75] Ibid. 6.

the word *demioergos* 'does not in origin refer to a craftsman as such
. . . it defines all the activities which take place outside the *oikos*
(household) for the benefit of the public'.⁷⁶ Now it may be true that,
*demioergos* in itself does not imply the notion of craftsmanship, but
the context in which the word occurs must surely be considered. The
fact that the bard is included in a list of people who have specialised
skills which can be of use to the community suggests that he too
possesses a certain skill. When Phemius has to justify his existence to
Odysseus he does so on the grounds that he is *autodidaktos*, a word
which clearly implies that there is at least an element of skill in the
poet's activity. At *Od.* xi. 368 Alcinous praises Odysseus for telling his
story ἐπισταμένως (that is, skilfully) like a bard. And, as I have
pointed out, the phrase κατὰ κόσμον used of Demodocus' song at *Od.*
viii. 489 refers as much to the construction as to the contents of the
song.⁷⁷

The importance of skill in poetry during the early period is also
apparent from the frequency of references to the teaching and learning of poetry, and from the repeated use of skill words vis-à-vis
poetry: οἶδα, ἐπίσταμαι, σοφός, σοφία, τέχνη.⁷⁸ Bruno Snell has shown
that the word ἐπίσταμαι in the early period means primarily 'know
(how)'.⁷⁹ Similarly οἶδα, τέχνη, σοφός and σοφία denote practical
ability and knowledge rather than 'wisdom'. Homer uses the word
σοφία only once, and in connection with a carpenter (*Il.* xv. 412).
And Hesiod uses the word of skill in seamanship (*Op.* 649) as well as
of Linus' musical skill (*fr.* 306). Craftsmen of many different varieties
are described as *sophos*—including poets.⁸⁰ Snell points out that

---

⁷⁶ *La parole*, 193–5.
⁷⁷ On the notion of poetic skill in Homer see especially Schadewaldt (n. 64), 70–5.
⁷⁸ For the teaching idiom see e.g. Hom. *Od.* viii. 481, 488, xvii. 519, xxii. 347; Hes.
*Th.* 22, *Op.* 662; Sol. *fr.* 13. 51. Cf. the idea that man learnt to sing from the birds:
Democr. *fr.* 154; Alcm. *frr.* 39, 40. For οἶδα see e.g. *Od.* i. 337; Alcm. *fr.* 40; Archil. *fr.*
120. 2. For ἐπίσταμαι see e.g. *Od.* xi. 368; Hes. *Op.* 107; Archil. *fr.* 1. 2; Sol. *fr.* 13. 52.
⁷⁹ *Die Ausdrucke für den Begriff des Wissens in der vorplatonischen Philosophie* (Berlin
1924), 81–3.
⁸⁰ See Snell (n. 79), 5–7, where he gives a list of σοφοί including seers, generals,
steersmen, doctors, coach drivers, wrestlers, cooks, and farmers. For σοφ- words of
poets, see e.g. Sol. *fr.* 13. 52; Ibyc. *fr.* 1. 23; Theog. 770, 995; Pi. *O.* ii. 86 and other
references cited by Lanata 83–5 (Pindar, of course, invests the terms σοφός and σοφία
with a new significance: in particular σοφός denotes for him a rare individual, set apart
from his fellows both by his inborn nature and by his communion with the gods);
Xenoph. *fr.* 2. 12; Ar. *Nu.* 547, *Pax* 797, *Lys.* 368. For a detailed study of the subject
see B. Gladigow, *Sophia und Kosmos* (Hildesheim, 1965).

*sophos* originally meant 'one who understands his craft': the emergence of *soph-* words to mean 'wisdom' in a more intellectual sense was a gradual process.

The use of the word *poiētēs* to mean poet[81] is evidently based on the notion of the poet as craftsman, but the evidence I have cited shows that this concept did not suddenly emerge from nowhere in the fifth century. In a fragment attributed to Hesiod (*fr. dub.* 357) poetic composition is likened to stitching:

> ἐν Δήλῳ τότε πρῶτον ἐγὼ καὶ Ὅμηρος ἀοιδοὶ
> μέλπομεν, ἐν νεαροῖς ὕμνοις ῥάψαντες ἀοιδήν.

Then first in Delos we bards sang, Homer and I, stitching song in new hymns.

The etymology of the words ῥάπτειν, ῥαψῳδεῖν, ῥαψῳδός and their precise meaning when applied to poets is uncertain, but clearly they involve an idea of craft.[82] Craft metaphors, as Svenbro rightly observes, become more frequent in the poetry of Bacchylides and Pindar—the poet is described not only as a stitcher and weaver of songs, but also as builder, carpenter or sculptor.[83] Svenbro argues that this use of craft metaphors is to be understood in terms of the professional poet's economic dependence on his patrons. Since what he produces is not tangible, the poet is in a weaker position than the craftsman as regards payment: he must therefore emphasize that his poetry is 'a form of merchandise' and portray his activity as a craft activity in order to be remunerated.[84] This theory sheds more light on Svenbro's own preoccupations than on Pindar. *P. v.* 72-6 indicate that Pindar was an aristocrat,[85] and the tone in which he addresses, for example, Thorax at *P. x.* 64-6 or Hiero at *P. i.* 85-94 suggests that he was on equal terms with his patrons rather than an inferior subject.[86] Pindar's craft metaphors reflect his attitude to his art, they

---

[81] Hdt. ii. 53; Ar. *Ach.* 654. See further e.g. Harriott 93-4. Similar terminology for the poet's craft occurs in Sanskrit and other IE languages. See M. West, 'Greek Poetry 2000-700 B.C.', *CQ* 23 (1973), 179 and bibliography there.

[82] For a sensible discussion see Harriott 94.

[83] See e.g. Bacch. v. 9-10, xiii. 223, xix. 8-10; Pi. *O.* vi. 1-4, 86-7, *P.* iii. 113, vi. 9, *N.* ii. 1-2, iii. 4-5, *I.* i. 14, *fr.* 194.

[84] *La parole*, 178-9, 187, 168-70.

[85] See Wilamowitz *Pindaros* (Berlin, 1922), 124; M. R. Lefkowitz, 'τὼ καὶ ἐγώ: The First Person in Pindar', *HSCP* 67 (1963), 229-32.

[86] See the further criticisms of St Fogelmark in his review of Svenbro, *Gnomon* 50 (1978), 13-24.

do not tell us about his social status. And whilst it is true that Pindar uses a large number of craft metaphors when speaking of his poetry, he says much more about his poetry in general than do his epic predecessors—a point not noted by Svenbro. He is more self-consciously articulate about his poetry—more self-conscious about his inspiration and genius as well as about his craftsmanship. Svenbro is not the only scholar guilty of one-sidedness in discussing Pindar's attitude to poetry. Grube, for example, claims that Pindar 'despises technique and training; everything in poetry is natural talent'.[87] This statement is misleading. Whilst Pindar does contrast the true poet who is a poet by nature ($\phi u \hat{a}$) with the poet who has merely been taught his craft,[88] he never denies the importance of technique in poetry. His frequent use of craft metaphors and his own evident concern with technique show that he regarded technique as a vital ingredient in poetry. But for the true poet mere technique is not enough.

## CONCLUSIONS

It was Plato who, so far as we know, first opposed the concepts of poetic inspiration and technique when he described inspiration as *enthousiasmos*. Even Democritus, who is often considered a precursor to Plato, evidently did not consider inspiration and technique as incompatible: Ὅμηρος φύσεως λαχὼν θεαζούσης ἐπέων κόσμον ἐτεκτήνατο παντοίων, 'Homer, being endowed with a nature subject to divine influences, constructed a fair work of poetry of every kind' (trans. Russell: DK *fr.* 21). In fact throughout early Greek poetry there seems to be an equal emphasis on craft and inspiration. If we are unable to accept this fact, it must be because we have certain pre-conceived notions about the concept of poetic inspiration and its relation to the idea of poetry as a craft. Doubtless the notion of inspiration originated from the poet's feeling of dependence on the divine. And this feeling corresponds to the belief of many poets throughout history that, as Dodds put it, 'creative thinking is not the work of the ego'.[89] But the idea of poetic inspiration in early Greece differs in a

---

[87] *Greek and Roman Critics*, 9.
[88] *O.* ii. 83–88. Cf. *O.* ix. 100–2, *N.* iii. 40–2.
[89] 81.

number of important ways from subsequent conceptions. It was particularly associated with knowledge, with memory and with performance; it did not involve ecstasy or possession, and it was balanced by a belief in the importance of craft. But although it therefore laid far more emphasis on the technical aspects of poetic creativity, it was nevertheless an idea essentially connected with the phenomenon of inspiration as we know it.

# 3
# Homeric Professors in the Age
# of the Sophists

N. J. RICHARDSON

## I. METRODORUS AND OTHERS

At the opening of Plato's *Ion* Socrates expresses his admiration for the rhapsodic profession in a characteristically ironic way:

I have many times envied you rhapsodes your art. Not only are you always dressed up in a way that accords with the dignity of your profession, and you cut the most imposing figures, but you are also required to spend your time on many good poets, and above all on Homer, the best and most divine poet of all; and you must have a detailed knowledge not only of his verses but also of his meaning (διάνοια). All this makes you an object of envy.

Ion agrees, saying this is the aspect of his art which has demanded the greatest effort of him, and he declares:

I think that I am the best exponent of Homer, and neither Metrodorus of Lampsacus nor Stesimbrotus of Thasos nor Glaucon, nor anyone else in the past has ever been able to express so many fine thoughts about Homer as I can.

He offers to give a display of his skill in eulogising Homer, a skill which deserves a gold crown from the Homeridae. Socrates politely postpones this, and embarks on his interrogation of the rhapsode, in order to discover what it means to be an expert on Homer. The conclusion is that the ability to be a eulogist of Homer depends not on technique but on divine inspiration.

It has often been remarked that much of the dialogue seems to be

This article represents a revised and extended version of a paper read to the Cambridge Philological Society on 14 November 1974. I should like to thank those who were present for some helpful and stimulating discussion, and also Professor Martin West for reading and commenting on the paper.

directed against general sophistic tendencies in the interpretation of poetry, and that Ion appears to be little more than a cover for the sophists.[1] One thinks, for instance, of the discussion in the *Protagoras* of Simonides' poem, and still more of the opening of the *Hippias minor*, where Hippias has just given an epideictic speech on Homer, and the dialogue continues with a discussion of the relative merits of the *Iliad* and *Odyssey*, and their leading characters. In the *Protagoras* also, Hippias is eager to give his epideictic speech on Simonides, but is discouraged from doing so by Alcibiades (347B).

But the authorities on Homer whom Ion mentions, Metrodorus, Stesimbrotus and Glaucon, are obscurer figures. What form, or forms, did their criticism take? A passage in Xenophon's *Symposium* (3. 5–6) seems to be relevant here. Niceratus, the son of Nicias, boasts that he was made to learn by heart the whole of Homer's poetry, i.e. the *Iliad* and *Odyssey*, by his father, in order that he should become a gentleman. Antisthenes drily observes that this makes him no better than the rhapsodes, who are the stupidest of all types of men. Socrates, however, comments that 'this is because they do not understand the hidden meanings (ὑπόνοιαι)'. But Niceratus 'has paid a great deal of money to Stesimbrotus, Anaximander and many others', so that none of their valuable teaching has escaped him.

Later on we learn what sort of subjects Niceratus himself considers that he is qualified to teach, by virtue of his knowledge of Homer (*Symp.* 4. 6–7). 'Let me tell you', he says, 'what benefits you will receive by associating with me. Doubtless you know that Homer, the wisest of men, has dealt with practically all human affairs in his poetry. So let anyone cultivate me who wishes to become an expert in domestic economy, public speaking or strategy, or to be like Achilles, Ajax, Nestor or Odysseus. For I am master of all these subjects.'[2] Once again Antisthenes ironically takes him up, asking if he is also an expert on kingship, because Homer praises Agamemnon's qualities as a king and general. Niceratus eagerly accepts this, and goes on to quote lines from Nestor's speech on charioteering (*Il.* 23. 335–7), and (as a joke) the phrase ἐπὶ δὲ κρόμυον ποτῷ ὄψον, 'and an onion as a relish for their drink' (*Il.* 11. 630), as further examples of the technical advice contained in the poems.

---

[1] For a useful discussion see H. Flashar, *Der Dialog Ion als Zeugnis platonischer Philosophie* (Berlin, 1958).     [2] Cf. Protagoras' claim at Pl. *Prot.* 318DE.

This takes us back to the *Ion*, where the same two examples are quoted (537AB, 538B), the second as an instance of medical knowledge, and Ion also insists at the end of the dialogue that Homer can teach one the arts of rhetoric and strategy (540Bff., 540Dff.). Although the general theme was no doubt conventional at the time (e.g. cf. Xen. *Mem.* 3. 1. 1–4, 2. 1–4, Pl. *Symp.* 174B, and Ar. *Ran.* 1034–6, for leadership and strategy), the correspondence is striking, and has suggested to some a connection between the two works. If so, the derogatory remark by Antisthenes about the rhapsodes could be influenced by the picture presented in the *Ion*.[3]

In both *Ion* and *Symposium* the main criticism is of the sophistic use of Homer as a compendium of ethical and technical knowledge. But what then is the significance of Socrates' remark about ὑπόνοιαι (hidden meanings)? The natural implication is that Stesimbrotus, Anaximander and others, whatever else they taught about Homer, claimed to interpret his ὑπόνοιαι. According to Plutarch (*Mor.* 19E), ὑπόνοια was the word used in earlier Greek for what was known in his time as ἀλληγορία (allegory). Plutarch is here talking of extensive allegorical interpretations of poetry, rather than using the word ἀλληγορία as a technical term of rhetoric, as it was often used. His statement is confirmed by Plato's *Republic* (378D), where immoral myths about the gods are rejected as unacceptable, whether they are composed ἐν ὑπονοίαις or ἄνευ ὑπονοιῶν 'in hidden meanings or without hidden meanings', because the young cannot distinguish what is ὑπόνοια and what is not. Amongst other things Plato mentions 'theomachies such as Homer composed', and it is in the context of allegorical interpretations of the theomachy in the *Iliad* that we are told that 'this form of defence is very old, and goes back to Theagenes of Rhegium' (Schol. B *Il.* 20. 67 = *Vors.* 8. 2). This takes one back to the late sixth century, and to the scholar who is described as the first to write about the poetry and life of Homer (*Vors.* 8. 1). However Theagenes may have interpreted the Homeric theomachy, Plato's words leave no doubt that allegorical interpretations of it were current by his time. He also mentions 'bindings of Hera by her son,

---

[3] Cf. Flashar, *Dialog*, 24 f., who also notes a parallel between *Ion* 535E5 and Xen. *Symp.* 3. 11. But Xenophon's text of *Il.* 23. 335–7 differs from Plato's, and both from our medieval texts. F. Dümmler, *Antisthenica* 29 ff., saw both the *Ion* and the *Symposium* passages as directed against Antisthenes, but failed to make a substantial case for this. See also F. Wehrli, *Zur Geschichte der allegorischen Deutung Homers in Altertum* (Diss. Basel, 1928), 69.

and precipitations of Hephaestus by his father when he was about to defend his mother from being beaten', as possible subjects for allegorical treatment.

One might, however, argue that ὑπόνοια (literally under-sense) could have a wider range of meaning than this, and include any interpretation which disregarded the obvious literal sense of a passage in favour of a more subtle way of taking the words.[4] The sophistic tricks which Socrates plays with the poem of Simonides might be an example of this, and a parallel could be found in the use of αἰνίττεσθαι (hint enigmatically) in the Platonic dialogues. In the *Theaetetus* (194Cff.) this refers to an allegorical interpretation of κέαρ (heart) in Homer as connected with κηρός (wax), thus 'hinting enigmatically that the soul is like wax'. But in the *Lysis* (214Bff.) the proverb 'god always draws like to like' is taken as hinting enigmatically that only good men can be truly friendly, since bad men are always 'at variance with themselves', and so cannot be described as ὅμοιοι (like). An even better example of this occurs in *Alicibiades II* 147Bff., where Socrates interprets κακῶς δ' ἠπίστατο πάντα 'and badly he understood all things' (of Margites) as meaning that 'it was bad for him to know all these things', because one cannot 'know something badly'. Here again he says that 'the poet αἰνίττεται (speaks enigmatically), just as virtually all other poets do'.

One might describe this sort of thing as a ὑπόνοια, but it is not allegory in the modern sense, whereby characters or whole scenes in a work of literature are taken as representing something other than what they appear to represent on the surface. One should remember that ἀλληγορία was also first used as a rhetorical term, which could include various forms of 'under-sense' such as extended metaphor, γνώμη (maxim), enigma, riddle and so on.[5] This might suggest that an interest in poetic ὑπόνοια developed as a by-product of the sophists' interest in rhetoric. But one might also suggest that it may be wrong to attempt to draw too hard and fast a line between detailed word-by-word analysis of a text with a view to eliciting its true meaning, and the more extended form of re-interpretation which seeks to reveal the

---

[4] ὑπόνοια normally means 'conjecture, suspicion, guess' (cf. LSJ s.v.). Cf. also E. *Ph.* 1133, where it refers to the symbolism of a shield-blazon, and Arist. *EN* 1128ª28, where it is used of 'innuendo' in modern comedy, as opposed to αἰσχρολογία (abusive speech).

[5] Cf. Philodemus, *Rhet.* I. 164, 174, 181 (Sudhaus), Demetrius, *On Style* 99 ff., 151, 243, Cic. *Or.* 94, 166 f., etc.

underlying purpose or hidden significance of whole scenes, or even of whole poems. In the language of Plato's day, both might be described as attempting to discover the ὑπόνοια, or what the poet αἰνίττεται (hints enigmatically).

It is generally agreed that 'the Sophists' used the former method, but in the case of the second there is some disagreement. Rudolf Pfeiffer, in his magisterial survey of ancient scholarship, has stated categorically that there is no trace of an interest in allegory on the part of the Sophists.[6] This question deserves, it seems to me, rather careful re-examination.

In the first place, as Pfeiffer himself notes,[7] the earliest Homeric 'scholar', Theagenes, appears to provide a counter-example to this kind of dichotomy. Apart from his alleged role as a pioneer of allegory, he is also said to have initiated the study of ἑλληνισμός (*Vors.* 8. 1A), i.e. of the correct usage of the Greek language, and he is also cited for a variant reading of *Il.* 1. 381 (*Vors.* 8. 3). And later, in the fourth century and Hellenistic period, we find evidence of a similar dual tendency, in the Derveni papyrus commentary on an Orphic *Cosmogony*, and in the work of Crates. As Pfeiffer again notes, the first of these contains a mixture of allegorical interpretation with etymology and the explanation of glosses, and it is probable that Crates also mixed textual criticism with allegory, rather than keeping the two separate (in his *Diorthotika* and *Homerika*).[8]

In the fifth century, the same seems to have been true of Metrodorus of Lampsacus, the first Homeric expert whom Ion mentions. As an allegorist he was notorious, but it is also likely that he gave a linguistic interpretation of the problematical lines *Il.* 10. 252–3, explaining that πλέων was ambiguous, and could mean 'full' as well as 'more'.[9] This involves a very strained reading of the text, which is not inconsistent with the highly fanciful tendency of Metrodorus' other interpretations.[10]

---

[6] *History of Classical Scholarship* (Oxford, 1968), 35 ff.

[7] *History of Classical Scholarship*, 11, 35.

[8] Cf. Pfeiffer, *History*, 237, 239.

[9] Schol. B *Il.* 10. 252 (= *Vors.* 61 A 5). Cf. Arist. *Poet.* 1461ª25, where this solution is mentioned.

[10] It is not clear what form of πλέως (or πλεῖος) Metrodorus wished to read, but he seems to have taken the phrase as meaning 'the full two parts of the night'. I see no reason to follow Jacoby (*FGH* 1, 522) in referring this interpretation to Democritus' pupil, Metrodorus of Chios, or to conjecture 'Zenodorus' (Horn ap. Diels, *Vors.* 61A5). In favour of Metrodorus of Lampsacus see Schrader, *Porphyrii Quaest. homericarum ad*

Metrodorus, however, was a pupil of Anaxagoras, and so is said to be 'not a Sophist' (Pfeiffer, *History*, 35) in the restricted sense of one who taught (especially rhetoric) for pay.[11] Or rather, we have no evidence that he was, although he is mentioned by Ion in the same breath as Stesimbrotus, who according to Socrates (Xen. *Symp.* 3. 6 above) did take money for his teaching about poetry. What of the major Sophists, such as Protagoras, Prodicus or Hippias? It may be worth remembering that according to Protagoras in Plato's *Protagoras* the early poets, such as Homer, Hesiod and Simonides, used their poetry as a 'cover' for their real purpose, i.e. sophistry (*Prot.* 316D πρόσχημα ποιεῖσθαι καὶ προκαλύπτεσθαι, 'adopted a disguise and worked under cover'; cf. 316E παραπετάσμασιν ἐχρήσαντο, 'they used screens'). This is rather like what Socrates says in the *Theaetetus* (180CD), in connection with the relativist doctrine and its alleged antecedents in *Il.* 14. 201 (= 302), that the ancients 'concealed this theory from the majority of men by means of poetry . . . whilst their successors in their greater wisdom reveal this truth openly, in order that even shoemakers may through hearing them understand their wisdom . . .' In other words, Protagoras' words could also be interpreted as a plea for allegorical treatment of poetry. The use of myths by Protagoras and Prodicus as vehicles for popular expression of their ideas is sufficiently well attested (Pl. *Prot.* 320C ff., Xen. *Mem.* 2. 1. 21 ff.), and although it is not the same thing as allegorical treatment of earlier poetry, it suggests a readiness to allow such an approach.[12] But it must be admitted that we have no actual examples of such interpretations of Homer by any of the major Sophists. What one can perhaps say is that their attitude to the poets as sophistic predecessors helped to create a climate of opinion in which less enlightened figures might pursue their own theories about Homer's 'true meanings'.

Metrodorus himself seems to stand in a class of his own, by virtue of his extremism. He interpreted the heroes of the *Iliad* as parts of the

---

*Iliadem pertinentium reliquiae* (Leipzig, 1880), 384, G. Lanata, *Poetica Pre-Platonica* (Florence, 1963), 247.

[11] On sophists and 'Sophists' see Guthrie, *History of Greek Philosophy*, III. 27 ff.

[12] Cf. also Prodicus' identification of the gods with objects in nature such as bread, wine, water, fire, etc. (*Vors.* 84B5 and E. *Ba.* 274 ff.). One might note too Pl. *Phdr.* 229C ff., where Socrates says that one might reasonably doubt the literal truth of the myth of Boreas and Oreithyia, ὥσπερ οἱ σοφοί (like the experts), and goes on to give a rationalist explanation, σοφιζόμενος (acting as an expert).

universe, and the gods as parts of the human body (*Vors.* 61A3-4).[13]
Agamemnon represented the αἰθήρ, upper air, Achilles the sun,
Helen the earth, Paris the air, Hector the moon, 'and the others
analogously'; whilst Demeter was the liver, Dionysus the spleen and
Apollo the bile. In other words, the whole poem was treated as an
allegorical representation of Metrodorus' own scientific theories. It is
possible to conjecture the lines on which these identifications were
made to fit the system of Anaxagoras.[14] The earth is at the centre of
the universe, maintained and surrounded by the air, as Helen is at
the centre of the Trojan War, embraced by Paris. The brightest of the
heavenly bodies, the sun and moon, revolve around the earth, as
Achilles pursues Hector about the walls of Troy. Achilles' armour is
described at that time as 'shining like the sun' (*Il.* 22. 134; cf. 19.
398). As the moon is robbed of her light by the sun, so Hector is killed
and stripped of this armour by Achilles.[15] The sun in turn is maintained by the αἰθήρ, which enflames and carries it round, as
Agamemnon instigates and maintains the war.

The other identifications presuppose the kind of analogy between
world and body, macro- and microcosm, which was especially
prominent in Anaxagoras' thought.[16] Apollo sends the plague in the
*Iliad*, and Anaxagoras' school was criticised by Aristotle for making
the bile the seat of acute diseases (59A105). Anaxagoras also held
that the tissues of the body were formed of dry and wet food, such as
bread and water (*Vors.* 59A46), and one remembers here Prodicus'
identification of Demeter and Dionysus with bread and wine (*Vors.*
84B5), echoed in the *Bacchae* (274 ff.). The liver and spleen were considered essential organs for life (cf. for example *Vors.* 64B6): hence,
perhaps, Metrodorus' other identifications. He may also have
identified Athene with the hands, and Zeus with νοῦς (mind) both in
man and the world (cf. *Vors.* 61A6 with 59A102).

Philodemus describes such theories as the work of madmen, and
Tatian also calls them very silly. It is indeed difficult to know whether

---

[13] For the complete text of Philodemus' reference see Mette, *Sphairopoiia* fr. 20.
[14] See especially W. Nestle, *Philologus*, 20 (1907), 503 ff. K. Reinhardt, *De
Graecorum Theologia Capita Duo* (Diss. Berlin, 1910), 79 ff., is less convincing. Cf. also
F. Buffière, *Les Mythes d'Homère et la pensée grecque* (Paris, 1956), 127 ff.
[15] Cf. S. *Tr.* 94-6 ὃν αἰόλα νὺξ ἐναριζομένα τίκτει κατευνάζει τε φλογιζόμενον ἅλιον . . .
(whom sparkling night brings to birth, herself despoiled, and lays to rest in blazing fire,
the sun . . .).
[16] Cf. Kirk and Raven, *The Presocratic Philosophers*, 385 ff.

they were intended to be taken seriously or not. One would also like to know what Anaxagoras himself thought of this type of thing. He is said by Favorinus to have been 'the first to demonstrate that Homer's poetry was about ἀρετή (virtue) and justice: and this argument was taken further by Metrodorus of Lampsacus, an acquaintance of his, who was also the first to study Homer's physical doctrine' (D.L. 2. 11 = *Vors.* 59A1§11). As Pfeiffer observes (*History*, 35 n. 3), this does not necessarily mean that Anaxagoras went in for moral allegory. Metrodorus, however, may have done so, for Philodemus mentions physical and moral allegory in the same breath when speaking of Metrodorus' identifications, although without actually naming him specifically.

It is possible that we have traces of another physical allegory by Anaxagoras' 'school', in the lines of Euripides' *Orestes* (982 ff.) where Electra sings of the sun as τὰν οὐρανοῦ | μέσον χθονός τε τεταμέναν | αἰωρήμασιν | πέτραν ἁλύσεσι χρυσέαισι φερομέναν | δίναισι βῶλον ἐξ Ὀλύμπου 'the rock suspended midway between heaven and Earth by hanging chains of gold, a clod from Olympus carried along in circling motion'. The sun is here identified with the rock suspended above Tantalus, who is hung midway between earth and heaven (cf. *Or.* 5 ff., 984 ff.), Hades being located in the air in accordance with fifth-century BC physics. The language, however, also recalls Anaxagoras' famous identification of the sun as a molten mass, and according to a later version Tantalus was actually punished for making this identification (*Vors.* 59A1 §8, 20a). But what about the 'golden chains' by which the sun is suspended? These must be explained by the passage in the *Iliad* (8. 18 ff.; cf. also 15. 18 ff.) where Zeus suggests that he might pull up gods and men, earth and sea, by a golden σειρή (rope) and leave all things suspended. This was itself the source of many later allegories,[17] and in the *Theaetetus* (153C) it is mentioned rather disparagingly by Socrates as the 'culminating evidence' in favour of the relativist theory. He says that the golden rope is 'nothing else but the sun', and 'as long as the revolving heaven and the sun are in motion, all things divine and human exist and are preserved, but if it were to stand still as though bound fast, all things would be destroyed and, as the saying goes, turned upside down'.

[17] Cf. P. Lévêque, *Aurea catena Homeri* (Paris, 1959), A. O. Lovejoy, *The Great Chain of Being* (Cambridge, Mass., 1957).

Here the golden rope is identified with the sun itself, but originally the sun should be suspended by golden chains, as in Anaxagoras' theory it is maintained by the fiery αἰθήρ. Zeus in the Homeric passage will have been taken as the Mind which directs the whole system, keeping all things in motion, or if he so chooses, bringing them to a standstill.[18]

This allegory must have aroused some interest, since it is referred to by both Euripides and Plato. It differs, however, from those of Metrodorus, in being based on a passage in Homer whose cosmological significance must have seemed rather obvious in ancient times. In fact, this and the similar passage about Hera's suspension in mid-air, bound by an 'unbreakable golden chain' (*Il.* 15. 18 ff.), might actually be the poetic relics of stories which were originally intended to have cosmological significance.[19]

The passage about the punishment of Hera is, in its turn, related to the story told by Hephaestus (*Il.* 1. 590 ff.), of how he was cast out of heaven by Zeus when he tried to defend his mother from being beaten (cf. 1. 591–3 and 15. 23–4). This is one of the myths which are mentioned in the *Republic* as receiving allegorical treatment.[20] Later, in the Homeric Scholia, various interpretations are offered of all these episodes, and they are also connected with the mention by Poseidon of the division of the world between himself, Zeus and Hades (*Il.* 15. 187–94). The underlying basis for these myths is taken to be the theory of the four elements, fire, air, earth and water, and it seems reasonable to assume that this was already the case in the fifth-century interpretations which Plato's reference in the *Republic* presupposes, as also in that of the golden chain in *Il.* 8. 18 ff. (where we have, besides αἰθήρ, earth and sea at verse 24, and air at 26). Empedocles' designation of the elements as Zeus, Hera, Aidoneus and

[18] A Pythagorean source for this allegory was suggested by Boyancé in *RÉG* 54 (1941), 155 f., 65 (1952), 347 f. But his assumption that Oenopides of Chios was influenced by Pythagorean ideas is questionable. Cf. W. Burkert, *Lore and Science in Ancient Pythagoreanism* (Harvard, 1972), 322. Note also that the Derveni papyrus commentary seems to show strong traces of influence from the school of Anaxagoras. Cf. R. Merkelbach, *Zeitschr. f. Pap. u. Epigr.* 1 (1967), 21 ff., W. Burkert, *Ant. u. Abendl.* 14 (1968), 93 ff. For other Euripidean instances of Anaxagorean theory presented in semi-allegorical form cf. *Vors.* 59A20b, 112 (E. fr. 944, 839 N.²).

[19] Cf. C. H. Whitman, *HSCP* 74 (1970), 37 ff., in favour of this view.

[20] Plato also mentions the 'bindings of Hera by her son' (i.e. Hephaestus), a non-Homeric myth which is linked to that of Hephaestus' fall and also similar to the binding of Hera by Zeus. On this see Page, *Sappho and Alcaeus*, 258 ff.

Nestis (cf. *Vors.* 31B6, and also 121-3) seems already to presuppose such allegorical interpretations, and paves the way for later ones.[21] What, then, of the other critics mentioned by Plato's *Ion* and Xenophon's Socrates? Both name Stesimbrotus of Thasos. The reference to ὑπόνοιαι in connection with him in the *Symposium* might suggest at first sight that he too was an allegorist, but as we have seen, the sense of this word cannot be pinned down with absolute certainty. Jacoby (*FGH* 11D p. 349. 15 ff.) rejects the assumption that he allegorised, because the extant fragments of his Homeric criticism (*FGH* 107F21-5) show no trace of such a tendency. He is followed by Pfeiffer (*History*, 35 f.).[22] Stesimbrotus is said to have taught Antimachus of Colophon (*FGH* 107T5), the first 'editor' of Homer's text,[23] and this suggests a philological bias. But as I have argued, this does not necessarily exclude other forms of criticism. In fact Stesimbrotus' interests were both varied and curious. He is best known as the author of a work on Themistocles, Thucydides son of Melesias and Pericles, often quoted by Plutarch (F1-11). This seems to have been a pamphleteering work, full of gossip and propagandist stories.[24] He also, however, wrote περὶ τελετῶν, *On Rituals* (F 12-20), and the fragments of this show an interest in the more recherché aspects of mythology connected with the mystery rituals of Dionysus, Demeter and related gods, which reminded Jacoby of 'Orphic' literature. We find an etymology of Dionysus (F 13), Διόνυξον . . . ὅτι σὺν κέρασι γεννώμενος ἔνυξε τὸν Διὸς μηρόν, 'Dionuxos . . . because being born with horns he grazed (*enuxe*) the thigh of Zeus'; an identification of Apollo (F 14), mentioned by Philodemus in the context of various 'allegorical' ideas of the gods in poetry (e.g. Zeus = αἰθήρ, Ge = Hestia etc.);[25] a report about Artemis, possibly as daughter of Ge, in the context of various myths of the enchainment of gods (F15); a description of Artemis and Athena as attendants of the Mother of the gods (F16; cf. E. *Hel.* 1301 ff., *Hom. Hy. Dem.* 424, Orph. fr. 49. 40 f.,

---

[21] The forces governing Empedocles' cosmic system, Love and Strife, are also, when taken at face value in earlier poetry, essentially what aroused the criticism of Xenophanes.

[22] Pfeiffer does not discuss the crucial *Symposium* passage. He also quotes Jacoby's statement that he was 'vom Beruf Rhapsode' (*History*, 343. 16). This seems to rest on a misunderstanding of Pl. *Ion* 530CD.

[23] On this 'edition' see N. G. Wilson, *CR* 19 (1969), 369.

[24] Cf. R. Meiggs, *The Athenian Empire*, 15 ff.

[25] Philod. *On Piety*, 22 f. (Gomperz). Cf. Anaxag. (?) 59A20b, E. fr. 944 (Hestia = Earth), and the Derveni papyrus, *Arch. Delt.* 19 (1964), 24, col. 18.

etc.); the statement that Zeus got his kingdom from his mother Rhea, and lost it when she gave it to Artemis and Athena (F 17); a story that the mole was blinded by Earth for ruining the crops (F 18; cf. the stories about Demeter's punishment of Ascalaphus or Ascalabus); and information about the Cabiri and the mysteries of Samothrace (F20).

This kind of interest in the mythology connected with mystery rituals and its possible implications seems to make Stesimbrotus a rather better candidate as Homeric allegorist, and all the more so if we bear in mind the sort of mixture of allegory, etymology and philology which we find in the Derveni papyrus.[26]

The actual fragments of Stesimbrotus' Homeric criticism are too scanty to tell us a great deal, but they do shed some light on the variety of his methods. Apart from the statement that Homer was a Smyrnaean (F22), there are three mentions of his views, all in the Homeric Scholia, in connection with problematical passages. Two of these involved celebrated Homeric problems, those of Nestor's cup and of the division of the world between Zeus, Poseidon and Hades. The construction of Nestor's cup formed the subject of later allegory, but we must beware of assuming that Stesimbrotus took this line here.[27] In fact, he discussed a separate question, concerning *Il.* 11. 636-7. The 'problem' was to explain why 'Nestor the old man' could lift the cup without difficulty, whereas others would have had trouble in doing so. Stesimbrotus said that it was 'in order that Nestor may plausibly (εἰκότως) seem to have lived many years: for if his strength remains and has not been withered by old age, it is reasonable (εὔλογον) that the extent of his life should be in accordance (τὰ τῆς ζωῆς εἶναι παραπλήσια)'.[28]

What this seems to amount to is a concern for the poet's technique for justifying his ἀπίθανα (implausibilities), or making them plausible. This fits well into the context of sophistic interest in techniques of persuasion, and it also anticipates Aristotle's discussion of the role of τὸ θαυμαστόν (the marvellous) and τὸ ἄλογον (the irrational) in epic (*Poet.* 1460[a]11-[b]2). There is no evidence of allegory here, but perhaps one could describe this attempt to clarify the poet's technical

---

[26] Cf. perhaps also Demetrius, *On Style* 101, τὰ μυστήρια ἐν ἀλληγορίαις λέγεται, the mysteries are spoken of in allegories (although this is in the context of rhetorical allegory).

[27] As Buffière does, *Les Mythes*, 135.

[28] Porphyry ap. Schol. B *Il.* 11. 636 (*FGH* 107 F 23).

motivation as a type of interpretation of ὑπόνοια, in the wider sense of 'hidden intention'.

The second instance is more difficult to analyse, as the text of the scholion which reports his view is corrupt.[29] The problem concerns the words τριχθὰ δὲ πάντα δέδασται (and in three parts have all things been divided) (*Il.* 15. 189), where πάντα (all things) was thought to conflict with the statement that 'earth and tall Olympus are still common to all' (193). The scholiast ascribes to Stesimbrotus an explanation which he says was followed by Crates, in the words πάντα οὕτως δέδασται, all things have thus been divided. As the scholiast also gives an allegorical explanation of the passage, in terms of the four-element theory, and as Crates is known to have favoured such interpretations, Curt Wachsmuth wanted to read ⟨ὅτι κατὰ στοιχεῖα⟩ πάντα οὕτως δέδασται '⟨that in accordance with the elements⟩ all things have thus been divided'.[30] But this would not really explain the problem under discussion here, and the allegorical passage comes under a separate lemma in the scholia. It is more likely that Stesimbrotus' solution was a purely linguistic one, as E. Maass suggested.[31] One of the solutions offered by the Townleian Scholia is to read τριχθὰ δὲ πάντ' ἃ δέδασται 'triple are all things *which* have been divided'. This kind of conjecture, involving a change of word-division or prosody, is mentioned by Aristotle (*Poet.* 1461ª21 ff.), and it was several times used by Crates (*Il.* 11. 754, 18. 489, *Od.* 4. 260).[32] If Stesimbrotus was responsible for this (of which we cannot of course be sure), it provides another example of the kind of uncritical ingenuity which was being applied to the text of Homer at the time, and of which Aristotle's discussion in chapter 25 of the *Poetics* gives us some idea.

[29] Schol. A *Il.* 15. 193 (= F 24) Ζεὺς δ' ἔλαχ' οὐρανὸν εὐρὺν ἐν αἰθέρι καὶ νεφέλῃσιν· γαῖα δ' ἔτι ξυνὴ πάντων καὶ μακρὸς Ὄλυμπος] πῶς δέ φησιν γαῖα . . . Ὄλυμπος; Κράτης ἐν δευτέρῳ Ὁμηρικῶν καὶ Στησίμβροτος· † πάντα οὕτως δέδασται. (And Zeus obtained for his share the broad heaven in the upper air and clouds: but earth is still shared in common by all, and so is tall Olympus] but how can he say 'earth . . . Olympus'? Crates in the second book of his *Homerika* and Stesimbrotus † 'all things have been divided'.)

[30] *De Cratete Mallota* (Diss. Bonn, 1860), 26, 44 ff.

[31] *Aratea* 176; cf. also J. Helck, *De Cratetis Mallotae studiis criticis quae ad Iliadem spectant* (Leipzig, 1905), 31 ff.

[32] Maass suggested reading in Schol. A *Il.* 15. 193 πάντ' ἃ - οὕτως - δέδασται, all things which thus have been divided, with psilosis (smooth breathing). He explained οὕτως (thus) as a parenthetic 'sic', but this is not used in this way by the Scholia. Helck explained it as meaning 'as in 190-2', but this also is not entirely satisfactory, and it remains a puzzle.

There is, then, no positive evidence that Stesimbrotus offered an allegorical interpretation of this passage. But as I have argued, such an interpretation was probably current by the end of the fifth century BC, and the fact that Stesimbrotus discussed the very trivial question of the supposed inconsistency of wording suggests that the passage was the subject of more general critical interest. We know that Crates combined textual discussion with a strong allegorical bias, and it is likely in view of his other interpretations that he also discussed the significance of *Il.* 15. 189 ff. for his cosmological views.[33] We cannot therefore dismiss the possibility that Stesimbrotus did the same thing, either here or elsewhere.

His final Homeric fragment suggests yet another line of approach. When Lycaon pleads with Achilles for his life, he says (*Il.* 21. 76) πὰρ γὰρ σοὶ πρώτῳ πασάμην Δημήτερος ἀκτήν, 'for with you first of all I tasted the grain of Demeter'. The early critics once again allowed themselves to be puzzled by this, thinking it to mean that Lycaon had not eaten bread until he met Achilles! Stesimbrotus' answer was that Lycaon was a foreigner, and so he had eaten only rough barley meal and not ground meal (ὅτι οἱ βάρβαροι ἄλφιτα οὐκ ἐσθίουσιν ἀλλ᾽ ἄρτους κριθίνους, 'that foreigners do not eat ground meal but barley loaves').[34] If this does little to increase our estimation for his good sense, it is nevertheless of some significance. An interest in heroic diet is something which we find again in Plato, fourth-century comedy, and of course Hellenistic scholarship (including, notably, Crates once again).[35] Stesimbrotus' explanation also shows an interest in cultural differences between Greece and other nations, which is typical of this period, and assumes that Greece in the heroic age was at a more advanced stage of civilisation than others. We find this awareness of cultural differences applied to the solution of Homeric problems also by Aristotle.[36]

These three fragments thus show that Stesimbrotus combined a

---

[33] Cf. Mette, *Sphairopoiia*, 26 f. n. 6, who holds this view.

[34] Schol. B *Il.* 21. 76 (= F 25). I assume that he interpreted the gloss ἀκτή (grain) as being connected with ἄγνυμι (I break) (cf. *Et. M.* s.v.), and that ἄλφιτα here means ground meal.

[35] Cf. Pl. *Rep.* 404Bff., Antiphanes fr. 273, Eubulus fr. 120 (Kock); Crates fr. 85A, ed. Mette, *Parateresis* (Halle, 1952); and for Aristarchus, see P. Hofmann, *Aristarchs Studien 'de cultu et victu heroum'* (Diss. Munich, 1905).

[36] Cf. *Poet.* 1461ª1 ff., frr. 160 and 166 (Rose), Pfeiffer, *History*, 69 f. Note, however, that unlike Stesimbrotus Aristotle uses a non-Greek (Illyrian) custom to explain a Greek practice at *Il.* 10. 152 f.

variety of types of approach characteristic of his period, including detailed textual criticism, an interest in epic vocabulary, awareness of cultural differences and developments, and concern for the poet's techniques of persuasion. All of this, as well as the combination of ingenuity and silliness which he displays, make Stesimbrotus typical of the age of the Sophists. At the same time, his interest in the mythology of τελεταί (rituals) together with the possible implications of Socrates' remark about his Homeric ὑπόνοιαι, suggests that he may have combined these lines of approach with some attempts at allegory. If so, he would be in a line of tradition running from (probably) Theagenes to Crates, on whom he seems to have had some influence.

Stesimbrotus is named by Socrates together with Anaximander, and it may be possible to suggest what sort of lines his study of ὑπόνοιαι followed. He is probably to be identified with the younger Anaximander of Miletus (*FGH* 9), whose *floruit* is placed by the *Suda* in the reign of Artaxerxes Mnemon (405–358 BC). This might mean that the mention of him in Xenophon's *Symposium* is anachronistic, but equally he may have been already active in Socrates' time. He is described as a historian writing in Ionic, but he is also said to have written a Συμβόλων Πυθαγορείων ἐξήγησις, *Explanation of Pythagorean Symbols* (*FGH* 9 T 1, *Vors.* 58C6). Jacoby identifies him with the Anaximander who wrote a Ἡρωολογία 'Account of heroes', from which Athenaeus quotes an Ionic form (F 1).[37] If all this is correct, Anaximander's interests (mythology, history, Pythagoreanism and Homeric interpretation) are not so dissimilar in their spread from those of Stesimbrotus. His *Explanation of Pythagorean Symbols* very probably gave metaphorical (or allegorical) interpretations of these curious prescriptions (originally ritual in character), on the lines of those given later, in Porphyry's *Life of Pythagoras* (42).[38] For example, μὴ καρδίαν ἐσθίειν, 'do not eat your heart', is interpreted as meaning 'do not hurt yourself by grieving', and στέφανον μὴ τίλλειν, 'do not shred a garland', as 'do not harm the laws (for they are the garlands of cities)'.

This makes it reasonable to suppose that Anaximander used a similar method in interpreting Homer. Most of the evidence for

---

[37] Heidel (*Proc. Amer. Acad.* 56 (1921), 241 ff.) wanted to ascribe this to the earlier Anaximander, but Jacoby rejects this. Corssen (*Rh.M.* 67 (1912), 249 f.) thought that the notice about the Pythagorean work confused him with Alexander Polyhistor, who wrote a work with the same title (*FGH* 273F94). Jacoby again disagrees.

[38] Cf. Burkert, *Lore and Science*, 166 ff.

Pythagorean exegesis of Homer comes from late antiquity, and it is difficult to determine how much if any of it dates back to the classical period.[39] Early Pythagorean disapproval of Homer and Hesiod is suggested by the story, told by Hieronymus of Rhodes in the third century BC (fr. 42 Wehrli), of Pythagoras' vision of their punishment in Hades on account of their lies about the gods. This would be in line with the criticisms of Heracleitus and Xenophanes. But this does not exclude the possibility of early attempts to interpret the poets in the light of Pythagorean ideas. The ἀκούσματα (oral instructions) (or σύμβολα) which seem to preserve much of the original kernel of Pythagorean lore, include some with a mythological character which already points in this direction, and they recall the similar mythical cosmology of Pherecydes, Pythagoras' reputed teacher.[40] Use of Homer, and possibly also interest in a Homeric 'problem', that of the number of agents of Patroclus' death (Il. 16. 849-50), is implied by the story of Pythagoras' claim to be the reincarnation of Euphorbus.[41] Later legend made Pythagoras himself the pupil of Hermodamas, a member of the Samian guild of rhapsodes claiming as their founder Creophylus of Samos, Homer's 'friend'.[42] It has also been suggested that Theagenes of Rhegium based his presumed allegorical view of the Homeric theomachy on Pythagorean ideas current in his homeland.[43] The theory of opposites on which he may have formed this interpretation could owe its inspiration to early Pythagoreanism, but this remains only a hypothesis.[44]

Early Pythagorean interest in the use of μουσική for therapeutic purposes is attested by Aristoxenus (fr. 26 Wehrli), and it is possible that this can be combined with the report that the Pythagoreans ἐχρῶντο ... Ὁμήρου καὶ Ἡσιόδου λέξεσιν ἐξειλεγμέναις πρὸς ἐπανόρθωσιν ψυχῆς 'used selected expressions of Homer and Hesiod for the restora-

---

[39] Cf. A. Delatte, *Études sur la littérature pythagoricienne* (Paris, 1915), 109 ff., and M. Détienne, *Homère, Hésiode et Pythagore* (Brussels, 1962). Neither is sufficiently critical.

[40] Cf. Burkert, *Lore and Science*, 170 ff., M. L. West, *Early Greek Philosophy and the Orient* (Oxford, 1971), 215 ff.

[41] Cf. Heracleides Ponticus fr. 42 (Wehrli), Call. fr. 191. 59, etc., and Porph. *VP* 26. For an ingenious explanation of this see Burkert, *Lore and Science*, 140 ff.

[42] Cf. Neanthes, *FGH* 84F29, Diog. Laert, 8. 2, etc., Burkert, *Mus. Helv.* 29 (1972), 74 ff.

[43] Cf. Delatte, *Études*, 114 f.

[44] See the discussion by Wehrli, *Zur Geschichte der allegorischen Deutung Homers im Altertum*, 88 ff. He compares Alcmaeon, *Vors.* 24B4.

tion of the soul'.[45] Later, Achilles' consolation of his troubled spirit by epic song was seen as a model for this.[46] In a similar way, the injunction not to eat the heart was connected with Thetis' words to Achilles (*Il.* 24. 128-9): τέο μέχρις ὀδυρόμενος καὶ ἀχεύων | σὴν ἔδεαι κραδίην . . .; 'how long in sorrow and mourning will you eat your heart?'[47]

Although this type of comparison derives from later sources it may suggest the lines along which Anaximander worked. If so, his interpretations were presumably primarily ethical, in contrast to the physical system of Metrodorus. Traces, however, of a Pythagorean use of mythology as a basis for physical cosmology in the fifth century BC may possibly be seen in the work of Philolaus, who was supposed to have made the heavenly bodies revolve around a central cosmic fire, which he called Hestia or Διὸς οἶκον καὶ μητέρα θεῶν βωμόν τε καὶ συνοχὴν καὶ μέτρον φύσεως ('the house of Zeus and mother of the gods and altar and maintenance and measure of nature', *Vors.* 44A16; cf. A17, B7). He also 'dedicated the angle of the triangle to four gods, Cronos, Hades, Ares and Dionysus', 'the angle of the square to Rhea, Demeter and Hestia', and 'that of the dodecagon to Zeus' (44A14). This curious *mélange* of mythology and geometry does not involve the reinterpretation of Homer, but it should be mentioned as another instance of the sort of thing found already in Pherecydes and Empedocles, and (if genuine) as creating a suitable background for such interpretation.[48]

One might also conjecture a Pythagorean origin for the connection of κέαρ in Homer with κηρός in Pl. *Theaet.* 194Cff. This is cited as evidence for the function of memory as the recipient of impressions (191Cff.), and is ascribed by Socrates to an unspecified group of people (cf. 194C4 φασίν). Later tradition emphasised the importance attached by the Pythagoreans to the training of memory, which was connected with their belief in reincarnation. If they were also the source of this interpretation of κέαρ, we should have another instance of Homeric allegory in this *milieu* at the time of Anaximander.

[45] Iambl. *VP* 164 (attributed to Aristoxenus by D.-K. *Vors.* I, 467). Cf. ibid. III, Porph. *VP* 32.

[46] *Anecd. Par.* 3. 56. Cf. also Chamaileon fr. 4 (Wehrli), Iambl. *VP* 198 (*Vors.* I, 471).

[47] Schol. A *Il.* 24. 129, Ps. Plut. *Vit. Hom.* II. 154, Eust. p. 1342. 13. For other examples of connections between the σύμβολα and Homer see Ps. Plut. *op. cit.* pp. 151-4, and Delatte, *Études*, 119.

[48] Cf. Burkert, *Lore and Science*, 337-50, in favour of the authenticity of the views attributed to Philolaus.

Speculation about the possible character of Anaximander's work strengthens the assumption that the ὑπόνοιαι of Stesimbrotus may also have involved allegory. The case is rather different with the last of the critics mentioned by Ion (not, however, by Socrates in Xen. *Symp*. 3. 6), Glaucon. In his discussion of 'problems' in the *Poetics* Aristotle refers to a critic of this name, who stated the sound but rather obvious principle that one should not assume a contradiction in the text on the basis of one's own particular interpretation of the passage in question, without considering alternative ways in which it might be taken (1461ᵃ33 ff.). The problem which Aristotle has just mentioned is that of Achilles' shield and Aeneas' spear (*Il*. 20. 267ff.). The spear goes through two layers of the shield, but is stopped by the gold layer. This would seem at first sight to indicate that the gold layer was at the centre, which could be thought to be inconsistent with the natural assumption that the gold was on the outside. It is not clear which of the various solutions later recorded was favoured by Aristotle, who simply says that one must consider the various possible interpretations of the words τῇ ῥ' ἔσχετο χάλκεον ἔγχος 'by which the bronze spear was checked' (*Il*. 20. 272).[49] Nor is it evident from Aristotle's words that Glaucon himself also discussed this particular problem. Buffière, however, assumes that he did, and suggests that he put forward the allegorical interpretation which occurs later, in Heracleitus' *Homeric Problems* (Ch. 51), whereby the five layers represent the five zones, the gold being the central torrid zone.[50] Unfortunately, his theory rests on a mistranslation of Aristotle's text, and can therefore be dismissed.[51] It is of course possible that Glaucon did discuss this problem, and that may be what led Aristotle to mention his general principle *à propos* of it, but if so there is no indication that he favoured an allegorical solution. It is also doubtful whether the theory of five zones was known as early as the fifth century BC, although Posidonius attributed its origin to Parmenides (*Vors*. 28A44a), and later doxographers to Pythagoras (Aët. 3. 14. 1).

One other Homeric interpretation can plausibly be ascribed to Glaucon, and this too points in another direction. It concerns the

---

[49] Cf. D. W. Lucas's discussion *ad loc*.

[50] Buffière, *Les Mythes*, 159 ff.

[51] He takes κατὰ τὴν καταντικρύ 'according to the opposite' at 1461ᵃ35 as '(la pique trouvant l'or) droit en face (d'elle)' (p. 162), which enables him to connect the reference to Glaucon which follows with the problem of the shield.

problem of Nestor's cup which was discussed by Stesimbrotus. This was evidently popular at the time, for Porphyry mentions a solution by Antisthenes, as well as others by *Glaucos* and Aristotle. It is very likely that we should read Glaucon here (cf. Schrader, *Porphyrii Quaest. Hom.* 1.168), and identify him with Ion's critic. His solution was that Nestor alone knew the trick for lifting the cup, by taking its handles on either side across the diameter.[52] This seems typically childish, but it was perhaps intended as an illustration of Glaucon's principle, that one should not assume only one interpretation to be possible, in this case that Nestor's superior ability was due to strength rather than skill.

It has sometimes been suggested (for example, by G. L. Huxley, *GRBS* 9 (1968), 52) that Glaucon should be identified with Glaucos of Rhegium, the late fifth-century writer of a work *On ancient poets and musicians*. After all, Theagenes also came from Rhegium! But in this case there is no doubt about the name Glaucos, and we should have to assume that where Glaucon occurs in both the *Ion* and *Poetics* this name is corrupt, which is unlikely.[53] Moreover, Ion mentions Metrodorus of Lampsacus and Stesimbrotus of Thasos, but simply Glaucon, and this perhaps indicates that he was an Athenian.[54]

If we look back over this discussion, we find that of the four Homeric critics mentioned one (Metrodorus) was definitely an allegorist, who also probably engaged in detailed linguistic interpretation; another (Anaximander) was very probably an allegorist; the third (Stesimbrotus) used a variety of methods, among which it is quite likely that allegory was included, as well as linguistic and textual criticism; whilst in the case of Glaucon no convincing case for allegory can be made.

---

[52] Γλαῦκος δὲ ὅτι κατὰ διάμετρον ἐλάμβανε τὰ ὦτα, ἐκ μέσου δὲ πᾶν εὔφορον (And Glaucos that he took the handles diametrically, and from the middle everything is easy).

[53] Cf. Hiller, *Rh.M.* (1886), 431 ff., Lanata, *Poetica Pre-Platonica*, 279 ff.

[54] Other scholars named Glaucon or Glaucos were: (*a*) Glaucon of Teos, who wrote on the art of delivery (Arist. *Rhet.* 1403ᵇ26). (*b*) Glaucon of Tarsus, who had views about the accentuation of μῆνις (wrath) (Schol. A *Il.* 1. 1); cf. Glaucos on θυμοραιστής (spirit-crushing) (Schol. BT *Il.* 16. 414). (*c*) Glaucon ἐν ταῖς γλώσσαις (in his *Glosses*) (Ath. 480F) cited for a Cypriot gloss. (*d*) Glaucos of Samos, an early writer on accentuation and prosody (*Gramm. Lat.* ed. Keil IV, 530. 10 ff., Schol. Pl. *Phaedo* 108D f., mentioned with Hermocrates of Iasos, who seems to have lived *c*.300 BC). None of these, I think, can be identified with our Glaucon.

All these four are shadowy figures, *tenues sine corpore vitae*, whose contribution to scholarship was too lightweight to leave any great impression on posterity. They help to fill in something of the background against which the larger figures such as Protagoras or Prodicus stand out, and give us an idea of the range of speculative methods applied to the interpretation of Homer at this period.

## II. ANTISTHENES

In the discussion about the use of Homer in Xenophon's *Symposium* Antisthenes played a part, questioning Niceratus' claims in a characteristically dry way. His own interest in Homer is attested not only by the two speeches of Odysseus and Ajax ascribed to him, but also by the long list of essays on Homeric subjects preserved by Diogenes Laertius (6. 17–18), as well as a number of fragments of his Homeric criticism.[55] These are of importance, and (as with Stesimbrotus) show him anticipating Aristotle's work on Homer in some respects. His well-known *dictum* (Dio, *Or.* 53. 4 = fr. 58 Decleva), ὅτι τὰ μὲν δόξῃ, τὰ δὲ ἀληθείᾳ εἴρηται τῷ ποιητῇ 'that some things have been said by the poet, i.e. Homer, in accordance with opinion, and others with truth', is probably to be interpreted as foreshadowing Aristotle's answer to criticism of objectionable passages in poetry by reference to contemporary belief (cf. *Poet.* 1460ᵇ35 ff. ὅτι οὕτω φασίν, . . . that this is what people say. . .).[56] He also shows an awareness of the important principle of *context*, or the need to consider the circumstances in which something is said, who says it and so on, which anticipates the later λύσις ἐκ προσώπου 'solution by reference to the character concerned'. For instance, in discussing the problem of the Cyclopes, who are called ὑπερφίαλοι (overbearing) and ἀθέμιστοι (lawless) (*Od.* 9. 106) and are said by Polyphemus to pay no heed to the gods (275 f.), yet enjoy a kind of Golden Age life under

[55] Cf. Fernanda Decleva Caizzi, *Antisthenis Fragmenta* (Milan–Varese, 1966), 19 f., 24 ff., 43 ff., and the valuable commentary *ad loc.* There is a review of this by Wehrli, reprinted in *Theoria und Humanitas* (Artemis Verlag, 1972), 167 ff. Cf. V. di Benedetto, 'Tracce di Antistene in alcuni Scoli all' "Odissea" ', *Studi italiani di filologia classica*, 38 (1966) 208–28.

[56] Note however that Antisthenes' view is said to have been followed up and elaborated by Zeno, and Zeno's method of interpretation of the gods was allegorical (frr. 166–7 von Arnim).

divine protection (107 ff., cf. 1. 70, 7. 206), Antisthenes said that only Polyphemus was unjust, and the fact that the others did not have to cultivate the earth showed their justice (fr. 53, Schol. *Od.* 9. 106). He probably argued here, as the Scholia do, that one should remember that it was Polyphemus who said that they were independent of the gods, and not the poet himself.[57]

In his essay περὶ ἐξηγητῶν (*On Interpreters*) he may have attacked the wilder speculations of some of his contemporaries, and it is tempting to see in Socrates' ironical remark about Stesimbrotus and others a sidelong glance at Antisthenes' own disapproval of their theories. There is no doubt that Antisthenes himself also used Homeric scenes and figures to illustrate his own ethical views, but on the question whether he went further, and indulged in allegory, there has been considerable dispute. The negative view was stated most forcibly by Tate, in answer to the arguments of Höistad.[58] Pfeiffer (*History*, 36 f.) follows Tate. Laurenti, however, has revived the arguments in favour of allegory.[59] Although I suspect that the battle may be over a phantom issue, the problem perhaps merits a further brief examination.

Laurenti argues that Antisthenes' monotheism must have led him to treat the gods allegorically.[60] It is true that he is said to have described ἔρως (love) as a disease which men call a god (fr. 108), but this on its own proves nothing about his interpretation of Homer. He also may have commented that Athene uses three forms of argument to restrain Ares at *Il.* 15. 121 ff. (fr. 56),[61] and this has connected with Democritus' explanation of Athene's title Tritogeneia as referring to the threefold nature of wisdom (*Vors.* 68B2).[62] This

---

[57] Fr. 52 (Schol. *Od.* 5. 211, 7. 257) makes a similar point about judging a speech by its context.

[58] Cf. *Eranos*, 49 (1951), 16 ff., 51 (1953), 14 ff.

[59] *Riv. crit. di storia della filosofia*, 17 (1962), 123 ff.

[60] Cf. fr. 39 A (Philodemus) παρ' Ἀντισθένει δ' ἐν μὲν τῷ Φυσικῷ λέγεται τὸ κατὰ νόμον εἶναι πολλοὺς θεούς, κατὰ δὲ φύσιν ἕνα 'And in Antisthenes' work *On what is Natural* it is said that by convention there are many gods, but by nature one'. Cf. frr. 39B–E, 40A–D. This must be related to his dictum about δόξα (opinion) and ἀλήθεια (truth) in Homer. Note that Zeno is also said to have adopted Antisthenes' monotheism (fr. 164).

[61] Tate, *CQ* 24 (1930), 6 n. 7, argues that this part of Schol. *Il.* 15. 123 is not a quotation from Antisthenes. I do not see how one can be definite about this.

[62] Is this a form of allegory? If so, it provides another instance of this linked to linguistic study. See, however, Philippson, *Hermes*, 64 (1929), 166 ff. (cf. Pfeiffer, *History*, 42 f.), against Democritus as an allegorist. Democritus also said that Eumaeus' mother was Penia (68B24), perhaps by contrast with his father Ctesios (*Od.* 15. 413 f.;

again on its own is too uncertain to be of much value. In the *Cratylus* (407A) Socrates says that 'most modern interpreters' of Homer identify Athene with νοῦς (mind) and διάνοια (thought). But even if Antisthenes did so, the allegory again lay very close to the surface here. In his Ἀθηνᾶ ἢ περὶ Τηλεμάχου '*Athena or On Telemachus*' he probably discussed her part in Telemachus' education (cf. Decleva, pp. 83 f.), but this need not necessarily have involved allegory. His view on the problem of Nestor's cup may bring us closer to this. He said that the reference was not to the cup's heaviness, but to Nestor's ability to carry his wine without getting drunk (fr. 55). In other words, he wished to interpret the lines metaphorically. This runs counter to the obvious sense of the words ἄλλος μὲν μογέων ἀποκινήσασκε τραπέζης, 'another man would have had difficulty raising it from the table' (etc.), and surely ranks as a ὑπόνοια. Its purpose is presumably to support Antisthenes' views on the evils of excessive drinking (cf. fr. 41 and Xen. *Symp.* 4. 41).

If we turn to the list of Antisthenes' Homeric works, we enter the realm of conjecture, but we may possibly get some guidance here from the way in which Socrates is often portrayed as using Homeric τόποι (commonplaces) by Xenophon and Plato. In the *Memorabilia* (1. 3. 7) he suggests, half-seriously as Xenophon says, that Circe's failure to transform Odysseus was due not only to Hermes' aid but also to Odysseus' own self-control and abstinence. Antisthenes may have made a similar point in his περὶ Κίρκης, *On Circe* (or perhaps his περὶ τῆς ῥάβδου, *On the Wand*), and echoes have been seen in Dio Chrysostom's eighth oration, a homily put into the mouth of Diogenes the Cynic, in which Circe is equated with pleasure in a similar way (8. 20 ff.).[63] This suggests that one might expect to find other parallels of this kind. Antisthenes wrote περὶ Πρωτέως (i.e. on

cf. Poros and Penia at Pl. *Symp.* 203B). Philippson (p. 175) argues that he must have meant that Eumaeus owed his virtues to his upbringing by Poverty, in a metaphorical sense.

   [63] Cf. J. Luloffs, *De Antisthenis Studiis Rhetoricis* (Amsterdam, 1900), 42 ff., and Decleva, pp. 84 f. Horace *Ep.* 1. 2. 23–6 is very close to Dio *Or.* 8. 25 and both may derive from a Cynic source (cf. Kiessling-Heinze *ad loc.*). Antisthenean influence has also been conjectured at Dio *Or.* 8. 33 (Heracles' encounter with Prometheus). Here Diogenes the Cynic makes Prometheus a sophist suffering from pride and ambition (τῦφος and φιλονικία). Cf. Antisth. fr. 27, where however Prometheus reproaches Heracles with worldliness, and frr. 97, 151–2 (Antisthenean condemnation of τῦφος). If this is correct, Antisthenes interpreted Prometheus' punishment allegorically.

Proteus in the *Odyssey*). The meeting of Proteus and Menelaus furnishes the Homeric Scholia with plenty of material for moral reflection (cf. Decleva, p. 84), and in particular the line (*Od.* 4. 392) ὅττι τοι ἐν μεγάροισι κακόν τ᾽ ἀγαθόν τε τέτυκται ('whatever evil and good have been done in your palace') was supposed to have been taken as a motto for moral philosophy by Socrates, Antisthenes, Diogenes, and even Aristippus (cf. Ant. fr. 176, Decleva *ad loc.*). This would do no more than make Proteus a prototype for the σοφός (expert), as Odysseus evidently was also for Antisthenes (frr. 51-2, 54). But the kernel of Antisthenes' admiration for Odysseus lay in his interpretation of the epithet πολύτροπος (of many turns) as referring to Odysseus' rhetorical adaptability, his skill in varying his style to suit different audiences (fr. 51). Such an ability to assume different 'characters' (cf. Antisthenes' work περὶ λέξεως ἢ περὶ χαρακτήρων, *On Style or On Characters*) reminds one of Proteus' power of transformation. Dionysius of Halicarnassus (*Dem.* 8) actually compares Demosthenes to Proteus, because he incorporated the virtues of all the styles, and he adds that Proteus probably really represents 'a subtle variation of style in a skilful man'.[64] It is tempting to suggest that Antisthenes may have made this comparison also. At the end of Plato's *Ion* the rhapsode, driven into a corner, takes refuge in the assertion that his art enables him to know ἃ πρέπει . . . ἀνδρὶ εἰπεῖν καὶ ὁποῖα γυναικί, καὶ ὁποῖα δούλῳ καὶ ὁποῖα ἐλευθέρῳ, καὶ ὁποῖα ἀρχομένῳ καὶ ὁποῖα ἄρχοντι, 'what a man ought to say, or a woman, or a slave, or a freeman, or a subject or a ruler' (540B). This sophistic claim is curiously reminiscent of the scholion (to *Od.* 1. 1) which reports Antisthenes' view on the meaning of πολύτροπος, quoting as illustration the story of Pythagoras' speeches in different styles to children, women, rulers and ephebes.[65] After Ion has made this assertion, and Socrates has undermined it, the dialogue ends with Socrates accusing him of behaving like Proteus, because he constantly changes his ground (541E)! Socrates makes the same comparison in the *Euthydemus* (288B), where the two sophists are said to be imitating Proteus, τὸν Αἰγύπτιον σοφιστήν (the Egyptian Sophist). This

---

[64] διαλέκτου ποικίλον τι χρῶμα ἐν ἀνδρὶ σοφῷ.

[65] It is not certain that this story was mentioned by Antisthenes, but it was known in the fourth century BC. (Dicaearchus fr. 33 Wehrli). Cf. Rostagni, *Studi italiani di filologia classica*, 2 (1922), 148 ff. (= *Scritti minori* 1. 1 ff.) for an interesting, if rather speculative discussion, and see also Decleva, p. 107, Burkert, *Lore and Science*, 115 n. 38 (who favours its inclusion in the Antisthenes fragment).

kind of playful comparison might be a reflection of a more serious attempt to portray Proteus as a mythical model for the ideal orator and sophist. Plato attacks the story of Proteus in the *Republic* (381Bff.) because it represents a god changing his form, and such criticism would give a suitable stimulus to the search for alternative interpretations.[66]

One might find another echo of this kind in the curious statement in the *Republic* (376 B) that good watchdogs have a philosophical nature, because they love those whom they know, and so are φιλομαθεῖς, fond of learning. This was taken up by the Cynics (cf. Elias *In cat.* III. 2 ff.), of whom Antisthenes was regarded (rightly or wrongly) as a forerunner.[67] One of his Odyssean works was περὶ τοῦ κυνός (*On the Dog*), and this presumably refers to Argos, who recognised Odysseus despite his disguise and then died. Argos' faithful endurance in the face of ill-treatment by those around him was a parallel to that of Odysseus, which Antisthenes seems to have admired as a prototype of his own ideal of indifference to circumstances.[68]

Antisthenes' few works on the *Iliad* included one περὶ ἡδονῆς (*On Pleasure*). This is at first sight a surprising title for a work on this poem. In Dio's homily of Diogenes, which I have mentioned already, the battle against pleasure is said to be a more difficult struggle than that fought over the Greek ships at Troy (*Or.* 8. 20 f., quoting *Il.* 15. 696, 711 f.), but that on its own is too general to be of much use. More specifically, Plato in the *Republic* (586C) compares the struggles of the deluded multitude over material pleasures to the battles over the phantom Helen, an image which was taken up by the Neoplatonists (cf. Buffière, *Les Mythes*, 410 ff.). Aristotle in the *Ethics* (1109^b7 ff.) says that we must 'feel towards pleasure as the Trojan

---

[66] Proteus was a popular subject of later allegory. Cf. Schol. *Od.* 4. 384, and Buffière, *Les Mythes*, 180 ff., 239, 339 ff., 552, 566 f.

[67] According to some he was called Κύων, Dog (Diog. Laert. 6. 13).

[68] Cf. E. Weber, *De Dione Chrysostomo Cynicorum sectatore* (Diss. Leipzig, 1887), 110 f., Luloffs, *De Antisthenis*, 58. Another parallel which does not seem to have been noted is that between Antisthenes' περὶ Ἀμφιαράου *On Amphiaraus* (cf. *Od.* 15. 244 ff.) and Ps. Plat. *Axioch.* 368A, where Prodicus is said to have quoted these lines in a speech in praise of death (because Amphiaraus was especially dear to Zeus and Apollo, and died before reaching the threshold of old age). Their use for this purpose surely involves a type of ὑπόνοια. Antisthenes wrote περὶ τοῦ ἀποθανεῖν, *On Dying*, περὶ ζωῆς καὶ θανάτου, *On Life and Death*, and περὶ τῶν ἐν Ἅιδου, *On Things in Hades*, and Alcidamas also wrote an ἔπαινος θανάτου, *Praise of Death*.

elders felt towards Helen, and on all occasions repeat their saying: for by sending her away like this we shall be less likely to go wrong'. He refers of course to the famous scene on the walls of Troy, when the old men comment on her fatal beauty, and add the prayer that she might return home and save them from further harm (*Il*. 3. 159 f.).

One wonders whether this type of comparison gave a lever to Antisthenes' discourse. One of his Odyssean pieces was περὶ Ἑλένης καὶ Πηνελόπης, (*On Helen and Penelope*). If he took Helen as a symbol for the fatal charm of pleasure, Penelope may have represented an image of the faithful labours of the philosopher. Another disciple of Socrates, Aristippus, is said to have compared those who had enjoyed the traditional curriculum of education without the study of philosophy to the suitors of Penelope, who possessed her servant-girls but not their mistress herself (Diog. Laert. 2. 79)![69]

The use of Homeric scenes and characters to illustrate one's views was already a commonplace activity in this period, and although this differs from allegory it created a way of thinking from which allegory might easily grow.[70] It is not possible to say definitely how far Antisthenes went in this direction. If we leave the game of speculating about his lost works and return to his quoted fragments, one of these at least (on Nestor's cup) shows that he was prepared to interpret a Homeric passage, whose literal sense was obvious enough, in a metaphorical way. His interpretation of πολύτροπος also shows a combination of linguistic analysis with the attempt to elicit a form of ὑπόνοια. All this, however, is very different from the system-building of Metrodorus, which seems designed more as a display of ingenuity, whereas Antisthenes' seriousness can hardly be doubted. οἶος πέπνυται, τοὶ δὲ σκιαὶ ἀίσσουσιν. ('He alone has sense, but they are shadows flitting to and fro.'). It is easy to see how the former type of approach brought the allegerists into early disrepute, whilst it is not unlikely that Antisthenean ideas about Homer are reflected in the work of Plato and later writers, such as Zeno and Dio Chrysostom.

In conclusion, we may say that all these approaches to Homer help to demonstrate the influence which he exercised over a crucial period

---

[69] The Neoplatonists took Penelope as an allegory of philosophy (Buffière, *Les Mythes*, 389 ff.).

[70] Cf. Wehrli, *Zur Gesch. d. alleg. Deutung*, 64 ff., for some valuable remarks on this.

in the development of Greek thought, when Scholarship was still in her infancy, ἀταλὰ φρονέουσα (thinking playful thoughts), and Philosophy had not yet come of age with Plato, but was still looking wistfully over her shoulder towards her origins in the world of myths and poetry.

# 4

# A Theory of Imitation in Plato's Republic[1]

## ELIZABETH BELFIORE

Plato's discussion of imitation in *Republic* 10 has often been called self-contradictory, or at least inconsistent with the treatment of *mimêsis* in *Republic* 3. It is argued, for example, that while *Republic* 3 banishes only some imitative poetry, *Republic* 10 opens with the statement that all imitative poetry has been excluded from the ideal state (10. 595a), but then nevertheless allows some forms of imitation, namely hymns and encomia (10. 607a).[2] Others claim that Plato fails to define important terms, such as 'imitation,' which he uses inconsistently. For example, critics have said that 'imitation' means 'impersonation' in *Republic* 3, but 'representation' in *Republic* 10.[3] The most extreme position is that Plato has no coherent concept of the imitation he attacks, but simply strings together a series of bad arguments.[4]

[1] This revision of my 1984 article contains minor stylistic changes and omits some references and Greek, but is substantially the same as the original. An excellent recent discussion of *mimêsis* is that of S. Halliwell, *The Aesthetics of Mimesis* (Princeton, 2002). Unless otherwise noted, all translations are my own.

[2] See especially C. Brownson, *Plato's Studies and Criticism of the Poets* (Boston, 1920), 88-94. More recently L. Moss, 'Plato and the *Poetics*', *Philological Quarterly*, 50 (1971), 533-42, argues against various attempts to reconcile books 3 and 10. For other surveys of views about the problem of consistency see also T. Gould, 'Plato's Hostility to Art', *Arion*, 3 (1964), 70-91; G. Sörbom, *Mimêsis and Art* (Stockholm, 1966), esp. 129-51; M. Partee, *Plato's Poetics* (Salt Lake City, 1981), 1-22; A. Nehamas, 'Plato on Imitation and Poetry in Republic 10', in J. Moravcsik and P. Temko (eds.), *Plato on Beauty, Wisdom, and the Arts* (Totowa, NJ, 1982), 47-78. Unless otherwise noted, I follow Burnet's OCT.

[3] For the view that Plato uses *mimeisthai* (to imitate) in several different senses see P. Vicaire, *Platon: Critique littéraire* (Paris, 1960), 221-5, and E. Schaper, *Prelude to Aesthetics* (London, 1968), 42-8. Some of those who hold that Plato uses *mimêsis* in the sense of 'impersonation' in *Republic* 3 and in that of 'representation' in *Republic* 10 are Brownson (above, n. 2) 92-3; F. M. Cornford, *The Republic of Plato* (Oxford, 1941), 324 n. 1; E. Havelock, *Preface to Plato* (Cambridge, Mass., and London, 1963), 20-6.

[4] See, for example, J. W. H. Atkins, *Literary Criticism in Antiquity* (Cambridge,

Numerous attempts have been made to resolve or explain these alleged inconsistencies. Some deny that Plato really means everything he seems to be saying,[5] or argue that book 10 expresses a different view from that of book 3 because it was written later.[6] Others believe that the apparent inconsistencies are due to the quite different aims of the two books.[7] Still others argue that Plato defines and discusses a good and a bad kind of imitation.[8] Or again, certain scholars claim that Plato's aesthetic theories in other dialogues can explain some apparent inconsistencies in the *Republic*.[9]

It has not been noticed, however, that *Republic* 3 and 10 contain a theory of imitation in the visual and poetic arts that is remarkably consistent and detailed in certain respects. In these books Plato defines, explicitly or by clear implication, many characteristics of different imitative arts and many relationships among these arts. This important area of definitions and relationships has never been adequately investigated.[10]

There are many indications of a consistently applied definitional strategy, with book 10. 595a–608b elaborating and explaining ideas briefly stated or merely implicit in book 3. 392c–398b. For example, the discussion of style (*lexis*) in the *Republic* 3 passage defines imitation as 'likening oneself to someone else' (3. 393c5–6), distinguishes genres of poetry from one another on the basis of their

1934), i. 48–51, and J. Annas, *An Introduction to Plato's Republic* (Oxford, 1981), 336–44.

[5] Representatives of this view are W. C. Greene, 'Plato's View of Poetry', *HSCP* 29 (1918), 56; A. H. Gilbert, 'Did Plato Banish the Poets or the Critics?', *Studies in Philology*, 36 (1939), 1–19; I. M. Crombie, *An Examination of Plato's Doctrines* (London, 1962), i. 147.

[6] This is the view of, for example, R. Nettleship, *Lectures on the Republic of Plato* (London, 1901²), 341, and G. Else, *The Structure and Date of Book 10 of Plato's Republic* (Heidelberg, 1972).

[7] Some interpretations along this line are those of W. Jaeger, *Paideia: The Ideals of Greek Culture*, trans. G. Highet (New York, 1943), ii. 215; R. G. Collingwood, 'Plato's Philosophy of Art,' *Mind*, NS 34 (1925), 163–4; Nehamas (above, n. 2).

[8] The best-known proponent of the view that Plato distinguishes between a 'good' and a 'bad' kind of imitation is J. Tate, ' "Imitation" in Plato's *Republic*', *CQ* 22 (1928), 16–23, and 'Plato and "Imitation" ', *CQ* 26 (1932), 161–9.

[9] See, for example, W. J. Oates, *Plato's View of Art* (New York, 1972) and W. J. Verdenius, *Mimêsis: Plato's Doctrine of Artistic Imitation and its Meaning to us* (Leiden, 1962).

[10] Vicaire (above, n. 3), 236–60, though he does not examine the *Republic* in sufficient detail, is one of the few who have undertaken a study of Plato's views on poetic genres.

use of imitation (3. 394b–c), and concludes with the condemnation
of one particular kind of imitation. *Republic* 10 opens with a reference
to the *Republic* 3 discussion of imitation. 'We did well . . . in not
admitting any [poetry] that is imitative [*mimêtikê*]' (10. 595a2–5)
and explicitly formulates the theory that the imitator imitates the
works of craftsmen, a view strongly suggested at *Republic* 3. 397e ff.
Definitions and relationships among the arts are as important in the
*Republic* 10 passage as they are in *Republic* 3. Plato begins the discussion of *mimêsis* in *Republic* 10 by asking for a definition of
'*mimêsis* in general', stating that this has not yet been adequately
given (10. 595c). Plato then suggests that this definition is given
within the next few pages, for he remarks, at 10. 599d3–4, that 'we
defined the imitator as the craftsman of an image (*eidôlon*)'. Book 10
goes on to define the subject matter of one kind of imitative poetry
(603c) and to give an account of the reactions of the audience to
different genres of poetry (605c–d). Throughout book 10 Plato is also
concerned with the relationship between painting and poetry and
with that between imitation and craftsmanship.

Nevertheless, Plato's views on the defining characteristics of the
imitative arts are, in *Republic* 3 and 10, often obscured by his not presenting them formally and explicitly. Classification is not, after all,
Plato's primary concern in these books, as it is in portions of his
*Sophist*, but is subordinate to ethical and psychological concerns. It
will therefore be helpful to reorganize Plato's material, collecting his
sometimes scattered remarks in *Republic* 3. 392c–398b and 10.
595a–608b, assigning a single label to each kind of imitative art and
explicitly describing relationships that Plato sometimes leaves his
reader to infer. The following examination begins with the most
general definition of imitation (Section I), proceeds to two important
kinds of imitation which Plato distinguishes and which we will call
'versatile imitation' and 'imitation with knowledge' (Section II), considers the two kinds of versatile imitation with which Plato is concerned: painting and poetry (Section III), and concludes with a study
of the genres of versatile poetry Plato mentions: epic, tragedy, lyric,
and comedy (Section IV). My study will, as far as possible, limit itself
to the two passages, *Republic* 3. 392c–398b and *Republic* 10. 595a–
608b, that form a structural and thematic unity.[11] The diagram outlines my procedure (Figure 1).

[11] This restriction means, for example, that I will not attempt to study Plato's views

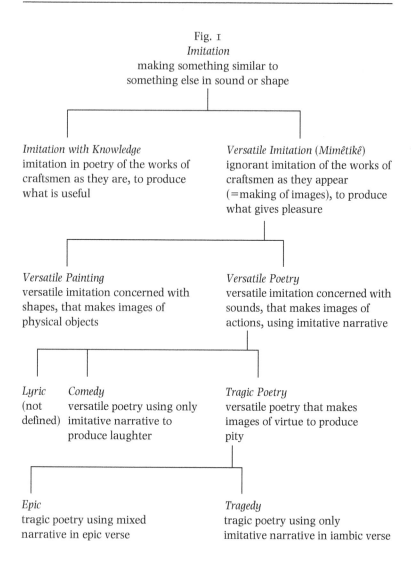

Fig. 1
*Imitation*
making something similar to
something else in sound or shape

*Imitation with Knowledge*
imitation in poetry of the works of
craftsmen as they are, to produce
what is useful

*Versatile Imitation (Mimêtikê)*
ignorant imitation of the works of
craftsmen as they appear
(=making of images), to produce
what gives pleasure

*Versatile Painting*
versatile imitation concerned with
shapes, that makes images of
physical objects

*Versatile Poetry*
versatile imitation concerned with
sounds, that makes images of
actions, using imitative narrative

*Lyric*     *Comedy*
(not       versatile poetry using only
defined)   imitative narrative to
           produce laughter

*Tragic Poetry*
versatile poetry that makes
images of virtue to produce
pity

*Epic*
tragic poetry using mixed
narrative in epic verse

*Tragedy*
tragic poetry using only
imitative narrative in iambic verse

on music, an important imitative art. For more comprehensive studies of *mimêsis* in
the works of Plato and other Greek writers see R. McKeon, 'Literary Criticism and the
Concept of Imitation in Antiquity', *Modern Philology*, 34 (1936), 1–35; H. Koller, *Die
Mimêsis in der Antike* (Bern, 1954); G. Else, ' "Imitation" in the Fifth Century', *CP* 53
(1958), 73–90 and *addendum* 245; Sörbom (above, n. 2).

## I. IMITATION

*Republic* 3. 393c5-6 gives the most comprehensive definition of imitation (*to mimeisthai*) found in the two passages: 'Is it not true that to make oneself similar to someone else in sound or in shape is to imitate that person to whom one makes oneself similar?' It has not been noticed that this passage anticipates some important features of *Republic* 10. First, it implies that since the imitator imitates by making something that is similar to something else in sound or shape, he is both an imitator of sounds or shapes and a maker of (other similar) sounds or shapes. Plato fails to spell this out, and it is of little importance in *Republic* 3. It does become significant, however, for an understanding of book 10, where Plato calls the imitator both an imitator of images (sounds or shapes), at 10. 600e5, for example, and a maker of images, at 10. 599a7.[12] In using the concepts of sound and shape to define imitation *Republic* 3. 393c5-6 also antici-pates *Republic* 10. 603b6-7, which distinguishes painting and poetry by their respective use of sight and sound.

*Republic* 3. 393c5-6 also anticipates another important concept of *Republic* 10: mistake. To imitate in sound (voice) is to make oneself similar to someone else in voice (3. 393c5-6), and this, Plato states at 3. 393c1-3, is to speak as though one were someone else. To speak as though one were someone else is, in turn, to try to make people believe that one is someone else (3. 393a8-b2), that is, to try to make people mistake one for someone else. Thus, to make oneself similar to someone else (to imitate someone else) is to try to make people mistake oneself for someone else. On the other hand, Plato writes, there is no imitation when the poet does not hide himself (3. 393c11-d2) or try to deceive us (3. 393a6-7).

In *Republic* 10 also, imitators try to make people mistake imitations for something else. At 10. 600e7-601a2, for example, an imitation is said to be mistaken for the truth by those 'judging from colors and shapes.'[13] In *Republic* 10, however, Plato does not follow the

---

[12] See Nehamas (above, n. 2), 62, for a good discussion of this aspect of *Republic* 10.

[13] Plato frequently stresses the imitator's ability to cause his audience to make mistakes. See, for example, *Republic* 10. 598c1-4, 598d2-3, 598e5-599a3, 601a4-b1, 602b1-4, 602c10-d4, 605b6-c4. On the kinds of mistakes involved, and on audience psychology generally, in *Republic* 10, see my 'Plato's Greatest Accusation Against Poetry', *Canadian Journal of Philosophy*, suppl. 9 (1983), 39-62.

linguistic usage of *Republic* 3, in which the relationship between artifacts and imitations is said to be one of similarity. This may be because he wishes to reserve the vocabulary of similarity for the relationship between artifacts and Forms; at least, artifacts are said to be 'such as that which is' at 10. 597a5. However we interpret this latter relationship, we should not confuse it with that between imitations and artifacts. Imitations are mistaken for artifacts, but artifacts are never mistaken for Forms in *Republic* 3 and 10. Further, Forms could not be imitated in the sense defined at *Republic* 3. 393c5–6, 'making similar in sound or shape,' for they do not have these sensible qualities. At *Republic* 5. 476b, for example, Plato explicitly distinguishes the Form Beauty from 'the beautiful sounds . . . and colors and shapes and everything that is crafted from such things.'

In one respect, however, 3. 393c5–6 might at least appear to contradict Plato's view of imitation in *Republic* 10 and elsewhere in *Republic* 3. Since it describes only a kind of imitation in which one human being uses himself (ἑαυτόν) to imitate another human being (ἐκεῖνον and ἄλλῳ are masculine), it cannot define the imitation of living things or of inanimate objects mentioned frequently in the two books (for example, at 3. 396b5–7, 3. 397a4–7, 10. 598a1–3). Many have in fact thought that Plato uses 'imitation' to mean 'impersonation' (in which a human being uses his or her own body to imitate another human being) in *Republic* 3, and to mean 'representation' (as when, for example, a painter imitates a bed) in *Republic* 10.[14]

This interpretation, however, risks imputing to Plato a distinction in which he is not interested. While it is true that in his *Sophist* (267a3–4) Plato distinguishes imitation using one's own body (acting, for example) from imitation using implements (painting, for example), in the *Republic* Plato not only ignores this distinction, he also fails to distinguish imitation of human beings from imitation of living things or of inanimate objects, shifting without warning from discussion of the one to the other. Thus, in *Republic* 3, Plato equates imitation of the sounds of animals and of natural phenomena with imitation of madmen (3. 396b5–9), and in *Republic* 10 he shifts unexpectedly from the painter who imitates the 'products of

---

[14] See above, n. 3.

craftsmen' (10. 598a2-3) to the painter who paints 'a shoemaker, a carpenter, the other craftsmen' (10. 598b8-c1). The masculines in 3. 393c5-6, then, do not have any theoretical significance and may be replaced by more general terms in a definition of 'imitation' (to mimeisthai). What Plato consistently means in Republic 3 and 10 is that 'To imitate is to make one thing (or person) similar to another thing (or person) in sound or shape.'

## II. VERSATILE IMITATION AND IMITATION WITH KNOWLEDGE

### A. Versatile Imitation (Mimêtikê)

Mimêtikê, 'versatile imitation,' is Plato's technical term for imitation of many things, and mimêtikos (pl. mimêtikoi), 'versatile imitator,' is the term for the practitioner of this art. That the -ikê forms of mimeisthai refer only to imitation of many things and that this helps to reconcile the account of Republic 3 with that of Republic 10 has been noticed only by Victor Menza, in an unpublished dissertation, to which the first part of this section owes much.[15]

Like other Greek -ikê words, mimêtikê designates an art or science, and mimêtikos refers to the expert in this art. It is likely that these terms were coined by Plato and first used by him at Republic 3. 395e1.[16] There, as Menza notes, Plato asks whether the guardian should be a mimêtikos, and immediately after, at 3. 395a2, he gives what amounts to a definition of this new term: 'A person will imitate many things and be a mimêtikos.' 'Will imitate many things' explains the new -ikê form: the mimêtikos is someone who imitates many things.[17] Although Plato also uses other forms of mimeisthai (to imitate) and its cognates in this way, mimêtikos always has this meaning in the Republic, and mimêtikê always designates the art of imitating many things.

---

[15] V. Menza, 'Poetry and the Technê Theory', Diss. Johns Hopkins 1972.

[16] This conclusion is based on the studies of P. Chantraine, Études sur le vocabulaire grec (Paris, 1956), 98; A. N. Ammann, -IKOΣ bei Platon (Freiburg, 1953); Else, 'Imitation' (above, n. 11); L. Brandwood, A Word Index to Plato (Compendia Series, 8 (Leeds, 1976).

[17] See Menza (above, n. 15) 132. Chantraine (above, n. 16), 141-2, notes that Plato often defines -ikê words as he introduces them.

Plato characterizes versatile imitation as imitation of many things, or as imitation of the works of craftsmen, or as imitation and making of images. I argue below that these different descriptions all refer to the same aspect of the imitator's activity.

1. *Imitation of Many Things*   In *Republic* 3, as Menza points out,[18] Plato condemns only the versatile imitator. The young guardians are not allowed to be *mimêtikoi*, imitating the many things (artisans, women, slaves, vicious people) they should not themselves become (3. 395d–396b), but they are allowed to imitate the one 'craftsman of freedom' (3. 395b8–c5) they are to become as adults. Plato also finds acceptable the poet who is an 'unmixed imitator of the good man' (3. 397d4–5), exiling only the poet who 'is able to become everything because of his cleverness and to imitate everything' (3. 398a1–2), that is, the *mimêtikos*.

*Republic* 10 is, as Menza notes, consistent with book 3 in condemning only the versatile imitator. The technical vocabulary at the opening of book 10 alerts us to the fact that versatile imitation alone is being considered: 'We founded the city well . . . when we did not admit all of it [poetry] that is *mimêtikê*' (10. 595a2–5). This is entirely consistent with book 3, which, as I have just shown, also rejected only the *mimêtikos*.[19]

Plato departs from this technical vocabulary when he goes on to ask what '*mimêsis* in general' is (10. 595c7). This departure is explained by the fact that, since 10. 595c–598c is a proof that the painter (or at least one kind of painter) is a *mimêtikos*, Plato does not want to use the technical term until the proof is complete. In this proof, Plato first compares the painter to a man who carries a mirror around everywhere. Because the man with the mirror does not try to deceive people, he is not an imitator,[20] although he resembles an imitator in that he 'makes' many things. He can make 'everything that

---

[18] Above (n. 15), 126–33.

[19] See Menza (above, n. 15), 252 and n. 1, p. 362.

[20] This difference between the man with the mirror and the painter is not usually noticed: see, for example, Partee (above, n. 2), 113–14; Annas (above, n. 4), 336; R. Cross and A. Woozley, *Plato's Republic* (New York, 1964), 274. There is no question of deception in *Republic* 10 until 598c, where the painter, 'if he is a good painter', is said to be able to deceive 'children and fools' by showing his works 'from a distance'. Imitation, unlike the act of carrying a mirror, requires skill and intent to deceive.

each of the craftsmen makes' (10. 596c2), 'every artifact,' 'everything that grows from the earth,' 'every living thing,' 'everything in the heavens,' and 'everything under the earth' (10. 596c4-9). Next, Plato establishes that the painter is an imitator (*mimêtês*, not *mimêtikos*) in an argument ending at 10. 597e10: 'We have agreed on the imitator (*mimêtên*).' Finally, Plato proves that painting imitates images and is, therefore, *mimêtikê* (10. 598a-c). The technical term *mimêtikê* reappears in this proof, at 10. 598b6, after which it is used frequently in the dialogue. Hereafter, the imitator book 10 condemns is the *mimêtikos*, who pretends to imitate and know 'everything' (for example at 10. 598c5-d1, 10. 598e1). At 10. 603a11, in fact, Plato replaces the earlier '*mimêsis* in general' with '*mimêtikê* in general.'

2. *Imitation of the Works of Craftsmen*   The many things the versatile imitator imitates are the many works of many kinds of craftsmen. That Plato's main concern is with craftsmanship has often been noted,[21] and is obvious from his constant opposition of imitator to craftsman. In *Republic* 10 the painter is said to be 'an imitator of that which those others make.' Plato then concludes: 'This, then, is what the tragedian also will be, if he is an imitator, and all the other imitators: someone who is by nature third from the king and the truth . . . Then we have agreed on the imitator' (10. 597e2-10). The painter is then said to imitate 'the works of the craftsmen as they appear' (10. 598a-b). Plato also writes that Homer will be shown to be a versatile imitator rather than a craftsman if he proves not to have done the deeds (*erga*) of different kinds of craftsmen (10. 599b3-7) but only to have imitated their words (10. 599c2). As I argue below (Section III.B.2), imitation of character (*êthos*) in *Republic* 10 is also imitation of the works of craftsmen who have knowledge of how to act wisely.

In *Republic* 3 also the versatile imitator imitates the works of craftsmen, although Plato is less explicit about this than he is in *Republic* 10. The ideal state of *Republic* 3 is founded on the principle of one man one work. There must be no 'double man' or 'manifold man' in this state, writes Plato, since 'each one does one work' (3. 397e1-2).

[21] Some good discussions of this topic are those of Menza (above, n. 15) and J. Moravcsik, 'Noetic Aspiration and Artistic Inspiration', in *Plato on Beauty, Wisdom and the Arts* (above, n. 2), 29-46.

Only in this state is the shoemaker a shoemaker and not a pilot in addition, the farmer a farmer and not a juryman as well (3. 397e4–7). For this reason, the person who can 'become all sorts of things and imitate everything' must be sent on his way (3. 398a–b), and the guardians must not be *mimêtikoi* (3. 394e–395d). Plato could only write in this way if he thought of the versatile imitator as someone who tries to imitate all the crafts. If the versatile imitator were himself a real craftsman, he would be doing one work, like the others. If, however, he were no craftsman at all, he would be an idler rather than a 'manifold man.' Instead, the versatile imitator is exiled because he is a pseudo-craftsman, a meddler in every sort of craft.[22]

3. *Making of Images*  That the *mimêtikos* is a pseudo-craftsman who imitates many things has been well understood in the literature, but Plato's concept of imitation of images (*eidôla*, sing. *eidôlon*) has been much misunderstood.[23] On my account, 'imitation of images' is simply a more accurate, technical term for 'imitation of many things' and 'imitation of the works of craftsmen.'

At *Republic* 10. 599d2–4 Plato remarks, as he cross-examines Homer, that the imitator has been defined: 'Dear Homer, if you are not third from the truth concerning virtue, the craftsman of an image, whom we defined as an imitator [*mimêtês*] . . .'. Since, as will be shown below (Section IV.C), virtue is the subject matter of only one kind of versatile imitator, Plato's question to Homer tells us that the *mimêtikos* (*mimêtên* obviously has this meaning here) has been defined as 'third from the truth, craftsman of an image.' Plato must be referring, first, to the argument ending at 10. 597e10 (above, Section II.A.2), where the imitator was agreed to be 'third from the truth' about craftsmanship. Next, 'craftsman of an image' at 10. 599d3 can only refer to 10. 597e10–598b8, where Plato introduced

---

[22] N. White, *A Companion to Plato's Republic* (Indianapolis and Cambridge, 1979), 96–7, notes that Plato's condemnation of imitative art in *Republic* 3 is based on his 'Principle of the Natural Division of Labor'. See also P. Shorey, *What Plato Said* (Chicago, 1933), 219, and B. Bosanquet, *A Companion to Plato's Republic for English Readers* (New York, 1895), 99 (cited by White, p. 97).

[23] For example, the images (*eidôla*) of *Republic* 10 have been connected with the images (*eikones*) of the Divided Line (*Republic* 6. 509–11) by, among others, H. J. Paton, 'Plato's Theory of *Eikasia*', *Proc. Aristotelian Soc.* 22 (1921–2), 69–104; S. Ringbom, 'Plato on Images', *Theoria*, 31 (1965), 95–6; J.-P. Vernant, 'Image et apparence dans la théorie platonicienne de la *mimêsis*', *Journal de psychologie*, 72 (1975), 136. Other common errors are discussed below, in this section.

the technical term *eidôlon* to explain 'in what way' (10. 598a7) the *mimêtikos* is able to make 'everything.' After it was agreed that the *mimêtikos* imitates not the Form but the works of craftsmen (10. 598a1-4), Plato asked whether he imitates these works 'as they are or as they appear' (10. 598a5), and explained this distinction in the paragraph at 10. 598a7-9: 'It's like this. A couch, if one sees it from the side or from the front or in any way whatsoever, does it differ at all itself from itself, or does it not differ at all but appears different?' The couch was then agreed not to differ but only to appear different (10. 598a10) and painting was said, at 10. 598b1-5, to imitate not 'that which is' but 'that which appears' (*to phainomenon*), and to be imitation of a 'phantasm,' not of 'truth.' The conclusion then followed: '*Mimêtikê* is, then, far from what is true, and, as it seems, for this reason makes everything, because it grasps some small part of each thing and that an image' (10. 598b6-8).

In this passage (10. 598a1-b8) *eidôlon* is a synonym of 'that which appears' (*to phainomemon*), of 'appearance' (*phantasma*), and of a thing 'as it appears' (*phainetai*). It is the opposite of 'that which is,' of 'truth,' and of a thing 'as it is.'

Plato distinguishes image from truth on an epistemological basis. The couch 'as it is,' or the truth about the couch, is the object of the craft knowledge of the user or of the true belief of the maker (10. 601c-602b). It cannot be perceived by the senses: the couch looks different no matter how one sees it (10. 598a7-9). The couch 'as it appears,' the 'appearance' (*to phainomenon*) or image, on the other hand, is the object of ignorant versatile imitation. The versatile imitator can imitate images 'although he does not know about the crafts of any of these [craftsmen]' (10. 598c1); he deceives the person who is 'not able to distinguish knowledge and ignorance, that is, imitation' (10. 598d4-5); he neither knows nor has right belief about what he imitates (10. 602a). His ignorance distinguishes him from the craftsman, and is a necessary condition for his imitation of images (10. 599a6-b7). The same contrast between *mimêtikos* and craftsman was strongly suggested at *Republic* 3. 394e-395b, where Plato stated that it was impossible to do or imitate many things well: only the ignorant person, he implied, could attempt to do this. At 10. 601b9-10 Plato clearly indicates the epistemological basis for his distinction between image and 'truth' when he characterizes the *mimêtikos* as someone who does not know the truth but only [perceives] the appearance: 'The maker of an image, the imitator, we say, knows nothing about the truth, but [perceives] the appearance' (*phainomenou*). The image, then, is sound or shape as perceived by someone ignorant of anything but sound and shape. The maker of images makes images that may be mistaken, by someone as ignorant as himself, for 'that which is.' 'That which is,' on the other hand, is a sensible artifact, a couch or a table, as understood by someone with knowledge of craftsmanship. The person with knowledge, like the *mimêtikos*, directs his attention to sensibles; however, by also 'looking to the Form' (10. 596b7), and consulting the user about what is truly fine (10. 601d8–e2), he has come to understand and not merely perceive sensible artifacts.

Because, then an image is *any* object perceived by an ignorant person, it is a mistake to think, as Else does, for example, that the *mimêtikos* will be better off if he happens to find a well-made artifact to imitate than if he imitates a poorly made one.[24] Plato's point is that even if, as in the examples in *Republic* 10, the 'model' is a well-made product of craftsmanship, the ignorant *mimêtikos* is only capable of grasping, imitating, and making images.

Another common mistake is to confuse imitation of images in *Republic* 10 with *phantastikê* (the art of making appearances) in the *Sophist* 235d–236c.[25] Plato distinguishes *eikastikê* (the art of making likenesses), which gives imitations the true proportions and colors of the originals (*Sophist* 235d6–e2), from *phantastikê*, which gives them the proportions that merely appear fine, 'letting the truth go' (*Sophist* 236a4–6). It makes, for example, the upper parts of very large statues proportionately larger, and the lower parts proportionately smaller than those of the originals (235e5–236a6). The products made by *phantastikê*, Plato writes, only appear to resemble what is fine 'because of our view from a poor position,' but if someone could 'view them adequately,' they would not appear to resemble the originals (236b4–7). Thus, while the *Sophist* distinguishes poor and good viewing conditions—good conditions being sufficient to tell us whether or not the truth is adequately represented—the *Republic* opposes an unchanging 'that which is,' that can be understood, to a constantly changing 'that which appears,' that can only be seen. The couch in *Republic* 10 apears different no matter how one sees it (10. 598a8), and one view is as bad as another. And again, unlike the *Republic*, which distinguishes imitation of images from imitation of that which is on the basis of craft knowledge, the *Sophist* makes no distinction between *phantastikê* and *eikastikê* on this basis: the two arts would require the same knowledge of the proportions of the original in order to make their respective products.

Once we have rid ourselves of these misunderstandings we can also see another of Plato's motives for introducing his concept of images. In *Republic* 3 Plato had characterized the *mimêtikos* as someone who imitates many different things. Now, Plato adds that the *mimêtikos* also imitates many different appearances of a single thing. He then uses this very demonstration of the apparent breadth of the field of the *mimêtikos* to prove its truly narrow scope, for he concludes that the *mimêtikos* does not really imitate 'everything' but only one thing over and over again: an image, which is a 'small part of each thing' (598b7). The versatile imitator's claim to universal skill has been neatly demolished.

Plato's concept of *mimêtikê* thus remains the same throughout *Republic* 3 and 10: versatile imitation is the ignorant making of images of the works of craftsmen as they appear. This concept is, however, elucidated only gradually. At first, the *mimêtikos* is said to be someone who imitates many things. These many things are then explicitly shown to be the works of craftsmen, and finally, to be these works 'as they appear,' that is, images as opposed to 'that which is.' The *mimêtikos* is consistently distinguished from the craftsman by his ignorance. He is ignorant of the truth about that which he imitates, and he leads others equally ignorant to mistake his images for 'that which is.'

Another distinguishing characteristic of *mimêtikê* is that it aims at producing pleasure. At 3. 397d6–8 Plato notes that the 'mixed man,' the *mimêtikos*, is pleasing, especially to boys and the crowd. *Republic* 10. 605d3 and 606b4 speak of the pleasure we get from imitations; 10. 607a5 refers to the 'sweetened Muse'; 10. 607c4–5 mentions 'that poetry and imitation [which is] devoted to pleasure,' and 10.

607d6–e2 asks the defenders of poetry to prove that it is not only pleasant but also useful.[26]

## B. *Imitation with Knowledge*

Plato's views on the possibility of a 'good' kind of imitation are much less clear and coherent than his theory of *mimêtikê*. He says very little about it, and when he does, he seems at one time to imply that there is or can be a good kind of imitation, while at another he appears to deny or ignore this possibility. Nevertheless, my analysis of *mimêtikê* is helpful here also. As I will argue, Plato's views on *mimêtikê* and craftsmanship imply that there cannot be a good kind of imitation (in the sense of 'imitation' defined above, Section I) in painting. In the case of poetry, however, his views do allow for a good kind of imitation, the antithesis of imitation of 'things as they appear.'

Those who argue for a Platonic theory of a 'good' kind of imitation[27] can point to a number of passages in *Republic* 3 and 10 in which Plato opposes the kind of imitation he condemns not only to craftsmanship but also to imitation of 'that which is,' or of the good. Thus, in *Republic* 3 he exiles the *mimêtikos*, but writes that 'if they [the guardians] imitate, they should imitate . . . brave, self-controlled, pious and free men' (3. 395c3–5). He also permits the poet who is an 'unmixed imitator of the good man' to remain (3. 397d4–5). Plato is most explicit about a good kind of art at 3. 401aff., a passage not included among those with which I am primarily concerned. Here, Plato commends poets who can 'put the image of the good character into their poems' (3. 401b1–3), and craftsmen who can 'track down the nature of the beautiful and the graceful' (3. 401c4–5), whether in painting 'images of living creatures' or in making houses (3. 401b5–6). In *Republic* 10 also, Plato opposes versatile imitation of the works of craftsmen 'as they appear' to the possibility of imitation of the works of craftsmen 'as they are' (10. 598a–b), and he contrasts imitation of the 'complaining character' with the possibility of imitating the 'wise and calm character' (604e).

In themselves, however, these passages offer little support for a

---

[26] On the opposition of pleasure and the useful in Plato's aesthetics see Moravcsik (above, n. 21), esp. 30, and V. Goldschmidt, 'Le Problème de la tragédie d'après Platon', *REG* 61 (1948), 23.                    [27] See above, n. 8.

Platonic theory of good imitation. In all of *Republic* 10 Plato says nothing about this kind of imitation except to deny that the *mimêtikos* engages in it. In the passage at 3. 395c he discusses this kind of imitation in merely hypothetical terms: '*if* they imitate . . .'. Again, in the passage at 3. 401a ff., *mimêsis* and its cognates occur only once, in a usage apparently quite different from that in the earlier discussion of *mimêtikê*.[28] The same passage calls both artists and craftsmen *demiourgoi* (craftsmen),[29] although elsewhere imitators and craftsmen are strongly contrasted. Thus, it is doubtful that Plato is discussing imitation at all at 3. 401a ff. What he is praising may instead be a kind of craftsmanship.

Plato's explicit statements offer even less evidence of a theory of a good kind of imitation in painting. The account of imitation and *mimêtikê* in *Republic* 3. 392c–398b is concerned solely with poetry, and while we find that the painter and musician are indeed said to produce imitations (3. 400a7, 401a8), no account is given of these products. In fact, Plato seems to be deliberately refusing to give such an account, for he leaves consideration of musical *mimêsis* up to the expert Damon (3. 400b), and he writes in only vague terms of grace and harmony in the visual arts (3. 401a1–8), saying nothing that might define grace and harmony and distinguish them from their opposites. Thus, no theoretical account of imitation in the visual arts, good or bad, is given in *Republic* 3.

In *Republic* 10 also Plato fails to give an account of imitation in the visual arts of 'things as they are.' Here, moreover, his more detailed account of *mimêtikê* and craftsmanship must imply that there cannot be a good kind of imitation in the visual arts.

At 10. 598a–c Plato makes the following claims:

1. The painter imitates the works of craftsmen (598a1–3);
2. Painting imitates the works of craftsmen not as they are but as they appear, and is imitation not of the truth but of that which appears (598a5–b5);

---

[28] At 3. 401a8 Plato writes that grace and harmony are 'kin and imitations' of the wise and good character. Although imitation of character in *Republic* 10 can involve the idea of mistaking one thing for another, it is hard to see how this can be true of the imitations of 3. 401a8.

[29] In *Republic* 10 the *mimêtikos* is called a 'craftsman', but he is always clearly just a 'craftsman of an image' (10. 599d3, for example), as opposed to a craftsman of the things we use. At 3. 401b3–4, however, 'the other craftsmen' indicates that Plato includes poets, painters, and house builders in the same category.

3. Therefore (ἄρα) *mimêtikê* is far from the truth and grasps only an image (598b6–8);

4. For example (οἷον) the painter will paint a shoemaker, a carpenter, though he does not know about the crafts of any of these people (598b8–c1).

In this passage Plato concludes (ἄρα, οἷον) that the *mimêtikos* in general and (at least one kind of) painter in particular are ignorant of craft knowledge of what they imitate. He arrives at this conclusion by arguing that the painter fails to imitate the truth about artifacts. Plato implies, then, that the person who could imitate the truth about artifacts would have craft knowledge about that which he imitates. Thus, the imitator of a couch 'as it is' would be a carpenter, who had knowledge (or true belief) about what makes a useful couch (10. 601c–602b).

If such an imitator existed, however, he could not, Plato also implies, imitate a couch 'as it is' by painting a couch. Plato insists that a painting of a couch is a couch, just like the artifact (10. 597b5–11). He also holds that:

1. All of the many things which we call by the same name have the same unique Form (10. 596a5–7); this Form has the same name (for example, 'couch') as the many of which it is the Form (10. 597b5–11).

2. The Form is that which determines what is the proper function (χρεία) of that of which it is the Form (10. 596b6–9, 601d4–6).[30]

From these views it follows that both the painting of a couch and the artifact must be judged by the same unique standard of function. But if, as we may reasonably assume, a couch functions as something to sleep on, *any* painting of a couch must, Plato's statements imply, be a useless couch, a mere apparent couch.

The same argument would apply to sculpture. If a sculpture does not have the functional characteristics of a couch, it must be an 'apparent couch.' If it does function perfectly as a couch, on the other hand, it could hardly be called an imitation of a couch.

Plato is not, however, committed to the same negative conclusion in the case of poetry. The craftsman of the things imitated by the poet

---

[30] For this interpretation of the Form of the Bed see N. R. Murphy, *The Interpretation of Plato's Republic* (Oxford, 1951), 238; Crombie (above, n. 5), 143–4; Moravcsik (above, n. 21), 38–9.

knows 'what pursuits make people better or worse' (10. 599d4-5) and makes products useful for this purpose. There is no reason why a poem could not have the same use as these products, if made by a craftsman. The poet would also be an imitator, however, if he tried to make people think he was another good man in different circumstances, instead of himself.

This interpretation of the poet who imitates things 'as they are' is supported by Plato's example at *Republic* 3. 396c. The good man, Plato writes, when he reaches in his narrative 'some speech or action of a good man,' wishes to 'relate it as if he himself were that person,' and he will not be ashamed of this kind of imitation (3. 396c5-8). But he does not wish seriously to liken himself to an inferior (3. 396d4-5). This is surely imitation in the same sense as that of 3. 393a-c: making oneself similar to (trying to make others mistake one for) someone else in sound or shape. Compare especially 3. 393a8: 'He speaks as if he were Chryses,' and 3. 396c7: 'relate it as if he himself were that person.'

The preceding analysis of the implications of Plato's theories implies that Plato would admit imitation of the good as a separate category of imitation in poetry, but not in the visual arts. Plato, however, says little to define this kind of imitation, mentioning it chiefly in order to contrast it with *mimêtikê*. For this reason, I conclude that his views imply that imitation of the good is the antithesis of imitation of 'things as they appear.' I will, then, define imitation of the good as imitation with knowledge, in poetry, of the works of craftsmen as they are, to produce what is useful.


### III. VERSATILE POETRY AND PAINTING

Plato distinguishes two kinds of *mimêtikê*, versatile painting and versatile poetry, according to medium and objects imitated.


### A. Medium

Plato explicitly distinguishes poetry and painting at 10. 603b6-7: 'that [*mimêtikê*] . . . concerned with sight, or that concerned with sound, which we call poetry'. The two media, sounds and shapes, of imitation in the most general sense (above, Section I) distinguish two kinds of *mimêtikê* from each other. Painting imitates and makes that which has color and shape. Although the distinguishing characteristic of versatile poetry is imitation and making of that which has sound, it also, of course, uses 'shapes,' *schêmata*, in the sense of gestures or motions (3. 397b2).

Strictly speaking, painting is just one kind of imitation concerned with shapes and colors. Weaving and embroidery are other visual arts mentioned (2. 373a7, 3. 401a2) but nowhere formally distinguished. Again, Plato seems to indicate that poetry is only one kind of imitation concerned with sound when he writes of 'those [imitators] . . . concerned with music, that is, poets and their helpers: rhapsodes, actors, dancers, and contractors' (2. 373b5–8), and when he distinguishes poets, rhapsodes, and actors at 3. 395a. These distinctions, however, are blurred in *Republic* 10. At 10. 605c10–d2 'Homer' would appear to be a rhapsode or actor performing the poems, but at 10. 600a10 and c1 'Homer' is the long-dead author of the poems. I will, then, ignoring distinctions among the various visual and musical arts, define versatile painting as that kind of *mimêtikê* that uses colors and shapes, and versatile poetry as that kind which uses, as Plato states at 10. 601a8, speech, meter, rhythm, and harmony.

### B. Objects Imitated

Both versatile painting and and versatile poetry imitate the images of the works of craftsmen, but each imitates those of a different sort of craftsman.

1. *Versatile Painting*   In most of Plato's examples, versatile painters imitate the images of artifacts. Plato first mentions tables and couches (10.596b1 ff.), then bits and reins (10. 601c6 ff.). However, there are indications that the versatile painter also imitates the bodies of living things. He is, after all, often called a *zôgraphos*, literally, a painter of living things. At 10. 598b9 he is said to paint a shoemaker and a carpenter, and 10. 601d4–6 suggests that living things, like artifacts, are objects of craftsmanship, since they also have excellence and beauty dependent on use. Just as a horseman knows what makes reins beautiful and useful, so he also knows what makes a horse beautiful and useful, and could, by breeding and

training, help to produce a useful animal. A versatile painter might, then, imitate this animal.

2. *Versatile Poetry*   It has long been recognized that the subject matter of (versatile) poetry is action, *praxis*, or more exactly, human beings acting.[31] Plato explicitly makes this point in *Republic* 10. 603c4–8: '*Mimêtikê* [sc. in poetry: 603c1] imitates, we say, human beings doing forced or voluntary actions, and as a result of this acting thinking they have fared well or ill, and in all these cases feeling pain or pleasure.' In a section of *Republic* 3 outside that with which I am primarily concerned Plato also mentions imitation of *lexis* (speech) or *praxis* (action) (3. 396c6). Plato then draws a distinction similar to that between forced and voluntary actions made at 10. 603c, writing that the ideal state should retain 'the harmony that would imitate the tones and accents of a brave man in warlike action and in every forced deed . . . and another harmony that would imitate his accents in a peaceful and not forced but voluntary action' (3. 399a–b).

A number of aspects of Plato's view that poetry is imitation of action become clear when it is treated as an integral part of the theory of the imitative arts with which I am now concerned.

First, Plato's concept of imitation of action in *Republic* 10 is anticipated by the definition of imitation (*to mimeisthai*) in *Republic* 3. 393c as 'making oneself similar to someone else in *sound* (or shape)' (above, Section I). This is evident from the fact that Plato uses 'sound' and 'action' interchangeably in *Republic* 10. Thus, he introduces versatile poetry, at 10. 603b6–7, as *mimêtikê* concerned with sound (κατὰ τὴν ἀκοήν) and then goes on to write that versatile poetry imitates action (10. 603c). Moreover, the analogy between versatile painting and versatile poetry in terms of vision and sound (10. 603b6–7) is restated at 10. 603d1–3 in terms of vision and action. In Plato's view, *praxis* (action), is essentially 'sound,' that is, the *logos* (speech), that communicates and expresses true or false human beliefs. Thus, at 10. 599c the 'imitator of medical speeches' is clearly

---

[31] πράττοντας, φαμέν, ἀνθρώπους . . . πράξεις . . . (10. 603c4–5). Contrast Aristotle, *Poetics* 6. 1450ᵃ16–17: ἡ γὰρ τραγῳδία μίμησίς ἐστιν οὐκ ἀνθρώπων ἀλλὰ πράξεως καὶ βίου. R. Dupont-Roc, 'Mimésis et enonciation', in *Écriture et théorie poétiques* (Paris, 1976), 11 n. 14, notes this difference in phraseology between Plato and Aristotle. See the excellent interpretation of this difference by G. Finsler, *Platon und die Aristotelische Poetik* (Leipzig, 1900), 42–3.

equivalent to the imitator of medical actions. In the *Republic*, Plato, unlike Aristotle, does not consider any formal properties of a plot in writing of imitation of action.[32] Even when he uses *logos* to mean 'story' rather than 'speech of a human being' he is concerned only with truth value. *Logoi* are true or false (*Republic* 2. 376e11), not plots with beginnings, middles, and ends.

Second, action is the subject matter of all versatile poetry, and not just of one kind.[33] Plato discusses versatile poetry as a whole ('that [imitation] concerned with sound, which we call poetry' (10. 603b6–7) just before he states, at 10. 603c, that versatile poetry imitates humans acting. He mentions pleasure as well as pain at 10. 603c: 'thinking they have fared well,' 'feeling pleasure,' and would thus seem to be thinking of comedy as well as tragedy. At 10. 606d1–3 Plato states that poetry arouses 'all the desires and pains and pleasures in the soul, which we say follow upon every action of ours.' That comedy, at least, is included in this generalization, is shown by Plato's statement at 10. 606c2–3 that 'the same account' (as that given of tragedy) applies to 'comic imitation.'

Finally, Plato treats actions, like artifacts, as works of craftsmen, which require knowledge to be made (done) well. This view was implicit in *Republic* 3's characterization of the guardians as 'craftsmen of freedom' (3. 395c1). In *Republic* 10 Plato is more explicit. First, he uses the same word, *erga* (works, or deeds) to refer to both the artifacts imitated by the versatile painter (10. 598a2–3) and the deeds imitated by Homer (10. 599b4–6), and he uses the terms *erga* and *praxeis* (actions) interchangeably at 10. 600a4–5. Again, he states, at 10. 598e, that the defenders of Homer and the poets say that 'these people know all the crafts and all human things concerning virtue and vice, and divine things.' He then states that he will not bother to question Homer concerning medicine or 'the other crafts' (10. 599b9–c6) but will instead examine whether Homer has knowledge of 'the greatest and finest things,' that is, generalship, government, and education (10. 599c6–d2). The makers of these actions or activities, Plato writes, use knowledge of 'what pursuits make

---

[32] At *Phaedrus* 268d4–5, on the other hand, he writes that tragedy is the 'proper arrangement' of parts.

[33] *Republic* 10. 603c is not a definition or description of tragedy, as has been thought, for example, by Dupont-Roc (above, n. 31), 7, and Goldschmidt (above, n. 26), 42.

humans better or worse' (10. 599d4-5) in the particular circumstances of war, government, and education. The poet, however, knows nothing about what he imitates, but only 'paints on the colors of each of the crafts with words and phrases,' whether he writes about generalship or about anything else (601a-b). Moreover, at 601d4-6, Plato includes actions with artifacts and living things as things whose virtue and beauty depend on use and of which there is a user and a maker. Now because pain and pleasure attend every action of ours (10. 603c, 606d) and because reacting appropriately to pain or pleasure also requires knowledge of what is good for humans (10.604b-d), acting well in *every* circumstance would seem to be, at least in *Republic* 10, a kind of craft, and all fine deeds (*kala erga*) would seem to be craft products. Plato suggests that acting well in painful circumstances is a craft when he compares it to medicine at 10. 604d1-2. This comparison also links the discussion of acting well (10. 603-4) with the previous (10. 599bff.) consideration of Homer's craft knowledge of medicine and other crafts.

Like other craft products, fine actions have two 'aspects': actions 'as they are,' and actions 'as they appear,' that is images. Like the versatile painters, the versatile poets imitate things 'as they appear,' making images (10. 605c3). They are 'imitators of the images of virtue and of the other things they write about' (10. 600e5-6).

In the sphere of action, just as in that of vision, Plato writes at 10. 603c10-d7, humans are at war with themselves, and have contrary elements in their souls at the same time (10. 603d2). For example, a 'good man' who loses a son will bear his misfortune 'most easily,' but he will nevertheless grieve (10. 603e3-8). When he is in the company of his equals he will fight and resist pain more, but when alone he will 'dare to say many things . . . and he will do many things he would not want someone to see him doing' (10. 604a1-8). We know, then, Plato writes, that there are two contrary things in his soul at the same time (10. 604b4). One part of his soul, which is ready to obey reason and law (10. 604b6-7, resisting pain (10. 604a10), is the 'wise and calm character (*êthos*), being always nearly the same itself to itself' (10. 604e2-3). Another, inferior, part, which draws him to pain (10. 604b1), is the 'complaining character' (10. 604e2). Plato concludes that the *mimêtikos* imitates only the complaining character, that 'furnishes much and varied imitation' and that he does not imitate the wise character because it is not easy to imitate or to understand when it is imitated (10. 604e1–6).[34]

Enduring the loss of a son, the action in Plato's example, is a craft product (*ergon*) made by a craftsman, the 'good man,' and it has two 'aspects,' corresponding to the carpenter's couch 'as it is' and 'as it appears.' The action 'as it appears' consists of the many sounds and movements that pain forces the man to make. Although he will give in to pain more in solitude, perhaps beating his breast and wailing, even in company he will be unable to avoid some outward signs of grief, such as a sorrowful expression and sighs. These signs of pain are the images imitated by the versatile poet. No matter when or where the ignorant *mimētikos* hears the good man who is enduring grief, he will grasp only these many and varied images. On the other hand, the action 'as it is,' the endurance of grief by a craftsman with knowledge, is resistance to and struggle against pain. This struggle remains the same, like the couch 'as it is,' and can only be understood and imitated by another craftsman.

Plato's example is of emotional reactions in tragic circumstances. However, because pain and pleasure attend all our actions (10. 603c6–7, 606d1–3), in comic and other circumstances as well, someone with knowledge will create craft products and will also exhibit outward signs of emotion that may be mistaken for 'that which is' by the ignorant. Certain kinds of actions also require other specific applications of knowledge: that of how to make people better in war, for example. The craftsmen of these actions or activities will not only give outward signs of emotion, they will also make sounds and movements that may be mistaken for the practice of their specific craft, for example, generalship. I will discuss imitation of this kind of action in Section IV.C.

In summary, Plato distinguishes two kinds of *mimētikē*, versatile painting and versatile poetry. Versatile painting imitates, and makes, visible things. It imitates the images of the works (*erga*) of those craftsmen who have knowledge of artifacts and living things. Versatile poetry, which is Plato's main concern, imitates and produces sound (speech) and imitates the images of the works of those craftsmen who are concerned with actions. Versatile poetry uses meter, rhythm, and harmony.

---

[34] *Ēthos* means both *dramatis persona* and 'delineation of character' in the visual arts (LSJ).

## IV. CRITERIA FOR DISTINGUISHING GENRES OF VERSATILE POETRY

Plato mentions four kinds of versatile poetry: epic, tragedy (together these are often called 'tragic poetry'), comedy, and lyric. Epic, tragedy, and comedy are distinguished on the basis of style (*lexis*), meter, actions imitated, and specific effects on the audience they aim at.

### A. *Style* (Lexis)

In all imitative poetry, whether *mimêtikê* or not, the poet of *Republic* 3 uses imitative narrative, that is, he 'makes his speech [*lexis*] similar to that of someone else' (3. 393c1–2). This is true in *Republic* 10 also, where sound is the medium of poetry and human speech is what imitative poetry imitates.

Different poetic genres, however, differ in their use of imitative narrative, that is, of dramatic dialogue. Plato lists three styles of speech: (1) 'plain narrative' (ἁπλῇ διηγήσει: 3. 392d5), narrative 'by report of the poet himself,' which the dithyramb uses exclusively (3. 394c2–3);[35] (2) 'imitative narrative' (3. 392d5), in which the poet speaks 'as though he were someone else' (3. 393c1), the kind of narrative tragedy and comedy use exclusively (3. 394c1–2); and (3) 'mixed narrative,' a combination of (1) and (2), used by epic (3. 392d6, 3. 394c4).

Plato then uses a second classification of styles of speech to distinguish the versatile poet from the non-versatile poet (3. 396b10–397d5). There are two 'unmixed' styles (3. 397d1–2): (4) plain narrative with little imitative narrative (3. 396e4–8), the style of the 'unmixed imitator of the good' (3. 397d4–5), and (5) 'imitation of everything' (3. 397a3), that is, either imitative narrative alone or imitative narrative with little plain narrative (3. 397b1–2). There is also (6) a 'mixed' style (3. 397c8–10, d6), a combination of (4) and (5). Plato accepts only the person who uses (4), the 'unmixed

---

[35] Plato's treatment of the dithyramb as purely narrative presents a problem, since it was in fact dramatic in the classical period. See the discussion of this problem by Vicaire (above, n. 3), 240–2. Partee (above, n. 2), 7, n. 15, calls attention to Plato's ambivalent attitude toward the dithyramb.

imitator of the good' (3. 397d4–5), and he bans the user of (5) and (6) on the grounds that the imitator of everything is a 'manifold man' who is not in harmony with the ideal state (3. 397d10–398b4). The *mimêtikos*, that is, the person who imitates everything, is, then, someone who uses (5), imitation of everything, or (6), which includes some (5).

It is obvious that these two systems of classification are very different.[36] Although Plato never attempts to clarify the relationship between them, it is possible to draw some conclusions with confidence. First, poetry that is *mimêtikê* must have at least some imitative narrative. Thus, the dithyramb, which does not contain any imitative narrative, cannot be *mimêtikê*. Again, since Plato classifies epic as *mimêtikê*, in *Republic* 10 (10. 602b9–10), and since (5) and (6) include some plain narrative, a genre may be *mimêtikê* even though it contains some plain narrative.

However, it is not possible to determine whether Plato would classify every poetic genre using only imitative narrative as *mimêtikê*. He states, in *Republic* 10 (602b9–10, 606c), that tragedy and comedy are *mimêtikê*, and (5), which is *mimêtikê*, includes some genres using only imitative narrative. But it is not clear whether (5) includes all genres of this kind. How would Plato classify a drama with only good characters? Nor do his remarks on styles of speech help to classify lyric. The genre's inclusion with epic at 10. 607a5, however, indicates that it is *mimêtikê*, and the fact that it contains much imitation of unworthy speeches and actions of men and gods points to the same conclusion.[37]

In sum, use of some imitative narrative is a necessary and sufficient condition for imitative poetry. It is a necessary condition for *mimêtikê*, but we do not have enough information to decide whether or not exclusive use of imitative narrative is a sufficient condition for

---

[36] For a helpful summary of Plato's discussion of the classifications of styles of speech see Cross and Woozley (above, n. 20), 272–3. Dupont-Roc's attempt (above, n. 31), 13–14 n. 51, to coordinate the two classifications is, though unsuccessful, worth noting.

[37] Brownson (above, n. 2) 94–6, argues convincingly against Stallbaum that Plato did not intend to admit all lyric into his ideal state when he allowed hymns and encomia. R. G. Collingwood, *The Principles of Art* (Oxford, 1938), 48, draws the erroneous conclusion that after Plato excludes all drama 'he finds himself left with that kind of poetry whose chief representative is Pindar'. A glance at the *Odes* (e.g. *Ol.* 1, *Pyth.* 4 and 9, *Nem.* 10) shows that Plato would have found little to choose between Pindar and Euripides.

*mimêtikê*. Plato is much less concerned with style than with imitation of images.

## B. *Meter*

Epic and tragedy differ in meter as well as style. At 10. 602b9-10, Plato speaks of 'those concerned with tragic poetry in iambic or epic verse,' naming the meters of tragedy and epic respectively. The same phrase also indicates that he often treats tragedy and epic as the same genre of 'tragic poetry.'[38] Plato is little concerned with meter and says nothing more about differences in meter.

## C. *Actions Imitated*

As was shown above (Section III.B.2), all versatile poetry imitates actions. Presumably, different genres imitate different kinds of actions, but Plato is specific only in the case of 'tragic poetry' (tragedy and epic). Tragedy and its leader Homer are said by their advocates to know 'all the crafts and all human things about virtue and vice, and divine things' (10. 598d7-e2). This list includes the entire range of the subject matter of tragic poetry. In the paragraph at 10. 599b9-e4, however, Plato says that he will not examine Homer on medicine and the other crafts (10. 599b9-c6) and proposes instead to question him about 'wars and generalships and the government of cities and the education of human beings' (10. 599c7-d1). These are the 'greatest and finest things' Homer writes about (10. 599c7). Plato then begins his questioning of Homer by asking him if he is someone with knowledge or merely an imitator, 'third from the truth concerning virtue' (10. 599d2-3). It is clear that 'virtue' refers to the 'greatest and finest things' just mentioned, that is, to a particular part of Homer's total subject matter. The less important crafts, such as medicine, are excluded, but important discoveries and inventions are included, at 10. 600a4-7. In the conclusion at 10. 600e, Homer and the poets are again said to be 'imitators of the images of virtue and of the other things they write about.'

---

[38] See also 10. 595b10-c2, 598d7, and 607a1-2, where Homer is called the 'leader of tragedy'. Havelock (above, n. 3), 8, notes that Plato does not distinguish between tragedy and epic. Vicaire (above, n. 3), 243-4, argues that this assimilation of the two genres in *Republic* 10 was a current idea taken up by Plato.

While it has been recognized that virtue (the 'greatest and finest things') in Homer's subject matter, my analysis suggests that, because Homer is the representative of only one kind of poetry, tragic poetry, virtue is the subject matter of this kind of poetry, marking it off from other kinds of poetry.[39] This inference is supported by some unnoticed features of Plato's use of the term *aretê* ('virtue' or 'excellence') in *Republic* 10. 598e–600e.

This section of the *Republic* deliberately plays on several different meanings of *aretê*. *Aretê*, in the technical, Platonic sense, refers to the order in the soul (*Republic* 4. 444d13–e2) and not to activity. In a less strict Platonic sense it can refer to useful actions done with knowledge of moral virtue, and would include activities such as enduring the loss of a son, which are certainly not among the 'greatest and finest' things Plato discusses in the passage at 10. 599c–600e. In the 'Homeric' sense, on the other hand, *aretê* is the virtue of someone with high social standing, successful in war and leadership.[40] *Aretê* in this sense is the subject matter of the epic poets who sing about the *klea andrôn* (the glorious deeds of men).[41] In showing that Homer is an imitator of the images of *aretê*, Plato is not concerned with the order in the soul but with that kind of *aretê* belonging to useful actions that he mentions at 10. 601d4–6. He plays on both the less strict Platonic sense and on the 'Homeric' sense of *aretê*. After restricting the scope of *aretê* to those activities in which 'Homeric' *aretê* is chiefly exhibited, he asks (10. 599d4–6) whether or not Homer had *aretê* in the Platonic sense, knowing what makes people better in public and in private. He then demonstrates that Homer did not have *aretê* in the 'Homeric' sense, because he was not remembered as a successful general or statesman but was 'much neglected in his own lifetime' (10. 600b9–c1). This allows Plato to conclude that Homer is an imitator of the images of *aretê* not only in the Platonic sense (he has no craft knowledge) but also in the

[39] Thus, virtue is not the subject matter of poetry in general, as is suggested, for example, by Else, *Structure and Date* (above, n. 6), 34.

[40] A. W. H. Adkins, *Merit and Responsibility* (Chicago and London, 1960), 32–3 defines 'Homeric' *aretê* in this way, and distinguishes it from a Platonic use of the term in which the cooperative excellences play a much larger part (chapters 13 and 14).

[41] Havelock (above, n. 3), 64, argues that the poets' subject matter is 'the mighty deeds of former men | And the blessed gods' (Hesiod, *Th.* 100–1). Compare Plato's statement at *Republic* 10. 598e1–2 that some people claim that Homer knows 'all human things concerning virtue and vice, and divine things', and see *Ion* 531c.

'Homeric' sense (he did not leave behind him memorials of fine works: 10. 599b6).[42]

*Aretê*, then, as it refers to the objects imitated by tragic poetry, retains much of its Homeric sense, but with a Platonic twist. Plato accepts the traditional view that tragic poetry is concerned with *aretê* in the sense of the important and memorable actions recorded by the singers of the glorious deeds of men. However, he insists that, because *aretê* depends on use (10. 601d4–6), true *aretê* requires craft knowledge of what is useful. A general with *aretê* in this sense is one of Plato's craftsmen of freedom, who uses for purposes of war his knowledge of what makes people better. Someone with no knowledge of this kind can only imitate the images of *aretê*: the shouting of commands, the waving about of weapons, all the sounds and gestures of someone who happens to be in charge of an army. He will also, I have argued, imitate the man's outward signs of emotion.

### D. Effects on Audience[43]

All versatile poetry aims at producing pleasure, but it can also arouse more specific emotions in the audience. *Mimêtikê*, Plato writes, arouses and increases all the desires and pains and pleasures in the soul (10. 606d1–7). Specifically, tragedy arouses pity (10. 606b3, c5) and comedy arouses laughter (10. 606c2–9). Although Plato links pity and fear elsewhere, in *Republic* 10 he says that tragic poetry arouses 'pity and praise' (10. 606b3) and omits fear.[44]

---

[42] In fact, Plato argues at 10. 598e–601a that Homer was not successful, not that he was ignorant. Because success is a criterion of Homeric, but not of Platonic *aretê*, Plato has only proved that Homer lacks Homeric *aretê*, not Platonic, as he leads the reader to believe. The demonstration that he lacks Platonic *aretê* is given in a later section of *Republic* 10 (603–6), when Plato argues that Homer represents 'a man claiming to be good, who laments out of season' (10. 606b2–3).

[43] For a detailed analysis of this topic see Belfiore (above, n. 13).

[44] *Republic* 3. 387c mentions shuddering ($\phi\rho\iota\kappa\eta$) as an effect of tragic poetry, but no mention is made of this reaction in *Republic* 3. 392c–398b or 10. 595a–608b. Although at 10. 606c5–6 pity and fear are indeed closely connected, fear is the reaction of reason to the desire for excessive laughter. Plato links pity and fear in the *Ion* (535c) and *Phaedrus* (268c–d), as does Gorgias in *Encomium of Helen* 9, a work with which Plato was certainly familiar. See M. Pohlenz, 'Die Anfänge der griechischen Poetik', *NGG* (1920), 167–72 = *Kleine Schriften II* (Hildesheim, 1965), 461–6, for a discussion of Gorgias' influence on Plato. Plato's omission of fear in *Republic* 10 may thus be deliberate and significant.

CONCLUSION

In *Republic* 3. 392c–398b and 10. 595a–608b Plato maintains a clear and consistent view of the relationships and distinctions among the visual and poetic imitative arts. To imitate in the most general sense is to make something similar to something else in sound or shape, that is, to try to make people mistake the imitation for something else. Plato distinguishes imitation in this general sense from a particular kind of imitation, imitation of many things, for which he invents a technical vocabulary, the -*ikê* forms of *mimêsis* (*mimêtikê*, *mimêtikos*). *Mimêtikê* alone is attacked in *Republic* 3 and 10. In *Republic* 10 Plato explains what he only suggests in *Republic* 3, that *mimêtikê* imitates craft products, in the sense of things made or done with knowledge of the useful. Then, introducing another technical term, *aretê*, Plato shows that *mimêtikê* can imitate and make only images, the works of craftsmen as they appear. He thus indicates that this art does not imitate many different things, but only one thing over and over again, an image. Plato also implies that there can be a kind of imitative poetry, different from *mimêtikê* in that it imitates with knowledge, but that there cannot be a kind of painting that imitates with knowledge. Plato adopts the traditional view that epic and tragedy, which he classifies as kinds of *mimêtikê*, are concerned with the 'greatest and finest things,' *aretê*. But his theory allows him to condemn them for imitating only the images of *aretê*, which are the mere sounds and shapes the ignorant associate with *aretê*. Finally, Plato holds that the aim of *mimêtikê* is to produce pleasure, and that the aim of tragedy is also to produce pity.

In sketching this outline of Plato's theory of the imitative arts I have deliberately left many problems unexamined, even in those sections of the *Republic* to which I have restricted my inquiry. My outline may nevertheless provide a useful tool with which to study some of these other problems. It will in any case have served its purpose if it has demonstrated that Plato's theoretical treatment of *mimêsis* in *Republic* 3 and 10 is, however obscurely presented, at least much more consistent and coherent than has often been thought.[45]

[45] I am indebted to George Sheets, Marcia Eaton, and the anonymous referees and editor of *TAPA* for their helpful criticisms of an earlier draft of this paper.

'Homeric' sense (he did not leave behind him memorials of fine works: 10. 599b6).[42]

*Aretê*, then, as it refers to the objects imitated by tragic poetry, retains much of its Homeric sense, but with a Platonic twist. Plato accepts the traditional view that tragic poetry is concerned with *aretê* in the sense of the important and memorable actions recorded by the singers of the glorious deeds of men. However, he insists that, because *aretê* depends on use (10. 601d4–6), true *aretê* requires craft knowledge of what is useful. A general with *aretê* in this sense is one of Plato's craftsmen of freedom, who uses for purposes of war his knowledge of what makes people better. Someone with no knowledge of this kind can only imitate the images of *aretê*: the shouting of commands, the waving about of weapons, all the sounds and gestures of someone who happens to be in charge of an army. He will also, I have argued, imitate the man's outward signs of emotion.

### D. *Effects on Audience*[43]

All versatile poetry aims at producing pleasure, but it can also arouse more specific emotions in the audience. *Mimêtikê*, Plato writes, arouses and increases all the desires and pains and pleasures in the soul (10. 606d1–7). Specifically, tragedy arouses pity (10. 606b3, c5) and comedy arouses laughter (10. 606c2–9). Although Plato links pity and fear elsewhere, in *Republic* 10 he says that tragic poetry arouses 'pity and praise' (10. 606b3) and omits fear.[44]

---

[42] In fact, Plato argues at 10. 598e–601a that Homer was not successful, not that he was ignorant. Because success is a criterion of Homeric, but not of Platonic *aretê*, Plato has only proved that Homer lacks Homeric *aretê*, not Platonic, as he leads the reader to believe. The demonstration that he lacks Platonic *aretê* is given in a later section of *Republic* 10 (603–6), when Plato argues that Homer represents 'a man claiming to be good, who laments out of season' (10. 606b2–3).

[43] For a detailed analysis of this topic see Belfiore (above, n. 13).

[44] *Republic* 3. 387c mentions shuddering (φρίκη) as an effect of tragic poetry, but no mention is made of this reaction in *Republic* 3. 392c–398b or 10. 595a–608b. Although at 10. 606c5–6 pity and fear are indeed closely connected, fear is the reaction of reason to the desire for excessive laughter. Plato links pity and fear in the *Ion* (535c) and *Phaedrus* (268c–d), as does Gorgias in *Encomium of Helen* 9, a work with which Plato was certainly familiar. See M. Pohlenz, 'Die Anfänge der griechischen Poetik', *NGG* (1920), 167–72 = *Kleine Schriften II* (Hildesheim, 1965), 461–6, for a discussion of Gorgias' influence on Plato. Plato's omission of fear in *Republic* 10 may thus be deliberate and significant.

that in the *Poetics* Aristotle sometimes presents to us the face of a formalist. I shall argue in the later part of this paper, however, that behind this appearance there may lie a more philosophically committed attitude to tragedy than is usually discerned there. In the first part, instead of rehearsing all the familiar Platonic arguments against tragedy I will adopt a somewhat oblique approach designed to foreground certain paradoxes that arise in Plato's engagement with the genre.[2] I want to suggest that while the differences between Plato's and Aristotle's views on tragedy are not insignificant, they have been allowed to obscure what may from a certain angle of vision turn out to be an affinity: the ostensible contrast between moralist and formalist may not after all be as clear-cut as it at first looks. My aim is to address the question of how the two philosophers reacted to tragedy as the medium of mythological images of human life, images constructed around a cluster of traditional religious ideas and consistently enough embodied in tragic poetry from Homer to Euripides, despite important differences between individual poets, to constitute a coherent challenge to the philosophers' views of the world, and especially their beliefs about the relation between virtue and happiness. I should emphasize that it is to the mythic patterns of Greek poetry, not to any independently defined critical theory, that I mean the terms 'tragedy' and 'tragic' to refer in all that follows.

In the myth of Er which concludes the *Republic* we are told how, when the moment came for souls to choose their next existence in the human world, the man who had drawn the first lot rushed forward and selected the life of the greatest tyrant. The folly and greed with which he acted prevented him at first from realizing that it was now his destiny (*heimarmenê*, 619c1)[3] to eat his own children and suffer many other terrible things. When a belated recognition of what he had chosen came upon him, he broke into gestures and cries of lamentation, 'blaming chance and the gods and everything rather than himself' (619b-c). If this anonymous figure is on one level representative of moral ignorance and irrationality in general (his

---

[2] I attempt a fuller examination of Plato's perspective on tragedy in 'Plato's Repudiation of the Tragic', in M. S. Silk (ed.), *Tragedy and the Tragic* (Oxford, 1996), 332–49, revised in my book *The Aesthetics of Mimesis: Ancient Texts and Modern Problems* (Princeton, 2002), 98–117.

[3] Cf. p. 126 below on the same word at *Phaedo* 115a3.

behaviour was not unique among the souls which Er witnessed, 619d1-3), he is also specifically reminiscent of the mythical Thyestes, whose life contained the two main details mentioned in the myth—the possession of tyrannical power, at least for part of his life, and the appalling fate of devouring his own children. Thyestes was a typical figure of the kind of Greek myth which lent itself to tragic treatment (we know of several plays about him, including works by Sophocles and Euripides),[4] a figure whose life embraced the experience of supreme power and status but also a collapse into extreme misery. It is unsurprising that Thyestes is cited twice in chapter 13 of Aristotle's *Poetics*, alongside Oedipus and others, as a paradigmatic subject for the tragic stage.[5] But it is equally telling that when Plato refers in book 8 of the *Laws* to the stories of Thyestes and Oedipus as exhibited in 'all the so-called seriousness of tragedy', he interprets them as instances of the just penalties that have to be paid for great offences.[6] Although Plato here refers to different details of Thyestes' life, his presentation of him, and even of Oedipus, as a character wholly responsible for all that happens in his life, is similar to the portrayal of the quasi-Thyestian soul in the myth of Er. In both places Plato is faithful to the principle laid down by Socrates at *Republic* 2. 380a-b that sufferings such as those of the Pelopidae (Thyestes' lineage) should be depicted as moral tales of deserved punishment.

Plato could hardly have been unaware of his anonymous figure's resemblance to Thyestes, and the description of the man's self-pitying behaviour after his recognition of his fate is surely designed to recall the critical observations made earlier in book 10 itself on the deeply emotional and emotive nature of tragic poetry. In both passages emphasis is placed on the extravagant grief that accompanies, or in the second case anticipates, a sense of extreme suffering;[7] in the one case we are dealing directly, in the other allusively, with material Plato considered characteristic of tragic drama and its Homeric prototype. It is therefore worth asking whether there is anything we can detect in this short passage of the

---

[4] T. Gantz, *Early Greek Myth* (Baltimore, 1993), 545-52, summarizes the evidence.

[5] 1453[a]11, 21; cf. 16. 1454[b]23.

[6] *Laws* 838c3-7; cf. the language used of tragedy at *Gorgias* 502b. Plato similarly moralizes tragic myths at *Laws* 11. 931b-c.

[7] See 605c-d, 606b, 619c, and cf. 3.387-8.

myth of Er which supplements the case made explicitly against
tragedy in the earlier parts of the book.[8]

Although Plato's anonymous soul lacks the stature of an
authentically tragic hero, it is significant that his story has enough of
the lineaments of a tragic myth to make it simultaneously evoke and
contradict the way that such a scenario might be handled by a poet
working within traditional religious categories. Plato dramatizes a
tension between free human choice and the combined limitations of
ignorance, on the chooser's part, and an externally imposed or
sustained necessity. The individual's responsibility seems to be
unequivocally stated in the terse words of the priest (*prophêtês*) who
speaks for Lachesis. 'A daimon will not be allotted to you; *you* will
choose your daimon . . . The responsibility is the chooser's; god has
no responsibility' (οὐχ ὑμᾶς δαίμων λήξεται, ἀλλ᾽ ὑμεῖς δαίμονα
αἱρήσεσθε . . . αἰτία ἑλομένου· θεὸς ἀναίτιος).[9] Already here there is a
problematic implication. Why, if a free choice is to be made, should
the question of a daimon arise at all? The paradox later hardens,
when all the souls have made their choices and go before Lachesis
herself, who assigns to each of them the daimon which it chose—a
daimon to fulfil the choices made (620d6–e1). The combined forces
of Necessity now fix as a portion of fate, a *moira* (620e4, cognate with
the earlier *heimarmenê*), what was supposed to originate as an
autonomous choice. This fact lends an ironic note to the earlier
description, already quoted, of the first soul's grief on his realization
of an irrevocable destiny (his complaints against 'chance and the
gods and everything rather than himself'), an irony heightened by
the use of the word *daimones* for 'gods' in this last phrase.

The irony, though, is double-edged. In the first place it operates
against the traditional and archaic view of humans as only partly in
control of their lives even in seeming moments of real freedom. The
moral perspective of the myth distances us from the self-pitying role

---

[8] Epicurus's friend Colotes of Lampsacus accused Plato of hypocrisy for attacking
tragic myths but writing in 'tragic' style himself in the myth of Er: for Colotes' complaint, with specific reference to the horrors at *Republic* 615d, see Proclus *In
Rempublicam* 2. 105. 23–106. 14 (ed. Kroll). Cf. D. Babut, 'L'Unité du livre X de la
*République* et sa fonction dans le dialogue', *Bulletin de l'Association Guillaume Budé*, 42
(1983), 31–54, at 48–54, on underlying connections between the myth of Er and the
work's earlier criticisms of poetry.

[9] 617e1–5; an affinity with Heraclitus fr. 119 DK (ἦθος ἀνθρώπωι δαίμων, 'character [is] a person's daimon') has often been remarked. On the significance of Plato's
daimon, and other points, see S. Halliwell, *Plato Republic 10* (Warminster, 1988), 184.

assumed by the anonymous figure, whose refusal of responsibility significantly echoes the words of Agamemnon in *Iliad* 19. 86-9:

> ἐγὼ δ' οὐκ αἴτιός εἰμι,
> ἀλλὰ Ζεὺς καὶ Μοῖρα καὶ ἠεροφοῖτις Ἐρινύς,
> οἵ τέ μοι εἰν ἀγορῇ φρεσὶν ἔμβαλον ἄγριον ἄτην,
> ἤματι τῷ ὅτ' Ἀχιλλῆος γέρας αὐτὸς ἀπηύρων.

*I am not responsible,*
*But Zeus and Fate and a Fury that walks in darkness,*
*Who cast a wild delusion on my mind in the assembly*
*On that day when I myself deprived Achilles of his prize.*[10]

Against this, however, there are disquieting suggestions lurking around Plato's attempt to turn religiously coloured concepts of necessity, a daimon, and fate into symbolic enforcements of the injustice contained within the individual's choice of life. It is precisely because the myth makes so much of (personified) *Anankê*, necessity, as the principle underpinning the system within which lives are selected and *daimones* allotted, that it becomes hard to trace the connection between the soul's choice and the resulting pattern of its embodied life. The dramatic frame of Plato's myth leaves the ideas of necessity and destiny with their full potency, yet its overt moral content *internalizes* responsibility within the human soul. The result is an irresolvable paradox. By trying to translate potentially tragic material into the substance of a moralistic fable, Plato is obliged to give a voice to the tragic outlook, to let it be heard at least in the background, even at the moment of its ostensible denial. In the attempt to employ inherited religious categories to dramatize the equation of injustice with unhappiness, an equation which in the *Republic* and the *Laws* he says that poets, contrary to much of their existing practice, should be compelled to affirm,[11] Plato nonetheless leaves the problem of undeserved suffering without resolution at the edge of his picture.

As a final comment on the paradoxical fate of the first soul in the myth of Er, I mention the question of pity, the canonically central

---

[10] Compare the refusals of responsibility at *Iliad* 3. 164, 19. 409-10, and *Odyssey* 1. 32, where Aegisthus, like the hasty soul of *Republic* 10, ignores a warning.

[11] *Republic* 2. 378d, 380a-b, 3. 392a-b, *Laws* 2. 660e-661c. The equation between justice and happiness would be worth asserting even as a lie or fiction (*pseudos*), *Laws* 2. 663c-d (cf. the converse principle at *Republic* 2. 378a, with Aristophanes, *Frogs* 1053).

tragic emotion. Socrates relates that some of Er's experiences in the
other world aroused pity in him (620a1). Is the hasty first soul a
fitting object of pity? It would surely cut right against the grain not
only of the myth's moral, but also of the *Republic*'s larger idea of
justice, to suppose that the quasi-Thyestean figure could be meant to
merit any real pity. He is taken to bring his own fate on himself; the
cause of it lies in his own soul. His sufferings will be a punishment,
and Platonic punishment is good for its subject. But, by the same
token, *whatever* happens to a soul in the eschatological world of the
myth ought to be an expression of perfect justice. There seems to be
little place for pity in Plato's universe.[12] Yet the fact remains that Er
feels some, and if we step to one side of the Platonic perspective we
may naturally suppose that he feels some of it for the first soul to
choose its next life, since it is made clear that the soul's choice
cannot be attributed to wickedness, and also that the prospective
consequences of its choice go far beyond the initial act of volition.
This unhappy man's fate is due to his ignorance of the nature of
goodness, despite his previous existence in a well-governed state; he
is hardly comparable to the incurably evil tyrants whose physical
punishment was gruesomely described earlier in the myth (615d–
616a). If Er were a good Aristotelian, he might well feel that he had
here witnessed a momentous tragic error, *hamartia*. Yet it is precisely,
if ironically, for his *hamartia* that Thyestes is said to deserve the just
punishment of death in the passage from *Laws* 8 (838c) which I cited
earlier. We can at any rate say, I think, that Er's pity is incongruous
with the total effect of his story; it is placed within the myth as
symptomatic of a mentality—a mentality potentially open to
tragedy—which the myth as a whole is intended to counteract. Yet
what reader can afford to condemn Er's reaction? Once again, Plato
hints at the possibility of tragedy at the very moment of his denial
of it: we shall shortly encounter something similar in one of his
greatest expressions of antagonism with the poets, the *Phaedo*.

    I have chosen to give some space to this short passage from the
myth of Er because through its oblique glance at a pattern of tragic

---

[12] Tragic pity is directly impugned at *Republic* 3. 387d and 10. 606b; at 7. 516c6,
518b2 (where the philosopher is momentarily like a compassionate Boddhisatva)
Socrates alludes to the possibility of philosophical pity for the prisoners in the Cave.
Elsewhere, sympathy for undeserved misfortune is touched on at *Laws* 11. 936b, for
orphans at 11. 926e, for strangers at 5. 729e6, for the unjust man (NB) at 5. 731c–d
and *Gorgias* 469a–b. Divine pity is mooted at *Laws* 2. 653c–d.

myth—with individual choice set against a background of divine compulsion and destiny—it crystallizes one element of Plato's challenge to the poets' vision of the human condition. Although this challenge is religious and metaphysical in reach, it also centres on the question of suffering, to which I now turn more specifically. The good man who suffers an apparent misfortune such as the loss of a son will, according to the Platonic Socrates of *Republic* 10, bear his grief with as much composure and self-discipline as possible. He will indeed, if he is capable of it, not grieve at all (603e). The reasoning part of his soul will tell him that it is not clear that the ordinary view of such things as evil is correct, that grief is useless, and that nothing in human life is anyway of much seriousness (604b–c). This passage comes from a discussion of dramatic poetry, which Plato here virtually equates with tragedy (he touches on comedy at the end, 606c), so that the relevance of these remarks to Greek tragedy is unquestionable. It is usual for treatments of this section of book 10 to put the main weight on what Socrates says about tragedy's capacity to excite and encourage emotions which are better kept in check: the observation at 606d that poetry waters and nourishes feelings which ought to be allowed to dry up is often rightly picked out as a telling formulation of Platonic objections to the psychological effects of art. But we should not concentrate on emotional symptoms to the exclusion of the morally false worldview which, according to the argument, underlies both the nature of tragic plays and the standard responses of audiences to them. Although Plato himself tends to emphasize the emotional indiscipline of tragic characters and their audiences, he indicates clearly that this is no matter of mere psychological hygiene, but one part of the soul's failure to grasp the truth about the good. Reason will tell the soul that life is not worth much in any case. We have heard this asserted before, in book 6, where Socrates asks: 'If a man has the vision of all time and all being, do you think it is possible that he will regard human life as of any real importance?'[13] This illegitimately rhetorical question rests on the thought that because the body and all that relates to it belongs to a sphere of existence which passes away, such things can therefore ultimately count for nothing.

It is from this metaphysical standpoint that Plato is able, in his

[13]   486a, later quoted by Marcus Aurelius, *Meditations* 7. 35. Compare e.g. *Laws* 7. 804b, 12. 959c, *Epistle* 7. 334e.

confrontation with tragedy, to work towards a radical denial of suffering: not a denial of the limited corporeal and psychological actuality of pain and grief, but a renunciation of the *significance* of suffering.[14] For the perfectly good person, it seems clear, 'suffering' could not matter; misfortune would be a purely external way of looking at the contingencies of existence, and one which could have no purchase on the reason-governed soul: the good *per se* is immune to external change (*Republic* 2. 380e–381b). At the opposite pole from this perfect specimen of philosophical goodness stands not the ordinary human being, deeply attached though he may be to life, but the tragic hero. The major characters of Homeric epic and Attic tragedy represent life lived at its heroic limits, a life which tests, in particular, the limits of suffering; and Plato's anxiety about such poetry reveals his awareness of this fact. The discussions of poetry in *Republic* books 2–3 and 10 form a continuity on this issue, if not on others. In both places normal human attitudes to misfortune are disputed through the questioning of poetry's depiction of such things in the lives of heroes. In book 3, when making precisely the same point as later about the good man's capacity to bear suffering impassively, Socrates castigates the Homeric portrayal of Achilles, of Priam, and even of Zeus in his mourning for Sarpedon (387d–388); in book 10 he contents himself with general references to the exhibition of such grief in Homer and tragedy.[15] The tragic hero differs from the ordinary person in being supposedly great and good, a presupposition that Plato's argument targets more than once in both books.[16] It is this combination of heroic status and merit with the display of an exceptional vulnerability to suffering—a combination which affirms the imbalance between excellence or virtue (*aretê*) and happiness (*eudaimonia*)—that makes the tragic hero the antithesis of Plato's good man. And in this connection it is important to notice that in book 10, at the climax of his attack on poetry, Plato recognizes the power of poetry to corrupt, as he puts it, 'even the best of us', apart from a very few (605c6–8): this immediately precedes the reference to tragic images of grieving heroes (605c10–d5) and it helps to

---

[14] Compare the readings of Plato's attitude to tragedy in H. Kuhn, 'The True Tragedy: On the Relationship between Greek Tragedy and Plato', *HSCP* 52 (1941), 1–40, 53 (1942), 37–88, and M. C. Nussbaum, *The Fragility of Goodness* (Cambridge, 1986), 122–35.

[15] 605–6; 603e refers back to 3. 387–8.

[16] See especially 3. 387d2, e9, 388a6, b4, 10.605d1, 606b2.

establish that it is tragedy's assertion of the place of suffering at the heart of the great life which Plato is set on contesting.

Despite the uncompromising cast of this aspect of the Platonic critique of tragedy, there are traces of equivocation on the point. Plato's moral idealism cannot be sustained wholly without regard to common experience. Various hints show that the existence of calamities is acknowledged as an inescapable feature of human societies, at least as at present organized. There will be no end to evils in the world, Socrates asserts in *Republic* 5 (473d–e), until philosophers become rulers, and the point is repeated in similar words in book 6 (501e). It is striking that, in criticizing the poets' portrayals of the gods in *Republic* 2, Socrates concedes that human life contains more evil than good, but his concern is to deny that the evil can be attributed to divine causes, as in the famous Iliadic passage about Zeus's two jars (379d). But does Plato purport to claim that suffering of misfortune would disappear if society were radically reformed along ideal lines? Certainly not in the envisaged society of the *Laws*, where the possible impact of chance and misfortune is occasionally acknowledged.[17] In *Republic* 3 Socrates goes so far as to contemplate the possibility of a type of drama whose subject-matter would draw on the good man's ability to withstand suffering and thereby to reduce it to insignificance. The issue comes up in the discussion of musical modes, where Socrates enquires about a mode suitable to accompany the artistic representation of fortitude in the face of danger, death, or other misfortune (399a–c). One might be inclined to interpret the drama of the good man's fortitude as a transitional art-form, a kind of reformed tragedy, on the road to the realization of the perfect society. But it seems doubtful whether Plato's idealism stretched to the belief that all suffering could ever be eliminated from life, whatever the organization of society, and so we find him, for example, referring to the fact that in the perfect state people will have a strongly unified sense of the misfortunes of individual citizens (*Republic* 5. 463e). There might always be a role, then, for art to dramatize the good man's courageous resistance to the material afflictions of earthly existence. It is an interesting question to ask just what Plato imagined that the ethos of such art might be. It could surely not coincide with existing scenes of tragic resilience such as,

---

[17] e.g. 9. 873c, 11. 924a, d, 926e, 928a, 929e, 936b, 944d.

say, Priam's visit to his son's killer in the *Iliad*, or Heracles' final acceptance of his fate in Euripides' *Heracles*, since in these and many other instances there is, quite apart from the presence of elements of naked grief and self-pity, no sense that the given misfortune can be reduced in significance, certainly not by comparison with some other-worldly scheme of things in which the corporeal will cease to matter. The Platonic 'tragedy', if one may call it that (see below on *Laws* 817), would presumably focus its attention on complete spiritual control over the bodily and psychological power of suffering. Could it do so, however, without allowing full dramatic weight to this power?

This question is certainly worth asking, for we have available a more direct approach to it than the brief and hypothetical passage from the *Republic* allows. We can look instead to the *Phaedo*, a work which ought to provide an appropriate test of Plato's attitudes to tragedy. The situation in the dialogue is one which would be susceptible to tragic treatment by someone who shared Plato's estimation of Socrates but not his metaphysics. In more than one passage of the *Republic* and the *Laws* Plato seems to take it for granted that the typical tragedy centres around an individual, a great or supposedly great man. Whether or not Socrates' life would meet the criteria of a heroic existence, his death posed an acute philosophical problem in Plato's mind. Could Socrates' death be in any sense a tragedy—an appalling rejection of philosophical goodness by the world, an index of some ineradicable flaw in things—as well as an overwhelming personal loss for those who loved Socrates? If we remember the passages in the *Republic* where it is the loss of a beloved person, and the grief-laden reaction to such loss, which is held up as the archetypal subject of tragic poetry, then it becomes more than a matter of biographical curiosity to ask whether Plato allowed the propriety of grief as a reaction to Socrates' execution. I do not claim to have a simple answer to this question, partly because it might reasonably be thought that only Plato's work as a whole, in all its complexity, could furnish one. But it seems appropriate to interrogate particularly the dialogue in which he comes closest to Socrates' death, and also closest to the type of philosophical 'tragedy' which he makes Socrates himself imagine in the *Republic*.

On one level, perhaps the most important level, the *Phaedo* is designed to rebut any simple view of Socrates' death as a tragic event; it is therefore at least misleading to observe without qualification, as Jowett does, that 'the *Phaedo* is the tragedy of which Socrates is the protagonist'.[18] It is unnecessary to show in detail how the dialogue's whole construction, with its strong conviction of the immortality of the soul and its emphasis on the need for the philosophical life to disentangle itself from the preoccupations of the body (death included), voices a denial of the possibility that the just man can truly suffer. We need here to appreciate that Plato could have held most if not all of the metaphysical beliefs that have been ascribed to him without denying the force and significance of misfortune in the world of the flesh. There is more than one conceivable way in which he might have endowed the good man's grief with spiritual reality and value, just as it supposedly is in some branches of Christian thought. Instead, he offers an apparently unqualified renunciation of suffering by making the Socrates of *Phaedo* demonstrate how a life of philosophical virtue, equivalent to yet transcending the heroic life of tragedy, can deprive suffering of all magnitude and meaning.

The dialectical and dramatic repudiation of suffering in the *Phaedo* at first looks so decisive that we might well conclude that Plato has gone even beyond the 'reformed' tragedy which Socrates imagines in *Republic* 3: we seem to be dealing not just with the spiritual mastery of suffering, but with its obliteration from the scheme of true values. Yet if this is so, it has to be recognized that Plato at least allows elements of a different view of Socrates' death to be glimpsed in the course of the dialogue. He does this partly on the level of argument, by giving Simmias and Cebes doubts about the immortality of the soul, doubts which communicate themselves to the rest of the company and concern future as well as already stated considerations on the subject.[19] To the extent that such doubts might be taken seriously, the possibility opens up after all of seeing the execution of Socrates as an unredeemed destruction of his life's value. More pointed, though, are the dramatic signals of what can be regarded, by reference to the critiques of the genre in the *Republic*, as typical tragic behaviour. The first of these is the dismissal of Xanthippe near the beginning of the piece (60a), echoed by a second dismissal of the

---

[18]  B. Jowett, *The Dialogues of Plato*[4] (Oxford, 1953), ii. 406. Kuhn, 'True Tragedy', 25, more aptly calls the *Phaedo* an 'anti-tragedy', as does Nussbaum, 'Fragility', 385.
[19]  88c; cf. 103c, 107b.

women near the end of the dialogue (116b). When Phaedo and his companions entered Socrates' cell on the day of his execution, Xanthippe let out a cry of grief and uttered a lament for the fact that this was to be the last time her husband and his friends would see one another. There are tragic parallels for this lament, whose self-consciousness might be thought particularly appropriate to drama.[20] Socrates gives simple orders for Xanthippe to be taken away, leaving scholars to speculate about what Plato might here be intimating about relations between husband and wife. But the moment should not be given biographical weight in that crude way; it is primarily a gesture which expresses Socrates' renunciation of the ties of life and the emotions which the prizing of these ties engenders. Later in the dialogue, Plato again refuses to allow any acknowledgement of suffering on the philosopher's part, this time by presenting a direct refusal of the conventions of mourning which he elsewhere identifies so closely with tragedy.[21] The contrast between his portrayal of Socrates and the characteristic Homeric-cum-tragic treatment of a hero's death is suggested by Socrates' own words at 115a, where he ironically borrows the language of the 'man of tragedy' (ἀνὴρ τραγικός),[22] who would talk fatalistically in terms of the summoning of destiny (heimarmenê, the word also used in the myth of Er, and at Gorgias 512e). Socrates thus spurns the posture of the self-pitying hero as humorously but resolutely as he does in the Apology, where he refers to and disdains the forensic convention of an appeal for mercy as the behaviour of one 'staging a pitiful drama' (τοῦ τὰ ἐλεινὰ ταῦτα δράματα εἰσάγοντος, 35b7). Plato uses more theatrical metaphors than any other classical Greek author; his usage reflects a consciousness of his own dramatic methods.[23]

Set against Socrates' capacity for unmoved acceptance of his death, and even for ironic humour, are the impulsive lamentations of Phaedo, Apollodorus and the rest of those present. Phaedo weeps, on his own later admission, not for Socrates but for himself (117c). This

[20] See e.g. Sophocles, Trachiniae 420-2, Oedipus Tyrannus 1071-2; Euripides Alcestis 163-4, 270-1, Hecuba 202-4, 409-14, Hippolytus 1097, Trojan Women 740-1, 761; for a Homeric archetype cf. Iliad 6. 407-13.

[21] At Phaedo 117d-e Socrates rebukes his companions by saying that it was to avoid scenes of lamentation that he had sent away the women (cf. the references to women and tragic laments at Republic 3. 387e, 398e, 10. 605e).

[22] On the interpretation of this phrase see my Aesthetics of Mimesis, 106-7 (where n. 17 should refer to the actor Hegelochus in Sannyrion fr. 8.4 PCG).

[23] See D. Tarrant, 'Plato as Dramatist', JHS 75 (1955), 82-9.

helps to bring out an implicit connection with Plato's critiques of tragedy in the *Republic*: what we are shown here is the self-regarding grief of one too attached to life, one whose emotions are incapable of suppression (117c–d). But we may be struck by a paradox here. Plato is himself dramatically portraying something akin to the type of behaviour he elsewhere rebukes the tragic poets for showing. It is true, of course, that Phaedo and the rest are presumably not to be treated as paragons of virtue, and their display of sorrow is therefore intelligible as a mark of inadequacy, in contrast to Socrates' perfect self-discipline. But the companions of Socrates are moved by a genuine love of him, and this seems to be something which Plato's whole project presupposes as admirable. And however much the emotion of the closing scene is subordinated to the central religious arguments of the dialogue, the fact remains that Plato's dramatic skills are used at the end to lend moving force to the view which Socrates' companions naturally take of their mentor's death. It is not that this final scene vindicates the tragic perspective which has already been so strongly contradicted by Socrates himself. But it does momentarily seem to *offer* it to the reader, and I find it hard to conclude that Plato was unconscious of this effect. Plato the tragedian has not been wholly suppressed by Plato the metaphysician.

I have tried briefly to suggest that the *Phaedo* stands as, among other things, a Platonic attempt to carry out the scheme of *Republic* 3. 399a–c and to dramatize the virtuous man's annulment of suffering and grief, but that this attempt involves Plato in the perhaps inescapable paradox that his own work includes and effectively employs some of the very features of tragedy against which his philosophical enterprise is directed, analogously to the way in which the myth of Er uses traditional religious categories in asserting the individual soul's responsibility for its destiny. In both these respects the *Phaedo* gives vivid form to the idea later found in the *Laws* that 'the finest and best life is the truest tragedy' (7. 817b). That idea, the boldest and most provocative of Plato's dramatic metaphors, occurs in a passage which sets up the philosophical life as an alternative to the life of the tragic hero and makes the writing of philosophy an alternative to the performance of tragic drama. This late passage is in a sense prefigured in the *Phaedo* itself, in Socrates' famous trope at 61a of philosophy as 'the greatest music' (*mousikê*, a term which embraces the musico-poetic arts in general), which is complemented

by his later attempt to produce a philosophical myth to rival that of
the poets. What we have in both places is explicit testimony to a
Platonic sense of being involved in a life-defining rivalry between
philosophy and poetry (the 'long-standing quarrel', *Republic* 10.
607b). The *Phaedo* as a whole can be read as perhaps the most
deliberate of Plato's attempts to sustain that rivalry against what he
rightly saw to be a coherent alternative to his own philosophy, the
tragic poets' view of the world as ultimately inhospitable to human
aspirations. Whatever the truth of the story that Plato composed
tragedies as a young man, we get glimpses as early as the *Apology* of
an interest in both measuring and contrasting Socrates with the
standards of mythical heroism, not only in the passage where
Socrates cites Achilles and the other 'demigods' who fought at Troy
for the virtuous fearlessness with which they faced death (28c–d),
but also in the closing section of the speech, where Socrates imagines
himself discoursing in Hades with 'other victims of unjust verdicts'
such as Palamedes and Ajax (41b), both of them prominent tragic
figures. As later in the *Phaedo*, Plato simultaneously and wryly
evokes a heroic model for comparison and yet also uses it as a foil to
Socrates, since the latter's anticipation of taking pleasure in con-
versing with Palamedes and Ajax (the latter, ironically, a figure
notorious for his *silence* in Hades)[24] serves as an expression of his
refusal to regard his own death as tragic. Here as in many later
passages, I think, we witness Plato's fascination with tragic myth, as
well as his rejection of it.

In moving from the dramatic and often ironic textures of Plato's dialogues to the rather colourless, dry world of Aristotle's treatise on
poetry, we experience a marked shift in style, tone, and approach.
Yet it has long been recognized that Aristotle carries over much from
Plato's treatment of poetry, subtly adapting what he borrows at
many points.[25] On the central issue of their attitudes to tragedy, however, there is a modern consensus that the two philosophers diverged
radically. It appears to many, indeed, that Aristotle did not simply fail
to accept Plato's religious and metaphysical reservations about

---

[24]  See *Odyssey* 11. 563–4, an episode echoed in the myth of Er at *Republic* 10. 620b.
[25]  A fuller analysis of this and other aspects of the *Poetics* can be found in my books
*Aristotle's Poetics* (London, 1986; repr. with new introduction, 1998) and *The Poetics
of Aristotle: Translation and Commentary* (London, 1987).

tragedy, but even considered such matters irrelevant to the critical evaluation of poetry. It is certainly remarkable (and, I shall argue, significant) that the *Poetics* largely neglects tragedy's religious dimension; and when the subject is broached in chapter 25, no one reading the book with the Platonic background in mind can fail to find arresting the passage where Aristotle seemingly dismisses the whole tradition of philosophical complaints (for which Xenophanes' name stands as a shorthand reference) about poetry's depiction of the divine. The dismissal is couched in a laconic manner typical of the *Poetics*: 'Perhaps it is neither moral nor true to say such things about the gods, and perhaps Xenophanes was right; but, anyway, people do say these things' (1460$^b$36-61$^a$1). This is actually offered as the solution of a critical 'problem'. As Lucas aptly comments, 'an answer less likely to satisfy Plato would be hard to imagine'.[26]

If this passage were taken to summarize Aristotle's entire view of the moral and religious components of tragedy, it would be futile to ask of the *Poetics*, as I have already asked selectively of Plato's critique of the genre, how it appraises tragedy as the vehicle of a powerful, heroically concentrated vision of life. But it would be premature to accept such a negative conclusion. I want instead to scrutinize the *Poetics*' doctrines of poetic form to see whether they may not imply more of a philosophically committed stance than at first sight looks likely.

A preliminary stage in the argument can be based on Aristotle's concept of a poetic *muthos*. The term *muthos*, together with a group of cognates, is found frequently in Plato's discussions of poetry. For Plato, as for Aristotle, (a) *muthos* is essential to poetry. Plato, however, consistently treats the narrative or dramatic content of a *muthos* as embodying a proposition or set of propositions (usually *false* propositions) about the world.[27] A story is thus always about something external to itself, and Plato regards a judgement on a story's truth or falsehood as a proper cognitive reaction to it. Because *muthoi* are assumed to convey propositions about the world, ethical assessments of their educational and cultural use are urgently called for. Aristotle takes over the term *muthos* but makes of it a virtually technical term to designate the formal object (the 'plot-structure')

[26] D. W. Lucas, *Aristotle Poetics* (Oxford, 1968), 239.
[27] See *Aesthetics of Mimesis*, 49–50, with my article 'From Mythos to Logos: Plato's Citations of the Poets', *Classical Quarterly*, 50 (2000), 94–112.

produced by the poet's art. He devotes the bulk of his analysis of tragedy in *Poetics* chapters 6–18 to an exposition of key concepts and principles relating to the *muthos*, including its structural coherence and unity (involving the schema of 'beginning, middle, end'), the deployment of its parts (especially 'reversal', *peripeteia*, and 'recognition', *anagnôrisis*, in the case of the 'complex' plot-type), and the handling of episodes and dénouement (*lusis*). It is to a large extent in and because of their divergent concepts of *muthos* that Plato and Aristotle are believed to take incompatible views of the religio-moral content of poetry. The *Poetics*' central chapters, it is commonly agreed, proceed as if the quasi-propositional status of a *muthos* had been discarded, to be replaced by a purely self-contained, 'aesthetic' notion of form.

To demonstrate the weaknesses of this common reading would require a lengthy argument, but some basic objections can be indicated here.[28] Much interpretation of the *Poetics* has suffered from the application of an extreme and falsifying polarity, of the kind characterized in my introduction, between moralistic and formalist views of poetry and art. Although such a polarity has roots in ancient criticism, it is not one with which the *Poetics* can be straightforwardly aligned, yet it has been employed both to support the didactic reading of the treatise standard among Renaissance and neoclassical critics, and to vindicate the formalist interpretation of the *Poetics* which, under the influence of a strong post-Enlightenment separation of moral and aesthetic values, has been dominant in modern times. In Aristotle's case this prejudicial polarity needs to be replaced by a framework which takes account of the philosopher's own nuanced conception of the relation between poetry and other forms of activity. Essential here is the statement of a kinship between poetry and philosophy at *Poetics* 9. 1451$^b$4-11, in a passage which furnishes clear evidence, supported elsewhere, of Aristotle's belief in the cognitive value of poetry and which is in itself sufficient to throw aestheticist interpretations of the treatise into grave doubt. Outright formalism is, in fact, inconceivable in a theory of poetry which relies as heavily as does the *Poetics* on the central category of mimesis. A poetic *muthos* may need to be judged by criteria which respect its

[28] For broader reflections on Aristotle's concept of poetic form see my article, 'Aristotle: Form and Unity', in M. Kelly (ed.), *The Encyclopedia of Aesthetics* (New York, 1998), i. 101-4.

status as an independent art, but independence from wholly external standards need not, and given mimesis *cannot*, entail complete autonomy or self-sufficiency: at *Poetics* 25. 1460$^b$13–15, which I quoted in my first paragraph, Aristotle says that poetic 'correctness' is not identical to, but not that it is entirely divorced from, that of other human practices. By his attribution to poetry of a concern with 'universals', enabling it to aspire to the condition if not the methods of philosophy, Aristotle acknowledges a more delicate relation between poetry and experience than a moralism–aestheticism dichotomy leaves room for. And it is the concept of a tragic *muthos* as the embodiment of 'universals' which reduces, without altogether eliminating, the discrepancy between Plato's and Aristotle's perspectives on the value of poetry. The implicitly propositional character of poetic *muthos* in Plato's scheme of criticism is converted by Aristotle into the possibility of correspondence between *muthos* and world at the level of 'universals'.[29]

But in order to come closer to an answer to the question whether a definite ethical standpoint or commitment can be identified in Aristotle's theory of tragedy, we need to focus on the properties of a tragic *muthos* posited in the *Poetics*. Fundamental among them is a 'change of fortune'. About the direction of the change—whether to or from great misfortune—the *Poetics* significantly vacillates;[30] but some sort of 'transformation' (*metabasis* or *metabolê*) is repeatedly assumed, and from it we can derive much else in the theory, including the tragic emotions and the design of the 'complex' plot. The distinctive themes of tragedy are therefore taken to be good and bad fortune, great prosperity (*eutuchia*) and adversity (*dustuchia*); these are the poles of success and failure between which the characters of tragedy move. I do not want immediately to tackle the old issue of why Aristotle apparently changes his mind between chapters 13 and 14 of the *Poetics* about the direction of the best tragic trans-

---

[29] I consider Aristotelian mimesis and universals more fully in 'Aristotelian Mimesis and Human Understanding', in Ø. Andersen and J. Haarberg (eds.), *Making Sense of Aristotle: Essays in Poetics* (London, 2001), 87–107; on universals compare J. Armstrong, 'Aristotle on the Philosophical Nature of Poetry', *Classical Quarterly*, 48 (1998), 447–55.

[30] This vacillation has often been played down, partly in order to make chapter 13 (where the *dustuchia*-ending is dominant) carry more weight than 14 (where the *eutuchia*-ending prevails); but outside these chapters the (final) direction of change is left open at 7. 1451$^a$13–14, 18. 1455$^b$28, and, by implication, 11. 1452$^a$31–2, 1452$^b$2.

formation, though I shall shortly return to this. Instead, I want to take the two basic types of tragic configuration, as specified in these chapters, and to ask of them in turn how they are related to the worldview projected by traditional tragic myth.

I propose to take chapter 14 first, since in itself it seems to me less problematic. Though the argument of this chapter leads Aristotle to a preference for plays in which extreme misfortune is threatened but averted, he does not relax his primary requirement that tragedy must elicit pity and fear; indeed, he re-emphasizes it at the start of this section (1453$^b$11–15). This looks somewhat paradoxical, since pity and fear have been defined as responses to misfortune (1453$^a$4–6), but it establishes that for Aristotle a plot in which, say, a killing within the family is narrowly avoided need not differ in emotional effectiveness from one in which the event does take place: the same sensitivities will be touched in the audience by the imminent prospect as by the actual occurrence. This is important, and it is linked to Aristotle's understanding of the tragic emotions; but what it does not explain is why a critic whose conception of tragedy revolves around pity and fear should have at any stage *preferred* such works to those in which the relevant kinds of deed are fully enacted. Even if Aristotle had not left apparently inconsistent judgements on the ideal tragedy in chapters 13 and 14, we would still have to account for the supposition that the drama of averted catastrophe could satisfy *better than any other* the tragic requirement of a pitiful and fearful change of fortune. It is pertinent but insufficient to show that such drama could make full use of reversal, recognition, and *hamartia*: that it could, in fact, fulfil all the requirements of the complex plot. It remains to find a consideration which could induce a preference, within the terms of Aristotle's theory, for the *Iphigeneia in Tauris* over the *Oedipus Tyrannus*.

When in the course of chapter 14 Aristotle describes the type of plot in which a terrible act, about to be committed in ignorance, is prevented by a scene of 'recognition', the phrase he employs for the act is ποιεῖν τι τῶν ἀνηκέστων, 'to perpetrate something incurable' (1453$^b$35). Aristotle uses the adjective ἀνήκεστος, 'incurable', nowhere else in the *Poetics*, and only once outside it (*Rhetoric* 2. 23, 1399$^b$4), but it is an apt word for the ultimates of suffering and evil: it is found with this force in several Greek authors.[31] It is ironic that

---

[31] Most interestingly for my purposes, Plato, *Republic* 10. 619a4, in a section of the

the word should occur just here within the *Poetics*, since it can apply only proleptically to situations of averted misfortune. Aristotle's averted catastrophe simply is not, in the end, a catastrophe; and if the requisite tragic emotions are to be aroused by essentially undeserved suffering, then although the imminent prospect of such suffering may successfully elicit them, it cannot do so in just the same way as the actuality.[32] Nor is it a matter of 'pure' emotion: the tragic emotions are related, on Aristotle's own theory, to the understanding of a total pattern of action. What the type of tragedy preferred in *Poetics* chapter 14 lacks is precisely the collapse into irreversible disaster. But it is just this extreme degree on the scale of unhappiness which belongs to many of the major tragic myths from Homer onwards. It is the kind of suffering which, as Aristotle himself observes of the misfortune of Priam in a passage from *Nicomachean Ethics* 1 to which I shall be returning, makes any possibility of happiness inconceivable (1. 9. 11, 1100ª8–9). While we must allow the title of tragedy, then, to the drama of averted misfortune, it cannot be tragedy of the same intensity, or with the same implications, as the tragedy of the 'incurable': for the prevention of what would otherwise have been irrevocable does not eliminate the possibility of *eudaimonia*, happiness, in either the traditional or the Aristotelian sense. I think we are therefore justified in regarding *Poetics* 14 as a prescription, in dramatic terms, for the avoidance of absolute or unmitigated tragedy. But before attempting to say more precisely what this might signify, we should examine the preceding chapter of the *Poetics*, since it might be thought to be the corollary of what I have just claimed: that we *do* there find an acceptance of ultimate, 'incurable' tragedy.

As a prelude to consideration of chapter 13, it is worth clarifying Aristotle's notion of the positive and negative fortune, *eutuchia* and *dustuchia* (or *atuchia*), which he sets up as the poles of tragic experience and which comprise the 'external goods' that define material and social prosperity or adversity. Plato's critiques of tragedy

myth of Er that anticipates the 'Thyestes' figure discussed in the first half of my paper, uses the phrase ἀνήκεστα κακά, 'incurable evils', with reference to the deeds of tyrants.

[32] We would expect there to be some difference in the balance of emotions, since fear specifically concerns prospects (*Nicomachean Ethics* 1115ª9, *Rhetoric* 1382ª21–2); but pity too can operate in advance of the relevant sufferings (*Rhetoric* 1382ᵇ25–6, 1386ª35–ᵇ1).

in *Republic* 2–3 and 10 had similarly addressed the genre's dependence on supposedly life-determining transformations of fortune.[33]
Working from the premise that material suffering was a misconception either on the level of causality (as with the hasty, Thyestes-like
soul's attempt to deny responsibility for its own evils) or on the level
of ethical evaluation (since bodily 'suffering' could hardly be regarded
as a real evil, if properly judged), Plato was able to suggest that the
portrayal of ostensible misfortune should be either eliminated from
poetry altogether or only admitted on condition that it be used to
show the virtuous man's ability to rise above it. Aristotle's mature
views on the relation between body and soul led to a more pragmatic
conception of the connections between virtue and bodily existence,
and enabled him to accept that happiness (*eudaimonia*) might be
partially dependent on the material circumstances of a life. I cited
above the passage from *Nicomachean Ethics* book 1 where Aristotle
comments on the destruction of Priam's happiness by his tragic
misfortune (his *tuchai*, 'strokes of fortune') and his wretched death.
*Eudaimonia* cannot make itself altogether independent of *eutuchia*.
Although, therefore, *eudaimonia* itself is mentioned only once in the
*Poetics* (6. 1450ª17–20), and that in a passage which some have
thought spurious, it is a reasonable inference from the choice of Priam
as an example in the *Ethics* that Aristotle takes tragedy's concern with
transformations from prosperity to adversity (and *vice versa*) to provide insight if not into happiness itself, then at least into the relationship of happiness to its material circumstances—the relationship
whose potentially tragic form Plato set himself to deny. Yet it is pertinent to my argument that in this same section of the *Ethics* we find
some equivocation on the relation between *eudaimonia* and *eutuchia*,
for having once conceded that fortune may destabilize happiness,
Aristotle comes back to the question in order to emphasize, in Platonic
fashion, the ability of the good man to endure misfortune without
diminution of his happiness.[34]

---

[33] See especially 3. 399a–c (referring to music but with clear implications for the
poetry that music would accompany), 10. 603c. *Gorgias* fr. 11. 9 DK shows that
related ideas (alongside a model of the audience's pity and fear) were already theorized
in the later 5th century.
[34] See *Nicomachean Ethics* 1099ª31–ᵇ8 and 1100ª4–9 for the original acknowledgement of the problem; Aristotle continues to wrestle with it at 1100ª32–
1101ª21. Nussbaum, *Fragility*, 327–36, offers an interpretation of this material,
including the Priam references.

Even if, then, Aristotle's philosophy did allow him to acknowledge the force of a type of tragedy whose meaning Plato could hardly countenance, it remains to be asked whether in his prescription for the finest tragedy, as he conceives of it in *Poetics* 13, it is this extreme case of vulnerability to the most devastating kind of misfortune which he has in mind. An immediately affirmative answer might seem to be warranted by the fact that Aristotle here cites the tragedy of Oedipus, by which he is likely as elsewhere to mean Sophocles' *Oedipus Tyrannus*; and if we were to set up a paradigm of Greek tragic myth, we could hardly exclude Sophocles' Oedipus from it. But such an answer would be unsatisfactory, since it fails to reckon with the interpretation of the Oedipus myth (as of other myths) implied by Aristotle's use of the word *hamartia*. My concern with this vexed term is limited here to its negative implications—hardly an inappropriate way of looking at its place in the theory, since its appearance in *Poetics* 13 is part of the conclusion to a train of thought that arrives at its goal, the definition of a tragic ideal, via a process of exclusion. As Aristotle says, formulating his plot-pattern in terms of a putative central figure, 'it is the person in between these who is left' ($1453^{a}7$), i.e. the type of hero who avoids the objections made against other types. It is therefore worthwhile asking exactly what Aristotle has discarded in his quest for the best tragedy.

For my present purposes the two significant exclusions are as follows (there are others which do not bear on my argument):

i. the downfall of the man who is *epieikês*, 'good' ($1452^{b}34-6$);
ii. the downfall of the (less than perfectly) good man for some reason beyond his control.

The second of these possibilities is not as such mentioned in *Poetics* 13, but I contend that it is nonetheless being excluded (or suppressed). Moreover, although there is a difference of moral degree between the two cases I have posited, they have something important in common. The given reason for Aristotle's rejection of the first case is that it would be *miaron*, 'disgusting' or 'repellent', to witness the downfall of the good man. The use of such a strong term of disapprobation (found nowhere in Aristotle's writings outside the *Poetics*) in itself justifies us in supposing that he has in mind a man of exceptional or perfect virtue, and it follows from this that the only conceivable cause of such a downfall, in Aristotle's scheme, would be a piece of blind misfortune, an *atuchêma*, something for which the victim could bear no responsibility.[35] If this is correct, then the two plot-patterns highlighted above have in common the exclusion of chance or the purely external impingement of misfortune. This makes good sense as an antithesis to *hamartia*, a term which suggests, however imprecisely, an action originating with the person who suffers its unforeseen or unintended consequences—an agent-centred concept, in other words. These two points, one positive and one negative, support the conclusion that Aristotle did not believe the best type of tragedy should deal with the accidental, arbitrary impingement of misfortune.

It is now possible to see grounds for my contention that there is an affinity between Aristotle's model of tragedy and one of the central Platonic objections to tragic myth, since in both cases we find an aversion to the stark tragedy of fate, chance, or—it must now be added—divine causation. The point becomes clearer if we reintroduce into the argument a factor mentioned earlier in my paper, the *Poetics'* neglect of the religious dimension of Greek tragedy. If it is true that Aristotle precludes chance from the best tragic plot (and there are further considerations which support the claim), this must be brought into conjunction with his disregard for the theology of tragic myth, since within the world of myth 'chance' (*tuchê*) has a religious status. Traditional Greek ways of thinking, as Aristotle himself acknowledges elsewhere, did not systematically distinguish between divine causation and the workings of *tuchê*.[36] In this context *tuchê* is a word of varied usage, quite capable of subsuming the forces of gods and fate; it is perhaps the word most simply expressive of the fatalism of Greek tragedy and its mythic material, since it has the widest applicability to situations in which what happens is conceived to have been inescapable and causally independent of the relevant agent(s). So it amounts to much the same thing for Aristotle to debar either chance or divine causation from his

---

[35] See *Nicomachean Ethics* 1135$^b$16-17, with T. Stinton, '*Hamartia* in Aristotle and Greek Tragedy', *Classical Quarterly*, 25 (1975), 221-54, at 226: Stinton's article remains the most important and subtle discussion of the whole subject of *hamartia*.

[36] Aristotle notes the religious view of *tuchê* at *Physics* 196$^a$5-7. An association between *tuchê* and the gods can be found at e.g. Hesiod, *Theogony* 360; Homeric *Hymn* 11. 5; Pindar, *Olympians* 8. 67, 12. 2, *Pythians* 8. 53, *Nemeans* 6. 24, Sophocles, *Philoctetes* 1326, Euripides, *Hercules Furens* 309, 1393, *Iphigeneia in Aulis* 1136; cf. the Thyestes-like soul at Plato, *Republic* 10. 619c5, quoted on p. 116 above.

ideal tragic plot. Either source of misfortune (or even of good fortune) would be equally hard to reconcile with his conception of tragedy as a genre which can dramatize, in quasi-philosophical fashion, 'universals' of human action and suffering, given that he explains these universals in terms of a tight causal nexus of human character and agency (9. 1451$^b$8–10).[37] Although, as we have seen, Aristotle allows popular religious attitudes to figure in chapter 25 as the solution to a general philosophical criticism of poetry, this is a very different matter from allowing such attitudes to determine the essence of the genre.

I promised earlier to avoid a full discussion of *hamartia*, but I ought to indicate very summarily here how I think it fits into my case. I take *hamartia* to be part of Aristotle's enterprise of producing a secular theory of Greek tragedy, and to stand as a philosophical attempt to reconcile the need for suitable tragic material (major, life-changing transformations of fortune) with a view of human experience from which the capricious and the mysterious are to be mostly excluded. *Hamartia* locates tragic action purely on the scale of human intention and moral responsibility; it ignores the religious scope of the world-view embodied in tragic myth. If, as we must assume, the concept of *hamartia* is consistent with the general thrust of the *Poetics*, then it must be compatible with the fundamental principle of 'necessity or probability' which Aristotle repeatedly invokes as his measure of dramatic coherence. *Hamartia* thus becomes a means of making catastrophe intelligible, but it does so, I maintain, only at the price of part of what makes existing Greek tragedy distinctive, which includes a sense that absolute tragedy can never be fully comprehensible.

It may be illuminating now to cast a second glance at chapter 14 of the *Poetics*. I noted earlier that, though there are apparent discrepancies between this and the preceding chapter, there are also shared assumptions, one of which is the possible operation, or even the necessity, of *hamartia* in the ideal plots of both chapters. In chapter 14 Aristotle envisages a plot of much the same nature as in chapter 13, involving an error which leads towards some calamity between close kin, the crucial qualification being now added that the action should stop short of the misfortune itself. There is really not so much separating these two ideal *muthoi* once one sees that for

---

[37] This is not to deny that sufferings caused by chance events could elicit pity: see *Rhetoric* 1386$^a$6–9, with *Aesthetics of Mimesis*, 223.

Aristotle both represent tragedies embedded in and caused by human ignorance or fallibility of some kind. If in the case of the first type the change of fortune is intelligible because attributable to a *hamartia*, then our understanding of such things (of the 'universals' of action and character which they convey) will be equally confirmed by the second type of plot, in which the recognition of what was previously mistaken is brought about before it leads to 'incurable' suffering. If Aristotle's emphasis is seen to fall throughout on the rational understanding of why tragedies come about, then chapter 14 does not involve an alien and surprising line of thought but an extension of the preceding argument; and its endorsement of plays of averted catastrophe can be regarded as the fulfilment of the aim of locating tragic causation firmly within the domain of human agency and fallibility. The experience of imminent misfortune is sufficient to allow the conditions and causes of *dustuchia* to come within the range of intelligibility, and at the same time to arouse powerful pity and fear, without the need for a display of 'incurable' suffering. Moreover, we can see that in the case of averted catastrophe Aristotle is just as likely as in chapter 13 to disregard the part played by divine causation in actual tragic *muthoi*. This is indirectly illustrated later in the *Poetics*, in chapter 17's summary of the plot-structure of Euripides' *Iphigeneia in Tauris*, a play which exemplifies the averted catastrophe ideal (and a work generally cited by Aristotle with as much approval as Sophocles' very different *Oedipus Tyrannus*).[38] It is striking that in his synopsis of the plot Aristotle omits most of the play's religious implications and asserts misleadingly that Apollo's part in Orestes' mission is 'outside the *muthos*' (1455[b]7-8). This is a telling redefinition of the play in such a way as to leave the foreground of supposedly probable human action intact, while downgrading the divine background which provides the larger and indispensable explanation of events. The secularization, or rationalization, of the myth is effected, as with much later Euripidean criticism, not by the playwright but the critic.

Any attempt at an economical reading of *Poetics* 13 and 14, it has

---

[38] Of the *Poetics*' six references to the *Iphigeneia* (11. 1452[b]6-8, 14. 1454[a]7, 16. 1454[b]31-5, 1455[a]18, 17. 1455[b]3-12, 1455[b]14-15) only one, the third, contains an element of criticism. The *Oedipus Tyrannus* is cited slightly more often, but on three occasions (14. 1453[b]31, 15. 1454[b]6-8, 24. 1460[a]28-30) it exemplifies less than ideal features.

to be admitted, will be open to objection and qualification, since Aristotle's train of thought in these sections is too compressed to yield to definitive solutions—a point of caution which particularly needs to be urged against many treatments of the *hamartia* problem. What I have offered here has hinged on just one question: what does each of these chapters imply about the essential pattern of a tragic transformation of fortune? The answer I have sketched has at least the merit of bringing the two chapters into a closer relation than many critics have been able to discern between them. There is, in fact, no good reason for the common assumption that chapter 13 represents the authoritative statement of the theory, with chapter 14 to be regarded as necessarily secondary and aberrant. I suggest, in short, that Aristotle's overriding interest is in tragic plots whose pattern of causality, however terrible its upshot, is susceptible to coherent understanding as well as being capable (for the very same reasons) of eliciting intense pity and fear: tragedy's finest material is conceived of as the pathology of human fallibility at its extremes. Understanding, where ethical action is concerned, may imply that in principle things might have been effected otherwise, that they might have been controlled so as to avoid misfortune. This is evidently so with the type of plot recommended in chapter 14, where the potentiality of preventing disaster is seen to be realized, yet without, it is supposed, reducing the force of the distinctive tragic experience. In these terms, there is an ultimately reassuring underpinning to Aristotle's reflections on tragedy: a conviction that, at any rate in the heightened mythical world of unified plot-structures (a world from which 'the irrational' is excluded),[39] tragic suffering lies within not beyond the limits of human comprehension. If Homeric and Attic tragedy may sometimes seem to intimate an awareness of how much falls outside those limits,[40] there is no trace of this in the *Poetics*. Aristotle himself was certainly able to see that a preference for a particular kind of tragic plot might stem from a desire to retain a basic moral acceptability in the genre; in chapter 13 he refers to the 'weakness' of audiences which like best the sort of play in which

---

[39] The exclusion of 'the irrational', τὸ ἄλογον (15. 1454ᵇ6–7, 24. 1460ᵃ28–9, 25. 1461ᵇ14–21), is the negative counterpart of the requirement for 'necessity or probability'. Divine agency and 'the irrational' are juxtaposed at 15. 1454ᵃ37–ᵇ8, as comparable defects in what one might call plot-logic.

[40] I give one account of this aspect of tragedy in 'Human Limits and the Religion of Greek Tragedy', *Journal of Literature and Theology*, 4 (1990), 169–80.

poetic justice is achieved, both good and bad agents getting their
deserts (1453ª30–5). Aristotle wants nothing so straightforward or
emotionally simple, but in a more subtle way, if my argument is
right, his own theory is designed to eliminate from tragedy, or to
redefine within it, some of those events with which rational moral
hopes and expectations cannot easily cope. The roots of this attitude
go deep in Aristotle's thinking, and I believe that the *Poetics*' scheme
of tragedy may be one symptom of a more general tendency in his
philosophy which has been described as a 'perception of conflict as
something to be avoided or managed'.[41] In making such a claim I
should stress that I am not attempting to convict Aristotle of a misunderstanding, but of a philosophical reinterpretation of tragedy.

Plato and Aristotle both believed, though with different emphases, in
a strong connection between virtue and happiness. One source of
conflict between their views and the myths of tragic poetry (Homeric
epic included) was a discrepancy in the idea of virtue (*aretê*) itself. But
even the philosophers were not unaffected by the traditional conception of heroism, and their own ethical ideals show a certain
affinity with it in the value they attach to such features as courage
and single-minded independence. Yet this degree of common ground
throws into relief the fundamental difference between tragedy and
the philosophers' ethical systems, for tragedy typically pictures a
world in which the relation of virtue to happiness is far from secure,
and perhaps even, at the heroic extreme, a desperate illusion.[42]
Plato's sense of this contradiction was acute and provided one of the
chief motivations behind his confrontation with tragedy, though I
tried earlier to suggest that he felt the pull of a tragic point of view so
clearly that at times he comes close to reinforcing it himself, at least
on the dramatic surface of his work. Aristotle's position, I have
argued, is equivocal, perhaps tantamount, and not only in *Poetics*
14, to his own, more nuanced denial of tragedy's profoundest fears.

---

[41] A. Macintyre, *After Virtue: A Study in Moral Theory* (London, 1981), 153; cf.
147–8 for some related thoughts on tragedy.
[42] See the brief but suggestive remarks of B. Williams, in M. I. Finley (ed.), *The
Legacy of Greece* (Oxford, 1981), 252–3, on the relation between the philosophers'
ethics and tragedy's sense of human insecurity; but when Williams writes of a sense
of significances, found in tragedy, which had 'disappeared ... perhaps altogether from
their [philosophers'] minds', I think he overlooks the tensions still to be traced in
their treatments of tragedy.

Aristotle could not be fully true both to tragedy and to his own philosophy, and I believe that his apparent rapprochement with tragic poetry may finally have to be regarded, against the background of that 'ancient quarrel' which so stimulated Plato, as more of an attempt to woo it over to philosophy's side than to meet it on its own terms. If so, Aristotle was not the last philosopher of whom this could be said.

# 6

# *Ethos and Dianoia:* 'Character' and 'Thought' in Aristotle's Poetics

## A. M. DALE

Among the most exciting of philosophical discoveries is that of a fundamental unity in apparently diverse phenomena, and Greek philosophy, which here made so great a contribution, was always susceptible of a slight intoxication at the idea. If all fields of human thought and the metaphysical scheme of the universe could be shown to be aspects of the same underlying reality, then it seemed that the same concepts should be transferable from one sphere of knowledge to another and illuminate each in turn. Under the heady influence of this notion, Plato, to his pupils' consternation, had run the philosophy of poetry into a cul-de-sac. Aristotle, scientist as well as philosopher, often uses the biologist's habits of observation, induction and classification to supplement the deductive approach, so that his conclusions usually end somewhere nearer than Plato's to what was commonly accepted as empirical reality. But the unity required by metaphysical thinking had to be satisfied too, and indeed it is the common experience of scholars that no one branch of Aristotle's multifarious activity is properly intelligible without some knowledge of the whole. Aristotelian ethics, politics, rhetoric, logic, metaphysic and natural science all make their contribution to Aristotle's theory of poetry; and it is perhaps not fanciful to detect in him some peculiar satisfaction in making the same terms do duty in different contexts. To us, with the lapse of 23 centuries and all the riches of comparative literature to draw upon, it has gradually become clear that the philosophy of poetry, as a branch of aesthetic,

Based on a lecture delivered during the visit [in 1959] of Professor and Mrs Webster (A. M. Dale) to Dunedin under the terms of the De Carle Lectureship, University of Otago.

must work out its own principles of analysis and cannot get very far so long as it keeps to concepts which illustrate the unity of all human thought. However appropriate and even profound some of Aristotle's overlapping terms of analysis may seem at first to be, however skilfully he modifies and adapts them to the realities of contemporary poetry as he saw it, they sometimes prove on closer examination imperfectly assimilated to this new context, and bear the faint, ineradicable traces of the different branch of inquiry for which they were originally devised. Yet we can often see how the peculiar characteristics of Greek poetry in Aristotle's own day gave these terms a contingent plausibility, and even propriety, which as universal currency they hardly possess. Thus for instance the new version of the metaphysical 'mimesis' theory, which Aristotle uses in order to reinstate poetry high in the scale of human activities after Plato's attacks, leads to an almost exclusive attention to the least subjective aspects of poetry: the most obviously mimetic form, the drama, gets fullest discussion and highest marks, epic comes second, with dithyramb a bad third and lyric either nowhere or subsumed vaguely under music. Now this *a priori* deduction from metaphysical principles is supported by the empirical facts of the contemporary scene, since the growing-point of new poetic life was to be found in the theatre, and Homer still remained an inexhaustible fount of inspiration, while *personal* lyric had not yet found its new Hellenistic forms, and, to judge by the trends evident at the turn of the fifth/fourth century, the intellectual content of *choral* lyric (including the choral lyric of drama) had become subordinate to the new music. Thus the theory appears as the product of a fusion of two methods of approach, the deductive and the empirical, and this fusion constitutes the essential character of the *Poetics*. To disentangle these two threads is a difficult and delicate operation, but in the process of trying we sometimes find clues to the understanding of Greek poetry and to the way it was understood by its own public.

The lines on which a subject such as poetry is to be discussed are in the Aristotelian method firmly laid down by analytic definition. Poetry has an essential nature—'mimesis', it can be classified into a limited number of 'kinds' or broad *genres* (epic, dramatic, etc.), each of which has its characteristic effect or function, and each of which can by scientific classification be subdivided into a certain number of 'parts', components, or one could say that poetry itself has a certain

number of parts, which are found in varying numbers and assort-
ments in its several kinds: thus epic has four parts, mythos, ethos,
dianoia, lexis, or Plot, Character, Thought, Diction, while tragedy
has these four, plus Spectacle (opsis) and Music. Now clearly this
analysis into component parts is of cardinal importance, since a
major part of the discussion is to be carried on in terms of these components. What is involved in the notion of such 'parts', and how do
we determine what they are? In the order of material objects the
problem is relatively simple; we can analyse the human body, for
instance, structurally into head, body and limbs, or physiologically
into bone, blood, skin, muscle, etc., or again chemically, and so on.
In each case the analysis if properly done is exhaustive and the whole
is the sum of the parts. But what do we mean by the 'parts' of
tragedy? Chapter 12 of our text of the *Poetics* shoots off into a sudden
digression on the 'quantitative parts' of tragedy—prologue, episodes,
choral odes, etc.; and here is firm ground: these sections will add up
to the whole of tragedy quantitatively considered. But the analysis
which shapes Aristotle's theory of tragedy is a qualitative one; it
divides poetry into its 'formative constituents', or again ($50^a8$) into
the parts which 'give a tragedy its quality'. And these parts we find
are precisely six in number, no more and no less—'every tragedy
therefore must have six parts . . . and no more'. How are they found,
and how do we know them to be exhaustive? They are somewhat
schematically arranged as given, one (Spectacle) by the manner of
the mimesis, two (Diction and Music) by its means, and three (Plot,
Character and Thought) by its objects, but this of course does
not answer the question. Aristotle expresses the result as a logical
deduction—'every tragedy *therefore* must have six parts', but the
premises when examined resolve themselves into a series of statements, which are clearly meant to be self-evident, except that ethos
and dianoia are rather perfunctorily derived from the fact that a
tragedy represents human beings in action, and the springs of
human action are two, ethos and dianoia—again a statement which
can be taken to command immediate assent, at least from the good
Aristotelian pupil who knows his *Ethics*.

How far can we agree that these six 'parts' are objectively present
and are the whole of tragedy's constituents? In the first place they are
not all ingredients in the same sense. Aristotle himself drops Music
and Spectacle as in some way less essential; they are present in a

performed tragedy but not in a read one. A read tragedy then is left with the same 'parts' as an epic poem: if the two are nevertheless not to be understood as identical forms of poetry, the reason is that Aristotle subsequently adds to his definition of tragedy the qualification 'acted, not narrated'. It is at once clear that the sum of the qualitative parts will not add up to the whole quality of a poetic form, and therefore 'part' is not altogether a good word, and 'exhaustive' is not to be too hard pressed. Of the remaining four, Diction, which together with Music is the *means* of mimesis, stands apart from the other three, which are bracketed together as the *object*. But even these three, Plot (or Story), Character, and Thought are not quite on the same plane; we find that Plot, which alone is a direct reflection of the 'universal', is all-pervasive, while Character and Thought seem to appear only in patches up and down the play; yet surely if they are merely logical and qualitative, not quantitative, 'parts', they ought not to be spatially determinable in this way. Further, Aristotle says the modern tragedians tend to produce plays which are 'characterless'. His editors are quick in his defence: 'Only relatively, of course', or 'Of course this only means, in Aristotle's own words, "without speeches expressive of character".' But the all-important question how ethos is present in a drama except in 'speeches expressive of character' is nowhere very clearly answered; and is it altogether satisfactory to have as an essential, major constituent of tragedy something which is liable to dwindle almost to vanishing point? The awkwardness is the less present to us in that thinking in English we are apt to let 'Character' melt imperceptibly into 'the characters', forgetting that our habit of referring to the people in a drama as 'the characters' itself originates in the *Poetics*, in that Aristotle speaks of τὰ ἤθη, 'the Characters', as well as of ethos, 'Character', though his definitions make it quite clear that he means something less by either than we mean by our terms. Still, let us keep clear of the *dramatis personae* and try what is usually called 'character-drawing', which is generally understood to be required to some minimum extent in every play and may be said to be more explicitly present in some parts than in others. But even this seems to be too wide for ethos in Aristotle's sense. His prescription for the ideal tragic hero is given under the heading of Plot, not of ethos. He restricts the word ethos to the moral as distinct from the intellectual characteristics of a person, the latter being constituted in the individual by dianoia. This however is apt to be a difficult distinction to draw. We have already seen that it belongs originally to an ethical context and its applicability to drama is not immediately obvious. Why just Character and Thought in particular? Why not reason and passion? or the material and the spiritual, or a dozen other arbitrary divisions of the human personality? For these two 'springs of human action' which 'determine the quality of a man and his success or failure' are hard enough to seize separately even in the ethical sphere, and the action that springs from them is usually one and indivisible; why then should we expect them to manifest themselves in human speech in separable quanta? If the answer is given that it is the dramatist's business to show how action is generated from these two sets of individual qualities, we might retort that what is of primary interest to the student of the ethics of individual conduct is not necessarily a paramount claim upon the dramatist, who is representing the *interplay* of human wills, a composite action, not a series of individual actions. In fact here Aristotle seems to have been carried away by the identity of the term 'action', $\pi\rho\hat{a}\xi\iota s$, for the action of a play, and for individual 'actions' or conduct in the ethical sense. One is tempted to picture Aristotle's Tragedy as a biological entity erupting into giant 'action' as a product of its autonomous ethos and dianoia. But even if we acquit Aristotle of such fantasies, at least we can say that the dramatist need feel no obligation to answer for his quotas of explicit 'character' and 'thought', since these are only arbitrarily selected abstractions from the whole compound of personality in action which he portrays.

If however we reunite ethos and dianoia into the single concept 'character' in the English sense of personality, we get a list of three constituents—Plot, Character, Diction—which does carry some sort of objective compulsion, in that their presence is implied in the definition of drama. Words, people to speak them, and something happening to those people; these are the irreducible minimum of which a drama is composed. But to accept them as components is not to say that they are necessarily the most satisfactory terms in which to analyse drama or to determine what makes a good drama. For one thing, it is only as abstractions that they are properly separable; as soon as we begin to give them a positive content they at once become intricately involved with each other. The Plot is what happens to these particular characters, including what they say to each other;

the characters have no existence except as working out this particular plot, and they are revealed, at least in read drama, solely by their words. The same applies to the dramatist's processes; he has not finished 'creating' his characters until he has put them through the whole of the action and selected every word they are to utter. And it may often happen that when we have discussed a particular drama in terms of its plot, its characters and its diction we are far from having exhausted its significance; for the *Agamemnon*, for instance, or any of Ibsen's plays of social criticism we should have to begin again from a different point of view.

These component parts, then, may enter into a general definition of drama, but for a discussion of what constitutes a good drama, or for rules of literary criticism by which to measure the achievement of a given drama or to attempt the writing of one, they are simply abstractions from which it is *possible* to set our angle in discussing the concrete whole. Other angles or starting-points may be equally or more profitable; we might for instance decide that the essence of drama is best given in terms of a relation between these components, that it shows 'character in action', or 'conflict'. But at least the meaning of these three terms, Plot, Character and Diction, is immediately obvious to us, and if Aristotle had in fact divided tragedy into these three components we should have recognised the obvious. Actually he produces four, with ethos and dianoia substituted for Character. So long as we leave these in a vague translation 'Character' and 'Thought' they may seem ordinary and relevant enough in a discussion of a drama, but the more we pursue them, the more elusive and lacking in self-consistency they seem to become; and the chief reason is, I think, that they are concepts taken over partly from the sphere of Ethics and partly from that of Rhetoric, and never wholly brought into line with each other or with the rest of the *Poetics*. Considered under Ethics, ethos and dianoia are both part of the individual make-up as, roughly, moral and intellectual qualities: they issue in action and determine a person's quality. But in fact only ethos is in the *Poetics* treated from this point of view. Psychologically, ethos is a more fundamental and abiding aspect of the personality than dianoia, which may indeed often be directed to giving others, by means of the spoken word, a misleading impression of the speaker's personality. Hence there are τὰ ἤθη, 'the Characters', related to individual persons, but never 'the Thoughts'. But also ethos, in the

singular, is defined as a declaration of προαίρεσις, 'will', 'purpose', or
moral choice on a given occasion 'when it is not obvious' (50<sup>b</sup>8),
where the mere course of the action is not enough for our understanding, and explicitness (in words) is required. In the *Poetics* the
distinction between implicit and explicit ethos, though never clearly
explained, is implied in those words 'where it is not obvious' and
54<sup>a</sup>18 '*if the words or the action* reveal some moral purpose'. There
is no corresponding distinction between implicit and explicit
dianoia because as we shall see dianoia is peculiarly the province of
the spoken word, of Rhetoric, so explicitness is its nature. No obligation is laid on the poet to make his dianoia characteristic of the
person uttering it, because by definition what is characteristic
belongs to ethos. It is not appropriate, says Aristotle, for a woman to
be clever, and he says it in his prescriptions for τὰ ἤθη. The dianoia in
the mouth of Oedipus must spring from Oedipus' situation; it is not
required to be expressive of Oedipus' nature. Such is the awkward
and indeed indefensible product of this dichotomy.

A divorce between Characters (in the English sense) and Plot has
put many difficulties in the way of critical analysis; the divorce
between ethos and dianoia, with some of the words spoken to be
allotted to the one, some to the other, and some to neither, is still
further from our notion of characters-in-action. Yet these distinctions are some sort of reflection of actual differences between Greek
and more modern tragedy, and indeed between Greek tragedy and
the New Comedy. In Menander every speaking part is 'a character'
and made to speak characteristically. In tragedy this kind of
'realistic' characterisation is slightly foreshadowed in the style of
speech occasionally given to anonymous humbler persons like the
Nurse in the *Choephoroe* or the Watchman in the *Antigone*, who are
thereby typified to some extent; on the other hand, some anonymous
figures, especially those Messengers called ἐξάγγελοι, may be left
deliberately blank of feature, uncharacterised; what they say simply
helps to explain or push on the story. So Aristotle's τὰ ἤθη do not
include every spoken part, but only those whose inner nature and
moral choices have some effect on the action. In the good tragedy, he
says in effect, there must be among the *dramatis personae* some who
have ethos, in whose qualities and impulses we are interested, and
who must therefore satisfy us by some degree of explicit self-declara-
tion. Moreover, even these central figures do not always speak

strictly 'in character'. Much confusion has been caused by modern
critics who insist on taking every utterance of an Oedipus or Ajax or
Medea as a bit of self-revelation. When it is essential for the audience
to understand the full magnitude of Alcestis' sacrifice for Admetus
Euripides commits the demonstration to Alcestis herself, without
thereby seeking to characterise her as rapt in the contemplation of
her own nobility—as a woman who would say that sort of thing,
nor Admetus as a husband who needed that sort of thing pointed out
to him. Von Blumenthal, in *Die Erscheinung der Götter bei Sophokles*,
is assuredly astray in seeing in Tecmessa's description of Ajax's
behaviour during his madness a female *penchant* for horrid details.
Nor is there in Greek tragedy much analysis of motive for its own
intrinsic interest, or for the sake of the completeness of a character in
the round. Alcestis' self-immolation for her husband's sake is so
essential to her traditional ethos, and so abundantly implicit in the
action of the play, that Euripides has seen fit, in the interests of his
conception of the whole shape of the play, to suppress in her speech
all eloquence in the expression of loving devotion. Explicit ethos is
required 'where it is *not* obvious'. Aristotle's isolation of ethos as
something intermittent which should not be left out of a play but
must be kept in its proper place does correspond to an actual and at
times slightly bewildering feature of Greek tragedy.

To modern ears, however, the most unfamiliar and the most
puzzling of these concepts is certainly dianoia. The 'Thought' of a
play might perhaps suggest to us its underlying theme, where there
is one, as distinct from its outer plot, or at least what the author himself is seeking to convey as the inner *meaning* of the action represented on the stage. Such 'Thought' is most easily detachable,
perhaps, where the poet has invented characters and situations to
illustrate or to symbolise what is in his mind, as Ibsen in *The Master
Builder*, or Shaw in *Major Barbara*, but it may also be conveyed in the
new interpretation of a given story, as in *Man and Superman*, or as the
story of Antigone is adapted by Jean Anouilh to demonstrate
Existentialist philosophy. Some such expression of the dramatist's
'Thought' can be disengaged from each successive new form given
by the Greek tragedians to the heroic myths, and is seen at its most
explicit, perhaps, in the choruses of the *Agamemnon*. But Aristotle
certainly means nothing of this kind; dianoia is given its position
among the essential parts of tragedy, not as a commentary on the

meaning of life, but as an essential function of the human mind issuing in action. Yes as we have seen it does not emanate from the nature of the speakers in the way that ethos does. What then are we to look for?

The word is used in a wide variety of senses in Greek—in almost every sense of our word 'thought', and with 'meaning' and 'intention' added. Its everyday, untechnical use appears for instance when Aeschylus in the *Frogs* (1058-9) claims that 'great thoughts must breed great words'; this is our ordinary notion of 'expressing thoughts in words'. In the *Sophist* (263 c2) Plato defines it as a process of thinking, a voiceless dialogue of the mind within itself, and such a dialogue issues in δόξα, an expressed opinion. Aristotle uses it in the general sense of 'intelligence' as a faculty in *Met.* 1025ᵇ25, and in one passage of the *Politics* (1337ᵇ9) it is 'mind' as opposed to 'body'. But there are one or two passages where Aristotle is using the word in a fairly general and untechnical sense which brings it nearer to the dianoia of the *Poetics*. In *Pol.* 1337ᵃ38 he says of education that it is not clear whether it should be directed chiefly to the intellect (dianoia) or the character (ethos), and in *Rhet.* III 16. 9 he contrasts dianoia with proairesis, advising the orator to let his words appear to come from the latter rather than the former, i.e. seek to appear good rather than clever. This is the same distinction as in the *Poetics*, between dianoia and the ethos which is shown in moral choices. How does this apply in the philosophy of poetry?

Dianoia (50ᵇ4) apparently comes third in order of importance of the six component 'parts'. There are three definitions:

(1) (50ᵃ7) Proofs and aphorisms are its manifestations.
(2) (50ᵇ11) It is used in proofs, refutations and generalisations.
(3) (50ᵇ4) It is a capacity for making all the relevant *points*, which in speeches is the function of the political art and of rhetoric.

The third of these is less different from the first two than it might appear. In *Rhet.* 1355ᵇ rhetoric is defined as the power to survey the whole range of apposite arguments to prove your point and convince your hearers. The generalisation is a very important type of argument, and it is from this point of view, as a means of Persuasion (πειθώ), not as a bit of distilled wisdom, that Aristotle thinks of the maxim or generalisation.

In Chapter 19, 56ᵃ33, there is a somewhat longer restatement which adds little to these definitions. [It remains to speak of Diction and Thought.] 'For Thought take what I have said in my *Rhetoric*; it belongs more strictly to that subject. To the sphere of Thought belong all the effects which have to be produced by means of the words. These effects consist of proving and confuting, rousing emotions— pity, fear, indignation and the like—and also exaggerating and mini- mising. Obviously the play's action has also to be compiled from the same ingredients when it has to give an impression of pity or fear or importance or probability, only here the effect has to be obvious with- out explanation [is this the play as a Biological Entity again?], whereas in the words it is the speaker who has to produce it, from what he says. After all, why have a speaker if the required effect is obvious without the words?'

The reason given for this perfunctory treatment of dianoia as com- pared with Plot, Character and Diction is that the subject has been dealt with at length in the *Rhetoric*. Although the actual word dianoia is not much used in the *Rhetoric* in any technical sense, we find (III 1. 7) that the art of rhetoric consists of dianoia *plus* diction in the sense of subject-matter and style, so that dianoia is in effect the whole content of rhetoric itself, and the aspects of it here summarised (in Chapter 19) are in fact a summary of that content (with one notable exception, to be discussed presently). This fact is of cardinal importance in Aristotle's interpretation of tragedy.

The insistence on the spoken word as the peculiar province of dianoia is noteworthy. The imperfect appropriateness of these concepts which Aristotle is using for the analysis of tragedy is nowhere more apparent than in the relation of the various 'parts' to the Word. Dramatic form implies that *everything* has to be conveyed by the spoken word—everything at least that Aristotle is concerned with in Plot, ethos, dianoia and Diction. But ethos (by Aristotelian definition, especially in the *Ethics*) is primarily something which a man is, rather than what he says or does, though both his words and his actions may be manifestations of it. Hence our uncertainties arising from the awkward distinction between τὰ ἤθη, The Characters, what the dramatic characters are, and their expressed ethos 'where it is not clear already'. With dianoia we come to some- thing which is (again by Aristotelian definition, this time from the *Rhetoric*) precisely the province of Eloquence, of the art of rhetoric. So the appeal here is not to the intellectual make-up of the personages as part of their nature, whether or not they come out with it in speech. The dianoia in a play *is* the eloquence of the personages, employed in putting their case on any occasion which requires it with all possible clarity and force. Their dianoia is the means by which an attitude of belief is produced in their hearers: they prove and disprove, exaggerate or gloss over, stir up emotions of pity, terror, indignation, calculated to influence belief. These phrases, 'an effect of plausibility', 'pity and terror', we have heard before in connection with the Plot, the chain of probable or necessary incidents generating pity and terror; yes, Aristotle seems to say, but that is not what I mean by dianoia, which is concerned only with the kind of persuasion that induces belief by means of *words* calculated for that end.

I come now to the one omission of which I spoke in the list of dianoia's functions in the *Poetics* as compared with the *Rhetoric*. In the *Rhetoric* eloquence is said to have three tasks: 'putting across', so to speak, your own ethos, rousing the desired emotions among your audience, and, its chief business, proving your case. In the *Poetics* the first of these is deliberately omitted, though in the *Rhetoric* the well-timed bit of self-revelation is recognised as an influential weapon of persuasion. (How many gifted speakers from Socrates downwards have opened their case with 'I am no orator as Brutus is'.) And in *Rhetoric* 1395$^b$13 general maxims, aphorisms, are shown to be particularly good examples of an argument which reveals the proairesis, the moral will, of the speaker, since they epitomise his attitude on the subject of the desirable; so if the maxims are morally edifying they make him appear χρηστοήθης, a good man. In the *Poetics* the aphorism is expressly kept aloof from the moral personality and brought under dianoia. In fact, of course, what we have called 'explicit ethos', the ethos 'where it is not obvious', ought to be *in the province* of dianoia, and it is only in that province that ethos can give the illusion of separability from the rest of the personality; but it cannot be put there because of the terms of Aristotle's definitions, so the issue has to be evaded or glossed over. If it be objected that we must here distinguish between a calculated piece of self-revelation introduced for a particular end by a speaker in an agonistic scene and the ordinary ethos appearing spontaneously as it were up and down the play, the answer is that Aristotle does not in fact make this distinction, and this brings us to a central difficulty in his whole treatment of dianoia.

At whom is the dianoia of a play directed? The other characters in a given scene? or the spectators? or both? Aristotle nowhere gives an answer or suggests that the question need arise. The whole subject is taken straight over from the province of Rhetoric and applied to tragedy without adaptation. In both, speeches are made, therefore the same rules of eloquence apply. The *Poetics* gives rules for good plot-construction, good character-drawing and good diction, but for good dianoia—'see my *Rhetoric*'. The summary of what dianoia sets out to achieve applies most obviously to scenes where there is a set debate, an agon, but not all rhetoric was agonistic. A lament, an appeal, even the careful portrayal of a situation, all require a capacity to find 'every possible persuasive point', and there is no suggestion of a difference between the reactions of the other dramatic characters and those of the theatre audience, or, what comes to the same thing, between what the poet wants to make *us* think and what the speaking character wants to make *his* hearers believe.

That such a difference is fundamental seems to us so obvious as to need no argument or illustration. But there is every reason why it should not have appeared so obvious to a Greek of the fourth century BC. Greek tragedy is a highly rhetorical form of art, much more so in the hands of Euripides than of his predecessors, and as far as we can judge the intensifying process continued with increased momentum in the fourth century. After a plunge into the turgid flood of Senecan drama we may indeed cool our heads with relief in the poetical sanity of Greek rhetorical tragedy, but rhetoric can be good as well as clever; it can present 'all the possible points' in so far as they are 'relevant and appropriate'. Apart from the large number of scenes in the extant plays which develop into a more or less formalised agon, there are still more which are half-agonistic, monologues addressed to the chorus, speeches in self-justification even though no opponent replies, carefully reasoned expositions of a point of view, all presented as if the speaker were out to convince an unwilling or sceptical listener who might otherwise have tended to believe the opposite. The Athenian theatre-audience was the same as that which listened in the Assembly or in the law-courts whether as judges or as spectators, and it would be only natural if their receptive attitude were the same in each context, when the rhetorical technique used by the speakers was so similar. It is obvious enough that such scenes as the dispute in the *Hercules Furens* between Lycus and Amphitryon as to the relative merits of bow and spear were written for an audience that loved a good debate for its own sake; but the manner extends to less obviously rhetorical subjects, as when in the *Trojan Women* Cassandra to comfort her mother 'proves' that fallen Troy is happier than the victorious Greeks:

$$\pi\acute{o}\lambda\iota\nu\ \delta\grave{\epsilon}\ \delta\epsilon\acute{\iota}\xi\omega\ \tau\acute{\eta}\nu\delta\epsilon\ \mu\alpha\kappa\alpha\rho\iota\omega\tau\acute{\epsilon}\rho\alpha\nu$$
$$\mathring{\eta}\ \tauο\grave{\upsilon}\varsigma\ \Mathcal{A}\chi\alpha\iotaο\acute{\upsilon}\varsigma$$

She is god-possessed, she says, but for so long she will hold the frenzy at bay and produce all the arguments. Or Hecuba, again, says 'Let me lie where I have fallen', and then goes on to show in detail that her sufferings are indeed 'fall-worthy', $\pi\tau\omega\mu\acute{\alpha}\tau\omega\nu\ \mathring{\alpha}\xi\iota\alpha$, ending with the rhetorical question 'Why then do you try to raise me up?' The controversy, the appeal, and the lament have their obvious counterparts in the context of Athenian public life; perhaps not only education and force of habit but the manner of the play's performance, as a competition before judges, and as an actors' as well as a poets' competition, and the great open-air theatre-scene itself, had their part in attracting so much of the play into the same sphere, in making the characteristic utterance of the main figures this argumentative presentment of a thesis. The temptation to listen to the dialogue of Greek tragedy as to a series of set pieces with a few looser interludes must have been strong, and the temptation to write it as such was clearly growing. Small wonder then that Aristotle referred the budding dramatist to his *Rhetoric* to learn how to write tragic speeches.

A great deal of Aristotle's analysis of tragedy, in spite of his obvious preference for Sophocles, is more appropriate to a form of drama nearer to that of Euripides but still further advanced in the same line of development. It is interesting to see how far his concept of dianoia helps us to understand Sophocles and how far it is misleading. The great agones are there, of course, though fewer than in Euripides and more carefully built into the structure of the plot: the decks, we might say, are less ostentatiously cleared for this type of display. There are also many non-agonistic speeches thrown into the characteristic rhetorical form, where the speaker is intent on making out a case; the audience to be convinced, or emotionally influenced, may be the other stage-figures, the spectators, or his own conscience, or all three; there is no cross-purpose here, and Aristotle's equation of the poet with the professional rhetorician who wrote speeches for his clients, and of the auditorium with the stage, can do no particular harm. The Greek tragic character often asks and answers his own questions, anticipates an imaginary opponent's objections, where in later Greek comedy or modern drama some minor, 'protreptic' figure would be put up to elicit replies. Self-justification is peculiarly apt to take this form, as for instance in the speech of Ajax (*Aj.* 457 ff.), beginning 'And now what must I do?' He examines the alternatives: 'Go home? Fall in battle under Troy?' He gives reasons for finding each of these inadequate. No, he says, 'I must attempt a deed which shall show me worthy of my birth and name', and ends with four maxims or generalisations which sum up his attitude to the moral decision he is making—to take his own life. Such dianoia is of course inextricably involved with ethos, and it is significant that the most perfect examples of this compound in English literature are to be found, not in drama, but in the dramatic monologues of Browning— for instance in that work of agonistic form, *The Ring and the Book*.

Self-justification again is the note of Antigone's famous, or notorious, explanation, in the course of her last lament, of her motives in burying Polynices (*Ant.* 904 ff.). Aristotle cites this in *Rhet.* 1417ᵃ29 when he is giving precepts for the handling of narrative in forensic oratory. Your version of events must be full of ethos; glimpses of your opponent's bad morals (proairesis) and your own good morals must constantly shine through. Don't let it appear that your statements are prompted by dianoia; keep them on the lines of moral choice. But if one of them sounds incredible, *then* add the reason. Sophocles provides an illustration in the passage from his *Antigone* 'that she cared more for her brother than for husband or children (proairesis); *for* these could be replaced if lost, whereas once father and mother were dead there was no hope of another brother (dianoia)'.

This is of course no use to us as a comment on this strange passage, adapted from an anecdote in Herodotus. What we find incredible is not that Antigone should have felt a duty to a brother more important than a duty to husband or children, but that she should at this point (just before her death) have chosen to justify her act on the grounds of such a preference—a purely hypothetical and gratuituous one, since she had no husband or children, and the only point of preferring a brother on the strength of his irreplaceability would be if it were a question of keeping him *alive* (as in the Herodotean version). It is the misapplied dianoia of the poet *behind* Antigone's ethic declaration and dianoetic explanation of it to which we object. It is true that Aristotle chooses his illustrations at their face value from the poets because the stories were universally known, and he is not here concerned with poetic propriety or an interpretation of Sophocles but with advice on rhetorical technique. Yet this is the treatise to which he refers the student of drama for the handling of dramatic speeches, and there is no suggestion that the objects and criteria of the one kind of eloquence are any different from those of the other. One might almost feel that this passage of the *Antigone* is an excellent illustration of the sort of passage a tragedian might write if he had followed Aristotle's teaching. At least the failure to keep these two spheres more clearly distinct might easily become a besetting weakness in Greek tragedy—and probably did so become in the fourth century BC.

The chief inadequacy of Aristotle's formula, however, is that it takes no account of the Sophoclean irony. In how many scenes does the whole conception rest upon the sharp distinction between the two audiences, the stage and the auditorium, instead of upon their equation! When Ajax deliberately sets out to deceive the Chorus as to his intentions in retiring with his sword to a lonely part of the beach, it is to this distinction that the gorgeous rhetoric of his great speech (*Aj.* 646 ff.) should be referred, not to the character of the hero. Ajax's moral will has been indicated clearly enough in the earlier speech already quoted (457 ff.), and that he should now falter in that grim resolution would be far more disturbing to our sense of the unity of his character than that he should act a whole-hearted deception. Yet he has to convince his stage-audience that he has so weakened, and all the resources of persuasive eloquence are deployed to this end, the majestic comparisons (no lesser parallels could serve for Ajax), the touch of shame, the suggestion of a solemn rite to be performed upon this malignant sword. 'Pray that my heart's desire may be fulfilled, bid Teucer look after my interests and yours, for I am going whither I must go, and perhaps you will learn that I have after all found salvation.' Every word is double-edged, and only once (667), in 'we will learn to revere the Atridae', does the mockery threaten to overreach itself. Magnificent poetry for an unworthy end? No, because every word spoken of the courses of Nature can be understood by us, the spectators, as by Ajax himself in his own heart, as true and applicable in a sense other, and more profound, than the obvious meaning they bear to his duped audience. This exploitation of 'the persuasive' on a double plane is Sophocles' method of adapting the dianoia of public life to the eloquence of tragedy.

# 7

# Aristotle on the Effect of Tragedy

## JACOB BERNAYS

### ENGLISH TRANSLATION BY JENNIFER BARNES

### INTRODUCTION BY JONATHAN BARNES

No sentence of Aristotle's has been more influential, or more contro-versial, than his definition of tragedy; and its last clause, which refers to the catharsis of the emotions and which determines Aristotle's conception of tragic action and the tragic hero, has been the object of a peculiarly strenuous debate. The best contribution to this debate was made by the erudite German, Jacob Bernays, and published in 1857.[1]

The Greek term *katharsis* sometimes means 'purification', and is applied in particular to certain religious rituals. Many scholars have supposed that tragic catharsis is a purification, and that tragedy (according to Aristotle) is essentially something which refines and improves our souls. Against this interpretation, Bernays argues that Aristotle has in mind a medical and not a religious use of the term *katharsis*. In medicine, catharsis is an operation of purgation, an operation effected by a laxative or an emetic. The purgation is worked upon the spectators of the tragedy. They—or some of them—have an excessive inclination to pity and to fear; the emotional pressure is painful and dangerous; the spectacle of tragedy stimulates and arouses precisely the feelings of pity and fear; and after the arousal

---

[1] J. Bernays, 'Grundzüge der verlorenen Abhandlung des Aristoteles über Wirkung der Tragödie', *Abhandlungen der historisch-philosophischen Gesellschaft in Breslau*, 1 (1857), 135–202; reprinted in J. Bernays, *Zwei Abhandlungen über die aristotelische Theorie des Dramas* (Berlin, 1880), 1–118. On Bernays see J. Glucker and A. Laks (eds.), *Jacob Bernays: Un philologue juif* (Cahiers de philologie, 16; Villeneuve d'Ascq, 1996). The English translation, by Jennifer Barnes, of the first part of Bernays's essay is a revised and corrected version of something first published in J. Barnes, M. Schofield and R. Sorabji (eds.), *Articles on Aristotle, 4. Psychology and Aesthetics* (London, 1979), 154–65.

and the emotional outflow which follows it, the spectators find themselves purged—they are drained and relieved. Thus tragedy offers not moral improvement but emotional relief. The theatre offers not a pulpit but a psychiatrist's couch. (And Bernays later became uncle-in-law to Freud.)

Aristotle does not suggest that tragic playwrights consider themselves, or ought to consider themselves, healers of souls; nor does he suggest that an audience deliberately goes to see *Oedipus* in order to find some sort of emotional relief: Aristotle is talking about the effects, not the aims, of the tragic theatre. But he evidently thinks that these effects, whether willed or not, are good, that catharsis is in itself something to be desired. And he thus defends tragedy against a heavy accusation: Plato had observed that tragic poetry has a powerful emotional effect on its hearers, and that in particular it evokes expressions of the weak and unmanly feelings. And Plato had inferred that all poetry should be strictly censored by the State and that much poetry should be forbidden. Aristotle admits that tragedy excites unmanly feelings; but he claims that this is an admirable and not an appalling effect—for the excitement works as a purge, alleviating rather than aggravating the audience's emotional malaise.

*Oedipus Rex* as *Exlax*. Fastidious readers, as Bernays feared, have been revolted by the medical diagnosis of catharsis. Theatre-going readers have wondered whether tragedies really do—or really did— act as emotional purgatives. And philosophical readers have found it strange of Aristotle to suggest that tragedy is, by definition and essentially, a form of rhubarb.

---

Aristotle's definition of the essence of tragedy at the beginning of the sixth chapter of the *Poetics* reads thus:

A tragedy . . . is an imitation of an action which is serious and complete, having magnitude, expressed in seasoned language, each of the kinds appearing separately in its parts, in a dramatic and not a narrative form, accomplishing through pity and fear the catharsis of such affections. ($1449^b24$-8)

In his *Hamburgische Dramaturgie* (no. 77) Lessing undertook to explain the definition by connecting it to Aristotle's remarks in the

*Rhetoric* about pity and fear, and to defend it against certain French and German misunderstandings. He did so with complete success—until he came to the last clause.

When he reaches these last six words, fraught with difficulty as they are, he advances with less certainty. He is caught up first by the word 'such (*toioutôn*)'. He tries to extricate himself in the following paragraph, which is scarcely compatible with the clear account of pity and fear which he has just given:

The word *toioutôn* refers only to the pity and the fear which have just been mentioned: tragedy should arouse our pity and our fear in order to purify these and similar passions—not all passions without discrimination. If he says *toioutôn* and not *toutôn*, 'these and such' and not 'these', that is in order to show [2] that by pity he means not just true pity but all philanthropic emotions, and that fear encompasses not just the shrinking from a future evil but also every similar emotion—including shrinkings from past and present evils (in other words, sorrow and grief). (ed. Fricke, pp. 328–9)

Again, *pathêmatôn* ('affections') means, in Lessing's view, precisely the same as *pathôn* ('emotions'); and although he scrupulously weighs every other term in the definition, he does not ask why, if both words have the same sense, Aristotle did not choose *pathôn* which he had already used of pity and fear in the *Rhetoric*.

Finally, Lessing translates *katharsis* as 'purification': he will 'only say briefly' what this purification consists in. On this capital question, however, everybody (even those 'who are equal to the task' and to whom Lessing appeals on a related topic in no. 83) would have liked a more detailed exposition—the more so because the closer delineation of *katharsis* which Aristotle himself deemed indispensable and which in the *Politics* he says he is reserving for the *Poetics* in fact nowhere appears in the extant text of the *Poetics*.

Lessing's explanation is this:

Since, to be brief, this purification consists in nothing other than the changing of the passions into virtuous dispositions, [3] and since according to our philosopher every virtue stands at a mid-point between two extremes, it follows that tragedy, if it is to change our pity into a virtue, must be capable of purifying us of both extremes of pity; and the same is true of fear. In relation to pity, tragic pity must purify the souls not only of those who feel too much pity but also of those who feel too little. In relation to fear, tragic fear must purify the souls not only of those who fear no evil at all but also of those who are upset by any evil whatever, however remote or improbable.

Again, in relation to fear, tragic pity must eradicate both what is too much and what is too little; and in relation to pity, tragic fear must do likewise. (no. 78, pp. 332–3)

It will be allowed that if such a 'changing of the passions into virtuous dispositions' is, in Aristotle's view, an *essential* feature of tragedy—as it is if he builds this sort of catharsis into his definition of its essence—then tragedy is for him *essentially* a moral matter. Indeed, given Lessing's analysis of the different levels of excessive and deficient pity and fear, we might think of tragedy as a reformatory which offers a means of correction for every unlawful form of pity and fear.

It goes without saying that nobody could have been less attracted to such an interpretation [4] than Goethe, who as he grew older showed himself ever more eager to eliminate teleology from his views on nature and on art. 'Music', he says in his *Nachlese zu Aristoteles Poetik*, 'music can have no more effect on morality than can any other art. Tragedy,' he continues—and he if anyone is qualified to speak on the subject—'tragedy and tragic novels do nothing to soothe the mind: on the contrary, they disturb it.' And he adds that Aristotle, 'who is in fact speaking of the construction of a tragedy, could not have in mind the effect, let alone the remote effect, which a tragedy might have on its audience' (*Gesamtausgabe*, xv (ed. W. Rehm), 897–900).

Thus Goethe, convinced that it was necessary to exclude any moral aim from the definition of tragedy, let himself be guided by this conviction when he came to interpret Aristotle and therefore wanted to divert catharsis away from the audience and on to the tragic character. To effect the diversion he offered the following translation: 'Tragedy is an imitation of an action which is serious and complete . . . which, after a passage through pity and fear, concludes by setting such emotions in equilibrium'. Scholars will not need to be told that the Greek words *di' eleou kai phobou perainousa . . . katharsin* cannot mean '*after* a passage through pity and fear *concluding in* catharsis', but only '*accomplishing* catharsis *through* pity and fear'. And Aristotelians, however uncertain they may be about the exact meaning [5] of *katharsis*, know from book 8 of the *Politics* that the word always refers to a process in the minds of those who see or listen to tragedy or music, and never to an equilibrium with regard to the action portrayed therein.

However easy it proved to dismiss Goethe's translation, the countless later scholars who have discussed Aristotle's definition have been unable to get round the serious objections to Lessing's view—objections which doubtless discouraged Goethe from accepting it. The most notable of these later scholars is Eduard Müller. After a careful survey of the several indications scattered through Aristotle's other works, he arrived at the following conclusion: 'Who can any longer doubt that the purification of pity, fear, *and* the other emotions consists in, *or at least* is very closely connected with, the transformation into pleasure of the pain which is attached to them?' (*Theorie der Kunst bei den Alten*, ii. 62, 377–88). But an attempt to define a concept by way of a disjunctive particle is always an awkward affair. And even if the second part of Müller's sentence, introduced by the word 'or', is correct, and we can accordingly say no more than that the transformation of pain into pleasure is *connected* with catharsis, nevertheless—and however intimate the connection may be—we are still justified in asking what catharsis *consists in*. It is surely not too bold to suppose that Aristotle intended by catharsis something determinate—not just a 'this or that'; [6] and if 'the tragic purification of the emotions' has become one of those many cultural catchphrases which delight the dilettante and dismay the philosopher, the responsibility for that really does not lie with Aristotle.

For the clouds which envelop the phrase as it occurs in the jargon of the connoisseur, and the scholarly efforts to characterize catharsis as a transformation of emotion into virtue or of pain into pleasure, have this in common: they forget how Aristotle himself presents catharsis—which he, after all, was the first to introduce into aesthetics as a *technical term*. Once this is forgotten, there is nothing to do but rely on the ordinary meaning of the verb *kathairô* and translate *katharsis* as 'purification'. And it then becomes inevitable to suppose that tragedy, as a purifying agent, works on the emotions, as objects to be purified, by way of operations more or less similar to those used everyday by housewives and by chemists as they separate the pure from the impure.

If we are to leave this cul-de-sac and return to the highway, our investigations must concentrate on the passage in the *Politics* to which I have already alluded—and which commentators on the *Poetics* have at any rate cited. If the passage is not quite as thorough as we might wish, it is at least by no means as brief as the definition in the *Poetics*. [7] Goethe seems to have heard only the vaguest rumours of the existence of this passage—no doubt from Herder, whose comments, it is true, can have aroused no expectation that it might be of use. Even Lessing, who once refers to it in passing (no. 78), oddly omits to follow it up—for anyone who has read the passage will find it still odder to suppose that Lessing knew the passage well and yet failed to realize its importance.

At this point in *Politics* 8. 7, Aristotle is attempting to show the place of the various musical harmonies in a well-ordered state:

We accept the division of melodies proposed by certain philosophers into ethical melodies, melodies of action, and emotional or inspiring melodies, each having, as they say, a mode corresponding to it. But we maintain further that music should be promoted for the sake not of one but of many benefits, that is to say, with a view to education, to catharsis (the word catharsis we use at present without explanation, but when hereafter we speak of poetry we will treat the subject with more precision)—and music may also serve for intellectual enjoyment, for relaxation, and for recreation after exertion. It is clear, therefore, that all the modes must be employed by us, but not all in the same manner. [8] Rather, in education the most ethical modes are to be preferred, but in listening to the performances of others we may admit also the modes of action and of emotion. For emotions such as pity or fear, or again enthusiasm, exist very strongly in some souls, and have more or less influence over all. Some people fall into a religious frenzy, and as a result of the sacred melodies—when they have used the melodies which excite the soul to mystic frenzy—we see them restored as though they had found healing and catharsis. Those who are influenced by pity or fear, and every emotional nature, must have a similar experience, and others too, in so far as each is susceptible to such emotions, and all receive a sort of catharsis and are relieved with pleasure. The cathartic melodies similarly give an innocent [9] pleasure. Such are the modes and melodies in which those who perform music in the theatre should be invited to compete. But since the spectators are of two kinds—the one free and educated, the other a vulgar crowd composed of mechanics, labourers and the like—there ought to be contests and exhibitions instituted for the relaxation of the second class too. And the music will correspond to their minds; for as their minds are perverted from the natural state, so there are perverted modes and highly strung and unnaturally coloured melodies. We receive pleasure from what is natural to us, and therefore professional musicians may be allowed to practise this lower sort of music before a lower type of audience. ($1341^b32-1342^a27$)

It was necessary to quote the final sentences of the passage, even though they do not deal directly with catharsis; for in them there is an incontrovertible proof of the distance which separates Aristotle from the thought of the last century, according to which the theatre is an offspring and a rival of the Church and an institution for moral improvement: Aristotle is resolutely determined to characterize the theatre as a place of amusement for the different classes of the general public. Whereas Plato zealously proscribes the newfangled [10] music which abandons ancient simplicity and is the source of every immorality (*Rep.* 424b; *Laws* 700, 797; cf. Cicero, *Laws* 2. 15. 38), Aristotle urges us to tolerate even the lower forms of music. Since there is a perverted audience which, given its nature, can enjoy only pop music, then at those festivals where it seeks pleasure and refreshment we should provide inferior music and not try to bore and improve with good. This view of the theatre unambiguously requires us to eliminate from theatrical catharsis anything which would give morality more weight than pleasure, which would make moral improvement the principal end and treat pleasure and amusement merely as the essential means to that end, as the honey on the brim of the glass which entices those who would have refused the medicine unsweetened.

And why should we approach theatrical catharsis from a moral or from a hedonistic standpoint, rather than from the standpoint which Aristotle himself adopts in the *Politics?* That is neither moral nor yet purely hedonistic: it is a *pathological* standpoint.

Aristotle's first example of actual catharsis, drawn from the common Greek experience of ecstasy, is pathological; and it is this which leads him to consider the possibility [11] of a similar cathartic treatment for all other emotions ($1342^a8-15$). Someone otherwise calm may be thrown into ecstasy by the Phrygian songs inherited from the mythical singer Olympus (that these are the principal 'sacred melodies' is shown by another passage in Aristotle and also by Plato); yet *after* they have heard or sung the intoxicating melodies, those who are possessed by ecstasy experience a feeling of tranquillity. Catullus, in his *Attis*, might have portrayed this had he, the most poetical of Roman poets, had as much understanding of enthusiasm as the most prosaic of Greek philosophers. After letting the passionate youth rave in Phrygian song, Catullus thinks he must chase him around the forest, and then, having exhausted him by these exertions, make him fall asleep, lost to the world and to himself until the following morning. The exercise was perfectly unnecessary: as soon as the boy's repressed ecstasy had poured itself forth in the madding song, it would have been spent and would have given way to a more thoughtful mood. In this way the poem would have sacrificed, at most, the versification of a sunrise: it would certainly not have lost any poetic value, and it would have gained infinitely in pathological truth—it would have represented the catharsis of enthusiasm.

If Aristotle's example is firmly fixed in the realm of pathology, so too are the expressions by which he attempts to elucidate the notion of catharsis. Those whose ecstasy has spent itself, he says, are 'restored as though they had found healing and catharsis' ($1342^a10$). [12] *As though*—hence not in sober fact, so that *katharsis* is no less metaphorical than *iatreia* ('healing'). Now we may set aside the wholly general sense of 'purification' for *katharsis*: this explains nothing precisely because of its generality; Aristotle could have had no occasion to add it *after* the much more concrete term *iatreia*; and, finally, it is so general that it would be absurd to precede it by the phrase 'as though', which marks out a metaphor. Taken concretely, the Greek term *katharsis* means one of two things: *either* an absolving from guilt by means of certain priestly ceremonies—a lustration; *or* a removing or alleviating of an illness by means of some medical therapy—a purgation.

Lambinus hit upon the first meaning in his translation of the *Politics:* he renders *katharsis* by *lustratio seu expiatio.* If this sixteenth-century Frenchman remains the only notable perpetrator of this error—more recently, when 'lustration through tragedy' had sprinkled its holy water over the mills of the Romantics, nevertheless no one dared to drown Aristotle in it—that is not entirely due to the brief words with which Reiz dismisses it in his edition of the last two books of the *Politics.* (The last two books according to the traditional ordering: Reiz himself established the correct ordering.) For this solid edition by the founder of the Leipzig school of classical scholarship has [13] not received the recognition it deserves. And yet no one who gives the matter two minutes' thought needs any outside help to realize how impossible it is that Aristotle, in a way quite foreign to his normal habits, should here have taken a technical philosophical term from the language of popular religion only to miss his real aim entirely. For he cannot have had in mind the ceremonies themselves—the incense and the ablution—but at best the emotional effects of these lustrations; and he must therefore have hoped to explain a perplexing emotional phenomenon—the calming of ecstasy by means of frenzied singing—by comparing it with another phenomenon no less perplexing, namely the feeling of release from guilt experienced by those who receive absolution. No one in his right mind could seriously credit Aristotle with so pointless and so evident a piece of verbal conjuring.

If, on the other hand, we understand *katharsis* in its medical sense—the only genuine alternative—all goes very well. *Katharsis* is then a special type of *iatreia*, the general term which precedes it: the ecstatic are calmed by orgiastic songs in the way in which the sick are cured by medical treatment—not any treatment, but one which employs cathartic means to purge the matter of the disease. Thus the puzzling piece of *emotional* pathology is explained: we can make sense of it if we compare it with a pathological *bodily* phenomenon. [14]

Next, at 1342ᵃ11, Aristotle mentions people who are susceptible to the emotions and for whom a catharsis similar to the orgiastic type is prescribed. He singles out by name—in an unmistakable reference to tragedy—those who are 'influenced by pity and fear', collecting all the rest under the general title of *pathêtikoi* ('emotional'). And he is able to find no word more suitable to stand alongside *katharsis* than 'relief' (*kouphizesthai*: 1342ᵃ14). Plainly, this can have no connexion with ethics, since in this momentary relief there is not even a return to a normal condition; and on the other hand the term in itself has so little to do with pleasure that in order not to omit this indispensable notion Aristotle is obliged to add 'with pleasure' to the verb 'relieved'. Thus Aristotle's purpose in using the term 'relief' can only be to make sense of the emotional process by comparing it with analogous bodily phenomena.

Let no one primly wrinkle his nose and allege that this reduces aesthetics to medicine. We are trying not to set out a complete definition of tragedy, but to give a methodologically sound interpretation of the words which Aristotle uses in *his* definition. If this road to the Muses' grove takes us past the temple of Asclepius, then that, in the eyes of Aristotelians, is just another proof that we are travelling in the right direction. The son of a royal doctor and himself a practising physician in his youth, [15] Aristotle did not exploit his inherited medical proclivities only in the rigorously scientific parts of his philosophy: his moral and psychological works, despite all the links which connect them to the *Metaphysics*, constantly reveal a lively concern for the physical side of things and a rejection not only of ascetisicm but also of any ethereal spirituality—something which is common among doctors and working scientists in any period but was rare among philosophers, even in Greece, once they had ascended into the heaven of ideas. Indeed, even in purely logical and metaphysical matters Aristotle clearly prefers to draw his examples from the realm of medical experience: where, for example, he claims that an unconscious teleology is found both in nature and in true art—that an artist does not ponder each step and yet never stumbles, that nature functions teleologically without becoming transcendent—no more suitable illustration occurs to him than the instinctive self-healing of the medical layman who, as though instructed by his illness itself, blindly seeks out the appropriate cure (see *Phys* 199$^b$31). If we accept the unequivocally medical analogy here, when we are dealing with the calm and healthy power of nature, we have still less reason [16] to reject an explanation of the term *katharsis* according to which strong emotional upheavals are compared to the phenomena of physical illness, simply on the grounds that such an explanation has a medical smell.

Such fastidious aversion to medicine apart, I cannot readily imagine any serious objection from those readers who have followed my examination of the passage in the *Politics*; and before turning to the doctrine of the *Poetics*, let me state clearly the purely terminological conclusions of the investigation so far: *katharsis* is a term transferred from the physical to the emotional sphere, and used of the sort of treatment of an oppressed person which seeks not to alter or to subjugate the oppressive element but to excite it, to draw it out, and thereby to effect a relief.

Aristotle makes it perfectly explicit that it is not the morbid matter but the unbalanced man who is the proper object of catharsis: those who fall into a religious frenzy, according to the *Politics* (1342$^a$11), experience healing and catharsis; those influenced by pity and fear must be relieved by a feeling of pleasure (1342$^a$15). Anyone who,

after such unequivocal statements, could still think it possible that
the definition in the *Poetics* should relate catharsis to a different object
must [17] have strange ideas about Aristotle's way with words.

Further, anyone prepared to countenance an inexplicable
violation of Aristotle's otherwise strict and determinate usage on the
grounds that it is attractive but by no means mandatory to interpret
the words *di' eleou kai phobou perainousa tên tôn toioutôn pathêmatôn
katharsin* by reference to the exposition in the *Politics* should recall
the unhappy circumstances in which modern readers find themselves when they try to overcome the difficulties of this sentence—
circumstances which Aristotle could not envisage and so could not
alleviate. In the complete *Poetics* (i.e. in the 'treatise on poetry' in two
books), he could confine his definition of tragedy within the limits
required by concision and brevity: the possibility of misunderstanding gave him no reason to expand his definition even by a few letters,
as long as it was conceptually complete and correct; for he had
sufficiently guarded against every such possibility by the supplementary explanations which he attached to its individual terms.
And for the term *katharsis*, in particular, the explanation—as the
promissory reference in the *Politics* shows—was as abundant as the
importance of the matter and the unfamiliarity of the term
demanded. The excerptor whom we have to thank and to blame for
the extant *Poetics* mercilessly excised the explanation: he had little
interest in pure philosophy, and he probably excised it precisely
because it was so comprehensive and so rich in purely philosophical
thought. [18]

The state in which this leaves us can be illustrated from other parts
of the definition. It begins with the claim that tragedy is 'an imitation
of an action which is serious (*spoudaios*) . . . expressed in seasoned
(*hêdusmenôi*) language *chôris hekastôi tôn eidôn en tois moriois*'. What
an intricate web of controversy would have been spun around these
last words, from *chôris* to *moriois*, had they not been immediately
followed by Aristotle's own interpretation, to the effect that different
kinds of 'seasoning' are separately applied to the different parts of a
tragedy, the language being enhanced in the choral passages by lyric
songs and in the dialogue by metre alone: 'Here by "seasoned
language" I mean that rhythm and song are superadded; and by
"the kinds appearing separately" I mean that some parts are worked
out only in verse, and others in song' ($1449^b29$-$31$).

Again, Bernhardy completely misunderstood the application to tragic action of the adjective 'serious (*spoudaios*)', simply because Aristotle's own explanation of this word does not immediately follow the definition but has already been provided a little earlier. Bernhardy thinks that a *praxis spoudaia* is an action which has 'a moral nature and value, in contrast with the physical events of epic' (*Grundriss der Griechischen Literatur*, ii. 687). Aristotle himself, however, refers to his earlier account of the origins of each type of poetry: [19] it is partly from this account, he says, that the definition of tragedy is derived ($1449^b23$). And in fact, from the second chapter of the *Poetics* onwards, Aristotle's exposition revolves mainly around the opposition between the serious (*spoudaios*) and the base (*phaulos*) or the ridiculous (*geloios*). What is serious is the subject of epic no less than of tragedy, which in the course of time absorbed epic ($1449^a2$); the base, on the other hand, is the subject of 'iambic' satire, which then in its turn developed into comedy, whose subject, the ridiculous, corresponds to the base. It is enough to consider the following passage: 'Just as Homer was the poet of poets in the serious style . . . so too he was the first to show us the forms of comedy by producing ⟨in the *Margites*⟩ a dramatic picture of the ridiculous' ($1448^b34$-9). We can no longer have any doubt about how Aristotle wished to characterize tragedy when he added the word *spoudaios*. He gave to tragedy the serious and to comedy the ridiculous not in order to avoid confusion with epic (which in his view is just as *spoudaios* and 'moral' as tragedy, and certainly not, in Bernhardy's anachronistic terms, 'physical'), but in order to draw a material distinction between tragedy and comedy where there is a formal identity. [20] In exactly the same fashion, tragedy and epic, whose matter is identical, are formally distinguished in that part of the definition which states that tragedy imitates 'in a dramatic and not a narrative form'.

In these cases misunderstanding cannot occur, or at least cannot prevail, because here even modern readers do not depend solely on the definition, but may take advantage of the supplementary explanations which Aristotle considerately offers. Each supplement removes one more veil from the draped definition, until it is finally revealed naked to the world—naked in every part save one. For in the case of catharsis, we are deprived—thanks to the excerptor—of that delicious advantage and must confront the definition in all its prim formality. We shall only understand it if, in place of Aristotle's own interpretation which has disappeared from the text of the *Poetics*, we use as a surrogate the passage in the *Politics* which, even if it does not exactly correspond to the definition, is for all that no less useful a guide to its central concept. Thus any explanations which are inconsistent with the terminological conclusions wrung from the *Politics*, however grammatically correct they are and however peacefully they may co-exist with modern aesthetic theories, [21] must be dismissed out of hand: they are grammatical, and they are aesthetically up to date; but they cannot possibly be right, i.e. Aristotelian. On the other hand, an interpretation which is proved on the touchstone of the *Politics*, however surprising it may seem to a modern aesthetician, may confidently be accepted as correct, as long as it is also linguistically admissible.

And in fact I do not think that any criticism can be made of the following translation of the words *di' eleou kai phobou perainousa tên tôn toioutôn pathêmatôn katharsin*: 'By ⟨arousing⟩ pity and fear tragedy alleviates and relieves such ⟨pitiful and fearful⟩ mental affections.' This translation allows itself no licence; in part, it satisfies the demands of an explanatory translation; in part it can be given a firm interpretative justification. It satisfies the demands, first, by choosing as a translation of *katharsis* not the ambiguous and unclear word 'purification' but rather—following Aristotle in the *Politics*—a term which insinuates a medical metaphor, and secondly, by borrowing from the same source the concept of 'alleviation' which Aristotle there couples with *katharsis*.

The translation does, however, require justification at one point—not in connexion with the delicate grammatical relation which holds between *pathêmatôn* and the verbal root of *katharsis*; [22] for we have dismissed any talk of the 'purification of the emotions', and the most pernickety grammarian could say nothing against our translation once *katharsis* is recognized as a medical metaphor—even if the same use of the genitive did not happen to be attested by examples in Aristotle, Hippocrates, and Thucydides. Rather, it is the translation of the word *pathêmatôn* by 'mental affections', with its implication of some standing or chronic condition, which requires justification. Of course, no one who knows Greek will deny that often, where it is not particularly important to mark the distinction, the choice between the forms *pathos* and *pathêma* seems to depend on the whim of the writer, on the mere stroke of his pen. But if it is ever incumbent on anyone to use words, and especially abstract words, with the greatest possible precision, then it is incumbent on a philosopher who is offering a definition; and it is incumbent on the reader of a definition to construe its meaning in the most precise way possible. Now a comparison of those passages in Aristotle where a relaxed use is improbable or impossible yields the following contrast: a *pathos* is the condition of a *paschôn* and designates the unexpected outbreak and overflow of an emotion; a *pathêma*, on the other hand, is the condition of [23] a *pathêtikos* and designates the emotion as inherent in the affected person, ready to break out at any time. Briefly, a *pathos* is a feeling, a *pathêma* a disposition to feel. Aristotle's lost explanation of catharsis will have indicated this in something like the following words: 'I mean by *pathêma* the condition of the *pathêtikoi*.' At any rate, he makes it abundantly clear in the *Politics* ($1342^{a}12$) that it is the *pathêtikoi*, those with a lasting disposition and a deep-rooted inclination to a certain emotion—in the case of tragedy, those disposed to feel pity and fear (*eleêmôn kai phobêtikos*), not those who are feeling pity and fear—who are to find in catharsis the means to indulge their inclinations in a 'harmless' manner. But once we take *pathêmatôn* in this sense, the definition in the *Poetics* and the account in the *Politics* are seen to be in complete agreement on the question of the proper objects of *katharsis*. In the *Politics katharsis* is expressly applied to people; the definition says that an alleviation or deflection of the disposition or inclination is brought about; and who could possibly regard the object—I mean the real, not the grammatical object—of catharsis as anything other than those who have these dispositions and are subject to these inclinations?

The harmony between the Aristotle of the *Poetics* and the Aristotle of the *Politics* is not the only advantage to be gained from taking *pathêmatôn* in its strict sense: [24] in addition, and without endangering the rigour of the definition, we may get past the little word *toioutôn*, at which even Lessing's usually confident step faltered and which caused later commentators to stumble gracelessly.

A logical thinker like Lessing must have been aware that an *et cetera*, which is what he thought *toioutôn* had to mean, would explode not only this but any definition; for a definition ought to delimit the defined concept as narrowly as possible, and an *et cetera* throws everything open. A definition which contains an *et cetera* will serve its function no better than a wall which contains gaps. But

Lessing thought that *toioutôn* could only mean *et cetera*; and so he sought to correct, as far as he could, the mistake which he thought Aristotle had made, by reducing to the smallest possible number the swarm of emotions which, in the train of pity and fear, were demanding 'purification' through tragedy. In the case of fear this seemed to work, more or less; for fear is the 'shrinking from a future evil', and Lessing thought that 'fear, *et cetera*' included shrinking from present and from past evils, i.e. sorrow and grief. But when we come to pity, this temporal distinction will not hold water: the unfortunate earn pity on account of past, as well as present and future troubles; and difference in time alters only the degree and not the nature—nor, [25] therefore, the name—of the sensation (*Rhet.* 1386$^b$1). Lessing's reaction to this betrays more clearly than anything else the fact that the relevant section of the *Dramaturgie*, though long mulled in his head, was penned in haste: he found himself obliged to write that 'pity and such' means 'pity and all philanthropic emotions'.

If Lessing left the door so wide open, it is hardly surprising that his successors pulled down the walls. One of the most recent commentators on Aristotle's definition glosses the words *tôn toioutôn* thus: 'He says "and such" because pity and fear are accompanied by many other feelings closely related to them, e.g. the emotions of *love* and *hate*, which, when they are conjured up in a tragedy, either arise from pity or fear, or are closely related to them', etc. But if that were really so, what childish games Aristotle would be playing with himself and his readers. The point and purpose of this part of his definition can only be that of *determining* the tragic emotions. At first we think that he has achieved this purpose, and admire the psychological genius with which from among all the feelings, emotions, and passions which teem in the human breast [26] he has selected two complementary emotions as the truly tragic ones—pity at the misfortune of others, and, inseparable from it, fear lest we meet with misfortune ourselves. Later, in chapters 13 and 14, we raptly follow Aristotle's rigorous examination of all the conceivable dramatic characters and situations: he accepts them as tragic or rejects them as untragic by a single criterion—are they or are they not capable of arousing precisely these emotions of pity and fear? Finally, we arrive at the conclusion which, in our *Poetics*, receives alas only summary expression: 'The poet must produce, by his imitation, the pleasure which comes from pity and fear' (14. 1453$^b$12). And yet after all this, we are now obliged to say that nothing serious was ever meant by that promising determination of the emotions; for the definition contains, apart from pity and fear, an *et cetera*, and it must be expanded to include sorrow, grief, philanthropy, love, and hate. Rather than allow ourselves to be trifled with in this way, let us see if the *et cetera*, like other will-o'-the-wisps, does not vanish when we get nearer to it.

For convenience, I quote the Greek words once again: *di' eleou kai phobou perainousa tên tôn toioutôn pathêmatôn katharsin.* Lessing remarks: 'he says *toioutôn* and not *toutôn*, "these and such" and not "these" . . .'. But Aristotle does not [27] say 'these and such'. If he wants to say that, he cannot do without the word 'and' in Greek, any more than Lessing can do without it in German: he must say *tauta kai toiauta*—and in fact he generally uses the fuller expression, *tauta kai hosa alla toiauta.* So here he would have said at least *toutôn kai toioutôn pathêmatôn.*

In fact, far from giving the commentators the vast arena offered by the words 'these and such', Aristotle does not even offer them as much space as the single word 'such' would allow. For the Greek for 'catharsis of such passions' is *tên toioutôn pathêmatôn katharsin*, with no article before *toioutôn*; and today, if not in Lessing's time, every reasonably complete dictionary will note that *toioutos* with the article can only refer to something already mentioned. Thus *ho toioutos* cannot be translated by 'such' in the sense of 'of that kind': if the simple demonstrative 'this' will not do, then 'such' can be tolerated provided that it is taken in a purely demonstrative sense. Just as in English, in order to avoid the tedious repetition of a word, we may use an anaphoric 'such' which does not in any way go beyond the conceptual limits of the term it picks up, so the Greeks, and in particular [28] Aristotle, liked to use the pronoun *ho toioutos.*

The most cursory glance at any of Aristotle's major works will turn up numerous examples of this usage; and even our *Poetics*, rudely shorn by the excerptor, provides several cases. One of them, only a chapter away from our definition, is proof enough by itself, and because it strikingly illustrates, from a different angle, the unvarying rigour of Aristotle's style, it may be briefly discussed.

Aristotle is describing the simultaneous development in the epic period both of grave and noble poetry and of jocular and satirical verse. Men with poetic talent, he says, were drawn, each according to his own character, in the one direction or the other: 'For the graver among them represented noble actions, and the actions of such personages; and the meaner sort the actions of the ignoble' ($1448^b25$). Aristotle thought that the material for satire, which is essentially subjective, is exhaustively described by the phrase 'the actions of the ignoble'. For epic, however, he sees two types of material. First, there are objectively 'noble actions', whether performed by the divine Achilles or by the divine swineherd. But even the most solemn epic poet may not limit himself to the portrayal of 'noble actions' and noble events, unless he is to become sublimely tedious: rather, as Plato explains in a similar connexion (*Rep.* 396d), he must accompany his hero [29] when 'he errs through sickness, or love, or even drunkenness'. And so, secondly, Aristotle recognizes that even intrinsically ignoble acts may be nobly described if they are performed by a heroic character who is in other respects noble and worthy of epic poetry. Aristotle links these two types of material— noble acts and acts of noble characters—in the closest possible way by giving to epic *tas kalas praxeis kai tas tôn toioutôn* as its object. Here no one will deny that *tôn toioutôn* simply picks up the preceding adjective *kalas*, modifying its grammatical form but leaving its conceptual content unaffected. In just this way, the words *tôn toioutôn* in our definition continue the sentence simply by picking up (and subjecting to adjectival transformation) the two preceding nouns *eleos kai phobos*. *tôn toioutôn pathêmatôn* means *eleêtikôn kai phobêtikôn pathêmatôn*.

Now that we have struck the putative *et cetera* from the list of controversial questions raised by our definition, the only problem is why Aristotle, since he means simply pity and fear, did not choose the simple demonstrative and write *toutôn tôn pathêmatôn*. This problem is, however, already solved for anyone who has been convinced by the interpretation of *pathêma* put forward above. For the words *eleos* and [30] *phobos* will lead a Greek to think first only of the *pathos*, the occurrent emotion of pity and fear, and not of the *pathêma*, the lasting affection. But Aristotle must be concerned with the latter if what he calls catharsis is to take place; and since the Greek language had not formed special nouns for the affections, as opposed to the emotions, of pity and fear, he was obliged to resort to circumlocution, using *pathêma* and the relevant adjectives. Aristotle could not *conceive* of the catharsis of the affections of pity and fear in any other Greek words than *eleêtikôn kai phobêtikôn pathêmatôn katharsin*; and so he had to *express* this in our sentence, which already contains the words *eleos kai phobos*, by employing a standard Greek abbreviatory device and writing *tôn toioutôn pathêmatôn katharsin*.

Is this interpretation, in which all the details balance and support one another, deceptive, or have we really solved the problem which the excerptor has made so much more difficult? Are the signals given in the *Politics* and our observations both of Aristotelian and of general Greek usage sufficient to establish an interpretation of the definition which is so indisputable and so universally compelling that we may assess its consequences without more ado? It would betray too optimistic a belief in the power of logic and method over the world in general and over the learned [31] world in particular if we imagined that a solution to a problem so ramified and so often discussed could win general acceptance so long as the grounds on which it is based remain purely logical and methodological. Anyone who is interested enough in the subject to have followed this discussion will surely have formed his own views on the question. In cases like this, there are few scholars who do not already belong to one party or another; and those whose opinion is already formed are not often convinced by an argument, however well constructed, which relies solely on evidence which is already well known. It is more likely that conviction will be achieved by the unexpected discovery of new pieces of evidence to fatten up the files. And indeed there is no reason to doubt that such new evidence might be found. The fact that the excerptor excised Aristotle's explanation of catharsis from our *Poetics* does not imply that it is irretrievably lost. In the course of time, the archives of Greek literature have fallen into disarray, and it is often wise not to look for things in their proper place but to poke around hopefully in the corners. We should not shy from the peculiar archival air which tends to gather in such dark places, and we must sometimes inhale a quantity of dust [32] before we can lay hands on the document for which we are searching.

# 8

# Literary Criticism in the Exegetical
# Scholia to the Iliad: A Sketch

## N. J. RICHARDSON

The Homeric Scholia are not the most obvious source for literary
criticism in the modern sense. And yet if one takes the trouble to read
through them one will find many valuable observations about poetic
technique and poetic qualities. Nowadays we tend to emphasize
different aspects from those which preoccupied ancient critics, but
that may be a good reason for looking again at what they have to
say.[1]

The contribution of the Alexandrian scholars has often been discussed, and I do not propose to deal with this here directly. In the
course of establishing the text of Homer Aristarchus in particular
recognized and made use of several important observations about
Homeric technique. The Venetus A Scholia give us much of our information about Aristarchus' views. But the other main Scholia, in
Venetus B, the Towneleian manuscript, and other related manuscripts, have much more to say about poetic and rhetorical aspects.
The question of the sources of all this material is a very complex one,
and except in the occasional cases where a particular scholar's name
is quoted, it is usually impossible to say from what precise period or
school of thought an observation derives. The principles of literary
criticism laid down by Aristotle in the *Poetics* have clearly had a
considerable influence, and so has the work of the Alexandrians
(although these Scholia sometimes defend a passage which
Aristarchus condemned). On these foundations has been built the
work of many other scholars. But it seems likely that the majority of

---

[1] I owe much to the suggestions and comments of Jasper Griffin, Doreen Innes and
Colin Macleod. It will be obvious that I am dealing with a vast and complex subject in
an impressionistic way, but I hope to suggest that it deserves more attention than it
has received.

the exegetical Scholia (as they are sometimes called) derive from scholars at the end of the Hellenistic and the beginning of the Roman period, who were consolidating the work of earlier critics. They contain some later material, notably extracts from the work on Homeric problems by Porphyry, inserted into the B Scholia in the eleventh century. But in general they seem to reflect the critical terminology and views of the first century BC and first two centuries AD.[2] These have their limitations, and one may feel that the vocabulary of critical terms which the Scholia use lacks flexibility and at times verges on the naïve: but within their limits they nevertheless show a lively appreciation of some fundamental aspects of Homer's art.[3]

## I. *Μῦθος* (PLOT)

In view of the ultimate derivation of much of the literary criticism in the Scholia from Aristotelian principles it is reasonable to begin an analysis with plot, and then go on to consider characterization and style. *Scale* and *unity* are the most important aspects of composition. The Scholia occasionally refer to the length of the poem as a fundamental epic feature, but they tend to take this for granted. The central part of the poem (from book 12 onwards), which for us can seem the most tedious, is long because of the complexity of the

[2] Cf. K. Latte, *Philologus*, 80 (1925), 171 (= *Kl. Schr.* 662), H. Erbse, *Beiträge zur Überlieferung der Iliasscholien* (Munich, 1960), 171-3, G. Lehnert, *De Scholiis ad Homerum rhetoricis* (Diss. Freiburg-Leipzig, 1896), 69.

[3] On sources and transmission see Erbse, *Berträge*, the preface to his edition of the Scholia, and M. Van der Valk, *Researches on the Text and Scholia of the Iliad* (Leiden, 1963), i. 414 ff. The most useful study of literary criticism in the Scholia is by M. L. Von Franz, *Die ästhetischen Anschauungen der Ilias-scholien* (Diss. Zurich, 1943). See also A. Roemer, *Die exegetischen Scholien der Ilias in Codex Venetus B* (Munich, 1879), R. Griesinger, *Die ästhetischen Anschauungen der alten Homererklärer* (Diss. Tübingen, 1907), A. Clausing, *Kritik und Exegese der hom. Gleichnisse im Altertum* (Diss. Freiburg, 1913), Lehnert, *De Scholiis*, and M. Schmidt, *Die Erklärungen zum Weltbild Homers und zur Kultur der Heroenzeit in den bT-Scholien zur Ilias* (Munich, 1976), 39 ff., who rightly criticizes Von Franz and Lehnert for excessive emphasis on Stoic origins. The Index to the Scholia by J. Baar (Baden-Baden, 1961) is useful, and should be consulted for full references to critical terms. My own references are not intended to be complete. I have taken most of my examples from the B and T Scholia, with some glances at A where relevant. I have not on the whole added illustrations from the other Scholia such as G. For further information on technical terms of rhetorical theory see H. Lausberg, *Handbuch der literarischen Rhetorik* (Munich, 1960).

fighting and the impossibility of narrating separate events simultaneously (ABT 12. 1; cf. BT 15. 390). At the beginning of book 13
one expects Achilles to return to the battle, as the wall has been
breached. But the poet 'creates length and variety by the inactivity of
Zeus' (BT 13. 1). The principle of *variety* (ποικιλία) is an essential
corollary of size, and this is very frequently invoked. The poet moves
from one type of scene to another in such a way that our attention is
not wearied. This is often a reason for introducing a scene in heaven.
Thus, for instance, the gods' council in *Il.* 4. 1 ff. gives 'dignity and
variety' to the narrative (BT 4. 1). Equally, the gods' interest and
interventions in the fighting make it more dramatic, and relieve the
monotony (BT 7. 17). The narrative of similar events is constantly
varied, especially in the case of the battle scenes, where single
combats and wounds are never allowed to become a monotonous
catalogue. Thus 'one should admire Homer's ability to describe
similar events without appearing to do so', as when Patroclus cuts off
the Trojans from the city, just as Achilles does later (BT 16. 394–5,
cf. 21. 3 ff.). Again, 'observe how often he refers to Patroclus' death,
without becoming monotonous' (BT 16. 689). Porphyry actually
mentions that Homer was criticized for his repetition of scenes and
speeches, and defends him against this (B 18. 309 = *Quaestiones
Homericae* I, ed. Sodano, No. 20). The sequence of battles in the poem
as a whole also displays this variety: 'after describing every type of
battle, in the plain, around the wall, and at the ships, he invented a
new kind in Achilles' combat at the river', and as the barbarians
alone are no match for Achilles and he does not want an anticlimax,
'he introduces the Theomachy and the battle with the river, taking
as a plausible pretext the choking of the river with the dead' (B 21. 1
= T 21. 18). The poet is essentially φιλοποίκιλος, fond of variety (BT
13. 219) and hence he also likes to contradict our expectations,
thereby increasing the dramatic effect (BT 7. 29, 13. 219, 14. 153,
18. 151, 22. 274).[4]

Related to the principle of variety is that of *relief*. The tension
of dramatic scenes and the sustained narrative of battle require

[4] For ποικιλία cf. also BT 5. 70, 143, 523, 6. 37, ABT 6. 71, B 8. 5 (Porphyry), T
10. 158, BT 11. 104, T 11. 378, 498, BT 11. 722–5, T 12. 129, BT 13. 1, 219,
340–2, 408, 14. 1, 147, 153, 476–7, T 15. 333, BT 15. 390, 16. 320, 339, 345,
593, 17. 306–7, 600, 18. 1, A 18. 314, ABT 20. 372, BT 20. 383, T 20. 397, BT 20.
463, T 20. 473, BT 21. 34, 24. 266.

interludes of a quieter nature. In particular, a gap in time in the main narrative is 'filled up' by another scene, which also provides a rest from the action. Thus, in book 1 Thetis leaves Achilles, promising to visit Zeus on the twelfth day, and in the middle of the verse (430) the poet turns to Odysseus' journey to Chrysa to return Chryseis to her father. By this judicious alternation of the two strands in the narrative he gives relief to his audience from monotony (BT 1. 430). This interweaving of strands is a fundamental feature of Homer's art.[5]

Another good example of relief is the mission of Hector to Troy in 6. 116 ff. The scenes in Troy offer a welcome contrast to the battle (Eustathius 650. 7 ff.), and the narrative gap caused by the journey of Hector is also filled by the meeting of Glaucus and Diomedes, which itself brings relief (BT 6. 119, 237). Eustathius points to the dramatic qualities of Hector's meetings with his family and with Paris and Helen, thereby answering the criticism that he should not be removed from the fighting at such a crisis (cf. BT 6. 116, Jachmann, *Homerische Einzellieder*, 1 ff.). Likewise in Book 14 the deception of Zeus gives new life to the narrative after the long scenes of battle (BT 14. 153). Changes of scene become more frequent when a crisis approaches, as for instance in the battle at the ships (BT 15. 390). This, however, is seen as a way of building up tension rather than relieving it.

The corollary to this alternation of narrative strands is the well-known principle governing the narration of *simultaneous events*, whereby in describing a complex scene the poet relates these events successively, and never goes back in time in his main narrative. The Scholia are well aware of this, as we have seen (BT 12. 1).[6] Aristotle had already made the basic observation about the freedom of epic in contrast to tragedy to build up a detailed picture of several events occurring together. This is one of the ways by which its scale is increased (*Poet.* 1459^b22 ff.).

The other main factor contributing to length is the introduction of *episodes* which are subsidiary to the main plot. Again, the Scholia

---

[5] Cf. BT 4. 539, 5. 693, 7. 17, 328, 8. 209, T 11. 599, BT 11. 619, T 13. 20, 168, BT 14. 1, 14. 114, 15. 362 (similes), 405, 16. 431, 666, 793, 17. 426, 18. 148, 22. 147.

[6] Cf. also ABT 10. 299, T 12. 199, A 14. 1, BT 22. 131, T 22. 437. Modern scholars have made great capital out of this simple principle. Cf. T. Zieliński, *Philologus Suppl.* 8 (1899–1901), 407 ff., D. Page, *The Homeric Odyssey* (Oxford, 1955), 65 ff., 77 n. 11, etc.

follow Aristotle's lead here (*Poet.* 1459ᵃ30 ff.). Homer's unity consists in his taking a single theme for his narrative, and drawing in other events wherever appropriate (AT 1. 1, B 2. 494, A 3. 237, T 11. 625). One can link this with another important observation about the way in which individual stories are related, that he states the main facts first and then goes back to causes and other related circumstances (BT 11. 671, Porphyry *ap.* B 12. 127). In one case (12. 127 ff.) this helps to explain what at first sight is a very confused order of narrative (see Leaf's note on 131, although he does not agree with Porphyry). Equally, the poet will often give a summary of what he is about to relate before going on to the detailed narrative (e.g. BT 11. 90–3; 15. 56 ff. which Aristarchus athetized); and he also briefly recapitulates before moving on to a new scene (BT 9. 1, 16. 1).

These devices help to bind the story together, and they introduce two other very important principles, those of *anticipation* and *foreshadowing*. This is related to the whole question of οἰκονομία, arrangement, i.e. the unified organization of a complex work. In modern terms, one might say that the *Iliad* as we have it is the product of long and careful premeditation, and the poet has the whole structure in mind from the beginning, just as we are told that Mozart could have a whole symphony in his mind from the start. The main plot moves forward with stately leisure, but the poet is always sowing the seeds of future events. This constant build-up of expectation helps to create the suspense and excitement which carry us forward to the climax of the work. The various battle-scenes which constitute the bulk of the poem are carefully ordered so as to form a progression towards the climactic scenes of Achilles' intervention, culminating in the fight with Hector. Thereafter the poem moves towards a close which is dramatically quiet but charged with emotion, like the ending of a tragedy. Thus episodes which may at first seem irrelevant to the main structure of the work are in fact architectonic elements contributing to the effect of the whole.

This is an elaboration of the Aristotelian view which the Scholia follow, and they do not put it so explicitly. But they do assume that the poet has a clear idea from the beginning of the direction in which his narrative is moving. It is particularly illuminating to see how they comment on the role of Patroclus in the poem. He is first mentioned at 1. 307, when Achilles returns with him and his companions to their tents after the quarrel. Here they note that his introduction at this early point in the narrative already prepares the way for his later intervention to plead with Achilles to return to the battle. Again the fact that Achilles entrusts Briseis to him (337) indicates their closeness, and his silence here (345) is picked up in the Embassy by the way he remains in the background, which suggests his gentleness (BT 1. 307, 337, 345). The Scholia compare his healing of Eurypylus, his distress at the Greek misfortunes, and the description of him as 'gentle' by Menelaus (17. 670). When we come to the series of events leading up to Patroclus' intervention, they are fully aware of the careful way in which this is prepared. The wounding of the heroes in book 11 leads to the Greek rout and battle by the ships (BT 11. 318, 407, 598).[7] Machaon goes back to the ships in his chariot when wounded, and so passes Achilles' view rapidly: Achilles therefore sends Patroclus to find out what has happened (BT 11. 512; cf. ABT 11. 604). Achilles has been watching the battle from his ship, clearly longing for the moment when he can return (BT 11. 600). Patroclus goes to Nestor, and this ensures that Nestor's eloquence will succeed where the Embassy had failed (AB 11. 611). Nestor's long story is designed οἰκονομικῶς, i.e. as part of the poet's plan, because this gives time for Eurypylus to return and meet Patroclus. This delays Patroclus and allows the poet to introduce the battle at the wall which follows (BT 11. 677–8, 809). Patroclus is respectful (αἰδήμων), and so he listens politely, in spite of the urgency of the situation. The wounding of Machaon has removed the doctor who could have treated Eurypylus, and so Patroclus does so instead (T 11. 833; cf. also BT 11. 813). His kindness leads him to stay with Eurypylus after treating him (BT 12. 1).

Finally, we return to Patroclus and Eurypylus at 15. 390, when the intervening great battle has made the Greek plight far more desperate and Patroclus' sympathy for them all the greater (BT 15. 390 and 12. 1). Later, after Patroclus' death, Hector drags his body in order to cut off his head and give the corpse to the dogs (17. 125–7). This barbaric intention is often overlooked, but the Scholia

---

[7] Cf. especially BT 11. 598: 'Having wounded most of the leaders except Telamonian Ajax he sent them back to the ships, Agamemnon, Diomedes, Odysseus, Machaon, Eurypylus, and Teucer in succession, in order that he may provide a plausible reason for the Achaeans' defeat. Then after bringing these back to the ships he devotes what follows to praise of Ajax, until Patroclus goes out to battle; and having killed Patroclus he returns to Ajax, until Achilles goes out to fight; and once he has brought him into the battle he ends the *Iliad* with his exploits.'

observe that it helps to justify Achilles' mistreatment of Hector's body (BT 17. 126-7). Whether or not Achilles is justified the motif surely does look forward to his retaliation.[8]

Thus, we can see that (unlike some modern critics) the Scholia are aware of the large-scale architecture of the poem. On a smaller scale, they are quick to pick up points of detail which anticipate what is to come in a subtle and unobtrusive way: for instance, when at 5. 662 Tlepolemus wounds Sarpedon, but 'his father (Zeus) *still* protected him from destruction' (BT); or when, after the Embassy, Diomedes says that the Greeks should fight next day, 'and Agamemnon himself among the foremost', which neatly anticipates his *aristeia* in book 11 (A 9. 709).[9]

Not only does the poet anticipate events later in the poem: he also looks forward to what is to come afterwards, the death of Achilles, the fall of Troy, and also some of the events in the *Odyssey*. The foreshadowing of Troy's fall helps to make the poem an *Iliad*, as do the references to earlier events in the war.[10] Their comment at 24. 85-6 is particularly fine (BT):

ἐπειδὴ μέλλει καταστρέφειν τὸν λόγον εἰς τὰς Ἕκτορος ταφάς, προλαβεῖν τι ἐπιχειρεῖ τῶν ἑξῆς καὶ τὸ κέντρον ἐγκαταλιπεῖν, ὡς ὁ κωμικός φησι, τοῖς ἀκρωμένοις, ὥστε ποθῆσαί τι καὶ περὶ τῆς Ἀχιλλέως ἀναιρέσεως ἀκοῦσαι καὶ ἐννοεῖν παρ' ἑαυτοῖς, οἷος ἂν ἐγένετο ὁ ποιητὴς διατιθέμενος ταῦτα.

Since he intends to close the story with the burial of Hector, he tries to anticipate to some extent the subsequent events, and to leave his sting, as the

---

[8] Cf. also BT 7. 79, 13. 831, 18. 176-80, Eust. 1098. 29 ff., 1136. 17 ff., 1136. 53 ff., and J. M. Redfield, *Nature and Culture in the Iliad* (Chicago, 1975), 169.

[9] For other references to οἰκονομία and anticipation (προσυνιστάναι, προοικονομεῖν, προαναφώνησις, πρόληψις, advance reference, anticipation, foreshadowing, advance notice, etc.) cf. T 1. 45, 213, BT 1. 242, 247, BT 2. 39, 272, 362, 375-7, 416, A 2. 718, B 2. 761, 787, 872, BT 3. 261, AB 3. 363, BT 4.2, 421, 5. 116, T 5. 348, BT 5. 543-4, 6. 116, 490-1, 516, 7. 125, 274, T 10. 274, 276, 332, AB 11. 17, BT 11. 45, T 11. 798, BT 12. 37, 113, 116, T 12. 228, 13. 241, 521, BT 14. 217, 15. 56, T 15. 64, BT 15. 258, ABT 15. 377, BT 15. 556, 594, 610, 16. 46, 71, 145, 752-3, 17. 215-16, 236, T 17. 351, BT 17. 695, A 18. 215-16. BT 18. 312, 372, 395, T 18. 418, A 18. 483, T 20. 7, 21. 515, 22. 5, 385, BT 23. 62-3, A 23. 616, etc. Cf. also Schol. G *Il.* 2. 36, 5. 674, 10. 336, 16. 71, and G. E. Duckworth, '*Προαναφώνησις* in the Scholia to Homer', *AJP* 52 (1931), 320 ff. As he points out, anticipation (προοικονομία) is really distinct from explicit foreshadowing (προαναφώνησις), although they are often confused in the Scholia.

[10] Death of Achilles: BT 1. 352, 505, 18. 88-9, 458. Fall of Troy and other later events: AT 2. 278, BT 6. 438, ABT 6. 448, BT 12. 13-15, T 13. 156, BT 13. 411, BT 15. 56, 21. 376, ABT 22. 61-2, G 12. 10. *Odyssey*: T 2. 260, ABT 4. 354, T 5. 561, T 10. 247, 252, 260, 12. 16, BT 24. 804.

comic poet says, in his audience, so that they should long to hear something also about the killing of Achilles, and should reflect on how effectively the poet would have described these events.

Anticipation of what is to come sustains the audience's interest, and the poet aims throughout to arouse his audience and keep them in a state of expectation or *suspense*. At the opening of his poem τραγῳδίαις τραγικὸν ἐξεῦρε προοίμιον· καὶ γὰρ προσεκτικοὺς ἡμᾶς ἡ τῶν ἀτυχημάτων διήγησις ἐργάζεται . . . (He has invented a tragic prelude for tragedies: for the description of misfortunes makes us attentive . . .) (AT 1. 1). The statement of the theme of the poem and summary of its tragic consequences are a model for the *proemium* of a work, arousing the expectations of the audience by the solemn grandeur of the subject (cf. Quint. 10. 1. 48). Likewise the invocation of the Muses calls attention to the importance of what is to follow, as well as inviting the audience to be less critical of the poet's own defects (AB 2. 484; cf. BT 11. 218, 14. 508, 16. 112, etc., Quint. loc. cit.). The introduction of Paris at the very opening of the fighting, challenging the Greeks, 'arouses the listener, as the cause of most dangers to others is himself the first to take the risk' (BT 3. 16). After the truce in book 7 Zeus thunders all night, planning trouble for the Greeks: thus προκινεῖ καὶ ἀγωνιᾶν ποιεῖ τὸν ἀκροατὴν ἐπὶ τοῖς ἐσομένοις ὁ ποιητής (The poet arouses the hearer in advance, and puts him in suspense about what is to come) (BT 7. 479).[11]

Creation of suspense is related to the poet's tendency to bring the action to a point of crisis and then provide a resolution. Aristotle had already observed this in connection with Agamemnon's testing of the army in book 2 (fr. 142; cf. Porphyry *ap.* Schol. B 2. 73). In book 8 Nestor is nearly caught by Hector when the Greeks are routed and one of his horses is wounded. Here the Scholia very observantly comment on the poet's use of language, which by calling Nestor 'the old man', and bringing up 'the fierce Hector', puts the listener in suspense (ἐν ἀγωνίᾳ). The use of the imperfect ἀπέταμνε (he was cutting away) and present participle ἀΐσσων (lunging), describing Nestor's desperate efforts to cut the horse free, brilliantly illustrate the weakness and slowness of the old man (ABT 8. 87). This fondness for cliff-hanging situations is noted again at 8. 217 (BT) when

---

[11] Cf. BT 8. 62, T 8. 470, BT 10. 38, 11. 604, 711, 12. 116, 297, 330, T 14. 392, BT 15. 594, 610, 16. 46, 431, AB 20. 443, BT 22. 274, T 23. 378, 383.

'Hector would have burnt the ships, if Hera had not inspired Agamemnon . . .'. The same applies to the crisis in book 11 when Odysseus is isolated by the Greek retreat and debates whether to stand or flee (T 11. 401, BT 412-13).[12] Such crises often require the intervention of a god to resolve them, anticipating the later *deus ex machina* 'god from the machine' resolutions of Greek tragedy. This applies to the scene in book 2, where the army rushes for the ships and Athene has to intervene: here the Scholia comment on Homer's invention of the μηχαναί (devices) used in tragedy (BT 2.156). Athene's intervention in the quarrel in book 1 is a similar case: εἴωθε δὲ εἰς τοσοῦτον ἄγειν τὰς περιπετείας, ὡς μὴ δύνασθαι παῦσαι ἄνθρωπον αὐτάς (he is accustomed to bring his dramatic reversals to the point where no human being is able to resolve them) (BT 1. 195; cf. 3. 380).

It will be clear by now that the Scholia follow closely the lead of Plato and of Aristotle in regarding Homer as the 'first of the tragedians'.[13] Not only was he the inventor of μηχαναί and περιπέτειαι (dramatic reversals).[14] He was also the first to use κωφὰ πρόσωπα (silent characters: the silent heralds at 1. 332: ABT) and children (BT 6. 468). The idea of Homer as a tragedian underlies much of the language used by the Scholia, especially when they are discussing vividly dramatic scenes and those which arouse emotion (πάθος, οἶκτος, ἔλεος, pathos, compassion, pity). τραγῳδεῖν (to represent in a tragic manner) and ἐκτραγῳδεῖν (to represent in a very tragic manner) are commonly used, although they often mean little more than 'to represent dramatically'.[15] When Agamemnon is compared to Zeus, this is an example of idealization, as in tragedy (ABT 2. 478). In the description of Hephaestus at work in book 18, δαιμονίως τὸν πλάστην αὐτὸς διέπλασεν, ὥσπερ ἐπὶ τῆς σκηνῆς ἐκκυκλήσας καὶ δείξας ἡμῖν ἐν φανερῷ τὸ ἐργαστήριον (in a wonderful

[12] Cf. T 11. 507, BT 12. 52, T 14. 424. K. Reinhardt, *Die Ilias und ihr Dichter*, 107 ff., discusses Homer's fondness for such situations.
[13] Cf. A. Trendelenburg, *Grammaticorum graecorum de arte tragica iudiciorum reliquiae* (Bonn, 1867), 70-85, L. Adam, *Die aristotelische Theorie vom Epos . . .* (Wiesbaden, 1889), 30 ff.
[14] For περιπέτεια cf. also AB 2. 484, BT 10. 271, 11. 464, 23. 65, and esp. BT 21. 34 πρῶτος οὖν τὸ τῶν περιπετειῶν εἶδος ἔδειξε, ποικίλον ὂν καὶ θεατρικὸν καὶ κινητικόν (Thus he was the first to show the form of dramatic reversals, which is complex and theatrical and moving).
[15] e.g. ABT 2. 73, BT 2. 144, T 7. 424, ABT 8. 428-9, T 13. 241, BT 17. 209 (τραγῳδίαν ἔχει, involves tragedy), 20.25.

way he himself has created the creator, as though he had rolled out onto the stage and clearly revealed to us his workshop) (BT 18 476). The moving and graphic portrait of Briseis in book 19 shows her with a 'chorus' of captive women, of whom she is the leader (BT 19. 282). Achilles' pursuit of Hector is prolonged, ἵνα ὥσπερ ἐν θεάτρῳ νῦν μείζονα κινήσῃ πάθη, so that as if in a theatre he may now arouse greater emotions (A 22. 201). On the other hand, when Agamemnon with a harsh and shocking speech persuades Menelaus not to spare Adrastus, they comment that such things as this killing are not shown on the stage in tragedy (BT 6.58). The rapidity of the announcement to Achilles by Antilochus of Patroclus' death also contrasts with the leisurely messenger speeches of tragedy (BT 18.20).[16]

Poetic invention obeys its own laws, as Aristotle had observed, and the Scholia are aware of this. They defend *poetic freedom* to 'follow the myths' however shocking or odd these may seem later. Thus, for instance, on the gods (ABT 8. 428-9; cf. BT 14. 176, A 18. 63):

ὅταν εἰς τὴν ἀξίαν ἀτενίσῃ τῶν θεῶν, τότε φησὶν αὐτοὺς μὴ κινεῖσθαι περὶ θνητῶν, ὡς οὐδὲ ἂν ἡμεῖς περὶ μυρμήκων· ὅταν δὲ ἐπιλογίσηται τὴν ποιητικήν, ἕπεται τοῖς μύθοις καὶ τὴν ὑπόθεσιν ἐκτραγῳδεῖ, συμμαχίας καὶ θεομαχίας παράγων,

when he considers the dignity of the gods, then he says that they are not moved by concern for mortals, just as we should not be concerned about ants; but when he is thinking about the poetic effect, he follows the myths and represents his theme in a tragic way, introducing alliances and battles of the gods.

At *Il.* 19. 108, on the problem of why Hera insists on Zeus swearing an oath when his word alone should suffice, they cite Aristotle (fr. 163 = Schol. A) for the view that within the framework of the story about the birth of Heracles it is natural for Hera to ask Zeus for an oath, as she wishes to be absolutely sure of the outcome. At *Il.* 14. 342-4 they distinguish three forms of poetic narrative, realistic, imaginatively convincing, and fantastic: ὁ μιμητικὸς τοῦ ἀληθοῦς, ὁ κατὰ φαντασίαν τῆς ἀληθείας (imitative of truth, in imagination of the truth) and ὁ καθ' ὑπέρθεσιν τῆς ἀληθείας καὶ φαντασίας (surpassing truth and imagination). The third includes such details as golden clouds in heaven, as well as the Cyclopes and Laestrygonians (BT).[17]

---

[16]  See also p. 201 on 17. 695 ff. and *Od.* 11. 563.
[17]  Cf. also Quint. 2. 4. 2, for this division of types of narrative. Criticism of Homer's fantasies was of course common (cf. 'Longinus' 9. 14, etc.).

Alternatively, the poet may reflect customs of his own time (B 3. 291, ABT 8. 284, B 10. 153 quoting Aristotle fr. 160; cf. *Poet.* 1461ᵃ1 ff.). This explains Achilles' dragging of Hector's corpse, a Thessalian practice (A 22. 397 and B 24. 15 quoting Aristotle fr. 166). They also quote Aristarchus' common-sense view that some things are due simply to chance inspiration (κατ' ἐπιφοράν) and one should not look for ulterior reasons for them: for instance the fact that the Catalogue of Ships begins with Boeotia (AB 2. 494), that Hector foresees Andromache carrying water for the Greeks in captivity, which led later poets to show her actually doing this (A 6. 457), and that Sleep is found in Lemnos by Hera (ABT 14. 231). Aristarchus had also formulated the important idea of τὸ σιωπώμενον (what is not mentioned) (or κατὰ συμπέρασμα, by implication), whereby the poet takes many things for granted or refers to them in passing, and one should not question them. Thus he mentions washing before a meal but not after, Athene gives her spear to Telemachus and never takes it back (*Od.* 1. 126 ff.), and so on (BT *Il.* 1. 449).[18] He does not aim to give a fully documented historical narrative, διδοὺς τοῖς ἀκροαταῖς καθ' ἑαυτοὺς λογίζεσθαι τὰ ἀκόλουθα, leaving his audience to work out for themselves what follows (BT 1. 449).[19] A corollary to this is the rhetorical technique for giving grandeur to a theme κατὰ συλλογισμόν (by inference), whereby an oblique reference leaves us to infer its size or importance, as when Zeus' nod alone makes Olympus tremble (T 1. 530), or Achilles' spear cannot be brandished by another hero (BT 16. 141-2).[20]

Such observations show a proper awareness of the distinctions between fictional and factual narrative, and they formed the conventional armoury for dealing with criticisms of the poet. They can be linked with the general rhetorical principle of πιθανότης (persuasiveness), the need for the narrative to be credible even where the poet is describing the extraordinary or miraculous. The role of the gods often serves this purpose: the speed of the assembly of the Greek army is ascribed to Athene's assistance (BT 2. 446); the killing of the chimaera is due to divine aid (BT 6. 183 τὸ ἄπιστον ἰάσατο, he cured

---

[18] Cf. A 2. 553, ABT 5. 127, A 5. 231, 6. 114, 11. 506, 12. 211, AT 16. 432, ABT 16. 666, ABT 17. 24, A 18. 356.

[19] Cf. Demetrius, *On Style*, 222 (quoting Theophrastus).

[20] Cf. BT 5. 744, 13. 127, 343, 15. 414, 24. 163, Quintilian 8. 4.21 ff. Homer's praise of Nestor's honey-sweet eloquence also subtly implies his own poetic charm, κατὰ συλλογισμόν (AB 1. 249)! Cf. BT 6. 357-8.

the implausibility), and so on.[21] But credibility is more often achieved by qualities which one would class under style, and can be considered more closely in that context.

## II. Ἦθος (CHARACTER)

Turning to characterization, we find that the Scholia are constantly aware of Homer's subtlety in this respect. They frequently comment on the way in which *speeches* reveal character, or observe that a particular thing is spoken or done ἠθικῶς (in character). Thus at 1. 348 διὰ μιᾶς λέξεως (i.e. ἀέκουσα) ὁλόκληρον ἡμῖν ἦθος προσώπου [of Briseis] δεδήλωκεν, by a single expression (i.e. 'unwillingly') he has shown us the whole character of this person (i.e. Briseis) (BT).[22] Different types of character speak in different ways: Hera's speeches are typical of a woman scorned (ABT 1. 542, BT 1. 553, 557; cf. BT 4. 20, ABT 4. 53, BT 8. 199, 201, 204); the speech of Andromache after Hector's death is in perfect imitation of a woman's character (BT 22. 477, 487), and Hecuba's virulent words about eating Achilles' liver are suitable to an old woman whose son has been killed and insulted after death (BT 24. 212). Again, when she begs Hector to drink wine and rest at 6. 260 this is typical of a mother (BT). They are quick to observe points of characterization of the individual heroes. Patroclus' gentleness has already been noted (cf. also BT 11. 616, 670, 677-8, 814, 12. 1, 19. 297). The poet's sympathy for him is shown by his use of *apostrophe* (direct address), addressing him in the vocative (BT 16. 692-3, 787; cf. Eustathius 1086. 49). He uses the same device for Menelaus: προσπέπονθε δὲ Μενελάῳ ὁ ποιητής, the poet is sympathetically inclined towards Menelaus (BT 4. 127; cf. 146, 7. 104, T 13. 603). The Scholia regard him as a moderate and gentle character (BT 6. 51, 62), who evokes the sympathy of his companions (BT 4. 154, 207, 5. 565, 7. 122). He is called a 'soft fighter' (17. 588), but this is said by an enemy and is not the poet's own view (ABT). His φιλοτιμία (love of honour) is

---

[21] Cf T 10. 482, A 18. 217, 230.

[22] Cf ABT 8. 85-7 (Nestor's physical weakness shown in action), and *Vita Sophoclis* § 21 for a similar comment on Sophocles. Homer and the tragedians seldom waste words on 'character sketches'. They know how to convey character in action and speech.

displayed in his dispute with Antilochus after the chariot-race (BT
23. 566).[23] Paris is contrasted with him, as cowardly, effeminate,
and disliked by his own people (BT 3. 19, AB 3. 371, Porphyry *ap.* B
3. 441 quoting Aristotle, fr. 150, BT 4. 207, 5. 565, 6. 509, etc.).
Agamemnon is also contrasted, as noble and commanding, but
arrogant and brutal: the Scholia reflect attempts to defend him from
criticism, as he is the Greek leader and so ought to be a model of kingship, but they cannot whitewash him entirely (cf. especially BT 1.
225, and T 1. 32, ABT 2. 478, BT 6. 58, 62). His defeatist speeches
to the army, suggesting return home, are interpreted as having a
covert intention which is the opposite of their apparent one (Porphyry
*ap.* B 2. 73, BT 2. 110ff., 9. 11, 14. 75).[24] This may be true of 2.
110 ff., but fails to convince us that Agamemnon is not being
portrayed as a weak and vacillating leader later.

Odysseus is a complex character who had always aroused much
debate. His intelligence and rhetorical skill were clear enough (BT 3.
212 ff., 9. 225 ff., 622, book 10 *passim*, etc.): but there were some
who detected signs of cowardice. In particular, in the Greek flight in
book 8 he did not stop to rescue Nestor: did he not hear Diomedes'
call, or did he hear and not respond (8. 97)? Aristarchus seems to
have thought that he heard, but others defended him (ABT 8. 97;
cf. BT 7. 168, ABT 8. 226, ABT 10. 139-40, T 10. 149, etc.).
Telamonian Ajax, on the other hand, is straightforward: honest,
open, and generous (BT 7. 192, 199, 226-7, 284, T 13. 77, B 13.
203, ABT 17. 645, A 17. 720), whereas his namesake the Locrian is
hot-tempered and boastful, faults for which he is duly punished (B
13. 203, BT 23. 473).

Achilles is the most difficult to assess. Homer will not let us forget
him in his absence, and these constant references not only anchor
the narrative to its central theme, but they also build up his importance (αὔξησις, aggrandizement), leading up to his return (BT 4. 12,
5. 788, 7. 113, T 11. 273, BT 11. 600, 13. 324, 16. 653). Plato and
Aristotle recognized his inconsistency (cf. Pl. *Hippias Minor* 369E ff.
and ABT 9. 309, Aristotle, fr. 168 and *Poet.* 1454[a] 26 ff.), and the
Scholia echo these criticisms and suggest answers (BT 18. 98, 24.

---

[23] That *apostrophe* is a sign of sympathy was argued independently by Adam Parry
in his sensitive analysis of the characters of Patroclus and Menelaus (*HSCP 76* (1972),
9 ff.).

[24] Cf. p. 201 below.

569). He is the noblest of the Greeks, but also cruel and ruthless: the Scholia have a hard time defending him, when the poet himself seems to disapprove of his brutality, especially in his revenge for Patroclus (cf. BT 11. 778-9, 20. 467, AB 22. 397, BT 23. 174). In the Embassy they characterize him as φιλότιμον, ἁπλοῦν, φιλαληθῆ, βαρύθυμον, εἴρωνα, fond of honour, simple, a lover of truth, indignant, self-critical (BT 9. 309), and view his great speech in answer to Agamemnon's offer as a masterpiece of nobility and angry pride (ABT 9. 429). The abruptness of the sentence-structure admirably conveys his emotions (A 9. 372, ABT 375 ff., 429). And yet, ἀεὶ δὲ πρὸς Ἀχιλλέα προσπαθῶς ἔχει, he is always sympathetic towards Achilles (B2. 692).

Lesser characters receive some attention: Menestheus' kindness, for instance, is noted (BT 12. 334-6). Antilochus is the first to kill a Trojan (4. 457 ff.), perhaps to honour him as he will not have an *aristeia* (scene of prowess) later, or because of his youthful boldness (BT). He is quick to help in a crisis, as when he goes to aid Menelaus (BT 5. 565): they were neighbours at home (BT 15. 568). His fondness for Patroclus is vividly shown by his speechlessness at the news of his death and the way he announces it to Achilles (BT 17. 695-8, 18. 18). His behaviour in the chariot race shows the character of a noble young man, over-eager for victory, but able to reconcile Menelaus to himself afterwards (BT 23. 543, 589, 591-2, 594).

On the Trojan side Hector receives most attention, and the Scholia give him a poor press. This is the extreme example of their general view that Homer wishes to present the Greeks as favourably as possible, whereas the Trojans are barbarians, and so are shown in a bad light. This notion (ἀεὶ φιλέλλην ὁ ποιητής, the poet is always favourable to the Greeks) seldom appears in the A Scholia, whereas it runs through the BT Scholia. In its more extreme form, therefore, it does not seem to derive from the Alexandrian scholars.[25] Although at times Homer undoubtedly shows more sympathy for the Greeks, they push this idea to absurd limits.[26] In particular, they often distort the way in which Hector is portrayed, claiming that he is arrogant, cruel, and cowardly. In the duel with Ajax they give all the credit to Ajax and none to his opponent, and in the battle which follows he is

[25] Cf. W. Dittenberger, *Hermes*, 40 (1905), 460 ff.
[26] Cf. J. T. Kakridis, *Homer Revisited* (Lund, 1971), 54 ff., who criticizes Van der Valk for supporting the view of the Scholia. See also Van der Valk, *Researches*, i. 474 ff.

tyrannical, boastful, and indecisive.[27] He blames others for his own mistakes, and his boasts and threats will rebound upon himself (BT 13. 768, 824, 831).[28] His successes are due to divine aid or good fortune (BT 15. 418, 644-5), and he is destroyed by his ambition and folly (BT 22. 91, 99). But as his death approaches we begin to feel more sympathy for him (BT 15. 610, ABT 17. 207-8), and Achilles' treatment of his corpse increases this, so that we are relieved when the gods protect it (BT 23. 184). There is a good deal of truth in all this, but it neglects those scenes which show Hector more favourably, and exaggerates the contrast between his behaviour and that of the Greek heroes.

The idea that the poet is always φιλέλλην leads to the assumption that he adapts his narrative in order to play down Greek disasters and magnify their successes (BT 7. 17, ABT 8. 1, BT 8. 2, 78, 131, 274, 350, 486-7, etc.). The audience's sympathies are all on the Greek side, and so they are pleased when they do well and sorry when things go badly.[29] This seems childish to us, but if we think of the reactions of any audience watching a war film we will soon realize that it was hard for the Greeks not to adopt this attitude.[30]

It is easier for us to sympathize with their admiration for the *realism* of Homer's characters. Truth to life is one of the fundamental virtues of Homer which they admire: the poet is ἄκρως μιμητὴς ἀληθείας, supremely good at representing reality (BT 5. 677). The scene of Hector's meeting with Andromache and Astyanax receives special praise, and when the child is scared of his father's helmet they comment that ταῦτα τὰ ἔπη οὕτως ἐστὶν ἐναργείας μεστὰ ὥστε οὐ μόνον ἀκούεται τὰ πράγματα ἀλλὰ καὶ ὁρᾶται· λαβὼν δὲ τοῦτο ἐκ τοῦ βίου ὁ ποιητὴς ἄκρως περιεγένετο τῇ μιμήσει, these verses are so full of vividness that one not only hears but also sees the actions: the poet took this from life and was outstanding in his representational ability (BT

---

[27] Cf. BT 7. 89-90, 192, 226-7, 284, 289, 8. 180-1, 197, 216, 497-8, T 515, BT 523.

[28] Cf. also BT 14. 366, 15. 346, T 15. 721, BT 16. 833, 17. 220, A 17. 225, 227, 240, ABT 17. 248, BT 18. 285, 293, 296, and Van der Valk, *Researches*, i. 475-6.

[29] This view is attributed to the scholar Pius (T 6. 234). His date is not known (*RE* IIA. 662), *pace* Van der Valk (*Researches*, i. 437 n. 120).

[30] There are parallels in the tragic Scholia (cf. Trendelenburg, *Grammaticorum*, 131). The historians were also criticized for lack of patriotism (Dionysius, *Thucydides*, 41; Plutarch, *De malignitate Herodoti*, On the Malice of Herodotus).

6. 468; cf. 472, 479).³¹ It is often such scenes of *pathos*, contrasting so strongly with the brutality of fighting, that arouse their approval (e.g. BT 22. 512, 24. 744). The power to portray emotion and evoke feeling is the most important link between Homer and tragedy, according with the Aristotelian view of tragedy as arousing 'pity and fear', and the Scholia are full of comments on Homer's ability to create sympathy in this way.³² One reason why the poem opens with the word 'Wrath' is ἵν' ἐκ τοῦ πάθους ἀποκαθαριεύσῃ τὸ τοιοῦτο μόριον τῆς ψυχῆς, in order that through this emotion he may purify such a part of the soul (AT 1. 1): here they echo the Aristotelian theory of κάθαρσις (purification). In the opening scene with Chryses the poet 'searches after pity by all means' (BT 1. 13–14). The presence of Priam and Hecuba as spectators of Hector's duel with Achilles increases the pathos and dramatic effect (B 3. 306). Words such as περιπαθῶς (in a moving way) are often used to describe such scenes (BT 4. 146, 153, 154–5, etc.).³³ ἦθος (character), and πάθος (emotion) are frequently combined (BT 4. 153, 6.411, etc.). The portrayal of Andromaché laughing amid tears is 'powerfully expressed and impossible to analyse' (δυνατῶς ῥηθὲν ἀνερμήνευτον), because of its conflicting emotions (ABT 6. 484). The poet himself sympathizes with his characters, minor as well as major ones, and sometimes even with inanimate objects. When Briseis tears 'her breasts and tender neck and lovely face' the poet 'seems to share in grieving at her disfigurement' (BT 19. 285). The death of Iphidamas (11. 221 ff.) admirably displays his narrative skill, for he divides the details of his autobiography, mentioning his marriage briefly to begin with, and only dwelling with sympathy on his loss of his new wife and her great value when he is killed (T 11. 226, 243, BT 242).³⁴ The scene of Andromache's lament when Hector has been killed is a masterpiece of pathos. Her quiet preparation of the bath for Hector's return, her ignorance of what has occurred, her reactions when she hears the sounds of lamentation, still uncertain of what has

³¹ For βιωτικῶν μιμητικὰ, things which represent life-like events, etc., cf. ABT 1. 547, BT 5. 370, 12. 342–3, A 18. 12; also 'Longinus' 9. 15, etc.

³² Cf. J. Griffin, 'Homeric Pathos and Objectivity', *CQ* NS 26 (1976), 161 ff. for a full and sensitive discussion.

³³ Also περιπαθές, παθητικῶς, very moving, in a moving way, etc. (see Baar s.v.).

³⁴ Cf. B 2. 692, BT 4. 127, 146, 7. 104, 13. 180, T 13. 603, ABT 16. 549, BT 16. 692–3, 775, 787, T 17. 301. At BT 15. 610–14 they defend these lines against rejection by Zenodotus and Aristarchus, observing that they show the poet's sympathy at Hector's impending death.

happened, the poignant recollection of happier times in the reference
to her wedding-veil, her fainting and narrow escape from death, and
her long speech, mourning her own fate and that of her child, with
all its touching and life-like details: all this makes a scene which
cannot be surpassed (ABT 22. 443-4, BT 448, 452, 465, 468, 474,
487 where they defend a passage condemned by Aristarchus, 500,
512). And just as the whole work began with the ominous reference
to the passion of anger, and a portrayal of the sufferings it caused, so
'he closes the *Iliad* with the greatest effects of pathos' (ἐπὶ πλείστῳ δὲ
ἐλέῳ καταστρέφει τὴν Ἰλιάδα), providing a model for orators in their
closing appeals (T 24. 746).

## III. Λέξις (STYLE)

After ἦθος and πάθος we should consider style. Naturally Homer was
regarded as a master of all the styles which later rhetorical theory distinguished (cf. Demetrius, *On Style* 37, Quint. 10. 1. 46 ff., Ps.-Plut.
*On the Life and Poetry of Homer* ii. 72 f.). Of these, the *grand or powerful style* might be expected to be most prominent. Demetrius sees
Homer chiefly as an exponent of this, and Homer is the prime model
of sublimity for 'Longinus'. The Scholia admire the grandeur or
solemnity of certain passages. Elevation is especially aided by introduction of divine scenes or the supernatural (e.g. ABT 2. 478, BT 4.
1, 439, B 7. 59, BT 10. 5, T 15. 599, T 18. 204, BT 20. 4, 21. 325,
23. 383). But heroic greatness of soul is also admired, as in Ajax's
famous prayer that they may die at least in daylight (ABT 17. 645-6;
cf. 'Longinus' 9. 10 where this example follows a series of passages
about the gods).[35]

Elevation of everyday scenes and actions by means of dignified
language is also frequently praised, and this is especially a feature of
similes (cf. BT 3. 385, 9. 134, 206, 13. 589, 14. 347, 16. 7, 17. 389,
570, 18. 346, 21. 12, 24. 266). More generally, the notion of
αὔξησις, aggrandizement, which runs through the Scholia, has an
important part to play here. As this means the art of making something seem more significant, it can refer to a large variety of devices.
Some of these are compositional on a large scale, for instance the

---

[35] On this 'hierarchy of sublime themes' see D. C. Innes, 'Gigantomachy and
Natural Philosophy', *CQ* NS 29 (1979), 165 ff.

aggrandizement of Achilles' combat by the Theomachy (T 21. 385). But others are more limited in scope. Similes, for example, are often regarded as serving this purpose. In general, the expansion of standard themes and addition of details adds to the importance of what is being described, or what is about to be described. Thus divine assemblies, 'typical scenes' such as those of arming, invocation of the Muses, an accumulation of similes and other devices can be used to signal a major episode, whilst details of wounds or a hero's background are used to draw special attention to a character or scene in the midst of the battle.[36] Powerful or striking effects are noted by the use of such epithets as δυνατός, δεινός, powerful, terrible, (e.g. ABT 6. 484, BT 14. 437, 15. 496, T 16. 283) or the terms ἔκπληξις, κατάπληξις, amazement, astonishment (BT 1. 242, 3. 182, T 18. 51; 20. 62, which is praised extensively by 'Longinus' 9. 6; BT 21. 388, which is quoted together with 20. 61 ff. by 'Longinus', 24. 630). But it is surprising that these terms are not more often used.

The *middle style* is rarely mentioned. The much-admired portrait of Briseis in 19. 282 ff. is said to be 'in the middle style' (μεσοῦ χαρακτῆρος) although it is also 'dignified, graphic, and pathetic' (σεμνῶς πέφρασται καὶ λίαν ἐστὶ γραφικός, τῷ δὲ μιμητικῷ συμπαθὴς καὶ γοερός, the description is dignified and very vivid, and in its realistic representation sympathetic and piteous: BT). The idea of κόσμος (ornament) may be relevant here (although it can have much wider uses). The Scholia are aware that this can serve a functional purpose. For example, their comment on the passage describing the return journey of the Greeks from Chrysa after the appeasement of Apollo is surely very acute (BT 1. 481): 'the poet shares in their joy and now paints a fair picture (καλλιγράφει) of their return-journey, in contrast to the journey out. He does the same in the case of Poseidon'. This must in fact be one reason why Homer expands in a

---

[36] Cf. BT 3. 182, 190, 4. 1, 2, 35, 153-4, 422, 435, 439, 452, 512, 5. 23, 70, 87, 543-4, 703, 801, T 6. 234, BT 6. 413, 499, 7. 208, 214, 8. 2, 77, 131, A 9. 14, ABT 11. 475, AB 11. 548, A 12. 4, BT 12. 23, T 12. 154, BT 12. 430, 465-6, T 13. 345, BT 14. 394-8, 15. 258, 312-13, 414, 16. 58, 98-9, 549, T 16. 810, BT 16. 814, AT 17. 260, BT 17. 671, 676, B 19. 388-91, BT 20. 213, T 21. 385, BT 22. 294, 371, AB 22. 443-4, BT 23. 222, 24. 214, 490. See also N. Austin, 'The Function of Digressions in the *Iliad*', *GRBS* 7 (1966), 295 ff., and G. M. Calhoun, 'Homeric Repetitions', *University of California Publications in Classical Philology*, 12 (1933), 1 ff.

lyrical way the 'typical scene' of a voyage at this point, whereas the
outward journey to Chrysa is very matter-of-fact.[37] The reference to
Poseidon is to his journey to help the Greeks at 13. 17 ff., another
lyrical passage which is said to be introduced for relief from the
battle (T 13. 20), whereas at 15. 218-19, when his forced departure
is described in only two lines, they say that Homer cuts short the
description, 'since it is with sorrow' (BT 15. 219). Again this shows
a sensitive awareness of the poet's subtle variation of 'typical scenes'
to suit the dramatic situation.

The Thersites-episode is seen as designed in part for comic relief
(ABT 2. 212; cf. Demetrius 163). In the Catalogue of Ships the
variety of epithets and formulae embellishes what would otherwise
be lifeless (B 2. 494).[38] They have a good comment on the death of
Otrynteides, whose life-history is described with lapidary pathos (20.
382 ff.): although this episode could be seen simply as an instance of
ποικιλία, it is particularly apt here, as the embellishment of the incident brings relief from the monotony of so many battles and killings,
and also shows that Achilles' first victim was not insignificant (BT
20. 383).

κόσμος is seen also as a function of the *similes*. The Scholia sometimes identify a single point of comparison and regard the rest as
ornamental (e.g. T 12. 41, or BT 21. 257, where the poet is said to
move 'from the powerful to the refined and flowery style': ἀπὸ τοῦ
ἀδροῦ ἐπὶ τὸ ἰσχνὸν ἔρχεται καὶ ἀνθηρόν).[39] More often, however, they
insist on the detailed and precise correspondence between simile and
narrative (see pp. 197-9 below).

The *plain style* is not often mentioned explicitly, but many features
which are supposed to characterize it are referred to. Occasionally the
*simplicity* of a passage is praised: Ajax's retreat at 16. 101 ff. makes a
vivid effect without the use of any rhetorical devices, the narrative
directly reflecting the action (BT). Priam's brief catalogue of the
horrors of a fallen city (22. 61 ff.) has no ornamental epithets to

---

[37] The Scholia also note that this is the only voyage described in the *Iliad*, and so
receives a good deal of attention (BT 1. 434 f.). Structurally, this scene provides an
effective contrast with the narrative of Achilles' anger.

[38] Cf. Dionysius, *On the Arrangement of Words* 16.

[39] Demetrius, however, praises 21. 257 ff. as an example of accurate and vivid
description (209). Cf. also BT 4. 482, T 11. 481, BT 17. 666, 22. 193. Demetrius
(129) chooses the simile at *Od.* 6. 105 ff. as an illustration of αἱ λεγόμεναι σεμναὶ χάριτες
καὶ μεγάλαι, what we call the dignified or stately kind of charm.

complicate its stark realism (BT). *Brevity* is often noted as effective: ἐν βραχεῖ δὲ πάντα πέφρασται, he has indicated everything briefly.[40] Thus, when Achilles sees the wounded Machaon passing his hut, and calls Patroclus out, Homer says of Patroclus κακοῦ δ' ἄρα οἱ πέλεν ἀρχή, and so this was the beginning of trouble for him (11. 604). This pregnant interjection by the poet 'puts the hearer in suspense to know what this trouble means, and begets attention by the brevity of the reference' (BT). Later they comment again on this passage: ἐναγώνιος δέ ἐστιν ὁ ποιητὴς καί, ἐὰν ἄρα, σπέρμα μόνον τίθησιν, the poet is dramatically engaged, and if he must do so, only sows a seed (T 15. 64). Likewise, rapidity is praised, as in Antilochus' announcement to Achilles of Patroclus' death: 'he gives the bad news quickly, in only two lines, and has revealed all briefly, the dead man, those who are fighting over him, his killer' (BT 18.20).[41] *Clarity* (σαφήνεια) is sometimes mentioned (e.g. BT 5. 70, σαφηνίζει, he makes clear, A 5. 9, AB 11. 548 as a function of similes, BT 4. 154, 11. 722-5). More often the term ἐνάργεια (vividness) is used to characterize a passage. On 4. 154 (χειρὸς ἔχων Μενέλαον, ἐπεστενάχοντο δ' ἑταῖροι, holding Menelaus by the hand, and his companions joined in his lament), in the context of Agamemnon's address to Menelaus after his wounding, they comment: ἄφελε τὸν στίχον, καὶ οὐ βλάψεις τὴν σαφήνειαν, ἀπολέσεις δὲ τὴν ἐνάργειαν, ἥτις ἐμφαίνει τὴν Ἀγαμέμνονος συμπάθειαν καὶ τὴν τῶν συναχθομένων ἑταίρων διάθεσιν, if you remove the verse, you will not harm the clarity, but you will destroy the vividness, which shows Agamemnon's sympathy and the disposition of his companions who share his grief (BT).[42] Again it is especially the similes which are said to have this quality of making the scene come to life before our eyes.[43]

[40] Cf. BT 1. 505, A 2. 765, 3. 200-2, BT 4. 125, 222, ABT 4. 274, BT 6. 460, 8. 87, T 10. 297-8, 314, BT 11. 239, 300, 13. 249, 15. 219, 496, 16. 112, T 16. 630, ABT 20. 372, BT 20. 395.

[41] Cf. also T 10. 409, BT 15. 6-7, 16. 293, 415-16, 17. 605, 20. 456, T 20. 460.

[42] Cf. also 6. 467-8, 10. 461, T 11. 378, AB 11. 548, BT 12. 430, 14. 438, 454, 15. 381, 16. 7, 17. 263, 389, 20. 394, 21. 526, 22. 61-2, 23. 362, 692, 697.

[43] Another related term is ἔμφασις, emphasis (cf. ἐμφατικῶς, expressively, which is similarly used, though different in origin), of any striking or vivid effect or expression: BT 1. 342, 2. 414, 3. 342, 4. 126, 5. 744, 8. 355, 9. 206, ABT 9. 374-5, BT 11. 297, 12. 430, 15. 381, 624, 740, 16. 379, ABT 17. 652-3, BT 21. 9-10, 361, 362, 22. 146, 24. 212. ἐνέργεια (vigour) can be used in a similar way (and the MSS confuse this with ἐνάργεια). Cf. esp. BT 12. 461: πανταχόθεν ἐκίνησε τὴν ἐνέργειαν, in every way he has evoked dramatic vigour, followed by a detailed catalogue of all the elements in the scene which make it so vivid and dramatic. Cf. also BT 10. 369, T 20. 48. Normally,

The other main quality of this style is said to be πιθανότης (persuasiveness), the ability to make one's narrative credible (cf. Demetrius 208, 221f.). We have already seen this associated with the use of divine interventions to account for extraordinary events, and the principle that one should not over-elaborate but leave one's audience to fill in some details themselves is also said to be an aspect of πιθανότης (Demetrius 222). πιθανότης is in fact an aspect of Homer's style in general, but it is especially shown in the way he gives realistic and circumstantial details of places or characters, as for example in the brief sketch of Simoeisius: ταῦτα δὲ εἶπε πολλὴν πίστιν ἐπιφέρων τῷ λόγῳ ὡς αὐτόπτης ὤν, in saying this he has given his description great credibility, as though he were an eyewitness (BT 4.473; cf. 470, 2. 673, T 11. 167, 772, BT 13. 171, 14. 225-7, T 16. 328). Elsewhere, a small touch gives life and persuasiveness to an incident, as when Odysseus forgets his whip after the killing of Rhesus (BT 10. 500), or when Patroclus routs the Trojans and the Greek ship is left 'half-burnt' (BT 16. 293-4). Extraordinary events, so often the material for criticism of Homer's credibility, are also defended, sometimes in a way which seems to us literal-minded: for instance, when Mydon falls on his head in the deep sand and remains there upside down, they give an elaborate explanation of how this could really happen (BT 5. 587)! On the other hand, when Achilles alone is nearly washed away by the river, they admit that this is ἀπίθανον, implausible, but follow the Aristotelian principle that its dramatic effectiveness is such that the hearer does not stop to reflect on its probability (BT 21. 269; cf. Arist. *Poet.* 1460ᵃ11 ff., especially 26f. and 35 ff.).

πιθανότης and ἐνάργεια are closely linked, and both depend on the power of *visualization* (cf. Arist. *Poet.* 1455ᵃ22 ff.). The visual or sometimes pictorial qualities of a scene are often noticed. The sacrifice on the shore at Chrysa is an 'impressive spectacle' (B 1. 316), the white fat mingling with the dark smoke φανταστικῶς, in an imaginative way (ABT 1. 317), and the poet 'paints a fair picture' of the return voyage (BT 1. 481). The famous nod of Zeus to Thetis was the inspiration for the works of Pheidias and Euphranor (AT 1. 528-30). The comparison of Menelaus' wounded thigh to ivory stained with

---

however, ἐνέργεια is used for personification of inanimate objects. These qualities could really be classified as well or better under the grand or powerful style, and this shows the essential artificiality of the whole system.

purple gives us an ὄψιν γραφικήν, vivid picture (BT 4. 141), and the scene of Hector smiling at his child and Andromache crying is also 'graphic' (BT 6. 405). The description of Hera dressing and making herself beautiful is contrasted with the work of artists who show women naked: Homer does not do so, but 'he has portrayed her in words more effectively than in colours' (BT 14. 187). Ajax's retreat in book 16 is 'more vivid than a painting', and the forceful repetition of words in 104–5 is not imitable by artists (BT 16. 104, T 107).[44] Another term to describe any especially vivid or striking image or visualization is φαντασία (imagination, imagery).[45] The famous scene before the Theomachy, when Zeus thunders, Poseidon shakes the earth, and Hades leaps up in terror, is an obvious example of φαντασία (T 20. 56; cf. 'Longinus' 9. 6). Quieter, but equally effective, is the portrayal of Thetis coming out of the sea 'like mist' (BT 1. 359). The opening of the fighting is marked by the appearance of the deities of war, Ares, Athene, and their associates Terror, Panic, and Strife, creating a μεγαλοπρεπὴς φαντασία, an impressive image (BT 4. 439), and Zeus holding his hand over Troy is another striking image of this kind (ABT 9.420). Such scenes involve gods (cf. BT 3. 385), but this is not always so, and vivid images of battle or contest have a similar effect (cf. BT 7. 62, 8. 62–3, 11. 534, 15. 712, 21. 3). Thus, the description of the chariot race in 23. 362 ff. is so well portrayed that the poet's audience see it as clearly as the spectators (BT; cf. Demetrius 209 f.).

The *similes* have already been mentioned several times, and many of the most appreciative comments of the Scholia concern them.[46] Their general functions are seen as contributing ἐνάργεια, αὔξησις, κόσμος, and relief from the narrative. Unlike many (but not all) modern scholars, however, the Scholia tend to regard the detailed elaboration of the similes as adding significantly to the effect of the scene with which they are compared, and they often admire their

---

[44] Cf. also A 3. 327, BT 4. 541, 5. 82, 6. 468, 10. 524, 11. 282, 12. 463–5, T 13. 11, BT 13. 281, 597, T 14. 285, BT 16. 470, T 17. 85, 136, 18. 586, BT 18. 603–4, 19. 282, T 20. 162, BT 21. 67–8, T 21. 175, BT 21. 325, 22. 61–2, 80, T 22. 97, 367, BT 22. 474, T 24. 163. Comparison between literature and the visual arts was common in antiquity. Cf. also R. W. Lee, 'Ut pictura poesis: The Humanistic Theory of Painting', *The Art Bulletin*, 22 (1940), 199 ff., for the development of such ancient parallels in the Renaissance.

[45] Cf. Quint. 6. 2. 29 ff., 'Longinus' 15 with D. A. Russell's commentary, and Von Franz, *Anschauungen*, 19 ff.

[46] For an extensive discussion see the work of Clausing (*Kritik*).

close correspondence or ἀκρίβεια (accuracy). For example, when
Athene deflects Pandarus' arrow and saves Menelaus, as a mother
deflects a fly from her sleeping child, they say: 'the mother indicates
Athene's favour towards Menelaus, the fly suggests the ease with
which it is swatted away and darts to another place, the child's sleep
shows Menelaus being caught off guard, and the weakness of the
blow' (BT 4. 130). In the same book the meeting of the two armies is
compared with the confluence of two mountain torrents (452 ff.).

Here you can hear the sound of the two rivers, and the whole description
adds to the effect (ηὔξησε) of the sound. For they do not flow through the
plains but from a mountain, thus creating not a flow but a rush of water; and
they come down to the same place, making the sound great by the
collision of their streams; and he adds 'from great springs', thus evoking a
harsh din by the quantity of the torrential water; and the hollow place which
receives them is called a μισγάγκεια (confluence of glens) making a harsh
*onomatopoeia* and adding to the threatening impression of the stream.
Perhaps also he has used a comparison with two rivers not only for greater
effect (αὔξησις), but also because there are two armies clashing with each
other. (BT)[47]

A simpler instance where they detect a correspondence which the
poet surely intended is in the comparison of the fall of Simoeisios,
who was born by the banks of the river Simoeis, to the fall of a tree
growing beside a river (BT 4. 484). When Hector pursuing the
Greeks is compared to a dog in pursuit of a single fleeing lion or wild
boar, they defend the details of the simile: Hector pursues them one
at a time, 'always killing the last man' (342), and the comparison is
primarily one of speed, the dog being quicker, but the Greeks are also
compared to the stronger and more valiant animal (ABT 8. 338). The
comparison of the retreating Ajax with a donkey being driven from a
corn-field by children is praised for its detailed correspondence (BT
11. 558). The simile suggests Ajax's contempt for the Trojans, and
their feebleness. The beast's greediness indicates his stubborn stand,
and the fact that he is grazing shows the slowness of Ajax's retreat.
The donkey is described as lazy and inured to much beating, having
had many sticks broken on his back: all this adds to the effect of
stubbornness. When the Greeks defending their gates are compared
by Asios to wasps or bees defending their homes on a road, the

---

[47] Cf. Virgil's echo of this simile, to describe Aeneas and Turnus raging over the
battlefield (*Aen.* 12. 523 ff.).

simile both shows their spirit and also is slightly derogatory, which is suitable in an enemy's mouth (BT 12. 167). When the Trojans pouring over the Achaean wall are like a great wave pouring over the sides (τοίχων) of a ship in a violent storm, they comment that ἀεὶ ἑαυτὸν παρευδοκιμεῖ ὁ ποιητὴς ταῖς ὁμοιώσεσιν· τί γὰρ ἐναργέστερον ἢ ἐμφαντικώτερον ἢ καθάπαξ συμφωνότερον ταύτης τῆς εἰκόνος; the poet always surpasses himself in his similes: for what could be more vivid or expressive or altogether appropriate than this image? (BT 15. 381). In the comparison of Patroclus to a marauding lion, wounded in the chest, 'whose valour brought his doom', they rightly admire this foreshadowing of Patroclus' death (BT 16. 752–3), and when Achilles' grief for Patroclus is compared to that of a lioness whose cubs have been stolen by a hunter, and who searches the glens for the man who has taken them, they note the appropriateness of this elaboration, suggesting Achilles' desire to take vengeance on Hector (BT 18. 318). Again, when his lament for Patroclus is like a father's for the death of his newly married son, this shows not only the depth of Achilles' love but also the poignancy of the loss, as the son had come of age and the father had lost not only his child but his hopes of grandchildren (BT 23. 222). These and many other examples[48] show their sensibility to the less obvious implications and wider resonance of the similes. It it easy to disparage this approach, as the product of a more sophisticated literary age, judging Homer by standards suitable for Apollonius Rhodius or Virgil. It would be more valuable to return to the *Iliad* itself, to see how often the Scholia do in fact appreciate more fully than we do the way in which similes enhance the poem.

They are also sensitive to what one might call the symbolic aspects of the similes: for example, when Hector's onslaught is like a reckless boulder bounding down a mountain, 'the barbarian and irrational onrush' is appropriately compared to an inanimate weight rolling onward unchecked (BT 13. 137; cf. 13. 39, etc.).[49] Another function of similes is to make visible what cannot easily be described or imagined, because of its extraordinary character. Hence they are

---

[48] Cf. ABT 2. 87, BT 3. 222, 6. 509, ABT 9. 4, BT 11. 113, ABT 12. 278, BT 12. 433, 13. 39, 137, 298, 14. 394–8, 15. 324, 618, 679, 690, 16. 406, 633, T 16. 756–7, BT 17.53, 61, 263, 434, ABT 17. 657, BT 17. 676, 747, 755, 18. 161, 207, B 18. 220, BT 20. 490, T 20. 495, BT 21. 12, 22, 522–3, 22. 199–201.

[49] On this see R. R. Schlunk, *The Homeric Scholia and the Aeneid* (Ann Arbor, 1974), 42 ff.

drawn from material familiar to the audience, and often from commonplace things, dignified by Homer's language, such as the child's sand-castle (BT 15. 362), or grasshoppers flying from a fire (BT 21. 12; cf. 16. 7, A 16. 364, BT 17. 389, 570). The Scholia are also appreciative of the relationship of different similes to each other, and of the way in which multiple similes are used to build up a complex picture (ABT 2. 455, BT 2. 480, 6. 513, AB 11. 548, T 12. 132, ABT 12. 278, BT 14. 394–8, 15. 618, 624, 17. 4, 133, ABT 17. 657, BT 20. 490).[50]

On the relationship of simile to *metaphor*, and the way in which metaphorical language may anticipate or answer a simile, there are some interesting observations by Porphyry (*Quaestiones homericae* I, ed. Sodano, Nos. 6 and 17 = B 11. 269, 4. 447). He notes that there can be an interchange of language between narrative and simile, as (for instance) when swarms of bees are called ἔθνεα, tribes, in a comparison with the Greek troops (2. 87), or κορύσσεται (raises its crested head) is used of a wave compared to the advancing army (4. 424), and vice versa where Achilles' voice compared to a trumpet is called ὄπα χάλκεον, a brazen voice (18. 222). Thus a 'cloud of foot-soldiers' immediately suggests and is followed by the simile of a storm-cloud moving over the sea, whose language in turn suggests the movement of troops, and a comparison of Penelope's cheeks wet with tears to melting snow brings in its train the metaphorical τήκετο καλὰ παρήϊα δακρυχεούσης, her lovely cheeks dissolved as she wept (*Od* 19. 205 ff.). This kind of interaction has attracted the attention of modern critics also.[51]

In their analysis of *speeches* they reflect the prevalent ancient view of Homer as a model for orators.[52] Thus the 'three styles' find their representatives in Odysseus, Nestor, and Menelaus (ABT 3. 212–16). The styles of the four speakers in the Embassy are well defined (BT 9. 622): Ὀδυσσεὺς συνετός, πανοῦργος, θεραπευτικός· Ἀχιλλεὺς θυμικός, μεγαλόφρων· Φοῖνιξ ἠθικός, πρᾶος, παιδευτικός· Αἴας ἀνδρεῖος, σεμνός,

---

[50] On this aspect see H. Fränkel, *Die homeríschen Gleichnisse* (Göttingen, 1921), and C. Moulton, *Similes in the Homeric Poems* (Göttingen, 1977).

[51] See especially the elaborate treatment of the whole subject by M. S. Silk, *Interaction in Poetic Imagery* (Cambridge, 1974). His note on ancient views of Homeric imagery does not mention Porphyry (211 f.). See also D. A. West, *JRS* 59 (1969), 40 ff. on interaction and transfusion in the similes in the *Aeneid*.

[52] See G. A. Kennedy, *AJP* 78 (1957), 23 ff., H. North, *Traditio*, 8 (1952), 1 ff.; and for a modern analysis D. Lohmann, *Die Komposition der Reden in der Ilias* (Amsterdam, 1970).

μεγαλόφρων, ἁπλοῦς, δυσκίνητος, βαθύς, Odysseus is clever, ingenious, courteous; Achilles passionate and noble-minded; Phoenix moralizing, gentle, didactic; Ajax courageous, dignified, noble-minded, simple, hard to move, deep. The Scholia also analyse their speeches in detail in accordance with rhetorical techniques (BT 9. 225 ff.). Speeches of persuasion are often interpreted as highly artificial and sophisticated, suggesting something covertly (λεληθότως), in contrast to their surface meaning. Thus Agamemnon's speech to the army in Book 2 is really intended as an encouragement to remain at Troy (BT 2. 110).[53] Helen's speeches are designed to win the Trojans' favour (Aristotle, fr. 147 *ap.* B 3. 237, BT 6. 344). Zeus and Hera bargain rhetorically with each other, emphasizing the extent of their concessions (ABT 4. 51). This approach may well seem out of place to us, but we recognize how much of Homer's individual invention is invested in the speeches. A particular device which is noted is the use of παραδείγματα (precedents, exemplary tales) or μῦθοι for persuasion or consolation, as in the reminiscences of Nestor and Phoenix:[54] their observations here are very pertinent, and they are quick to note not only the parallelism of the Meleager story with Achilles' situation, but also the relevance to this of what Phoenix says of his own past life (448 ff.).[55] Notice too their first-class observation about *silence*, when Antilochus is speechless at the news of Patroclus' death: πανταχόθεν ἐπεσημήνατο τὸ πένθος, μάλιστα δὲ ἐκ τοῦ μηδὲ πυθέσθαι τὸν τρόπον τῆς τελευτῆς. γίνεται οὖν ἡ σιωπὴ παντὸς λόγου μείζων, he has indicated his sorrow by every means, but above all because he does not even ask about the manner of his death. Consequently his silence is more powerful than any speech (BT 17. 695–8). There is a similar comment on Ajax's famous refusal to answer Odysseus at *Od.* 11. 563: δῆλον οὖν ὅτι καὶ τῶν παρὰ τραγῳδοῖς λόγων βέλτιον αὐτοῦ ἡ σιωπή, thus it is clear that his silence is better even than the speeches in the works of the tragic poets.[56] The dramatic effect of these episodes has some bearing on the question of silences in tragedy.[57]

[53] Cf. BT 14. 75, and [Dionysius of Halicarnassus], *On Contrived Speeches* (*Opuscula* 2. 310 ff.) and p. 188 above.
[54] BT 1. 262, 7. 132, 155, 9. 448, B9. 452, 480, BT 9. 527, 11. 670, 717, 785–6, A 18. 117, BT 24. 601–2.
[55] Cf. Austin, 'Function'.
[56] Cf. 'Longinus' 9.2, and W. Bühler, *Beiträge z. Erklärung der Schrift vom Erhabenen*, 15 ff.
[57] Cf. O. Taplin, 'Aeschylean Silences and Silences in Aeschylus', *HSCP* 76 (1972), 57 ff.

There are many other features of Homeric style and technique on which the Scholia have useful observations to make, and I will mention here only a few which seem to me particularly valuable. It was Aristarchus who first observed the well-known Homeric principle of ὕστερον (or δεύτερον) πρότερον, the later (or second) one first, itself only one form of the device of ring-composition, whereby the items in a list are picked up and repeated in reverse order.[58] Aristarchus, however, also noted contrary examples, and a collection of these by Epaphroditus is quoted by the Towneleian Scholia (15. 6-7).[59] They seem to reflect controversy over this point, saying ὅτι καὶ πρὸς τὸ πρῶτον ὑπαντᾷ ὁ ποιητής, note that the poet also answers the first point (i.e. the reverse of ὕστερον πρότερον), although this is obviously wrong. They also note instances of chiasmus, a related structural device (e.g. T 22. 158), and antithesis (e.g. BT 12. 417 ff., where there is also chiasmus). Complex sentence structure and parenthesis are observed (e.g. BT 3. 59, A 17. 608, and also A 2. 745, P. Oxy. 1086. 115 on 2. 819 ff., etc.).[60] A particularly involved example, with a parenthetic expansion of thirteen lines, is noted in Achilles' speech at 18. 101 ff. (BT; cf. Leaf ad loc.). They also observe the use of asyndeton and extended paratactic sentence-structure in speeches of anger (BT 3. 50-3). Asyndeton has perhaps never been used more effectively than where Hector in his last fight loses his spear and calls to Deiphobus for another:

στῆ, δὲ κατηφήσας, οὐδ' ἀλλ' ἔχε μειλινὸν ἔγχος.
Δηΐφοβον δὲ κάλει λευκάσπιδα μακρὸν ἀΰσας·
ἤτεέ μιν δόρυ μακρόν· ὁ δ' οὔτι οἱ ἐγγύθεν ἦεν.    (22. 293-5)

He stood downcast, for he had no other ashen spear.
And he called to Deiphobus with his white shield, giving a loud cry:
He asked him for a long spear: but he was nowhere near him.

Here they comment: ἡδέως χρῆται τῷ ἀσυνδέτῳ· ἀλλὰ καὶ τῇ ἐπιφορᾷ (repetition) ἐλεεινότατον, he effectively makes use of the asyndeton; but he also evokes great pathos with the repetition (T 22. 295).

Repetition and anaphora can be used for effect in many ways. The most famous rhetorical example was that of Nireus, with its

---

[58] Cf. A 2. 629, 763 and P. Oxy. 1086 i. 11 ff., A 4. 451, 7. 276, AT 11. 834-5, A 12. 400, T 15. 330-3, A 24. 605, Cicero ad Att. 1. 16. 1, and S. E. Bassett, HSCP 31 (1920), 39 ff.
[59] Cf. A 2. 621, 6. 219, T 15. 330-3, 16. 251, 22. 158.
[60] Cf. Schmidt, Erklärungen, 36-8.

double epanalepsis and asyndeton (2. 671ff.; cf. Arist. *Rhet.*
1414ᵃ2ff., Demetrius 61-2, A 2. 671). When the confused noise of
the advancing Trojan army is compared with the cries of cranes, the
triple repetition of κλαγγή (cry, scream) emphasizes the continual
din (ABT 3. 5). When Andromache foretells Hector's death, the
repetition of the pronoun 'you' suggests her love and dependence (BT
6. 411). In the description of Ajax's retreat, the insistent repetition of
different parts of βάλλειν to strike (βάλλοντες ... βαλλομένη ... βάλλετο:
striking ... being struck ... was struck) creates a powerful effect (BT
16. 104).⁶¹ Epanalepsis of a half-line, which occurs only three times
(20. 371-2, 22. 127-8, 23. 641-2), each time with what seems to
be a slightly different purpose, is noted in the first case as emphasizing the force of fire and strength of iron, in the second as suggesting
the long-drawn-out conversation of the young man and girl (ABT
20. 372, BT 22. 127).⁶² Repetition in a catalogue of an emphatic
word or simply of connective particles is recognized as a feature of
archaic style (T 10. 228, BT 17. 216-18).⁶³

A different form of repetition is that of *formulaic epithets*. Milman
Parry acknowledged that Aristarchus had already recognized the
general or formulaic character of many epithets, in cases where they
did not seem to fit the immediate context.⁶⁴ The BT Scholia and
Porphyry echo his views, although they are aware of other attempts
to explain such cases (e.g. BT 8. 555). Eustathius also has a good
comment on the use of θρασὺν Ἕκτορα 'bold Hector' at 24. 786
(1376. 12): 'the poet preserves the fine epithets for the heroes in a
dignified way, even when they cannot act in accordance with them,
and in this way as it were keeps them as treasures (κειμήλιοι) for
them'. At the same time we can now see that Parry was too vigorous
in denying that such epithets could ever have a more specific effect.
We can also sympathize with such comments as that on 21. 218,
where Scamander complains that his lovely waters (ἐρατεινὰ ῥέεθρα)

---

⁶¹ Cf. also 2. 382-4, 'Well let a man sharpen his spear, well set his shield,/ Well let
one give a meal to his swift-footed horses/ Well let one look about his chariot and have
a care for warfare' for *epanaphora* and *homoeoteleuton* together (ABT 2.382). L. P.
Wilkinson observes that anaphora is relatively rare in Homer, and hence all the more
striking when it does occur (*Golden Latin Artistry* (Cambridge, 1966), 66 f.).

⁶² Eustathius regards such repetition as spontaneous (ἐνδιάθετος) and realistic
(1211. 44, 1321. 44).

⁶³ See also Demetrius, *On Style* 54, Dionysius of Halicarnassus, *On the Arrangement
of Words* 16 (*ad fin.*), on repetition and variation in the Catalogue of Ships.

⁶⁴ Cf. *The Making of Homeric Verse* (Oxford, 1971), 120ff.

are choked with corpses: 'the epithet is well-used to show that it is waters of such quality which are polluted' (BT). Parry unjustly criticized this comment (p. 120). He ought to have noted that this phrase is in fact unique in Homer!

Another important aspect of Homeric language which ancient scholars appreciated was the poet's tendency when using rare or archaic words to add a phrase which explained their sense, or alternatively to suggest their *etymology* by a related word, as with ἤτοι ὁ κὰπ πεδίον τὸ Ἀλήϊον οἶος ἀλᾶτο, then did he go wandering alone about the Aleian (Wandering) Plain (6. 201). Porphyry has a long discussion of this, which begins with the famous statement that as Homer often explains himself one should interpret him by his own evidence (Ὅμηρον ἐξ Ὁμήρου σαφηνίζειν, interpret Homer from Homer) and he lists many other examples.[65] This Homeric technique of etymology has been seen as a kind of foreshadowing of later scholarly work on epic language.[66]

The Scholia also observe the poet's ability to *invent names* for his characters which suit their situation. Thus the daughters of Agamemnon in 9. 145, Chrysothemis, Laodice, and Iphianassa, all have names appropriate to a ruling family (ABT). Aristarchus noted that the poet was ὀνοματοθετικός (an inventor of names).[67] Interest in Homeric names goes back at least to Prodicus, who observed that Bathycles was so-called because of his father Chalcon's wealth in bronze (T 16. 594 f.).[68]

IV. SOUND AND RHYTHM

Finally, there is an aspect of Homeric verse which seldom receives the attention it deserves, whereas the Scholia have many useful observations on it. This is sound and rhythm.[69] The modern

---

[65] Schol. B 6. 201 = *Quaestiones Homericae* I, No. 11. Cf. also A 6. 200, T 7. 278, A 9. 137, BT 13. 281, 14. 176, T 14. 178, ABT 14. 518, T 15. 536.

[66] Cf. Pfeiffer, *History of Classical Scholarship*, i. 3 ff.

[67] Cf. A 5. 60, A 6. 18, AT 12. 342, etc.

[68] Note also Democritus, D.-K. 68 B 24: Eumaeus' mother was called Penia! As Eumaeus' father is called Ctesios (*Od.* 15. 414), it looks as if Democritus intends an allegory like that of Poros and Penia as parents of Eros.

[69] In general see W. B. Stanford, *The Sound of Greek* (University of California Press, 1967), who discusses the views of ancient critics such as Dionysius of Halicarnassus, and also Wilkinson, *Golden Latin Artistry*, 9 ff.

tendency to pay special attention to the traditional or formulaic character of the verse does not encourage sensitivity to the way in which the poet fits sound to sense in particular contexts, whereas the ancient emphasis on *mimesis* naturally led to appreciation of this. The Scholia often note the *harshness* or rough sound of lines or phrases, e.g.: BT 2. 210, αἰγιαλῷ μεγάλῳ βρέμεται, σμαραγεῖ δέ τε πόντος, roars on the mighty shore, and the sea resounds (simile); BT 2. 463, κλαγγηδὸν προκαθιζόντων, σμαραγεῖ δέ τε λειμών, as they settle down with loud cries, and the meadow resounds (simile); BT 3. 358 = BT 7. 252, καὶ διὰ θώρηκος πολυδαιδάλου ἠρήρειστο, and through the richly patterned breastplate it thrust its way, where the last word 'suggests the force of the blow'; B 13. 181 ὣς πέσεν, ἀμφὶ δέ οἱ βράχε τεύχεα ποικίλα χάλκῳ,[70] thus he fell, and about him rang his armour patterned with bronze; BT 16. 792 χειρὶ καταπρηνεῖ, στρεφεδίνηθεν δέ οἱ ὄσσε, with the flat of his hand, and his eyes whirled round, where the unusual compound of στρέφω (turn) and δινέω (whirl) is said to produce a harsh effect, again suggesting the force of the blow; BT 23. 30, πολλοὶ μὲν βόες ἀργοὶ ὀρέχθεον ἀμφὶ σιδήρῳ, many shining oxen bellowed around the iron, where ὀρέχθεον(bellowed) imitates their bellowing; BT 23. 396, θρυλίχθη δὲ μέτωπον ἐπ' ὀφρύσι . . . (and his forehead over his eyebrows was shattered) where θρυλίχθη (was shattered) describes the face shattered in the crash, and at 23. 392 they also comment on the imitation of the sound of the breaking chariot in ἵππειον δέ οἱ ἦξε θεὰ ζυγόν, and the goddess broke his horse's yoke (BT), presumably referring to the harsh brevity of ἦξε (broke).

It is especially the similes which produce such effects, and of these most commonly the sea and river scenes. Thus of 13. 798 f.

> κύματα παφλάζοντα πολυφλοίσβοιο θαλάσσης,
> κυρτὰ φαληριόωντα, πρὸ μέν τ' ἄλλ', αὐτὰρ ἐπ' ἄλλα

blustering waves of the surging sea, swollen, foam-crested, some in front, and others behind,

they say that by the harshness of composition of the letters the poet imitates the noise, and the similar endings of the words also contribute to the effect of incessant waves, whilst παφλάζοντα

---

[70] Cf. *Od.* 21. 48–9, ἀνέβραχεν . . . ἔβραχε (roared about . . . roared) of doors, quoted at B 8. 393 on πύλαι μύκον, the gates bellowed where μύκον (bellowed) is also said to be 'onomatopoeic'.

(blustering) especially imitates their sound, κυρτά (swollen) their size, and φαληριόωντα (foam-crested) their colour (BT). At 15. 624 ff.

λαβρὸν ὑπαὶ νεφέων ἀνεμοτρεφές· ἡ δέ τε πᾶσα
ἄχνη ὑπεκρύφθη (etc.)

raging, wind-nourished by the clouds, and all the ship is covered by spray

the κόμπος (roaring) and ψόφος (din) of the language 'do not allow one to see the ship, hidden as it is by spray' (BT 15. 625). In the simile of the flooded rivers pouring down to a junction in the hills, already discussed, the language suggests the din:

ὡς δ᾽ ὅτε χείμαρροι ποταμοὶ κατ᾽ ὄρεσφι ῥέοντες
ἐς μισγάγκειαν συμβάλλετον ὄβριμον ὕδωρ
κρουνῶν ἐκ μεγάλων κοίλης ἔντοσθε χαράδρης,
τῶν δέ τε τηλόσε δοῦπον ἐν οὔρεσιν ἔκλυε ποιμήν·
ὡς τῶν μισγομένων γένετο ἰαχή τε πόνος τε.   (4. 452 ff.)

And as when torrential rivers flowing down from the mountains
unite their mighty waters in a confluence of glens
from great well-heads, within a hollow ravine,
and the shepherd in the mountains hears their roar from far away:
just so as they mingled together was their shouting and trouble.

This is achieved especially by the harsh sound of some of the words, such as μισγάγκειαν (confluence of glens) (BT).[71] The most celebrated of these similes was 17. 263 ff., which was supposed to have caused Plato (or Solon) to burn his poetry in despair:

ὡς δ᾽ ὅτ᾽ ἐπὶ προχοῇσι διιπετέος ποταμοῖο
βέβρυχεν μέγα κῦμα ποτὶ ῥόον, ἀμφὶ δέ τ᾽ ἄκραι
ἠϊόνες βοόωσιν ἐρευγομένης ἁλὸς ἔξω,
τόσσῃ ἄρα Τρῶες ἰαχῇ ἴσαν . . .

and as when at the mouth of a river rain-fed from heaven,
a great wave roars against the current, and on either side the jutting
headlands boom as the salt sea spews outside,
so great was the shout with which the Trojans advanced . . .

Here the sea's rush meets the water pouring from the river, swollen by rain, and the echo of their roar is expressed in ἠϊόνες βοόωσιν (headlands boom), with the *diectasis* (metrical extension) of the verb (BT).[72]

---

[71] Cf. p. 188 above, and also Dionysius 16.
[72] Cf. Arist. *Poet.* 1458[b]31, Dionysius 15.

A similar effect is produced in 14. 394 (T): οὔτε θαλάσσης κῦμα τόσον βοάᾳ ποτὶ χέρσον, neither does the sea's wave roar so loud upon the shore. This shows that *diectasis* was not necessarily merely a metrical device, but could also be artistic. Likewise they find that the metrical lengthening of the last word in 7. 208, σεύατ᾽ ἔπειθ᾽ οἷός τε πελώριος ἔρχεται Ἄρης, then he rushed forward as giant Ares advances (simile), suggests the appearance and broad advance of Ajax (BT). Demetrius (48 and 105) finds grandeur in the harshness of sound of 16. 358, Αἴας δ᾽ ὁ μέγας αἰὲν ... (and mighty Ajax always ...) and vigour in the 'cacophony' of 12. 208, Τρῶες δ᾽ ἐρρίγησαν, ὅπως ἴδον αἰόλον ὄφιν, the Trojans shuddered, as they saw the writhing snake, a στίχος μείουρος, tapering verse (verse which tails off) which the Scholia also admire as expressing the consternation of the Trojans by its sudden ending (T)![73]

Long vowels in themselves can help to create an effect of size or grandeur, as in 12. 134, ῥίζῃσιν μεγάλῃσι διηνεκέεσσ᾽ ἀραρυῖαι, fixed fast by their great downstretching roots (simile; BT), and 12. 339–40, βαλλομένων σακέων τε καὶ ἱπποκόμων τρυφαλειῶν καὶ πυλέων ... (as shields were battered and horse-crested helmets and the gates), where the repeated genitive endings are emphatic (T).

The Scholia are quick to pick up other instances of *mimesis* and *onomatopoeia* in single words and phrases, such as λίγξε (twanged) of a bow's twang (BT 4. 125), ἀποβλύζων (dribbling out) of a child bringing up wine (BT 9. 491), βαμβαίνων (chattering) and ἄραβος (chatter) of chattering teeth (A 10. 375), καρφαλέον ... ἄϋσεν (rang drily) of a shield whose rim is struck by a spear (BT 13. 409), αὖον ἄϋσεν ἐρεικόμενος (rasped drily as it was rent) of a bronze corslet torn by a spear (BT 13. 441), λάκε (cried) of armour struck by swords and spears (T 14. 25), ἀνεκυμβαλίαζον (fell tumbling over), a βουβῶδες ῥῆμα (booming expression) which suggests chariots being overturned (BT 16. 379), and χρόμαδος (grinding) of wrestlers' teeth (ABT 23. 688).[74] They also consider that ἀγκαλίδεσσι (in the dear arms) suits

---

[73] On 'cacophony' see also Demetrius 219, where he quotes as vivid *Od.* 9. 289 κόπτ᾽ ἐκ δ᾽ ἐγκέφαλος χαμάδις ῥέε, δεῦε δὲ γαῖαν, he cut, and the brain flowed out, and wetted the ground, and *Il.* 23. 116 πολλὰ δ᾽ ἄναντα κάταντα πάραντά τε δόχμιά τ᾽ ἦλθον, and often upwards and downwards and sideways and crossways they went.

[74] Cf. Demetrius 94 and 220, quoting σίζε, sizzled (*Od.* 9. 394) and λάπτοντες γλώσσῃσι, lapping with their tongues, (*Il.* 16.161). Demetrius admires Homer's ability to imitate sounds and to create new words. Dionysius (16) mentions βρέμεται (roars) and σμαραγεῖ (crackles) (*Il.* 2. 210), κλάγξας (shrieking) (12. 207), ῥοῖζον

the smallness of the child being held in his nurse's arms (ABT 22.
503), and (ingeniously) that *tmesis* (word-division) can imitate the
idea of an axe cutting in ἵνα τάμῃ διὰ πᾶσαν (cuts the sinew wholly in
two) (BT 17. 522), or of a lion tearing a bull to pieces in λέων κατὰ
ταῦρον ἐδηδώς (a lion which has eaten a bull entirely) (BT 17. 542).
In the second case they point out that this was not metrically necessary, as one could have said ταυρὸν κατεδηδώς (a lion which has
entirely eaten), and they compare Anacreon's διὰ δὲ δείρην ἔκοψε
μέσην (he cut the neck in two in the middle), and κὰδ δὲ λῶπος ἐσχίσθη
(wholly the cloak was slit, fr. 441 Page).

*Smoothness* and *euphony* were much discussed in antiquity, and
although the Scholia notice such effects less often they have a few
observations of this sort.[75] Conjunctions of vowels were thought to
create a liquid sound, as in 22. 135

> ἢ πυρὸς αἰθομένου ἢ ἠελίου ἀνιόντος (BT)
>
> either of blazing fire or of the rising sun

or 22. 152

> ἢ χιόνι ψυχρῇ, ἢ ἐξ ὕδατος κρυστάλλῳ (BT)
>
> or frozen snow, or water turned to ice.[76]

When the death of Euphorbus is compared to the fall of an olive tree
(17. 53 ff.) they acutely observe the contrast between the smoothness
of sound in the first part and the harshness of the pathetic close (BT
17. 58):

> οἷον δὲ τρέφει ἔρνος ἀνὴρ ἐριθηλὲς ἐλαίης
> χώρῳ ἐν οἰοπόλῳ, ὅθ' ἅλις ἀναβέβροχεν ὕδωρ,
> καλὸν τηλέθαον· τὸ δέ τε πνοιαὶ δονέουσι
> παντοίων ἀνέμων, καί τε βρύει ἄνθεϊ λευκῷ·
> ἐλθὼν δ' ἐξαπίνης ἄνεμος σὺν λαίλαπι πολλῇ
> βόθρου τ' ἐξέστρεψε καὶ ἐξετάνυσσ' ἐπὶ γαίῃ ...

---

(whistle) and δοῦπον (thud) (16. 361), and ῥοχθεῖ (crashes) (*Od.* 5. 402). Quintilian
cites λίγξε βιός (the bow twanged) and σίζ' ὀφθαλμός (his eye sizzled) as 'justly admired'
(1. 5. 72).

[75] See esp. Demetrius 68 ff., Dionysius, *passim*, Stanford, *Sound of Greek*, esp. pp.
48 ff.

[76] Cf. Demetrius 69 ff. (citing Αἰακός, χιών, Αἰαίη, Εὔιος, ἠέλιος, ὀρέων, Aiakos,
snow, Aiaiē, Euios, sun (Helios), of mountains, etc.). On the other hand, a concur-
rence of long vowels between two words could produce an effect of grandeur and
strain, as in the famous passage in the *Odyssey* about Sisyphus (cf. Demetrius 72,
Dionysius 20, Schol. *Od.* 11. 596, Eust. 1701. 55, 1702. 19-23).

and as a man nourishes a flourishing shoot of olive
in a lonely place, where plenty of water wells up,
fine and healthy; the breaths of all the winds
shake it, and it is laden with white flowers:
then suddenly a wind comes with a mighty tempest
and uproots it from its trench and lays it flat on the ground . . .

Special *rhythmic or metrical effects* are also noticed. When Zeus' nod
makes Olympus tremble the speed of the syllables in the dactylic line

κρατὸς ἀπ' ἀθανάτοιο, μέγαν δ' ἐλέλιξεν Ὀλυμπον

from his immortal head, and he made great Olympus tremble

suggests the speed of Zeus' movement, and especially the trembling
of the mountain (ABT 1. 530). The brevity of ἆλτο δ' ὀιστός (and the
arrow sprang) and κόψε (cut) suggests speed (BT 4. 125, 12. 204).
They also note that 12. 381 is entirely dactylic, although apparently
for no special reason (BT).[77] The A Scholia observe that 11. 130 is
wholly spondaic:

Ἀτρείδης· τὼ δ' αὖτ' ἐκ δίφρου γουναζέσθην.

The son of Atreus: and those two supplicated him from their chariot

They must therefore have scanned Ἀτρείδης (Atreides) as three
syllables. They compare *Od.* 21. 15, and add that such lines are
rare and metrically unattractive.[78] *Il.* 23. 221 is also noted as
δωδεκασύλλαβος, having twelve syllables, i.e. spondaic (T):

ψυχὴν κικλήσκων Πατροκλῆος δειλοῖο.

invoking the spirit of wretched Patroclus

Here the heavy rhythm is obviously appropriate.
*The structure of the line* also receives occasional notice. 3. 182

ὦ μάκαρ Ἀτρείδη, μοιρηγενές, ὀλβιόδαιμον

O blessed son of Atreus, child of fate and favourite of fortune

is unusual because 'the expression of praise is built up in a climactic
way, each word being a syllable longer than the last' (BT). This
'rhopalic' (club-shaped) verse is used at the other end of classical

---

[77] So in fact is 12. 380 also. Dactylic lines such as 6. 511, 13. 30, 20. 497, 24. 691
are probably intended to suggest speed. Cf. also *Od.* 11. 598 (Sisyphus' stone again),
*Hom. Hy. Dem.* 89, 171, 184, 380.
[78] Cf. Demetrius 42, on spondaic rhythms in prose.

poetry by Ausonius for a whole Christian poem of 42 lines beginning 'Spes, Deus, aeternae stationis conciliator' (O God, our hope, provider of our eternal home). There is no doubt that Priam's exclamation is a unique and impressive line (the last two words of which occur nowhere else in Greek literature), whether or not the poet was aware of the special structure which he was producing.

Three-word lines are also rare and striking.[79] The Scholia note an instance at 11. 427. Others are 2. 706, 15. 678, *Od.* 10. 137, 12. 133a, *Hom. Hy. Dem.* 31, *Hy.* 27. 3, Hes. *Op.* 383. Most of these begin with αὐτοκασίγνητος (very own brother) or a similar compound of κασίγνητος (brother).

Pauses (and perhaps also caesurae) already attracted some attention at an early stage. A pause after a trochee in the fifth foot is not permitted (A 12. 49, BT 12. 434), and a pause after the first long syllable of the fifth foot is rare (A 15. 360; cf. Maas, *Greek Metre*, § 88).[80] A pause after the trochee in the second foot is also considered unusual in Homer (A 1. 356).[81]

Finally, I have noticed one interesting instance of a remark about *recitation*. When Patroclus arms for battle they say that this passage should be recited quickly, to imitate his haste to prepare for the fight (T 16. 131). As the lines are largely formulaic, this could presumably be done without fear that the audience would lose track of the sense.

[79] Cf. S. E. Bassett, *CP* 12 (1917), 97 ff. and my notes on *Hom. Hy. Dem.* 31. See also Bassett, 'Versus tetracolos', *CP* 14 (1919), 216 ff.

[80] This provides added support for Aristarchus' condemnation of 24. 556, although this fact is not mentioned by the Scholia. 557 is also metrically suspect (cf. Leaf). Aristarchus' reading at *Il.* 9. 394, γυναῖκά γε μάσσεται (will surely seek for a wife) avoids the rare trochaic caesura in the fourth foot which occurs with γυναῖκα γαμέσσεται (will give a wife in marriage) (Maas, *Greek Metre*, § 87), but we do not know why he preferred this reading.

[81] It is not clear whether the Scholia distinguish properly between word-break and pause. According to Aulus Gellius (18. 15) it was Varro who first noted the main caesura in the third foot, although it seems that metricians before him had already observed that the central part of the hexameter seldom consisted of a single unit of sense. See Bassett, *The Poetry of Homer* (University of California Press, 1938), 145 ff., and *CP* 11 (1916), 458 ff. (where he shows that Arist. *Metaph.* 1093[a]30 f. does *not* refer to the caesura).

# 9

## Stoic Readings of Homer

A. A. LONG

How did the Stoics read Homer? Common sense suggests that the
question must be complex. The evidence confirms this. Are we asking about Zeno or Posidonius? Should we mention Aristo's brilliant
parody of Homer's line about the Chimaera (*Il.* 6. 181) to mock the
Academic philosopher Arcesilaus (Diogenes Laertius 4. 33)? Or
Strabo's ingenious efforts to demonstrate Homer's geographical
expertise? Or Epictetus's remark that the *Iliad* is nothing but an idea
(φαντασία), because it would not have occurred if Paris and Menelaus
had not made their respective mistakes in regard to Helen (*Discourses*
1. 28. 10 ff.)? Stoic philosophers, like all educated Greeks, knew
Homer intimately and could use him as they saw fit. Were they also,
however, united in their acceptance of a general theory about the
meaning and interpretation of the epics and the philosophical value
of these poems from a Stoic viewpoint? The question cannot be
settled decisively from the surviving words of the early Stoics, but
modern scholars are not deterred from arriving at a virtual consensus about how it should be answered. Their theory, generally
asserted as a fact, is that Stoic philosophers, beginning around 300
BC with Zeno, the founder of the school, interpreted Homer himself as

In drafting and revising this paper, I have been helped by many people. It would not
have become even an embryonic idea but for the invitation from Bob Lamberton to
write on this topic. Before the paper was read to the Princeton conference, Tom
Rosenmeyer gave me detailed criticisms and encouraged me in my heresies. Like all
the conference participants, I benefited from the excellent discussions our work
received. Subsequently, Alan Bowen, Denis Feeney, and Jim Porter sent me further
comments, all of them trenchant and helpful, which I have tried to absorb and answer,
and I learned much from further discussion of the paper by audiences at Leiden and
Utrecht Universities. I am also grateful to Glenn Most, who gave me a copy of his fine
study 'Cornutus and Stoic Allegoresis' before it appeared in *ANRW* 2/36/3 (1989),
2014–65. Finally I thank my colleagues at Leiden University for housing me so
graciously during the final work of revision, and the National Endowment for the
Humanities, which provided me with a fellowship at this time.

a crypto-Stoic. In this paper I shall cast doubt on this theory and offer a different interpretation of the Stoics' generic interests in Homer.

According to this received opinion, the Stoics took Homer (and other early Greek poets, especially Hesiod) to have a correct understanding of the world—its physical structure and processes, its god(s), its basic causes and purposes—a correct understanding because it coincided with the Stoics' own philosophy of nature.[1] Thus, so the theory goes, the Stoics interpreted certain episodes in Homer, for instance the story at the beginning of *Iliad* 15 that Zeus punished Hera by hanging her from the sky by a golden chain, as deliberately *disguised* references to astronomy and natural phenomena. Crucial to this theory is the supposition that Homer often *means* something other than he *says*. Homer, the Stoics are supposed to have thought, really understood the world in the Stoics' way; but because he was a poet, he does not express Stoicism directly. He composed, in other words, on two levels: On the surface he offers an epic narrative about the deeds of gods and heroes, but what he is *really* talking about, and understands himself to be talking about, is the physical world in a sense acceptable to Stoic philosophers.

We can sum up this theory by the term 'allegory', taking allegory in its standard ancient definition: 'saying what is other—i.e., saying or meaning something other than what one seems to say.'[2] The Stoics, we are asked to believe, took Homer to be an allegorist; they interpreted the epics 'allegorically' because of assumptions that they made concerning the poet's philosophical understanding and methods of composition. That is the theory I propose to contest, but

---

[1] Because the theory, as I call it, has been taken to be a fact, no publication that I know of seeks to prove it, and I have to confess to endorsing it myself in 'Stoa and Sceptical Academy', *Liverpool Classical Monthly*, 5/8 (1980), 165-6. Characteristic statements of it can conveniently be found in Phillip De Lacy, 'Stoic Views of Poetry', *American Journal of Philology*, 69 (1948), 241-71 esp. 256-63, and in Rudolf Pfeiffer, *History of Classical Scholarship: From the Beginnings to the End of the Hellenistic Age* (Oxford, 1968), 237, which I discuss below. Some qualified dissent is offered by Peter Steinmetz, 'Allegorische Deutung und allegorische Dichtung in der alten Stoa' *Rh.M.* 129 (1986) 18-30; cf. also J. Tate, 'Plato and Allegorical Interpretation [2]', *CQ* 24 (1930), 7-10. The other studies that I have found most helpful are Glenn Most's article 'Cornutus and Stoic Allegoresis', and Fritz Wehrli, *Zur Geschichte der allegorischen Deutung Homers in Altertum* (Diss. Basel, 1928). For further references see the bibliographical citations given by Steinmetz and Most.

[2] Cf. Heraclitus, *Quaest. Hom.* 5. 2, and Anon., Περὶ ποιητικῶν τρόπων under ἀλληγορία in *Rhetores Graeci* 3. 207. 18-23 (Spengel). In the second passage, allegory is exemplified by the 'idea of devil' as signified by the word *snake*.

its proponents have never, to the best of my knowledge, made its implications fully explicit. Part of the difficulty of understanding what the Stoics were doing arises from the vagueness of the modern claim that they allegorized Homer.

Allegory is a very complex notion. Some preliminary clarification of it can be reached once we recognize that a text might be called allegorical in a strong sense or in a weak sense.[3] A text will be allegorical in a *strong* sense if its author composes with the intention of being interpreted allegorically. Familiar examples of such texts are Dante's *Divine Comedy*, Spenser's *Faerie Queen*, and Bunyan's *Pilgrim's Progress*. Such texts require their reader to take them allegorically; they are composed as allegories. A text will be allegorical in a *weak* sense if, irrespective of what its author intended, it invites interpretation in ways that go beyond its surface or so-called literal meaning. Examples include the stories of Pandora's box in Hesiod and Adam and Eve in Genesis. Such stories, as we today read them, seem to signify something general about the human condition which is quite other than their narrative content; but they are weak allegories because, in these cases, the allegorizing is a contribution by us, the readers, and not something that we know to be present in the text as originally constructed. In some sense, all literary interpretation is weak allegorizing—our attempt to say what a narrative *means*.[4] As we shall see in detail later, Heraclitus, the author of *Homeric Problems*, interpreted Homer as a strong allegorist. Yet even Heraclitus did not take Homer to be the author of an 'allegory'. As a literary genre, allegory is scarcely attested in antiquity before Prudentius (fourth century AD). Medieval and later allegories need to be put on one side in considering the scope of allegorizing in classical antiquity.

---

[3] The distinction is my own but influenced by the work of others, especially Maureen Quilligan, *The Language of Allegory* (Ithaca, NY, 1929), who (25–6) acutely distinguishes allegorical narrative from allegoresis, 'the literary criticism of texts'. See also D. Dawson, *Allegorical Readers and Cultural Revision in Ancient Alexandria* (Berkeley, 1992). For good remarks on the Greek terminology and recognition of how it may differ from 'allegory in the modern sense,' cf. N. J. Richardson, 'Homeric Professors in the Age of the Sophists' (Chapter 3 in this volume).

[4] Cf. Northrop Frye, *Anatomy of Criticism: Four Essays* New York, 1957), 89, and Robert Lamberton, who observes, in *Homer the Theologian* (Berkeley, 1986), 20, that allegorical interpretation 'can comprehend virtually the whole of what we call "interpretation" beyond mere parsing.'

According to the theory I propose to reject, the Stoics as a school took
Homer to be a strong allegorist in the way just explained. Instead, I
shall argue, it is doubtful whether they even took themselves to be
allegorizing *Homer's* meaning, i.e., interpreting the epic narratives,
in a weak sense. As the paper develops, I will offer a different account
of the Stoics' generic interest in Homer, and also, by the way, in
Hesiod. Before we come to grips with the details, something needs to
be said about why the question matters: What is at stake in our asking how the Stoics read Homer?


II


Homer was *the* poet for the Greeks. Children learned large parts of
the *Iliad* and *Odyssey* by heart as part of their primary education.
All Greek literature and art, and just about all Greek philosophy,
resonate against the background of Homer. Throughout classical
antiquity and well into the Roman Empire, Homer held a position in
Mediterranean culture that can only be compared with the position
the Bible would later occupy. The comparison is important if we are
to understand why, from as early as 500 B.C., the status and meaning of Homer were central questions for philosophers. Like the Bible
for the Jews, Homer offered the Greeks the foundation of their
cultural identity. Such texts, however, can only remain authoritative
over centuries of social and conceptual change if they can be brought
up to date, so to speak—I mean they must be capable of being given
interpretations that suit the circumstances of different epochs.[5]
When read literally, Homer was already out of date—physiologically
and ethically unacceptable—for the early Ionian thinkers Xenophanes and Heraclitus. It was probably their criticism that evoked
the first so-called allegorical defence of Homer. In the fifth century,
Metrodorus of Lampsacus (frs. A3–4 D–K) 'interpreted the heroes of
the *Iliad* as parts of the universe, and the gods as parts of the human
body. Agamemnon represented the αἰθήρ, Achilles the sun, Helen the
earth, Paris the air, Hector the moon.'[6] Crazy though this kind of

---

[5] The point is well stated by Albert Henrichs, 'Philosophy, the Handmaiden of
Theology,' *Greek, Roman and Byzentine Studies*, 9 (1968), 439.
[6] Cf. N. J. Richardson, 'Homeric Professors', p. 68 above. Tatian (Metrodorus fr. A3
D–K) describes Metrodorus as 'converting everything to allegory' (πάντα εἰς ἀλληγορίαν
μετάγων).

allegorizing seemed to many in antiquity, Metrodorus was not alone in his style of interpretation. Plato a few decades later (*Theaetetus* 153c) makes Socrates refer ironically to a proposal that the golden chain (with which Zeus challenges the other Olympians to a tug-of-war, *Il.* 8. 18–27) is 'nothing else but the sun.'

Metrodorus and his like seem to have taken Homer to be a strong allegorist—a poet who was really au courant with scientific theories but who chose to disguise them in a misleading narrative. Why would anyone suppose that a poet would do such a thing? Plato (*Protagoras* 316d) makes Protagoras say that Homer, Hesiod, and Simonides were really sophists—possessors and teachers of practical wisdom—who used poetry as a 'cover' for their real purposes in order to avoid unpopularity. Plato is probably ironical again here, but the kind of explanation he ascribes to Protagoras is essential to anyone who proposes, against the evidence of historical change, that an ancient author actually *intends* to give a contemporary message or a message that differs from the literal sense of his text. The message must be covert, esoteric, allegorical in the strong sense— and yet, somehow or other, open to the expert interpreter to disclose.

Later antiquity reveals many examples of such allegorical readings. One of the most famous is that of the Neoplatonists who interpreted the *Odyssey* as a spiritual journey through the Neoplatonic universe. Another example is the Jew Philo of Alexandria's interpretation of whole episodes in the Pentateuch, for instance Noah's construction of the ark, by means of Stoic and Platonic concepts. The author I want to focus on is the Heraclitus (not the famous Ephesian philosopher) who wrote a work called *Homeric Problems—Homer's Allegories Concerning the Gods*.[7] Nothing is known about this man's life or background or precisely when he wrote. His work probably dates from the first or second century AD.

Heraclitus announces his purpose very clearly at the beginning of his book. He intends to rescue Homer from the charge that his account of the gods is blasphemous. He states his primary point in his second sentence: 'If Homer was no allegorist, he would be completely impious.'[8] That is to say, if Homer's apparent meaning is his real

---

[7] The text has been excellently edited in the Budé series by Félix Buffière, *Héraclite: Allégories d'Homère* (Paris, 1962).

[8] Ὅμηρος] πάντα ἠσέβησεν, εἰ μηδὲν ἠλληγόρησεν.

meaning, his gods are violent, sexually corrupt, the very reverse of moral exemplars. As Heraclitus knows very well, Plato had banned Homer from his ideal state for just this reason. By interpreting Homer as a strong allegorist, Heraclitus sets out to save Homer from Plato's criticism (and also from Epicurean disparagement). He proceeds systematically through the epics, book by book, to illustrate Homer's 'allegorizations concerning the gods.' One example will suffice because Heraclitus's methods are monotonously similar. The 'theomachy'—the battle between the gods in *Iliad* 21—is not to be taken literally; rather, the warring gods are to be interpreted as natural elements and heavenly bodies: Apollo is the sun, Poseidon is water, Hera is air, etc. What Homer is really talking about in this passage is cosmology.

For Heraclitus, allegory is not an importation by the interpreter; it is not the interpreter's reading of a text but central to the text's, or rather, to the author's intent. He characterises allegory as 'a trope that consists in saying one thing but meaning something different from what one says' (5. 2), or a disjunction between 'what is said' (λεγόμενον) and 'what is thought' (νοούμενον, 5. 16). As justification for applying it to Homer, he gives examples from other poets— Archilochus's use of a storm at sea to signify the perils of war and Anacreon's image of a frisking horse as a way of insulting a girl-friend (5. 3–11). These examples, from our point of view, are cheating. They are metaphors, not allegories; or, if you want to say that all metaphors are allegories, then Homer is an allegorist (because he uses metaphors) but not the kind of allegorist Heraclitus needs to prove. However, Heraclitus is not interested in Homer's metaphors, but in his supposedly deliberate treatment of the gods as veiled references to natural phenomena. This is evident, for instance, in the following quotations: 'Homer conceals his philosophical mind,' 'the hidden truth in [Homer's] words,' and '[Homer] has signified to us the primary elements of nature.'[9] Heraclitus knows there are obvious objections to reading Homer in this way. He defends his position by alleging that philosophers such as Heraclitus, his Ephesian namesake, and Empedocles use allegory, and so there should be nothing surprising if the poet Homer does so too (24. 8).

Heraclitus's allegorical reading of Homer can rest there for the

---

[9] ὑποκρύπτεταί τις Ὁμήρῳ φιλόσοφος νοῦς (26. 3); τὴν ὑπολελησμένην ἐν τοῖς ἔπεσιν ἀλήθειαν (6. 5); ὑπεσήμηνεν ἡμῖν τὰ πρωτοπαγῆ στοιχεῖα τῆς φύσεως (23. 14).

present. We now come to the Stoics. Scholars have generally supposed that Heraclitus was a Stoic or that he at least followed Stoic precedent in his allegorization of Homer.[10] If that were so, and if (as was also supposed), Heraclitus was transmitting a Stoic reading of Homer that had been orthodox for centuries, there would be nothing to argue about: the Stoics will have interpreted Homer as a strong allegorist. Why does correctness on this point matter? If the standard theory is correct, the Stoics will have been primarily responsible for authorizing the allegorical interpretations of literature that we find in Philo, the Neoplatonists, and others because the Stoics were far and away the most influential philosophers during the Hellenistic and early Roman period. In that case, we learn something very important concerning both Stoicism and the interpretation of Homer. However, to anyone who respects the Stoics as serious philosophers this finding should be unwelcome. The Stoics were rationalists and they were also empiricists. They don't talk nonsense, and it is frankly non-sensical to suppose that Homer was a crypto-Stoic. In addition, what motivation could the Stoics have for such an enterprise as Heraclitus is engaged in? Why should it matter to them to save Homer's theo-logical credit at the cost of claiming, against all reason, that he is a strong allegorist?[11]

However, if Heraclitus were an orthodox Stoic, that would seem to settle the question. In fact, as Félix Buffière, the latest editor of Heraclitus, has carefully argued, there are no good grounds for thinking that Heraclitus was a Stoic.[12] Although he often draws on

---

[10] This is particularly evident in P. De Lacy's influential study, 'Stoic Views of Poetry', (see n. 1 above).

[11] No satisfactory answer to this question has been proposed, as G. Most recognizes in a careful discussion of the 'motivations' of Stoic 'allegoresis,' 'Cornutus and Stoic Allegoresis', 2018–23. The favorite answer is that the Stoics wanted Homer's support for their own philosophy. If, however, they had to allegorize Homer in order to make him appropriately Stoic, their procedure was egregiously circular, as Most points out. There is no evidence that the Stoics took Homer to be a philosopher or a Stoic sage. Indeed, Seneca, *Epistle* 88. 5, pokes fun at the whole idea of Homer's being a philo-sopher of any persuasion, including a Stoic. The joke would be in bad taste if the school of his allegiance had allegorized the poet in the way commonly proposed, though Seneca's position is compatible with the Stoic interpretation of Homer's poetry as a φιλοσόφημα, which Strabo (1. 2. 7) takes to be universally accepted.

[12] F. Buffière in *Héraclite: Allégories d'Homère*, pp xxxi–xxxix. Buffière's detachment of Heraclitus from Stoicism is unknown to or ignored by Michael Hilgruber, 'Dion Chrysostomos 36 (53), 4–5 und die Homerauslegung Zenons,' *Museum Helveticum* 46 (1989), 15–24. Hilgruber, 22, invokes Heraclitus in order to support his claim that Dio Chrysostom's account of Zeno ad loc. refers to Zeno's allegorization of Homer.

Stoic physics for the cosmology that his allegories ascribe to Homer, that alone does not make him a Stoic; by this date Stoicism has become a lingua franca for technical writers who are not themselves Stoics. In addition, Heraclitus includes doctrines that are non-Stoic and inconsistent with orthodox Stoicism.[13] Buffière concludes that Heraclitus was not affiliated with any specific philosophical school, and his arguments seem to me utterly convincing.[14]

There is a further crucial point that he does not make. If Heraclitus were simply drawing upon Stoic orthodoxy, his whole essay would be redundant and disingenuous. Because he does not support his approach to Homer by any appeal to the Stoics or, for that matter, to other authorities, the obvious implication is that he takes himself to be doing something not readily accessible in the way the standard theory would have us suppose. We are in no position, then, to infer from the work of Heraclitus that official Stoics interpreted Homer in his manner. He offers no confirmation for the theory that the Stoics took Homer to be a strong allegorist.

Unquestionably, Homer was important to the Stoics. The founding fathers of Stoicism—Zeno, Cleanthes, Chrysippus, none of whom were from mainland Greece—developed a philosophy that would appropriate, as far as possible, traditional Greek culture. Contrast the Athenian Epicurus, who rejected Homer as part of his radical program to abandon all παιδεία (*Epicurea* 228-9 Usener). The Cypriot arriviste Zeno could not have been more different. He wrote five books of *Homeric Problems* (Diogenes Laertius 7. 4), perhaps his most extended work on any subject.

Zeno's work on Homer is totally lost. The one thing we can say about it for certain is that he discussed standard philological cruxes, which reminds us that Homeric philology had just become extremely

---

[13] e.g., he invokes Plato's tripartite psychology (17. 4-18. 8) in order to explain various lines in the *Odyssey* and, unlike the Stoics, locates rationality in the head (19. 1-19). The Stoic doctrines that he uses he takes over without acknowledgement or attributes to 'the greatest philosophers' (22. 13; cf. 25. 2), citing Stoics only once by name (33. 1) for their interpretation of Heracles.

[14] He notes that many of Heraclitus's allegories recall interpretations current before the Stoics—'Les stoïciens ne sont donc qu'un des derniers chaînons de la grande chaîne' (xxxvii)—and sums up Heraclitus's relation to Stoicism by saying (xxxix), 'La teinte de stoïcisme qu'il offre par endroits, n'est rien de plus, chez lui, qu'un vernis récent sur un meuble ancien.' Because Buffière accepts the traditional doctrine on Stoic allegoresis, he has no vested interest in detaching Stoicism from Heraclitus.

fashionable through the work of scholars in Alexandria.[15] In the case of Chrysippus, some few generations after Zeno, there survive eight examples of his work on Homer (cf. n. 15). They are all emendations to the text or grammatical explanations. In none of them does he draw upon doctrinaire Stoicism. He contributes intelligent philology, and the Homeric scholia record this, mentioning his name alongside the famous grammarian Aristarchus. Like all educated Greeks, of course, the Stoics had lines of Homer and other poets in their heads which they could use to make an ethical point and to show that their philosophy accorded with 'the common conceptions' of people. Although the voluminous writings of Chrysippus have not survived, we possess fragments of them in which some seventy lines of Homer are quoted. In all of these, Chrysippus cites Homer in order to support a Stoic doctrine—for instance the mind's location in the heart—and in all cases he takes Homer literally, not allegorically.[16]

For what reason, then (apart from the misconception concerning Heraclitus), have scholars propagated the belief that the Stoics took Homer to be a strong allegorist? The principal reason is a misleading focus upon just one text, to the neglect of all evidence that tells a rather different story. I will illustrate the point by reference to Rudolf Pfeiffer in his highly influential *History of Classical Scholarship from the Beginnings to the End of the Hellenistic Age*.

Pfeiffer (237) writes, 'Orthodox Stoics were necessarily allegorists in their interpretation of poetry.' He does not explain what he means by allegorist, though without elucidating the terms he writes of 'genuine allegory' and 'true allegorist.' Pfeiffer justifies his claim about the Stoics with a selective quotation in Latin from Cicero's *De natura deorum* 1. 41: [Chrysippus] 'volt Orphei Musaei Hesiodi Homerique fabellas accommodare ad ea quae ipse . . . de deis immortalibus dixerat, ut etiam veterrimi poetae . . . Stoici fuisse videantur.' As translated, this says, 'Chrysippus . . . wanted to fit the

---

[15] For the evidence, cf. *Stoicorum Veterum Fragmenta* (Stuttgart, 1974): *SVF* 1. 275 (Zeno's proposal to emend 'καὶ Ἐρεμβούς to Ἀραβάς τε, *Od.* 4. 84), and *SVF* 3. 769–77 (von Arnim's collection of passages documenting Chrysippus's interpretations of Homer). For discussion, cf. P. Steinmetz, 'Allegorische Deutung', 19–21, 26–7. A recently published papyrus of a commentary dealing with passages from *Odyssey* 11 probably includes Chrysippus's name; cf. *Corpus dei papiri filosofici greci e latini* (Florence, 1989), 421 (Chrysippus 5T).

[16] The point is made by P. Steinmetz, 'Allegorische Deutung', 27.

stories of Orpheus, Musaeus, Hesiod, and Homer to his own statements about the immortal gods [namely in his first book *On the Nature of the Gods*] in order that even the most ancient poets . . . might seem to have been Stoics.' Pfeiffer leads his readers to suppose that this is a totally objective remark about the Stoics. But it is not. Actually, it is a piece of anti-Stoic polemic by the Epicurean spokesman in this Ciceronian book, and we know Cicero's source for it. Cicero got the remark from the Epicurean philosopher Philodemus, but Cicero himself has subtly altered the original. What Philodemus said is this: 'Chrysippus just like Cleanthes tries to harmonise the things attributed to Orpheus and Musaeus, and *things* in Homer, Hesiod, Euripides and other poets' with Stoic doctrine.[17] The 'things' in question, as Philodemus indicates, were divine names and myths *transmitted by the poets*. Philodemus, hostile to Stoicism though he is, does not imply that Chrysippus took Homer and the other poets to be crypto-Stoics or strong allegorists. This is an addition by Cicero on behalf of his Epicurean critic.

Cicero, or his source, also adds to Philodemus a very damning clause that Pfeiffer omits; the full Latin text reads, 'in order that even the most ancient poets, *who did not even suspect this* [*qui haec ne suspicati quidem sunt*] might seem to have been Stoics.'[18] There, in a nutshell, we have the principal basis for the modern theory about the Stoics' allegorical interpretation of Homer—a text that, in reality, is a Ciceronian distortion of Epicurean polemic.[19]

Still, one may retort, there must be some foundation to the Epicurean criticism. There is, as we shall see, but ancient philosophical polemic did not operate with any rules of fair play. Before taking the

---

[17] Philodemus, *De pietate*, col. vi (ed. in Albert Henrichs, 'Die Kritik der stoischen Theologie im PHerc. 1428', *Cronache Ercolanesi*, 4 (1974), 17): ἐν δὲ τῷ[ι] δευτέρ[ωι] τὰ εἰς Ὀρφέα [καὶ] Μουσαῖον ἀναφερ[όμ]ενα καὶ τὰ παρ᾽ [Ὁ]μήρωι καὶ Ἡσιόδω[ι] καὶ Εὐριπίδῃ καὶ ποιητα[ῖ]ς ἄλλοις [ὧ]ς καὶ Κλεάνθης [πει]ρᾶται σ[υ]νοικειοῦ[ν] ταῖς δόξ[αι]ς αὐτῶ[ν]. This passage is often overlooked when the Cicero text is cited, and Cicero's divergence from it has never, to the best of my knowledge, been noted.

[18] I read *sunt* rather than *sint*, which would most naturally make the relative clause a comment by Chrysippus. *Sunt* is reported as a reading of some mss. by the Loeb editor of Cicero's *De natura deorum*, though it is not recorded in the Teubner edition or that of A. S. Pease ad loc.

[19] For other examples of unqualified reliance on Cicero's comment here, cf. J. Tate, 'Cornutus and the Poets', *Classical Quarterly*, 23 (1929), 42; S. Weinstock, 'Die platonische Homerkritik', *Philologus*, 82 (1926-7), 137; P. Steinmetz, 'Allegorische Deutung', 27; M. Hilgruber, 'Dion Chrysostomos', 19. n. 33: P. De Lacy. 'Stoic Views of Poetry', 263, actually referring to Cicero, *De nat. deor.* 1. 36.

Epicurean critique of the Stoics at face value, we should let the Stoics speak for themselves. Cicero himself provides us with one means of doing so in a passage he writes for the Stoic Balbus in book 2 of his *De natura deorum*. As we shall see, this passage does not sit well with the traditional account of Stoic allegoresis, and it is generally ignored in discussions of the subject. Before setting it alongside the Epicurean critique just examined, we need to consider what is unambiguously attested concerning the Stoics' attitude to early Greek poetry.

## III

So far as Homer is concerned, the Stoics' interest in his poems was plainly complex. As I have mentioned, Zeno and Chrysippus contributed to Homeric philology; and we also know that Zeno had views about the whole corpus of Homeric poetry because he judged the *Margites* to be a youthful work by the poet (*SVF* 1. 274). But our central question is the Stoics' approach to early Greek poetry generically. For if they interpreted Homer allegorically, they also approached Hesiod in the same way. The question of how, in general, the Stoics interpreted passages in Homer is a question about what they thought early Greek poetry could contribute to the history of ideas.

Contexts in which we learn about this are not philological or literary, but theological and cosmological.[20] Like the Epicureans, the Stoics were much concerned with the anthropology and aetiology of religion. Both schools found elements of truth in traditional Greek religion but saw them as overlaid by superstition and myth. The Epicureans thought people were right to picture the gods in human form but wrong to involve them in the world. Stoics took the opposite view. They rejected anthropomorphic gods but retained a divine presence throughout nature. As theologians and cosmologists, they took on the task of studying Greek mythology for traces of their own views. This prompted them to investigate the factors that led people to conceive of gods in the first place. A doxographical summary shows the role they assigned to poetry in this study.[21]

---

[20] This point is well taken by G. Most, 'Cornutus and Stoic Allegoresis', 2025–6.

[21] Ps.-Plutarch, *De placitis philosophorum* 879c–880d = Aetius, *De placitis* 1. 6 = *SVF* 2. 1009. The importance of this neglected testimony was brought to my attention by F. Wehrli, *Zur Geschichte der allegorischen Deutung*, 52–3.

The author attributes to the Stoics three 'forms' that have mediated reverence for the gods:

The physical is taught by philosophers, the mythical by poets, and the legislative is constitued by each city.[22] The entire discipline has seven divisions. The first one deals with phenomena and the heavens. People got a conception of god from the sight of the stars; they observed that these are responsible for great harmony, and they noticed the regularity of day and night, winter and summer, risings and settings, and the earth's production of animals and plants. Therefore they took the sky to be a father and the earth a mother . . . father because the outflow of waters is the same type of thing as sperms, and mother because of her receiving the waters and giving birth. . . . To the second and third topic they [the Stoics] distributed gods as benefactors and agents of harm—as benefactors Zeus, Hera, Hermes, Demeter, and as agents of harm Poinai, Erinyes, Ares. . . . The fourth and fifth topics they assigned to things and to passions, as passions Eros, Aphrodite, Pothos and as things Hope, Justice, Eunomia. As the sixth topic they included the poets' inventions (τὸ ὑπὸ τῶν ποιητῶν πεπλασμένον). For Hesiod, because he wanted to construct fathers for the generated gods, introduced such progenitors for them as 'Koios and Krios and Hyperion and Iapetos' (*Theogony* 134);[23] hence this topic is also called myth. The seventh topic is . . . [here I summarise] apotheosized men who were great benefactors, such as Herakles.

In this sophisticated and perceptive passage, myth and poetry are mentioned as just one of many sources of theological notions. The text does not say that Hesiod—the one poet named—really understood the gods to be different from what he said they were. It simply registers the fabricated character of his account, and his wish to construct divine genealogies.

A much fuller statement of the same topics is to be found in Cicero, *De natura deorum* 2. 63–72. After dealing with the apotheosized humans, Cicero's Stoic spokesman Balbus turns to myth and poetry, and he adds a central point omitted by the doxographical text. Stories

---

[22] Dio Chrysostom 12. 44 adopts a version of this tripartite division, substituting ἔμφυτον for φυσικόν and then adding a fourth category in order to accommodate the plastic arts.

[23] I translate the received text, Ἡσίοδος γὰρ βουλόμενος τοῖς γενητοῖς θεοῖς πατέρας συστῆσαι εἰσήγαγε τοιούτους αὐτοῖς γεννήτορας, "Κοῖον κτλ." Von Arnim in *SVF* 2.1009 prints θεούς, an emendation of the transmitted text by Hermann Diels (*Doxographi Graeci* (Berlin, 1975), 296) and also accepted by J. Mau in the Teubner edition of Plutarch, *Moralia* V, fasc. 2, Pars 1 (Leipzig, 1971), but sense and flow of the Greek are against this. The Titans named are from the first generation of gods and are sires of gods themselves; cf. Hesiod, *Theogony* 404.

such as Hesiod tells, for instance the castration of Ouranos by Kronos and the fettering of Kronos by Zeus, are utterly erroneous and stupid. However, that story is actually a fictional and superstitious perversion of an intelligent and correct understanding of certain natural phenomena ('physica ratio non inelegans inclusa est in impias fabulas'): that the highest entity, the aether, does not need genitals in order to procreate, and that Kronos, i.e., χρόνος ('time'), is 'regulated and limited.'[24]

Cicero's Stoic spokesman is not interested in saving the veracity of poets including Homer. He dismisses anthropomorphic gods—and their involvement in the Trojan war—as absurd (*De nat. deor.* 2. 70). What he commits himself to is a theory of cultural transmission, degeneration, and modification. At some time in the remote past, on this view, certain people intuited basic truths about nature. They expressed these, however, in a symbolical mode that was easy to misinterpret as independently valid.[25] Hence the emergence of misleading myths. The task of the Stoic interpreter of religious history is to identify and articulate the correct beliefs that directly gave rise to such myths but are not evident in their superficial narrative content. Far from suggesting that Homer and Hesiod were proto-Stoic cosmologists, this passage implies that the poets propagated misleading myths as if they were truths.

Cicero's Balbus, giving the official Stoic view, does not match well with the Epicurean account in *De natura deorum* I. 41, the passage on which Pfeiffer and others chiefly rely for their theory about the Stoics' allegorization of Homer. Here, in the Stoics' own account, nothing is said about what *Homer or Hesiod themselves meant*. The Stoics are interested in their poems as *sources* of pre-existing, prephilosophical views of the world—what we may call 'true myths,' which in the later poems take on a narrative life of their own and are thus misunderstood.[26]

---

[24] Cicero twice uses *voluerunt* in *De nat. deor.* 2. 64 to refer to the meaning intended by those who developed the 'physica ratio non inelegans.' He does not imply that this meaning was understood by those who told the 'impias fabulas.'

[25] 'Videtisne igitur ut a physicis rebus bene atque utiliter inventis tracta ratio sit ad commenticios et fictos deos? Quae res genuit falsas opiniones . . .'.

[26] When referring back to these Stoic activities, the Academic critic of the Stoics (*De nat. deor.* 3. 63) does not refer to their 'allegorization' of the *poets* but to their pointless efforts 'to rationalize the mendacious stories and explain the reasons for the names by which each thing is so called' ('commenticiarum fabularum reddere rationem, vocabulorum cur quidque ita appellatum sit causas explicare').

The two pieces of evidence I have just analyzed give a clear and coherent account of the Stoics' generic interests in early Greek poetry. However, they can be supplemented by something else, which, until recently, had been curiously neglected in the discussion of this whole topic.[27] From the first century AD there survives an entire book by the Stoic philosopher Cornutus, entitled *Compendium* (Ἐπιδρομή) *of the Tradition of Greek Theology*. Cornutus wrote this work, as he remarks, for young students. His topic is the transmitted names, epithets, cults, and myths pertaining to particular divinities. He draws on poetry, especially Hesiod's, simply because poetry is a primary vehicle for the transmission of theology.

Cornutus has a methodology for analyzing his data. It is not allegory (to which he never refers) but etymology. He assumes (as the earliest Stoics had also assumed) that the Greek gods have the names and epithets that they do—'earthshaking Poseidon,' etc.—because in their original usage these names represented the way people understood the world. Etymology, that is, analysis of the original meaning of names, enables the Stoic philosopher to recover the beliefs about the world held by those who first gave the gods their present names. From our modern perspective, Stoic etymologies often seem fantastic. From the same perspective, we have to say that the Stoics were far too bold in relying on etymology as they did and in presuming a coincidence between the original meaning of divine names and aspects of their own philosophy of nature. More on this point later. What I want to emphasize now is that etymology is not the same as allegory, although allegories may make use of etymology. Etymology offers explanations of single names and phrases—atomic units of language, as it were. But to have allegory, it seems, we need a whole story, a narrative—Pandora's box, the Garden of Eden, etc. Only rarely does Cornutus offer an interpretation of any extended episodes in early Greek poetry.[28] He is an etymologist, not an allegorist.[29]

[27] G. Most's study, 'Cornutus and Stoic Allegoresis', has ensured that Cornutus will not be neglected in the future. Although Most endorses the notion of Stoic 'allegoresis,' what he understands by this seems to be largely compatible with the thesis of my paper.

[28] The points I have just made are well developed in D. Dawson, *Allegorical Readers and Cultural Revision* (Berkeley, 1992).

[29] Contrasting Cornutus's methodology with that of Heraclitus, F. Buffière notes, 'Cornutus ne s'attarde guère aux allégories proprement dites et ne se limite point aux données d'Homère, pour les dieux qu'il étudie,' *Héraclite*, p.xxxi. An interesting feature

Cornutus's etymologies are based upon the same cultural assumption that we found just now in Cicero. Greek poetry is not the bottom line for recovering primitive beliefs about the gods and cosmology. Behind the earliest Greek poetry, and distortedly present in it, are ways of understanding the world whose basic correctness the Stoic interpreter, through etymology, can reveal. Cornutus's principal source is Hesiod, and he also refers to Homer a number of times. Fortunately for our purposes, he is explicit about his approach to poetic texts and about his methodology. In section 17 (Lang), Cornutus begins by noting the number and variety of myths generated among the ancient Greeks and other peoples. As an example he takes two stories from Homer: Zeus's suspending Hera by the golden chain (*Il.* 15. 18–24) and Thetis's support of Zeus against the rebellion of the other Olympians (*Il.* 1. 396–406). Of the first of these he writes, 'The poet seems to cite (or, possibly, pervert, παραφέρειν) this fragment of an ancient myth, according to which Zeus was fabled to have suspended Hera from the sky with golden chains, since the stars have a golden appearance, and to have attached two anvils to her feet, i.e., evidently earth and sea, by means of which the air is stretched down and cannot be removed from either of them.' Cornutus bases his interpretation on the traditional etymology of ἀήρ, 'air,' as Hera.[30]

Cornutus then adduces the second myth, that of Thetis, and says: 'Clearly each of these gods was privately plotting against Zeus continuously, intending to prevent the world's origin. And that would have happened if the moist had prevailed and everything had become wet, or if fire had prevailed and everything had become fiery, or if air had prevailed. But Thetis, who disposes everything properly, positioned the hundred-handed Briareus against the gods mentioned— Briareus, who perhaps controls all exhalations from the earth.' For this interpretation Cornutus relies on etymologies of the names

of Cornutus's etymological analysis, as G. Most points out, 2027–8, is his frequent mention of and refusal to choose betwen alternative etymologies.

[30] Cosmological readings of this passage are ancient. F. Buffière thinks they may go back to the time of Anaximenes, *Les Mythes d'Homère*, Paris, 1956, 115–17. Socrates cites a version in Plato, *Theaetetus* 153c, and ἀήρ is found in *Cratylus* 404c. Heraclitus (40) elaborates the interpretation along the same lines as Cornutus but conjoins it (41. 1) with an allegorization of Hera's oath (*Il.* 15. 36–7), where he also locates the four elements; thus he thinks himself entitled to say that: 'Homer continuously allegorizes them' (41. 12).

Thetis (τίθημι) and Briareus (βορά and αἴρειν). Thus he finds germs of
Stoic cosmogony in Homer's story, but he does not suggest that
Homer himself did so.[31]
Immediately following this passage, Cornutus gives the following
instruction: 'One should not conflate myths, nor should one transfer
names from one to another; and even if something has been added to
the transmitted genealogies by people who do not understand what
the myths hint at (αἰνίττονται) but who handle them as they handle
narrative fictions, one should not regard them as irrational.[32]
Cornutus is addressing would-be students of the history of religion.
Not unlike a modern ethnographer or cultural anthropologist, he
warns against tampering with the recorded data. He recognizes that
the data, as transmitted, may distort the original beliefs that he takes
to underlie existing myths, but the problems of transmission are not
sufficient to rule out recovery of the myths' original rationale. In the
next part of this section, he turns to Hesiod's 'mythical' cosmogony
and interprets its details in terms of Stoic physics. He concludes with
these remarks: 'I could give you a more complete interpretation
of Hesiod's [genealogy]. He got some parts of it, I think, from his
predecessors and added other parts in a more mythical manner,
which is the way most of the ancient theology was corrupted.'[33]
Reading this passage in the light of Cornutus's previous instructions,
we can see that Hesiod is one of the people who made inappropriate
additions through his failure to see the theological physics implicit in
his inherited material. For Cornutus neither Homer nor Hesiod is a
crypto-Stoic. Both are the transmitters of myths.

    In his interpretation of those myths, Cornutus intends to elucidate
neither the scientific acumen of Homer and Hesiod nor their poetic
intentions. He is interested in what we might call proto-myth, myth

---

[31] Heraclitus (25) explains this story as an allusion to the eventual destruction of
the world by deluge or conflagration, which are, of course, Stoic ideas.
[32] Cornutus 27. 19 Lang: δεῖ δὲ μὴ συγχεῖν τοὺς μύθους μηδ᾽ ἐξ ἑτέρου τὰ ὀνόματα ἐφ᾽
ἕτερον μεταφέρειν μηδ᾽ εἴ τι προσεπλάσθη ταῖς παραδεδομέναις κατ᾽ αὐτοὺς γενεαλογίαις
ὑπὸ τῶν μὴ συνιέντων ἃ αἰνίττονται, κεχρημένων δ᾽ αὐτοῖς ὡς καὶ τοῖς πλάσμασιν, †ἀλόγως†
τίθεσθαι. Tom Rosenmeyer has convinced me that the sense requires ἀλόγους
(referring to μύθους) and I translate the text accordingly. Cornutus, as Rosenmeyer
notes in written comments he gave me, is 'talking about methods of looking at myth,
not about the mentality of the one who looks at the myth.'
[33] I give the Greek of the concluding parts of this translation, Cornutus 31. 14–17
Lang: τὰ μέν τινα, ὡς οἶμαι, παρὰ τῶν ἀρχαιοτέρων αὐτοῦ παρειληφότος, τὰ δὲ μυθικώτερον
ἀφ᾽ αὑτοῦ προσθέντος, ᾧ τρόπῳ καὶ πλεῖστα τῆς παλαιᾶς θεολογίας διεφθάρη.

detached from narrative context in a poem, myth as interpretable evidence of pristine cosmological beliefs. At the end of his book, he tells its young addressee to realize that 'the ancients were not nobodies but competent students of the world, and well equipped to philosophize about it via symbols and riddles' (Cornutus 76. 2–5 Lang).[34] Does Cornutus take the wise ancients to have been deliberate allegorists—practitioners of indirection—and to be identical with the early Greek poets? Surely not. He is saying that proto-myth, in the sense just explained, is the form in which the ancients expressed their serious thoughts about the world. The Stoic exegete seeks to recover these by removing the veneers created by poetic fictions and superstitions.

The evidence of Cornutus, an official Stoic, tells decisively against the evidence of Heraclitus, a contemporary perhaps but a dubious Stoic at best. Thus far we have found no shred of evidence from unimpeachable Stoic sources to suggest that Stoics in general interpreted Homer allegorically or took Homer himself to be an allegorist. They had many interests in Homer; insofar as they asked themselves what cosmological truths he expressed, they took themselves to be interpreting pre-Homeric myths within the poem, not the poem's narrative content or Homer's own knowledge or purposes.[35]

---

[34] Cornutus 76. 2–5 Lang: οὐχ οἱ τυχόντες ἐγένοντο οἱ παλαιοί, ἀλλὰ καὶ συνιέναι τὴν τοῦ κόσμου φύσιν ἱκανοὶ καὶ πρὸς τὸ διὰ συμβόλων καὶ αἰνιγμάτων φιλοσοφῆσαι περὶ αὐτῆς εὐεπίφοροι. It is not necessary to take Cornutus's words to endorse Posidonius's controversial position on the existence of full-fledged philosophers in the Golden Age (Seneca, Epistle 90. 4 ff.). For discussion of Stoic views on cultural history, cf. G. Most, 'Cornutus and Stoic Allegoresis', 2020–3, and Michael Frede, 'Chaeremon der Stoiker,' ANRW 2/36/3 (1989), 2088. Strabo (10. 3. 23) makes a similar point to Cornutus, but he also emphasizes the difficulty of extracting primary theological truths from mythical material that is not internally consistent. The passage is mentioned by R. Lamberton, Homer the Theologian (Berkeley, 1986), 26.

[35] The thesis I am advancing has affinities with the positions of both P. Steinmetz, 'Allegorische Deutung', and G. Most, 'Cornutus and Stoic Allegoresis,' though I differ from both of them in my view of the Stoics's attention to myth rather than poetry. Most (2023–36) criticizes Steinmetz for attacking a straw man, 'allegorical interpretation of poetry as poetry'; but Steinmetz has good reason to do this within the context of the traditional theory, because it enables him to shift the focus of the Stoics' interests to the myths incorporated by the poets. However, Steinmetz continues to think (23), incorrectly I believe, that the Stoics took themselves to be uncovering via etymology the poet's meaning. Most, though he writes of the Stoics' allegoresis of poetry, comes close to my position when he notes (2026 n. 80), 'The figures of mythology ultimately have an explanation in terms of physical allegoresis which is their ἀλήθεια; but in many details this has been misunderstood, presumably already by the poets themselves, and the result is the δόξα of superstition.'

At this point, however, an obvious question arises. It may seem that my account of the Stoics' interpretative interests in Homer and Hesiod has merely pushed matters one stage further back. The new theory saves the Stoics from taking Homer to be a crypto-Stoic, but it does so at the cost of positing crypto-Stoics prior to Homer—the original enlightened ancients whose names for the gods display their correct understanding of nature. That challenge demands an answer and I will give it at the end of the paper. For the present, I want to leave it in abeyance because some further evidence requires consideration.

IV

So far, my case against the standard theory of the Stoics as allegorists of poetic meaning has largely rested on the following points: rejection of Heraclitus as an official Stoic, rejection of the polemical evidence of the Epicurean in Cicero, and reliance on the three witnesses who explain the Stoics' interest in the myths expressed in poetry. This material is all relatively late within the history of Stoicism. What reason do we have for thinking that it correctly represents the views of the earliest Stoics, the founders of the school? Is it not possible that they, or some of them, were allegorists as the standard doctrine proposes, and that it is Cicero's Stoic spokesman and Cornutus who are aberrant?[36] I cannot decisively disprove this suggestion because what we know of Zeno, Cleanthes, and Chrysippus on this matter is so fragmentary, but the evidence we have seems to offer nothing unambiguously in its favour.

First Chrysippus. It was he, above all, who represented orthodoxy for later Stoicism. As I have already said, his eight recorded contributions to Homeric exegesis are all philological. I also pointed out

[36] This is the view of J. Tate, 'Cornutus and the Poets,' but only so far as Cornutus is concerned, because Tate overlooks Cicero, De nat. deor. 2. 63–72. Tate claims that earlier Stoics believed 'Homer and Hesiod to have been original thinkers, who expressed sound doctrine in the mythical style proper to the primitive times in which they lived.' The evidence he cites to support this is our old favourite, Cicero De nat. deor. 1. 41, and other indirect testimonies—Strabo 1. 1. 10 and 1. 2. 9, Dio Chrysostom 55. 9 ff., and Heraclitus. Yet Cornutus himself, apart from his coherence with the other Stoic evidence discussed above, says that his book is only a summary of works by earlier philosophers (Cornutus 76. 6–8 Lang).

that in all cases where he cites Homer in support of a doctrine he takes Homer's text at its surface or literal meaning. The only cosmological allegory he is known to have advanced concerns not a text but a painting. There was a famous and obscene painting at Argos that showed Hera fellating Zeus (*SVF* 2. 1071–4). Chrysippus explained this (do we know he was utterly serious in doing so?) as an interaction between the two Stoic principles, Zeus/god and Hera/matter. Interestingly enough, this interpretation does not invoke the standard Stoic etymology, Hera/ἀήρ.

When it was a question of choosing between interpretations of a myth, Chrysippus was skillful at exploiting the literal sense of a passage. He wanted to show that Hesiod's account of Athena's birth from the head of Zeus does not contradict the Stoic doctrine of the heart as the mind's center.[37] 'Some people,' he says, 'take this story to be a symbol of the mind's location in the head.' But they fail to attend properly to Hesiod's text. Chrysippus notes that Hesiod gives two versions of Athena's birth and that a common feature of both is Zeus's swallowing of Metis.[38] So Athena is generated from Metis, present in the belly of Zeus, and not *simpliciter* from the head of Zeus. Therefore, the myth in Hesiod confirms Chrysippus's view on the central location of the mind. This piece of exegesis may be overingenious, but it approaches the text in ways that are scrupulous, closely argued and even, perhaps, ironical.

Galen characterises Chrysippus's practice here in language that modern scholars conventionally call allegorizing.[39] But Galen has correctly seen that what interests Chrysippus is the interpretation of a myth, and *interpretation* is a much better term than *allegorization* for what Chrysippus is doing. Chrysippus does not take himself to be identifying a gap between surface meaning and hidden meaning. His interpretation demythologizes Hesiod but it does so in ways that retain the obvious link in the text between Metis as goddess and μῆτις as a word signifying intelligence.

Next Zeno. In his fifty-third oration, 'On Homer,' Dio Chrysostom

---

[37] Galen, *De plac. Hipp. et Plat.* 3. 8. 1–28 = *SVF* 2. 908–9.

[38] Chrysippus's text of the *Theogony* included lines that modern scholars excise; cf. fr. 343 Merkelbach-West.

[39] Cf. *De plac. Hipp. et Plat.* 3. 8. 34 on Chrysippus's concern to explain the ὑπόνοιαι of myths.

speaks briefly about Zeno's judgment of the poet. Dio's context is this: Most philosophers and grammarians are unequivocal in their admiration of Homer. Plato, however, although sensitive to Homer's charm, criticizes the poet severely for his myths and statements about the gods. This is not an easy matter to assess. Did Homer err, or did he merely 'transmit certain physical doctrines present in the myths according to the custom of his time'?[40] Dio seems to allude to the Stoic theory of cultural transmission and not to Heraclitus's treatment of Homer as an allegorist. He then observes that Zeno wrote on both Homeric poems and found nothing to criticize in them. Zeno's object, according to Dio, was to save Homer from the charge of self-contradiction. He did this by showing in detail that Homer wrote 'some things in accordance with opinion (δόξα) and other things in accordance with truth (ἀλήθεια).'[41] Dio then notes that Antisthenes anticipated Zeno in this approach to Homer. It was Zeno, however, and others including Zeno's follower Persaeus, who expounded Homer in this way, point by point. Unfortunately, Dio gives no example of Zeno's procedure. We are left to infer what apparent inconsistencies he sought to remove and how he did so.

Given Dio's context, the inconsistencies should above all include apparently incongruent statements in Homer about the gods. If Zeno harmonised these by distinguishing 'opinions' from 'truths,' he presumably wanted to show that Homer's treatment of the gods is epistemologically complex, containing both identifiable truths and identifiable fables or falsehoods. Coherence would be established by distinguishing these two modes of discourse and by appropriately assigning passages to (false) opinion or to truth. There is good reason to attribute this procedure to Antisthenes. He distinguished, as the Stoics later did, between the many gods of popular religion and a single divinity in nature (Cicero, *De nat. deor.* 1. 32). Ethically impeccable passages in Homer about the gods collectively or about Zeus in particular could seem to justify the application of this distinction to the poet.

There is no good evidence that Antisthenes offered physicalist

---

[40] Dio Chrysostom 53. 5: πότερον Ὅμηρος ἥμαρτε περὶ ταῦτα ἢ φυσικούς τινας ἐνόντας ἐν τοῖς μύθοις λόγους κατὰ τὴν τότε συνήθειαν παρεδίδου τοῖς ἀνθρώποις. Cf. Cicero *De nat. deor.* 2. 64, 'physica ratio non inelegans inclusa est in impias fabulas.'

[41] Dio Chrysostom 53. 4 (*SVF* I. 274): ὁ δὲ Ζήνων οὐδὲν τῶν Ὁμήρου ψέγει, ἅμα διηγούμενος καὶ διδάσκων ὅτι τὰ μὲν κατὰ δόξαν, τὰ δὲ κατὰ ἀλήθειαν γέγραφεν, ὅπως μὴ φαίνηται αὐτὸς αὑτῷ μαχόμενος ἔν τισι δοκοῦσιν ἐναντίως εἰρῆσθαι.

allegories of the Homeric gods in the manner of Metrodorus of Lampsacus.[42] His well-known interest in the figures of Odysseus, Ajax, and Herakles was ethical. Is allegory implied by or consonant with Zeno's use of the distinction between truth and opinion? Many have thought so,[43] but there are strong reasons for doubt. Fritz Wehrli states the obvious objection: 'It is false to take this as evidence for allegory since allegory creates truth out of everything mythical.'[44] His point is that Antisthenes and Zeno would not have distinguished between Homer's true and opining statements if they had taken the opining ones to express covert truths.

Peter Steinmetz goes a step further than Wehrli: 'It is unclear how physico-cosmological allegory or psychological-ethical allegory could help in resolving inconsistencies between two Homeric passages.'[45] Steinmetz interprets Zeno's concern as philological. On this view, Zeno was primarily interested in close textual analysis of Homer—in resolving apparent inconsistencies such as the description of Ithaca as 'low' and 'very high' in adjacent words (Od. 9. 25).

It is highly likely that Zeno's five books of Homeric Problems did address such points. We have no evidence that this work included allegorization, and Steinmetz could have helped himself to an additional point. Cicero tells us, on Stoic authority, that the separation of proto-science from legend and superstition was treated more fully by Cleanthes and Chrysippus than by Zeno (De nat. deor. 2. 63). It can hardly, then, have formed a major part of his five-book work Homeric Problems. However, Steinmetz's strictly philological reading of Dio's testimony will not do. That interpretation does not fit Zeno's distinction between 'truth' and 'opinion,' nor does it chime with Dio's theological context.

The most obvious point was made by J. Tate in an article written sixty years ago: The distinction between 'truth' and 'opinion' or fiction was a commonplace in the interpretation of Homer.[46] Strabo

[42] Cf. F. Wehrli, Zur Geschichte der allegorischen Deutung, 65 ff.; N. Richardson, 'Homeric Professors', 80–6 in this volume; M. Hilgruber, 'Dion Chrysostomos', 15–18.

[43] Cf. M. Hilgruber, 'Dion Chrysostomos', who is the latest to take Dio's text to refer to Zeno's allegorizing, but in my opinion he fails to overturn the arguments of Tate (cf. n. 46 below). He adduces no new evidence for the thesis and saddles himself with a view of the passage that makes Zeno, but not Antisthenes, an allegorist of Homer.

[44] F. Wehrli, Zur Geschichte der allegorischen Deutung, 65.

[45] P. Steinmetz, 'Allegorische Deutung', 20.

[46] 'Plato and Allegorical Interpretation [2]' CQ 24 (1930), 7–10. Tate's view is summed up in these remarks of his ad loc.: 'As spokesman for the multitude [Homer]

uses it (I. 2, etc.) to save Homer's credit as a geographer against Eratosthenes' opinion that the poet is entirely concerned with fiction. According to Strabo, Homer regularly combines truth and falsehood (I. 2. 7–9, I. 2. 19, etc.). In addition, the poet sometimes overlays truths with a mythical covering to flavour his style and enchant his audience. Strabo is confident, too confident, that he can remove Homer's mythical accretions and exhibit the kernel of his factual knowledge. He treats Homer as fully in control of his (Strabo's) distinction between truth and falsehood; perhaps Zeno did so too. However, Strabo does not maintain, as Heraclitus does, that Homer's myths are regularly reducible to covert truths.[47]

Another author who can illuminate Zeno's approach to Homer is Plutarch. In his essay *On How to Study Poetry*, Plutarch rejects astrological and cosmological allegory as the way to clear Homer from the charge of representing the gods immorally (19e–20a). In this context he is clearly talking about the likes of Heraclitus, but he does not name the Stoics. For Plutarch one correct response to this charge is to recognize that Homer includes 'healthy and true theological doctrines' and others 'that have been fabricated to excite people' (20 f.). Setting the former against the latter enables the poet's own voice to be distinguished. This comes as close as possible to the simplest interpretation of Zeno's distinction between 'truth' and 'opinion.'

A second recommendation of Plutarch is also relevant to the Stoics' procedures. He emphasizes the importance of recognizing how poets use the names of the gods (23a). Sometimes a divine name is to be taken as a direct reference to the god himself. Frequently, however, poets use the names of gods, by metonymy, to refer to impersonal states of affairs—for instance, Zeus to denote fate or fortune, Ares to signify war, Hephaestus to signify fire. Plutarch does not call this allegory and nor would I. The second kind of usage does not invoke a hidden meaning. It is a transparent application of

---

may contradict the truths he knew and expressed elsewhere. But this contradiction is only apparent, for in this case it is not Homer who is wrong but the multitude whose views he is expressing.' Diogenianus criticizes Chrysippus for his selective quotations from Homer, which obscure the fact that Homer does not consistently support Chrysippus's doctrine that everything is fated; cf. Eusebius, *Praeparatio evangelica* 6. 8. 1–7.

[47] For a well-balanced account of Strabo's treatment of Homer, cf. D. M. Schenkeveld, 'Strabo on Homer', *Mnemosyne*, 29 (1976), 52–64.

names, and one that belongs to the Greek language from its recorded beginnings. Plutarch offers it as a way of 'correcting' most of the seemingly out-of-place statements made in Homer about Zeus (24a). Plutarch may have drawn heavily on Stoicism in his writing of this essay. However that may be, Zeno could certainly have availed himself of Plutarch's two procedures in his process of removing apparent inconsistencies from Homer. Unlike allegory, these procedures clearly fit his distinction between truth and opinion, and both are set by Plutarch within a theological context, as Dio's citation of Zeno requires.

Before we leave Plutarch, a further word on his approach to Homer is in order. He has no time for allegorical euhemerism, as we have seen. Yet, as far as I know, Plutarch never launches any attack on allegorical interpretation of poetry by the Stoics.[48] Because his knowledge of Stoicism was second to none, and because he uses every opportunity to make fun of Stoic extravagances, his silence on this point should embarrass proponents of the standard theory about the Stoics, represented by R. Pfeiffer, as 'necessarily allegorists in their interpretation of poetry.'

## V

However Zeno read Homer, he certainly sought to demythologise Hesiod by means of etymology.[49] What survives of Zeno's work on the *Theogony* has close affinities with Cornutus. Zeno interpreted Hesiod's χάος as primal water, deriving the word from χύσις or χέεσθαι (*SVF* I. 103–4), meaning 'pouring'. He identified four of Hesiod's Titans (children of Earth and Heaven) with cosmic powers, justifying this by etymology, and treated the names of the Cyclopes similarly (*SVF* I. 100, 118). Above all, he set a pattern for later Stoics in explaining the names of the Olympians as primary allusions to the physical elements—Hera/air, Zeus/aither, Hephaestus/fire, etc. Like Cornutus, Zeno seems to have focused on divine names and epithets rather than the extended episodes of the poem.

---

[48] Plutarch does complain (*De aud. po.* 31e) about the 'childishness' or 'irony' Cleanthes exhibits in his physicalist etymology of ἄνα Δωδωναῖε (see main text below). Immediately later he criticizes Chrysippus for an implausible, but not physicalist, etymology of Κρονίδης.

[49] Cf. P. Steinmetz, 'Allegorische Deutung', 21–3.

It seems quite credible that Zeno applied this approach to Hesiod, as he is said to have done (Cicero, *De nat. deor.* 1. 36), but not to Homer.[50] Unlike Homer, Hesiod has an explicit cosmogony. His divine genealogies include many items that we today would call abstract powers or that have a straightforward reference to physical phenomena. His narratives are much simpler than Homer's. The whole tenor of his work is descriptive rather than dramatic. As modern studies of myth and the beginnings of philosophy have shown, Hesiod lends himself to treatment as a pioneer in speculative thought.

Homer was more hallowed and more complex. He had been interpreted allegorically long before the Stoics, but not with results that any major thinker took seriously. For Cornutus's theology Hesiod is far more significant than Homer. Cornutus does show, however, that Stoicism by his time was accommodating some cosmological interpretations of episodes in the *Iliad*. Peter Steinmetz is probably right to give Cleanthes the credit or discredit for adumbrating these.[51] In Cleanthes' case, unlike that of Zeno, we have clear evidence of reading isolated words in Homer through Stoic eyes. Cleanthes derived ἄνα Δωδωναῖε, 'O lord of Dodona,' an invocation of Zeus in the *Iliad*, from ἀναδίδωμι, and related this to the Stoic doctrine of air vaporising from the earth (*SVF* I. 535). He wanted to make Atlas's epithet in *Odyssey* I. 52 ὀλοόφρων, 'mindful of everything,' instead of 'malevolent,' ὀλοόφρων, in order to indicate Atlas's providential concern for the world (*SVF* I. 549). And he interpreted the mysterious plant μῶλυ (*Od.* 10. 305) as signifying 'reason,' deriving it from the verb μωλύεσθαι, 'to relax' (*SVF* I. 526).[52] Thus he could explain why μῶλυ protected Odysseus from the passions that Circe exploited in his followers.

This is not allegory, as Heraclitus uses it, but etymology. For Heraclitus it is crucial that Homer means something different from

---

[50] P. Steinmetz makes this point, loc. cit.

[51] P. Steinmetz, 'Allegorische Deutung', 23-5.

[52] According to Apollonius Sophistes, the source of this evidence, 'Cleanthes says that reason (λόγος) is signified allegorically (ἀλληγορικῶς).' The absence of any offical Stoic account of 'allegory' makes it likely that this is a scholiast's report of Cleanthes rather than his own verbatim statement. In any case, as I have tried to emphasize throughout, the important point is not the ancient terminology applied to Stoic interpretations but whether they should be termed *allegorical* from our perspective. Sometimes ἀλληγορέω is simply synonymous with ἑρμηνεύω; cf. Metrodorus fr. A6 D–K with Plutarch, *De Iside* 363d.

what he says—that he intends his stories to be taken not literally but as *covert* references to natural phenomena. No such assumption is required by Zeno or Cleanthes. Their explanations of divine names are based upon etymologies whose validity is quite independent of anything Homer or Hesiod may have thought. For all we know, Cleanthes may have supposed that Homer wrote ὀλοόφρονος. His emendation could have aimed at restoring a truth not evident to Homer but familiar to Homer's wiser predecessors.

## VI

The lines between poetry and myth and between poetic meaning and mythological interpretation are fine ones to draw. It would be a mistake to presume that the Stoics never overstepped them or that they always tried to keep them apart. Nonetheless it does appear that we have failed to distinguish between the Stoics' interest in myth and their understanding of literature. They were well aware that poets combine truth *and* fiction at the surface level of meaning. As students of Hesiod, they will have known *Theogony* 27–8, where the poet himself seems to alert his audience to the fact that he is about to recite just such a combination. What passes under the name of Stoic allegorizing is the Stoic interpretation of myth. The Stoics seem to have recognized that *myths are allegories*, stories told in order to explain problematic features of the physical world. They thought that elucidation of these myths could help to confirm their own understanding of nature. Interpretation of the meaning and composition of Homer or Hesiod per se was not their concern. As even the hostile Philodemus says (*De Pietate* col. vi), 'It was *things* in Homer and Hesiod' that Chrysippus tried to harmonise with Stoic doctrines. The things in question were divine names and myths transmitted by the poets, and not the poets' own use of these. By taking the latter to have been the Stoics' concern, we have come to believe that they advertised Homer and other early poets as proto-Stoics.

The evidence I have reviewed—drawn from Stoics and not their detractors—tells decisively against the pertinence of this assessment. Some Stoics, though perhaps not Zeno, used Homer among other poets as a source of myth pertaining to cosmology. They did this as students of natural theology, believing, most reasonably, that divine

names and epithets and myths *are* serious evidence of how early
people interpreted the world. They assumed, less reasonably, that
etymology is the best device for recovering the beliefs of the primary
users of names and that etymology could line up those beliefs with
some of their own views on nature. They had enough confidence in
their own cosmology and human rationality to presume that many
of their own findings were not original; this was naive perhaps, but
it is an approach that should appeal to cultural historians and
anthropologists. In all of this, the Stoics treated early Greek poetry as
ethnographical material and not as literature in, say, an Aristotelian
sense.

So, to conclude, has my revision of the standard theory merely
pushed the problem one stage further back, so that instead of Homer
and Hesiod being crypto-Stoics that role is now being played by the
anonymous mythmakers who preceded them? I think not. For one
thing, on my explanation, the ancient sages are not crypto-Stoics.
They are not deliberately concealing truths about nature in misleading myths. Myth, in the theory I am offering, *is* the early people's
mode of interpreting the world. Second, up to quite a large point, the
Stoics were right about this. Many Greek myths *are* cosmological—
ways of ordering the physical world. To have had the insight to see
this is greatly to the Stoics' credit, and gives them a theory very
different from the standard one that Homer's epic narrative is a Stoic
cosmology in disguise. Many anthropologists take allegory to be
central to a myth's mode of signification. The Stoics clearly had an
inkling of this. They did not make the mistake of supposing that a
myth's meaning is identical either to its function in a larger story (the
personification of concepts) or to a secret message inscribed by the
storyteller.

Allegory, so we are often told today, covers everything written. All
texts are codes, no meaning is objective or stable, authorial intentions do not count, what *we* find in a text *is* what the text says.
Although this modern fashion might seem to suit the Stoics, they
should firmly reject it. Their hermeneutic is fundamentally historicist. That is why it depends on etymology, the search for original
meanings. Independently of the Stoics, the idea had developed that
Homer was his own allegorist; the task of the exegete then became
one of demonstrating Homer's knowledge of philosophical truths.[53]

[53] This practice seems to be well under way by the end of the fifth century, on the

This is the position of Heraclitus, and it is also evident in that curious work, attributed to Plutarch, *On the Life and Poetry of Homer*.[54] Once Homer was his own allegorist, he could be turned into any philosopher one liked, as he is by pseudo-Plutarch. The scene was set for Neoplatonist allegorical readings.

The contribution of Stoicism to this was partly substantive but also accidental and indirect. It was substantive because the Stoics had shown how to give cosmological readings to certain myths by etymologizing the names of their divine agents. Their philosophy of nature is a strong presence in Heraclitus. But an element of accident is also evident there. Stoicism simply was the most powerful philosophy in his time. If Heraclitus was to use philosophy as the way of exonerating Homer, he had to turn to the Stoics. Mutatis mutandis, the same holds for Philo's allegorical readings of Scripture. These do not make him a Stoic. The Stoic contribution is indirect for the reason I have emphasized throughout this paper—the shift from interpreting the earliest poets' myths as sources for archaic beliefs to interpreting Homer as an allegorist.

evidence of Metrodorus of Lampsacus, and it can also be observed in the Derveni papyrus, whose author takes Orpheus to have had access to truths about the world which he then clothed in enigmas; cf. Jeffrey S. Rusten, 'Interim Notes on the Papyrus from Derveni,' *Harvard Studies in Classical Philology*, 89 (1985), 121–40. In comments on the original draft of this paper, which he kindly sent to me, Denis Feeney wrote, 'If it was possible in the fifth century to talk of Homer as someone who expressed truth in veiled ways, then the Stoics' later discretion in using him only as a source for early belief is even more striking.' I agree. But, apart from the arguments I have advanced, it would be quite unlike their philosophy in general if the Stoics had simply appropriated an earlier, but highly contentious, approach to Homer. What I am proposing has much in common with Aristotle's view of mythically clothed truths about astronomy (see especially *Metaphysics* 12. 1074[b]1), but a comparison with Aristotle is too large a subject to be pursued here.

[54] Until recently, the most accessible edition of this work was the Teubner edited by G. N. Bernardakis (*Plutarchus Moralia VII* (1896), which contains the Plutarchan spuria). Now, however, this has been replaced by J. F. Kindstrand's new Teubner ([*Plutarchus*] *De Homero*). The author of *On the Life and Poetry of Homer* sees no difficulty in making Homer the source of contradictory doctrines, for instance Stoic ἀπάθεια and Peripatetic μετριοπάθεια (cf. sections 134–5), and the inspiration of all the most famous philosophers. Thus he entirely fits Seneca's sarcastic critique (cf. n. 11 above).

# IO
# *Epicurean Poetics*

## ELIZABETH ASMIS

If one were to ask people to rank the contributions made by the Epicureans to philosophy, I would not be surprised if poetic theory were near the bottom of most people's lists, or altogether missing, whereas poetry itself might well be at the top. The ancient quarrel between philosophy and poetry seems to have played itself out in an extreme paradox in Epicureanism. Epicurus has the reputation of being the most hostile to poetry of any Greek philosopher. But some of his later followers were clearly devoted to poetry, and one of them, Lucretius, achieved a remarkable reconciliation between philosophy and poetry.

In this paper, I propose to investigate the road between Epicurus and Lucretius. What were Epicurus' views, and to what extent did his followers adopt, modify, or jettison his views? We know that in other areas Epicurus' followers went to great lengths to show that their views were consistent with those of their leader. The more innovative they were, it seems, the more they insisted on their orthodoxy. The problem of orthodoxy became especially acute at the time when Zeno of Sidon was head of the Epicurean school at Athens, about the end of the second century to the early 70s BC.[1] The period of Zeno and his immediate followers is also a time when the Epicureans showed

From the paper read 25 October 1990, at Boston University as part of the 13th Annual Boston Area Colloquium in Ancient Philosophy.

[1] The problem of orthodoxy is well attested in the areas of epistemology and ethics, as well as rhetoric and poetry. On epistemology, see Asmis 1984, esp. pp. 220–4. When Zeno of Sidon was head of the Epicurean school there was a very acrimonious debate among Epicureans on who observed Epicurus' teachings about whether rhetoric is a craft. This debate is discussed in detail by Sedley 1989; see also Asmis 1990: 2400–2. In his work Περὶ παρρησίας, (fr. 45. 8–11 Olivieri), Philodemus sums up the loyalty of Epicurus' followers in a statement which is virtually an oath of loyalty: καὶ τὸ συνέχον καὶ κυρι|ώτ[α]τον, Ἐπικούρωι, κα|θ᾽ ὃν ζῆν ἡ⟨ι⟩ρήμεθα, πει|θαρχήσομεν ('the basic and most important [principle] is that we will obey Epicurus, according to whom we have chosen to live').

an especially strong interest in poetry. Zeno and his student Philodemus of Gadara both offered comprehensive criticisms of poetic theories; and while Lucretius' great poem on the nature of the universe overshadows all contemporary poetry, Philodemus' epigrams are among the most elegant examples of this genre. There are just a few, well-known bits of evidence about Epicurus' views on poetry. But these testimonies, in conjunction with the much larger and partially unfamiliar body of evidence concerning the later period, suggest that there is greater continuity between Epicurus and his followers than has been thought.

The allegorist Heraclitus (about the first century AD) pairs Epicurus with Plato as a detractor of Homer, while charging him with deriving his doctrines from the great poet. Heraclitus accuses Epicurus of condemning all of poetry, not just Homer; and he describes Epicurus as 'purifying himself (ἀφοσιούμενος) from all of poetry at once as a destructive lure of fictitious stories.'[2] He also charges that, although Epicurus condemned poetry, he was a 'Phaeacian' philosopher who, by misinterpreting Odysseus' words to Alcinous, stole from Homer the notion that the supreme good is pleasure.[3] Another late author, Athenaeus, associates Epicurus with Plato as someone who expelled Homer from cities.[4]

But Epicurus' hostility to poetry is not as simple a matter as Heraclitus and Athenaeus make out. According to Heraclitus, the Homeric words that Epicurus misinterpreted were:

> . . . ὅταν εὐφροσύνη μὲν ἔχῃ κατὰ δῆμον ἅπαντα,
> δαιτυμόνες δ' ἀνὰ δώματ' ἀκουάζωνται ἀοιδοῦ
> τοῦτό τί μοι κάλλιστον ἐνὶ φρεσὶν εἴδεται.

> When joy possesses all the people,
> and banqueters throughout the house listen to the singer,
> this seems to my mind most beautiful.[5]

Heraclitus has omitted three lines, coming just after mention of the singer, in which Odysseus describes the abundance of food and drink at the banquet. The whole passage is:

---

[2] *Homeric Problems* 79 and 4 (= U 229), including at 4: ἅπασαν ὁμοῦ ποιητικὴν ὥσπερ ὀλέθριον μύθων δέλεαρ ἀφοσιούμενος.
[3] *Homeric Problems* 79 = partly at U 229.
[4] *Deipnosophistae* 5. 187c = U 228.
[5] *Homeric Problems* 79. These lines correspond to *Odyssey* 9. 6–7 and 11.

οὐ γὰρ ἐγώ γέ τί φημι τέλος χαριέστερον εἶναι
ἢ ὅτ' ἐυφροσύνη μὲν ἔχῃ κατὰ δῆμον ἅπαντα,
δαιτυμόνες δ' ἀνὰ δώματ' ἀκουάζωνται ἀοιδοῦ
ἥμενοι ἐξείης, παρὰ δὲ πλήθωσι τράπεζαι
σίτου καὶ κρειῶν, μέθυ δ' ἐκ κρητῆρος ἀφύσσων
οἰνοχόος φορέῃσι καὶ ἐγχείῃ δεπάεσσι·
τοῦτό τί μοι κάλλιστον ἐνὶ φρεσὶν εἴδεται εἶναι.

For I say that there is no more pleasant fulfilment than when joy possesses
all the people, and banqueters throughout the house listen to the singer,
sitting next to each other, and alongside the tables are full of bread and meat,
and the wine-pourer draws drink from the mixing-bowl and brings it and
pours it into cups. This seems to my mind to be most beautiful.[6]

According to Heraclitus, Epicurus failed to notice that Odysseus was
driven by necessity to praise his host's way of life. What Heraclitus
fails to notice himself is that, in the very lines he has cited, Odysseus
is praising the joy of listening to the songs of a poet.

Odysseus' words to Alcinous are among the most famous passages
of poetry in antiquity.[7] Because they were thought to propose a view
of the goal (τέλος) of life, they received much philosophical attention.
Plato cited only Homer's description of food and drink, omitting the
lines dealing with the singer, to illustrate the inadequacy of Homer's
ethics.[8] Aristotle cited only the lines dealing with the singer as evidence that Homer believed that music is an appropriate leisure time
activity.[9] Later authors associated the whole passage with Epicurean
hedonism. Some, like Heraclitus, accused Epicurus explicitly of
taking his hedonism from Homer.[10] More perceptively, Seneca
derides the attempt to turn Homer into an Epicurean or any other
philosopher. Seneca also describes the ostensible 'Epicurean Homer'

---

[6] *Odyssey* 9. 5-11.
[7] The history of these verses, dubbed Homer's 'golden verses,' is discussed by
Kaiser 1964: 213-23.
[8] *Republic* 3. 390a-b.
[9] *Politics* 1338ª27-30.
[10] These references have been gathered by Bignone 1936; see also Kaiser 1964,
220-1. Athenaeus (*Deipnosophistae* 12. 513a-c), quoting the entire passage at *Odyssey*
9. 5-12, writes that 'Odysseus seems to be the leader for Epicurus' notorious pleasure';
then he cites a defence of Odysseus similar to that of Heraclitus. Likewise, ps-Plutarch
(*De vita et poesi Homeri* 2. 150) claims that Epicurus was misled by Odysseus' words to
propose pleasure as the goal of happiness. A scholiast on *Odyssey* 9. 28 and Eustathius
(p. 1612, 10) also claim that Epicurus took the goal of pleasure from Homer.
Exceptionally, the scholiast approves of Epicurus' notion of the goal, with the observation that he extended the Homeric goal to all circumstances of life.

as one who praises peace, banquets, and songs.[11] Implicitly, the entire later tradition associates the full measure of Homeric conviviality, including poetic entertainment, with Epicureanism.

Although the charge of plagiarism is hardly plausible, it is not implausible, as Bignone has argued, that Epicurus cited Odysseus' words in his own writings.[12] Despite his reputation for being unlearned, Epicurus was not averse to citing verses for his own ends. Epicurus seems to have quoted a couple of verses from Sophocles' *Trachinians* to illustrate his claim that we naturally avoid pain.[13] He might well have cited the famous Homeric verses to explain his complementary doctrine that we all naturally seek pleasure. By doing so, he would have staked a position within a philosophical tradition; nor need he have imputed any special insight to either Odysseus or Homer. If Epicurus did cite the passage, it is unlikely that he excluded poetic entertainment from the life of pleasure.

Plutarch is our main witness for Epicurus' attitude to poetry. He subordinates the charge that Epicurus shunned poetry to the general charge that he rejected all intellectual pleasures. In his treatise *It is impossible to live pleasantly according to Epicurus*, Plutarch alleges that both Epicurus and Metrodorus berated their intellectual forebears, including the poets, in the most abusive language. Two terms cited by Plutarch, apparently of the milder sort, are 'poetic confusion' (ποιητικὴ τύρβη) and 'the foolish statements (μωρολογήματα) of Homer.'[14] Plutarch accuses the Epicureans of rejecting both historical investigation, including the study of poetry, and the

---

[11] Seneca (*Epistle* 88. 5): nam modo Stoicum illum faciunt . . . modo Epicureum, laudantem statum quietae civitatis et inter convivia cantusque vitam exigentis ('they sometimes make him a Stoic . . ., sometimes an Epicurean who praises the condition of a government that is at peace and passes life among banquets and songs'). In a lighter vein, Lucian (*Parasite* 10-11), quoting 'banqueters sitting next to each other' and 'alongside the tables are full of bread and meat,' suggests that Epicurus stole from Homer the goal of the parasite.

[12] Bignone 1936: 270-3, holds that Epicurus cited the verses polemically to show, against Aristotle, that the type of enjoyment praised by Odysseus is not the supreme good; instead, Bignone proposes, Epicurus wished to show that the supreme pleasure is the absence of pain and anxiety, that is, catastematic pleasure. In response to Bignone, Giancotti 1960: 83-4, argues that Epicurus cited the verses in partial agreement with Odysseus; for Epicurus approves of the kinetic pleasure of listening to songs and consuming food and drink, even though this is not the supreme good, catastematic pleasure. A passage in *PHerc.* 1012 (see below, n. 18) suggests that Epicurus cited Odysseus' words as expressing a commonplace opinion.

[13] Diogenes Laertius 10. 137 (= U 66).

[14] 1087a = U 228.

mathematical studies of geometry, astronomy, and harmonics.[15] As an example of Epicurean philistinism, Plutarch cites a statement from Metrodorus' *On Poems* : 'Don't worry,' Metrodorus said, about admitting that you don't even know 'on whose side Hector was, or the first lines of Homer's poetry, or the middle'.[16] Plutarch also reports that the Epicureans urged their students to 'hoist sail' in order to flee intellectual pleasures. In particular, he notes, Epicurus' entire entourage urged Pythocles not to 'envy the so-called liberal education'; and they praised a certain Apelles for having kept himself entirely 'pure' (καθαρόν) of learning.[17] These admonitions can be traced to Epicurus' own writings. Epicurus urged Pythocles in a letter: 'Flee all education, hoisting sail'.[18] According to Athenaeus, Epicurus' words to Apelles were: 'I call you blessed, Apelles, because you set out for philosophy, pure of all education.' Athenaeus adds that Epicurus was himself 'uninitiated in the educational curriculum.'[19]

The sail boat in Epicurus' *Letter* is an allusion to the boat in which Odysseus sailed past the Sirens.[20] In another treatise, *How a young person should listen to poets*, Plutarch explicitly associates the Epicurean hoisting of sails with the Homeric episode by asking: should we protect the young against the deceptions of poetry by

---

[15] 1092d–1094d.

[16] 1094d–e

[17] 1094d, including: ὅπως οὐ ζηλώσει τὴν ἐλευθέριον καλουμένην παιδείαν.

[18] 10. 6 (= U 163): παιδείαν δὲ πᾶσαν, μακάριε, φεῦγε τἀκάτιον ἀράμενος. Quintilian (12. 2. 24) also quotes this advice. It is possible, as Bignone 1936: 282-3 has suggested, that Epicurus included a polemic against Homer in the same letter to Pythocles. *PHerc.* 1012, whose author was conjectured by Crönert to be Demetrius the Laconian, contains an address to Pythocles, together with an attack on Homer, as follows (col. 48. 8–13): Ὅμη|ρος μὲν γὰρ οὐδὲν πλῆον | περὶ τῶν τοιούτων διέ|γνωκεν ἤπερ ο[ἱ] λοι[πο]ὶ ἄν|θ[ρω]ποι, ἡμεῖς δ[έ], ὦ Πυθό|κλ[εις ... ('Homer recognized nothing more about such matters than the rest of mankind, but we, Pythocles . . .') The text is fr. 70 of Enzo Puglia's new edition of fragments, 1980: 49. Bignone argued that Demetrius excerpted not only the address to Pythocles from Epicurus' letter (as is generally agreed), but probably also the preceding remarks on Homer. Puglia's new text strongly supports this suggestion. The issue under discussion is Homer's notion of enjoyment, as indicated by the word [ἀπό]|λαυσιν at lines 4–5. The claim that Homer knew no more than the rest of mankind also occurs in the arguments against grammar which are attributed by Sextus Empiricus 'especially' to the Epicureans (*Adv. math.* 1. 285 and 299, see below).

[19] *Deipnosophistae* 13. 588a (= U 117), including: μακαρίζω σε, ὦ Ἀπελλῆ, ὅτι καθαρὸς πάσης παιδείας ἐπὶ φιλοσοφίαν ὡρμήσας.

[20] The Sirens' song was commonly taken to symbolize the attractiveness of learning in general and poetry in particular; see Kaiser 1964: 109-36.

plugging their ears with wax (as happened to Odysseus' men), forcing them to flee poetry 'by hoisting the sails of an Epicurean boat'; or should we protect them by binding them and straightening their judgment with reason (Odysseus' choice)?[21] The same Siren imagery is implicit in the description of poetry as a 'destructive lure,' which the allegorist Heraclitus attributes to Epicurus. Heraclitus' entire description of Epicurus as 'purifying himself' (ἀφοσιούμενος) from this lure seems to be based on the same well-known core of testimonies cited by Plutarch and others. The purity demanded by Epicurus has a religious aspect; and Athenaeus responds to it by calling Epicurus 'uninitiated.'

Plutarch shows that Epicurus' opposition to poetry is part of a larger issue, education. Like Plato in the *Republic*, Epicurus believed that the whole traditional educational system, with its teaching of Homer and other poets, was a corrupting influence that prevented a person from achieving happiness. Epicurus also rejected the alternative curriculum proposed by Plato in the *Republic*, with its purged poetry and rigorous program of mathematics. Epicurus aimed to replace both types of education with Epicurean philosophy. Accordingly, he assured his students that it was an advantage not to be educated; and, unlike most philosophers, he welcomed the uneducated, both young and old, to his school.

But Plutarch's testimony, too, is ambivalent. Embedded within his attack is evidence that Epicurus was, in part, hospitable to poetry. On the one hand, Plutarch notes, Epicurus claims in his *Questions* (Διαπορίαι) that the wise person is a 'lover of sights (φιλοθέωρον) and enjoys hearing and seeing Dionysiac performances (χαίροντα . . . ἀκροάμασι καὶ θεάμασι Διονυσιακοῖς) as much as anyone'; on the other hand, Epicurus does not permit musical or philological inquiry even over drink, but in his work *On Kingship* (Περὶ βασιλείας) 'recommends even to music-loving (φιλομούσοις) kings that they should put up with military narratives and vulgar jesting at parties rather than with lectures on musical and poetic problems.'[22]

---

[21] *De poetis audiendis* 15d.

[22] *Non posse suaviter vivi* 1095c (= U 5 and 20): φιλοθέωρον μὲν ἀποφαίνων τὸν σοφὸν ἐν ταῖς Διαπορίαις καὶ χαίροντα παρ' ὁντινοῦν ἕτερον ἀκροάμασι καὶ θεάμασι Διονυσιακοῖς, προβλήμασι δὲ μουσικοῖς καὶ κριτικῶν φιλολόγοις ζητήμασιν οὐδὲ παρὰ πότον διδοὺς χώραν, ἀλλὰ καὶ τοῖς φιλομούσοις τῶν βασιλέων παραινῶν στρατηγικὰ διηγήματα καὶ φορτικὰς βωμολοχίας ὑπομένειν μᾶλλον ἐν τοῖς συμποσίοις ἢ λόγους περὶ μουσικῶν καὶ ποιητικῶν προβλημάτων περαινομένους. ταυτὶ γὰρ ἐτόλμησεν γράφειν ἐν τῷ Περὶ βασιλείας . . .

Plutarch thinks that these two positions are contradictory: how can the Epicureans care so much about musical performances, if they shut their ears to discussions about musical and poetic matters, such as musical modes, poetic styles, and so on?[23] In a manner that is typical of him, Plutarch has juxtaposed two excerpts that are not really in conflict with each other. In his *Questions*, Epicurus challenges a distinction made by Plato in the *Republic*.[24] Socrates argues that ordinary lovers of sights (φιλο-θεάμονες) and lovers of hearing (φιλήκοοι) differ from philosophers (φιλόσοφοι) in that the former chase the sights and sounds of sensible things, whereas philosophers seek the wisdom of knowing things in themselves. The lovers of sounds, especially, are strangely unphilosophical, as Glaucon observes: they are unwilling to participate in discussion and 'run around all the Dionysiac festivals' instead, 'as though they had rented out their ears to listen to all the choruses.' True philosophers, Socrates proposes, are lovers of sight in the special sense of being lovers of the sight of truth.[25] Using φιλοθέωρος as a synonym for φιλοθεάμων, Epicurus responds to Plato's distinction by contending that the wise person loves the sights and sounds of Dionysiac festivals as much as anyone.[26] The Epicurean wise person does not forsake the objects of sense perception in the pursuit of truth; for wisdom consists precisely in enjoying sensory experiences and having correct opinions about them. Epicurus agrees that the wise person loves the sight of truth, but insists that the love of truth encompasses the love of visual spectacles and auditory performances.

In this confrontation with Plato, Epicurus gives clear approval to the enjoyment of musical and poetic performances. In the second half

Diogenes Laertius (10. 120) paraphrases the first claim as follows: μᾶλλόν τε εὐφρανθήσεσθαι τῶν ἄλλων ἐν ταῖς θεωρίαις ('[the wise person] delights more than others in spectacles').

[23]  *Non posse suaviter vivi* 1095e–1096c.

[24]  *Republic* 5. 475d–476b. This attack on Plato is further evidence that Epicurus studied Plato's dialogues.

[25]  475d–e.

[26]  Boyancé 1947: 91–2 suggests that Epicurus' attitude to Dionysiac festivals is a concession to established religious practice, rather than an endorsement of poetic performances: the Epicurean, he proposes, will participate in religious festivals, even though he does not share the ordinary person's beliefs; cf. Obbink 1984: 607–19. Although the terms φιλοθέωρος, θεωρία, and θέαμα can apply to religious spectacles, there is no reason to suppose that their scope is restricted to religious worship here. As was customary, Epicurus regularly uses forms of θεωρ- to refer to visual or mental viewing in general.

of Plutarch's indictment, Epicurus rejects an entirely different use of leisure time, listening to lectures on musical and poetic problems. These are lectures given by musicologists and grammarians or literary 'critics,' experts who, according to Epicurus, make no contribution to happiness.[27] By contrast, Epicurus approves of philosophical inquiry about music and poetry. According to Diogenes Laertius, Epicurus held that the wise person 'alone would discuss music and poetry correctly.'[28] Epicurus himself wrote a book, not extant, *On Music*; and his friend Metrodorus, as we saw, wrote *On Poems*.[29] In advising kings to put up with military talk and buffoonery at parties rather than with musical and literary criticism, Epicurus does not advocate the former kind of entertainment, but suggests merely that it is more tolerable than the latter. Military talk, we may guess, might be useful for kings, even though a party is hardly the proper occasion for it, and buffoonery might be pleasant, whereas musicology and philology are neither. In his work *Symposium*, Epicurus showed that appropriate subjects of discussion at parties are indigestion, fever, wine, and sexual intercourse—all topics that are useful for party-goers to know about.[30] But Epicurus does not imply here or elsewhere that one should fill one's leisure time with nothing but useful discussion. It is significant that he does not advise 'music-loving' kings to give up music; he urges them only not to waste their time listening to learned discussions about it.

Although Plutarch regards Epicurus' notion of entertainment as incredibly crude, his testimony indicates that Epicurus had a clear-cut position. Epicurus distinguished between two uses of poetry, education and entertainment, and condemned poetry wholesale as education, while welcoming it as entertainment. Plutarch charges Epicurus with just one type of inconsistency: excluding musical and

---

[27] Plutarch pairs the 'critics' with the musicologists (*Non posse suaviter vivi* 1095c, see n. 22 above). There is a fine line between 'grammarians' and 'critics.' As Sextus Empiricus shows (*Adv. math.* 1. 93), grammar included poetic criticism. Some who called themselves 'critics' held that grammar is subordinate to 'criticism'; among them, Crates held that, unlike the grammarian, the 'critic' must be experienced in 'all knowledge of speech (λογικῆς ἐπιστήμης)' (*Adv. math.* 1. 79).

[28] Diogenes Laertius 10. 121.

[29] Another friend of Epicurus, Colotes, discussed poetry in his work *Against Plato's Lysis*. It is difficult to extract any information from the few relevant fragments; see Crönert 1906: 6–12; and Mancini 1976: 61–7, esp. 61–3.

[30] U 56–63.

literary learning from the appreciation of music and poetry. But Epicurus' dichotomy suggests a more serious inconsistency. How can the two uses of poetry, education and entertainment, be compartmentalized so neatly as Epicurus supposes? Is it possible for a person to derive enjoyment from poetic performances without being contaminated by morally bad subject matter? Plato did not think so. Epicurus seems to believe optimistically that one can. Presumably, Epicurus held that it is a sufficient protection to come to a poetic performance with a philosophically trained mind. Epicurus adopted an analogous position concerning religious ritual: the Epicurean participates in it freely, while discounting false religious beliefs. Both positions betoken a strong faith in human rationality.[31]

Unlike Plato, Epicurus did not propose to use a purified type of poetry as a propaedeutic to philosophy or happiness. Nor did he consider poetic form appropriate for teaching philosophical doctrines. In his list of things that the Epicurean wise person will and won't do, Diogenes Laertius reports that, although the wise person alone would speak correctly about music and poetry, he would not practice the composition of poems,[32] and that he would leave behind prose writings.[33] As the writings of Epicurus and his circle amply illustrate, the wise person uses prose, not poetry, to instruct others. What prevents Epicurus from making poetry a handmaid to philosophy is again, I suggest, his rationalism. Although there is no doubt that Epicurus and his followers practiced irrational indoctrination, it was Epicurus' aim to persuade his students by an appeal to their intellectual powers, or, as he conceived it, by philosophical examination. He sought to mould their character by undisguised opinions, approved by a mental act of judgement on the part of each person. To this end, he required clarity as the only quality of good speech.[34] It is the function of clear speech to communicate clear opinions that are verifiable by each student on the basis of sensory experience. False tales, mimetic experience, public speeches are all rejected as educational tools because they do not engage a person in a clear vision of

---

[31] Ronconi 1963 argues that there is an irreconcilable conflict between Epicurus' theory, which makes him repudiate all of poetry, and his practice, whereby he cites poetry and recommends Dionysiac festivals.

[32] Diogenes Laertius 10. 121 (= U 568).

[33] Diogenes Laertius 10. 120 (= U 563): συγγράμματα καταλείψειν.

[34] Diogenes Laertius 10. 13.

the truth.[35] What produces a happy life is 'sober reasoning' in all circumstances;[36] and this depends on having a clear view of human nature, as imparted by the clear speech of philosophy.

Granted that the wise person will not use poetry to instruct others, why should he or she not compose poems for private enjoyment? There is some confusion about Epicurus' prohibition in the text of Diogenes (10. 121). All the manuscripts have: [τὸν σοφὸν . . .] ποιήματά τε ἐνεργεῖν οὐκ ἂν ποιῆσαι. Since the combination of the two infinitives is ungrammatical, all editors have accepted Usener's emendation of ἐνεργείᾳ for ἐνεργεῖν. According to Usener, Epicurus' meaning is that, whereas the wise person has poetic ability, he won't use this ability 'in actuality.'[37] This interpretation makes sense only if we understand the wise person's poetic ability in the very restricted sense of an ability to judge a poem philosophically: the wise person knows all that it is useful to know about poems, but he does not have the expertise that a practicing poet has. The wise person, therefore, does not compose poems 'in actuality'—that is, not at all. Epicurus might have justified this absolute prohibition on the ground that the toil of learning the poetic craft outweighs the enjoyment of practicing it; or he might have held that the wise man will have nothing to do with an inherently deceptive mode of expression.

But Diogenes' report admits of another interpretation. This is to take either ἐνεργείᾳ, as emended, or ἐνεργεῖν, understood as a gloss on ποιῆσαι, in the sense of 'being busy at,' or 'making a practice of,' or 'practicing energetically'—meanings primarily associated with the corresponding adjective ἐνεργός and adverb ἐνεργῶς. In that case, Epicurus is not prohibiting the wise person from dabbling in the composition of poetry, but only from busying himself with it or practicing it in the manner of a professional poet. I shall return to this possibility.

In the centuries after Epicurus, his followers both defended and revised his position that poetry is to be rejected as education and welcomed as entertainment. Cicero signals a major shift in his book *On Ends*. He taunts his young friend Torquatus, a confirmed

---

[35] According to Diogenes Laertius (10. 120), the wise person 'will not make panegyric speeches' (οὐ πανηγυριεῖν). See further De Lacy 1939.

[36] *Letter to Menoeceus* 132 (νήφων λογισμός).

[37] Usener briefly explained: 'copia et facultas poeseos non minus in sapiente est, etsi carmina non facit'. The contrast between the sage's ability, including his ability as a poet, and his actual practice is well attested in Stoicism (*SVF* 3. 654-6).

Epicurean, by pointing out that he, Torquatus, is devoted to history, poetry, and literature in general, whereas his master, Epicurus, shunned these studies and was altogether uneducated.[38] Torquatus comes to Epicurus' defence by asserting that, according to Epicurus, 'there is no education except that which contributes to the learning of happiness' (*nullam eruditionem esse . . . nisi quae beatae vitae disciplinam iuvaret*). There is no reason why Epicurus should have spent his time reading the poets, 'in whom there is no solid usefulness but only a childish delight' (*in quibus nulla solida utilitas omnisque puerilis est delectatio*) and whom, Torquatus admits, he reads at the urging of Cicero. Nor is there any reason, Torquatus continues, why Epicurus should have wasted his time on the Platonic curriculum of 'music, geometry, arithmetic and astronomy.' For unlike 'the art of life,' or practical philosophy, none of these arts contributes anything to happiness. Torquatus concludes that Epicurus is not uneducated (*ineruditus*), but those are who think they should study into old age what it is disgraceful for them not to have learned as children (*pueri*).[39]

Cicero's presentation is based on well known doxographical material. Similarly to Plutarch, he accuses Epicurus of rejecting all learning, as divided into literary studies and mathematics. But there is an important difference: the Roman Torquatus does not shun traditional studies as Epicurus is said to have done and to have advised others to do. As though aware of his failure to follow Epicurus' example and precept, Torquatus makes Cicero responsible for the deviation.[40] At the same time, Torquatus admits that literary

---

[38] *De finibus* I. 25-6 and 71-2. Cicero appears to use *indoctus* (I. 26 and 72) and *ineruditus* (I. 72, cf. *parum . . . eruditus* at I. 71) as synonyms, corresponding to Greek ἀπαίδευτος.

[39] *De finibus* I. 71-2: Qui quod tibi parum videtur eruditus, ea causa est quod nullam eruditionem esse duxit nisi quae beatae vitae disciplinam iuvaret. An ille tempus aut in poetis evolvendis, ut ego et Triarius te hortatore facimus, consumeret, in quibus nulla solida utilitas omnisque puerilis est delectatio, aut se, ut Plato, in musicis, geometria, numeris, astris contereret, quae et a falsis initiis profecta vera esse non possunt et si essent vera nihil afferrent quo iucundius, id est quo melius viveremus;—eas ergo artes persequeretur, vivendi artem tantam tamque operosam et perinde fructuosam relinqueret? Non ergo Epicurus ineruditus, sed ii indocti qui quae pueros non didicisse turpe est ea putant usque ad senectutem esse discenda.

[40] Giancotti 1959: 24; and 1960: 69-76, holds that there is total agreement between Epicurus and his followers, including Cicero's Torquatus. He suggests that Epicurus and his followers alike condemned only certain poems—those that present myths and appeal to the emotions—as having no utility, whereas they admitted other

and mathematical studies do not contribute to happiness, and that the study of poetry in particular is without 'solid utility' and nothing but a 'childish delight' (*puerilis delectatio*). The latter phrase recalls Plato's proposal in the tenth book of the *Republic* to set aside the 'childish love' (παιδικόν . . . ἔρωτα) of poetry.[41] Torquatus does not set it aside; and he is uncomfortably aware that, whereas Epicurus spent his time in the serious pursuit of philosophy instead of literary and mathematical studies, he is devoting much of his time to a trivial pursuit.

This difference between Torquatus and Epicurus suits Cicero's polemical purpose. Throughout the discussion, Cicero aims to show that Torquatus' professed Epicureanism is incompatible with robust Roman values, as exemplified by Cicero himself. At the same time, Cicero's literary portrait of Torquatus stands for real Epicureans at Rome who were devotees of Epicurus and poetry at once; and we might expect some of them to resist the charge of deviating from their master. How would they defend their study of poetry, without the help of Cicero? Another look at Cicero's exposition suggests a possible defence.

Cicero's Torquatus presents a tightly constructed argument whose major premiss is a definition of 'education' (*eruditio*) as 'that which contributes to the learning of happiness.' Torquatus attributes this definition to Epicurus himself. Accordingly, neither the traditional curriculum nor that of Plato counts as 'education'; the only education in the proper sense is philosophy. The other studies, such as the 'childish (*puerilis*) delight' of poetry, are properly the pursuits of childhood: it would be disgraceful for children (*pueri*) not to occupy themselves with them; but they do not make a person educated. To put the point in Greek, the curriculum of so-called liberal studies is παιδεία only in the etymological sense of being the occupation of children, παῖδες; it is not παιδεία in the proper sense in which education is a training for happiness.

The definition of education is not exemplified in the extant sayings of Epicurus, but might be said to capture his intent.[42] It is clearly a

poems as having utility. This interpretation is in conflict, among other things, with Torquatus' blanket characterization of poetry as having no 'solid utility' (as pointed out by Boyancé 1960: 442).

[41] *Republic* 608a.

[42] Apart from the testimonies that have been cited, *Vatican Saying* 45 is the only

philosophical reinterpretation of the commonplace notion of education.[43] Using the new definition, Epicurus' followers could argue that
when Epicurus urged Pythocles to 'flee all education, hoisting sail'
(παιδείαν δὲ πᾶσαν . . . φεῦγε τἀκάτιον ἀράμενος), he meant: don't be
misled into thinking that what commonly passes for education is
education; shun this spurious education and turn instead to real
education. According to this interpretation, Epicurus was, in effect,
using the term παιδείαν in quotation marks. Plutarch confirms this
hypothetical exegesis by paraphrasing Epicurus' command to
Pythocles as 'do not envy the so-called liberal education.'[44] What
Epicurus did not mean, on the other hand, according to this exegesis
is: avoid so-called liberal studies altogether. So long as a person
shuns these studies as an education, he is free to enjoy them as a
leisure-time activity or, to use the Aristotelian term, as διαγωγή.
Epicurus' admonition to 'hoist sail' does not mean, therefore, as
Plutarch mistook it, that one should shut one's ears to poetry and all
other learning. There is another option: it is possible to flee the
Sirens, as Odysseus did, by experiencing the charm of their song
while escaping its destructive influence. What one needs as a defence
is the only true education, Epicurean philosophy.

It would not be surprising if Cicero was not convinced by this
exegesis. The plain meaning of the testimonies is that Epicurus urged
his followers to get away from traditional and Platonic education
altogether. The hypothetical exegesis, however, proposes nothing
that might not be held to agree with Epicurus' views. His approval of
poetry as an enjoyment provides an opening for the acceptance of
poetry as a leisure-time occupation, or διαγωγή, alongside the serious
pursuit of philosophy. Epicureans like Torquatus could argue that
they really do emulate Pythocles and Apelles, and even Epicurus, in
the only way that matters: they keep themselves pure of so-called
education by giving serious attention only to philosophy. Epicurus'

extant text in which Epicurus uses the term παιδεία. Epicurus shows his contempt for
those who flaunt their learning by observing that the study of nature, φυσιολογία, does
not make people boast or show off 'the education that is an object of rivalry among the
many' (τὴν περιμάχητον παρὰ τοῖς πολλοῖς παιδείαν).

[43] Cicero uses the ordinary definition at 1. 26, when charging Epicurus with being
uneducated: est enim [Epicurus] . . . non satis politus iis artibus quas qui tenent
eruditi appellantur ('[Epicurus] is not sufficiently polished in those arts whose possession causes people to be called educated').

[44] See above, nn. 17 and 18.

followers are quite willing to admit a difference between Epicurus' practice and their own: he did not 'waste' his time in poetry and other so-called liberal studies, whereas they spend time in such pursuits. But this difference, as Torquatus shows, does not amount to a difference in the estimation of these studies. Historically, the difference might be explained by the fact that Epicurus is the philosophical leader and they are the followers: as leader, he gave them the protection they need; and as followers, they may exploit it.

Sextus Empiricus provides a further glimpse of how Epicurus' followers related poetry to philosophy. In agreement with Cicero's Torquatus, Sextus reports that Epicurus held that learning (as ordinarily understood) makes no contribution to wisdom.[45] We have already seen that one type of learning rejected by Epicurus is the criticism of poetry as practiced by the grammarians. According to Sextus, the grammarians tried to show the usefulness of their discipline by arguing that, whereas poetry contains many 'starting-points' (ἀφορμάς) for wisdom and happiness, these truths cannot be discerned adequately without the light shed by the grammarians. The ethical precepts of the philosophers, the grammarians maintained, are rooted in the ethical sayings of the poets; and this is true even of Epicurus, who stole his most important doctrines from the poets.[46] As the allegorist Heraclitus and others confirm, Epicurus had a reputation for stealing from the poets. With obvious reference to the Platonic expulsion of poets from cities, the grammarians also claimed that poetry is useful and even necessary for the welfare of cities.[47]

Against the grammarians, Sextus cites a series of objections which he says are due 'especially' to the Epicureans.[48] In these arguments, poetry is analysed as harmful in three ways. First, although poetry contains some worthwhile statements, these are outweighed by many more statements that are harmful. Since poetry does not supply demonstrative proofs (ἀποδείξεις), which would allow listeners to distinguish between good and bad, listeners incline toward the worse course.[49] Second, whereas philosophers and other prose-writers teach what is useful by pursuing the truth, poets aim at

---

[45] *Adv. math.* I. I; cf. *Adv. math.* 6. 27 (= U 229b).
[46] I. 270-3.
[47] I. 275-6.
[48] I. 299: τὰ μὲν ὑπὸ τῶν ἄλλων λεγόμενα . . . καὶ μάλιστα τῶν Ἐπικουρείων. Sextus distinguishes these arguments from his own Pyrrhonist arguments.
[49] I. 279-80.

all cost to move the soul (ψυχαγωγεῖν), and since falsehood moves the soul more than truth, poets pursue falsehood rather than the truth.[50] Third, poetry is a 'stronghold of human passions,' inflaming anger and the desire for sex and drink.[51] These arguments allow that poetry may occasionally be useful. But poetry can be useful only when the language is clear.[52] Moreover, even if it is occasionally useful for cities, it is not necessary to their welfare; nor, if it is useful for cities, does it follow that it is useful for individuals.[53]

Because they view poetry as predominantly false and harmful, we might expect Sextus' opponents of grammar to brand poets in general as corrupters of humankind and to join with Plato in banning all except morally useful poetry. Instead, they recognize a way of rendering poetry harmless: whereas grammar cannot bring any aid to poetry, philosophy can cancel out the harm and even extract some utility from it. For philosophy can distinguish the good from the bad in poems by supplying proofs. Whereas poetry unaided is harmful, it is harmless and can even be of some small moral benefit when joined by philosophy.

In this partnership, philosophy extends its help to poetry without being dependent on it in any way. 'Genuine philosophers,' Sextus' opponents of grammar claim, do not use the poets as witnesses; instead, their own argument is sufficient to persuade.[54] This is an attack not only on the grammarians, but also on the Stoic propensity to cite poets in support of their doctrines. The attack is reinforced by the claim that the assumptions of poets are far worse than those of ordinary individuals. Examples of how bad the beliefs of the poets are include the castration of Uranos by Cronos and the subjugation of Cronos by Zeus—stories defended by the Stoics by allegorical inter-pretation.[55] This implicit attack against the Stoics agrees with the Epicureans' rejection of allegorical explanation. Epicurus, it is argued, did not steal any doctrines from the poets: for his teaching is fundamentally different from that of the poets; or, if there is a resem-blance, what is admirable is not the mere assertion, but the philo-sophical proof; or the belief is shared by Epicurus with all of mankind, not just the poet.[56]

Although these arguments are clearly indebted to Plato and

[50] I. 296-7.  [51] I. 298.  [52] I. 278.
[53] I. 293-5.  [54] I. 280.  [55] I. 288-91.
[56] I. 283-6.

although Sextus may well have gathered his material from a variety of sources, the overall content and cohesiveness of the arguments show that the Epicurean school is indeed the main source of the arguments, as Sextus states.[57] The demand for clear speech, the distinction between civic and private life, the view that poetry does much harm, and, in general, the claim that learning is useless for happiness, are all fundamental tenets of Epicureanism. Sextus does not name any particular Epicurean; but we can go a little further in trying to pinpoint his source. The view that there is little or no utility in poems, and that poems inflame the emotions, is argued in detail in the writings of Philodemus of Gadara (c. 110-40 BC).[58] In his book *On Music*, Philodemus is concerned primarily with the utility of music; but in the course of his discussion he has much to say about the utility of poems. With a systematic review of poems that are sung, he maintains that they have little or no utility, and that they do much harm by intensifying the emotions. Against an opponent, probably the Stoic Diogenes of Babylon, who agreed with Plato that music has the power to produce orderliness or disorder of the soul, he argues at length that if there is any moral utility in songs, it lies in the poems—or lyrics—not in the musical accompaniment, and even then it is small. The harm done by poems, moreover, can be very great. Marriage songs, for example, are no more useful than cookery; if there is a moral benefit, it comes from the poems, not the music, and then it extends to only a few (if indeed marriage can be said to be a good).[59] Love songs do not help the passion of love either by the music or by the poetry; in the case of most people, most poems inflame it.[60] In particular, Ibycos, Anacreon, and the like corrupted the young with the thoughts expressed in their love songs.[61] Also, poems that are sung as dirges generally do not heal grief, but most often intensify it.[62] Concerning poems in general, Philodemus brings

---

[57] Apart from the general claim that the poets state many morally harmful beliefs, the most conspicuous debt to Plato is the charge that poetry is a stronghold of the passions (as designated by the Stoic term πάθη), with the bipartite division of passions into anger and the desire for food and drink.

[58] Philodemus' views on poetry are discussed in more detail in Asmis 1991.

[59] *On Music* 4, col. 5. 25-37 Neubecker.

[60] *On Music* 4, col. 6. 5-8; I understand 'poems' (from lines 4-5) with ὑπὸ τῶν πλείστων (line 7).

[61] *On Music* 4, col. 14. 7-13. Anacreon is cited likewise by Sextus Empiricus (*Adv. math.* 1. 298) as a poet who 'inflames' the 'love-maddened.'

[62] *On Music* 4, col. 6. 13-18.

his greatest indictment against poetry in his work *On Piety*, where he charges the poets, along with philosophers and others, of holding beliefs about the gods that are 'impious and harmful to humans.'[63]

In the fifth book of *On Poems*, Philodemus extends to all poems the claim that there is little utility in them, while showing that they have a goodness that is independent of the utility of their subject matter. Against Heraclides of Pontus, who followed Plato in demanding that poems be both useful and pleasing, he objects that

he eliminates (ἐκρ[απ]ίζει, literally 'expels with the rod') from goodness the most beautiful poems of the most famous poets because they provide no benefit whatsoever; in the case of some poets [he eliminates] most poems, and in certain cases all poems.[64]

Echoing the Presocratic Heraclitus, who demanded that Homer and Archilochus be expelled (ἐκβάλλεσθαι) from the contests and flogged (ῥαπίζεσθαι),[65] Philodemus uses the compound verb ἐκραπίζει to show his disapproval of Heraclides' censoriousness. If utility is admitted as a criterion of a good poem, Philodemus argues, a large proportion of the most beautiful poems of the most famous poets will not qualify as good. Philodemus restates his objection later in book 5 in a survey of poetic theories that he owes to his teacher Zeno of Sidon.[66] Using the same verb ἐκραπίζειν, which occurs only in these two places, he now rejects the requirement for poetic utility in general on the ground that it

eliminates (ἐκραπ[ίζ]ει) many wholly beautiful poems, some containing what is useless, others containing what is not . . . and prefers many that are worse, as many as contain beneficial or more beneficial thoughts.[67]

Philodemus agrees with Zeno that utility is absent from many utterly beautiful poems and is not a requirement of good poetry. He

---

[63] *On Piety*, PHerc. 247. 7 = fr. 48, p. 20 Gomperz.

[64] *On Poems* 5, col. I. 10-18 Jensen: . . . τὰ κάλ|λιστ[α] ποιήματα τῶν [δο|κιμ[ω]τάτων ποιητῶ[ν | διὰ τὸ μηδ' ἡντινοῦν | ὠφελίαν παρασκευ[ά-]|ζειν, ἐνίων δὲ καὶ [τὰ | πλε[ί]οστα, τινῶν δὲ πά[ν] |τα [τ]ῆς ἀρετῆς ἐκρ[απ]ί|ζει.

[65] DK 22 B 42.

[66] Philodemus introduces his survey by saying that he will refute the opinions found in Zeno (*On Poems* 5, col. 26. 19-23). Zeno classified these opinions for the purpose of criticism and may be assumed to be responsible for the analysis as a whole, including the objections.

[67] *On Poems* 5, col. 29. 8-17 Jensen: . . . πολλὰ τῶν παν[κά-]|λ[ων] ἐκραπ[ίζ]ει ποιημά|των τὰ μέ[ν ἀ]νωφελῆ, | τὰ [δὲ οὐδ' ἀνωφελ]ῆ περι|έχοντ[α, καὶ π]ολλὰ πρ[ο|κρίνει τ[ῶ]ν ἡττόνων, | ὅσα τὰς ὠφελίμους ἢ τὰς | ὠφελιμωτέρας, περιειλη|φε.

obviously places a high value on poems that have no utility, and thereby shows why an Epicurean might wish to devote time to poetry, despite its moral deficiencies.

Like Sextus' opponents of grammar, Philodemus considers it the function of prose, not poetry, to be useful. Although the thrust of his argument in *On Music* is that any moral benefit associated with music comes from the words of songs, not the music, he does not consider poems suited for moral instruction. One reason, as Philodemus shows in an argument against the Stoic Cleanthes, is that poetic expression blunts any moral message that a poem might have. Against Cleanthes' claim that melody reinforces the moral impact of a poem and makes the thoughts more useful, Philodemus argues that melody not only fails to enhance but actually weakens the moral utility of the thoughts because the pleasure, as well as the special qualities of the sounds, distract the listener, because 'the words are expressed continuously and not naturally,' and so on.[68] The same argument applies to poems without music; in their case, too, the moral force of a poem is weakened by the attendant pleasure, the peculiarity of the sounds, and the unnatural diction. In general, Philodemus believes, poetic expression is not as clear as prose. He points out in *On Poems* that not every kind of clarity is permitted to poets nor does the permitted kind seem to fit all thoughts.[69] In agreement with Sextus' opponents of grammar, he draws a distinction between poems and 'demonstrative discourses' (ἀποδεικτικοὶ λόγοι).[70] The kind of clarity that poems lack most conspicuously is the clarity of philosophical demonstration; and since this is an indispensable tool of moral instruction, the usefulness of poems is severely limited.

It follows that if ever poems are useful, prose would have been more useful. In *On Music*, Philodemus is not at all persuaded that the many examples of how poets stopped civil strife with their songs are historically accurate. But if Stesichorus and Pindar did indeed persuade their fellow citizens to put aside their differences, Philodemus writes, they did so by speech (λόγων) put in poetic form, not by the melodies; and 'they would have succeeded better if they

---

[68] *On Music* 4, col. 28. 16–35; cf. 26. 9–14. At col. 15. 5–7 Philodemus claims that music, like sexual pleasure and drink, distracts a person from paying attention to the misfortunes of love.

[69] *On Poems* 5, col. 28. 26–32.

[70] *On Poems* 5, col. 29. 33–6.

had tried to dissuade them by prose.'[71] Of prose, the best kind is philosophical prose, whose job it is to teach what is morally correct. Music, Philodemus points out, cannot console the distraught lover at all; only the words (λόγος) can do so.[72] Words, moreover, overpower sexual passion by 'teaching what is futile, harmful, and insatiable.'[73] The words of a song can do some teaching. But the teaching of moral truths is clearly the special prerogative of philosophical prose, using 'demonstrative discourses' to show, among other things, that unless a limit is placed on desires, they are insatiable and cause great unhappiness. Philodemus therefore suggests that instead of contributing music toward the acquisition of 'erotic virtue,' as Diogenes of Babylon seems to have claimed, the Muse Erato contributed 'poetry or, better still, philosophy.'[74] Since 'everything has been attributed to the Muses', Philodemus reasons, we might as well make Erato responsible for contributing philosophy to the virtue identified as 'erotic' by the Stoics. For music does not contribute one bit toward helping people who are in love. Poetry can help a little; but it can help only to the extent that it agrees with philosophy, which alone can show the full truth about love.

In his own quarrel with poetry, Philodemus agrees with Plato that poets have said 'vulgar, bad, and contradictory' things about every virtue. If they were to have knowledge about virtue, Philodemus adds, 'they would not have this knowledge as poets ([κ]αθ' ὃ ποιηταί), let alone as musicians.'[75] Moral knowledge belongs to the philosopher; it belongs to poets—and here Philodemus parts with Plato— to create beautiful poems, whether morally beneficial or not. Drawing the same distinction between the proper function and an incidental attribute of a poem, Philodemus claims in his Zenonian survey of poetic theories in *On Poems* that 'even if [poems] benefit, they do not benefit as poems (κα[θὸ πό]ηματ').'[76] Philodemus agrees with Sextus' opponents of grammar that it is not the aim of poetry to present the truth; hence, if poetry does impart moral truths, this is incidental to its function. Because it is not the job of the poet to

---

[71] *On Music* 4, col. 20. 7-17.
[72] *On Music* 4, col. 15. 1-5.
[73] *On Music* 4, col. 13. 16-24.
[74] *On Music* 4, col. 15. 15-23.
[75] *On Music* 4, col. 26. 1-7, including: οὐ | μὴν ἀλλ' οὐδὲ [κ]αθ' ὃ ποιη|ταὶ ταῦτ' εἰδεί[εν] ἄν, οὐχ ὅτι|καθ' ὃ μουσικοί.
[76] *On Poems* 5, col. 29. 17-19: κᾶν ὠφελῇ, | κα[θὸ πο]ήματ' οὐκ ὠφε|λεῖ.

discover or impart truths, the philosopher will not use the poet as a witness. In his work *On Rhetoric*, Philodemus picks out a favorite poet of many philosophers in order to make this point: 'How would a philosopher pay attention to Euripides, especially since he has proof (πίστιν) whereas Euripides does not even bring in proof?'[77] These similarities between Philodemus' position and Sextus' account suggest that Sextus may have drawn directly on Philodemus or one of his circle. Such a conjecture receives some support from the fact that in his book *Against the Musicians* Sextus cites a series of arguments that coincide even more closely with arguments found in Philodemus' *On Music*.[78] Philodemus, we know, was strongly indebted to his teacher Zeno, whom he greatly admired; and, as we have seen, in *On Poems* he used a summary of poetic theories prepared by Zeno.[79] Zeno wrote a work *On Grammar*, as well as a work *On the Use of Poems*, which are not extant.[80] A powerful and original thinker, Zeno was remarkably adept at gathering material for his arguments from many sources and marshalling them in tight array against his opponents. It is plausible, therefore, that Zeno was the primary source of Sextus' arguments.[81]

[77] *On Rhetoric* HV[1] v. 5, col. 27. 10–14 (Sudhaus v. 1, p. 262): καὶ πῶς Εὐριπίδει φιλόσοφος | ἂν προσέχοι καὶ ταῦτα μη|δὲ πίστιν εἰσφέροντι | πίστιν αὐτὸς ἔχων; The type of proof used by a philosopher is demonstrative proof, ἀπόδειξις; πίστις is 'proof' in a wider sense, which includes the proofs used by rhetoricians and, at times, poets. In Sextus' arguments, Euripides is called 'the philosopher of the stage' and he is said to have held more reasonable views about the gods than Homer or Hesiod (*Adv. math.* 1. 288–9).

[78] *Adv. math.* 6. 19–37. This section consists of the 'more dogmatic', non-Pyrrhonist arguments against music (as announced at 6. 4). Gigante 1981: 215–21, showed that there is a close agreement between this section and Philodemus' *On Music*, and conjectured that Sextus is here indebted directly to Philodemus.

[79] Many of Philodemus' writings contain summaries or transcriptions of Zeno's teachings; and some are derived entirely from him. Zeno had a strong interest in literature as well as in mathematics and logic. In addition to *On Poems*, Philodemus' other major work on literature, *On Rhetoric*, contains extensive excerpts from Zeno's writings.

[80] *PHerc.* 1005, col. 10, contains a list of Zeno's works, including περὶ γραμματικῆς and περὶ ποιημάτων χρήσεως. *PHerc.* 1012, whose author is thought to be Demetrius the Laconian, contains two references to Zeno that may have been derived from Zeno's *On Grammar*; see Angeli and Colaizzo 1979: 76. There are no other testimonies about Zeno's *On Grammar*.

[81] Crönert (1906: 119) previously suggested that Sextus' Epicureans are οἱ περὶ τὸν Ζήνωνα and that Sextus used Zeno's *On Grammar*. Crönert supposes, unnecessarily in my view, that Sextus derived his knowledge of Zeno's work from Aenesidemos. It is possible that Demetrius the Laconian, an associate of Zeno and Philodemus, also participated in the debate on the usefulness of poetry. *PHerc.* 1014 is entitled

Cicero, Sextus, and, above all, Philodemus show that at the end of the second century and in the first half of the first century BC the Epicureans reconsidered the relationship between poetry and philosophy. Although we have very little evidence about Epicurus, the testimonies suggest that whereas Epicurus emphasized the harmful educational influence of poetry and the need to replace poetic teaching by philosophy, his followers took the more hospitable view that it is not the function of poetry to teach and that philosophy may form an alliance with poetry, in which both pursuits achieve their own ends. In this partnership, the serious study of philosophy gives licence to Epicureans like Torquatus to spend their leisure time in the enjoyable, though fundamentally useless, study of poetry. As a sign of this more conciliatory view, Cicero's Torquatus describes poetry as having 'no solid usefulness' (*nulla solida utilitas*). Torquatus recognizes that only philosophy can bring happiness; but since philosophy can render the enjoyment of poetry harmless, there is no reason why he should not indulge in this delight, which may even bring a little incidental moral benefit. Since Epicurus, too, admitted poetry as a form of enjoyment, there is no contradiction with Epicurus' doctrine; but a new place is given to poetry as a study subordinate to philosophy.

Philodemus is the outstanding example of a Greek Epicurean who conjoined the pursuit of poetry with philosophy. But he went considerably further than Cicero's Torquatus in the value he placed on poetry. As we have seen, Philodemus held that poetry can do much harm. In particular, he agreed with Epicurean tradition that Homer said many foolish and harmful things. His book *On Piety* (Περὶ εὐσεβείας) contains striking examples of how Homer propagated false and pernicious beliefs about the gods.[82] But Philodemus also believed that Homer provides beneficial moral guidance for rulers. In fact, Philodemus devoted an entire treatise to showing that Homer offers

'Demetrius' *On Poems 2*', and has been attributed to the Laconian by the most recent editor, Costantina Romeo 1988. It is debatable, however, whether the author is the Laconian or the first-century BC. Peripatetic; see Romeo, 1988, 21–5. The extant text shows a detailed acquaintance with Greek poetry and includes excerpts from Homer, Euripides, and others.

[82] For example, he denounces Homer's description of Ares, son of Zeus, as 'mindless, lawless, murderous, a lover of strife and of battle' (*On Piety*, PHerc. 1088, 10 = fr. 95. 22–8, p. 46 Gomperz). Other examples of Homeric impiety occur at fr. 37, p. 9 Gomperz; fr. 63, p. 34 Gomperz; and fr. 145, p. 59 Gomperz.

good advice on how to rule. The treatise is *On the Good King according to Homer*; and it has generally been regarded as an anomaly among Epicurean texts. In this work, which is dedicated to Piso, the father-in-law of Caesar and a leading politician himself, Philodemus proposes to extract from Homer 'starting-points . . . for the correction of positions of power' (ἀφ[ορμῶν] . . . εἰς ἐπανόρθωσιν δυνα⟨σ⟩τε[ιῶν]).[83] With numerous examples from the whole range of human Homeric rulers—Odysseus, Nestor, Agamemnon, Achilles, Hector, Alcinous, Telemachus, the suitors, and others—and even some divine rulers, Philodemus gives a detailed analysis of how a ruler should behave both in peace and in war. It looks as though, contrary to Epicurus' alleged expulsion of Homer from the city, Philodemus has led him back.

Whereas Torquatus' devotion to poetry as something pleasurable but fundamentally useless can readily be regarded as an extension of Epicurus' position, the view that Homer is morally useful seems a reversal. Philodemus does bring Homer back into the city—the Roman city—as a politically useful poet; and this is a major turning point in the history of Epicurean poetics. Yet this apparent reversal can also be seen to fit a tradition of interpretation which claims to be faithful to Epicurus' thought. In particular, it fits the view that philosophy may ally itself with poetry in such a way as to illuminate the truths that are found incidentally in poems. Philodemus recognizes that Homeric poetry contains a great deal that is harmful, not just in its theology, but also in its depictions of the misuse of power, notably by Achilles, and most of all, by the suitors. But, according to Philodemus, Homer also shows, through Nestor, Odysseus and others, how the misuse of power is to be corrected. These 'starting-points for the correction' of power need to be illuminated by the philosopher—not anyone else; and this is the job that Philodemus undertakes for Piso, a Roman ruler who is in a position to practice what he is taught.[84] As philosophical interpreter of Homer, Philodemus guides Piso through a reading of Homer by drawing attention to statements that are morally beneficial. The treatise is unique as an example of Epicurean literary criticism, according to which the only legitimate critic is the philosopher, distinguishing

---

[83] Col. 43. 16–19 Dorandi.
[84] At col. 25. 20 Dorandi, Philodemus refers to himself as a 'philosopher.'

what is morally valuable from what is morally harmful. Although Philodemus' procedure resembles that of other philosophers, the theoretical underpinning is wholly different. He does not use the poet as a witness for moral truths, but identifies truths on the basis of his own philosophical understanding.

Philodemus, therefore, extends Epicurus' acceptance of poetry by admitting it not only as a pleasant, but also as a morally useful, pastime. He also made another extension, which concerns the enjoyment of poetry. For the most part, Philodemus seems to follow Epicurus closely on how poetry is to be enjoyed. Indeed, much of what he says about the pleasure of listening to poetry looks like an amplification of Epicurus' remarks. In his book *On Music*, Philodemus mentions that the Homeric poems 'have indicated, as they ought to, that music is appropriate at parties.'[85] One obvious piece of evidence is Odysseus' speech to Alcinous. I suggested earlier that Epicurus may have quoted the words; Philodemus surely has them in mind, and may be following Epicurus. Homer, of course, attests that not just music, but the recitation of poems is appropriate at parties; and Philodemus agrees with him. Philodemus approves of Diogenes of Babylon for admitting Homer, Hesiod, and other poets to the entertainment at parties, even though he does not approve of Diogenes' reasons.[86] Philodemus proposes, in effect, to recreate the good cheer of Homeric parties by bringing in Homer himself, together with other early poets and their successors, as singers of tales; and this position is not essentially different from that of Epicurus.

Just as Epicurus recommends the enjoyment of Dionysiac festivals, so Philodemus points out that there is an abundance of public entertainments for one's listening pleasure; indeed, he observes, there is such great scope for participating in them that one can easily get tired of them.[87] Like Epicurus, Philodemus restricts participation to being a member of the audience, in the belief that the acquisition of technical musical skill adds nothing to happiness. The availability of public shows, Philodemus points out, makes it futile to toil at learning musical skills oneself; only the small-minded, who have nothing worthwhile to do, think they need to toil at learning music in order to get enjoyment for themselves.[88] Musical learning and practice, Philodemus argues, are toilsome and 'shut us out from the things

---

[85] *On Music* 4, col. 16. 17–21.     [86] *On Music* 4, col. 17. 2–13.
[87] *On Music* 4, col. 37. 16–29.     [88] *On Music* 4, col. 37. 8–15.

that are most decisive for prospering.'[89] What is most decisive for happiness is, of course, the study of philosophy; but Philodemus presumably also has in mind the companionship of friends. The 'continuous inactivity of the person who sings in boy-like fashion or is busy at playing the lyre (κιθαρίζο[ντ]ος ἐ[ν]εργῶς),' Philodemus implies, excludes the activity of friendly social intercourse.[90] Expertise in musical theory is no less an obstacle to happiness than skill in performance, since it requires practice for its perfection.[91] Philodemus supports Epicurus' ban on musical and literary lectures by commenting that 'to have something to say [about music] at parties and other gatherings' is 'not demanded of all . . . and may even be laughed at if a philosopher should do it.'[92] In general, 'it is vastly better to have good cheer (εὐθυμίαν) than uselessness (ἀχρηστίαν) by giving a display or working out some other detailed interpretation.'[93]

These warnings against musical expertise would seem to apply just as much to poetry. But there is a problem. Philodemus not only studied poetry and wrote about it as a philosopher; he also composed poetry. In one of his epigrams, he calls himself μουσοφιλής, 'beloved of the Muses'; and although he might well have extended the meaning of this term to include service to the Muse of philosophy, he draws attention specifically to his poetic creativity. For he promises his addressee Piso, to whom he dedicated *On the Good King according to Homer*, that Piso will hear 'things far sweeter than [in] the land of the Phaeacians' at the party to which Philodemus invites him.[94] Piso, we may guess, loved Homer; and Philodemus, it appears, places himself ever so ironically among the successors of Homer himself. Philodemus composed only light epigrams; but he displays considerable

---

[89] *On Music* 4, col. 37. 31-4: τῶν κυριωτά|των πρὸς εὐετηρίαν ἐκκ[λ]εί|ουσαν.

[90] *On Music* 4, col. 37. 36-9.

[91] *On Music* 4, col. 38. 22-6; Philodemus claims that the required practice 'removes [us] from the things that tend toward happiness.'

[92] *On Music* 4, col. 38. 12-19.

[93] *On Music* 4, col. 38. 25-30: καὶ μυρί[ωι κ]ρεῖτ|τ[ον ἔχ]ειν τὴν εὐ[θυ]μίαν | ἢ τὴν ἀχρηστίαν ἐ[πι]δει|κ[ν]υμένου[ς ἢ τ]ῶν ἄλλων | τι τῶν ἐκ τῆς διεξόδου π[ε]||ραίνοντας. The verb περαίνειν is also used by Plutarch in his report of Epicurus' prohibition of musical and poetic lectures (*Non posse suaviter vivi* 1095c, see n. 22). Although the verb is commonplace, it is possible that Philodemus and Plutarch are drawing on the same text by Epicurus.

[94] *Palatine Anthology* 11. 44. David Sider drew my attention to the reference to the Phaeacians; please see his commentary.

poetic skill. How could he justify this activity if Epicurus did indeed prohibit the wise person from composing poems?

At this point I would like to return to the alternative interpretation of Epicurus' prohibition. It is possible that Philodemus and others interpreted Epicurus to mean that the wise person does not make a practice of composing poetry: unlike the lyre-player who plays ἐνεργῶς, keeping himself busy with this activity, the wise person does not busy himself with composing poetry. If he composes poetry, he does so as an amateur, not a professional. Accordingly, he does not spend a great deal of effort at acquiring the skill, so that the pleasure of exercising the skill is not outweighed by the toil; nor does he deprive himself of any opportunities for happiness, or of any 'good cheer' at parties. This interpretation could have been placed on either an original prohibition phrased simply as ποιήματά τε οὐκ ἂν ποιῆσαι or on a prohibition augmented by ἐνεργείᾳ.[95] Whatever the original wording, it is unlikely that Epicurus meant to leave a loophole for poetic composition. But his followers might reasonably have argued that he did not intend his prohibition to apply to the amateur efforts of someone who practices poetic composition only incidentally, not 'as a poet.'

If Philodemus justified the composition of poems as an amateur pleasure, this is a further extension of the acceptance of poetry as a leisure-time occupation, or διαγωγή. The amateur composer does not use poetry for the serious purpose of instructing others. To educate others, he uses prose, just as Epicurus demanded. Philodemus' own writings exemplify this demarcation between prose and poetry. His epigrams might have some incidental moral utility, but they are not intended to teach.

Philodemus, then, represents a new kind of Epicurean, who studies poetry with enjoyment and even profit, and who may even compose poems as a pastime. This Epicurean is cast in a new mould, but one which is carefully calculated to fit the standard established by Epicurus. But there is also a wholly different new Epicurean. Lucretius exploited the seductive beauty of poetry to educate others and spared no labor to make poetry a suitable vehicle for philosophical instruction. By combining the two uses of poetry, education and enjoyment, that Epicurus had kept strictly apart, Lucretius

---

[95] See p. 247 above. If Epicurus wrote the simple prohibition, a later interpreter may have added ἐνεργεῖν as a marginal explanation which subsequently crept into the text.

seems to preclude any way of reconciling his approach to poetry with that of Epicurus. Lucretius does not, however, use poetry without offering a defence of his method; and this defence may be regarded as his own novel exegesis of Epicurus' views on poetry. In a famous image, Lucretius compares himself to a doctor who smears honey around the cup of bitter medicine in order to trick the child into drinking the healing potion. The reason for this trickery, Lucretius explains, is that the doctrine of Epicurus generally seems 'too cheerless' (*tristior*) to people who are not acquainted with it.[96] Lucretius proposes to use poetry as a lure to attract the ordinary person to Epicurean philosophy. But this is not all. Lucretius does not regard poetry simply as a necessary device, dictated by the antipathy of his audience. Instead, what makes him so enthusiastic about his work is that poetry makes a positive contribution to the presentation of philosophy. Not only does its sweetness differ from the bitterness of the doctrine, but also its clarity differs from the obscurity of Epicurus' discoveries. Lucretius takes great pleasure in his poetic toil 'because I fashion such lucid songs about an obscure subject matter' (*quod obscura de re tam lucida pango/carmina*).[97] As he assures Memmius, he will not spare any labor 'in seeking by what words and what song I may be able to spread clear light over your mind.'[98] Lucretius aims to dispel the darkness of his listeners' ignorance by illuminating the discoveries of Epicurus with the language of poetry.

In claiming clarity for his verses, Lucretius asserts, paradoxically, a continuity of his method of teaching with that of Epicurus. Whereas Epicurus assigned clarity to prose alone, Lucretius now claims this quality for poetry. If poetry has clarity, it is an entirely appropriate vehicle for imparting philosophical truths. Lucretius is so intent on proving the suitability of poetry as a philosophical medium that he does not shun any technical difficulties; indeed, he goes out of his way to give a full presentation of philosophically difficult material. His poem is a 'demonstrative discourse' (ἀποδεικτικὸς λόγος), aiming to move the soul (ψυχαγωγεῖν) in such a way as to lead

---

[96] *De rerum natura* I. 936-50, including (943-5): quoniam haec ratio plerumque videtur / tristior esse quibus non est tractata, retroque / volgus abhorret ab hac.

[97] I. 933-4.

[98] I. 143-4: quaerentem dictis quibus et quo carmine demum / clara tuae possim praepandere lumina menti.

it to the truth. In combining what other Epicureans kept apart, Lucretius reaffirms the traditional link between divine inspiration and poetic expression. Lucretius symbolizes his source of inspiration by Venus, a deity who represents both his love for Epicurus and the expression of this love in his poetry. If called to account by Epicurus for using poetry to instruct others, he might reply: 'You have inspired me to attempt a feat that no one has tried before: to illuminate your teachings in poetry. I do not deviate from your path; but you have shown me a path by which I may lead others to a clear vision of your divine truth.'

We do not know whether Lucretius associated with Philodemus and his friends. There is no sign in Philodemus' writings that he ever conceived that a poem such as Lucretius' might be compatible with Epicurus' teachings. Yet I suspect that if he ever came to know Lucretius' poetry, he would have been so impressed by its exceptional beauty and clarity that he would have welcomed Lucretius as an associate in his own efforts to spread Epicureanism to the Romans.[99]

REFERENCES

This list also includes some useful items that were cited by David Sider in his important response to the preceding discussion. That response can be found in the Proceedings of the *Boston Area Colloquium in Ancient Philosophy*, 7 (1991), 94-103.

Angeli, A., and Colaizzo, M. (1979) 'I frammenti di Zenone Sidonio', *Cronache Ercolanesi*, 9: 47-133.
Asmis, E. (1984) *Epicurus' Scientific Method* (Ithaca NY).
——(1990) 'Philodemus' Epicureanism', in W. Haase (ed.), *Aufstieg und Niedergang der römischen Welt*, 2/36/4 (Berlin), 2369-2406.
——(1991) 'Philodemus' Poetic Theory and *On the Good King* according to Homer', *Classical Antiquity*, 10: 1-45.
Bignone, E. (1936) *L'Aristotele perduto e la formazione filosofica di Epicuro* i (Florence).
Boyancé, P. (1947) 'Lucrèce et la poésie', *Revue des Études Anciennes*, 49: 88-102.

---

[99] I am very grateful to Dirk Obbink for many helpful comments on an earlier draft of part of this paper.

——(1960) Review of Giancotti 1959, in *Revue des Études Anciennes*, 62: 441-5.

Clay, D. (1983) *Lucretius and Epicurus* (Ithaca).

Courtney, E. (1991) *The Poems of Petronius* (Atlanta).

Crönert, W. (1906) *Kolotes und Menedemos* (Munich).

De Lacy, P (1939) 'The Epicurean Analysis of Language', *American Journal of Philology*, 60: 86-90.

De Witt, N.W. (1939) 'Epicurean doctrine in Horace', *Classical Philology*, 34: 127-34.

Disch, H. (1921) *De poetis Aevi Augusti Epicureis* (Bonn).

Dorandi, T. (1990) 'Filodemo: Gli orientamenti della ricerca attuale', *Aufstieg und Niedergang der Römischen Welt*, 2/36/4: 2328-68.

Ferguson, J. (1990) 'Epicureanism under the Roman Empire', *Aufstieg und Niedergang der Römischen Welt* 2/36/4: 2257-2327.

Fraenkel, E. (1957) *Horace* (Oxford).

Gerhard, G. A. (1909) *Phoinix von Kolophon* (Leipzig and Berlin).

Giancotti, F. (1959) *Il Preludio di Lucrezio* (Florence).

——(1960) 'La poetica epicurea in Lucrezio, Cicerone ed altri', *Ciceroniana*, 2: 67-95.

Gigante, M. (1981) *Scetticismo e Epicureismo* (Naples).

——(1986) 'Biografia e dossografia in Diogene Laerzio', *Elenchos*, 7: 34-44.

——(1990) *Filodemo in Italia* (Florence).

Gigante, M., and Capasso, M. (1989) 'Il ritorno di Virgilio a Ercolano', *Studi Italiani di Filologia Classica*, 7: 3-6.

Gigon, O. (1986) 'Das dritte Buch des Diogenes Laertios', *Elenchos*, 7: 133-82.

Griffin, M., and Barnes, J., eds. (1989) *Philosophia Togata: Essays on Philosophy and Roman Society* (Oxford).

Kaiser, E. (1964) 'Odyssee-Szenen als Topoi', *Museum Helveticum*, 21: 109-36 and 197-224.

Mancini, A. (1976) 'Sulle opere polemiche di Colote', *Cronache Ercolanesi*, 6: 61-7.

Maresch, K. (1987) *Koelner Papyri (P. Koeln) 6 = Papyrologica Coloniensia*, 7: 26-51.

Mejer, J. (1978) *Diogenes Laertius and his Hellenistic Background* (Wiesbaden).

Naumann, H. (1938) 'Suetons Vergil-vita', *Rheinisches Museum*, 87: 364-9.

Nisbet, R. G. M., and Hubbard, M. (1970) *A Commentary on Horace's Odes Book 1* (Oxford).

Obbink, D. (1984) 'POxy. 213 and Epicurean religious ΘΕΩΡΙΑ', *Atti del XVII Congresso Internazionale di Papirologia* (Naples), 607-19.

Puglia, E. (1980) 'Nuove letture nei PHerc. 1012 e 1786 (Demetrii Laconis opera incerta),' *Cron. Erc.* 10: 25-53.

Romeo, C. (1988) *Demetrio Lacone, la poesia* [PHerc. 188 e 1014] (Naples).

Ronconi, A. (1963) 'Appunti di estetica epicurea', in *Miscellanea di Studi Alessandrini in memoria di Augusto Rostagni* (Turin), 7–25. Reprinted 1972 as 'Poetica e critica epicurea', in *Interpretazioni letterarie nei classici* (Florence), 64–90.

Rostagni, A. (1961) 'Il *De Morte* di Vario', in *Virgilio Minore* (Rome), 391–404.

Saller, R. (1989) 'Patronage and Friendship in Early Imperial Rome', in A. Wallace-Hadrill (ed.), *Patronage in Ancient Society* (London), 49–62.

Sedley, D. (1989) 'Philosophical Allegiance in the Greco-Roman World', in Griffin and Barnes 1989: 97–119.

——(1976) 'Epicurus and his Professional Rivals', in J. Bollach and A. Laks (eds.), *Études sur l'Épicurisme antique* (Lille), 119–59.

Sider, D. (1995) 'The Epicurean Philosopher as Hellenistic Poet', in Obbink (ed.), *Philodemus and Poetry* (Oxford), 42–57.

Ungar, R. (1870) *Varii de morte eclogae reliquiae* (Halle).

White, P. (1978) 'Amicitia and the Profession of Poetry in Early Imperial Rome', *Journal of Roman Studies*, 68: 74–92.

# I I

# *Rhetoric and Criticism*

## D. A. RUSSELL

The words 'rhetoric' and 'rhetorical influence' come readily enough to the tongue when people talk of Greek and Latin literature, but all too often a great vagueness hangs about them; one is seldom sure whether they are being used historically with reference to certain facts of ancient education or as terms of abuse for some 'insincerity' or 'artificiality' in literature which the speaker invites us to deplore. My object here[1] is to supply a few facts about the ancient rhetoricians and their intentions, and then to add some observations about the relevance of what they were doing to our own understanding of the ancient writers. Most of what I say is about Greek rather than Latin rhetoric, but I shall of course draw on Latin material, which, for some parts of the subject, is both more abundant and more intelligent than what survives in Greek. Richard Volkmann, on whose great book[2] we still depend, confessed that the only way by which he came to understand what rhetoric meant to the ancients, and to feel that he had in his hands an 'Ariadne's thread' to the labyrinth, was by the repeated reading of Quintilian.

## I. HISTORICAL OUTLINE

The history of Greco-Roman rhetoric may be said, very schematic-ally, to fall into three periods: the age of the sophist, the age of the

[1] This paper is based on one read to the Oxford Classical Society in Trinity Term 1965. I have tried to handle some of the same topics briefly in articles on *Rhetoric* and *Literary Criticism* for the 2nd and 3rd editions of the *Oxford Classical Dictionary*.

[2] *Die Rhetorik der Griechen und Römer*, 2nd edn. (Leipzig, 1885). The recent book of George Kennedy, *The Art of Persuasion in Greece* (London, 1963), provides an excellent introduction to the Greek part of the subject, down to and including Dionysius of Halicarnassus. See also D. L. Clark, *Rhetoric in Greco-Roman Education* (New York, 1957); M. L. Clarke, *Rhetoric at Rome* (London, 1953).

philosopher, and the age of the rhetor. The last was ten times as long as either of the others.

By the age of the sophist I mean the period down to c.390, when Isocrates and Plato began, in their different ways, to revalue rhetoric. If we may believe Aristotle,[3] the story begins in Sicily. There, the fall of the tyrannies in the fifth century was followed by social and political upheaval. Old patterns of power and influence disappeared, new democratic ones emerged. In such a situation, success and often personal safety depended much on a persuasive tongue. Friends and wealth might be lost, but the eloquent man (like the trained soldier in other sorts of troubles) carried his treasure and his defence around with him. The earliest teachers, both in Sicily and in Athens, were practical men, not much interested in the principles of their art, though perhaps inclined to make something of a mystery of its technical terms. To them belongs the doctrine of how to divide your speech into parts: prooemium, narrative, argumentation, epilogue. Plato[4] was amused by their refinements: confirmation ($\pi\iota\sigma\tau\omega\sigma\iota\varsigma$), supraconfirmation ($\epsilon\pi\iota\pi\iota\sigma\tau\omega\sigma\iota\varsigma$), sub-demonstration ($\upsilon\pi o\delta\eta\lambda\omega\sigma\iota\varsigma$), subsidiary laudation ($\pi\alpha\rho\epsilon\pi\alpha\iota\nu o\varsigma$). Each part of the speech has its function and appropriate manner. These early teachers also discussed the uses of the argument from probability ($\dot{\alpha}\pi\dot{o}$ $\tau o\hat{\upsilon}$ $\epsilon\dot{\iota}\kappa\acute{o}\tau o\varsigma$), the mainstay of the Athenian litigant with a poor case: 'of course he was near the harbour when he was killed; he was much too drunk to get any further.'[5] This topic seemed elementary to later rhetoricians, and not much is heard of it in this form; but the theory of the divisions of a speech remained a live subject, debated (for example) between the two great rival sects of the Augustan age, the Theodoreans and the Apollodoreans.[6]

The leading figure of the early period was Gorgias.[7] Himself $\delta\epsilon\iota\nu\grave{o}\varsigma$ $\lambda\acute{\epsilon}\gamma\epsilon\iota\nu$[8] he claimed to make others so too. One of the ways he did so is

---

[3] Reported by Cicero, Brutus 46 = L. Radermacher, Artium Scriptores (a thorough collection of pre-Aristotelian texts on rhetoric), A. V. 9.

[4] Phaedrus 266d.

[5] Cf. Antiphon v. 26. This speech (On the Murder of Herodes) is the best example of early forensic technique.

[6] D. A. Russell on 'Longinus' 3. 5 (edition Oxford, 1964).

[7] Texts in Radermacher, Artium, B VII: Helena, ed. O. Immisch (Bonn, 1927). See now G. M. A. Grube, The Greek and Roman Critics (London, 1965), 16ff.

[8] Plato, Meno 95c.

full of significance for the future: he displayed his skill on themes which had no practical importance. Two pieces of his of this kind survive; one, the *Encomium of Helen*—Ἑλένης μὲν ἐγκώμιον, ἐμὸν δὲ παίγνιον (an encomium of Helen, but my piece of play)—is a work of real importance in the history both of rhetoric and of criticism. The serious part of it is a rhetorician's apologia, an encomium of λόγος, where λόγος is made to include not only public speech but poetry and other kinds of discourse. Poetry (§ 8) induces in its hearers pity, fear, desire, indeed vicarious emotion of all kinds. And these effects— which cannot fail to call to mind the *Poetics*—are, Gorgias implies, due to the λόγος to which the poet has added metre—not to the metre itself. Hence his definition: τὴν ποίησιν ἅπασαν καὶ νομίζω καὶ ὀνομάζω λόγον ἔχοντα μέτρον (Poetry as a whole I consider, and call 'Logos with metre'). This idea, that poetry differs from prose only in the addition of metre, becomes in fact standard among the rhetoricians.⁹ Moreover (§ 13), the function of λόγος is to persuade or charm; the victim of persuasion (Helen) is the victim of a sort of aggression, and therefore not blameworthy. And this persuasion is to be found not only in practical (political or forensic) situations but in scientific discourse (τοὺς τῶν μετεωρολόγων λόγους) and in philosophy: for here too (this no doubt shocked Socrates) the aim is not to seek the truth but to convince opponents. It is this comprehensiveness in Gorgias' claim which is specially important. The essence of the rhetorical attitude to literature is that *every* form of λόγος, verse or prose, is a form of persuasion, and is to be judged by its effectiveness for this purpose. The consequences of Gorgias' manifesto were incalculable, in criticism as well as in education.

By 'the age of the philosopher' I mean that of Isocrates, Plato, and Aristotle. In their different ways all three faced the problem of the amorality of rhetoric. Though Gorgias had not admitted this, others had; and the ordinary citizen, confronted by δεινότης ('expertise') in court, had little doubt that it was a menace not only to his interests but to his moral code. This is why speakers so often take pains to deny expert training; Euxitheos, the defendant in a speech of Antiphon,¹⁰ is made to say: 'If I put any point well, credit this to my truthfulness rather than to my expertise (ἀληθείᾳ . . . δεινότητι).'

---

⁹ Cf. e.g. Hermogenes, *de ideis* 2, p. 389. 22 Rabe: ποίησις = πανηγυρικὸς (i.e. epidictic) λόγος ἐν μέτρῳ. Aristotle's different view (*Poetics* 1) did not affect this tradition.                                                                    ¹⁰ 5. 5.

Isocrates' solution was to develop the teaching of rhetoric into a moral and political training; he called it φιλοσοφία ('philosophy'), to the scandal of Plato and his school, who were giving the word a new meaning. Whatever we call it, it was meant to be a school of citizenship. Isocrates argued that by training people in general moral or political issues he taught them not only εὖ λέγειν (to speak well) but εὖ φρονεῖν (to have good thoughts); he added, as an incidental recommendation of his system, that his finished graduate would in fact be more effective in debate because of the authority his character would command. Isocrates' teaching methods make a sympathetic impression. He would discuss his own work with his pupils as well as their exercises; and he conceived the relationship between pupil and teacher as a lifelong one, of use to both.[11] Later philosophical and rhetorical schools, all the way down to the Neoplatonists on the one hand and Libanius[12] on the other, show the endurance of these practices in ancient education.

To Plato, of course, neither earlier rhetoric nor the teaching of Isocrates offered a path of wisdom; it was a 'department of flattery'.[13] His most serious discussion is in the *Phaedrus*, in a passage[14] where he turns from negative criticism to offer a sketch of a possible 'scientific' rhetoric. In this the analogy with medicine is very clear. The orator needs to know 'the varieties of the human mind'; he must understand what sort of argument is convincing to what sort of audience; and he must know how to recognize in real life the moment when such-and-such a rule ought to be applied. It was this suggestion in the *Phaedrus* that Aristotle worked out in his own *Rhetoric*. The legend[15] of how he gave afternoon lectures in the Academy on the subject, in competition with Isocrates, is at least an apt invention. One feels in reading the *Rhetoric* that Aristotle is showing the professionals that he didn't think their game very important, but he could in fact play it (like other games) better than they could themselves. We may doubt his usefulness as a practical teacher; as a theoretician he is unrivalled. He took the old, cynical hints about

---

[11] Isocrates often speaks of his pupils and his aims as a teacher; see. e.g. *Philippus* 17 ff., *Antidosis* 178 ff.; Grube, *Greek and Roman Critics*, 38 ff.

[12] *Autobiography*, ed. A. F. Norman (Oxford, 1965), pp. xx ff. More is known about Libanius' relations with his pupils than about any other teacher in antiquity.

[13] *Gorgias* 462 e ff.

[14] 271 c ff.

[15] See Cic. *de oratore* iii. 141.

'probability' and parallel instances and developed them into a—
still cynical—system of 'arguments' and 'examples' (ἐνθυμήματα,
παραδείγματα). He took the outline sketch in the *Phaedrus* and filled
in the blanks with the same shrewd and uncomplimentary attention
to human foibles that he shows in the *Ethics*. Most important, he laid
the foundations of the theory of style, discussing its excellences
(ἀρεταί), the differences between speaking and writing, metaphor,
and what he calls ἀστειότης ('urbanity', Lat. *urbanitas*)—the quality
that makes a remark telling. It could easily be argued that all later
rhetoric is a commentary on Aristotle.

Educational systems have a wonderful power of survival. Greek
rhetoric outlasted Attic oratory by something like a thousand years.
Only for a brief moment of this time, in Cicero's Rome, were the real
rewards in power and influence accessible to the orator.

It is doubtless an accident that the best comprehensive guides to
ancient rhetoric which we have—*ad Herennium*[16] and Quintilian—
are Latin; Greek text-books were constantly being written. But there
seems little doubt that it was the Roman stimulus, in the second and
first centuries BC, that gave new life to the system. When Caesar or
Pompey, Antony or Octavian attended the lectures of a Greek rhetor,
it *may* have been a red-letter day for the Roman, but it certainly was
for Apollonius or Theodorus the rhetor. The Romans were eager to
learn; more important, their world was the real one. Through them
the Greek intellectual exercised, or felt he might exercise, worthwhile power.

He might continue to feel this, in a sense, under the principate; but
he was no longer preparing his pupils for the political exercise of
rhetoric, only for its quieter uses in law and administration. We need
not question the justice of the common first-century complaint[17] of
the consequent withdrawal of rhetoric from life and its increasing
preoccupation with clever fantasy, even if in the age of Augustus the
practice of *declamatio* engaged some notable minds.[18] There is an air
of unreality even about Quintilian for all his monumental common
sense. On the Greek side, the important feature of this period is the

---

[16] Caplan's Loeb edition is a particularly valuable introduction to the whole subject.
[17] e.g. 'Longinus' 44.
[18] The elder Seneca's declaimers include Livy and Ovid. His *controversiae* and
*suasoriae* have often been discussed: convenient edition by H. Bornecque (Garnier
series), best introduction in S. F. Bonner's *Roman Declamation* (Liverpool. 1949).

gradual literary revival: the rise, in the first and second centuries AD, of an archaizing, but very lively, literature. Written in classical Attic, intended for public performance, and directed at the educated in every city, the works of the second-century sophists reflected the cultural unity of all readers of Homer and Demosthenes from the Euphrates to Hadrian's Wall. To this age belong most of the extant *rhetores Graeci*.[19] Notable among them are Hermogenes, an infant prodigy in the days of Marcus Aurelius and author of a series of text-books much used and commented on down to the sixteenth century, and the two writers περὶ ἐπιδεικτικῶν ('on epideictic speeches') who pass under the one name of Menander and give fascinating recipes for public speeches and even poems suitable for such occasions as marriages, deaths, and the arrival of the provincial governor on tour. In due course, the imperial writers themselves, from Aristides to Libanius, faded into the past and became classics; the Byzantines continued for a millennium to write commentaries on them.[20]

## II. THE SYSTEM

That it is possible at all to attempt an 'outline of rhetoric' is due to the extreme conservatism of the teachers; the subject remained substantially the same from early Hellenistic times. To a large extent this was the achievement of Aristotle and Theophrastus; the loss of Theophrastus' writings on rhetorical and critical subjects is probably the most serious gap in our knowledge. It was not so much Aristotle's detached and philosophical approach that survived as the way in which he arranged the subject. The basic scheme of most later treatises seems to be in origin Peripatetic:

(i)    content (εὕρεσις, *inventio*, Aristotle's πίστεις);

---

[19] The nineteenth-century collection by C. Walz and the three-volume selection by L. Spengel have not been completely replaced by modern critical texts; the Teubner *Rhetores Graeci* by H. Rabe and others contains some important works (e.g. Hermogenes and *Prolegomenon Sylloge*), but its completion is far off. See also: D. A. Russell and N. G. Wilson, *Menander Rhetor* (Oxford, 1981); M. Heath, *Menander: A Rhetor in Context* (Oxford, 2004) and *Hermogenes on Issues* (Oxford, 1995); and Hermogenes, *On Types of Styles*, tr. C. W. Wooten (Chapel Hill, 1987).

[20] The history of Latin rhetoric in late antiquity and the Middle Ages is of course outside the scope of this survey. Brief account in E. R. Curtius, *European Literature and the Latin Middle Ages* (London, 1953), 62–78.

(ii)   arrangement (οἰκονομία, *ordo*);
(iii)  diction or style (λέξις, ἑρμηνεία);
with the two practical appendixes:
(iv)   delivery (ὑπόκρισις);
(v)    mnemonics (μνήμη, *memoria*).[21]

Εὕρεσις is *inventio*; it is not 'invention' if by that we imply some degree of imaginative creation. It is simply the 'discovery' of what requires to be said in a given situation (τὰ δέοντα εὑρεῖν), the implied theory being that this is somehow already 'there' though latent, and does not have to be made up as a mere figment of imagination. It is the poet, *qua* myth-maker, who is allowed, as part of his licence (*licentia*, ἐξουσία) to make things up; and even he, in serious genres at least, ought not to exercise the privilege too often. Thus in the *Aeneid* Virgil sets out to reproduce, and sometimes to fill out, the tradition he has inherited; he rarely permits himself to invent episodes or characters,[22] and his ancient commentators religiously tried to minimize the occasions when he seems to do so. When Cornutus[23] found himself unable to trace the *historia* behind the account at the end of book iv of how Iris cut the hair from Dido so that she could die, he commented: 'adsuevit poetico more aliqua fingere, ut de aureo ramo'. The Golden Bough remains unexplained; the *quaestio* raised by the lock of hair was solved by Macrobius by a reference to Euripides' *Alcestis* (73), and one more place where 'free invention' had seemed to occur was eliminated. The nature of ancient *inventio* and its difference from modern invention are of the first importance. Not only did the concept circumscribe the poet in ways we find surprising, but it actually liberated the historian, by giving him very much the same range; this is why most ancient historians feel free to fill out the tradition with speeches, standardized accounts of embassies or battles, likely motivations, and other manifestations of 'the probable' (τὸ εἰκός). Both poet and historian operate within rules which were originally rhetorical.

---

[21] Ancient speakers either spoke *extempore* or wrote out their speeches and learnt them by heart, speaking without them. Revised versions were then prepared. When Cicero tells us (*pro Plancio* 74) that the first speech he made in the senate after his return 'propter rei magnitudinem dicta de scripto est', he implies that it was exceptional; he was being specially careful not to put a foot wrong.

[22] R. Heinze, *Virgils epische Technik* (4th edn. Darmstadt, 1957), 239 ff.

[23] In the first century AD. See Macrobius, *Saturnalia*, 5. 19. 2.

The rhetorical teaching of *inventio* undoubtedly sharpened the mind. The large and involved subject of στάσεις (*status, constitutiones*) is a good example. This was an early Hellenistic invention, due to Hermagoras of Temnos.[24] Στάσις is a difficult word to translate: we may perhaps think of it[25] as the 'stance', 'position', or 'approach' which we adopt in order to grapple with a problem or an adversary. The στάσεις λογικαί ('logical times')—as distinct from those concerned with the interpretation of law—were four in number: στοχασμός (*coniectura*), ὁρισμός (*definitio*), ποιότης (*qualitas*), μετάληψις (*translatio*). The 'conjectural approach' is simply inquiry into fact: a man is found with a dead body in a lonely place; he is naturally accused of murder; but did he do it? The 'approach by definition' consists in asking whether the alleged act falls under the definition of the crime—was it murder? A standard example of this *status* was Demosthenes' speech against Midias, which turned on whether the insulting blow was merely ὕβρις ('wanton violence') or—because the incident happened at the Dionysia—ἀσέβεια ('impiety'). The 'approach by quality' is, as it were, a further line of defence: granted the deed was done and it falls under the definition of the crime alleged, was it nevertheless expedient or honourable? And if even this failed, one might have recourse to 'transference', as Cicero did in defending Milo; the orator uses this *status* when he argues that the case should be brought at another time, or before another court, or against another defendant.

Cicero knew these doctrines, and used them;[26] the Attic orators, so far as we know, did not though Antiphon's *Tetralogies* show that the basic categories were understood. But since the light of nature often suggested to them arguments which fall under one or other of the στάσεις, later rhetors could find fulfilment in commenting on them from this point of view.

Had rhetoric remained always a practical science, style (λέξις) would no doubt have played a much smaller part in it than it did. The ordinary needs of litigation are pretty well met if the essential virtues

---

[24] Fragments edited by D. Matthes (Teubner); see Kennedy, *Art of Persuasion*, 303 ff. The doctrine underwent considerable modifications later.

[25] Cf. fr. 10 d Matthes.

[26] Sensible and useful 'interpretations' of some of Cicero's speeches (e.g. *pro Milone*) are given in C. Neumeister, *Grundsätze der forensischen Rhetorik* (1964), 34 ff., 82 ff.; see also F. Solmsen, 'Cicero's First Speeches: A Rhetorical Analysis', *TAPA* 69 (1938).

(ἀναγκαῖαι ἀρεταί) of correctness, clarity, and propriety are understood and practised. But there are obvious reasons for the importance in fact accorded to λέξις. One is the tendency, going back to the very early days, for teachers of rhetoric to take all literature, including poetry, as their province; the other is the concentration, in much Hellenistic and Roman literature, on novelty of expression or conceit rather than on large-scale originality of idea or approach. The rhetorical discussion of style (the λεκτικὸς τόπος), as we see it (e.g.) in Quintilian Books viii and ix, comprises three main topics: the use of individual words, the organization of words, and what are called 'figures'. The first of these is λέξις in its narrowest sense of 'diction'. It comprises rules for the use of various special sorts of word—especially foreign words, new coinages, and metaphors—not only with reference to clarity and correctness but from the point of view of the 'tone' which a word can itself import into a context. Words could lend 'dignity' or 'charm'—μεγαλοπρέπεια or ἡδονή. They did it, or so Theophrastus thought,[27] sometimes by their sound, sometimes by their pleasing or dignified significance. They 'illuminate' and 'adorn': *illustrant et exornant orationem.*

The organization of the words is called σύνθεσις, *compositio.* Given the comparative freedom of Greek from rigid logical or syntactical rules of order, and the traditional association in music and poetry of certain rhythms with certain effects and emotional tones, this was bound to become an important subject. It comprised sentence-structure, hiatus, rhythm, the affective quality of certain sounds. One special treatise on it survives, that of Dionysius of Halicarnassus;[28] difficult as it is, this is one of the most rewarding books of Greek criticism.

Finally, figures (σχήματα). By this were meant[29] abnormal (παρὰ φύσιν) configurations of thought or words: rhetorical question, for example, where we cast the *thought* into a new shape (σχῆμα), or hyperbaton, where we displace a *word.* This is the most tortuous of the branches of rhetoric; as Alexander[30] plaintively says (using, by the way, the trope *litotēs* to say it), there is οὐχ ἡ τυχοῦσα δυσκολία

---

[27] Demetrius περὶ ἑρμηνείας 173; cf Cic. *de oratore* 3. 150 ff.
[28] Ed. W. Rhys Roberts. See now Grube, *Greek and Roman Critics,* 217 ff.
[29] D. A. Russell on 'Longinus' 16–29, for the distinction between 'figures' and 'tropes' and for some bibliography.
[30] Spengel, *Rhetores Graeci,* iii. 7.

('no ordinary difficulty') in talking about these things, for there was a great dispute whether figures were infinite in number or merely incomprehensibly many. Nevertheless, ancient discussions of figures from time to time show useful insights, because they involve the close analysis of individual passages. Perhaps the best Greek writing on σχήματα is the famous chapter (16) in which 'Longinus' introduces the subject. He takes a single example—Demosthenes' οὐκ ἔστιν ὅπως ἡμάρτετε . . . μὰ τοὺς Μαραθῶνι προκινδυνεύσαντας τῶν προγόνων[31] ('You cannot have been wrong . . . by those of our forefathers who risked their lives at Marathon!')—and shows how it transforms the subject and affects the hearer, and how different it is from the formally similar passage of the comic poet Eupolis which is said to be its origin (σπέρμα). 'It is not simply making an oath which lends grandeur; it is the where and the how, the occasion and the purpose.' These words convey two warnings: not to be seduced by the knowledge of a 'source' into misinterpreting the 'derivative'; and not to imagine, when we have been clever enough to give some feature of style its rhetorical name, that it is the feature, rather than the context and occasion, which produces the effect. Rhetorical question, apostrophe, and so on are ways of drawing special attention to what is said; they do not as a rule indicate *why* it is important.

Most of the Greek books on λέξις in its wide sense are concerned to describe different types of writing (χαρακτῆρες, εἴδη, ἰδέαι, *genera dicendi*). The history of these concepts is extremely complicated, and by no means fully known.[32] Most often we hear of three 'styles': ἁδρός ('grand'), ἰσχνός ('thin'), and some kind of intermediate— either a desirable mean between the two extremes or a distinct 'ornamental' or 'smooth' style (γλαφυρός, ἀνθηρός). In Demetrius, however, there are four χαρακτῆρες; Hermogenes' ἰδέαι, if we count both the main concepts and the subordinate, number about a dozen.[33] It is very difficult to compare one scheme with another, or to relate the concept of χαρακτῆρες to that of 'virtues of diction'

---

[31] *de corona* 208: stock example of σχῆμα ὀμοτικόν, see Goodwin ad loc.

[32] See, e.g., G. L. Hendrickson in *AJP* 25 (1904), 125 ff. and 26 (1905), 249 ff.; F. Quadlbauer in *Wiener Studien*, 71 (1958), 55 ff.; Kennedy, *Art of Persuasion*, 278 ff.; Greek and Roman Critics, 107 ff.

[33] For Demetrius see G. M. A. Grube's translation (*A Greek Critic: Demetrius on Style* (Toronto, 1961); for Hermogenes, D. Hagedorn, *Die Ideenlehre des H.* (1964). For Hermogenes see Wooten's translation (n. 19 above), and I. Rutherford, *Canons of Style in the Antonine Age* (Oxford, 1998).

(ἀρεταὶ λέξεως). The only author who tries to go into the logical problems raised by the subject is Hermogenes, and he does not get very far. It is best to be very cautious about the development; I will confine myself to two general points. (i) The χαρακτῆρες, at any rate in later Hellenistic and Roman theory, are seldom just a matter of diction, or indeed of diction plus σύνθεσις plus figures. They are best described as tones or qualities of writing, involving the choice not only of words but of subject. Thus Demetrius usually puts what he has to say under the three heads of διάνοια ('meaning'), λέξις, and σύνθεσις. 'Longinus' pays great attention to 'sublime thoughts' and 'emotion' before proceeding to the λεκτικὸς τόπος, to which he clearly attaches less importance. Similarly Hermogenes. (ii) However great the refinement the basic distinction of tones is into two: high and low, grand of and everyday. Even Hermogenes' ἰδέαι fall into two groups: those 'contributing to grandeur':

σεμνότης (gravity, solemnity);
τραχύτης (asperity, harshness);
σφοδρότης (vehemence);
λαμπρότης (brilliance);
ἀκμή (full vigour, climax of energy);
περιβολή (amplitude);

and those 'contributing to charm':

κάλλος (beauty);
γλυκύτης (sweetness);
δριμύτης (piquancy);
γοργότης (rapidity);
ἦθος (character).[34]

The confrontation itself is in essentials at least as old as Aristophanes. The ἀγών ('contest') between Aeschylus and Euripides in the Frogs contains all the points in nuce: contrast of language between the remotely heroic and the realistically emotional, the metaphors from building and medicine which later became a staple feature of critical vocabulary.[35]

It is difficult to think of any one more distinctive feature of the

---

[34] On some meanings of the difficult term ἦθος, see J. F. Lockwood, CQ 23 (1929), 180 ff.; D. A. Russell on 'Longinus' 9. 15. Hermogenes' primary concern is with the orator's power to make a sympathetic impression.

[35] πυργώσας ῥήματα σεμνά, Frogs 1004; οἰδοῦσαν . . . ἴσχνανα, ibid. 940-1.

ancient view of literature than this contrast. It appears in various
guises throughout Greek and Roman criticism. One of its guises is the
antithesis between ἦθος (*mores*, character as in 'character part') and
πάθος (*animi motus*, emotion). Aristotle[36] contrasts the *Iliad*, a poem
of high emotion (παθητικόν), with the *Odyssey*, a poem of moralizing
and realism (ἠθικόν); 'Longinus' (9. 13-14) develops this. In the *Iliad*,
he says, elevation never fails, there is a continuous outpouring of
emotion; the *Odyssey*, on the other hand, deals with real life (βίος),
and is a sort of comedy of manners (κωμῳδία ἠθολογουμένη). Here
ἦθος, comedy, and realism are set against πάθος, tragedy, and things
higher than the ordinary experiences of human life.

There lies behind this contrast an even more fundamental
principle: the view of literature as public statement, requiring
different levels of formality, different uniforms, as it were, for different
occasions. This is what the aesthetic (and also moral and social) law
of decorum (τὸ πρέπον) demanded. Ancient writers and readers
accepted it instinctively, and greeted breaches of etiquette, such as a
low word in a solemn context, with horror and disgust.[37]

III. SOME RHETORICAL EXERCISES

The instruction in rhetorical schools did not of course consist wholly
of theoretical lectures. Books like περὶ ἰδεῶν and περὶ ὕψους are
advanced work, and imply much earlier study, much of which was
done by practical exercise. If we ask ourselves what is most likely to
have influenced the future writer, the answer that suggests itself is
'the exercises rather than the theory'. So let us look briefly at some of
these.

We possess a number of books of preliminary exercises
(προγυμνάσματα, *praeexercitamina*), as well as both Greek and Latin
μελέται or *declamationes* of a more advanced kind. The προγυμνάσματα
formed a recognized sequence. The boys began by writing animal
fables, and then slightly more ambitious narratives (διηγήματα).
Having mastered this, they proceeded to anecdotes (χρεῖαι) and
maxims (γνῶμαι); these were exercises in the development of a single
theme. The technique thus learned could then be used in a variety of

---

[36] *Poetics* 1459ᵇ14.
[37] 'Longinus' 43 provides examples.

more ambitious exercises involving composition on a rather larger scale: refutation and confirmation of arguments, commonplaces, encomium, invective, comparison. It looks as though the vital stage was the elementary essay-writing technique of χρεία and γνώμη; an example will show what this was like.[38] *Crimine ab uno disce omnes!*

*How to Treat a Maxim (γνώμη, sententia)*

Take the example:

> Οὐ χρὴ παννύχιον εὕδειν βουληφόρον ἄνδρα.[39]
> Not all night long should men of counsel sleep.

Proceed as follows:

   (i) Praise the author briefly.
  (ii) Give a simple paraphrase of the maxim: 'The man who bears responsibility ought not to sleep all night'.
 (iii) State a reason: 'For the leader must always be engaged in thought, and one does not think while asleep'.
  (iv) State the contrary:[40] 'If there is nothing wrong with a private citizen's sleeping all night, it is obvious that the ruler should stay awake'.
   (v) Make a comparison: 'As helmsmen stay awake to take thought for the common safety, so should rulers'.
  (vi) Give an example: 'Hector did not sleep, but lay awake thinking, on the night he sent Dolon as a spy to the ships'.
 (vii) Quote a corroborative opinion.[41]
(viii) Pronounce an exhortation: 'In our day-to-day affairs, we too must show care and watchfulness'.

Repeated practice in this sort of thing would naturally make amplification by paraphrase and contrast and illustration by com-

---

[38] [Hermogenes], pp. 8 ff. Rabe; Latin version (which I have drawn on) in Priscian, p. 554 Halm (*Rhetores Latini Minores*). For a general account of these exercises see D. L. Clark, *Rhetoric*, 177–261, and see now G. A. Kennedy's translation of the *Progymnasmata* (Atlanta: Society of Biblical Literature, 2003).

[39] *Iliad* 2. 24.

[40] Obscure, and slightly different in the Latin version. Key terms (βουληφόρος, εὕδειν) are replaced by their opposites.

[41] The Latin gives Sall. *Cat.* 2. 8: 'multi mortales dediti ventri atque somno indocti inculteque vitam sic ut peregrinantes transiere'.

parison and example almost instinctive: they are of course very common procedures both in prose and in poetry.[42]

Only when he had completed the preliminary course would the student proceed to declamation, i.e. to the *controversiae* and *suasoriae* we know best from the elder Seneca. This is comparatively familiar ground. 'A maiden captured by pirates is sold as a prostitute; she refuses to let her clients have their money's worth, and kills a soldier who attempts to rape her. Acquitted of murder, she is sent home, and applies for a post as priestess, for which chastity is a necessary qualification. Discuss.'[43]

## IV. CONCLUSION

Unreality, fantasy, mechanical technique: it is easy to make fun of the grotesque skeleton of the rhetorical tradition, less easy to imagine what the living creature was like and what it meant to the sensitive and intelligent. But only if we can stand back from the detail and do this can we hope to use our knowledge to illuminate our own understanding of ancient literature.

Though the rhetors nowhere state a critical theory, they do imply one. If a literary work may be said[44] to have three references—to the universe, to the writer, and to the audience—Greek rhetorical theory, like the Renaissance criticism which descends from it, thinks the audience-reference by far the most important. Next comes the reference to τὰ πράγματα, last and least the personal experience of the writer. This is not to say that the Greeks overlooked this third aspect of things altogether; but the familiar doctrine of the inspired poet, whether it is given a religious or a psychiatric turn, tells us nothing about poems as an expression of personality, but only that the poet is an odd case and performs well only when he loses control of his conscious mind. The Wordsworthian 'spontaneous overflow of powerful feelings' is alien to ancient criticism, whether or not it is true of the experience of any ancient poet. When ancient writers

[42] Two random (not perfect) examples from Horace: *Odes* 3. 4. 65–80, the γνώμη *vis consili expers mole ruit sua*; 2. 10. 1–12, the precept of moderation.

[43] *Controversiae* 4. 2. Bonner, *Roman Declamation*, gives a good account of the declamations, their influence and their critics.

[44] Cf. M. H. Abrams, *The Mirror and the Lamp*, ch. 1.

speak of a coherence between utterance and the whole personality—
*talis oratio qualis vita*[45]—they do so in a moral sense; from before
Plato to Seneca and beyond there is a strong tradition that innovations and affectations in style are both symptoms and causes of moral
decadence.

The consequences of this 'audience-orientation' are many. One is
the attention paid to propriety, rules, genres,[46] literary uniforms, and
so on. Another is the tendency to subsume poetry under the general
head of λόγος, as λόγος ἔχων μέτρον. This was strengthened by the
facts of Greek literary history, in which poetry in early ages performed various didactic and persuasive functions which later
belonged to prose: the elegiac exhortations of Solon (fr. 2 Diehl) and
the prose of Demosthenes had the same aim of convincing the *demos*
and forcing it to act. Aristotle is almost alone in trying to make a
distinction between imaginative and other writing which is different
from the formal one between prose and verse; later criticism
generally neglected his attempts. It remained in the hands of the
rhetors, who regarded poets and orators as playing essentially the
same game, except that the aims of the poets were more frivolous and
they enjoyed greater freedom in vocabulary and invention. The
chapter by 'Longinus' (15) on φαντασία ('visualization'), by which
he means the vivid conjuring up of a scene, illustrates the rather
curious consequences of this attitude. Poetical φαντασία is a matter
of sheer imagination: Orestes seeing the Furies, Phaethon riding
dangerously through the sky. The rhetorical variety, on the other
hand, must be rooted in fact and argument. When Hyperides said,
defending his proposal to liberate the slaves, 'it was not the proposer
that drew up this decree, it was the battle fought at Chaeronea', he
is not only painting a picture, he is arguing a case. It is this grip on
the immediate occasion, the sense of urgency and reality, which
marks off the orator. Poetry is characterized negatively, by the
absence of this, rather than positively.

But of course it does not follow, because the critics judged all
writing as persuasion, that the poets thought of it like that. We must
make here an obvious distinction. When we speak of 'rhetorical
influence' on literature we may mean one of two quite different

---

[45] Seneca, *Epist. mor.* 114. 1.
[46] For a short account of this concept, R. Wellek and A. Warren, *Theory of Literature.* (1949: Peregrine Books edition 1963), ch. 17.

things. In Hellenistic and Roman literature we mean the direct influence of rhetorical teaching. When a commentator points out figures in Virgil, we can be confident that Virgil saw them too, and perhaps even gave them the same names. With the earlier literature the question is different. The usefulness of rhetorical comment rests not on any fact in the history of education, but on the extent to which the principles the rhetors used are based on a correct view of the aims and methods of the early poets themselves. Now the existence of the poetic genres, which are not critics' inventions but poets' traditions of work, and also the importance of occasion and ceremonial in the development of all Greek art, are, I think, indications that the rhetors were in fact rightly interpreting the intentions of the poets, and were following a natural tendency of their race, not imposing an alien way of thought. It is this which gives ancient rhetorical criticism a certain value beyond the range of the literature influenced by the actual teaching of rhetoric. Not only Virgil and Ovid, but Homer and Sappho, thought of what they were doing primarily in terms of persuasion, conviction, 'putting something across'.

It would seem to follow[47] that we must make a clean break with the 'Romantic' view that 'sincerity' in the sense of correspondence with the writer's personal experience is the unique hallmark of good poetry. There is nothing new, either in classical studies[48] or in general literature,[49] in making this stand; however, it is perhaps worth making it again, since it still seems to shock people to say that it is not only impossible but generally irrelevant to inquire into the vicissitudes Catullus and Propertius went through in their amours. Yet this is so; and it is connected with the same attitudes which led to the development and dominance of rhetoric. We should think even of Catullus and Propertius as something like dramatic poets; their business is to represent convincingly the personality (ἤθη) and emotions (πάθη) of a man in love—a man, however, whose emotions and

---

[47] So long as we assume that criticism (and not only history) must take account of the intentions of poets.

[48] See e.g. H. F. Cherniss, *Me in versiculis parum pudicum*, reprinted in *Critical Essays on Roman Literature: Elegy and Lyric*, ed. J. P. Sullivan (London, 1962), 15–30.

[49] To quote a standard text-book (Wellek and Warren, *Theory*, ch. 7). 'There is no relation between "sincerity" and value as art. The volumes of agonizingly felt love poetry perpetrated by adolescents and the dreary (however fervently felt) religious verse which fills libraries are sufficient proof of this.'

fantasies are unusually rich and varied, taking life and colour from tradition as well as from the world around. If the lover were not so thought of, the poetry would not be worth writing. What we cannot say, and ought not to ask, is whether Catullus and Propertius do this out of insight into the feelings of others or out of their own experience; we like to think the latter, but even so the experience will be remembered and generalized, gathered and separated into a series of episodes bearing little relation to the time-sequence of its original form. There is of course a problem about what to say when a poem seems to us splendid, life-like, and convincing; I am suggesting that we ought not to say it seems 'sincere' if by that we imply that the discovery of some biographical fact might confirm or destroy the judgement. What we can say—and say within the traditions of ancient criticism—is what 'Longinus'[50] says of Euripides: 'The writer's soul rides in Phaethon's chariot and shares the dangers and the flight of his horses.'

[50] 15. 4, cf. 15. 2 for a similar idea.

# 12
# Theories of Evaluation in the Rhetorical Treatises of Dionysius of Halicarnassus

## D. M. SCHENKEVELD

### I

It is well known that in his rhetorical writings Dionysius of Halicarnassus offers many examples of what can be called practical criticism. His methods in applying this kind of criticism need no illustration, nor is it necessary to remind the readers of his categories, like e.g. the types and the virtues of style. All these aspects have been abundantly[1] studied.

Only to a much lesser extent has attention been given to a more theoretical aspect of his criticism, namely his theory of evaluation[2]. It is true, Dionysius does not spend much time on this subject, but on several occasions he offers statements which, put together, seem to suggest that he possessed such a theory. For in the passages concerned he enters into questions such as 'Which man is competent to

[1] See S. F. Bonner, *The Literary Treatises of Dionysius of Halicarnassus* (Cambr. Class. Stud. 5; Cambridge, 1939; repr. 1969), and the latest account by G. Kennedy, *The Art of Rhetoric in the Roman World* (Princeton, 1972), 342–63.

[2] More or less important are the studies of F. Nassal, *Aesthetisch-rhetorische Beziehungen zwischen Dionys und Cicero* (Diss. Tübingen, 1910), esp. 37–40; O. Immisch, *Horazens Epistel über die Dichtkunst* (Philol. Suppl. 24/3; Leipzig, 1932), esp. 62–72; M. Pohlenz, Τὸ πρέπον, NGG (1933), esp. 62–5 and 71 ff.; W. Steidle, *Studien zur Ars Poetica des Horaz* (Würzburg, 1939; repr. Hildesheim, 1967), esp. 60–2; G. Pavano, *Sulla cronologia degli scritti retorici di Dionisio d'Alicarnasso, Acc. di Sc. Lett. e Arti di Palermo* IV/3/2/2 (1942), 14 ff.; G. Pavano, *Dionisio d'Alicarnasso critico di Tucidide, Acc. di Scienze di Torino* 68 (1938), 10 and 23; G. Pavano, *Saggio su Tucidide* (Palermo, 1958); Karin Pohl, *Die Lehre von den drei Wortfügungsarten* (Diss. Tübingen, 1968), esp. 81–90. I have not been able to see the typewritten thesis of P. Costil, *L'Esthétique littéraire de Denys d'Halicarnasse* (Paris, 1949).

evaluate literary works?', or 'Does sound evaluation rest upon a rational or an irrational basis?'

The aim of this article is to interpret the relevant texts, and to investigate if they constitute a coherent theory of evaluation. It is not my intention to trace the history of the various ideas and notions which are discussed by Dionysius, except in one case.

The texts are taken from different writings of Dionysius: it became apparent during my research that the problem of their chronological order[3] has no bearing on my subject.

## II

A passage from *On Thucydides* forms the starting-point, because there Dionysius mentions the various groups of people able to criticize a work, the tools by which they do so, and their specific objects. In his judgment on Thucydides' performances in the department of style Dionysius quotes the account of the last battle between the Athenians and the Syracusans (*Hist.* 7. 69-72) and adds this remark:

*Text I* (On Thucydides *27, i. 543-5 Usher*)

This and narratives like it seemed to me admirable and worthy of imitation, and I was convinced that in such passages as these we have perfect examples of the historian's sublime eloquence, the beauty of his language, his rhetorical brilliance, and his other virtues. I was led to this conclusion when I observed that every soul is won by this style of writing, since it offends neither our irrational faculty (*to alogon tès dianoias kritèrion*), which is our natural instrument for distinguishing the pleasant (*ta hèdea*) from the distasteful, nor our rational faculty (*to logikon kritèrion*), which enables us to judge individual technical excellence (*to kalon*). Nobody, even the most inexperienced student of political oratory, could find a single objectionable word or figure of speech, nor could the most expert critic with the utmost contempt for the ignorance of the masses find fault with the style of this passage: the taste of the untutored

---

[3] Cf. Pavano, *Cronologia*, and Kennedy, *Art of Rhetoric*, 344.

majority and that of the educated few will be in agreement, for surely those laymen, and there are many of them, will find nothing base, tortuous or obscure to offend them, while the rare expert with his specialised training will find nothing ill-bred, humble or uncultivated. But the rational faculty (*to logikon kritèrion*) and the irrational one (*to alogon kritèrion*) will combine in one voice; and these are the two faculties with which we properly judge all works of art.[4]

Several points require our attention here, as they will return repeatedly:

(a) Dionysius distinguished between the irrational faculty of the mind (*to alogon kritèrion*) and the rational faculty (*to logikon kritèrion*);

(b) The irrational faculty is an innate function ('our natural instrument') and presumably present in the layman, whereas the rational faculty belongs to the expert and does not come naturally to him;

(c) The irrational capacity is concerned with what is pleasant (or distasteful), the rational one with what is excellent in each individual art;

(d) Both capacities are necessary, and we are not allowed to neglect either of them;

(e) Dionysius first speaks of *psychagôgia* ('every soul is won') and he then distinguishes the two capacities. Evidently, the expert, too, undergoes a 'psychagogic' experience. The nature of this feeling Dionysius does not define. Elsewhere the word often does not mean more than 'entertainment', but in *On Demosthenes* 22 (323 Usher, for instance) Dionysius compares the way he is influenced by Demosthenes with the experiences of the Corybants and other *mystai*. Consequently in our passage *psychagôgia* may come close to 'ecstasy'. Clearly, however, all people who read literary texts will undergo this experience.

Notwithstanding the remarks (a)–(e), several other points still remain obscure, especially the question of the range of the two capacities, and that of a possible preference for one of them.

[4] All translations of Dionysian texts have been taken over from the Loeb edition with translation by Stephen Usher, *Dionysius of Halicarnassus Critical Essays*, 2 vols. (1974–85). Several times I slightly modified these, especially in the case of technical terms.

To some extent other passages will provide the answers.

### Text II (On Thucydides 34, i. 565 Usher)

But those who keep an impartial mind and examine literature in accordance with correct standards, whether they are endowed with some natural power of appreciation or have developed their critical faculties (*kritèria*) by help of instruction . . .

### Text III (On Thucydides 4, i. 471 Usher)

I need not say that the layman is as competent a judge of many things as the expert—those things which are apprehended by the irrational senses (*aisthèsis alogos*) and the feelings—and that these are the faculties (*kritèria*) which all forms of art aim to stimulate and are the reason for its creation.

In these passages the judgment of the layman, again, is accepted as valid, although Text II first speaks of the examination of literature with correct standards, and only then is the distinction made between a natural capacity and one reinforced by instruction. The principle underlying these specific rules Dionysius does not elucidate, but we may suppose that art (*technè*) is meant. In this matter, however, Dionysius nowhere gives a clear answer to our queries.[5]

In Text IV he quotes from Plato's *Menexenus* 236D and adds that as to their understanding, some words could have been left out, but not for their sound:

### Text IV (On Demosthenes 24, i. 335 Usher)

Who would have criticized it (viz. the passage with some words left out) for obscurity? But perhaps the form that we have sounds better and is more impresssive? Quite the contrary: its dignity has been removed and destroyed. It needs no reasoning to learn this: every reader is aware of it through his own feelings, for it is the senses, untutored by reason (*alogoi aisthèseis*), that decide in all cases what is distasteful and what is pleasant, and they need neither instruction nor persuasion in these matters.

This passage points to the ear as the proper instrument for evaluation, and this sense-organ stands in no need of instruction. The ear

---

[5] This explanation implies a contradiction. For an interesting example of the same kind, see Bonner, *Literary Treatises*, 45 f.

seems to be self-sufficient and it acts on a non-logical basis. Dionysius even extends the scope of his remark to non-literary achievements, for he speaks of the senses in the plural. At other times he repeats this observation, especially in relation to the visual arts.[6]

Now we have found that, in matters of evaluation, the ear has an important place, it will cause no surprise to come across similar passages. In Text V he gives advice how to understand the compositional style of Demosthenes.

## Text V (On Demosthenes 50, i. 429 Usher)

First consider its melody, of which the most reliable test is the instinctive feeling (*alogos aisthèsis*): but this requires much practice and prolonged training.

Here Dionysius asks us to judge Demosthenes by the latter's most outspoken characterictics, in the first place by his melodiousness. In this case the ear is the best judge, which statement implies that a rationally based judgment is not needed here. Such a judgment is even explicitly excluded in Text IV, 'it needs no reasoning to learn this'. Passage V contains an additional remark, which seemingly contradicts earlier statements. In Text IV instruction and persuasion were said to be dispensable, whereas in this passage the instinctive feeling (*alogos aisthèsis*) of the ear appears to need much practice and prolonged instruction. Has Dionysius shifted his ground here? Such a shift is itself not impossible, but I think that we have to explain this matter differently. Dionysius means by 'instruction' instruction based upon logic, i.e. a process whereby one can explain what is being done. 'Practice', on the other hand, points to practical training which gives one the 'knack' which makes one sensitive without any rational explanation being offered.[7]

The next passage once again underlines the importance of the ear, in this case in matters of *actio*.

## Text VI (On Literary Composition 23, ii. 203 Usher)

The ear's instinctive feeling (*to alogon tès akoès pathos*) testifies (how to read a passage from Isocrates).

---

[6] Cf. Pohlenz, *NGG* 63 ff.
[7] See also the end of Text VII.

Another Dionysian passage says something more. Shortly before Dionysius had remarked that one of Lysias' most outstanding characteristics is his 'charm' (*charis*). This feature is 'a quality which is beyond description and too wonderful for words. It is very easy and plain for layman and expert alike to see' (*On Lysias* 10, i. 39 Usher). Lysias' charm eludes rational explanation, like other fine qualities which are difficult to express in words, such as physical beauty, good melody, and what is called 'timeliness' (*kairos*). Then Dionysius continues as in Text VII.

### Text VII (On Lysias *11, i. 39–41 Usher*)

In each case it is our senses (*aisthèsis*) and not our reason (*logos*) that provide the key. The advice which teachers of music give to those wishing to acquire an accurate sense of melody and thus to be able to discern the smallest tone-interval in the musical scale, is that they should simply cultivate the ear, and seek no more accurate standard of judgment (*kritèrion*) than this. My advice also would be the same to those readers of Lysias who wish to learn the nature of his charm: to train the irrational senses (*alogos aisthèsis*) by patient study over a long period and by feeling without thinking (*alogon pathos*).

Because 'timeliness' (*kairos*) is mentioned here, this passage may be followed immediately by Text VIII.

### Text VIII (On Literary Composition *12, ii. 87 Usher*)

However, I think we must in every case keep good taste (timeliness, *kairos*) in view, for this is the best measure of what is pleasurable (*hèdonè*) and what is not . . . Indeed, the nature of the subject is not such that it can be covered by an all-embracing, technical method of treatment, nor can good taste in general be pursued successfully by science (*epistèmè*), but only by opinion (*doxa*).

All these passages confirm and expand the interpretation of the first text. The irrational sense-perception is a matter of innate capacity, and, therefore, it is found in laymen. The irrational senses can be trained, not imparted by logical instruction. The phenomena it judges have to do not only with the acoustic aspects of literary works, but with general features, such as καιρός, as well. These objects are also called 'what is pleasant' (*ta hèdea*) or 'distasteful' (*ochlèra*), as distinct from 'what is excellent' (*kalon*). In all these matters, it seems that the irrational judgment is the only one that counts.

### III

This last conclusion still leaves an important question unanswered. It has not yet become clear whether ultimately one faculty of judgment (*kritèrion*) is more decisive than the other, whether e.g. the irrational judgment may overrule the rational evaluation, or whether, somehow or other, Dionysius, after all, prefers a judgment based upon the *ratio*. From the foregoing passages we know that both faculties (*kritèria*) are necessary (see Text I: 'the two faculties by which we judge all works of art' V.) Other texts, such as VII and VIII, however, seemed to suggest that in the case of timeliness (*kairos*) and other crucial matters the irrational feelings decide what, from a literary point of view, is written well. Moreover, we cannot deny that timeliness (*kairos*) is in Dionysius' eyes of the utmost importance.[8] So far, we do not seem to err in having ascertained that the ultimate decision lies with the irrational sense (*alogos aisthèsis*). Dionysius reinforces this conclusion in *On Lysias*, when he discusses the method for distinguishing the genuine speeches of Lysias from those falsely ascribed to him.

*Text IX* (On Lysias *11, 1. 41 Usher*)

Whenever I am uncertain as to the genuineness of any speech that is attributed to him, and find it difficult to arrive at the truth by means of the other available evidence, I resort to this virtue of style to cast the final vote. Then, if the writing seems to be graced with those additonal qualities of charm, I deem it to be a product of Lysias' genius, and consider it unnecessary to investigate further. But if the style is devoid of grace and beauty, I view the speech with a jaundiced and suspicious eye, and conclude that it never could be by Lysias. I do not strain my instinctive feeling (*alogos aisthèsis*) beyond this.

In the cases of authenticity, when other indications are lacking, the decisive factor is an aesthetic one, viz. the presence of Lysianic charm. Dionysius provides us with examples of this method too. The speech *About the Statue of Iphicrates*, though an impressive example of rhetorical ability, lacks the specific Lysianic charm, and therefore is spurious. Up to this point, Dionysian practice is in harmony with his

---

[8] Cf. the survey by Pohlenz, ibid.

theory, but then he adds, inconsistently (12, i. 43 Usher); 'but the blatancy of its spuriousness only forced itself upon me when I came to calculate its date.'[9] For another speech, *On the Betrayal of Iphicrates*, he follows the same method, although he now says that the absence of Lysianic charm made him suspicious. The decisive matter, however, is again the chronological incongruity.

We can say that Dionysius professes to have an aesthetic method, but hesitates to apply it. In the ultimate analysis, his *ratio* has the upper hand.

## IV

At this point the reader may object that the foregoing conclusion is valid only for non-aesthetic problems, and go on to suggest that in aesthetics proper Dionysius finally prefers the irrational judgment. But even there, problems arise, especially when we try to decide a question so far left out of discussion. For what has Dionysius in mind when in Text I he assigns to the irrational faculty (*alogon kritèrion*) judgment upon what is pleasant (*ta hèdea*) and to the rational one (*logikon kritèrion*) that upon what is beautiful and excellent (*ta kala*)? The contents of the words *hèdea* and *kala* are still obscure, and have to be ascertained before we can proceed. More than once Dionysius offers a theoretical exposition of these concepts, several times, indeed, outside the context of *alogos aisthèsis*. Scholars have studied these expositions to a great extent: a *communis opinio*, however, has not been arrived at. The lack of this finds its finest illustration in the discussions on a non-Dionysian passage, viz. Horace, *Ars poetica* 99–100:

> *Non satis est pulchra esse poemata: dulcia sunto,*
> *Et quocumque volent animum auditoris agunto.*

It is not enough for poetry to be beautiful; it must also be pleasing and lead the hearer's mind wherever it will.

C. O. Brink, following Tate, and A. Rostagni, take *pulchra* as 'well made, quae placent recto iudicio' in opposition to *dulcia*, which

---

[9] Cf. 12, i. 41–3 Usher: Using, then as my main criterion simply that the speeches of Lysias are composed in a pleasing style, I have come to suspect many of the speeches which have been commonly regarded as genuine.

means 'emotionally effective'.[10] O. Immisch, however, explains these words as 'erhaben', 'angenehm', respectively, and does not interpret them as opposite terms, but rather as complementary.[11] Both groups of interpreters refer to our Texts X and XI (to be quoted later on), Rostagni also quotes Text I, thereby implying that the notions of pleasant-beautiful (*hèdea-kala*) in all three passages are the same. This latter view of Rostagni's is held by other scholars, such as P. Geigenmueller[12] and F. Nassal.

### Text X (On Demosthenes, *47, i. 419 Usher*)

Virtually every work, whether it is created by nature or mothered by the arts, has two objectives, pleasure and beauty.

Practically the same thought is expressed in Text XIa.

### Text XIa (On Literary Composition *10, ii. 69 Usher*)

It seems to me that the two most important effects which those who write both poetry and prose should aim at are attractiveness (*hèdonè*) and beauty (*to kalon*). The ear craves for both of these.

In Text XI*b* Dionysius subsumes various terms under the two main 'ends'

### Text XIb (On Literary Composition *11, ii. 71-2 Usher*)

Under attractiveness (*hèdonè*) I list freshness, charm, euphony, sweetness, persuasiveness and all such qualities; and under beauty impressiveness, solemnity, seriousness, dignity, mellowness and qualities like them.

This further definition of the two main 'ends' makes it clear that beauty (*to kalon*) tends towards the archaic-rough aspect of literary composition, whereas attractiveness (*to hèdu, hèdonè*) corresponds to the melodious-smooth aspect. Accordingly, in *On Demosthenes* 47 Dionysius explicitly links *to hèdu* with the smooth mode of composition, and *to kalon* with the severe style of composition. So there exists

---

[10] C. O. Brink, *The 'Ars Poetica'* (Cambridge, 1971), 183–4; A. Rostagni, *Arte poetica di Orazio* (Turin, 1930; 1946), *a.l.*

[11] Immisch, *Horazens Epistel*, 62 ff., cf. Steidle, *Studien*, 61 ff.

[12] *Quaestiones dionysianae de vocabulis artis criticae* (Diss. Leipzig, 1908), 34 f.

a clear distinction between the two 'ends', *hèdone* and *to kalon*, but both are to be sought after, as is stated in Text XI*a*: 'the ear craves for both of these'. Indeed, the whole of *On Literary Composition* is one continuous argument that, at least in matters of shaping words and sentences, the trained ear takes an important place, if not the only one. This trained ear decides whether the result of composition may be called *pleasant* and *beautiful*.

This observation, viz. that *to kalon* as well as *to hèdu* belongs to the province of the ear, has a great bearing on the following discussion. For when we return to the first text and try to apply our last conclusion to it, a confusion arises. Let us suppose that the words *kalon-hèdu*, used in both texts, denote the same contents. In that case, Text I assigns *to kalon* not to the province of the irrational feelings (*alogos aisthèsis*), whereas Texts X and XI do. To explain this further, the application of what is said in Text I to the theory of the modes of composition leads to the conclusion that the rough composition with *to kalon* as its 'end' can only be apprehended by the rational faculty (*to logikon kritènon*). This conclusion completely contradicts the whole argument of *On Literary Composition*. Consequently, we have to conclude that the words *kalon-hèdu* of the various passages denote something different.

This inference, which, incidentally, is not new,[13] does not imply that the two distinctions have nothing in common. Such a view seems very unlikely, indeed. But what do they have in common? Various interpretations have been given, of which those of Steidle and Pavano seem to be the more attractive.[14] According to Steidle, Dionysius, within *ta hèdea* (the pleasant), the domain of emotions, distinguishes between *to hèdu* (that which is pleasant and attractive) and *to kalon* (that which is impressive). Text IV apparently strengthens this interpretation, because it mentions 'dignity' and impressiveness, words usually connected with *to kalon* in the same breath as *to hèdu*. It also states that their absence is detected by the irrational feeling (*alogos aisthèsis*), the sense-perception, which, as we know from Text I, judges what is pleasant (*ta hèdea*). The conclusion is obvious: there exists a department, called *to kalon*, which has nothing to do with the other one (viz. *to hèdu*). This latter one

---

[13] Pohl, *Lehre*, 82. My disagreement with her exposition (42–4) on some points (see *Mnemos.* 1974), is of no importance here.
[14] Cf. esp. Steidle, *Studien*, 60 n. 55.

comprises the emotionally perceived effects of *to kalon* and *to hèdu* respectively, and the first one, *to kalon*, comprises 'die mit dem *logikon* (the rational faculty) fassbare künstlerisch-technische Vollkommen-heit' (p. 60 n. 55).

This interpretation, however convincing it seems to be, is marred by one omission, because it does not define what exactly is techni-cally and artistically perfect, and where one can find it. Not, pre-sumably, in the composition of words, for the very work on composition discusses 'alle(n) vom Kunstwerk ausgehende(n) und mit der *alogos*, *aisthèsis* wahrnehmbare(n) Reiz' and nothing else. Further, it is not easy to see that the other part of the stylistic domain (*lektikos topos*), the choice of words, will be for us the place to look, in so far as in the first chapter of *On Literary Composition* Dionysius calls composition much more difficult than the choice of words. *A priori* we would expect on the basis of this statement that the technically perfect element would be found in the realm of the composition. But this expectation is not fulfilled.

So it seems that the rational faculty is excluded from the stylistic domain, because there is no place for its beauty (*kalon*). Perhaps it will function in the domain of contents (*pragmatikos topos*). In this area Dionysius distinguishes between invention (*heuresis*) and arrangement (*oikonomia*): he assigns invention to nature (*phusis*), and puts arrangement under art (*technè*) (*On Thucydides* 9, i. 481 and 34, i. 563 Usher). Must we therefore conclude that the proper domain of the rational faculty is arrangement, and that we may expect to find 'what is beautiful in each art' there?

This conclusion is, of course, absurd, but seems inevitable, pro-vided we apply Steidle's interpretation to our subject. Dionysius would never subscribe to such a view. Its consequences would be that, for the greatest part, his instruction in rhetoric is non-technical. But this view he expressly denies, e.g. in his definition of rhetoric: 'rhetoric is a technical capacity' (ii. 197. 2 U.-R.). To find a way out of these difficulties I have tried another solution than Steidle's. This solution is that the distinction of Texts X–XI on the one hand, and those of Text I on the other, overlap in this way: when evaluating, the layman and the expert first judge a literary text by means of their irrational perception and establish by this means the presence, or absence, of what is pleasant (*ta hèdea*). This being done, the expert takes over, practises his specific skill, founded on *logos*, and ascertains, on a scientific basis, the technical perfection of the text. According to this interpretation, *to hèdu* and *to kalon* of texts X–XI will be judged twice, first, by the irrational feeling (*alogos aisthèsis*) and then by the rational faculty (*logikon kritèrion*). This explanation comes close to that of Pavano, expounded in his articles and his commentary on *On Thucydides*. According to Pavano, Dionysius ultimately prefers the expert's judgment and assigns the first place to the rational faculty (*to logikon kritèrion*), for the irrational feeling (*alogos aisthèsis*) leads to judgment, opinion (*doxa*) only, not to science (*epistème*). Pavano rightly stresses the context of Text II, where Dionysius opposes the blind admirers of Thucydides, who do not judge soberly, but 'under hypnosis'.[15] This fact has to be taken into account when we explain his statements. Pavano then concludes:

> Si deve intendere dunque che qui Dion. non allinei il criterio logico all'altro, per completare il quadro delle funzioni del critico; ma egli lo invoca come il necessario correttivo dell'altro e contro coloro che, per essersi abbandonati al sentimento senza controllo, hanno finito, come qui dice, per perdere la luce della ragione, o come altrove vuole, per smarrire la via della verità.

This interpretation of Pavano's, coupled with my attempt to define the place of *ta hèdea-to kalon* in relation to the rational and irrational faculties has much in its favour. For it seems plausible, that, especially when arguing against critics who 'lost their reason', Dionysius plays down the role of the irrational feeling (*alogon aisthèsis*) in favour of the rational judgment, which acts as a corrective of the irrational faculty (*alogon kritèrion*). When Dionysius does not have to contend with such critics, we would expect him to lay more stress on the role of the irrational judgment. This he does indeed, even to such an extent that he says of timeliness (*kairos*), the most important feature of all in literature: 'timeliness (good taste) cannot in general be pursued successfully by science, but only by opinion' (Text VIII). This exclusion of science (*epistème*) which amounts to the neglect of the rational judgment, however, is completely unexpected. Here Dionysius does not so much weaken his previous point of view but rather ignores it.

Thus, when accepting Pavano's explanation we appear to come across another incongruity, which is not easy to explain away. This

---

[15] *On Thucydides* 34, i. 565. Cf. 565, 'His admirers are suffering from the same sort of infatuation', and 563, 'Those who have admired Thucydides immoderately'.

incongruity, moreover, is increased in the last passage to be discussed, Text XII.

## Text XII (On Dinarchus 7, ii. 269-71 Usher)

Generally speaking, two different forms of imitation can be found with regard to ancient models: one is natural, and is acquired by intensive learning and familiarity; the other is related to it, but is acquired by following the precepts of art. About the first, what more is there to say? And about the second, what is there to be said except that a certain spontaneous charm and freshness emanates from all the original models, whereas in the artificial copies, even if they attain the height of imitative skill, there is present nevertheless a certain element of contrivance and unnaturalness.

For a better understanding of the point of this passage it is necessary to take its context into consideration. When advising on how to decide the authenticity of many speeches ascribed to Lysias, Hyperides, Demosthenes, and Dinarchus, Dionysius states that Dinarchus is not 'the inventor of an individual style by which one can recognize him with accuracy, except in this way: he displays many examples of imitation and of difference from the original models of the speeches themselves' (*On Dinarchus* 6, ii. 267 Usher). Such a model for Dinarchus was Demosthenes ('the Demosthenic style, which he imitated most of all', *On Dinarchus* 5, ii. 265 Usher). But Demosthenes himself was also an imitator (ibid. 267, 'Demosthenes [. . .] selected the best features of all writers'). Now, in our passage Dionysius summarizes this matter of *mimesis* and the relationship between the archetypes, which themselves are the result of *mimesis*, and their imitation. The difference between these two groups appears to lie in the presence of a certain spontaneous charm and freshness of the archetypes and a certain element of contrivance and unnaturalness in the imitations, acquired by following the precepts of the art. For our subject this passage implies that it is possible to determine the presence of such a *charis*, and at the same time that this is done by the irrational judgment. For, as we have seen before, the irrational feeling (*alogos aisthèsis*) decides on charm and freshness, features apparent in the archetypes. This conclusion has as a consequence that the most beautiful works are evaluated ultimately by the irrational faculty (*alogon kritèrion*) and that judgment on works which 'smell of the lamp' and are inferior is passed by the rational faculty (*logikon kritèrion*), and is arrived at by science (*epistème*). But this function of the mind, according to Pavano at least, has a more important place than opinion (*doxa*). Once more, the discrepancy is present.

## V

So all attempts to find an explanation covering all the passages fail, and a coherent theory of evaluation is impossible to detect. Taken in itself, each distinction may be workable and have a value of its own, but it concerns a subject which at other times is looked at from another point of view. When the several points of view are combined, confusion appears to reign.

The causes of this confusion can partly be traced, but to go deeper into these would mean a lengthy treatment, which is out of place here. One instance, therefore, may suffice.

I have before tried to show that the interpretation of Steidle, which subsumed the group pleasant-beautiful (*hèdu-kalon*) of Texts X–XI under *ta hèdea* of Text I, was not acceptable, because it led to the conclusion that, in the field of *lexis* at any rate, no place was left for the rational judgment, in so far as its most difficult part, the composition of words, was wholly and exclusively judged by the irrational perception of the ear. If we suppose that Dionysius did not have this opinion about *synthesis*, the situation would have been different, for in that case some part of it could have been saved for the rational judgment to operate upon, and Steidle's interpretation would have been cogent.

However, Dionysius did adhere to this opinion, because in this respect he followed the theories of *hoi kritikoi*. These theories I discussed in an earlier article,[16] the main argument of which may be summed up as follows: *hoi kritikoi*, a group of critics, at least some of them, laid all emphasis on the composition of words, to the neglect of the other parts of rhetoric. In this field they advocated the irrational judgment, and carried forward their argument as far as the final conclusion that the contents of a literary work are unimportant, or rather, their value is defined by that of the composition, and are

[16] '*OI KPITIKOI* in Philodemus', *Mnemos.* 4/21 (1968), 176–214. Cf. Pohl, *Lehre*, 145–59. See now R. Janko, *Philodemus On Poems, Book One* (Oxford, 2000), ch. 5.

judged upon by the irrational judgment. Dionysius took over the greater part of their argument, but he did not accept their final conclusion. He could not do so without impairing his belief in the goal of his rhetorical teachings. For him that goal is a rhetoric which is useful for the free citizen. He continuously calls his rhetoric a 'philosophical' or 'political' rhetoric, thereby following Isocrates, whose speeches Dionysius praises as the finest examples to obtain excellence in behaviour (*On Isocrates* 4, i. 115 Usher)—an important criterion to him is the usefulness of a literary work. In the case of historiography, too, Dionysius is attentive to the usefulness of a historical subject. It is true, in the *Letter to Gnaeus Pompeius* 3 (ii. 373) the purpose of choosing a subject is defined as to select a noble subject which will please the readers, but Dionysius condemns Thucydides for choosing a 'bad subject'. More clearly he explains his point of view in the introduction to the *Roman Antiquities* (i. i. 2): 'I am convinced that (all historians) ought, first of all, to make choice of noble and lofty subjects, and such as will be of great utility to their readers' (trans. E. Cary, Loeb edition). Even in *On Composition* we come across traces of this moral view of literature. In the first chapters Dionysius mentions the possibility (3, ii. 25 Usher) that a good arrangement of words lends attractiveness to verse and prose alike; conversely, a bad composition may destroy the value of the thought expressed. Nowhere does he say that a wrong thought still works, provided it is clothed in a beautiful arrangement.[17] Evidently, Dionysius holds the view that thought must be useful. This being so, he cannot follow the *kritikoi* in their final conclusions, but adopts their theories to a certain point only. By doing this, however, he appears not to realize that their starting-point, viz. the exclusive importance of the composition of words, which because of its euphony is to be judged by the ear only, must have an adverse effect on his other views, e.g. his view concerning the goal of his rhetorical teachings.

## VI

The explanation proposed here will give no cause for surprise, as it fits in with the view which we arrive at when studying other aspects of Dionysius' rhetorical writings. The longer we do so, the more

---

[17] For a different view cp. Isocr., *Euag.* 191a.

we will be convinced that he may well seem to operate within a coherent system, but in reality he discusses isolated aspects of a rather vaguely defined whole: he appears to lack a consistent view of the foundations of his literary criticism. In this article inconsistencies have been detected which make it impossible to arrive at a coherent theory of Dionysius. The same discovery can be made for other aspects, *e.g.* the theory of types of style, the very use of the word *synthesis* (composition), not to speak of the confusion which appears when in *On Literary Composition* the distinction of *hèdu-kalon* is developed.[18]

We would do Dionysius an injustice if we suggested that he is the only ancient rhetorician who was inconsistent: he, like many other ancient rhetoricians, stands in a tradition which contains many contradictory theories. Even Aristotle, who approached rhetoric from a rigorously philosophical point of view, gets into trouble when discussing the style of a speech. Like Dionysius, other rhetoricians became stuck the moment they left the purely philosophical plane: nevertheless, they claimed that their job was a real art (*technè*) with a logical basis and a logical structure. This claim, it is well known, they put forward against their rivals in educational matters, the philosophers, who maintained that rhetoric had a merely empirical structure. The rhetoricians borrowed from various philosophical systems—directly or indirectly—several theories, which could be adapted to isolated problems, but caused confusion when fitted into the rhetorical system as a whole.[19]

POSTCRIPT

Reactions to this article are to be found in: Cynthia Damon, 'Aesthetic Response and Technical Analysis in the Rhetorical Writings of Dionysius of Halicarnassus', *Museum Helveticum*, 48 (1991), 33–58; Koen Goudriaan, *Over Classicisme. Dionysius van Halicarnassus en zijn program van welsprekendheid, cultuur en politiek*, PhD Vrije Universiteit te Amsterdam, 2 vols. (Amsterdam, 1989), 142–54 (cf. the English summary ii. 685–6). Also in the following article, which I have not seen: F. Donadi, 'Il "bello" e "il pacere" (osservazioni sul *De compositione verborum* di Dionigi di Alicarnasso', *Stud. ital. filol. Class.* 79 (1986) 42–63.

[18]   See Pohl, *Lehre*, 81 ff.
[19]   See G. Kennedy, *The Art of Persuasion in Greece* (Princeton, 1963), 321 ff.

# 13
# *Longinus: Structure and Unity*

## DOREEN C. INNES

Longinus, as I shall follow convention in terming the author of *On the Sublime*, uses the formal structure of a textbook. He begins with preliminaries, where he introduces main themes, and analyses related neighbouring faults. He lists five sources of the sublime, promises to analyse the characteristics of 'each type', καθ' ἑκάστην ἰδέαν τούτων (8. 1), and continues to remind us of this schema. Thus figures 'follow next in their due place' (16. 1 ἐφεξῆς τέτακται), and word-arrangement is 'the fifth of the headings contributing to the sublime which I set out at the beginning' (39. 1 ἡ πέμπτη μοῖρα τῶν συντελουσῶν εἰς τὸ ὕψος, ὧν γε ἐν ἀρχῇ προὐθέμεθα). The final chapter is a surprise in its unusual form, a reported dialogue between an unnamed philosopher and Longinus, but, as we shall see, its contents form a satisfying climax.

Textbook structures elsewhere offer a sequence of preliminaries, analysis under formal headings and final appendices,[1] but Horace's *Ars Poetica* is a particularly interesting parallel. Horace similarly starts with key themes (artistry, unity and propriety) and neighbouring faults (1–37). He then analyses poetry under the three headings set out in 38–41 (arrangement, diction and content), and adds a formally distinct section on the poet's aims and virtues (295 ff.). Yet Horace in practice subverts this formal superstructure; he deliberately blurs transitions (where indeed *is* the transition to content?[2]). Instead he highlights a set of interlocking key themes; and he ends, like Longinus, with a grand finale, which reiterates key

[1] Appendices are partly the equivalent of modern footnotes, but see below on 43 as an example of more organic use in Longinus.

[2] The favoured candidates are 119 and 153. But note the term *res* (subject matter) already in 73 ff. on the link of metre and content (and indeed already 49). This fits Horace's emphasis on the interlocking relationship of words and content (38–41, cf. 311).

themes and provides an insight into reasons for failure—the picture of the undisciplined mad poet, who claims freedom but lacks *ars*. Longinus also subverts *his* carefully constructed superstructure. To take the most obvious problem, why is there no independent analysis of the second of the five sources, emotion?—precisely the source which is the most original and whose exclusion by Caecilius evokes immediate polemic and justification (8. 2-4). The long lacuna in 9. 4 must make us cautious, but the transition at the end of 15 is crucial, since 15. 12 formally concludes the first source on sublimity of thought, and 16. 1 formally introduces figures as the next logically following topic. Yet 15. 12 makes no mention of emotion. The most stimulating attempt to solve this notorious problem is by Donald Russell (1981). Yet I doubt the five-source schema of 8. 1 can have only a temporary purpose, part of a careful preparation for a defence of Plato. Some formal explanation will have been given in the long lacuna beginning in 9. 4, and my own favoured explanation is that the second source, 'vehement and inspired emotion' (8. 1 τὸ σφοδρὸν καὶ ἐνθουσιαστικὸν πάθος) is primarily and typically found in conjunction with the first source. Great thought, we are told, is often found without emotion, and Longinus immediately offers an example and suitable contexts, but, significantly, he gives no example of suitable emotion without greatness of thought. He also (8. 2) excludes low, ignoble emotions, such as pity, grief and fear, and what he particularly recommends is the opposite, 'noble emotion', τὸ γενναῖον πάθος, a type which will combine emotion and nobility of thought, and it is this which more than anything will inspire our speech (8. 4). Emotion as a source of sublimity on its own without nobility of thought will be a very curious beast—though it will presumably cover the ecstasy of madness. I explore this question elsewhere (Innes 1995). But whatever the details of his explanation, I accept that Longinus preserved the validity of his five-source superstructure throughout the work[3] and presented emotion as a source which is important but only rarely, if ever, autonomous.

It is also often claimed that 15. 12 is an incomplete summary of 9-15: it includes imitation and imagination, the topics of 13. 2-15, but it omits sublimity from density of detail in 10 (and can therefore also omit emotion, a very dubious argument). But I agree with

---

[3] He has, for example, already written two books on arrangement, but for his present project 'necessarily' (ἐξ ἀνάγκης) he includes some brief discussion (39. 1).

Mazzucchi (1990) that 10-13. 1 are not on sources of sublimity but on methods of intensifying thoughts—by concise selection and by expansion (αὔξησις), methods which Longinus aptly distinguishes by his use of vocabulary, amassing words beginning συν- and ἐπι- respectively. Mazzucchi rightly compares the distinction of thoughts and approaches, ἔννοιαι and μέθοδοι, in Hermogenes (e.g. 218-19 Rabe).

One final detail on formal structure: 43, on petty diction, is formally an appendix out of due order (diction was discussed in 30-8). It can be defended simply as an appendix, and it runs on smoothly enough from the preceding topic on faults of arrangement. But I suggest a more integral function. It concerns failure of the sublime and acts as a gliding transition to the final chapter on reasons for a lack of sublimity. After the paean of praise of sublimity in the digression in 33-6 (also of the power of word-arrangement in 39), the discussion of the fifth source has already moved towards an emphasis on negative aspects, (1) an absence of the first source, sublimity of thought (good arrangement can compensate for that lack, 40. 2-3), and (2) 'what makes arrangement petty' (41-2; note that 41 begins μικροποιόν, 'what makes *petty*'). Then 43 provides a further example of such pettiness, this time 'pettiness in diction' (μικρότης τῶν ὀνομάτων). This all sets the scene for the final chapter on what is effectively pettiness of nature, that absence of sublimity of thought which causes the current dearth of sublime writers. If we also look back over the whole structure, 41-3, placed near the end, are on opposite faults of technique, and thus balance the account of neighbouring faults of thought (and emotion) which comes near the beginning, in 3-5.

The apparent anomalies of structure are therefore part of a careful scheme, and as Longinus himself says (20. 3 of a flurry of anaphora and asyndeta), 'thus his order is disordered, and his disorder conversely contains order', οὕτως αὐτῷ καὶ ἡ τάξις ἄτακτον καὶ ἔμπαλιν ἡ ἀταξία ποιὰν περιλαμβάνει τάξιν. Longinus did not wish us to forget or disregard the textbook structure, but he did wish us also to see its limitations, and I follow Donald Russell closely in his emphasis on gliding transitions and the way in which one section is linked to the next by common themes. My own aim is to examine ways in which that structure of five apparently divisible categories is subverted in ways which emphasise a view of sublimity as an organic whole. The omission of emotion as a separate category of analysis is in itself a signal of that approach.

Take the most important formal transition, from the innate to the technical sources, the same passage which we have already examined for its omission of emotion (15. 12). Longinus uses a typical textbook transition of the type 'so much for "x", now for "y"', but in 16. 2 ff. he blurs that formal distinction by launching directly into an analysis of the Marathon oath of Demosthenes (18. 208), in which he continues the emphasis on the primacy of the two innate sources. The example is also about Chaeronea, as is the last example in the previous chapter (15. 10), thus resuming the noble idea of fighting for freedom. Then too, like Homer (9. 7), Demosthenes presents men like gods (16. 2 'deifying . . . like gods', ἀποθεώσας . . . ὡς θεούς, 16. 3 'immortalising', ἀπαθανατίσας). The Marathon oath also picks up the theme of *mimesis*, the creative emulation of a predecessor. It illustrates the irrelevance of merely verbal *mimesis* (16. 3 Eupolis is not Demosthenes' source), and so reminds us of the true *mimesis* of spirit which he championed in 13. 2–14, and which, in another gliding transition, he then illustrated under the next topic, imagination, where Euripides emulates an idea of Aeschylus and improves it,[4] by turning an over-grotesque personification of a building feeling ecstasy into the sublime notion of a whole mountain sharing ecstasy at the epiphany of Dionysus (15. 6). Key themes of greatness of thought and *mimesis* thus continue past the formal transition to analysis of technique—and, as we shall see, they continue through to the end, into 44.

Also significant is the choice of Demosthenes as the first example within the technical sources, since it heralds his prominence generally within the technical sources; contrast the leading role played earlier by Homer, who provides the first examples of the first source (8. 2 and 9. 2). Yet it is also Demosthenes who is the first author named in the whole work (2. 3; cf. 1. 2, the first quotation, a passage probably assumed by Longinus to be by Demosthenes). He is also already highlighted within the first source: his dense intensity of style is distinguished from those of Plato and Cicero (12. 3–5), and it

---

[4] Russell (1981: 79–80) terms the Euripides example 'a partial success'; but compare the similar reaction of nature to the epiphany of Poseidon, a passage explicitly admired in 9. 8. For Aeschylus' less successful personification of a building, compare Longinus' disapproval in 4. 6 of Plato's personification of walls left 'to sleep and not rise up' (Pl. *Lg.* 778d).

is Homer, Plato and Demosthenes who are the prime models for
*mimesis* (14. 1; cf. 36. 2). But it is Demosthenes[5] more than the other
two who combines the two innate sources and who best illustrates
the ideal partnership or ἀλληλουχία of nature and technique (36. 4;
cf. 2. 2-3, 22. 1)—and it is this partnership which dominates
Longinus' analysis of the technical sources—and which, likened to
that between light and shade (17. 2), significantly concludes the
analysis of Demosthenes' Marathon oath, the first example to appear
under the technical sources.

At the end of the treatment of figures there is another formal
conclusion, but it is no mere textbook transition. It succinctly
summarises the relationship of emotion to sublimity in a memorable
antithesis: 'emotion is as much a part of sublimity as ethos is of
pleasure' (29. 2 πάθος δὲ ὕψους μετέχει τοσοῦτον ὅποσον ἦθος ἡδονῆς).
The significant placement emphasises the importance of emotion,
πάθος. Emotion, as we were told in 8. 2-4, is important but not
always necessary, and within each of the other four sources
Longinus sets next to each other examples with and without emotion
(e.g. love and storms in 10. 1-6, or the varied series in 23, 32 and
40). Emotion has, however, been particularly prominent within the
treatment of figures (e.g. 19-21 on asyndeton; note also 38. 3 where
Longinus recommends emotion 'as I said before also in the use of
figures'). Longinus therefore aptly ends his analysis of figures by
recalling the importance of emotion.[6] This key theme is what
matters, not what can be casually dismissed as 'so much unnecessary technical detail' (29. 2 ἐκ παρενθήκης τοσαῦτα πεφιλολογῆσθαι).[7]

Digressions similarly emphasise main themes, as they may elsewhere, as in Sallust's *Catiline* and *Jugurtha* (e.g. *Cat.* 36. 4 ff. and *Jug.*
37 ff.), Cicero's *Brutus* (esp. 181 ff. and 284 ff.) and Horace's *Ars
Poetica* (e.g. 60 ff.). These are no purple patches, they serve as focal
points, asserting or reiterating main themes. So Russell (1981: 73):

---

[5] Demosthenes also fits Longinus' primary interest in oratory: he aims to produce a
work of use to 'those active in public affairs', πολιτικοὶ ἄνδρες (1. 2, cf. 17.1); note also
his use of 'the orator', ὁ ῥήτωρ, in 9. 3, 11. 2.

[6] It may also be significant that emotion is absent from the immediately preceding
analysis of the figure of periphrasis (28-9. 1). This is a figure particularly open to
misuse, even in Plato: Longinus may implicitly suggest that it is safer to use figures
with emotion.

[7] He similarly disdains unnecessary multiplication of examples, 22. 4; contrast
Caecilius (1. 1, 4. 2).

'the most carefully composed and memorable parts of the book . . .
[they] are discursive additions to the scheme, and not integral to it,
though they clearly are integral to the author's general purpose'.
Lacunae preclude certainty, but the extant text offers a striking
pattern. All the digressions are in the form of comparisons, all focus
on the nature or φύσις of the author, and they move from comparison
of two works by a single author (Homer's *Iliad* and *Odyssey* in 9.
11-15), to comparisons of similar and contrasting authors
(Demosthenes and Plato, Demosthenes and Cicero in 12. 3-5); and
from individual admired models of the past to the more general and
crucial digression on the nature of genius and flawless mediocrity in
33-6.

Patterns of imagery provide yet another form of unity.[8] Take, for
example, the image of competition for victory and the first prize (key
terms are those referring to first place, victory and competition, e.g.
πρωτεύειν/τὰ πρωτεῖα, τὰ νικητήρια and ἀγών).[9] Thus at the beginning
and end of the work the sublime is what wins first place for authors
(1. 3, 44. 2); in our mimesis of past masters we contend like athletes
for first place (13. 4); and within a network of competitive imagery
within the genius/mediocrity digression, Hyperides is a good all-
rounder, who is often second but never gets the top prize (34. 1), and
it is Demosthenes who is always victorious over orators of every age
(34. 4); we are all, finally (35. 2 ff.), born as competitors or
spectators, marvelling at nature as if at a great festival and stirred to
go beyond normal horizons to gain the eventual prize of victory (τὰ
νικητήρια) from eternity itself (36. 2).

A particularly prominent source of imagery is provided by the
mighty forces of nature such as light, sun, thunderbolts, fire, rivers
and sea. These too come to a climax in the genius/mediocrity digression (33-6). Longinus here richly exploits and pulls together imagery
which he has previously used of particular authors, most notably in
the digressions: so Homer is the Ocean, and the stream from which
Plato draws (9. 13, 13. 3); Plato is himself a broad sea, and he flows

---

[8] I shall not here give parallels for what are traditional areas of imagery, such
as Homer as Ocean, Demosthenes as thunderbolt. I am also selective, omitting in
particular imagery from vocabulary of inspiration, e.g. 8. 4, 13. 2, 16. 2. For a useful
list of the most colourful images, see Matelli 1987, 183-90, for parallels see the
commentaries of Russell 1964 and Mazzucchi 1992.

[9] See 1. 3; 13. 4; 14. 2; 33. 1; 33. 4; 34. 1; 34. 4; 35. 2; 36. 2; 44. 2.

smoothly (12. 3, 13. 1), whereas Demosthenes is like a rushing
torrent of emotion (32. 1). Water imagery links all three of Longinus'
main models for our imitation, and in 35. 4 this imagery comes to a
climax, as Ocean and great rivers represent all great writers of
genius, and are set above small, useful streams which do not evoke
instinctive awe and admiration.[10]

A still more pervasive nexus of imagery is that of light, fire, sun
and thunderbolts. Demosthenes is a thunderbolt, as is the impact of
sublimity itself (12. 4, 1.4), whereas Cicero is a spreading fire, which
also blazes but has greater mass (12. 4). Where there is powerful
imagination 'the factual aspect is concealed since it is *encircled by
light*' (15. 11 τὸ πραγματικὸν ἐγκρύπτεται περιλαμπόμενον); and, in an
extended series of images in 17. 2, if it is 'encircled by the light' of
grandeur, artifice 'sinks out of sight' (περιλαμφθεῖσα . . . δέδυκε), and
the brilliant light of Demosthenes' passion hides the artifice of his
figures, just as (in a double simile from nature and art) 'dim lights
disappear in the surrounding light of the sun' (τὰ ἀμυδρὰ φέγγη
ἐναφανίζεται τῷ ἡλίῳ περιαυγούμενα), or, in a painting, light throws
the rest into shade. The sun is an apt symbol for the supremacy of
nature or φύσις, but it also links Demosthenes back to Homer whose
*Iliad* is like the bright noonday sun, the *Odyssey* like the setting sun,
still grand but less intense (9. 13). The link is all the stronger if
Longinus asks us to remember that the sun's supremacy over other
stars had been applied to Homer in an epigram of Leonidas (*AP*. 9. 24
= 30 Gow–Page).[11]

Light and fire imagery then, like water imagery, comes to a climax
in 33–5, and in a triple crescendo it also marks the end of three
successive stages of the digression: (1) flawed genius is superior to
flawless mediocrity, and the quick succession of examples ends with
Pindar and Sophocles: both show flawed genius, 'they blaze
vehemently but are often inexplicably extinguished' (33. 5 ἐπι-
φλέγουσι τῇ φορᾷ, σβέννυνται δ' ἀλόγως πολλάκις); (2) so too, in an
extensive comparison of two specific authors, Hyperides is inferior to

---

[10] Longinus inverts Callimachean praise of small springs; but for possible polemic
also against the plain-style Atticism praised by Caecilius, note that imagery of such
streams is also applied to prose authors: so Plato's plain style is pure like the clearest
springs (D.H. *Pomp.* 2) and Lysias is 'more like a pure spring than a great river' (Quint.
*Inst.* 10. 1. 78).

[11] The comparison itself is common, e.g. Quint. *Inst.* 8. 5. 29, Lucr. 3. 1044 (of
Epicurus), and see Nisbet–Hubbard (1970) on Hor. *Carm.* 1. 12. 48.

Demosthenes, and the climax of the praise of Demosthenes is that we are blinded as 'he thunders and dazzles us' with his brilliance (34. 4 καταβροντᾷ καὶ καταφέγγει); and then (3) in the culminating image of the whole digression, we marvel not at small fires but at the fires of heaven—or at Etna's volcano, where the earth's convulsions throw up rivers of fire,[12] a final image which no doubt deliberately combines both fire and water (35. 4).

The rich use of imagery within the digression in 33–5 is in itself striking, and is particularly apt, since it is a digression within an analysis of imagery, the use of metaphor and simile.[13] It also exploits and brings to a climax strands of imagery which are almost absent from the final chapter.[14] This will be deliberate: they come to their own separate climax in 33–5,[15] and there is a different focus with a correspondingly different range of imagery in 44.

Why, asks the philosopher in this final chapter, do sublime authors no longer exist? Why do we have authors able only to persuade and please?[16] Is it the lack of political freedom (44. 1)? In reply, Longinus reaffirms that the author's own nature is the prime source of sublimity (44. 6 ff.). To create sublime literature even in an age of moral decline, we must not let our inborn potential greatness of thought wither away, but aim at posterity. Longinus thus fulfils his opening promise to show how we may 'develop our nature' to produce sublimity (1. 1 τὰς ἑαυτῶν φύσεις προάγειν), that we should nurture a mind (cf. e.g. 9. 1) which despises desires such as wealth

---

[12] Rivers are in themselves a banal image to describe the flow of lava (e.g. [Arist.] *Mu.* 4. 395b); but Longinus shows his own literary claims to join the list of sublime authors with a deliberate echo of Pindar (*P.* 1. 21 ff.; cf. 33. 5) and the suggestion of violent disruption on the vast scale he admires in Homer in 9. 6, ἀναρρηγνυμένης μὲν ἐκ βάθρων γῆς, 'when the earth is broken apart from its depths'.

[13] Longinus is, as often, his own example: see Innes 1994, 36–53, esp. 48 ff.

[14] Minor isolated use: 44. 3 ἔπαθλα, συνεκλάμπει, and νάματος; 44.6 καταβυθίζουσι; 44. 10 ἐπικλύσειαν.

[15] Hypothetically, the lacuna in 37. 1 (a continuation of the analysis of metaphor) might include further examples of such imagery: if so, it would remain true that imagery from natural phenomena has some restrictions on its use, since it is virtually absent from what precedes the first and follows the last lacuna, 1–9. 4 and 38–44. The lacuna in 9. 4 also prevents us from knowing if the imagery found in both 9. 1–3 and 44 was further supported in the lacuna (an attractive notion), but it remains significant within our extant text that the same imagery links two passages at structurally important points on the crucial importance of greatness of thought.

[16] Sublimity evokes a strong emotional impact, stronger than persuasion or pleasure, and it rejects the merely smooth or elegant: on this key theme cf. 1. 4; 3. 4; 10. 4; 10. 6; 15. 9; 21. 1; 29. 2; 33. 5; 39. 1.

(cf. 7. 1), and looks upwards[17] to seek what is immortal (44. 8; cf. e.g. 36. 3 and especially 36. 1, where sublimity raises us up towards the greatness of god's mind). In short, it aims beyond the ephemeral to the whole of eternity, πρὸς τὸν αἰῶνα (44. 9; cf. 1. 3; 4. 7; 9. 3; 14. 3; 34. 4; 36. 2).

These themes also conclude two patterns of imagery, (1) freedom, slavery and imprisonment, and (2) pregnancy, births and growths. Both appear also in 9. 1-3, before the huge lacuna in 9. 4, and it may seem significant that they appear precisely at the beginning of the discussion of the first source, greatness of thought—the very absence of which is seen as the key to the loss of sublimity at the very end of the work, in 44.

Imagery of freedom runs throughout the final chapter: first (44. 1-5), the philosopher laments the loss of political freedom as a prison which stunts the sublime; he looks to *external* causation and the imagery is of imprisonment and maiming of the *body*; then Longinus in reply (44. 6 ff.) looks to the freedom of the *mind* or spirit, and uses imagery of *internal* freedom. This recalls 9. 3 where slavery of the mind is incompatible with sublimity, since 'those who think the petty thoughts of *slaves*' (μικρὰ καὶ δουλοπρεπῆ φρονοῦντας) cannot produce anything worthy of eternity. This enslaved mind is in contrast to the sublime mind which is 'as if *pregnant* with noble excitement' (9. 1 ὥσπερ ἐγκύμονας . . . γενναίου παραστήματος), and we can compare such a truly creative mind with the mind which is absorbed in ephemera, and will, 'as it were, miscarry and certainly *bring nothing to term* with regard for *the view of posterity*' (14. 3 ὥσπερ ἀμβλοῦσθαι, πρὸς τὸν τῆς ὑστεροφημίας ὅλως μὴ τελεσφορούμενα χρόνον). These aborted stillbirths contrast with the true pregnancy of inspiration (13. 2), where the creative stimulus of a predecessor is like the inspiration which fills the Delphic Sibyl and makes her '*pregnant*' (ἐγκύμων) with the divine power. The vivid image is a natural development from the pervasive vocabulary of creativity, especially γεννᾶν, γόνιμος, ἐντίκτω (all three of which appear in 44[18]); so for example (7. 2) the audience feels 'as if it has itself created what it has heard' (ὡς αὐτὴ γεννήσασα ὅπερ ἤκουσεν). False creation is analogously described as like the false hollow swellings of the body (3. 4

---

[17] Cf. Pl. *R.* 586aff., quoted in 13. 1.
[18] Cf. γεννᾶν 2. 1; 5; 6; 15. 1; 15. 12; 18. 2; 38. 4; 44. 7; 44. 11; γόνιμος 8. 1; 31. 1; 44. 3; ἐντίκτω 16. 3; 44. 7.

and 7. 1), and in music it effects 'bastard copies and likenesses of persuasion, not legitimate activities, as I said, proper to human nature' (39. 3 εἴδωλα καὶ μιμήματα νόθα ἐστὶ πειθοῦς, οὐχὶ τῆς ἀνθρωπείας φύσεως, ὡς ἔφην, ἐνεργήματα γνήσια).

All this imagery is richly expanded in 44, where Longinus explains the loss of sublimity in terms of the stunting of the mind, as false emotions are allowed entry and then in turn, in exotic genealogical fantasy, create succeeding generations of further false offspring, such as desire for wealth and pleasure: as a result our innate potential withers away. These images include some deliberate vocabulary echoes of previous passages: thus the false offspring produce their own still worse children, who are 'not their bastard offspring but entirely legitimate' (44. 7 οὐ νόθα ἑαυτῶν γεννήματα ἀλλὰ καὶ πάνυ γνήσια; cf. 39.3 quoted above); men no longer look up, no longer have concern for the view of posterity (ὑστεροφημία), and it is now destruction which is brought to term (44. 8 τελεσιουργεῖσθαι; cf. 14. 3 quoted above).

One final image in 44 is that of judgement in the lawcourt, 44. 9: such imagery has appeared earlier: in 14. 2 we must imagine the scrutiny of our work by great authors of the past as if at a lawcourt or theatre where they are judges (κριταῖς) and witnesses of sublimity; and in 33. 4 sublime authors get 'the vote of first place' (τὴν τοῦ πρωτείου ψῆφον) for their greatness of thought; I suggest that this image recalls the role of the true literary critic, especially Longinus himself, as just such a judge or κριτής. Literary judgement too must be free and truthful (cf. 1. 2; 7. 4; 34. 1). References to his own judgement frame the genius digression (33. 1 and 36. 4), and Caecilius, by contrast, is the critic biassed by the two emotions of prejudiced hostility and favouritism (32. 8).[19] The free judgement of the true critic is thus part of the wider notion of that inner freedom of mind which Longinus champions in 44. We are, he continues (44. 9), as if 'taken prisoner' (ἠνδραποδισμένοι), so can we expect to find still 'any free judge of greatness' (ἐλεύθερόν τινα κριτὴν τῶν μεγάλων)? Are we to be ruled or free, 'let out as if from a prison', ὥσπερ ἐξ εἱρκτῆς ἄφετοι (44. 10)?

The final chapter also points up the pervasive intertextuality, as theory, imagery and quotation all support each other in reinforcing

[19] The two emotions are described as ἀκρίτοις: may this difficult and disputed word mean 'lacking true judgement' or 'not appropriate to a true critic'?

key ideas. Escape from prison was an example in 15. 9 (D. 24.
208), and it is the concluding image cited from Plato's elaborate imagery of
the body in *Timaeus* 65c–85e, when the soul is 'released free' from
the body (32. 5 μεθεῖσθαι τε αὐτὴν ἐλευθέραν; note that 'free' is the
final and emphatic word in the sentence). Quotations which
implicitly or explicitly assert the value of freedom are also more
generally pervasive, such as those illustrating the fight of Greece
against Persia or Athens against Macedon (15. 10; 16. 2 ff.; 22. 1–2;
32. 2).[20]

I have briefly indicated the use of such patterns of examples elsewhere (Innes 1994, 44–5; 49); thus Homer is a sun (9. 13), so
compare the previous examples of the light of creation ('let there be
light and there was light'), followed by the light Ajax demands to let
him fight (9. 9–10);[21] I suggest here some more instances, restricting myself to Longinus' favoured area of the mighty forces of nature:
Cicero and Demosthenes are like fires (12. 3–4), and Homer's
madness (9. 11) is compared to a destructive fire raging in the
mountains; note too that the fire is raging in the mountains, and
mountains are among the great natural phenomena of the earth, like
Etna's fiery volcano in 35. 4, the Aloadae piling mountain upon
mountain to build a path to heaven (8. 2), and the response to a
god's epiphany that 'the whole mountain shared the ecstasy' (15. 6
πᾶν δὲ συνεβάκχευ' ὄρος; cf. 9. 8 when at Poseidon's epiphany 'the
high mountains and woodland trembled', τρέμε δ' οὔρεα μακρὰ καὶ
ὕλη).

Another example from nature is the image of stormwinds to
suggest Demosthenes' forcefulness (20. 3 ὡς αἱ καταιγίδες): compare
forceful winds and storms in several quotations, especially 10. 4–7,
where some are successful, as in Homer's storm (10. 5), in contrast
to the failures of the *Arimaspeia* and Aratus (10. 4 and 6), which are
then immediately followed by the successful shipwreck in
Archilochus (10. 7). Outside this tight nexus of four successive

---

[20] On these examples as part of the heroic spirit, see Segal 1987, 207–17, esp.
215–6. For Longinus it is freedom of mind or soul which characterises an Ajax or a
Demosthenes.

[21] The examples also contribute gliding transitions between traditional categories
of sublime thought (cf. Hermog. *Id.* 243 f. Rabe): gods, the divine and the heroic.
Longinus avoids the formal use of textbook subdivisions but offers examples from each:
cosmic disruption by gods, cosmic creation of light, and heroic demand for god to
create light.

examples illustrating failure and success, add 9. 14 on the successful storms of the *Odyssey*, and the failure in detail of Herodotus' storm (43. 1; but the thought, significantly, was a good one). Winds appear specifically in the storms cited from Homer (like Homer, it is forceful) and Herodotus (it gets tired!), and, to add another example of failure, the description of Boreas, the north wind, is said to be confused and lacking forcefulness (3. 1): the thought is good but taken to an extreme of bombast. I could add examples of heaven and far horizons (8. 2; 9. 4-5; 9. 6; 9. 8; 9. 9; 15. 4), all examples of the first source, nobility of thought, and all mirroring sublimity's own transcendence of the ordinary horizons of the cosmos (e.g. 35. 2 ff.); but let me conclude: Longinus is his own best example, whether we consider the microcosm of minor points of technique such as 18. 1 (the topic of rhetorical questions is introduced by rhetorical questions) or the macrocosm of overall unity. Longinus may seem concerned only with examples of sublimity from short passages or poems, but he himself illustrates, on a larger scale, the unity he praised in 10. 1: to select 'what is most appropriate', τὰ καιριώτατα, and to combine them densely 'to be able to form a single body', καθάπερ ἕν τι σῶμα ποιεῖν δύνασθαι.[22] *On the Sublime* has true unity from interlocking key themes, examples and imagery, and the apparently separate limbs of the five sources (8. 1) themselves merge together, a symbol of that single cohesive organic unity.

REFERENCES

Innes, D. C., 'Period and Colon; Theory and Example in Demetrius and Longinus', in, W. W. Fortenbaugh and D. C. Mirhady (eds.), *Peripatetic Rhetoric after Aristotle* (RUSCH 6; New Brunswick, NJ, and London, 1994), 36-53.
——Longinus, Sublimity and the Low Emotions', in Doreen Innes, Harry Hine and Christopher Pelling (eds.), *Ethics and Rhetoric* (Oxford, 1995).
Matelli, E., 'Struttura e stile del περὶ ὕψους', *Aevum*, 61 (1987), 131-247.
Mazzucchi, C. M., 'Come finiva il περὶ ὕψους?', *Aevum Antiquum*, 3 (1990), 143-62.

[22] Here again we see linking use of imagery and quotations. The Sappho quotation which follows itself illustrates unity of body and soul (10. 2-3; compare the body/tabernacle examples from Xenophon and Plato in 32. 5 ff.); and for imagery drawn from the body compare 11. 2; 21. 2; 30. 1; 40. 1; 43. 5.

Mazzucchi, C. M., *Dionisio Longino Del Sublime* (Milan, 1992).

Nisbet, R. G. M., and Hubbard, Margaret, *A Commentary on Horace, Odes I* (Oxford, 1970).

Russell, D. A., '*Longinus*', *On the Sublime* (Oxford, 1964).

——'Longinus Revisited?' *Mnemosyne*, 34 (1981), 143–55.

Segal, C., 'Writer as Hero: The Heroic Ethos in Longinus, On the Sublime', in J. Servais (ed.), *Stemmata: Mélanges de philologie, d'histoire et d'archéologie grecques offerts à Jules Labarbe* (Liège and Louvain-la-Neuve, 1987), 207–17.

See now also

Innes, D. C., 'Longinus and Caecilius: Models of the Sublime', *Mnemosyne*, 55 (2002), 259–84.

Whitmarsh, T., *Greek Literature and the Roman Empire: The Politics of Imitation* (Oxford, 2001), 57–71.

# 14

# The Structure of Plutarch's
# How to Study Poetry

## D. M. SCHENKEVELD

### I

In his treatise *How the Young Man Should Study Poetry* (commonly abbreviated to *How to Study Poetry*)[1] Plutarch shows the ways of using poetry as an introduction of young children to the study of philosophy. In dealing with the relationship between poetry and philosophy he takes his place in a long series of authors on this subject, and it is not difficult to trace his allegiance to or controversy with foregoing writers. When e.g. he says (15A) 'now it is neither useful nor perhaps possible to keep boys of the age of my Soclaros or your Cleandros away from poetry', he clearly reacts against Plato's views expressed in *Republic* 377A–398B, whereas he follows the same author in detecting many dangers in poetry. Traditional are also his views on poetry being based on imitation and containing much fiction and untruth.

However, the purpose of this article is not to trace Plutarch's views back to earlier authors[2], but to look at this treatise as an independent work, especially at its structure.

On the surface this structure looks very simple. First comes the

---

[1] Most translations have been taken over from the Loeb edition (*Plutarch's Moralia I with an English translation by Frank Cole Babbitt*, 1st printing 1927). Some, however, come from Russell's translation of chs. I–V in D. A. Russell and M. Winterbottom, *Ancient Literary Criticism* (Oxford, 1972), 507–30.

[2] See for this subject G. von Reutern, *Plutarchs Stellung zur Dichtkunst. Interpretation der Schrift 'De Audiendis Poetis'* (Ph.D. diss. Kiel, Gräfenhainchen, 1933), and K. Ziegler, 'Plutarchos von Chaironeia', *RE* 21 (1951), 804–7 (2nd edn. Stuttgart, 1964, 168–71). For Plutarch's position in the classicist views on μίμησις see now H. Flashar, *Die klassizistische Theorie der Mimesis*, in *Le Classicisme à Rome* (Entretiens sur l'Antiq. Class. 25; Geneva, 1979), 78–97 and 106.

introductory letter to Plutarch's friend Marcus Sedatius, who, just as
the author, has a young boy to educate. Then the treatise proper
starts with an introduction to the subject (15B-16A), after which
Plutarch gives two chapters concerning theoretical aspects (16A-
18F), followed by practical discussions in chs. IV-VI (19A-25A).
Ch. VII again has a theoretical content, and after a reference to this
('Now since this is so'), ch. VIII turns to the practical lessons again.
These are continued up to the end of ch. XIII (35E), while the final
chapter looks like a conclusion, and contains many similarities with
the introductory chapter).[3]

   This picture of the structure of the treatise already presents us with
one problem, viz. the position of ch. VII. In his text Plutarch does not
state the reason for turning back at this place to a theoretical discussion, but just ends ch. VI with a formula of conclusion and transition
('This, then, is enough on this subject'), which is followed by the
opening phrase of ch. VII ('There is a fact, however, which we must
recall to the minds of the young not once merely, but over and over
again . . .').

   Other questions also arise, such as that of the role of the theory of
chs. II-III and VII in the practical chapters. For an answer to these
and other questions we must investigate the treatise more closely,
and try to detect, as it were, a deep structure under the surface.

   Such an attempt has been undertaken in recent times by two
scholars, Heirman and Valgiglio,[4] whereas in earlier studies[5] we
sometimes find hints, but no more than these. The results of Heirman
and Valgiglio diverge widely, on the distinction of the main parts of
the work as well as in their views on the position of ch. II. To
Heirman ch. VII is 'a recapitulating condensation of both Ch. II and
Ch. III', and he divides the treatise from ch. II up to ch. XIV into two
parts, II-VI and VII-XIII. The second part he views as being similar
in procedure to the first, but on a deeper level (pp. 23 f.). So in his
analysis ch. VII acts, as it were, as a pivot, and the whole work

---

   [3] The current division into chapters is modern, and other divisions are possible. In
general, however, the modern chapters start at places where Plutarch made an
incision; this is specifically the case in chs. II, III, VII, VIII, IX, X-XII and XIV. Therefore we may keep to the current distinctions.
   [4] L. J. R. Heirman, *Plutarchus, 'De Audiendis Poetis'*. Introduction-Translation-
Commentary (Ph.D. diss. Leiden, The Hague, 1972), and E. Valgiglio, *Plutarco, De
Audiendis Poetis*. Introduzione, testo, commento, traduzione (Turin, 1973).
   [5] e.g. Von Reutern, *Plutarchs Stellung*, 31 and 84.

contains the following four parts: ch. I (two introductions), II–VI, VII–XIII, and, finally, XIV.

Independently from Heirman's work Valgiglio presents a different picture, as his scheme shows (p. lviii): 'Cap. 1: Introduzione. I) Elementi negativi: Cap. 2. Cap. 3: al quale sono legati, come opportuno completamento, i capp. 4, 5, 6, e, come appendice, i capp. 7, 8, col quale ultimo si può dire che faccia corpo il cap. 9. II) Temi di passaggio: Capp. 12 e 10. III) Elementi positivi: Capp. 11, 13 e 14'. In this scheme ch. VII has a subordinate place and is put together with ch. VIII, whereas chs. X and XII form the transition between the negative and positive parts.

Both divisions have their stronger and weaker points, as will appear later on. Heirman is right in putting ch. VII in a prominent place, but he neglects the gradual change from negative to positive views of poetry. On this aspect Valgiglio is better, but he puts too strong an accent here. Moreover it is wrong to put with the latter scholar a caesura after ch. IX and to neglect the differences in subjects treated in chs. IV–VI, VIII–X and XI–XIII. The latter omission explains Valgiglio's rather curious isolation of ch. XII from its surrounding chapters, but does not justify it.

One could proceed with expressing more objections to Heirman's and Valgiglio's views, but an extensive treatment of these would lead away from a more profitable approach, viz. a consideration of Plutarch's treatise itself. In the meantime, it will have become evident that any treatment of the structure of *How to Study Poetry* has to explain the relation between the theoretical and practical chapters[6] and to account for the position of ch. VII as well as to offer a clear picture of the structure in general.

2

When tackling this task, we should not forget that Plutarch has not written a theoretical dissertation on the nature of poetry, but a very practical guide for an educator and his son. In ch. 1, 15B, he says: 'I beg that you will take them and peruse them, and [. . .] impart them to Cleander' (the son of the addressee). In other words, the young boy

---

[6] To call chs. II–III and VII 'theoretical' and the other chapters 'practical' antici-pates my argument.

also is expected to read this treatise. We would, therefore, be surprised if Plutarch had composed a dry exposition only. *A contrario* it seems reasonable to suppose that the practical chapters are the most important parts of the whole treatise. In accordance with this supposition I shall first investigate these chapters, and turn to the theoretical ones later on (§ 3), whereafter the relations between the two groups will be studied (§ 4), the fifth paragraph offering the conclusions.

The practical lessons of chs. IV–VI start already at the end of ch. III (18E/F 'If then we remind our sons etc.'). Here the words 'with the idea of of investing mean and unnatural characters and persons with unnatural and mean sentiments' together with 'the suspicion felt against the person in question discredits both his actions and words' admit of a distinction between characters (persons) on the one hand, and action and words on the other. Plutarch first shows the ways in which to deal with actions and words in chs. IV–VI (19A 'concerning what is expressed'; 19C 'In like manner also, the poet comments upon actions'; 19D, 'adding a sort of verdict of his own to what is done or said'; 19E 'declarations and opinions concerning the words of the text . . . from the actions themselves'). By doing so he has chosen a method of concentrating the reader's mind on *single* passages without any recurrence to their larger context. This especially becomes clear from 20C onwards, when single lines are compared with other single lines. It is also important to note that in the beginning of ch. IV Plutarch says that we must give close attention 'to any indication the poet gives that he disapproves of what is being said'. Disapproval of statements and actions in poetry takes here the first place.

The method chosen follows a definable course. At first single passages with objectionable opinions and actions are discussed. At 20C ff. conflicting statements are compared with one another ('the mutual contrarieties of the poets') but the larger context is kept out of consideration yet. So we see that Plutarch starts with the most simple reading and ascends, one might say, to the higher level of comparison, at which level the young boy has to develop his inventiveness. This appears from the various remedies offered in order to protect the boy's mind against bad influences. They range (see also § 4) from choosing the better opinion of two conflicting lines which stand in immediate vicinity to countering a wrong statement with one chosen from the writings of another author. The last remedies ask for more knowledge, now of a more technical kind, for the reader has to pay attention to some significant words and to the shift in meaning a word has undergone between Homer's time and nowadays.

So here, too, we meet with a further step in the gradually proceeding confrontation of the reader with more intricate problems. On the whole, however, he has not yet progressed beyond reading single passages. It seems a plausible inference that so far Plutarch's method of presentation reflects the reading course of children,[7] and that the passages under discussion are taken from anthologies and other collections.[8]

As has been stated before, ch. VIII starts the second main part of the practical lessons. Here a considerable shift of attention occurs, for Plutarch now treats the characters of outstanding personages in poetry.[9] These had already been mentioned in ch. III, but no more than that. In ch. VIII Plutarch shows that these kings and heroes are a mixture of good and bad qualities, just as people in ordinary life. Therefore, the young reader must not imagine that e.g. because Achilles is a hero, all his actions and words are accordingly admirable; on the contrary, he should be on the alert for wrong opinions and deeds of these characters too. Just as in previous chapters, Plutarch quotes again many individual lines, but these are not to be considered in isolation, for they are examples illustrating the poetical portrayal of characters. So this discussion presupposes that the reader is now reading complete works or lengthy passages, and the lines under discussion are considered in their context.[10]

---

[7] Cf. 14E, where Plutarch mentions books young people like to read, probably (so Heirman, *Plutarchus* 25) in an ascending order: Aesop's *Fables*, *Tales from the Poets*, Heraclides' *Abaris*, and Ariston's *Lycon*. All these books are characterised as 'doctrines about the soul which are mixed with the mythology'. Babbitt's '*and* (my italics, DMS) philosophical doctrines etc.' creates a fifth category, but this is based on the wrong insertion of 'and' (*kai*) in the Greek text. Consequently, his note *a* is misleading.

[8] Cf. Russell–Winterbottom, 506: 'Plutarch drew many of them (sc. his quotations) from existing collections, not from first-hand readings'. See also H. I. Marrou, *Histoire de l'éducation dans l'Antiquité* (Paris, 1960⁵), 210, about anthologies as the first texts to be read at school.

[9] Cf. Von Reutern, *Plutarchs Stellung*, 85 f.: 'Ein Unterschied gegenüber der vorher gesuchten Didaskalia liegt darin, dass hier keine Dogmen und Gnomen herauskristallisiert werden, sondern die homerischen Helden werden einfach auf gut und böse beobachtet'.

[10] It is another matter, of course, whether this is done correctly. At 27C–E on Odysseus' reactions when awakening on the shore of Ithaca it is not.

At 28A editors mark the start of a new chapter (IX), and indeed at
this place the point of view is changed again. Here the emancipation
from the authority of the poets becomes the subject, but the introductory phrase 'Now in all cases it is useful to seek after the cause of
each thing that is said' indicates to my mind that this chapter is an
appendix to the foregoing discussion on the apparent authority of the
characters.[11] This explanation is strengthened by the fact that in ch.
X we are back again at the theme of 'good and bad characters and
personages' (28E–F). These are now considered under the heading of
'differences' between various types and peoples, what they promise
and how they react, etc. So in chs. VIII and X (with ch. IX as an
appendix) Plutarch uses again a progressive method in first treating
individual characters and then comparing them by pointing out
characteristic differences.

In chapter X (29B) he had already broadened his scope by referring
to virtues and vices as such, but had come back to their relation to
the personages in poetry. From ch. XI (30D) onwards he focuses on
these mental qualities in general and looks first for passages which
are uttered with a view to inspiring courage, justice and self-
restraint. At 32A the fourth cardinal virtue, 'understanding', comes
as the most divine and kingly quality, from which all other virtues
are derived.[12] In the next chapter (XII) the vices form the basis for
treatment, when Plutarch shows how to draw profit from passages
suspected of base and improper conduct or how to rewrite them. In
ch. XIII the virtues form the framework again, when the reader is
admonished to apply the good advice of a particular line to other
situations. After this discussion based on virtues and vices (30D–
35C) Plutarch ends by stressing the two important results of carefully
reading poetry, viz. an attitude of moderation and magnanimity
(35D).

So far we have seen that the practical chapters (IV–VI, VIII–XIII)
are structured on three principles, viz. (a) single passages with statements and actions, looked at in isolation or in comparison with
others (IV–VI), (b) characters in poetry, viewed in the same ways
(VIII–X), and, finally, (c) virtues and vices mentioned in poetry

---

[11] So too Valgiglio, p. lvii.
[12] Cf. Valgiglio, p. xlviii. Heirman, *Plutarchus*, 9 f., lists seven virtues one has to
acquire and seven corresponding vices one has to overcome. But there he is talking
about the whole treatise, not about this chapter with its technical division.

(XI–XIII). Within each section a progression in the difficulty of the subject-matter was detected. This broadening of the subject in the various chapters, taken together and in each section, must be the outcome of a deliberate method of Plutarch and looks in agreement with his purpose, to offer an introduction into reading poetry. We had also observed a gradual progress in the reading material from single passages to complete books or lengthy parts. But this aspect of reading is not Plutarch's main concern, for when discussing virtues and vices he is looking at isolated lines again.

In ch. I already Plutarch had stressed the need of going slowly when one wishes to acquaint children with the study of philosophy, for they take more delight in 'what does not seem philosophical or serious at all' (14E). He admits that children are more readily impressed by poetry, that this may contain bad opinions; he rejects, however, the possibility of excluding poetry from their education both on practical grounds and from a utilitarian point of view (15A). On the contrary, he shows the way to turn their minds by means of poetry towards philosophy, whereby poetry is an introductory exercise in philosophy (15F). With these thoughts of Plutarch in mind we understand better why he proceeds from loose statements in ch. IV to the discussion of moral virtues and vices in chs. XI ff.

His intentions are kept up in the final chapter (XIV). There the young reader is to be taught that many poetic lines agree in content with well-known philosophical tenets. This theme is developed, and Plutarch ends his treatise by reiterating his main purpose, 'the young man has need of good pilotage in the mattter of reading, to the end that in a spirit of friendship and goodwill and familiarity he may be convoyed by poetry into the realm of philosophy' (37B). So ch. XIV is not so much the conclusion, in the sense of a summary,[13] but rather the climax of the treatise. Not before he has gone through poetry and has ascended to the level of virtues and vices, is the young boy taught that what he has done in the final stages comes down to a study of philosophy.

---

[13] Heirman, *Plutarchus*, 20–2, lists many similarities between chs. I and XIV; not all of these are to be classified as such.

3

The structure of the practical chapters being laid bare, it is time to turn to a consideration of the theoretical chapters II–III and VII. Ch. II has as its main point that in poetry much fiction (untruth, *pseudos*) is present, either by deliberate intent or unintentionally. The latter case is the more frequent and dangerous. The young reader must therefore keep in mind that poetry is not much concerned with truth, and that in many cases the truth is hard to track down, even for philosophers. By doing so the child will be less inclined to pay attention to poets in these matters. In ch. III Plutarch is still talking about the means to steady the reader's mind, but he changes the focus, for he now stresses the point that poetry is mimetic.[14] It may be praised for its power of imitation, but this praise does not necessarily lead to praise of the bad acts which are imitated, or, as Plutarch puts it (18D), 'For it is not the same thing at all to imitate something beautiful and something beautifully.' Examples clarify all statements, and, as we have seen, the final words of this chapter gradually lead over to the practical lessons of chs. IV ff.

The purpose of the two theoretical chapters thus appears to be, not to philosophise *in vacuo*, but to impress on the reader's mind that poetry may, and often does, contain wrong opinions and acts, and that this fact stems from its nature of being mimetic. It is in accordance with these views that Plutarch predominantly mentions wrong opinions and actions, and does not point out that his theory also admits of poetic passages being right. It seems as if his first concern is to wean away the young men from poetry with a bad influence and to make them critical towards the reputation of poets in order to clear their minds for more positive views. Chs. IV–VI pursue this approach, the theme continuously being how to counter wrong statements in poetry.[15] Here too, the existence of right

---

[14] Mimetic of what? Plutarch does not state this clearly, but the answer must be 'of reality' (*alètheia*). Not before ch. VII is this word used in this sense ('the imitation that does not show an utter disregard of reality', 25C). The dual meaning of *alètheia* ('truth' and 'reality'; cp. *pseudos*, 'untruth' and 'fiction') should be kept in mind. Babbitt sometimes neglects this, e.g. at 25D, where he translates 'when poetic art is divorced from the truth'. A better rendering would be something like: 'apart from the aspect of being realistic the art of poetry etc.'

[15] In these chapters many wrong opinions are discussed and only a few actions. Cf.

opinions is taken for granted, but not explained. At the same time it is evident that these chapters have more links with the second chapter on fiction (*pseudos*) than with the third on imitation.[16] The latter one was just necessary in order to account for the occurrences of fiction.

An explanation of why poetry may voice right opinions does not come before ch. VII. One will remember that chs. VIII–XIII discussed poetic characters as a mixture of good and bad qualities, whereafter the good qualities, the virtues, were treated separately in a general way. So from a didactic point of view Plutarch would have been remiss if he had tackled this subject of good (and bad) qualities without first setting out why they can occur in poetry. This function is fulfilled in ch. VII, and here the theory of mimesis is deepened. Now, Plutarch seems to think, it is time to proceed and pursue the theme of poetry as imitation of reality to a greater extent. Even then, however, he restricts himself to rather simple statements, to what the young reader needs to know, viz. that poetry imitates reality, and therefore imitates characters which show bad and good qualities (25B; note the order), but he does not elucidate these statements.[17]

4

So far the relations between the theoretical and the practical chapters could have been taken thus that the chapters on theory provide the tools by which one can deal with poetry in practice. These tools, however, have a rather restricted use, for the theory in chs. II–III does clarify why wrong opinions occur, but not how to counter them. The proper tools to do so are offered in chapters IV–VI only. These lack a theoretical basis in so far as Plutarch does not explain why they, and not others, have been chosen. Nevertheless, some system is present here. As one will recall, the main theme here is how to deal with lines containing wrong opinions and bad acts. The solutions offered are:[18]

the scheme in § 4. Dr Slings, probably rightly, supposes that this preponderance is linked to the use of anthologies.

[16] Cf. Von Reutern, *Plutarchs Stellung*, 21.

[17] As far as I can see, Valgiglio does not explain why ch. VIII should belong to the theoretical part. The first phrase of this chapter precludes this view.

[18] Valgiglio's scheme is almost the same, except that ch. IV (21D–22A) is put after VI, 25B (and IV, 19B even after 30C).

A. The poet himself gives hints (19A),
   1. in the case of opinions (19A),
      *a.* beforehand (19A),
      *b.* in closing lines (19D),
   2. in the case of actions (19E).
B. The poet does not give hints. Then we must
   1. take from his own works a line with a better opinion, which is found
      *a.* in immediate vicinity (20C) or
      *b.* at a distance (20E), or we
   2. take from the works of other excellent authors a better opinion (21D).
C. We may also pay attention to single words which blunt the bad effects of a passage (22B).
D. Another method is to look at the changes in the meaning of key-words (22C).

The chs. VIII–XIII stand in the same relation to ch. VII as IV–VI do to II–III. They have their own divisions, which have not been prepared in ch. VII. These divisions are not as clear-cut as in chs. IV–VI, but we may detect a sort of scheme in ch. VIII, when Plutarch discusses the way to deal with wrong and right opinions of characters. From 27A 'Now in these cases the difference is manifest; but in cases where Homer's judgement is not made clear' it appears that in the foregoing the problem was treated under the heading of 'the difference between good and bad opinions is clear, so the choice is easy' (A). This first part, I think, starts at 26AB. The second part is formed by 27A–E, under the heading of 'the difference is obscure' (B), and 27E–28A acts as an appendix on the specific position of the tragedians. Ch. X, which again discusses characters in poetry, has their differences as its main theme, but lacks a definite scheme and looks like an arbitrary enumeration of several differences to be considered. The same is true *mutatis mutandis* for the remaining chapters. Notwithstanding this lack of clear classifications of the various tools to be used, however, the relation to ch. VII is evident: this chapter provides the general background, and no more than this, against which in the practical chapters Plutarch applies his tools, not announced before. For this very reason it is advisable not to speak of theory being applied in the following chapters, but only of a theoretical basis for practice.

5

The analysis carried out has laid bare an underlying structure of the work. This deep structure appeared to have been laid out carefully and with an eye to the needs of the young readers as to its main parts. In its practical chapters *How to Study Poetry* starts with the more easily solvable problems and gradually proceeds towards its goal, the study of philosophy. The theoretical chapters provide the general background but avoid to give specific rules of interpretation. These have been reserved for the practical lessons, where a multitude of examples illustrate these rules. This method of demonstration by example must have been pleasant to the young reader, more than a dry enumeration, and seems the result of deliberate composition on Plutarch's part. One might even go one step further, and be inclined to link the rather haphazard collection of rules (the tools) with a desire of Plutarch not to hinder the young reader with too precise a set. We have already seen that in chs. VIII–XIII, especially in the later chapters, not much of a scheme could be detected. But a closer inspection of chs. IV–VI reveals an almost similar inconsistency, for the introduction of what in § 4 are called sections C and D comes as a surprise. Moreover, when Plutarch arrives at section A2 (the poet himself gives hints in the case of actions), he has recourse to the device that 'in Homer, this kind of instruction is tacit; but it affords a useful kind of reinterpretation for the most severely criticized myths' (19E). The set of tools is a rather haphazard collection of rules, gathered without much consistency. It is, however, wrong to derive the nature of this collection from a deliberate choice by Plutarch, for this supposition implies that he could have proceeded in a more consistent way. But in his other works he does not do so either, and it is very improbable that he could have done so. For in the rest of ancient critical works we meet with a similar lack of consistency. Even when clear classifications form the basis of such treatises as for example ch. 25 of Aristotle's *Poetics*, Dionysius' writings, the remains of Aristarchus' activities, we are in the dark why for these lines this method of exegesis has been chosen and for others a different one. By inference, therefore, I conclude that Plutarch's set of rules was not selected with a view to the youthfulness of his readers. One can only say that he eschews the more technical terms, such as 'solution of the problem in the text by looking at the person speaking'.

A final remark concerns the addressee of the treatise and its reading public in general, in addition to what has been said at the beginning of § 2. Plutarch's ultimate purpose is that young people come to the study of philosophy, but he addresses in the first place the father of a young son, his friend M. Sedatius, and so all fathers and educators. This appears from the introductory remarks (such as 15B and 15F–16A), and from other passages where he speaks about what 'we' should do for the young ones, up till the closing sentence with the word 'pilotage' (37A). But his instructions to the educator are immediately transferable to the child, for they follow a course intelligible to him. Plutarch, therefore, could safely ask Sedatius to peruse himself the treatise and, after approval, to share it with his son Cleander (15B). To put it in modern terms, the textbook for the pupil and its companion, the instructions for the teacher, are here put together.

### POSTCRIPT

A modern study of Plutarch's views on poetry is L. Van Der Stock, *Twinkling and Twilight. Plutarch's Reflections on Literature* (Verhand. Kon. Akad. van Wetensch., Lett. en Schone Kunsten van België, Klasse d. Lett. 54-145, Brussels, 1992).

# 15

# 'Ars Poetica'

## D. A. RUSSELL

Quintilian[1] alludes to this poem as *ars poetica or liber de arte poetica*. The manuscript tradition, instead of associating it with the *Epistles*, gives it a separate place, in company with the *Odes* and *Epodes*. Its differences from the *Epistles* are in fact more significant for its understanding than its resemblances to them. It is very much 'a treatise with *Dear so-and-so* at the beginning'.[2] Its length, its didactic formulae, the recurrent addresses to the Pisones in the manner of Lucretius' to Memmius, and especially its very technical content, mark it out as an experiment. Perhaps it was the last of the great innovator's new creations; for, though the arguments about its date[3] are indecisive, there is much to be said for a late one, after the last book of the *Odes*. Porphyrio's identification of the Piso father with the future *praefectus urbi*[4] (48 B.C.-A.D. 32) may be right after all: he could well have had, by his late thirties, two sons old enough to be thought interested in poetry.

What Horace is attempting is, to put it as briefly as possible, a poem on poetics. Both halves of this description, however, need to be clarified. Despite *nil scribens ipse* (306), where Horace speaks as the non-practising theorist, the *Ars*, like the *Epistles* and *Satires*, is composed on poetical principles. Transitions and movements of thought

---

The literature on the *Ars* is vast. Most recent, and much the most useful guide, is C. O. Brink's *Horace on Poetry* (vol. i, *Prolegomena*, Cambridge, 1963; vol. ii, *Commentary*, 1971). This chapter was written in the main before Brink's *Commentary* was available: I have not made any substantial changes in the light of it. See also G. W. Williams's review of Brink's first volume, *JRS* 54 (1964), 186-96; and P. Grimal, *Horace: Art Poétique* (Les cours de Sorbonne, 1966). My attempt at a prose translation is in D. A. Russell and M. Winterbottom, *Ancient Literary Criticism* (Oxford, 1971), 279-91.

[1] Praef. 2, 8. 3. 60.
[2] Cf. Demetrius, 228: συγγράμματα τὸ χαίρειν ἔχοντα προσγεγραμμένον.
[3] For discussion see R. Syme, *JRS* (1960), 12-20.
[4] Tacitus, *Ann.* 6. 10.

depend on verbal association and emotional tone rather than on logical or rhetorical arrangement. The choice of topics and the degree of elaboration accorded to them is determined, as in Lucretius or the *Georgics*, more by the poetical potential or viability of the theme than by the need to give a certain weight to a certain matter because of its place in an overall pattern of argument or precept. Second, the subject of this eccentric didactic poem—as far removed from the norm of the *Georgics* as Ovid's *Ars* was to be—is not poetry, but poetics: the body of theory formulated, largely out of earlier insights, by Aristotle and his successors, and current in Hellenistic times in a variety of handbooks and summaries.

Porphyrio, of course, informs us that Horace drew specially on one such handbook: 'congessit praecepta Neoptolemi τοῦ Παριανοῦ de arte poetica, non quidem omnia sed eminentissima' ('he gathered together the precepts of Neoptolemus of Parium on the art of poetry—not all of these, but the most important ones'). We naturally view this with scepticism, mindful of the exaggeration with which ancient scholarship was wont to proclaim discoveries of derivation and plagiarism. We do not believe Servius when he tells us that *Aeneid* IV comes *paene totus* from Apollonius' *Argonautica*, because we can check the facts. Why then should we believe Porphyrio here? A fair analogy; but even Servius does not lie, he only exaggerates. Porphyrio should be given the credit of a right, or at least plausible, diagnosis. What little we know in other ways of Neoptolemus supports the case. But suppose we had Neoptolemus *in extenso*: is it likely that this would further our understanding of the *Ars* more than, say, Varro's *De re rustica* furthers our understanding of the *Georgics*?[5] The poem before us does not after all look at all like a versified treatise. Nor, on all the analogies that ancient literature affords, was it written to make poets of us or the Pisones, Its aim surely was to please us and compliment them.

Yet (l. 343)

> Omne tulit punctum qui miscuit utile dulci.

> The man who combines pleasure with usefulness wins every vote.

Is not Horace trying to do this too? Of course; but in a way that needs

---

[5] Varro indeed is better placed to help us, for he tells us facts of ancient rural life which we need to know. The theorist Neoptolemus unlocks no such stores of otherwise unattainable knowledge.

defining. Peripatetic treatises on poetics tended to have a certain lay-out, resting on general theory: basically, it would seem, the principle of Aristotle's *Rhetoric* (not to be found in the *Poetics*) that content and argument should be discussed independently of form and language. This simple division into 'what is to be said' and 'how it is to be said' goes back anyway to Plato, for we find it in the moral critique of poetry which he makes in *Republic* II and III.[6] It exists in more sophisticated forms in the Hellenistic critics: the famous ποίημα/ποίησις distinction in Neoptolemus is one of these, for ποίησις (the act of composing a whole poem) deals with the entire business of plot, and ποίημα (the work of making verses, or the verses so made) involves the entire topic of the linguistic medium.[7] Now Horace does indeed recognize this *res/verba* division (40 ff.). And he naturally dis-cusses vocabulary at some length in some places, and plot at some length in others. But he does not submit his exposition to it as a principle of division of the material, as a textbook writer would. Even if one supposes (and there is plausibility in this) a shift from form to content at l. 118, it is heavily overlaid: simplicity and variety, with which the poem begins, are topics of content; vocabulary and metre, matters of form, recur often enough in the latter part, from l. 232 onwards. The most significant point of technical arrangement in the poem is the simple one, often observed, that the whole of the last part (from about l. 295) is devoted, not to the poet's works, but to his person and function in society. The caricature at the end is of the mad, disorganized poet; the caricature at the beginning, which it seems to balance, is of the chaotic, disorganized work of art. Now we know that Philodemus criticized in Neoptolemus the tripartite division of the subject ποίημα/ποίησις/ποιητής.[8] It is an obvious and captious point, not untypical of much ancient polemic, that a poet is not a species of poetry. But however unfair Philodemus' argument, we need scarcely doubt that this is how Neoptolemus divided the matter. In following him, Horace not only reproduced a textbook order of things, but (far more important) opened his own way to satire and moral interest.

I shall return to this point. In all other respects, the process of turn-ing poetics into poetry manifestly did not depend on a given articu-lation of the subject. What was far more important to Horace was the

---

[6] *Rep.* 392.    [7] See esp. Brink, *Horace*, 59 ff.    [8] Ibid. 58.

richness of the topics built into the system. These we may group in two sets of three. The first set consists of certain ideas which were of basic importance in Aristotelian theory and its Hellenistic developments: unity, propriety (*decorum*), the historical development of the *genres* and in particular of drama. The second comprises themes to which Horace seems to have devoted more space than we might have expected: the importance of *ars* compared with *ingenium*—a presupposition of anyone who writes an *ars*;[9] the commitment of the poet not only to conscientious workmanship but to socially valuable moral principles; and the difference between Roman attitudes and Greek. These latter points arise mainly in the last part of the poem; they represent the most serious lesson it has to teach. For towards the end the 'poem on poetics' seems to become more hortatory. It is not indeed a protreptic to poetry. The Pisones might well find it rather a warning off (372-3):

> Mediocribus esse poetis
> non homines, non di, non concessere columnae.

> Neither men nor gods, nor bookshops allow poets to be mediocre.

It is difficult to write a sentence about the *Ars*, especially one which claims to paraphrase it, without acute diffidence. Problems posed, solved or dissolved by four centuries of scholarship have resulted in a neurotic confusion unexcelled even in classical studies. It is easy to see how this has happened. Here is a poem the content of which has seemed peculiarly important in every age when European literature has looked back to its classical roots. It is also a poem of great delicacy and allusiveness. There is a sort of printing in two tones which reveals different legends as you turn it towards or away from the light. A lot of the *Ars* is like that. Lines and sections read quite differently according to what you hold in mind from the context, and whether you look forwards or back. Analysis is therefore almost always controversial. Anyone who undertakes to guide a party round the poem is likely to be pointing out things that are not there, and missing things that are. Nevertheless, some sort of paraphrase is the only help worth having. So I attempt one.

'While he teacheth the art, he goeth unartificially to work, even in the very beginning'[10] wrote a seventeenth-century critic, following

---

[9] Cf. 'Longinus' 2.    [10] H. Peacham, *The Compleat Gentleman* (1622).

Scaliger's damning phrase, *ars sine arte tradita*. But the caricature of the Scylla-like monster with which the poem opens is in fact not without art. An introductory comparison, often quite bizarre, is a common exordium, for example, in works of popular philosophy like Plutarch's. It attracts attention, and relates the subject to something outside it—a good move to excite interest. Here, by relating poetry to painting, Horace makes a special point: both are forms of imitation, traditionally paired together. Painting, said Simonides, is silent poetry.[11]

When unity and disunity are in question, Horace thinks particularly of epic: so here, so also below in ll. 136-52. A grand enterprise is spoilt by a superfluous description (*ecphrasis*), however pretty it may be. A 'purple patch', in fact, involves a breach not only of unity but of *decorum*, since this implies the consistent maintenance of a single tone of discourse. But the main point in all this paragraph is unity: it is emphasized by two more parallels, from painting and pottery (19-22), and by the analogy of other literary vices.

These last lines (24-31) deserve a closer look. The general principle they convey is that the effort to achieve some good quality often leads us into a bad one: brevity into obscurity, smoothness into flabbiness, grandeur into bombast, caution into dullness—and variety into absurdity. This is standard literary theory, based ultimately on the Aristotelian doctrine of 'mean' and 'extremes'.[12] The way out of the danger is afforded by *ars*; this alone enables us to distinguish success from failure. Horace's economy is noteworthy: in a few lines, he reminds us of the traditional 'three styles'—grand, slight and smooth—as well of the traditional justification of *ars* and the relation of the question of unity to the more general one of technique. At the same time he elaborates on his theme with charm and humour: on the *ecphrasis* (17-19), on the unsuccessful sculptor in bronze (32-5), on beautiful black eyes and hair (37).

Alternation between fullness and brevity is a feature of the poem, one of its chief techniques of variety. This is perhaps to be regarded as a Hesiodic inheritance, for the *Works and Days*, a much-studied model for the Alexandrians, is like this: brief gnomic wisdom alternates with set pieces of description. Nowhere is this technique clearer

---

[11] Plutarch, *Moralia*, 346F.
[12] See e.g. 'Longinus' 3, Demetrius, 114, [Cicero] *ad Herennium* IV, for 'adjacent faults' of various kinds.

than in the next part of the *Ars*. First, a fundamental *praeceptum*: choose your subject within your powers (38–40). This is elaborated only to the extent of being said twice over, with a certain amount of metaphor (*umeri*) and anaphora (*quid . . . quid . . .* ). From competent choice of subject will follow both style and arrangement (40–1). These two are taken up in reverse order: arrangement of material briefly (42–5),[13] vocabulary at length. Characteristically Augustan is the emphasis laid on ingenious word-combination (*iunctura*, σύνθεσις) as the road to distinction and novelty. It could be a veiled compliment to Virgil, whose detractors turned this notion on its head to speak of the insidious affectation (*cacozelia*) inherent in his use of common words.[14] The theory of poetic vocabulary involved various topics: foreign words or 'glosses,' metaphors and neologisms. Horace chooses only the last. It has no doubt a special relevance to Latin, where the conscious expansion of vocabulary on Greek lines was an active issue. More important, it leads to a general topic with a moral aspect: the dependence of vocabulary on usage (*usus*) and the consequent mortality of words. The conventional exemplification of *debemur morti nos nostraque* (61) takes us for a while away from the critic's lecture to the world outside.

At l. 73 comes a sharp break. The entertaining survey of metres in relation to genres looks wholly forward, to the *discriptas . . . vices operumque colores* of l. 86. Metre is the principal *differentia* of genre. But ll. 86–8 seem at first sight to look both ways: not only back to the metres but on to ll. 89–98, to the differentiation of tragedy from comedy by language, and the circumstances in which each may sometimes usurp the other's manner. It is a question of some importance whether this apparent double face is really there. The passage on metre is incomplete without ll. 86–7. It is the same sort of economical incorporation of background theory that we saw in ll. 25–8, and like that passage is futile without its conclusion. On the other hand, the passage 89–98 has a completeness in itself. It does not need the generalization, though it may be held to illustrate it. We should, I think, be careful not to seek connections where they are

[13] Or to 44, if Bentley's transposition of *hoc amet, hoc spernat . . .* to follow *in verbis . . . serendis* is right, as (e.g.) Vahlen, Kiessling-Heinze, and Brink maintain.

[14] Donatus, *vita*, 44: 'novae cacozeliae repertorem, non tumidae nec exilis [i.e. not arising from the common perversions of the grand and simple styles] sed ex communibus verbis atque ideo latentis.'

not. Hesiod reminds us that chains of *gnomai* often have loose or broken links. A reading of the ancient technical treatises—notably Demetrius, *On Style*—should warn us further that even these works are often lacking in logical order. In interpreting this passage, we should allow for some deliberate disjointedness: paragraph not (as some editors) at l. 85, but at ll. 88, 91, 92, 98.

All this is about drama. Epic has slipped from sight, the other genres appear only incidentally as examples of the diverse *colores*. This concentration is typical of Peripatetic criticism. It becomes more and more pronounced as the *Ars* proceeds. From now on, the whole of the poem (up to l. 295) is concerned with drama, except for ll. 131-52, an encomium of Homer which is an evident digression. It is a natural and proper conclusion from this that the scope of the poem is something different from a critique of the contemporary Augustan literary scene. However important those lost masterpieces, Varius' *Thyestes* and Ovid's *Medea*, may have been, they were marginal to the Augustan achievement. Strange if Horace did not know this too. The literary scene, which is his subject for example in the *Letter to Augustus* (*Epist.* II. 1), is not the topic here: here it is the theory that he takes as his material.

Diction, said the textbooks,[15] should be appropriate to emotion, character and circumstance. Horace follows this pattern: emotion (99-111), circumstance (112-13), character (114-18)—in the usual technical sense of the determinate *ēthos* of a particular sort of person. Much of the detail of this discussion is known to be part of the technical tradition. With ll. 114-17, we rightly compare the censure of Aristophanes in Plutarch:[16] 'You could not tell whether it is a son talking or a father or a farmer or a god or an old woman or a hero.' What remains puzzling is probably traditional also: the mysterious Colchian, Assyrian, Theban and Argive (118) will also have a history in lost books of poetics.

Line 119 comes in abruptly:

> aut famam sequere aut sibi convenientia finge.

> Either follow tradition or invent a consistent story.

Read without context, this advice has a more general application than to features of character. Indeed, as we read on, it proves to

---

[15] Cf. Aristotle, *Rhetoric* 3. 7.
[16] *Moralia*, 853D. The parallel confirms the reading *divus* in 114.

include plot. But at the moment Horace disguises the shift. He exemplifies his maxim from the field of which he has just been speaking. Just as farmer, nurse and hero had to have appropriate language, because their character is a datum, so the known heroes of mythology must be represented in their accepted colours. A nontraditional character, on the other hand, has merely to obey the law of internal consistency. Now non-traditional *stories*—here is the shift of subject, masked by the common element of breach with tradition—are in fact the clothing of general statements about action and personality in particular forms. *Proprie communia dicere* (128), much disputed, is a more philosophical way of expressing the process more superficially seen by Aristotle as 'adding names'.[17] This is a difficult matter. Better therefore to use traditional stories—but make them your own by distinctive treatment. To illustrate this Horace turns to epic, and gives us an encomium of Homer, in just those respects which most attracted Hellenistic craftsmen—or for that matter Virgil: his sense of how to begin, the plunge *in medias res*, the limitation of the subject, the selection of the poetically viable, the grasp of overall unity. The last point (152) brings us back to the theme of Horace's own exordium. The recollection gives emphasis and a sense of pause, as at the completion of a movement. But the whole passage is, of course, something of a digression. It is a virtuoso piece too: everyone remembers its highlights, the proverbial mouse (139), the alliterative *cum Cyclope Charybdim* (145), the *in medias res* (148).

So back to the stage, to an audience willing to endure to the epilogue (153-5). And back also to the portrayal of character. We seem to be in the situation of ll. 125-8; we are now to hear in more detail how the dramatic *persona* should be maintained. As a teaching example, Horace chooses the Ages of Man. He gives us four:[18] but he bases himself a good deal on the three Ages described from the orator's point of view by Aristotle.[19] Thus Aristotle says of the young:

They are full of desire and liable to do what they desire. Among bodily desires they are most inclined to follow that of sex, in which they have no self-control. They are changeable and fickle in their desires, which they form quickly and give up quickly.

[17] *Poetics*, 1451[b]10.
[18] Cf. in general F. Boll, *Die Lebensalter*, *Neue Jahrbücher*, 31 (1913), 89-146, reprinted in *Kleine Schriften zur Sternkunde des Altertums* (Leipzig, 1950).
[19] *Rhetoric* 2. 12-14.

All this comes to half a line:

> cupidusque et amata relinquere pernix
> Eager and quick to abandon the objects of his love. (165)

At the same time, there is much in Aristotle for which Horace finds no place: the confidence and hopefulness of the young, their mercifulness, bashfulness, and freedom from disillusion. It is partly of course that these qualities are of interest to the orator, who needs to know how to influence such characters, more than to the poet who has just to represent them; but it is noticeable also that Horace's description has a more satiric tinge, at once vivid and censorious. His timid and grumbling old men, too, show something of this, though the basic features of their character are already in Aristotle. In all this, the poeticizing of the subject involves not only selection but a marked change of tone from the clinical to the satiric.

This connected development is followed, for contrast, by a series of *praecepta* on points of dramatic art. Deliberately not linked, these *praecepta* are varied by the mock-heroic summaries of legends in ll. 185-7, and by the expansive account of the moral attitudes appropriate to a chorus in ll. 196-201.

A taste of such material evidently suffices. If we look ahead, we glimpse a motive for it: the overpowering importance of techniques and observance of the proprieties, which is shortly to be illustrated in a very striking way.

But no signs yet of what is coming. Only a quite natural transition from the chorus to the accompanying music (202). But not the music as it is now: a historical perspective unexpectedly appears. It is a moralist's view of things, Platonic rather than Aristotelian, associating prosperity with luxury and, in some sense, decadence. Aristotle,[20] it is true, had noted that pipe-playing was introduced into education after the Persian wars; and also that changes in musical taste were liable to come from the demands of an uneducated audience. But there is another element in Horace's account of the theory that moral decline and luxury were associated: the audience of the later period was no longer *frugi castusque* (207). It is reasonable therefore to think of Plato, of the 'vile theatrocracy' condemned in the *Laws*.[21]

---

[20] *Politics* 1341a28, [b]15.      [21] 700A-701B. But see Cicero, *De Legibus* 2. 38.

Horace had handled this topic of fifth- and fourth-century cultural history elsewhere, in the Letter to Augustus.[22] Here he divorces it from its historical setting. At the same time he touches it with a master hand: *vino diurno* (209), the matching of oracular style with sense in ll. 218–19. It is yet another set piece; but not complete in itself, since it is essential logical preparation for what follows.

The licentious audience of post-war Greece needed special titillation at the end of the day;[23] satyr-plays, performed at the end of sets of tragedies, provided it. This is to choose one of two rival accounts of the development of drama: not Aristotle's,[24] according to which tragedy grew as a refined form of the satyr-play, which is seen as something more primitive; but a later and commoner one[25] in which Pratinas, a successor of Thespis, invented satyr-plays as a new variety. Horace's choice—which may also be Neoptolemus'—is poetically apt, and it is more important to see this than to wonder about the historical judgment behind it. The story of prosperity and moral laxity leads up to the new discovery, and the new discovery leads to what is evidently the end-point of the whole development: namely, advice on how to write this peculiar genre.

Now there may of course be circumstances which, if known to us, would reduce our astonishment at this move. The Pisones may have burned with ambition to conquer even this literary corner for Rome. Horace may have thought that this was a desirable step in the progress of Augustan literature. Alexandrian satyr-plays, such as the *Lityerses* of Sositheos, may have been notable in themselves or have attracted the attention of the theorists whom Horace follows. It is in this last point, I am inclined to say, that the heart of the matter lies. Satyr-drama aroused special theoretical interest. In its classical form, it was burlesque in content, but tragic in language and metre. This intermediate status called for definition, for a close analysis of metre and style in terms of decorum. It is the consequent rather complicated play with critical concepts that Horace here turns into thirty lines of poetry.

It is a study in balance and the Aristotelian mean. The serious and

[22] *Epist.*, 2. 1. 93 ff.
[23] Cf. ll. 154–5 for the idea of 'keeping' the audience till the end of the performance.
[24] *Poetics* 1449ᵃ20, if this is the right interpretation of ἐκ σατυρικοῦ μεταβαλεῖν. Cf. also Dioscorides, *Anth. Pal.* 7. 37. 1–6.
[25] *Suda*, s.v. 'Pratinas'.

the humorous must be blended in such a way that heroic characters, already introduced in the serious plays, neither disgrace themselves nor soar above human ken. Satyr-drama is tragedy on holiday, as it were; it is not comedy, for its characters, after all, are divine. It will not eschew metaphor, but it will depend for its distinction on arrangement rather than on unfamiliar language (240-4). This last point is a little strange: it is not true of classical satyr-drama, which has a good deal of exaggerated diction. But Horace is presumably legislating for a refined form of the genre. Finally, the humour must steer clear of the erotic and the indecent. We aim at a respectable audience (248-50).

It would be wrong to suppose that just because this topic occupies a comparatively large space, it is proportionately important in the thematic structure of the poem. We could not after all make a case for this for the Ages of Man. But it would be wrong too to regard the satyr-section as a mere episode. It is too central for that—and not only in position, though it may well be significant that it comes plumb in the middle of the poem. As an illustration of the vital importance of knowledge and technique, it touches the heart of the poem's subject. Moreover, it seems to close a distinct phase in the argument. Little has been said so far to refer us specifically to the Roman situation: ll. 49-58, on vocabulary, seems the only significant exception. With the halfway mark passed, and the satyr-section out of the way, this is to change. Roman problems are dominant in ll. 251-94, prominent also in the rest of the poem.

The organization of ll. 251-94 is not easily missed, and it is important to recognize it. The tongue-in-cheek beginning, as if we did not all know what an iambus was, may mislead for a moment; but it soon becomes obvious that its function is solely to prepare for the point that traditional Roman metrical technique has a crudity and heaviness which are nowadays unforgivable. Modern taste should not accept a Plautine standard of metre—any more than a Plautine standard of humour. Where Rome has done well is in enterprise: not only has she followed Greeks in the successive inventions of tragedy and comedy (275-84), but ventured outside Greek range into historical and Italian plays. Where she fails is in technique: *limae labor et mora*. This alone, apparently, prevents Rome from achieving the traditional praise of the Greeks. Other considerations to come may modify this; but for the moment, the argument seems complete, and the formal address to the Pisones (291-4) both emphasizes the importance of what is said here and signals the end of the main part of the poem.

But even this break, though the most meaningful in the whole composition, is not complete. There is a bridge. Technical perfection in the work has had its emphasis. In what follows, Horace examines the balance of the poet's make-up, and the relation of *ars* to *ingenium* in him. The last part of the poem thus parallels and complements the earlier parts in various ways. None the less it has its independence: it is certainly *de poeta*, and the common comparison with the account of the perfect orator with which Quintilian closes the *Institutio* is an illuminating one. Two features, of very different kinds, give an air of separateness. One is the element of caricature. A welcome butt has presented himself: the poet who relies on his 'genius'. This unpleasing eccentric now keeps cropping up: ll. 295-302, 379-84, 416-18, and especially ll. 453-76. He brings with him a more satirical tone, evident notably in the 'friend and flatterer' development of ll. 422-52. But, second, we have for the first time in the poem an apparent formal division of the material (307-8):

[i]   Unde parentur opes, quid alat formetque poetam,
[ii]  quid deceat, quid non, [iii] quo virtus, quo ferat error.

(i) where the poet's resources come from, what nurtures and forms him, (ii) what is proper and what not, (iii) in what directions excellence and error lead.

The most influential person to take this seriously was Eduard Norden.[26] His identification of (i) with ll. 309-32, (ii) with ll. 333-46, (iii) with l. 347-end, has been much disputed. But it grows on one; and it, or something like it, must be right.

(i) There is certainly truth in the first part. Here there are three interconnected themes: the practical need of the poet—especially the dramatist—for a knowledge of ethics, and particularly the detailed, preceptive ethics which comes, for example, in treatises *de officiis*; the triumph of a piece that gets character and moral sentiments right over one that is technically competent but trivial; and the supporting instance of Greece, whose immortal literature is grounded on a moral character free from all greed save greed for fame. This, I think, is the

---

[26] *Hermes*, 40 (1905), 481-525.

point of the brilliant classroom scene of ll. 325 ff.; Horace is answering an objection which he imagines, but does not spell out: the objection that the emphasis on *mores* in ll. 319-22 seems to conflict with the admiration for Greek technique which is axiomatic in the poem. His answer is that what has been said needs some supplementing: the Greek miracle did not really depend solely on technique, but also on moral qualities, on a generosity and unworldliness not natural to dour, money-grubbing Rome. That meanness is inimical to the growth of literature is a common enough thought: we may compare the last chapter of *De Sublimitate*,[27] where the link between avarice (φιλοχρηματία) and the loss of true standards of excellence is worked out in some detail.

(ii) The reconciliation of the aims of pleasure and utility (333-46) attaches loosely to what precedes: *prodesse* relates to the effect of the *speciosa locis . . . fabula*, *delectare* to that of the melodious nonsense. But this section has its own coherence. It is a neat, spare little exercise in balances and antitheses: ll. 335-7 take up *prodesse*; ll. 338-40 *delectare*; ll. 341 and 342 repeat the pair; l. 343 states the solution and l. 344 repeats once again: a bland compromise reconciles ψυχαγωγία (charm) and διδασκαλία (instruction) as it does *ingenium* and *ars*.

(iii) But at l. 346 comes a more decided break. We find a string of propositions: (*a*) small faults are venial; (*b*) some poetry bears careful and repeated inspection; (*c*) it's no use being a mediocre poet, though it may be some use being a mediocre lawyer; (*d*) keep your work eight years before publishing. At first sight, there are contradictions in this, if one takes it all as a recipe for good writing. But it is a whole, and a familiar one. 'Longinus', with different emphasis, combines similar elements: small errors are venial (33-6); great writing sustains repeated study (7); no one would wish to be Apollonius rather than Homer (33).

The appeal to Piso (366), taken up in l. 385, seems to add emphasis to an attitude which, despite the disavowal of obsessive perfectionism, remains somewhat discouraging. Poetry is here a luxury art, and can be compared with the accessories of a good dinner (374-6); we therefore exact a higher standard of perfection than we would in something one might be obliged to do, like speaking in public in a lawsuit. Consequently, if the well-born Roman

---

[27] 'Longinus' 44. 6-7.

attempts it, he should put his efforts aside, submit them to rigorous
and friendly critics, and only publish them after long reflection and
revision. There may be examples of amateurs who rush in (384-5);
these are much to be deprecated.

Piso might surely ask: Why then should I bother to write at
all? The answer to this, and the counter as it were to all this discouraging perfectionism, appears in ll. 390-407. The connection
here, once again, is a suppressed question, a matter of an imaginary
debate, not a textbook sequence of headings. The answer is that the
reason for not feeling ashamed of taking endless trouble is that poetry
is a very grand thing—a great civilizing force in human history. This
is a splendid section: precise, delicate, urbane, steering clear both of
the banal and of the pompous. Horace begins with an allegorical
version of two myths: Orpheus' taming the savage beasts represents
his suppression of cannibalism—or rather, perhaps, of meat-eating;
Amphion's miraculous building of Thebes represents (presumably)
the power of music to produce order in minds and in society.
Lawgiving was thus the first achievement of the ancient *vates*;
martial excitement, moral advice, flattery and entertainment
followed—in that order.[28]

The ideal poet begins to take shape. A scrupulous but unpedantic
craftsman, a balanced moralist and a shrewd observer, he takes his
trade seriously because he understands its place in human history.
But, by the terms of the poem, he is also a Piso. It is part of the transposition of 'poetics' which the composition of the *Ars* involved that
the perfect poet should have the special features of a young Roman
nobleman. As the portrait proceeds, this becomes clearer. He must
beware of flatterers. Here (419-52) follows a standard topic of ethics,
the distinction of flatterer and friend,[29] with a standard Hellenistic
illustration.[30] Individuality is given by the reminiscence of Quintilius,
the transposition of Aristarchus' obelizing procedures to the critic-
friend, and especially by the important *sententia* at the end (451-2):

> hae nugae seria ducent
> in mala . . .

> these trifles lead to serious troubles . . .

[28] A verbal—but hardly significant—contradiction of 1. 377: *animis natum . . .
poema iuuandis*.

[29] See especially Plutarch's *De adulatore et amico*.

[30] Diodorus, 20. 63. 1.

What makes poetry important to a Piso is that his hobby may make him ridiculous. The critic-friend must do his duty.[31]

The final episode of the poem is pure caricature: the enemy is mercilessly traduced; he is not worth keeping alive; goodness knows what impiety has damned him to writing verses; he is a dangerous lunatic—and his recitations spell death.

Set this conclusion side by side with the exordium, and it prompts an observation which may help to bring out the unity of the whole. We began with a monstrous poem; we end with the pseudo-poet who might write it. The *Ars*, with its many facets, the shimmering surface that catches so many different lights, admits of course many observations on this level. But this one is worth more than a moment's pause. It brings out two essentials of the process that turned poetics into this sort of poetry. It reminds us that the *poiēma*, the thing made, could never be material for a poem without the maker, without his emotions and morals, his credibility, his honesty. Only by bringing in the artist could the 'art' be made to live. And second, this particular sort of poem, like the *Satires* and *Epistles*, needs something to laugh about, and, perhaps more important, someone to laugh at. It is the madman who sticks in our mind most, it is the caricature that brings the complicated and allusive artfulness of the whole poem most vividly to life.

The *Ars* is one of those *aurei libelli* treasured in medieval and Renaissance education as containing a particularly potent distillation of the wisdom of antiquity. That it is, in its own right, a subtle, bold and, on the whole, successful poem matters far less historically than its doctrinal content and its apparent utility as a model of a kind of humorous didactic piece. It was for long the most accessible source of the basic tenets of classical criticism: the doctrines of propriety and genre, and the underlying assumption that the poet, like the orator, sets himself a particular task of persuasion and is to be judged by his success in bringing it off. The history of its influence is therefore long and complex; all I can do here, by way of appendix, is to indicate a few points of entry and give a few illustrative extracts from some of the less accessible places.[32]

---

[31] Not to do so would be to yield to a pernicious inhibition, what Greek moralists called δυσωπία: cf. *pudens prave* (l. 88).

[32] See, besides the standard general histories of criticism: J. E. Spingarn, *A History*

From the early Middle Ages, Horace was a curriculum author, and
no part of him was more studied than the *Ars*, with its valuable
literary lore and its impeccable morality. Medieval poetics, very
much an art of the schoolroom, was inevitably much influenced by
it: poetical *artes* sprang up which, however different in content, owed
their being in the last resort to Horace.[33] In the Renaissance, imitation took a different road. Girolamo Vida's *Poeticorum Libri III*
(1527)[34] is a notable landmark. It was the most famous and
successful didactic of the age. Formally, nothing could be much less
like the *Ars*. Vida's model is the *Georgics*, his ideal poet is Virgil. There
is nothing of Horace's play with theory. Vida's concern is straightforwardly didactic—to teach Virgilian composition, by precept and
still more by example. But there are passages of Horatian inspiration,
and the basic assumptions of the *Ars* are there. Here, for example, is
how Vida handles what is in effect Horace's advice on epic prooemia
(ii. 18-21, 30-9):

> Vestibulum ante ipsum primoque in limine semper
> prudentes leviter rerum fastigia summa
> libant et parcis attingunt omnia dictis
> quae canere statuere: simul caelestia divum
> auxilia implorant, propriis nil viribus ausi . . .
> incipiens odium fugito, facilesque legentum
> nil tumidus demulce animos, nec grandia iam tum
> convenit aut nimium cultum ostentantia fari,
> omnia sed nudis prope erit fas promere verbis:
> ne, si magna sones, cum nondum ad proelia ventum,
> deficias medio irrisus certamine, cum res
> postulat ingentes animos viresque valentes.
> principiis potius semper maiora sequantur:
> protinus illectas succende cupidine mentes
> et studium lectorum animis innecte legendi.

Before the courtyard, on the very threshold [*Aeneid* 2. 469!], the wise always

*of Literary Criticism in the Renaissance* (New York, 1908); B. Weinberg, *History of
Literary Criticism in the Italian Renaissance* (Chicago, 1961); M. T. Herrick, *The Fusion
of Horatian and Aristotelian Literary Criticism, 1531-1555* (New York, 1946).

[33] On Matthew of Vendôme's *Ars versificatoria* and Geoffrey of Vinsauf's *Poetria
nova*, see F. J. E. Raby, *Secular Latin Poetry*, ii. 30, 122; E. Faral, *Les arts poétiques du
XIIᵉ et XIIIᵉ siècle* (Paris, 1923); J. de Ghellinck, *L'essor de la littérature latine au XIIᵉ
siècle* (Brussels, 1946), ii. 243 ff.

[34] Many editions down to the eighteenth century. An excellent English verse translation was made by Christopher Pitt (1725).

dip lightly into the essentials of the story, and touch on everything they have resolved to sing with a few, sparing words. At the same time, they beg the heavenly help of the gods, for they venture nothing by their own strength. ... When you begin, avoid causing disgust; have no bombast about you, but soothe your readers' willing ears. At this point it is out of place to talk grandly or in a way that displays too much polish. It will be quite proper to set out everything, almost, in the barest words; if you sound a loud note now, when you have not yet reached the battle, you may well fail ridiculously in the middle of the encounter, when the story demands great courage and powerful strength. Let what follows always be greater than the beginning. Forthwith inflame the captive mind, with eagerness, and bind the zeal to read upon your readers' hearts.

Neologisms are another Horatian theme (iii. 267–84):

> Nos etiam quaedam idcirco nova condere nulla
> religio vetat indictasque effundere voces.
> ne vero haec penitus fuerint ignota suumque
> agnoscant genus et cognatam ostendere gentem
> possint, ac stirpis nitantur origine certae.
> usque adeo patriae tibi si penuria vocis
> obstabit, fas Graiugenum felicibus oris
> devehere informem massam, quam incude Latina
> informans patrium iubeas dediscere morem.
> sic quondam Ausoniae succrevit copia linguae:
> sic auctum Latium, quo plurima transtulit Argis
> usus et exhaustis Itali potiuntur Athenis.
> nonne vides mediis ut multa erepta Mycenis,
> Graia genus, fulgent nostris immixta, nec ullum
> apparet discrimen? eunt insignibus aequis
> undique per Latios et civis et advena tractus.
> iamdudum nostri cessit sermonis egestas:
> raro uber patriae tibi, raro opulentia deerit.

No scruple therefore forbids us to invent some new words, and utter sounds unspoken before. But let them not be altogether unknown: let them acknowledge their ancestry, be able to show their relationships, and rely on an origin in some certain race. If the poverty of our native vocabulary obstructs you very much, it is right to import from the happy shores of Greece some shapeless mass which you can mould on a Latin anvil and command to unlearn its native ways. This is how the resources of the tongue of Ausonia grew of old. This is how Latium was developed. Use transferred many things there from Argos; Italians won the plunder of an exhausted Athens. Do you not see how many words, stolen from the heart of Mycenae,

Greek in origin, gleam amid our own? They show no difference; in like
uniform, citizen and stranger move through the realms of Latium. Our
language's poverty has long since yielded; rarely will the rich soil of your
country, rarely its wealth fail you.

But the best parts of Vida are perhaps the most independent. The long
development on sound and sense towards the end of book III begins
with a reminiscence of Horace, but soon moves away into a sensitive
lesson in Virgilian artistry (iii. 365–76):

> Haud satis est illis utcumque claudere versum,
> et res verborum propria vi reddere claras:
> omnia sed numeris vocum concordibus aptant,
> atque sono quaecumque canunt imitantur et apta
> verborum facie et quaesito carminis ore.
> nam diversa opus est veluti dare versibus ora
> diversosque habitus, ne qualis primus et alter,
> talis et inde alter, vultuque incedat eodem.
> hic melior motuque pedum et pernicibus alis
> molle viam tacito lapsu per levia radit:
> ille autem membris ac mole ignavius ingens
> incedit tardo molimine subsidendo.

It is not enough for them to round off the line anyhow and to make the
subject clear by the correct force of the words. They suit everything to
harmonious verbal rhythms and imitate the subjects of their song in sounds,
with apt shapes of words and a poetical expression diligently sought. For one
has as it were to give the lines different expressions and different guises, so
that the first is not followed by another and then another of the same kind,
moving along with the same look on its face. One is speedier of foot and wing
and gently glides over its smooth way with silent motion: another, of mighty
limbs and mass, moves more sluggishly, pausing in its slow effort.

Vida, for all his limitations and pedagogic tone, deserves more attention than he gets. With his concern for practice rather than theory,
he follows in a sense in the line of the medieval *artes*; but his
Virgilianism and his skill in mimicry are new. Writing in the 1520s,
he was still comparatively unaffected by the more profound and
speculative poetics that developed from the renewed study of
Aristotle.

   It was inevitable that, as a source for theory, Horace should take a
back seat once the *Poetics* became familiar. He is very much a subsidiary source to the great theorists, a Minturno or a Castelvetro. But

he did of course remain popular, and at a somewhat humbler level we see much of his influence in the latter part of the century. G. Fabricius (*De Re Poetica*, 1560) drew up a list of forty-one propositions derived from the *Ars*, with some from the *Epistles* and *Satires*. This proved a popular compendium: William Webbe's *Of English Poetry* (1586) reproduces it.[35] Two of the great literary manifestos of the age also clearly owe a good deal to Horace: du Bellay's *Deffence et Illustration de la langue françoise* (1549) and Sidney's *Apology for Poetry* (1583).[36] But in the field of scholastic poetics, Scaliger's negative judgment was important (*Poetics*, 1561, preface):

> Horatius Artem quam inscripsit adeo sine ulla docet arte ut Satyrae propius totum opus illud esse videatur.
>
> Horace, in what he entitled the *Art* [*of Poetry*], teaches with so little art that the entire work seems to be closer to a satire.

And he himself made little use of the *Ars*. Explicitly, or more often tacitly, he criticizes its viewpoints on various matters. His rhetorical prescriptions for the appropriate portrayal of different national characteristics (3. 17)[37] and of the Ages of Man (3. 15) rest on other sources. For the latter topic, he returns conspicuously to the chapters of Aristotle's *Rhetoric* from which Horace departed.

It is probably broadly true that in the seventeenth century the *Ars* was more important as a poetic model than as a source of critical theory. In England, it attracted Ben Jonson both as commentator (the commentary is lost) and as translator.[38] In France, it served as the model of the most Horatian and most famous of its imitations—

---

[35] Text in G. Gregory Smith, *Elizabethan Critical Essays*, i (Oxford, 1904), 290 ff. (English), 417 ff. (Latin).

[36] The standard editions give the necessary information: Sidney is ibid, i. 148 ff., for du Bellay see the edn. of H. Chamard (Paris, 1945). In du Bellay, note especially: 2. 4. 'Ly donques et rely premierement . . . feuillete de main nocturne et journelle les exemplaires grecs et latins: 2. 4 te fourniront de matière les louanges des Dieux et des hommes vertueux, le discours fatal des choses mondaines, la solicitude des jeunes hommes, comme l'amour: les vins libres, et toute bonne chere: 2. 6 ne crains donques . . . d'innover quelques termes . . . avecques modestie toutefois . . .' Du Bellay's Latinisms were severely attacked in a pamphlet published in 1550, 'le Quintil Horatian', which takes its title from Horace's critic-friend.

[37] Cf. *AP* 118. Only *Assyrii* occur of Horace's examples. It is tempting to cite some of the rest: 'Germani fortes, simplices, animarum prodigi, veri amici, verique hostes. Suetii, Noruegii, Gruntlandii, Gotti, beluae. Scoti non minus. Angli perfidi, inflati, feri, contemptores, stolidi, amentes, inertes, inhospitales, immanes . . .'

[38] *Works*, ed Herford and Simpson, viii. 303 ff.

Boileau's *Art Poétique* (1674). Boileau's Horatianism is not primarily
a matter of the direct allusions, numerous and interesting as these
are.[39] It is far more that his insistence on correctness and technique
overlaps a good deal, though not completely, with Horace's doctrine
of the relation of *ars* and *ingenium*; and that his particular brand of
urbanity found the model of the Horatian satire congenial and
reasonably well within grasp. There is a difference of tone: more
courtliness, less vigour; less conciseness; more obvious order in the
layout. But essential Horatian qualities remain, as they do also in
Pope's *Essay on Criticism*, where a new slant is given to the traditional material (Vida's as well as Horace's) by concentrating on the
function and person of the critic—now not just a friendly and frank
Quintilius, but a new sort of professional man.

Horace, we may suspect, would have enjoyed the parodies of himself, or at least some of them, that were a vogue in the eighteenth
century. They presuppose the close familiarity with the *Ars* that its
use in education so long assured. I quote two excerpts from William
King's *Art of Cookery* (1709).[40] First, the Ages of Man (214 ff.):

> If you all sorts of persons would engage,
> Suit well your eatables to ev'ry age.
>    The fav'rite child, that just begins to prattle,
> And throws away his silver bells and rattle,
> Is very humoursome, and makes great clutter
> Till he has windows[41] on his bread and butter;
> He for repeated suppermeat will cry,
> But won't tell mammy what he'd have or why.
>    The smooth fac'd youth that has new guardians chose,
> From playhouse, steps to supper at The Rose,
> Where he a main or two at random throws:
> Squandering of wealth, impatient of advice,
> His eating must be little, costly, nice.
>    Maturer Age, to this delight grown strange,
> Each night frequents his club behind the 'Change,
> Expecting there frugality and health
> And honor, rising from a Sheriff's wealth . . .

---

[39] e.g. 1. 11 (*AP* 38); 1. 64 (*AP* 31); 1. 77 (*AP* 343); 1. 190 (*AP* 424); 3. 6 ff.
(origin of tragedy); 3. 124 (*AP* 125); 3. 269 ff. (*AP* 136 ff.); 3. 375 ff. (ages of man—
omits childhood); 4. 26 (*AP* 372); 4. 71 ff. (the good critic); 4. 135 ff. (civilizing effect
of poetry).

[40] For the author's character, see Johnson's *Life*.

[41] i.e. patterns made with sugar on the bread.

But then, old age, by still intruding years,
Torments the feeble heart with anxious fears:
Morose, perverse in humor, diffident,
The more he still abounds, the less content;
His larder and his kitchen too observes,
And now, lest he should want hereafter, starves;
Thinks scorn of all the present age can give,
And none, these threescore years, know how to live.

And this is what King (331 ff.) makes of *Ars*, ll. 270–84:

Our fathers most admir'd their sauces sweet
And often ask'd for sugar with their meat;
They butter'd currants on fat veal bestow'd
And rumps of beef with virgin-honey strow'd.
Inspid taste, old Friend, to them who Paris know
Where rocambole, shalot, and the rank garlic grow.
Tom Bold did first begin the strolling mart
And drove about his turnips in a cart;
Sometimes his wife the citizens would please
And from the same machine sell pecks of pease:
Then pippins did in wheelbarrows abound,
And oranges in whimsey-boards went round.
Bess Hoy first found it troublesome to bawl
And therefore plac'd her cherries on a stall;
Her currants there and gooseberries were spread
With the enticing gold of gingerbread:
But flounders, sprats and cucumbers were cry'd
And ev'ry sound and ev'ry voice was try'd.
At last the law this hideous din supprest,
And order'd that the Sunday should have rest,
And that no nymph her noisy food should sell
Except it were new milk or mackerel.

These *jeux d'esprit* are a proof of the familiarity of the *Ars* to the educated. There is another proof too, perhaps more striking and still with us—the number of phrases of the work that have penetrated our ordinary speech: 'purple patch' (15), *sub iudice* (78), *in medias res* (149), *laudator temporis acti* (173), the mountain giving birth to the mouse (139), Homer nodding (359). All Horace's works have earned this kind of testimony: the *Ars* has it to a rather special degree.

# 16

# Ovid on Reading: Reading Ovid.
# Reception in Ovid, Tristia 2

BRUCE GIBSON

In this chapter I propose to consider Ovid's poem as a document of literary criticism, which offers us a striking treatment of the role of the audience in reception.[1] Ovid's concerns are twofold: on the one hand he is concerned with the ostensible manner in which his own works have been read, but he also discusses a wide range of other texts, and, in doing so, offers readings of them, which, I will argue, illustrate the open-ended nature of reception and meaning.

Now, undoubtedly we are sometimes too willing to label works as 'anti-Augustan' or 'Augustan', as if that was all that could be said about them;[2] the glib use of such terms often seems to obscure more complex and more interesting questions (the *Aeneid* and the *Georgics*

I would like to thank the Editorial Committee of *JRS*, Alessandro Barchiesi, Rolando Ferri, Don Fowler, Stephen Heyworth, Andrew Laird, John Moles, and Tony Woodman for their invaluable comments and suggestions.

[1] For an introduction to the history of reception, see J. P. Tomkins, 'The Reader in History: The Changing Shape of Literary Response', in J. P. Tomkins (ed.), *Reader-Response Criticism from Formalism to Post-Structuralism* (1980), 201-32. See also the collection of essays edited by U. Eco, *Interpretation and Overinterpretation* (1992).

[2] On the use of these terms in relation to Ovid, see the discussion and bibliographic material of S. G. Nugent, '*Tristia* 2: Ovid and Augustus', in K. A. Raaflaub and M. Toher (eds.), *Between Republic and Empire: Interpretations of Augustus and his Principate* (1990), 239-57, at 241; A. Barchiesi, *Il poeta e il principe: Ovidio e il discorso augusteo* (1994), 34-6; G. D. Williams, *Banished Voices: Readings in Ovid's Exile Poetry* (1994), 154-8; T. Habinek, *The Politics of Latin Literature* (1998), 3-14. For a theoretical treatment of the issues, see D. F. Kennedy ' "Augustan" and "Anti-Augustan": Reflections on Terms of Reference', in A Powell (ed.), *Roman Poetry and Propaganda in the Age of Augustus* (1992), 26-58, while G. K. Galinsky, *Augustan Culture: An Interpretive Introduction* (1996), 225, 244-6, draws attention to the need to see 'Augustan' as a term with a wider frame of reference than that of agreement (or disagreement) with the views of the *princeps*. Note also the important article of F. Ahl, 'The Art of Safe Criticism in Greece and Rome', *AJPh* 105 (1984), 174-208.

are familiar examples). But with Ovid, however, such issues are at least raised by the poet himself, since the exile poems do deal with his attitude to Augustus, and the twin possibilities of writing poetry which can offend the emperor, or which can please him.[3] Now while Ovid's famous explanation of the causes of his exile as 'carmen et error' (*Trist.* 2. 207) may perhaps be a smokescreen[4]—he adduces the *Ars Amatoria* as his fault in order not to have to go into the details of what the *error* was that had offended Augustus—*Tristia* 2 must still be considered on its own terms; Ovid writes as if it is possible for Augustus to be offended by his poetry, and therefore the issue is an important one. For example, he seems to offer an 'Augustan' reading of the *Metamorphoses* to Augustus himself at *Tristia* 2. 557-62.[5]

> atque utinam reuoces animum paulisper ab ira,
>   et uacuo iubeas hinc tibi pauca legi,
> pauca, quibus prima surgens ab origine mundi
>   in tua deduxi tempora, Caesar, opus!
> aspicies, quantum dederis mihi pectoris ipse,
>   quoque fauore animi teque tuosque canam.

And would that you would recall your mind from its anger for a little while, and, when you are at leisure, order a few lines from here to be read to you, the few lines in which I have led down my work which starts from the first origin of the universe to your times, Caesar. You will see how much heart you yourself have given to me, and with what favour I sing of you and of your family.

In the last two lines Ovid proclaims that he regards his *Metamorphoses* as a work which affirms the emperor and his family. But perhaps the crucial word in the whole passage is *pauca* ('a few lines') which not only jokingly refers to the whole fifteen books of the *Metamorphoses*,[6] but also evokes a particular passage, the passage which

---

[3] The reciprocal relationship between Augustus' edict of relegation, described as 'tristibus . . . uerbis' (*Trist.* 2. 133) and Ovid's exile poetry, *Tristia*, is noted by Habinek, *Politics*, 155-6.

[4] For this view see most recently Galinsky, *Augustan Culture*, 269.

[5] On the issue of 'Augustanism' in the *Metamorphoses*, see e.g. B. Otis, *Ovid as an Epic Poet* (1966), 145, 302-5, 329; G. K. Galinsky, *Ovid's Metamorphoses: An Introduction to the Basic Aspects* (1975), 210-17; P. Hardie, 'Questions of Authority: The Invention of Tradition in Ovid *Metamorphoses* 15', in T. Habinek and A. Schiesaro (eds.), *The Roman Cultural Revolution* (1997), 182-98.

[6] On 559-60 see D. R. Shackleton Bailey, 'Notes on Ovid's Poems from Exile', *CQ* 32 (1982), 390-8, at 393, who construes *surgens* as neuter. It is, however, perfectly possible to take *surgens* as masculine, referring to Ovid himself; for the sliding relation

brings the poem down to the time of Augustus and concludes by
describing the metamorphosis of Julius Caesar into a star (*Met.* 15.
843–50),[7] before proceeding to an encomium of Augustus, who is
said to surpass Julius Caesar (15. 850–70); the passage concludes
with Ovid's pious wish that the day of Augustus' ascent to heaven be
long postponed. It is in the light of *pauca* that we should perhaps consider the last two lines of my quotation from *Tristia* 2. Ovid asks the
emperor to consider how much heart he has given to him (that is,
encouragement to composition), and with what favour Ovid is
singing of him and his family. Perhaps the answer is not so much as
we might think.[8] Ovid asks Augustus to measure his attitude to the
emperor on the basis of *pauca*, which at first sight seems encomiastic:
the poet does not wish to bother Augustus; who is burdened with
more weighty cares (this point, recalling Horace's treatment of
Augustus in *Epist.* 2. 1, is made at *Trist.* 2. 213–38). *Pauca* might
moreover suggest that only a few lines of the text are needed to prove
Ovid's loyal credentials, so full of tributes is it.[9] However, in spite of
Ovid's earlier claim that there are many testimonies to his loyalty
in the *Metamorphoses* (*Trist.* 2. 63–6),[10] there are only a few lines

between an author and his text, compare the discussion of *Tristia* 2. 5 below, at p. 350.
On the relation between this passage and the opening of Ovid, *Metamorphoses* 1, see A.
Barchiesi, 'Voci e istanze narrative nelle Metamorfosi di Ovidio', *MD* 23 (1989),
55–97, at 91, who notes the subtle change from 'ad *mea* perpetuum deducite tempora
carmen' (*Met.* 1. 4) to 'in *tua* deduxi tempora, Caesar, opus' (*Trist.* 2. 560).

[7] On this passage see e.g. Otis, *Ovid*, 303–4; Galinsky, *Ovid's Metamorphoses*, 259.

[8] Contrast however F. G. B. Millar, 'Ovid and the *Domus Augusta*: Rome Seen from
Tomoi', *JRS* 83 (1993), 1–17, at 8, who regards this passage and the references to the
*Metamorphoses* as straightforward panegyric: 'Looking back in *Tristia* II on his poetic
achievement before his exile, Ovid, if anything, rather underestimates how profoundly
shaped by Augustan loyalism this work had been (555–62).'

[9] Cf. *Trist.* 2. 61–2 (on the *Ars Amatoria*): 'quid referam libros, illos quoque, crimina
nostra, / mille locis plenos nominis esse tui?' and the discussion of Barchiesi,
*Il poeta* 22–3; Williams, *Banished Voices*, 172.

[10] Note especially *Trist.* 2. 66: 'inuenies animi pignora multa mei'. Galinsky, *Ovid's
Metamorphoses*, 219 regards *Trist.* 2. 63, 'inspice maius opus', as an echo of Virgil,
*Aen.* 7. 44: 'maius opus moueo'. This argument is even more convincing if one
compares Ovid's use of *maius opus*, at *Am.* 3. 1. 24 to refer to the possibility of writing
tragedy. At *Trist.* 2. 63 Ovid is also referring to *Met.* 15. 750–1, 'neque enim de
Caesaris actis / ullum *maius opus*, quam quod pater exstitit huius', where Julius
Caesar's greatest achievement is his (adoptive) paternity of Augustus; on this passage
of the *Metamorphoses*, see further S. Hinds, 'Generalising about Ovid', in A. J. Boyle
(ed.), *Ramus: Critical Studies in Greek and Roman Literature 16. Imperial Roman Literature
I* (1987), 4–31, at 24–6. Note also *Fasti* 5. 567–8, 'spectat et Augusto praetextum
nomine templum, / et uisum lecto Caesare maius opus', where Mars is looking at

referring to the emperor, those in book 15 and the lines in book 1 (*Met* 1. 204–5) which compare the gods' reaction to Jove's intended flood to the response of mortals to the attack on Julius Caesar, before adding 'nec tibi grata minus pietas, Auguste, tuorum / quam fuit illa Ioui', 'Nor was the piety of your subjects less pleasing to you, Augustus, than the piety of the gods was to Jove.' When we consider the totality of the fifteen books of *Metamorphoses*, it seems a little strange that the emperor is asked to determine Ovid's loyalty and enthusiasm from the handful of lines where Ovid does mention him.[11] The centrality of reception as a concern for Ovid is brought out in the reference to a passage at the very end of the work. Apart from the brief mention in book 1, Augustus would have had to have read through all the intervening books before finally reaching the passage which Ovid points to, unless he were to order someone else to read the passage to him; we shall see later that Ovid was at least willing to countenance the possibility that Augustus might not have had much time for poetry anyway.

Whether or not one accepts the more questioning undercurrents of my analysis of the passage from the *Tristia*, it is hard to deny that Ovid does open up for us questions of political allegiance, 'anti-' or 'pro-' Augustan.[12] Furthermore, in a typically Ovidian fashion, the political status not only of the *Metamorphoses* but also of the address to Augustus in *Tristia* 2 is called into question.

In this chapter I intend to examine Ovid's views on readership and reception in the *Tristia*. As we have seen, the task is a complex one, and I hope that one point which will emerge is the extent of the writer's own inconsistency. Along the way, I may well both flirt with

Augustus' temple to Mars Ultor. Other occurrences of *maius opus* in Ovid are *Ars Am.* 3. 370, *Rem.* 109, and *Met.* 8. 328.

[11] S. J. Heyworth, 'Notes on Ovid's *Tristia*', *PCPhS* 41 (1995), 138–52, at 146 n. 39: 'less than 2 pages reveal the *Metamorphoses* as shaped by Augustan loyalism, without mention of any episode between 1. 205 and Aeneas in book 13!'

[12] H. B. Evans, *Publica Carmina: Ovid's Books from Exile* (1983), 11: 'Yet the problem of Ovid's attitude to Augustus cannot be ignored in any examination of the exile poetry. As proponents of the non-political Ovid have observed, the poet did not give major emphasis to imperial themes in his earlier works. The Ovidian concordance reveals that by far the largest number of references to Augustus appear in the books for [*sic*] Tomis. This is not surprising when we remember the main themes of the exile poetry, Ovid's defense of his conduct and appeals for imperial mercy.' Contrast however Williams, *Banished Voices*, 162 (on *Tristia* 2): 'To take sides with the self-caricature of the poet against his caricature of the emperor may be to enter into the spirit of the poem, but it is not criticism.'

and cross swords with such alluring monsters as intentionalism and biographical criticism.

Ovid begins his second book of exile poetry by asking himself why he is having anything to do with literature and books, when it is literature which has caused him to endure such suffering. This division between the author and his work need not occasion particular surprise: in the first poem of *Tristia* 1 Ovid sent his book to Rome, lamenting that this was a journey forbidden to him, while in *Tristia* 3. 1 the entire poem is a monologue spoken by the book. In *Tristia* 2 this dichotomy, which will be a running theme, is brought to our attention at the poem's outset. Consider the following passage (*Trist.* 2. 5–8):[13]

> carmina fecerunt, ut me cognoscere uellet
> omine non fausto femina uirque meo:
> carmina fecerunt, ut me moresque notaret
> iam pridem emissa Caesar ab Arte mea.

My songs have brought about that men and women should wish to know me, which portended nothing good for me. My songs have brought about that Caesar should censure me and my way of life from the *Ars Amatoria* which had already been published.

The language could not be more explicit. His *carmina* ('poems') are the reason for present attitudes to himself. The author is here a passive figure; it is his poems which have independently caused people to wish to know him, and it is his poems which have caused Caesar's response to the *Ars Amatoria*. Elsewhere (*Trist.* 2. 207) Ovid ascribes his downfall to 'carmen et error'; here, in anticipation of the later passage, he gives a fuller picture of the relation between author and text. In particular, notice the shifting role of *me* in these four lines. In the first couplet, Ovid speaks of how his songs have made men and women wish to get to know him. The pairing 'femina uirque' suggests that Ovid has his erotic verse in mind, and here *me* seems synonymous both with the poetry, and with Ovid himself.[14]

---

[13] On the textual difficulties of this passage, see G. Luck, *P. Ovidius Naso. Tristia Band 1* (1967), 14; Heyworth, 'Notes', 139–40.

[14] Compare, for instance, Propertius 1. 7. 13: 'me legat assidue post haec neglectus amator', where *me* stands for the text of Propertius. Note also Ovid, *Ars Amatoria* 1. 2, 'hoc legat et lecto carmine doctus amet', where *me* is found as a variant for *hoc* in some manuscripts. Regardless of whether *me* or *hoc* is the text Ovid wrote, the variant strikingly illustrates a hesitation as to whether or not to equate a text with the author.

Whereas in the first couplet Ovid remarks that his songs have caused people to know him, or his songs, in the next couplet he speaks specifically of his personal experience of Augustus' reaction. There are thus two types of *I* in this passage; what is most striking is that Ovid does not say 'I have been responsible' (on either interpretation of *I*). Instead he uses the third person; it is his poems which are responsible.

This distinction between poet and poetry anticipates the position adopted later in *Tristia* 2. 353-6:

> crede mihi, distant mores a carmine nostro—
> uita uerecunda est, Musa iocosa mea—
> magnaque pars mendax operum est et ficta meorum:
> plus sibi permisit compositore suo.

Believe me, my morals are different from my song—my life is modest, my Muse is playful. The greater part of my works is lying and feigned: it allowed itself more licence than its composer.

Now the whole issue of personae in ancient literature is one which is currently being debated, but, without at this stage entering into the debate, one can at least say that in this passage there is an attempt to draw a distinction between an author and the character of his works. For this type of defence[15] one may compare for instance Catullus' approach to this same distinction between a poet and his works in Catullus 16. 5-6: 'nam castum esse decet pium poetam / ipsum, uersiculos nihil necesse est', 'For a pious poet himself should be chaste, but his verses need not be so at all.'[16] Luck in his commentary notes several similar passages elsewhere in Ovid's exile poetry and in other authors.[17]

A line of enquiry which may perhaps be revealing, however, is an examination of the argument which Ovid uses in reaching the position outlined at *Tristia* 2. 353-6. The poet does not simply pass off without argument the assertion that a poet's work has nothing to

---

[15] Nugent, '*Tristia* 2' 251, speculates that Ovid's claim to personal virtue may glance at Augustus' own immoralities.

[16] On the complexities of Catullus 16 see D. L. Selden, 'Ceveat Lector: Catullus and the Rhetoric of Performance', in R. Hexter and D. L. Selden (eds.), *Innovations of Antiquity* (1992), 461-512.

[17] See e.g. *Trist.* 1. 9. 59-60, 3. 2. 5-6, *Ex Ponto* 2. 7. 47-50, 4. 8. 19-20, Martial 1. 4. 8, 'lasciua est nobis pagina, uita proba', with Citroni's commentary ad loc. and G. Luck, *P. Ovidius Naso. Tristia Band* 2 (1977), 131-2.

do with his personal morality.[18] The passage is the culmination of a complex argument, which is concerned as much with the role of an audience in a text's reception as with the designs of the author. After introducing the twin motifs of *carmen et error*, and declining to speak of the latter (on the grounds that he has no wish to renew Augustus' wounds) at *Tristia* 2. 207-10, Ovid then begins the defence of his *carmen*. The argument begins strikingly with a passage pointing out that Augustus has higher concerns to deal with than poetry (*Trist.* 2. 213-18):[19]

> fas ergo est aliqua caelestia pectora falli?
> et sunt notitia multa minora tua;
> utque deos caelumque simul sublime tuenti
> non uacat exiguis rebus adesse Ioui,
> de te pendentem sic dum circumspicis orbem,
> effugiunt curas inferiora tuas.

Can it therefore be right that heavenly minds are in some way deceived? Indeed there are many things which are beneath your attention; and just as Jove, when he watches over the gods and lofty heaven at the same time, does not have the leisure to be engaged in trivial matters, in the same way more insignificant matters escape your concern, when you survey the world which depends upon you.

Here (and an ironical reading of this passage is possible), Ovid asserts that it is possible for 'caelestia pectora' to be deceived, or tricked, *falli*,[20] a word which opens up the by no means simple possibility of 'misreading'.[21] Ovid continues by reminding the emperor that he has responsibilities for such provinces as Pannonia and Armenia,[22] before concluding this section as follows (*Trist.* 2. 237-40):

[18] See A. Barchiesi, 'Insegnare ad Augusto: Orazio, *Epistole* 2, 1 e Ovidio, Tristia II', *MD* 31 (1993), 149-84, at 176-8.

[19] For comparison with the opening of Horace, *Epist.* 2.1, see Barchiesi, 'Insegnare', Barchiesi, *Il poeta*, 20-1, and Williams, *Banished Voices*, 180-1. See also P. Cutolo, '*Captatio* ed apologia in *Tristia* II', in I. Gallo and L. Nicastri (eds.), *Cultura, poesia, ideologia nell'opera di Ovidio* (1991), 265-86, at 277-8.

[20] John Moles suggests to me the possibility that *falli* may evoke the *Dios Apate* in *Iliad* 14.

[21] The issue of misreading is discussed by Eco, *Interpretation*, 45-88. Eco argues (52) 'that we can accept a sort of Popperian principle according to which if there are no rules that help to ascertain which interpretations are the "best ones", there is at least a rule for ascertaining which ones are "bad"'. This positivism is challenged by R. Rorty, ibid., 89-108.

[22] See Habinek, *Politics*, 151-69, who sees Ovid's representation of Tomis and the Roman frontier in the exile poetry as a discourse of colonization.

mirer in hoc igitur tantarum pondere rerum
te numquam nostros euoluisse iocos?
at si, quod mallem, uacuum tibi forte fuisset,
nullum legisses crimen in Arte mea.

Am I therefore to be surprised that under this burden of mighty matters you
never unrolled my frivolities? But if you by chance had had the leisure,
which I would prefer, you would have read no crime in my *Ars Amatoria*.

In the first place Ovid even suggests that Augustus may never have
had time to read the *Ars Amatoria*, since he was so burdened with the
cares of Empire.[23] Note the emphasis placed on reception here; it is as
if Ovid is ascribing to Augustus the construction of a negative 'reading' of the *Ars Amatoria* without having 'read' the text. Secondly, he
argues, if Augustus had had the leisure to read the *Ars Amatoria*, he
would not have found any *crimen* ('crime') in the *carmen* (poem).[24]
Again the burden of interpretation falls on the reader of the poetry;
instead of saying, 'I have not written a wicked poem', Ovid invites
Augustus to find out for himself its contents and implications.[25]

He continues by conceding that the poems are not worthy to be
read by Augustus, but then maintains that the charge of incitement
to adultery is invalid (*Trist.* 2. 243–6), which then allows him to
quote (with slight adaptation[26]) the lines from the *Ars Amatoria* (1.
31–4) warning married women to keep away from his poetry. Again

---

[23] Nugent, '*Tristia* 2', 250–1, argues that the issue of whether Augustus read the
*Ars Amatoria* is 'a no-win situation proposition for Augustus'.

[24] Barchiesi, *Il poeta*, 22–3, argues that 'Il punto è che, se Augusto avesse avuto
tempo, avrebbe trovato le parole "*nullum* [. . .] *crimen*" nell *Ars*, il *carmen* che per lui è
un *crimen: inque meo nullum carmine crimen erit* (1,34 "e nella mia poesia non ci sarà
alcun capo d'accusa"). L'argomento è circolare (e serpentino). Questo testo non è
incriminabile perché dice a chiare lettere: "Io non sono un testo incriminabile".' See
also Barchiesi, 'Insegnare', 166–7.

[25] Nugent, '*Tristia* 2', 251, detects a different emphasis: 'Thus does Ovid prescribe
Augustus' reading and, with the extended revisionist reading of earlier texts, foist his
own readings upon Augustus. Again Ovid recommends a specific reading of his own
works to Augustus: ' "Just open my books and you'll see what a role you play there,
how I really value you".'

[26] On the alteration of *Ars. Am.* 1. 33, 'nos Venerem tutam concessaque furta
canemus' to 'nil nisi legitimum concessaque furta canemus' (*Trist.* 2. 249) see
Barchiesi, 'Insegnare', 166, who notes on the same page that the alteration to the text
of the *Ars* reinforces the earlier implication that Augustus was not an attentive reader.
One might make the further point that such an alteration itself illustrates the independence of text from author: a text cannot only be misunderstood, but even altered
(although, paradoxically, it is here the author, Ovid, who is altering his own text). See
also Williams, *Banished Voices*, 206–9.

the issue of reception is raised, and Ovid draws attention to the problematic nature of addressing a particular work to particular readers; it is all very well to restrict a work to those who are not married, but anyone can still read the poem. This issue is, of course, relevant to *Tristia 2* itself as well; the work is addressed to Augustus, but what are the likely responses of other readers of the text? This point is made by the poet himself, perhaps because mere quotation of the lines in the *Ars Amatoria* prescribing the readership of the poem was unlikely to suffice as a defence. Ovid gives the argument which would be likely to be used against him (*Trist.* 2. 253–6):

> 'at matrona potest alienis artibus uti,
>     quoque trahat, quamuis non doceatur, habet.'
> nil igitur matrona legat, quia carmine ab omni
>     ad delinquendum doctior esse potest.

'But a matron can make use of skills intended for others, and has something from which she can draw conclusions, although she is not being taught to.' Then let matrons read nothing, because any poem can make them more learned in debauchery.

In the second couplet, the kernel of Ovid's position in *Tristia 2* is revealed. Instead of asserting that the poet's life and his works can be quite different in terms of their moral character, he adopts quite a different position, since he is prepared to challenge that first premise that a poet's work can be morally corrupting. His response is the brilliant assertion that every poem, 'carmine ab omni', can lead to the corruption of a married woman, so that such women are to read nothing at all. Here we see Ovid arguing that it is in fact possible for any such reader to construct her own 'immoral' reading from the text.

The succeeding lines exemplify such readings of poetry, and stress the paramount role of the individual reader (*Trist.* 2. 259–64):

> sumpserit Annales—nihil est hirsutius illis—
>     facta sit unde parens Ilia, nempe leget.
> sumpserit 'Aeneadum genetrix' ubi prima, requiret,
>     Aeneadum genetrix unde sit alma Venus.
> persequar inferius, modo si licet ordine ferri,
>     posse nocere animis carminis omne genus.

She will have picked up the *Annales*—nothing could be more manly than them—and of course she will read how it was that Ilia became a parent.

When she has first picked up 'the mother of the Aeneadae', she will ask how bountiful Venus became the mother of the Aeneadae. I will show below, if only one is permitted to relate it in order, that every kind of poem can corrupt the mind.

Even the most austere literature, such as Ennius' *Annales* (also mentioned at *Trist*. 2. 423–4), or Lucretius' didactic poem can nevertheless contain elements which could be harmful to the reader. Notice again Ovid's habitual interest in the reception of texts: the reader has physically to pick up the books in question; the reader of Lucretius is imagined as asking how it is that Venus can be called the 'mother of the Aeneadae'.[27] There is a slight but important distinction between the first two couplets. In the first couplet, the reader is envisaged simply as passively reading the tale of Ilia and Mars. In the second, however, reading the text involves not mere acceptance of its contents, but questions raised in response to it; the married woman reads the phrase 'Aeneadum genetrix' and then asks about its implications in a parody of mythological curiosity and learning. It is a pleasing irony that it is didactic poetry, a type of poetry which teaches its readers and is hence in a position of authority, which Ovid imagines as producing this more involved and independent response from the reader; the didactic nature of Lucretius' poem itself evokes a *frisson*, since Ovid's 'harmful' work, the *Ars Amatoria*, is also didactic. Lucretius is moreover a peculiarly appropriate example for burlesque in this fashion, since his poem had included in book 4 a celebrated passage on the dangers of love (4. 1037–1287). Indeed, one might even argue that Ovid is parodying one of his own methods in the *Ars*, the technique whereby possible questions from the audience are anticipated. Compare, for instance, the episode in *Ars Amatoria* 1. 375–80 where Ovid responds to an imaginary question

---

[27] The couplet referring to Lucretius also tellingly illustrates the unstable nature of signs and meaning. 'Aeneadum genetrix' in the first line signifies the works of Lucretius, here represented by the opening words. In the second line, the same pair of words literally refers to the 'mother of the Aeneadae' (itself a paradoxical idea, since Aeneas is her son). The shift in meaning between the first and second lines of the couplet mirrors the fluidity and uncertainty of a text's reception; Ovid imagines a reader rebelling and asking awkward questions right at the inception of the Lucretian text. Cf. Barchiesi, *Il poeta*, 22–3, on 'nullum . . . crimen' in *Trist*. 2. 240 and 2. 247–50. On first words of literary works, see S. J. Heyworth, 'Horace's *Ibis*: on the Titles, Unity, and Contents of the *Epodes*', in *PLLS*, 7 (1993), 85–96, at 85–6; P. G. McC. Brown, 'An Interpolated Line of Terence at Cicero, *De finibus* 2. 14', *CQ* 47 (1997), 583–4 with n. 3.

on whether it is a good idea to take his own precepts on winning over the mistress's maid so far as actually to sleep with her.

Ovid then restates his case that every type of poem can be harmful (263-4), before making explicit the obvious argument that everything which can be harmful can of course be beneficial as well (*Trist.* 2. 265-8):

> non tamen idcirco crimen liber omnis habebit:
>   nil prodest, quod non laedere possit idem.
> igne quid utilius? siquis tamen urere tecta
>   comparat, audaces instruit igne manus.

But not for that reason will every book be guilty. Nothing is advantageous, which does not also have the potential to cause harm. What is more useful than fire? Yet if someone is preparing to burn down buildings, he equips his daring hands with fire.

After saying that not every book has *crimen*, Ovid continues by expounding the ambiguous status of various *exempla*. Thus fire is immensely useful, but can be used for the destruction of buildings. Similarly, the medical arts can be both beneficent and malign in their influence, whilst a sword can be put to different uses by travellers and by bandits. The *exempla* illustrate the point that such things as fire possess no intrinsic moral value; such value is assigned to them as a consequence of the use to which they are put; in the same way it is possible for meaning to be determined by a reader. The poet then returns to his true subject matter, the status of literature (*Trist.* 2. 273-6):

> discitur innocuas ut agat facundia causas;
>   protegit haec sontes, inmeritosque premit.
> sic igitur carmen, recta si mente legatur,
>   constabit nulli posse nocere meum.

Eloquence is learned so that it may conduct blameless cases; it protects the guilty and overwhelms the innocent. In the same way, therefore, my poem, it will be agreed, can harm nobody, if it is read with the right mind.

Just as eloquence can be put to good uses in the law courts, so will it be agreed that his poem will not cause any harm, *recta si mente legatur*.[28] Here *recta . . . mente*, which evokes the Stoic phrase ὀρθὸς

---

[28] The Stoic implications of *recta mens* (recalling ὀρθὸς λόγος) are noted by G. Luck, *P. Ovidius Naso. Tristia Band*, 2 (1977), 123, and Williams, *Banished Voices* 164. For

λόγος, as noted by Luck and Williams, does not, I would argue, refer to the process of finding a right or single interpretation of a text, but to the morality of the reader. Ovid does not say that if a person reads a text *recta . . . mente*, he or she will find the true meaning; instead he argues that such a person will not be corrupted. The issue is one of the *consequences* of, and not the nature of, reading. There is a possible objection, which Ovid meets effectively by asserting that the power of his poetry has been much exaggerated anyway (*Trist.* 2. 277-8):

> 'at quasdam uitio.' quicumque hoc concipit, errat,
>     et nimium scriptis arrogat ille meis.

'But a poem corrupts some women.' Whoever thinks this is wrong, and ascribes too much power to my writings.

From here Ovid points out (*Trist.* 2. 279-300) that spectacles and such places as theatres and even temples can nevertheless be places for love;[29] a reader of his works might recall that he had suggested such places as suitable for finding a girl at *Ars Amatoria* 1. 59-100, 3. 387-98.[30] Once again, just as he had envisaged a reader asking how it was that Venus came to be called 'Aeneadum genetrix' in Lucretius, so too does Ovid show the same type of interest in *responses* to phenomena: thus standing in the temple of Jove engenders the thought that the god has had many love affairs with mortal women; similarly, in the temple of Juno, one can reflect on the many rivals ('paelicibus') who caused the goddess pain (*Trist.* 2. 289-92). After other examples of dubious behaviour among the gods, Ovid then reiterates his view that 'omnia peruersas possunt corrumpere mentes: / stant tamen illa suis omnia tuta locis' ('All things can corrupt perverse minds, yet all those things remain safe in their own contexts') in *Tristia* 2. 301-2. The first line of this couplet affirms the point that all things can be dangerous, but Ovid then modifies his position, remarking that nothing need be dangerous if it is in its

---

Ovid's argumentation here, compare also the discussion of good and bad speech at Plato, *Phaedrus* 258d, which commences with a recognition that the writing of speeches is not in itself shameful, and Gorgias' defence of rhetoric as a morally neutral skill at Plato, *Gorgias* 456c6-457c3; see further E. R. Dodds's 1950 commentary on the *Gorgias*, and B. Vickers, *In Defence of Rhetoric* (1988), 84-120.

[29] On this passage see Barchiesi, *Il poeta*, 23-4, Williams, *Banished Voices*, 165, 201-4.
[30] Williams, *Banished Voices*, 202.

proper place, thus allowing himself to renew his claim in the following couplet that the *Ars Amatoria* in any case included a warning that
it was written only for those who were courtesans, *meretrices*. This
claim about place, or context, having a limiting effect on reception is
in any case a spurious one; the discussion of such thoughts spring-
ing to mind in *temples* has already shown this. Reception cannot be
controlled.

It will already have become clear that the argumentation of *Tristia*
2 is shifting and sometimes elusive. Having returned to his defence
that the *Ars Amatoria* in any case included a warning, Ovid now
pursues this motif, pointing out that if a woman enters a place from
which she has been barred by a *sacerdos*, the responsibility for that
act is hers. In itself this argument is without mischief, yet it continues
in much more daring vein (*Trist.* 2. 307-8):

> nec tamen est facinus uersus euoluere mollis;
> multa licet castae non facienda legant.

But it is not however a crime to unroll tender verse. Chaste women may read
of many things which they may not do.

Here the poet draws a distinction not between the morals of the
*author* and his text, but between the morals of the text and its *reader*.
If the reader is a chaste woman, there is no difficulty in her reading
a work which deals with behaviour which she is not to imitate (*non
facienda*). In the ensuing section Ovid illustrates his point with a series
of *exempla* where again the emphasis is on the *response* to particular
sights: thus a matron can behold naked women without being
corrupted, whilst the Vestals are able to behold courtesans. This
allows him to continue by arguing (*Trist.* 2. 313-14) 'at cur in nostra nimia est lasciuia Musa, / curue meus cuiquam suadet amare
liber?' 'But why is there too much licentiousness in my Muse, or why
does my book persuade anyone to love?' Here Ovid not only develops
his argument that it is impossible to argue that a book is morally bad,
but also alludes to the earlier passage (*Trist.* 2. 277-8) where he
warned against ascribing too much efficacy to his poetry.

The sequel is a frivolous confession of repentance, explained in
terms of Ovid's failure to write on various epic subjects (*Trist.* 2.
317-36), such as the Trojan war, Thebes, or even the legendary
Roman past, or the more recent exploits of Augustus.[31] These

---

[31] Ovid's *recusatio* of an epic on Augustus is discussed by Williams, *Banished Voices*,

examples will be significant later on in the book. Ovid explains, however, that his talent was designed for work on the smaller scale (327–8): 'tenuis mihi campus aratur: / illud erat magnae fertilitatis opus', 'I plough a scanty field—that was a task for great fecundity', so that epic projects were beyond him. Unfortunately erotic verse proved to be as congenial to the poet's talent as it was conducive to his downfall. In lines 345–52 he imagines Augustus' argument that he has given instruction in nefarious conduct. The rejoinder, that 'quodque parum nouit, nemo docere potest', 'no one can teach what he knows badly', then leads into an assertion that no husband has had cause to doubt a child's paternity on Ovid's account, which is immediately followed by his exposition, in 353–6, that his poetry is separate from his morals, a passage to which I have already referred. The language of *Tristia* 2. 352 'ut dubius uitio sit pater ille meo', 'so that a father should be uncertain because of my fault', echoes the distinction between Ovid the person and Ovid the poet which occurs at the beginning of *Tristia* 2: *uitio . . . meo* ('my fault') could simultaneously refer to a hypothetical act of adultery committed by the poet himself or the action of another adulterer; in both cases it is, for the sake of argument, envisaged that the woman has been corrupted by his literary work.

In 357–8 Ovid continues in enigmatic vein:[32]

> nec liber indicium est animi, sed honesta uoluptas:
> plurima mulcendis auribus apta feres.

Nor is a book an indication of the mind but an honourable pleasure. You will say many things that are suitable for soothing the ears.

The fact that the book may confer pleasure is not in itself an indication of the author's intent or character. However, there is an oddity in this position, since the present book, *Tristia* 2, is nothing if not an attempt to demonstrate an *indicium animi*, Ovid's intention not to corrupt his readers. The paradox of Ovid's position here is that, in keeping with the distinction in 353 between his morality and his

190–3, who notes the link with *Amores* 2. 1 where Ovid renounces epic (and Jove) in favour of love. See also S. Stabryla, 'In Defence of the Autonomy of the Poetic World (Some Remarks on Ovid's "Tristia" II)', *Hermes*, 122 (1994), 469–78, at 473–4.

[32] In 357, though other manuscripts read *uoluntas* ('will') two manuscripts (EV) have *uoluptas*, a reading favoured by Williams, *Banished Voices*, 170 n. 39 and J. Diggle, 'Notes on Ovid's *Tristia*, Books I–II', *CQ* 30 (1980), 401–19, at 417–18. *uoluptas* seems preferable, since it accords well with 'mulcendis auribus' in 358.

poetry, between *mores* and *carmine nostro*, he argues that one cannot discern the *animus* of an author from his book. However, what Ovid is doing in *Tristia* 2 is precisely to give an 'indication of his mind'.[33] This draws attention to the ironic use of a literary mode as a means for communicating what purports to be biographical information about the state of Ovid's mind.[34]

In the section which follows Ovid then discusses and offers readings of a range of poets. As well as constituting part of his defence, I would argue that these readings are also illustrative of earlier intimations that it is possible for a text to be read in any way the reader wishes. Ovid begins with some simple references to earlier authors, and interprets their characters and lifestyles from their writings. On the theory that poetry is an index of character, Accius the tragedian would then be 'savage' (*atrox*), Terentius would be 'gregarious' (*conuiua*), while the writers of martial epic would be 'aggressive' (*pugnaces*) (*Trist.* 2. 359-60). Yet, curiously enough, if this same principle were to be applied, Ovid in *Tristia* 2 would be contrite and desiring to appease Augustus. Ovid's ostensible concern, however, is a defence of his erotic works, and in the next couplet (*Trist.* 2. 361-2) he makes the obvious point that he is by no means the first poet to have treated the subject of love. The next four lines (*Trist.* 2. 363-6), however, include a deft sleight of hand:

> quid, nisi cum multo Venerem confundere uino,
>     praecepit lyrici Teïa Musa senis?

---

[33] For the legal flavour of *indicium*, note such idioms as *indicium postulare* (to seek pardon by informing) and *indicium profiteri* and *indicium offerre* (to offer information): see *OLD* s.v. *indicium* 2b.

[34] Nugent, ('*Tristia* 2'), 253: 'In the context of Ovid's exilic work, however, the assertion is devasting, for it directly contradicts Ovid's stance throughout the entire corpus of his exilic poetry—namely, that his poetry of exile is a direct reflection of his life in exile. More specifically, the assertion undermines the claim to credibility that this apologia itself might have.' Cf. Williams, *Banished Voices*, 171: 'But Ovid's defence leaves him with a new problem. He defends the *Ars* by appealing to the benefits of a reading which is alive to the disjunction between poet and poetic persona; but he invites us to believe that in lines 353-8 poet and poetic persona are one. His defence can only stand if it is read without the kind of literary sophistication which that defence calls for to vindicate the *Ars*.' The point is also made by Barchiesi, *Il poeta*, 18. The problems of interpreting a text whose author is still living are discussed by Eco, *Interpretation*, 72-88. Typical of his approach is the following observation (73): 'At this point the response of the author must not be used in order to validate the interpretations of his text, but to show the discrepancies between the author's intention and the intention of the text.'

> Lesbia quid docuit Sappho, nisi amare, puellas?
> tuta tamen Sappho, tutus et ille fuit.

What did the Tean Muse of the old lyric poet teach, except the mingling of Venus with much wine? What did Lesbian Sappho teach girls, except how to love? Sappho, however, was safe, he also was safe.

Here, in a complete reversal of his earlier claim that the poet does not impart moral instruction, he alleges that Anacreon and Sappho both gave instruction in love, and nevertheless came to no harm.[35] The argument is all the more striking because Ovid here imparts a didactic purpose (which he had denied in his own poetry) to the non-didactic love poems of Anacreon and Sappho. The same criticism (or judgement) could of course be applied to the *Amores*, to say nothing of the *Ars Amatoria*, actually cast as a didactic poem. Once again we may observe the elusiveness of Ovid's argumentation; here he is concerned with the argument that others wrote love poetry and were unaffected by the practice. It is an especially bold stroke to accuse Sappho and Anacreon of the charge which Ovid has been most keen to rebuff in the earlier part of his argument.

Ovid then continues with Callimachus and Menander (*Trist.* 2. 367–70):

> nec tibi, Battiade, nocuit, quod saepe legenti
> delicias uersu fassus es ipse tuas.
> fabula iucundi nulla est sine amore Menandri,
> et solet hic pueris uirginibusque legi.

Nor, Callimachus, did the fact that you yourself often confessed your love affairs in verse to your reader cause you harm. No play of pleasant Menander is without love, and it is the custom for him to be read by boys and girls.

Once again the poet deftly modifies his previous stances and arguments. In his own case he was anxious to assert that his life was by no means unchaste, despite the contents of his poems (*Trist.* 2. 353–6). Here, however, he wilfully adopts a biographical mode of reception, interpreting Callimachus' poems as confession ('delicias uersu fassus es ipse *tuas*'), a mode of reading which he explicitly rejects for his own poetry. Once again Ovid declines the absolutism of a consistent approach, thus illustrating the open-endedness of

---

[35] Note that an unpunctuated text of 365 allows equal priority to the alternative meaning: 'What did Lesbian Sappho teach except to love girls?'

reception. The couplet on Menander is also shrewdly cast. All of the comedian's works have an amorous element in them, 'but it is the custom for him to be read by boys and girls'. Luck in his commentary notes the similarity with the opening stanza of Horace's third book of *Odes*: 'As priest of the Muses I sing to girls and boys songs not heard before', 'carmina non prius / audita Musarum sacerdos / uirginibus puerisque canto', but declines to make further comment. The echo seems to have two possible effects: on the one hand, it mischievously recalls a solemn passage from Horace and applies it to the comedies of Menander. The second possibility is that it draws attention to an actual similarity between Menander and Horace. Although it is not true to say that every poem by Horace contains erotic elements, Ovid's reminiscence is a reminder that the songs addressed by Horace in book 3 to 'uirginibus puerisque' include not only such weighty works as the six so-called 'Roman odes', but also works on lighter subjects (such as *Odes* 3. 7, 3. 9, 3. 10, 3. 12, 3. 26, 3. 28); the shift in tone from *Odes* 3. 6 to 3. 7 is particularly notable.

In *Tristia* 2. 371–80, Ovid again modifies a position he had adopted earlier. Whereas in 2. 317–36, he was lamenting his failure to write mythological epic on the grounds that such subjects would have been far safer, here Ovid shows that it is possible to offer radical readings even of works such as the *Iliad*.[36] Again I draw attention to the language of evaluation (*Trist.* 2. 371–4):[37]

> Ilias ipsa quid est aliud, nisi adultera, de qua
>     inter amatorem pugna uirumque fuit?
> quid prius est illi flamma Briseidos, utque
>     fecerit iratos rapta puella duces?

What else is the *Iliad* itself, except an adulteress, about whom there was a fight between her lover and her husband? What does it have before the passion felt for Briseis, and how a stolen girl made the generals angry?

Instead of saying 'What is the *Iliad* but a poem *about* an adulteress?', Ovid implies an even deeper level of moral corruption by saying,

---

[36] Williams, *Banished Voices*, 193, suggests that Ovid portrays Homer's epics 'as if they were Hellenistic love-romances'.

[37] Compare Propertius 2. 8. 29–36 for a similarly erotic treatment of the *Iliad*; see also Propertius 2. 1. 49–50; D. T. Benediktson, 'Propertius' elegiacization of Homer', *Maia*, 37 (1985), 17–26. See also S. Hinds, 'Essential Epic: Genre and Gender from Macer to Statius', in M. Depew and D. Obbink (eds.), *Matrices of Genre: Authors, Canons and Society* (Cambridge, Mass., 2000), 221–44, at 229.

'What is the *Iliad* but an adulteress, about whom there was a fight between her lover and her husband?' (Note that *Ilias* can mean 'Trojan woman' as well as 'Iliad', and that in the phrase 'pugna uirumque', which superficially recalls Virgil's 'arma uirumque' from *Aen.* I. I, 'uirumque' here means husband, not man). This approach gives primacy to the whole Trojan legend, rather than the *Iliad*'s own declared subject, the anger of Achilles, here dealt with in the second couplet. Even the 'anger of Achilles' does not escape alteration. In Homer, we hear first of all of the anger of Achilles, at the beginning of the poem, and then hear of the quarrel between Agamemnon and Achilles, which is then followed by Agamemnon's decision to console himself for the loss of Chryseis by taking Briseis from Achilles. Ovid's reference to the opening of the *Iliad* humorously reverses the sequence of the epic, where we hear of anger as the subject, and then hear of Achilles' *achos* (pain) at the loss of Briseis (*Iliad* I. I88), a pain which is as much connected with the dishonour incurred by Achilles as the loss of Briseis; Ovid however asks 'What comes before the passion felt for Briseis?', as if that passion is the very subject of the epic.

In the four lines on the *Iliad*, Ovid offered a reading where love was the principal theme of the work. Similarly with the *Odyssey* (*Trist.* 2. 375–80):

> aut quid Odyssea est nisi femina propter amorem,
>   dum uir abest, multis una petita procis?
> quis nisi Maeonides Venerem Martemque ligatos
>   narrat, in obsceno corpora prensa toro?
> unde nisi indicio magni sciremus Homeri
>   hospitis igne duas incaluisse deas?

Or what is the *Odyssey*, except one woman sought on account of love by many suitors while her husband is away? Who but Homer tells of Venus and Mars bound together, their bodies caught in the shameless bed? How, except through the testimony of great Homer, would we know that two goddesses grew hot with passion for their guest?

Just as the *Iliad* was an adulteress, and not about one, so too is the *Odyssey*, in pointed refutation of its actual title and opening word (Ἄνδρα, 'man', *Od.* I. I), 'a *woman* sought on account of love by many suitors while her husband is away'. Here one is reminded of wives in love poetry who are similarly sought, and have, or have not, given way.[38] Even if one wished to assign primacy to Penelope in the *Odyssey*, a more conventional reading of the epic might have concluded that the poem was 'a woman who *resisted* many suitors, while her husband was away'.[39] Ovid does not go so far as to say 'resisted', and the moral status of Penelope is not made explicit. The examples of the *Odyssey* and *Iliad* show how the reception of a text is not in the hands of the author; the type of reading offered here, burlesque though it may be, demonstrates the power of a reader.

In 377–8, Ovid then mentions the tale of Ares and Aphrodite, which appears in *Odyssey* 8. 266–366. The couplet is a subtle one. In the first place, there is an immediate rejoinder to Ovid's question, 'Who but Homer narrated the tale?' The answer is that it is not Homer but Demodocus, the blind Phaeacian singer, who gives the story, which is merely reported by Homer; Ovid thus assigns blame to Homer, even though Homer did not present the tale in his own person. Homer's representation of Demodocus' song about Aphrodite and Ares becomes a moral failing, and the same is true for Homer's testimony of the passions of Calypso and Circe for Odysseus (*Trist.* 2. 379–80):

> unde nisi indicio magni sciremus Homeri
> hospitis igne duas incaluisse deas?

How, except through the testimony of great Homer, would we know that two goddesses grew hot with passion for their guest?

There is a pleasing irony in the language here. *indicio . . . Homeri* of course refers to evidence supplied by Homer, but *indicio* also recalls *Tristia* 2. 357, 'nec liber indicium est animi'. Ovid of course rejects the idea that a book's morals are those of its author, but if one does accept the notion, then the amours of Circe and Calypso are related *indicio . . . Homeri*, 'through a revelation of Homer'. In other words, Homer's narratives of Circe and Calypso could, on such a theory of literature and morality, be considered as evidence for his character.[40]

---

[38] Cf. e.g. Propertius 3. 12, Horace, *O.* 3. 7 and 10, Ovid, *Am.* 3. 4. 23–4.

[39] Note that Agamemnon, at *Odyssey* 24. 196–8 predicts that the immortals will ensure *Penelope's* lasting fame in a song. There have been several recent treatments of the *Odyssey* centred on Penelope: see e.g. M. A. Katz, *Penelope's Renown: Meaning and Indeterminacy in the Odyssey* (1991), N. Felson-Rubin, *Regarding Penelope: From Character to Poetics* (1994).

[40] Compare Hermesianax *fr.* 7. 27–34 Powell for an erotic interpretation of Homer's biography on the basis of his poems.

After demonstrating the possibilities for erotic reinterpretation of Homer that are open to a reader,[41] Ovid shifts his attention (381–410) to the genre of tragedy, and points out (382) that it always contains the 'materiam . . . amoris', illustrating his case with such examples as Hippolytus, Canace, Pelops, Medea, Tereus, Thyestes, Scylla, Clytemnestra and Aegisthus, Bellerophon, Hermione, Atalanta, Cassandra, Danae, Andromeda, Semele, Haemon (the beloved of Antigone), Alcmena, Admetus, Theseus, Protesilaus, Iole, Deidameia, Deianeira, Hylas, the *Iliacusque puer* (either Ganymede or Troilus), concluding breathlessly as follows (*Trist.* 2. 407–8):[42]

> tempore deficiar, tragicos si persequar ignes,
> uixque meus capiet nomina nuda liber.

I will run out of time, if I run through the loves of tragedy, and my book will scarcely contain the bare names.

Tragedy is an ingenious genre for Ovid to use. The erotic nature of many of its plots could be denied by nobody. Nevertheless, tragedy reminds us of what the poet does in his discussion of epic, the appropriation of high genres into the realms of love poetry.

For the moment, however, the discussion continues with lesser works, such as the Milesian fables of Aristides, Eubius' shadowy work on the methods required for procuring abortion, to say nothing of more explicitly pornographic works such as the *Sybaritica* of Hemitheon of Sybaris (*Trist.* 2. 413–18):

> iunxit Aristides Milesia crimina secum,
> pulsus Aristides nec tamen urbe sua est.
> nec qui descripsit corrumpi semina matrum,
> Eubius, inpurae conditor historiae,
> nec qui composuit nuper Sybaritica, fugit,
> nec quae concubitus non tacuere suos.

---

[41] Williams, *Banished Voices*, 193–4, offers a different emphasis, seeing these rereadings of Homer as simply being Ovid's reply to Augustus' reading of Ovid's poetry: 'If Augustus has been critically naive and one-sided in his evaluation of the *Ars Amatoria*, then Ovid can be equally one-sided and simplistic in his assessment of the Homeric poems, as well as of Greek tragedy and the poets he mentions in lines 363–470.'

[42] Williams, *Banished Voices*, 198, interprets this list as a reminder to Augustus that 'poetry can immortalise persons other than the poet himself'. Ovid's characteristic overstating of his case in *Tristia* 2 with sheer weight of examples is noted by Williams, *Banished Voices*, 194.

Aristides joined together the Milesian crimes, but he was not, however, exiled from his own city. Nor did Eubius, who wrote on abortions, the writer of an impure enquiry, go into exile, nor the author of the recent *Sybaritica*, nor the women who did not keep quiet about their own love-making.

The effect of this rather odd sequence of works listed by Ovid after his discussion of tragedy is a disarming one; it is almost as if he gives the impression of scraping the barrel in a search for works which have love as their subject. Aristides, the author of Milesian fables, who was not exiled, gives an ironic contrast with that other Aristides, Aristides the Just, who was ostracized. Mention of Eubius (which one suspects would not have been especially tactful given Augustus' concern to encourage larger families), and then works which were downright pornographic seems in fact to be a weak argument, since Ovid seems to be comparing himself with works much more dubious even than his own *Ars Amatoria*. But before leaving such Greek authors, it is worth noting the innocuous transition from them (*Trist.* 2. 419-20):

> suntque ea doctorum monumentis mixta uirorum,
> muneribusque ducum publica facta patent.

And these works are mixed up with the memorials of learned men, and have become publicly available due to the generosity of leading men.

This reminds us that such works are readily available in the libraries which have been endowed for the public; the most notable example was of course Augustus' Palatine library. There is an implicit contrast with the treatment which Ovid fears will be meted out to his *Tristia* in *Tristia* 1. 1. 69-98 where he advises his work not to hope to find a place on the Palatine; the same motif can also be found in *Tristia* 3. 1 as well. Moreover *muneribusque ducum* is a pointed reminder that leading men, including Augustus, have themselves been involved in the dissemination of such texts; it is as if the blame does not just lie upon the head of an author. *Publica facta patent* too stresses the role of reception, the need for an audience to exist for such poetry, as well as hinting that there may well be a considerable demand; one recalls that *Tristia* 2 began with the poet remarking on the manner in which he was known to men and women because of his poetry (5-6).

Now to the Latin authors and Ovid's readings of them. He starts by mentioning Ennius and Lucretius for their martial and cosmological poetry, a seemingly innocuous beginning.[43] However *ut* clauses in lines 423-6 on these authors lead to the *sic* which introduces four lines on Catullus and his poetry (427-30). Again, the detail of the language is important; the *ut* clauses followed by the *sic* clauses are a strikingly simple, yet effective means to hint at the parity and equivalence shared by the two forms of poetry. We have already seen how Ovid annexed tragedy to the realm of the erotic; now, by a different tactic, he increases the respectability of amorous writing by suggesting that it is purely a difference of interest and subject matter which distinguishes the work of a Catullus from that of an Ennius or a Lucretius. Moreover, the implied similarity further enforces the points previously made by Ovid both about annalistic epic and Lucretius' poem (259-62), where he drew attention to such erotic elements as Ilia and the opening phrase of Lucretius, 'Aeneadum genetrix'.[44]

Lines 429-30 refer to Catullus' love poetry, 'in quibus ipse suum fassus adulterium est', 'in which he confessed his own adultery', *suum* again emphasizing an actual coincidence between the biography of the poet and the contents of his poetry. In the ensuing list of Roman love poets which follows the reflexive adjective is similarly used of Calvus, 'detexit uariis qui sua furta modis' (*Trist.* 2. 432), and Varro of Atax (*Trist.* 2. 440), 'non potuit Veneris furta tacere suae'. The point is simple: this draws attention to poets whose scandalous lives and loves have informed their own poetry. Ovid, on the other hand, has already established a contrast between his personal morality and the conduct described in his amatory works.[45] One may make the further point that Ovid in his exile poetry goes to great lengths to heighten the sense of his personal morality by writing not about Corinna or some other mistress, but about his wife, previously not mentioned in his poetry. Her regular appearances in the exile poetry can in part be seen as an attempt by Ovid to demonstrate his own virtues—the poems addressed to his wife show an exemplary form of married life and fidelity, and though she did not accompany him into exile, a typical *exemplum* of marital steadfastness, on the grounds

---

[43] The ironic aspects of Ovid's presentation of Ennius and Lucretius are perceptively discussed by Barchiesi, *Il poeta*, 15-18.

[44] Barchiesi, *Il poeta*, 16-17.

[45] Note also Ovid's earlier account of his balanced and moderate lifestyle (*Trist.* 2. 89-116), discussed by Williams, *Banished Voices*, 162-3.

that she could do more for him by working for his return in Rome, Ovid is nevertheless keen to portray her as the equal of such heroines as Penelope, who had patiently endured their husbands' absences; for this, see e.g. *Trist.* 1. 6. 19–22, 5. 14. 35–40, *Ex Ponto* 3. 1. 105–13. Mention of Roman love poets who had written about their love affairs stands in pointed contrast to Ovid's presentation of his own private life in the *Tristia*, where he is able to enjoy the reflected glory of his wife's pious devotion.[46]

The remaining poets mentioned in lines 427–46 reinforce the argument, though one may pick out such details as the implication of personal immorality in such phrases as 'Cinnaque procacior Anser' (*Trist.* 2. 435). Note, however, that once again the direction of Ovid's argument has shifted. Whereas he began his account of Greek love poets by pointing out that Anacreon and Sappho came to no harm as a result of their compositions, it becomes apparent in lines 445–6 that Ovid is not interested in a mere enumeration of Latin love poets; the example he chooses, Gallus, is a curious one, since Gallus did incur the displeasure of his imperial master and indeed committed suicide. What does Ovid have to say of him? (*Trist.* 2. 445–6):

> non fuit opprobrio celebrasse Lycorida Gallo.
> sed linguam nimio non tenuisse mero.

Nor was it a disgrace for Gallus to have celebrated Lycoris, although it was a disgrace not to have held his tongue under the influence of excessive wine.

The curiously negative language 'non fuit opprobrio' seems to draw attention to Gallus' punishment; Augustus is reminded of a poet whom he did not punish on poetic grounds.[47] The enigmatic second line of the couplet seems to set even Gallus' offence in a trivial light (compare Ovid's reference to 'temerati crimen amici' at *Am.* 3. 9. 63), perhaps awkwardly suggesting a parallel for Ovid's *error* of sight, which supposedly was a contributory factor in his fall.

The *frisson* engendered by the mention of Gallus is immediately emphasized in the following lines (*Trist.* 2. 447–64) which move on

---

[46] Cf. R. G. M. Nisbet, ' "Great and Lesser Bear" (Ovid *Tristia* 4. 3)', *JRS* 72 (1982), 49–56, at 56: 'Most curiously of all, and surely deliberately, he [Ovid] professes an Augustan ideal of marriage, even if the celestial pattern is marred by the imperfections of earth.'

[47] On Gallus' gossip about Augustus, see Dio Cassius 53. 23. 5, J. -P. Boucher, *Caius Cornélius Gallus* (1966), 49–54.

from Gallus, a love poet who caused no offence in his non-didactic poetry but was punished on other grounds, to Tibullus, here represented as a didactic poet of love, an exaggeration of the pose of *praeceptor amoris* which is found in the elegiac poets. Tibullus stands in contrast to Gallus not just because of his survival, but also because he actually, as Ovid represents him, gives instruction, as opposed to description of love. The poem of Tibullus to which Ovid is alluding is Tibullus 1. 6, where the poet suspects that Delia has betrayed him with another. In *Tristia* 2. 447-58, Ovid incorporates, in some places with extremely close echoes, motifs from Tibullus 1. 6, a poem where Tibullus upbraids a *mari complaisant*. The presentation of the poem is, however, quite different from Tibullus', which despite its cynical premise, is, if it is didactic, imparting lessons from which the wronged husband may benefit: Tibullus, in a jokingly confessional mood, admits some of the tricks of the trade to the husband. Ovid however uses the poem in quite a different way. Note especially the following couplet (*Trist.* 2. 449-50):

> fallere custodes idem docuisse fatetur,
>     seque sua miserum nunc ait arte premi.

The same poet tells of teaching how to deceive guardians, and says that now he is wretchedly overwhelmed by his own skill.

As has been noted by Barchiesi and Williams, this seems a neat rewriting of Tibullus 1. 6. 9-10:

> ipse miser docui, quo posset ludere pacto
>     custodes: heu heu nunc premor arte mea.

I myself taught how one could beguile guardians: alas, alas, now I am overwhelmed by my own skill.

But there is a difference.[48] Tibullus' lesson to Delia is not explicitly said by him to have been couched in a literary form, and may be regarded as part of the fiction of the poem. Ovid, by contrast, himself presented such instruction to his mistress in a literary form (*Am.* 1. 4), so that the charge against Tibullus would in any case fall on

---

[48] On Ovid's use of Tibullus 1. 6 see Barchiesi, 'Insegnare', 171-2; Williams, *Banished Voices*, 195-6. In a curiously biographical moment Williams argues (195) as follows: 'It is not too fanciful to believe that Tibullus' telling complaint *heu heu nunc premor arte mea* (1. 6. 10) is what first led Ovid to select the poem as eminently suitable for reproduction in *Tristia* 2.'

himself. But there is more. In his treatment of Tibullus, Ovid is applying the same criteria which he rejected in *Tristia* 2. 353-6, where he
drew a distinction between a poet's moral life and his poetic output.
Here, with Tibullus, Ovid brilliantly contrives to have both sides of
the argument: Tibullus the poet is found guilty of morally corrupt
teaching in his poems, on the basis of biographical evidence which is
itself gathered from Tibullus' poetry. The evidence that Tibullus
assumed a *poetic* didactic role is gleaned neither from the poetry of
Tibullus nor from other evidence pertaining to his life, but Ovid's
*docuisse fatetur* implies that Tibullus was all these things anyway.
Moreover the passage also has implications with regard to the theme
of reception: the anecdote about Tibullus illustrates that poet's
failure to control the reception of his own text, and his inability to
prevent it being read and used in a way which was not to his own
advantage.

Similarly a couplet relating to Propertius (*Trist.* 2. 465-6):

> inuenies eadem blandi praecepta Properti:
> destrictus minima nec tamen ille nota est.

You will find the precepts of beguiling Propertius are the same: but he was
not affected with even the smallest mark of censure.

Once again the allegation of *praecepta*, actual teaching and instruction. And indeed, Propertius did express the wish that he would be
read by neglected lovers (1. 7. 13), 'me legat assidue post haec
neglectus amator', but he is nevertheless not a teacher of love on
quite the same scale as Ovid.[49]

Mention of Propertius, and Tibullus before him, allows Ovid to
return to his own role as a poet, and to affirm his canonical status
within the history of Roman poetry (*Trist.* 2. 467-70):

> his ego successi, quoniam praestantia candor
> nomina uiuorum dissimulare iubet.
> non timui, fateor, ne, qua tot iere carinae,
> naufraga seruatis omnibus una foret.

I followed these poets, since kindness tells me to hide the names of those
currently alive. I confess that I did not fear that there would be one shipwreck where so many ships had sailed, where everyone else had been saved.

---

[49] On the didactic elements in Propertius, see A. L. Wheeler, 'Propertius as
Praeceptor Amoris', *CPh* 5 (1910), 28-40.

Ovid's treatment of Tibullus and Propertius has two functions, as now emerges. On the one hand, he associates himself with their love elegies (a type of composition which he himself essayed), and on the other hand, by misrepresenting their compositions as being more didactic than they really are, he is able to argue that such writings did not result in their punishment. More striking is the first couplet of the passage I have just quoted, where Ovid refrains from naming any contemporary poets, ostensibly on the grounds that he needs to hide them (in keeping with his general practice of concealing names in the *Tristia*, if not the *Epistulae ex Ponto*). However, the couplet also serves another purpose; it is a reminder that Ovid is not the only poet of his type—there are, indeed, others of his kind writing in Rome. *Servatis omnibus* ('Everyong else had been saved') in the second couplet makes the same point even more insistently.

And indeed, Ovid continues, just as there have been those who have written of love with impunity, so other dubious activities have received attention: as is well known, the list of *artes* and games begins provocatively with dice (*Trist.* 2. 471-92), a pastime dear to Augustus (Suetonius, *Div. Aug.* 71).[50]

After observing (*Trist.* 2. 495-6) that out of so many poets he is the sole example 'quem sua perdiderit Musa', 'whom his own Muse destroyed', Ovid continues by arguing that such forms as the mime, which frequently contain adulterous plots, are tolerated, and, with Ovid's typical interest in reception, watched by all classes and ages (*Trist.* 2. 501-2):

> nubilis hos uirgo matronaque uirque puerque
> spectat, et ex magna parte senatus adest.

These mimes are watched by marriageable girls, married women, men and boys, and most of the Senate is there.

After pointing out that a spectacle may be even more corrupting than something which is heard, Ovid suddenly points out Augustus' own role (*Trist.* 2. 509-16):

---

[50] On the link between games and poetic *lusus* see Williams, *Banished Voices*, 204-5, who notes the appearance of gambling in the *Ars Amatoria*. On the whole passage see also J. Gómez Pallarès, 'Sobre Ovidio, *Tristia* II, 471-492', *Latomus*, 52 (1993), 372-85, who interprets (380-1) the reference to poems written on 'fucandi cura coloris' (*Trist.* 2. 487) as an allusion to Ovid's own *Medicamina faciei femineae*.

> inspice ludorum sumptus, Auguste, tuorum:
>   empta tibi magno talia multa leges.
> haec tu spectasti spectandaque saepe dedisti—
>   maiestas adeo comis ubique tua est—
> luminibusque tuis, totus quibus utitur orbis,
>   scaenica uidisti lentus adulteria.
> scribere si fas est imitantes turpia mimos,
>   materiae minor est debita poena meae.

Look at the expenditure on your spectacles, Augustus; you'll read that many such things have been bought by you at a high price. You have often looked on these things, and put them on to be looked at—your gentle majesty is indeed everywhere—and with your eyes, which the whole world makes use of, you have unconcernedly beheld adulteries on stage. If it is right to compose mimes which imitate shameful conduct, a lesser punishment is needed for my material.

Here Ovid implicitly puts Augustus in the role of both author and audience of his own spectacles in the memorable line 'haec tu spectasti spectandaque saepe dedisti'. Of course, on the superficial level, there is an element of daring in these lines, since he is associating Augustus with adulterous spectacles in the theatres, and there is a tradition of Augustus himself as a notorious adulterer (Suetonius, *Div. Aug.* 69). *Lentus* too strikes a chord, suggesting the lingering pleasure of an emperor in such scenes.[51] More significant than all this, however, is the fact that Augustus is open to censure either on the grounds which the poet represents the emperor as using against him (putting temptation in the way of others), or in Ovid's terms, because Augustus is a spectator of something which is immoral. This passage is a good example of the complexities in examining Ovid's attitudes to Augustus, even in a poem which is ostensibly an attempt to win over the emperor's clemency.

*Tristia* 2 often recapitulates material; his comments on the effects of looking at visual images in *Tristia* 2. 521-8 need not detain us. However, immediately afterwards, Ovid returns to the theme of poetry, repeating in *Tristia* 2. 529-32 his own inability to write epic. This, however, is at once followed by the most powerful literary

---

[51] For *lentus* in a sexual (but metaphorical) context, cf. Catullus 28. 9-10: 'o Memmi, bene me ac diu supinum / tota ista trabe lentus irrumasti'. Cutolo, '*Captatio*', 281-2 with n. 38, sees a link with Virgil's description of Tityrus as 'lentus in umbra' (*Ecl.* 1. 4), with the intriguing possibility of a contrast between Augustus, linked to Tityrus, and Ovid, compared implicitly with the exiled Meliboeus.

subversion in the whole poem, a triumphant interpretation of the *Aeneid* in erotic terms (*Trist.* 2. 533–6):[52]

> et tamen ille tuae felix Aeneidos auctor
> contulit in Tyrios arma uirumque toros,
> nec legitur pars ulla magis de corpore toto,
> quam non legitimo foedere iunctus amor.

And yet that fortunate author of your *Aeneid* brought arms and the man into Tyrian beds, and no part from the whole work is more read than love joined in an illegitimate union.

The pointed possessive *tuae* heightens the sense of an *ad hominem* criticism of Augustus.[53] In the second line, *arma uirumque*, the opening of the *Aeneid*, is humourously juxtaposed with 'in Tyrios . . . toros', referring to Aeneas' dalliance with Dido at Carthage.[54] Even more weighty, however, are the implications of the second couplet, where Ovid, returning to the theme of reception, makes the damning point that *Aeneid* 4 and its narrative of Dido's passion for Aeneas is the most popular part of the *Aeneid*.[55] Once again Ovid draws attention to the independence of the reader and the possibilities of interpretation which are open to all, his most potent literary example, the *Aeneid*, reminding us that there are many who only read it in portions.[56]

---

[52] For Ovid's use of the *Aeneid* in the *Metamorphoses*, see e.g. Galinsky, *Ovid's Metamorphoses*, 217–51; J. B. Solodow, *The World of Ovid's Metamorphoses* (1988), 110–56.

[53] Cf. Barchiesi, *Il poeta*, 18: 'L'*Eneide* prediletta dal principe e appropriata dal discorso augusteo (*tuae*) ha portato fortuna a Virgilio, *felix* perché opposto a Ovidio che scrive *tristia* per colpa dell' *Ars amandi*; eppure anche li c'è una storia d'amore di un certo tipo. La legge della pertinenza, il *decorum*, è stata violata perché l'epica, fattasi impura, potesse aprirsi a un tema erotico che dona successo e popolarità a Virgilio.' Cutolo '*Captatio*', 283, sees in this passage of the *Tristia* an allusion to Horace, *Epist.* 2. 1. 245–7: 'at neque dedecorant tua de se iudicia atque / munera, quae multa dantis cum laude tulerunt, / dilecti tibi Vergilius Variusque poetae'. On the generic implications of this passage, see Hinds, 'Essential Epic', 230–1.

[54] For reworkings of *arma uirumque* in Ovid's works, see Barchiesi, *Il poeta*, 5–14, 25–6. Ovid's 'toros' recalls Aeneas speaking his narrative of his wanderings 'toro . . . ab alto' (Virgil, *Aen.* 2. 2), and Dido's dying words, spoken 'os impressa toro' (*Aen.* 4. 659).

[55] For the popularity of Dido, see Galinsky, *Ovid's Metamorphoses*, 248, who also notes that Ovid treats the episode only briefly in the *Metamorphoses*.

[56] Note that Augustus himself is recorded as having heard readings of portions of the *Aeneid* (*Vita Donati* 32); cf. Ovid's own suggestion (*Trist.* 2. 557–60, discussed above) that Augustus arrange to have the panegyric passage at the end of the *Metamorphoses* read to him as an excerpt. Note also J. Masters, *Poetry and Civil War in Lucan's Bellum Civile* (1992), 222, on Vacca's account of Lucan's recitation to Nero:

What then are the implications of *Tristia* 2? What insights into the
reading of poetry does it offer?

In the first place I would wish to emphasize Ovid's elusiveness, and
willingness to deviate from his own lines of argument. As I hope to
have shown, *Tristia* 2, though it argues a general defence, cannot be
pinned down, since Ovid is constantly changing his own criteria.
Thus he gives us in *Tristia* 2. 353-6 a typical argument that a poet's
morals should not be judged according to those exhibited in his
works, yet both in terms of other poets, such as Catullus and Calvus,
and in terms of himself, Ovid is inconsistent, since he regards other
love poets as putting their own lives into their poetry, while his claim
that a book is not an *indicium animi*, is refuted by his own attempts in
a literary setting to show an *indicium animi* of his own to Augustus.

A point which does emerge from the text, however, is the liberation of the audience.[57] On the one hand, this is a liberation from the
author, and a recognition that an author cannot tell his audience
how they are to interpret a text.[58] Thus Ovid is constantly drawing
our attention to the process of reception. In the example I have just
mentioned, he shows how a selective reading of *Aeneid* 4 is possible,
one that indeed is so selective as to ignore the rest of the poem; one
may compare the even more selective 'reading' of the *Ars Amatoria*
which Ovid ascribes to Augustus, a reading dependent on the

'Lucan may indeed have published or recited three books in advance of the rest, pre-
cisely *because* he was conscious of the fact that Virgil had done similarly with the
Aeneid.' On Augustus' literary tastes, see Suetonius, *Div. Aug.* 89; R. Syme, *The Roman
Revolution* (1939), 460, 484-5; Galinsky, *Ovid's Metamorphoses*, 211-12; Williams,
*Banished Voices*, 181.

[57]  On the audience of *Tristia* 2 itself, see T. Wiedemann, 'The Political Background
to Ovid's *Tristia* 2', *CQ* 25 (1975), 264-71, at 271, who makes the important point
that *Tristia* 2's readership extends beyond the notional addressee of the poem,
Augustus, and suggests that the poem 'was not intended for Augustus' eyes at all; it
was meant to influence the circle of educated Roman aristocrats to whom Ovid's other
poems from Tomoi were addressed, and Ovid hoped that *they* would be the ones who,
recognizing the absurdity of Augustus' grounds for exiling Ovid, would do their best
to see that he was recalled'.

[58]  For discussion of the idea that a text can simultaneously be read in two ways, see
Demetrius of Phalerum, *De elocutione* 291, with Ahl, 'Art', 195; Otis, *Ovid*, 305;
Barchiesi, *Il poeta*, 21; Williams, *Banished Voices*, 157-8; Hinds, 'Generalising', 25: 'If
he [Ovid] was subversive in his writing (as I believe he was), how could he possibly
proceed but by indirection and nuance? In any but the most powerful or the most reckless of Romans, publicly voiced anti-Augustanism must needs be a rhetoric of
ambiguity and innuendo. Every passage ever written by Ovid about Augustus admits
of a non-subversive reading but that is not in itself a refutation of Ovidian subversion.'

emperor not having read the text and on an enemy of Ovid's giving a misleading account of it to Augustus (*Trist.* 2. 237-8, 2. 77-8). Similarly, Ovid's account of the process of interpretation of Lucretius' 'Aeneadum genetrix' takes no account of Lucretius' intentions when using the phrase; what matters is that a reader may be moved to speculate on how it was that Venus became the mother of the Aeneadae.

But Ovid does not just imply that the reader is independent of the author.[59] In effect he posits another type of independence as well, independence from external forces such as the emperor. Instead of offering the defence, or assertion, that Ovid's work would survive anything (cf. the end of the *Metamorphoses* for this, and the extraordinary assertion in *Tristia* 3. 7. 47-8 that Augustus has no power over his *ingenium*[60]), Ovid adopts a different, but equally potent tactic, implying that it is not possible for Augustus to control interpretation.[61] Thus even a temple, perhaps one of the ones restored by

---

[59] Note that Ovid even countenances the possibility that the *Tristia* themselves may give offence to a reader at *Trist.* 1. 1. 22 (addressed to his book): 'ne, quae non opus est, forte loquare, caue.' Ovid's despatch of his book to Rome without him in *Trist.* 1. 1 can be compared with the discussion in Plato, *Phaedrus* 275d of the defencelessness of the written word. Note also the language of control used by Eco, *Interpretation*, 83, in discussing his failure to prevent interpretations of the title of his novel, *Foucault's Pendulum*, as a reference to Michel Foucault, despite the fact that the pendulum of the title was the work of Léon Foucault: 'But the pendulum invented by Léon was the hero of my story and I could not change the title: thus I hoped that my Model Reader would not try to make a superficial connection with Michel. I was to be disappointed; many smart readers did so. The text is there, and perhaps they are right: maybe I am responsible for a superfical joke; maybe the joke is not that superficial. I do not know. *The whole affair is by now out of my control.*'

[60] *Trist.* 3. 7. 47-8: 'ingenio tamen ipse meo comitorque fruorque: / Caesar in hoc potuit iuris habere nihil.' Compare Tacitus' comments on the folly of imperial bookburning (*Ag.* 2. 1-2, *Ann.* 4. 35. 5). For censorship during Augustus' reign, see Seneca, *Contr.* 10 pr. 4-5 (on T. Labienus), Dio Cassius 56. 27. 1 (anonymous pamphlets), Suetonius, *Caligula* 16, Tacitus, *Ann.* 1. 72 (Cassius Severus), Suetonius, *Div. Aug.* 36 (ending of publication of the *acta senatus*). Though Syme, *Roman Revolution*, 486-7, refers to 'stern measures of repression against noxious literature' towards the end of Augustus' reign, there is perhaps a danger of overestimating the nature and extent both of such literary and intellectual opposition to Augustus and of the emperor's responses; see now K. A. Raaflaub and L. J. Samons, II, 'Opposition to Augustus', in K. A. Raaflaub and M. Toher (eds.), *Between Republic and Empire: Interpretations of Augustus and his Principate* (1990), 417-54, at 436-47, who rightly draw attention to the ancient evidence for Augustus' lenience in such matters. As Syme notes, the *Ars Amatoria* was not suppressed. See also M. Citroni, *Poesia e lettori in Roma antica* (1995), 431-5, 440-2.

[61] One might, however, contrast the opening poem of the third book of the *Tristia*, where his book describes its failure to gain admission to the temple libraries of Rome

the emperor, can lead a woman to improper thoughts; similarly even
Augustus' *Aeneid, tuae* . . . *Aeneidos,* can be read in a fashion which
neglects everything except the tale of Dido and Aeneas in *Aeneid* 4.
The possessive adjective *tuae,* suggesting Augustus' control over the
*Aeneid,* is introduced at the very moment where the emperor's failure
to control the reception of perhaps the most Augustan text, Virgil's
*Aeneid,* is also demonstrated.[62]

Thus *Tristia 2* is important not only as Ovid's defence of his own
poetry. As I hope to have shown there are a number of inconsistencies in his argument, inconsistencies that perhaps represent weakness,[63] but a kind of elusive and paradoxical weakness; Ovid uses the
poem to assert his own mastery not just as a poet but also as a reader:
hence the brilliant series of 'readings' of various texts which he offers.
Undoubtedly there are other confrontational strands in the argument, such as the cheeky reference to Augustus' role as the giver of
corrupting *ludi* and a player of dice, which seem to criticize the
emperor. What I hope to have shown, however, is that that confrontation hinges on Ovid's interest in the reception of texts, and the
conferring of power on readers rather than authors.[64] If Ovid is
challenging the emperor in *Tristia 2,* under the guise of attempting to
appease his wrath, we would do well to remember that he is conscious of the role of his readers as well.

(*Trist.* 3. 1. 59–80). The book, however, ends up in private hands: perhaps a more
dangerous form of reception? Cf. F. Kermode, 'Freedom and Interpretation', in B.
Johnson (ed.), *Freedom and Interpretation: The Oxford Amnesty Lectures 1992* (1993),
46–68, at 46: 'There is obviously a close relation between liberty of interpretation and
political liberty in general.'

[62] Ancient rhetorical theory (in Demetrius of Phalerum and in Quintilian) of
ambiguity as a mode to be used when addressing tyrants is usefully discussed by Ahl,
'Art', 186–92; Williams, *Banished Voices,* 159–60. See also M. Dewar, 'Laying it on
with a Trowel: the Proem to Lucan and Related Texts', *CQ* 44 (1994), 199–211, for
a sceptical response to ironic readings of Lucan's opening address to Nero.

[63] See further S. G. Owen, *P. Ovidi Nasonis. Tristium Liber Secundus* (1924), 55;
Wiedemann, 'Political Background', 271; Nugent, '*Tristia,* 2', 243–4. Note however
the verdict of R. Syme, *History in Ovid* (1978), 222: 'a fine piece of work, lucid,
coherent, and forceful, worthy of a great orator or a good historian'. For analysis of
the rhetorical structure of the poem see Owen, pp. 48–54; G. Focardi, 'Difesa,
preghiera, ironia nel II libro dei *Tristia* di Ovidio', *SIFC* 47 (1975), 86–129, at
87–105; Stabryla, 'Defence', 471.

[64] Williams, *Banished Voices,* 168, sees the shift between author and reader in terms
of responsibility, rather than power.

REFERENCES

Ahl, F. (1984) 'The Art of Safe Criticism in Greece and Rome', *AJPh* 105: 174–208.

Barchiesi, A. (1989) 'Voci e istanze narrative nelle Metamorfosi di Ovidio', *MD* 23:55–97.

——(1993) 'Insegnare ad Augusto: Orazio, *Epistole* 2,1 e Ovidio, *Tristia* II', *MD* 31:149–84.

——(1994) *Il poeta e il principe* (Bari).

Bartsch, S. (1994) *Actors in the Audience: Theatricality and Doublespeak from Nero to Hadrian* (Cambridge, Mass.).

Benediktson, D. T. (1985) 'Propertius' Elegiacization of Homer', *Maia*, 37: 17–26.

Boucher, J.-P. (1966) *Caius Cornélius Gallus* (Bibliothèque de la Faculté des Lettres de Lyon, 11; Paris).

Brown, P. G. McC. (1997) 'An Interpolated Line of Terence at Cicero, *De finibus* 2. 14', *CQ* 47: 583–4.

Citroni, M. (1995) *Poesia e lettori in Roma antica* (Bari).

Cutolo, P. (1991) 'Captatio ed apologia in *Tristia* II', in I. Gallo and L. Nicastri (eds.), *Cultura, poesia, ideologia nell'opera di Ovidio* (Pubblicazioni dell' Università degli studi di Salerno, Sezione Atti, Convegni, Miscellanee, 33; Naples), 265–86.

Dewar, M. (1994) 'Laying it on with a Trowel: The Proem to Lucan and Related Texts', *CQ* 44: 199–211.

Diggle, J. (1980) 'Notes on Ovid's *Tristia*, Books I–II', *CQ* 30: 401–19.

Eco, U. (1992) *Interpretation and Overinterpretation* (Cambridge).

Evans, H. B. (1983) *Publica Carmina: Ovid's Books from Exile* (Lincoln, Nebr., and London).

Felson-Rubin, N. (1994) *Regarding Penelope: From Character to Poetics* (Princeton).

Focardi, G. (1975) 'Difesa, preghiera, ironia nel II libro dei *Tristia* di Ovidio', *SIFC* 47: 86–129.

Galinsky, G. K. (1975) *Ovid's Metamorphoses: An Introduction to the Basic Aspects* (Oxford).

——(1996) *Augustan Culture: An Interpretive Introduction* (Princeton).

Gómez Pallarès, J. (1993) 'Sobre Ovidio, *Tristia* II, 471–492', *Latomus*, 52: 372–85.

Habinek, T. (1998) *The Politics of Latin Literature* (Princeton).

——and Schiesaro, A. (eds.) (1997) *The Roman Cultural Revolution* (Cambridge).

Heyworth, S. J. (1993) 'Horace's *Ibis*: On the Titles, Unity, and Contents of the *Epodes*', in *PLLS*, 7: 85–96.

——(1995) 'Notes on Ovid's *Tristia*', *PCPhS* 41: 138–52.

Hinds, S. (1987) 'Generalising about Ovid', in A. J. Boyle (ed.), *Ramus:*

*Critical Studies in Greek and Roman Literature*, 16/1 *Imperial Roman Literature*, 4–31.

Hinds, S. (2000) 'Essential Epic: Genre and Gender from Macer to Statius', in M. Depew and D. Obbink (eds.), *Matrices of Genre: Authors, Canons and Society* (Cambridge, Mass.), 221–44.

Katz, M. A. (1991) *Penelope's Renown: Meaning and Indeterminacy in the Odyssey* (Princeton).

Kennedy, D. F. (1992) ' "Augustan" and "Anti-Augustan": Reflections on Terms of Reference', in A Powell (ed.), *Roman Poetry and Propaganda in the Age of Augustus* (London), 26–58.

Luck, G. ed. (1967 and 1977) *P. Ovidius Naso. Tristia* (Wissenschaftliche Kommentare zu griechischen und lateinischen Schriftstellern; 2 vols. Heidelberg).

Masters, J. (1992) *Poetry and Civil War in Lucan's Bellum Civile* (Cambridge Classical Studies, Cambridge).

Millar, F. G. B. (1993) 'Ovid and the *Domus Augusta*: Rome Seen from Tomoi', *JRS* 83: 1–17.

Moles, J. L. (1990) 'The Kingship Orations of Dio Chrysostom', *PLLS* 6: 297–375.

Nisbet, R. G. M. (1982) ' "Great and Lesser Bear" (Ovid *Tristia* 4. 3)', *JRS* 72: 49–56.

Nugent, S. G. (1990) '*Tristia* 2: Ovid and Augustus', in K.A. Raaflaub and M. Toher (eds.), *Between Republic and Empire: Interpretations of Augustus and his Principate* (Berkeley, Los Angeles and Oxford), 239–57.

Otis, B. (1966) *Ovid as an Epic Poet* (Cambridge).

Owen S. G. (1915) *P. Ovidi Nasonis Tristium libri quinque. Ex Ponto libri quattuor. Halieutica. Fragmenta* (Oxford).

——(1924) *P. Ovidi Nasonis Tristium liber secundus* (Oxford).

Raaflaub, K. A., and Samons, L. J. II (1990) 'Opposition to Augustus', in K.A. Raaflaub and M. Toher (eds.), *Between Republic and Empire: Interpretations of Augustus and his Principate* (Berkeley, Los Angeles, and Oxford), 417–54.

Selden, D. L. (1992), 'Ceveat lector: Catullus and the Rhetoric of Performance', in R. Hexter and D. L. Selden (eds.), *Innovations of Antiquity* (New York and London). 461–512.

Shackleton Bailey, D. R. (1982), 'Notes on Ovid's Poems from Exile', *CQ* 32: 390–8.

Solodow, J. B. (1988). *The World of Ovid's Metamorphoses* (Chapel Hill, NC, and London).

Stabryla, S. (1994) 'In Defence of the Autonomy of the Poetic World (Some Remarks on Ovid's "Tristia" II)', *Hermes*, 122: 469–78.

Syme, R. (1939) *The Roman Revolution* (Oxford).

——(1978) *History in Ovid* (Oxford).

Tomkins, J. P. ed. (1980) *Reader-Response Criticism from Formalism to Post-Structuralism* (Baltimore).

Vickers, B. (1988) *In Defence of Rhetoric* (Oxford).

Wheeler, A. L. (1910) 'Propertius as Praeceptor Amoris', *CPh* 5: 28-40.
Wiedemann, T. (1975) 'The Political Background to Ovid's *Tristia* 2', *CQ* 25: 264-71.
Williams, G. D. (1994). *Banished Voices: Readings in Ovid's Exile Poetry* (Cambridge Classical Studies, Cambridge).

# 17

# Reading and Response in
# Tacitus' Dialogus

## T. J. LUCE

Since the Renaissance scholarly investigation of Tacitus' *Dialogue on
Orators*, or *Dialogus de oratoribus*, has focused chiefly on placing
the work in its historical and literary context. For a long time authenticity was an issue.[1] When at last most had agreed on Tacitean
authorship, the question of the date of composition came to the fore.
The year AD 81 was long favored: that is, the last months of Titus'
reign before the accession of Domitian.[2] The Ciceronian, or rather
neo-Ciceronian, style was the chief reason for postulating an early
date: Tacitus needed time to make the 180-degree turn to the
completely different style of his maturity. But Leo in a famous review
article of 1898 established that genre determines style: since Cicero
was Tacitus' model for a dialogue by historical personages on an
oratorical topic, a Ciceronian style was clearly appropriate, if not
obligatory.[3] Leo favored a date after Domitian's death, and most have

I wish to thank A. J. Woodman for his helpful comments on an earlier version of this
paper.

[1] Heubner gives a succinct review of the question in Güngerich (1980: 191–2), as
does Hass-von Reitzenstein (1970: 7–9); cf. Merklin (1991: 2259–61). For earlier
views see Gudeman (1914: 1–10). Doubters included Beatus Rhenanus, Lipsius, J. F.
Gronovius. As late as 1962 Paratore continued to hold out (1962: 101–69): Titinius
Capito is his choice. Some regard the question as still unsettled: e.g. Bardon (1953)
and Hass-von Reitzenstein (1970: 8). Some have identified the *Dialogus* with
Quintilian's lost *De causis corruptae eloquentiae* (*On the Causes of the Corruption of
Eloquence*), e.g. L. Herrmann (1955: 349–69).

[2] Tacitus at *Agr.* 3. 2 implies that he wrote nothing during Domitian's reign. On the
general question, see Heubner in Güngerich (1980: 195–6). D'Elia (1979) would date
it between 78 and 89.

[3] Leo (1898: esp. 172–83), a review of Gudeman's 1st edn. (in English) of the
*Dialogus*, which appeared in 1894. In the 2nd edn. of 1914 (in German) Gudeman
persisted in dating the work to 81.

followed him since. But the precise time after the emperor's assassination is still a lively question. Murgia and Barnes reckon the *Dialogus* as Tacitus' first work, written in 97, before the appearance of the *Agricola* and *Germania* in the next year.[4] Others are willing to put it as much as a decade or more later. Many opt for 102, the suffect consulship of the dedicatee, Fabius Iustus.[5]

Historical questions were also investigated during these years, such as the identity of the participants, the dramatic date, and references in the text to persons and events.[6] Nor was the literary background slighted: models, antecedents, and allusions were identified and lists were drawn up. Most significant is the debt to Cicero; the borrowings in language, subject matter, setting, and dramatic technique are extensive.[7]

Finally, the state of the text presented challenges, both the many errors and garblings of the Latin and the lacunae. The gap after chapter 35 has provoked much discussion: was it short or long and did it contain a speech by Secundus?[8]

As for the subject matter, most have interpreted it in light of its literary heritage and in the context of the debate about literary

[4] Murgia (1980, 1985), followed by Barnes (1986), but for reasons mostly different from those of Murgia.

[5] Murgia (1980: 99-100) and Barnes (1986: 229-32) review the chief opinions of their predecessors. See also Heubner in Güngerich (1980: 195-6). Kappelmacher (1932) first argued for 102: dedications to a consul in office are common—cf. Woodman (1975: 274-5). Syme (1958: 670-3) would put it in 102 or 'some four or five years later'.

[6] On the date and the interlocutors, see Heubner in Güngerich (1980: 196-200); on the interlocutors, Barnes (1986: 236-7).

[7] Hass-von Reitzenstein (1970) devotes her valuable monograph largely to Tacitus' debt to Cicero's dialogues (see pp. 5-6 for an overview). Güngerich in his commentary (1980) notes the many allusions and parallels. See also the useful collection in Gudeman (1914: 85-98).

[8] Barnes (1986: 226-8) mentions some of the textual problems that recent scholars have dealt with. On the lacuna after ch. 35 Merklin (1991: 2271-5) and Heubner in Güngerich (1980: 193-4) review the manuscript evidence and modern discussion, as do Hass-von Reitzenstein (1970: 106-11) and Bringmann (1970: 165-6, 177-8), to which add Murgia (1979), who argues for the loss of a single folium, equivalent to two and a half to three pages in the Teubner text; contra Merklin (1991: 2275). Brink (1989: 495) regards the argument for a long lacuna that included a speech for Secundus 'by now as a dead duck'; cf. Barwick (1954: 4 n. 1, 33-9). Steinmetz has recently argued (1988: 342-57) for a short speech for Secundus, equivalent to some seventy lines in the Oxford Classical Text, in which Secundus explains the decline as the result of the natural law of growth and decay, as at Sen. *Contr.* 1 Praef. 7. Steinmetz's arguments do not persuade me.

decline, which was carried on by many writers during the first century AD. On both counts the work appeared to be derivative— lively and brilliantly realized, to be sure, but at bottom traditional in style and form, conventional in argument.

First, let us consider the form, which owes as much to Cicero as does the style. Parallels with the *De oratore* (*On the Orator*) in particular are numerous and striking. In both works the setting is the home of an older man who has made his mark in oratory and public life (Crassus/Maternus). The dramatic date is put more than twenty-five years in the past (91 B.C./A.D. 75). The author, now in middle age, was in his teens when the dialogue took place; he took no part in the discussion, but simply reports what the various speakers said on the subject of oratory.[9] Among the interlocutors are two teachers of the author in his youth (Crassus, Antonius/Aper, Secundus), whom he used to attend in the forum, the courts, and as a visitor to their homes. The man at whose domicile the dialogue is set is the commanding figure, the one to whom the climactic speech of the dialogue is given. The next most important interlocutor is a crusty orator (Antonius/Aper) who argues against the *communis opinio* of the others. They characterize him as habitually taking the opposite side in debate and maintain that he really does not believe what he says. There are other speakers, including an aristocratic younger man (Caesar Strabo/Messala) who accepts the task of discussing a major aspect of the practice of oratory. The setting of the sun puts an end to the discussion. As the participants prepare to depart, they make good-humored jibes at one another, and vow to continue the discussion another day.

Just as the form and style are traditional, so also the subject matter—which is, one might say, even hackneyed. During the first century AD many people acknowledged the fact of oratory's decline and inquired into its causes.[10] Some carried on the debate in the larger context of the vicissitudes and decline of artistic talent generally. We see the issue discussed in Velleius Paterculus (1.

---

[9] Cicero does not represent himself as present. His friend, Cotta, reports the whole of the two-day conversation to him (*De or.* 1. 26-9, 3. 16).

[10] Heldmann (1982) treats the topic for both Greece and Rome; at 255-86, 294-9, he discusses Tacitus and the *Dialogus*. See also Caplan (1944); Kennedy (1972: 446-64); Fantham (1978: 111-16); Heubner in Güngerich (1980: 201-2); cf. Barnes (1986: 233-4). Even Cicero at *Tusc.* 2. 5 spoke of a decline.

16-18), the elder Seneca (*Controuersia* 1, praef. 6-10), Petronius (1-2, 88), the younger Seneca (*Epistulae* 114, esp. 1-2), the elder Pliny (*Naturalis Historia* 14. 1. 3-7), Quintilian (*Institutio Oratoria* 8. 6. 76), the younger Pliny (in a sour mood, *Epistulae* 2. 14), and the author of *On the Sublime* (44), if that work is to be dated to the first century AD, as some think.[11] Tacitus comes toward or at the end of the debate.

The introduction to the *Dialogus* is brief (1. 1-5. 2: some three pages in a modern text) and its conclusion briefer—less than ten lines (42). The main body consists of three pairs of speeches, each pair devoted to a different topic.[12] The domestic setting, many realistic touches, and deft characterization help to soften and distract from the underlying formality of structure. The interaction seems spontaneous, while the argument gives the impression of moving forward in an uncontrived manner.[13] The speeches themselves, however, are long and rather monolithic.

Tacitus first introduces the subject: his friend, Fabius Iustus, has often asked him[14] the reasons for the decline of oratory at Rome (1. 1-4). He then sets the scene (2. 1-5. 2): in the company of two admired teachers, Marcus Aper and Iulius Secundus, he arrives at the home of Curiatius Maternus. On the previous day Maternus had recited a new tragedy he had written, entitled *Cato*. It created quite a sensation, for it expressed sentiments that were said to have offended those in power. The three come upon Maternus in his bedroom, the manuscript of the offending *Cato* in his hands. Secundus requests him not to court danger so openly: please revise the *Cato*, he asks, by removing the objectionable passages. The result will be not a better *Cato*, but at least a safer one. Maternus declares he will do no such thing. In fact, he is now rapidly putting the final touches to it because he wants to get on with a new tragedy he has in mind, entitled

---

[11] For a first-century AD date, see e.g. Goold (1961—Augustan), Russell (1964: 185), Kennedy (1972: 369-77); for a later date, Williams (1978: 17-25), Heldmann (1982: 286-93; he argues that ch. 44 refers to the *Dialogus*), Barnes (1986: 233).

[12] On the structure, see Barwick (1929: 106-8), Häussler (1969: 46-50), Bringmann (1970).

[13] Hass-von Reitzenstein (1970) illustrates the many parallels, allusions, and imitations of the Ciceronian dialogues in setting and dynamics, especially *De oratore*, *De re publica*, and *De natura deorum*. On the interconnections that she sees Tacitus forging from speech to speech, see e.g. pp. 58, 63, 144-58.

[14] For the request as a *topos*, see Janson (1964: 117-20).

*Thyestes*: he darkly remarks that whatever *Cato* had failed to say, *Thyestes* will.[15]

At this juncture the subject of the first pair of speeches (5. 3–13. 6) is naturally introduced: whether oratory or poetry is to be preferred. Aper rebukes Maternus for giving up his career as an orator and barrister in favor of writing poetry. He argues for oratory and against poetry on the grounds of utility, pleasure, and fame. At the end, he, like Secundus, appeals to Maternus to stop his poetic activity. He has nothing against poets, he assures his listeners: for those who do not have the talent to be orators, poetry is a creditable fallback. At the end, he, like Secundus, makes a personal appeal to Maternus. Do not, he asks, flirt with danger by speaking on behalf of Cato: speak, rather, on behalf of beleaguered friends who need your help in the courtroom. In his rebuttal (11. 1–13. 6) Maternus criticizes contemporary oratory; poetry, he says, enables him to retreat from the hurly-burly of public life into the 'groves and glades' of poesy (*nemora et luci*).[16]

The unexpected arrival of the young aristocrat, Vipstanus Messala, introduces the subject of the second pair of speeches: namely, whether ancient or modern orators are better (14. 1–16. 3). All men are agreed, Messala asserts, that there has been a decline in oratory, and he—Messaia—has long pondered the reasons why. Secundus and Maternus urge him to give his thoughts on the question. Before Messala can begin, Aper says that he will not let the moderns be condemned without a hearing and go undefended. The second phase of the *Dialogus* is thus launched (16. 4–26. 8).

[15] The subjects of these tragedies offended because they treated the themes of tyranny and liberty. See Syme (1958: 104, 110); Heldmann (1982: 257–71). For their probable connection with the downfall of Helvidius Priscus in 74–5 at the hands of Eprius Marcellus (Dio 65. 12, 13. 1a; Suet. *Vesp.* 15), see Syme (1958: 104 n. 4, 211–12). Tacitus reports earlier clashes in 70 at *Hist.* 4. 5–8, 43; cf. *Dial.* 5. 7.

[16] Twice Tacitus uses the phrase *nemora et luci* to refer to the retreat by the poet into the quiet of the countryside to compose (9. 6, 12. 1). Scholars are divided as to whether the *Dialogus* is being referred to by Pliny in a letter to Tacitus of about 107 (*Ep.* 9. 10. 2). Some believe that the phrase is so common (*ut ipsi dicunt*, 'as they themselves say': *Dial.* 6.9) that no such allusion can be meant: e.g. Sherwin-White (1966: 487–9); Güngerich (1980: 36–7, seconded by Heubner at 192). Along with others, such as Jones (1968: 135–6), R. Martin (1981: 59), and Murgia (1985: 176 and n. 16), I believe that Pliny is indeed alluding to the *Dialogus*. It is precisely because of the use of the phrase by others (*ut ipsi dicunt*) that, when Pliny identifies it with Tacitus particularly, something special must be meant: not a phrase thrown out in conversation but, more probably, in a published work where the phrase stands out by emphatic use, as it surely does in the *Dialogus*.

Aper declares that he is tired of the knee-jerk reaction of so many contemporaries in preferring the old to the new (18. 3). Simply because something is fresh and different does not automatically make it worse. What's more, just what *is* 'old' (*antiquus*)? How old does a thing have to be to qualify? Why, when you look over the whole of history, Cicero lived yesterday, so to speak: he is our contemporary on the long view. Aper then turns to the question of taste: our present age is the product of an ever improving, an ever more sophisticated refinement. He has great fun skewering the faults of the older orators whom the others admire, particularly Cicero.

Maternus turns now to Messala (24. 1–3), twice requesting him not to give a defense of the ancients—for, he says, they need none—but to say why he thinks oratory has declined. Messala says he will do so, but is immediately drawn into a defense of the old-time speakers Aper had criticized (25. 1–26. 8). Messala scoffs at the moderns for their effeminate, histrionic, meretricious habits of speaking. Aper, he charges, named the ancient orators one by one—Cicero, Calvus, Asinius, and so on—but he named not a single modern. Who are these paragons, anyway, he wants to know? Who is the modern Cicero? our Caesar? our Calvus? By God, declares Messala, if Aper won't name names, I will!

Maternus breaks in (27. 1–3). Spare us, spare us, he pleads (27. 1–3), for there can be no question that oratory has declined. What we want to know is why. This marks the end of the second pair of speeches. We are now launched on the last pair: why oratory has declined (28. 1–41. 5).

The chief cause of the decline, in Messala's view (28. 1–35. 5), is cultural and educational: he outlines both the careless way young children are now brought up in the home and the defective manner of educating them when they go to school.

The lacuna after chapter 35 contained the end of Messala's speech and the beginning of the last speech by Maternus. This final speech (36. 1–41. 5) offers a different reason for oratory's decline: namely, the changed political circumstances between the late republic and the empire of AD 75.[17] The best kind of oratory, asserts Maternus,

---

[17] Brink (1989: 485, 493, 497) claims that Maternus' speech does not give a proper cause: 'its main function . . . appears to be to refute Messala's *causa* by implication' (p. 485); 'Maternus too denies decline, or admits it only in a manner of speaking (*Dial.* 41). Hence again no aetiology is called for; the subject of the dialogue is

flourishes in times of political turmoil, when life-and-death issues are at stake and when danger and upheaval threaten. Such was the late republic of Cicero's day. But we now live in a period of security and tranquillity, he asserts, in which the emperor has pacified eloquence along with everything else. In short, if oratory is to be great, it requires a particular sort of environment; it is a historically determined phenomenon. In a striking conclusion he declares that had those present been born in the days of the collapsing republic, they would have been pre-eminent orators, and if the men of those days had been transported to the present, moderation and self-restraint would have been their lot. It is not possible to enjoy great fame and great security at the same time.[18]

Most readers have relied on Tacitus' chief literary model, Cicero, in understanding the *Dialogus*. The roles of Maternus and Aper, in particular, have been interpreted in the light of their Ciceronian counterparts. The character who speaks for Tacitus is believed by many to be Maternus,[19] just as in the *De oratore* Crassus is Cicero's acknowledged spokesman (1. 120). It is clear, for example, that Tacitus himself is convinced of the fact of oratory's decline, as he states in the opening sentence: the question is not whether there has been one, but why. And when at 27. 1 Maternus puts a stop to the debate between Aper and Messala on the primacy of the ancients and the moderns by asserting that as far as he is concerned the ancients were unquestionably better, he can be taken to be expressing Tacitus' view. Moreover, many believe that Maternus' retirement from forensic activity in order to take up literary pursuits mirrors a similar decision by Tacitus. After his prosecution with Pliny of the peccant governor Marius Priscus early in 100 we hear of no further

---

invalidated: the orators of the day are as competent as they can be—in the conditions of the day, which have their own advantages' (p. 497). But this confuses what is potential with what is actual: contemporary orators have the potential to be great, but the political climate prevents that potential from being realized. Oratory itself has declined and no great orators exist at present.

[18] Two popular arguments explaining decline have no place in the *Dialogus*, or are touched on lightly: the general collapse of morality together with the growing spread of luxury (e.g. Sen. *Contr.* 1, praef. 6-10; Sen. *Ep.* 114. 1-2; Pliny *NH* 14. 1. 3-7), and the biological explanation that all things go through cycles of growth and decay (e.g., Cic. *Tusc.* 2.5); cf. Williams (1978: 49). At *Ann.* 3. 55. 5 Tacitus shows interest in the latter idea but is wary about the former.

[19] See e.g. Barwick (1929: 107-8) and (1954: 17-18, 23-4, 30), Syme (1958: 111 and n. 3), Kennedy (1972: 518); cf. Bringmann (1970).

oratorical endeavors on his part. Maternus gave up the forum for poetry, it is argued, Tacitus for history.[20] Then again, Maternus' final speech seems to many a tour de force, sweeping past the cultural and educational explanation offered by Messala to argue that both the flourishing and the decline of oratory depend on the political conditions of an age. In the debate on the cause of decline, this argument is unique; it may be original to Tacitus. Based as it is on a historical perspective, it seems particularly fitting for Tacitus to hold at this point in time, when he was preparing to write, or was in the course of writing, the *Histories*. To many readers the *Dialogus* thus ends on a note of impassioned eloquence that transcends the earlier arguments in power and persuasion. In sum, just as Crassus is Cicero's spokesman in the *De oratore*, so with Maternus in the *Dialogus*.

As for Aper, his role is viewed as devil's advocate.[21] Scholars have compared his role with that of Antonius in the *De oratore*, who at the conclusion of the first day's debate is accused of not believing what he has said (1. 263), and who, at the start of the second day, admits that this indeed was true (2. 46). Comparable also is the role of Furius Philus in the *De re publica*, who agrees to argue the case that no state can be governed without doing injustice, although he does not himself believe it.[22]

Finally, Messala. In explaining his role critics have looked not so much to a Ciceronian model as to issues contemporary with Tacitus. The arguments given to Messala, especially those in his second speech, which attributes the decline of oratory to a decline in education and cultural values, are evidently quite close to Quintilian's views as expressed in his lost treatise *De causis corruptae eloquentiae*.[23] Many see in Messala's role a critique, if not a polemic, by Tacitus against the views of Quintilian, both those concerning the causes of the decline as expressed in the *De causis*, and the rather optimistic

---

[20] Pliny *Ep.* 2. 11, esp. sec. 2. Cf. Kappelmacher (1932: 127), Syme (1958: 109-11, 672), Hass-von Reitzenstein (1970: 152-4). I myself believe that the evidence for the parallel is weak and that the case does not stand up; so also Bringmann (1970: 167 n. 25) and R. Martin (1981: 65-6), cf. Heldmann (1982: 286 n. 208a). Maternus' decision to abandon public life seems particularly at odds with Tacitus' praise for those who serve the state well, despite the dangers and difficulties: *Agr.* 42. 4, *Ann.* 4. 20. 2.

[21] Cf. Hass-von Reitzenstein (1970: 131-43).

[22] See Cic. *De re p.* 2. 70 (cf. Aug. *Ciu. Dei* 2. 21) and 3. 8. Philus' task is described as *improbitatis patrocinium* ('dishonest advocacy').

[23] See Barwick (1954: 8-18) and Brink (1989: esp. 484-8).

assessment of the health of contemporary oratory that he made a few years later in the *Institutio Oratoria* (10. 1. 122).

The preceding sketch, admittedly selective and incomplete, has attempted to characterize the general approach many have taken in interpreting the *Dialogus*. The approach is from the outside in: from the conventions of style, genre, and form on the one hand, and from the debate on the decline of oratory and literature carried on in the first century, on the other.

In the past few decades, however, some critics have felt increasingly uneasy about the validity of much of this standard interpretation; close examination of the text has revealed disturbing inconsistencies, contradictions, and illogicalities. Certain of these 'imperfections' had been noticed by some earlier scholars, but for the most part they were glossed over or explained away. In recent years, however, the discovery of inconsistencies and contradictions seems to have grown exponentially in number: the entire fabric of the *Dialogus* appears shot through with them. Yet so far discussion has been piecemeal, focusing on this or that passage or, more commonly, on one or other of the interlocutors, while explanations to account for these problems have been divergent and at odds with one another. In the remainder of this chapter I will argue that many of the perceived difficulties are related to one another because they have a common cause: the nature of the argumentation in the *Dialogus*. But first it will be necessary to illustrate the nature of the inconsistencies and contradictions, and to review some of the explanations that have been advanced to account for them.

### SOME PROBLEMS AND SOLUTIONS

Let us begin the discussion with Aper. A minor problem must first be addressed: is Aper a devil's advocate? That is, does he express views that he personally does not hold? The parallels with Antonius in the *De oratore* and with Philus in the *De re publica*, discussed previously, suggest that this is the case.[24] Yet Antonius and Philus tell us straight out that they do not believe what they say. Aper never does. To the end he makes no concession: the last words of the *Dialogus* are given

---

[24] Cf. Hass-von Reitzentein (1970: 27).

to him, and, though said in jest, they suggest that he is as prepared to defend modern oratory as ever.[25] It would thus appear that Aper in the dramatic scenario Tacitus has devised is genuinely convinced of his position. This is a small but suggestive difference from the Ciceronian model.

But what is the reader to believe? Isn't it significant that Aper is charged with acting as devil's advocate no less than four times, twice by Messala and twice by Maternus (15. 2, 16. 3–4, 24. 2, 28. 1)? Doesn't this suggest that, even if the reader thinks Tacitus depicts Aper as believing what he says, the reader should think twice about believing it himself? Not necessarily. Charging one's opponent with not believing in his case has a long and honorable pedigree in ancient rhetoric. Cicero uses it against opponents on a number of occasions. It is a rhetorical ploy to unsettle one's opponent and make his case seem weak. Whether his case is really weak must be decided on other grounds.[26]

Yet the question of Aper's sincerity is eclipsed by the following: as noted earlier, Tacitus in the opening sentence says that the question Fabius Iustus has posed is why oratory has declined. Whether it has declined is not mentioned as an issue: decline is taken for granted. And, as has been also noted earlier, Maternus at 27. 1 states his firm conviction that decline has in fact occurred. So it would appear after all that Aper's defense of the ancients cannot be convincingly sustained: the other interlocutors do not believe it and Tacitus himself does not believe it.[27] What, then, is Aper doing in this dialogue?[28]

[25] *Dial.* 42. 2.

[26] For example, Cicero's treatment of the young Atratinus (*Cael.* 1–2); cf. Luce (1986: 150 and n. 20). A common variant was to charge the prosecution with failing to realize the true implications of the charges that have been brought, as at Cic. *Lig.* 10. 12–13. I must confess, however, that repeating the charge four times seems to be rather overdoing it, and the repetition may be intended to invite the reader to believe in it; note, too, that Aper does not contradict the charges when Maternus claims he does not believe what he says (24. 2) or when Messala declares that what he will say is what they all believe (28. 1).

[27] Whenever we date the *Dialogus*—97, 102, or later—Tacitus' views on the poor health of oratory cannot be complimentary to Pliny. If 102 or later, it would be deflating to Pliny's amour propre, especially in connection with the *Panegyricus*: cf. Syme (1958: 112–15), Murgia (1980: 121–2), Barnes (1986: 244). If in 97, we must suppose that Pliny in his later correspondence on oratorical matters and fame chose never to refer to Tacitus' published verdict that modern oratory was less great and brought correspondingly less fame than in earlier days (cf. *Epp.* 1. 20, 2. 11, 7. 20, 9. 14); cf. *Dial.* 7. 4 (Aper is speaking) with *Ep.* 9. 23. 2–3.

[28] In the *De re publica* Laelius is made to assert that Philus' habit of arguing the

In an article of 1975 Deuse set out the dilemma more clearly and faced its implications more forthrightly than any of his predecessors.[29] For Deuse it is highly significant that Maternus interrupts Messala's rejoinder to Aper, since an impasse has been reached and feelings are running high. This is done, Deuse argues, because Tacitus wants to illustrate that discussions of aesthetic preference are subjective and emotional. Why eloquence has declined lends itself to rational analysis; whether it has declined does not. Thus we find no real rebuttal to Aper's thesis. Maternus cuts off Messala's rejoinder and moves the discussion at once to the causes of decline. Deuse concludes, first, that Tacitus, who was convinced of the decline of oratory, must necessarily present an ambivalent picture of a man who defends the merits of contemporary eloquence, and, second, that when a person is convinced of the superiority of modern rhetoric, rational discussion and a conclusion logically arrived at are not possible. This, for Deuse, is what Tacitus is trying to convey in dramatic terms in the *Dialogus*.

Now, it may well be true that for Tacitus *de gustibus non disputandum*, and that this belief is illustrated in the *Dialogus*. But the Aper–Messala exchange takes up a third of the work; in fact, Aper has a greater share of speech than any other character. Why devote so much space to a man whose main position Tacitus considers untenable, and whose lengthy remarks lead to the banal conclusion that 'there is just no accounting for taste'? I myself am not convinced that Deuse has fully explained the presence of the middle pair of speeches in the *Dialogus*.

Next, Messala. In his long speech on education he compares the defective methods of the moderns with the admirable training of Cicero's day. His two chief points are these. First, modern training is extremely narrow in comparison with the earlier period. Back then students of oratory knew about law and philosophy; they read widely in literature and history; they even swotted up subjects like geometry, music, grammar, and physical science. From this broad

opposing case is based on his conviction that by this method the truth is most easily discovered (3. 8). Could this explanation be applicable to the *Dialogus*? It would not seem so, at least on the level of the dramatic scenario: Aper, unlike Philus, never admits he disbelieves what he says, and no interlocutor suggests, as Laelius does, a reason for his acting as he does (see also *De or*. 1. 26 3). Cf. Hass-von Reitzenstein (1970: 37–43).

[29] Deuse (1975), commended by Heubner in Güngerich (1980: 198).

learning Cicero's marvelous eloquence wells up and overflows, says Messala (30. 5). But nowadays ignorant students are content to acquaint themselves with a few rhetorical tricks: they know very little. Messala's second objection is that students in Cicero's day were quickly introduced to the real world: they chose certain eminent speakers and followed them about into the courts, the forum, and the senate, experiencing firsthand the heat of debate about real issues, some of great moment. Contemporary students, on the other hand, learn within the confines of the classroom, declaiming on unreal subjects before an audience composed of their peers, youths as ignorant and inexperienced as they. Ravished maidens, rewards to tyrannicides, incestuous mothers: these are their subjects. The real world has no place in their curriculum.

A powerful indictment of the present and a heady commendation of the past! But there is something skewed in Messala's picture. His description of education in Cicero's day derives chiefly from Cicero's own writings, especially the *Brutus* and the *De oratore*;[30] however, what Cicero describes there is an ideal, not what education was in fact like in his time[31] (it goes without saying that Cicero believed that he himself came closest to realizing this ideal). Many of Cicero's speakers in the *De oratore*, including Antonius and even his brother Quintus (1. 5), to whom the work is addressed, doubt that such wide accomplishments are really necessary, much less possible. And Crassus, who speaks for Cicero, and even Cicero himself in the prefaces to the first two books of the *De oratore* (1. 16-22, 2. 5-7) concede that few have the drive or the ability to acquire such broad learning. Tacitus thus has Messala convert Cicero's sketch of an ideally educated orator into a description of the actual educational attainments of the age as a whole.

Messala's remarks present the reader with a number of other problems, of which I will mention two. The first is that declamation and its unreal subjects were not restricted to the young in their classrooms. Their elders indulged in them with gusto, as the reminiscences of the elder Seneca testify. Asinius Pollio and Messala Corvinus, whom Messala in his first speech cites as exemplars of bygone eloquence, appear regularly in Seneca as declaimers (e.g.,

---

[30] Brink well argues that some of this Ciceronianism is really neo-Ciceronianism refracted through the spectacles of Quintilian (1989: 488-94).

[31] Cf. Barwick (1929: 87-90), Brink (1989: 490-1, 494).

*Controuersia* 3 praef. 14, *Suasoria*. 6. 27). We find Pollio, for example, speaking on 'The Madman Who Married His Daughter to a Slave' (*Controuersia* 7. 6. 12, 24). Pirates (1. 6. 11, 7. 14), ravished maidens (2. 3. 13, 19; 4. 3), and disinherited sons (1. 6. 11; 4. 5; 7. 14) are frequent subjects in the cases he argued. So dedicated was Pollio to declamation, Seneca tells us (4 praef. 2–6), that he performed only three days after the death of a son.[32] The second problem is this. Messala describes (34–5) how modern youth, shut up in their schools, have next to no experience of life beyond the schoolroom walls, whereas students in the late republic attended great orators in public, even following their mentors to their homes, where they enjoyed private conversation and informal instruction. Now this is exactly how Tacitus, at the start of the *Dialogus* (2. 1), tells us he learned oratory from Aper and Secundus. Moreover, this custom continued long after Tacitus' youth in the 70s. We read in the letters of Pliny of many young men attending him both in public and as visitors to his home. As for Tacitus, he had a coterie of youthful aspirants; it was from their number that Pliny hoped a candidate might be found as a teacher for the new school in Comum that he had endowed.[33] In short, both the picture that Messala presents of education in Cicero's day and the picture he gives of his own are one-sided and overstated. What, then, are we to make of his role in the *Dialogus*?

Let me now turn to Maternus, in whose words we find equally marked peculiarities and contradictions. In his first speech he defends his decision to abandon his forensic career for poetry on the grounds that contemporary oratory is used as an offensive weapon to attack one's opponents for financial gain. Its most successful practitioners are men of evil character whose eloquence he calls 'bloody' (*sanguinans*, 12. 2), since it often ends in the victim's death on a capital charge (he is referring to informers, or *delatores*, and their victims).[34] At the end of his remarks (13. 5) he again describes public life, which he is forsaking, as tumultuous and dangerous. Yet

---

[32] In addition, Maternus points out (38. 2) that one of Asinius Pollio's most famous speeches, *Pro heredibus Vrbiniae*, was delivered during Augustus' reign before the centumviral court, which was the premier court of the empire.

[33] *Ep.* 4. 13. 10 (AD 104/5). See Sherwin-White's note (1966: 289). Cf. also *Epp.* 6. 11, 23, 29; 7. 9; 9. 13. 1. Contrast, however, the pessimistic picture in *Ep.* 2. 14.

[34] See Winterbottom (1964: 90–4).

in his final speech he characterizes the political climate of the present day as one of peace, security, and good order (41. 4):

Why is there need for long speeches in the senate when the best men quickly agree? Or for numerous speeches to the people, when the inexperienced masses do not decide matters, but a supremely wise individual? Or for prosecutions voluntarily undertaken, when wrongdoing is so rare and inconsequential? Or for speeches in defense that are intemperate and provoke resentment, when the emperor's pardon may come to the aid of the accused in his peril?

Contrast, too, this rosy picture with Tacitus' unfavorable estimate of so many aspects of the principate in his historical writings.

Attempts to resolve the discrepancies between Maternus' two speeches have diverged greatly. The views of three scholars are illustrative. Reitzenstein[35] early in the century believed on the basis of Maternus' last speech that Tacitus early in his career, when he wrote the *Dialogus*, was a confirmed believer in the desirability of the principate, but that pessimism increasingly came over him in later years as he worked his way through the *Histories* and *Annals*. On the other hand, Köhnken believes that because the pessimistic view of the principate in Maternus' first speech is similar to the picture we find in the historical writings, the first speech must reflect Tacitus' real opinion. The last speech is thus for Köhnken pure irony: demolitionary in effect and intention.[36]

The third explanation is that of Williams in his book *Change and Decline*,[37] in which he emphasizes more strongly than anyone else to date the many contradictions that inhere in the person and remarks of Maternus. To explain the particular discrepancy between the hostile description of the principate in Maternus' first speech and the positive picture we find in the last, Williams argues that the first part of the *Dialogus* describes conditions at the time of the dramatic setting, AD 75, whereas the last speech describes conditions when Tacitus was writing, AD 102. In 75 the *delatores* were much in evidence. The previous year Eprius Marcellus had brought down his old antagonist, the Stoic Helvidius Priscus, who was soon

---

[35] Reitzenstein (1915: 226–52 = 1967: 70–96).
[36] Köhnken (1973: 32–50). Heubner in Güngerich (1980: 208) terms Köhnken's view irrefutable (unwiderleglich). Cf. Heldmann (1982: 280, 285).
[37] Williams (1978: 26–51).

after put to death, possibly in that very year.[38] Four years later Marcellus fell: implicated in a conspiracy in the last months of Vespasian's reign. This is the political situation in which we find ourselves in the first part of the *Dialogus*, Williams believes. The happy days of Trajan's new reign, however, are what are being described in Maternus' last speech. In support of this interpretation Williams cites Tacitus' favorable remarks on the new dispensation at the start of the *Agricola* and Pliny's assertion in the *Panegyricus* (34–5) that the days of the *delatores* were over: Trajan had 'abolished' them.[39]

The explanation does not convince me.[40] I find it difficult to believe a priori that the *Dialogus* suffers from the sort of chronological schizophrenia that Williams describes. Without warning, the reader is catapulted forward twenty-seven years. In partial support of his thesis Williams claims that all historical references to 75 are confined to the early part of the Dialogus. This is untrue. At 37. 2, in the middle of his final speech, Maternus mentions an edition of eleven books entitled *Acta* and three entitled *Epistolae* being put out by Licinius Mucianus. Now the elder Pliny mentions that Mucianus was dead by the year 77, when Pliny published his *Natural History* (32. 62). In the *Dialogus* Mucianus is still alive, as the phrase *a Muciano contrahuntur* ('are being gathered by Mucianus') shows. In short, Maternus' last speech is fixed in the 70s, not in 102.

Another contradiction deserves emphasis. Maternus argues that the orator's world is one of blood and peril, the poet's of peace and safety. Yet the reverse is true. It is not an orator who has offended those in power, but a writer of tragedies. Maternus is in danger, and his friends are worried for him. Secundus urges him to remove the offending passages from the *Cato* (3. 2), Aper to realize the danger he is in: he cannot plead as an excuse the quiet and security of the poet's

---

[38] See Syme (1958: 104 n. 4; cf. 211–12): 'the modern Cato.'

[39] The word is Williams's (1978: 36). One cannot, however, 'abolish' delation per se: *crimen deferre* is the only way in law that a charge may be brought (then, too, one man's *delator* might be another man's patriot). Certain restrictions might be enacted (cf. Suet. *Titus* 8. 5), or certain extralegal abuses curbed (although Pliny in that curiously heated passage at *Pan.* 34–5 is remarkably short on specifics). It is instructive that Aquillius Regulus, notorious *delator*, half-brother of Messala (*Dial.* 15. 1), and Pliny's *bête noire*, was untouched by Trajan's punitive measures (nor does Vibius Crispus seem to have been affected by those of Titus). Cf. Winterbottom (1964: 93–4).

[40] Nor Murgia (1980: 118, 121–2).

life when he takes on the emperor.[41] On the other hand, the orator's world as Aper presents it at the end of his speech is one of compromise and little risk-taking (10. 6-8). The orator may be excused because he fulfills an obligation when he helps a friend in trouble and because his words are spoken on the spur of the moment; the poet may not be excused because he voluntarily chooses his subject and what he writes is premeditated.

At the end of his first speech Maternus makes a series of wishes: that when he dies he may not have more wealth than he may safely leave to the heir of his choice (he alludes to the prospect of imperial confiscation if he does not leave the emperor a share); that the statue on his tomb may be happy and ivy-crowned, not worried and grim; and 'as for my memory, let there be no resolution in the senate or petition to the emperor' (i.e., should he die condemned or under a cloud).[42] The repeated references early in the *Dialogus* to the offense Maternus has given to the powerful and to the concern that his friends express for his safety and, above all, this highly charged conclusion to his first speech strongly suggest that Maternus soon after met an untimely end.[43]

Most scholars, such as Deuse, Köhnken, and Williams, have tended to concentrate on particular passages or persons to explain the difficulties they find in the text. A few have given explanations of wider applicability; these might be dubbed the 'psychological factor' and the 'ambivalence factor' (or a combination of both). Those favoring psychology believe that the conflicted and conflicting facets of

[41] *Dial.* 10. 7. I believe that the emperor is being referred to; denied by Gudeman (1914: 259).

[42] The translation is that of Church and Brodribb (1942) (13. 6). Güngerich (1980: 58) and Talbert (1984: 365 n. 14) do not believe that the references here are to public memorials. But why would anyone use such language for a private memorial? (Take whose advice about what? Make what request and from whom?) See Barnes (1986: 239-40).

[43] So also Syme (1958: 110-11), Cameron (1967), Hass-von Reitzenstein (1970: 37), Williams (1978: 34), Murgia (1980: 122). Barnes (1986: 238-44) identifies the interlocutor with the Curiatius Maternus of a Spanish inscription published in 1973 (*AE* 283) and with the Maternus put to death by Domitian in 91 or 92 (Dio 67. 12. 5). I believe that the death of the Maternus of the *Dialogus* must have come shortly after the dramatic date. The worry repeatedly expressed by his friends seems premature for a death that was to come sixteen or seventeen years later, especially for a man already into middle age, as he seems to be in the *Dialogus*. Dio's language does not suggest to me a poet reciting tragedies, but an orator declaiming a speech, an activity that Maternus is represented as renouncing in 75.

Tacitus' own personality are mirrored in the opposing interlocutors and the opposing arguments. Two examples of the psychological approach are Keyssner and Häussler. Keyssner argued that Tacitus' portrayal of Aper and Maternus reflects the tug-of-war in his own psyche, and that Maternus' discrepant views of the present— dangerous versus safe, free versus unfree—arise from inner conflict that Tacitus could not resolve himself.[44] Some thirty years later Häussler described the dilemma according to psychological and character types: 'Tacitus is the historian Maternus (not the dreamy utopian), Tacitus is the moralist Messala (not the old-fashioned reactionary), and Tacitus is the literary critic Aper (not the superficial utilitarian).'[45] What we as readers are to do, according to Häussler, in the *Dialogus* and in the historical writings, is to separate out the admirable qualities—moral, psychologyical, aesthetic, intellectual, and so on—from the unadmirable ones. Each character is clothed in a wrapping that needs to be removed in order to find the essential person beneath; here, he argues, is where we will find what Tacitus really thinks and admires.[46] Now, there may be merit in this approach, but Häussler does not explain what this wrapping is, why it is there, and how much needs to be removed before we get to the real stuff beneath.

Still other critics resort to generalities when attempting to explain the *Dialogus*. Goodyear is a representative of the 'ambivalence factor': 'The thought of the *Dialogus* accords well with that of a historian who wavers between nostalgia for the past and realistic acceptance of the present. In a word, its elusiveness and ambivalence are eminently Tacitean.'[47] Certainly 'elusive' and 'ambiguous' are popular terms in Tacitean criticism, and with reason. Still, they do not help us much in explaining the actual problems we encounter in interpreting the *Dialogus*. Even Williams resignedly observes toward the end of his analysis: 'Consequently it is not easy to say what finally emerges.'[48] Klingner in a famous article argued that Maternus in his last speech cannot be supposed to express fully his real opinions about the principate, much less be a spokesman for the views of Tacitus. For all

[44] Keyssner (1936: 94-115, esp. 108).
[45] Häussler (1965: 235).
[46] Häussler (1965: 248-9), cf. Luce (1986: 144-9).
[47] Goodyear (1970: 16).
[48] Williams (1978: 45).

that, Klingner believed, Maternus sees the unresolvable dilemma between the freedom enjoyed under the republic, together with its accompanying violence, and the repression under the empire, together with the settled conditions it brought. Tacitus, concludes Klingner, is not Maternus, but he felt the same antinomy as does the character he created.[49]

## THE ARGUMENTATION

It is often stated or assumed that once Tacitus had decided to write on oratory, the dialogue form as we see it in Cicero was an obvious choice, if not obligatory.[50] Yet Quintilian, that committed Ciceronian, eschewed it. He preferred didactic exposition of the sort we find in the *Institutio*, which doubtless also characterized the lost *De causis corruptae eloquentiae*; it is a form well suited to Quintilian's personality and profession. A discussion of oratory in dialogue form was therefore not obligatory. On the other hand, it was clearly congenial to the temperament and manner of Tacitus, especially the opportunity to create a dramatic scenario involving historical personages at a particular moment in time: compare, for example, the remarkable exchange between Seneca and Nero in book 14 of the *Annals* (53-6). Much excellent work has been done to illustrate Tacitus' debt to Cicero in the *Dialogus*. Yet as instructive as these results are, the similarities tend in people's minds to overshadow the differences between the two authors. And it is in these differences, more than in the imitation and borrowings, that the deeper significance of the *Dialogus* is to be found.[51]

---

[49] Klingner (1961: 492-4).

[50] Barnes (1986: 235) argues that, in part, Tacitus chose the dialogue form and set it in 75 to refute Quintilian's assumptions about the health of oratory 'without needing to refer to Quintilian at all.' I am not convinced that Tacitus aimed chiefly to criticize Quintilian, even in the speeches of Messala (see subsequent discussion).

[51] Perhaps the most striking difference is seen in Maternus' climactic speech, where he argues that oratory flourishes in times of political turmoil; this flatly contradicts Cicero's claim that oratory is the product of a well-ordered and peaceful state. The verbal parallels could scarcely be more pointed: compare 40. 2, 'est magna illa et notabilis eloquentia alumna licentiae, quam stulti libertatem uocant, comes seditionum, effrenati populi incitamentum,' with *Brut.* 45, 'pacis est comes otique socia et iam bene constitutae ciuitatis quasi alumna quaedam eloquentia,' and *De or.* 2. 35, 'languentis populi incitatio et effrenati moderatio.' See Koestermann (1930: 415-21), Bringmann (1970: 171-4), R. Martin (1981: 63-4). Caplan's statement

One of these differences is the nature of the argumentation, which is unlike that in any of the ancient writers of dialogue who have come down to us. For example, in Plato, generally speaking, the conversational form involves the interlocutors in a common search into a complex, abstract question; the search proceeds by stages toward the truth, but not attaining it with sufficient certainty to warrant expounding it as dogma. Sometimes one or more of the interlocutors remain to the end unconvinced by Socrates' position. In Cicero, on the other hand, who claimed to be writing *Aristotelio more*, 'in the Aristotelian manner,' the truth is already ascertained.[52] The dialogue form permits this truth to be expounded in a dramatic way and for other opinions to find expression.[53] But in the end the various parts fall together into a single system. In the extensive prefaces to each book of the *De oratore*, for example, Cicero tells his brother Quintus what his own beliefs are and that Crassus is his spokesman (1. 120). All the interlocutors of the *De oratore* are in agreement when the long disquisition comes to a close. Moreover, some topics are discussed in an informal, piecemeal manner, marked by casual and occasionally frequent interruptions.[54]

Tacitus' manner is wholly different. He sets out six speeches arranged in three antithetical pairs. Each speech has been composed according to the formal rules of rhetoric. The first speech by Aper illustrates this formal structure. He begins with a *partitio*, or statement outlining the topics that he will cover: utility, pleasure, and fame—*utilitas, uoluptas, fama* (5. 4). Each *topos* comes up in order and is formally introduced, the first by 'nam si ad utilitatem uitae . . .' (5. 5), the second by 'ad uoluptatem oratoriae eloquentiae transeo' (6. 1), the third (7. 3) by 'fama et laus cuius artis cum oratorum gloria comparanda est?' The main body, or *tractatio*, of the speech over, Aper then selects, in standard rhetorical fashion, some *exempla*

(1944: 318) that 'Cicero's thought is not necessarily in conflict with that of Tacitus' interlocutor' seems to me to be controverted by the facts and by the language.

[52] Cic. *Fam.* 1. 9. 23; cf. *Att.* 13. 19. 4. Shackleton Bailey (1977: 315) cites *Acad.* 2. 119, adding 'mainly continuous exposition in well-rounded periods as opposed to Platonic conversation.'

[53] At *De or.* 1. 206, for example, we learn that what Antonius is about to say will express the opinion of Crassus also. Cf. Hass-von Reitzenstein (1970: 34, 74–5).

[54] Hass-von Reitzenstein (1970: 75–82, 91–4) analyzes the variety of techniques that Cicero used for the different types of dialogues he wrote. The *Dialogus* is closest to the *De oratore*, she argues. For Cicero's own comments, see *Att.* 4. 16. 2–3.

by way of illustrative proof: in this case, the contemporary orators Eprius Marcellus and Vibius Crispus. In power, wealth, and fame few can beat these fellows, Aper asserts. He next launches his *refutatio* (9. 1–10. 2) by arguing, as one might anticipate, that poetry cannot match oratory in respect to utility, pleasure, or fame. In his *conclusio* (10. 3–8) he concedes that, for those who do not have the talent for oratory, poetry is a creditable substitute: a lesser form of *eloquentia*, in fact. At the end he makes an appeal to Maternus to give up his defense of *Cato*: it is dangerous, and Aper is worried for him. The appeal is cast in the form of the rhetorical figure of *anteoccupatio*, in which Aper anticipates arguments Maternus might use in his coming defense and rebuts them now.[55]

Each, speech is formally structured, therefore. There are no interruptions;[56] each person finishes what he has to say before anyone else begins. Nor do the speeches show in any systematic way where opposing views are in error. Only on particular points (such as the naming of Marcellus and Crispus as exemplars of great orators, to which Maternus objects) do they respond to one another.[57] Nor are concessions made, since they are a sign of weakness.[58] No one, for example, says: 'Well, you might be right on this point; so let's push the discussion forward on this basis.' There is no dialectical progress. The job of the speaker is to defend a point of view with an appearance of full certainty, using all the weaponry from the rhetorical arsenal that he can muster.

It should be clear what type of argumentation is being deployed in the *Dialogus*. It comes from the courtroom and from the *suasoriae* and *controuersiae* as practiced in the schoolroom and the halls of adult declamation. The speaker voluntarily takes up, or is assigned, a point of view or a client, either for defense or for attack. Speeches in the

---

[55] *Dial.* 10. 5, 7. See Güngerich (1980: 43).

[56] The one at 27. 1 is the exception; but note that Messala is allowed to speak in defense of the ancients for quite a while before being cut off (25, 1–26. 8). The statement at 16. 4 is not an interruption by Aper of Messala, who has not yet begun to speak, but a pre-emption. At 32. 7 Messala voluntarily ends, and is then urged by Maternus to continue with another phase of his subject, which he does at 33. 4.

[57] Cf. the comments of Hass-von Reitzenstein (1970: 110 and n. 317).

[58] The passage at 10. 8, to be discussed, is not a concession by Aper to an argument by Maternus, who has not spoken yet, but is an admission that a modern orator who wishes to play it safe will not go on the offensive as prosecutor (as do the *delatores*, Marcellus and Crispus, who are cited as the exemplars of the modern successful orator).

Roman historians come from the same rhetorical workshop. The subjects of the *suasoria* were, after all, historical figures at certain crises in their careers: for example, 'Cicero Deliberates Whether to Beg Antony's Pardon' (Seneca, *Suasoria* 6). Sometimes, by a perverse twist of fate, the bizarre topics of the *controuersia* appeared in real life. Take this case, which might well have been the subject of an actual *controuersia*. The Law says: An uncle may not marry his niece, for this is incest. The emperor Claudius declares his intention of marrying Agrippina. You, now, are picked to speak for the defense. This, of course, is what L. Vitellius finds himself doing in book 12 of the *Annals* (5–7). Or, more notoriously, this case: the Law says: A son shall not kill his mother, for this is matricide. In book 14 (10–11) of the *Annals* the unenviable task of defending the son is given to Seneca. Tacitus gives us an outline of Seneca's arguments in a letter to the senate that he composed for Nero. The historian has, however, two criticisms. It is instructive to note what he alleges bothers him and what does not. Not the plea that Nero killed his mother in self-defense after she had tried to have him assassinated (such a claim must form the basis of the defense in order to justify matricide). Not the list of outrages that she was alleged to have committed since the days of Claudius, and which her loyal son had spent much time over many years trying to conceal, or at least to palliate (some of which were true, others believed to be true). No, what bothered Tacitus was, first, the account in Nero's letter of the collapsed boat (14. 11). Was anyone so simpleminded as to believe that this happened by accident, as Seneca claimed? And, second, was anyone so simpleminded as to believe that a woman, after being wounded in what was claimed to be an accident at sea, would send a single man with a dagger through the ranks of soldiers that guarded the emperor to assassinate him? Tacitus is bothered less by the fact that the whole defense of the matricide was a tissue of inventions, which it patently was, than by Seneca's failure to make the inventions cohere and seem credible. In the face of the enormity of matricide, the connoisseur of rhetoric is alert to the plausibilities.

Putting one's case in the best light requires selectivity: what to include and what to leave unmentioned. Then again, certain facts and illustrative examples will, like objects positioned for a photograph, be spotlighted from flattering angles.[59] In addition,

---

[59] Cf. Martin and Woodman (1989: 31).

heightened colors will be applied, including whiteners to one's own case, blacking to that of the opponents.

Selectivity of argument in the *Dialogus* is everywhere present, both on a small and large scale. An example of the former comes in the debate between Aper and Maternus on the primacy of oratory versus poetry. When Aper maintains that oratory is superior to poetry in respect to utility, pleasure, and fame, Maternus counters him on the topics of pleasure and fame, but quite naturally does not mention utility. Were he to try to make a case for poetry's utility in first-century Rome, it would simply not be credible. On a larger scale we see selectivity in the overall picture of oratory that is given in the first and last speeches, especially concerning delation and *delatores*. In Aper's first speech in praise of oratory he does not directly touch on the subject; when he cites Marcellus and Crispus as examples of successful modern orators, he does not mention or hint at the real reason for their success (which would destroy the effect he is trying to achieve). It is left to Maternus in his reply to do that (12. 2, 13. 4-5). The end of Aper's speech is particularly striking (10. 3-8), for here, when the subject of danger versus safety reemerges, he makes two concessions, the first apparent, the second real. First, he allows that poetry is a form of *eloquentia* (10. 3-5): however, it is a lesser form of *eloquentia*, and Maternus, who has the ability to scale the heights of eloquence in oratory, should not be content to rest on the lower slopes with the poets (10. 5). Second (at 10. 8), he concedes that considerations of safety require the contemporary orator to defend friends who are in trouble, rather than to go on the offensive in the role of prosecutor (as the *delatores* did).[60] The circumspect modern orator will therefore confine himself to 'private disputes of our own age'. He will, in effect, be content to rest at an elevation somewhere below the summit of true eloquence. This concession does not fit well with the picture of oratory that he sketched earlier in his speech.

Maternus argues in his last speech that the greatest orations in Greece and Rome were political in nature (37. 6-8): Cicero's fame rests, for example, not on his defense of Quinctius or of Archias, but on the Catilinarians, the defense of Milo, the Verrines, and the Philippics. Speaking on civil cases in the modern centumviral court,

---

[60] *Dial.* 10. 8.

he argues, limits the speaker in subject matter and freedom of expression (38. 2-39. 3). Maternus' case requires that he underestimate the possibility of great oratory in civil cases (yet on balance most ancients—and moderns—would probably agree with his judgment about the primacy of political oratory). Conspicuous by its absence in this speech is any reference to the activity of the *delatores*. Maternus cannot mention them because they do not fit with his speech's picture of the contemporary world as an age of security and little wrong-doing (41. 4).[61]

Exaggeration, like selectivity, is everywhere present in the argumentation of the *Dialogus*. In the first debate between Aper and Maternus, Aper argues that the poet gets little respect (9. 1-10. 2). He has a great deal of fun (9. 3-4) describing how the harried poet, after sweating over his verses day and night for a year, is forced, when it comes time to give a recitation, to pressure friends into attending. At his own expense he fits out an auditorium, rents the seats, and gets the programs ready. His reward? At the recitation he is greeted with a scattering of applause and a few empty-headed bravos; within two days no one remembers a thing about it. An amusing picture: selective in the unflattering details it includes, and exaggerated, although not overly so. The scenario is based on believable elements (compare the first satire of Persius). At the same time, Aper foresees an argument that Maternus might use in rebuttal: the recent gift of 500,000 sesterces from the emperor Vespasian to the poet Saleius Bassus, Secundus' best friend (9. 5). Aper must pre-empt that argument now (*anteoccupatio*), before Maternus gets to it. How to do this? Well, says Aper, the 500,000 is certainly marvelous and generous. But how much better it would be if Bassus earned his own keep, rather than being beholden to the liberality of others.[62]

Maternus' description of the poet's world is more exaggerated than

[61] On the narrow focus of this last speech, despite its fundamental brilliance, see Heldmann (1982: 274).

[62] *Dial.* 9. Aper's language implies that the poet must play up to the emperor from a position of dependency. Earlier at 8. 3 he had argued that the orators Marcellus and Crispus, by contrast, stood on an equal footing in their friendship with Vespasian, who well knew they brought to the friendship something he could never give them (i.e., their oratorical talent). The logic here is obviously defective, both because without the emperor neither orator would have much standing, and because Vespasian is as unable to give Bassus his poetic talent as Marcellus and Crispus theirs in oratory.

Aper's picture of the harried poet. Poetry emerged in the far-distant days, he says, of a golden age. There were no orators then because there were no wrongdoers for orators to defend.[63] Poets in those days were the vehicles of divine utterance; they even broke bread with the gods. Maternus cites as examples Orpheus and Linus. He concedes that all this may seem to Aper 'excessively mythological—and made up' ('fabulosa nimis et composita,' 12. 5). Well, yes. And Maternus' examples should make us think twice also, for while the *fame* of Orpheus and Linus is indisputable, their poetic careers were scarcely such as to give one confidence about the repose and security that the poetic calling is supposed to entail. What happened to Orpheus and Linus was not pleasant. And, of course, there is Maternus himself. It is he, and no orator, who has offended those in power and who will not abate his freespokenness. His is a retreat not from danger, but into it. The utopian world of the poet that he depicts seems particularly unreal in the face of the perilous situation his poetry has put him in at the present moment.[64]

When educated people heard speeches such as those in the *Dialogus*, therefore, they judged them on two broad levels. On one, they listened as knowledgeable practitioners and as connoisseurs, looking for ingenuity and plausibility: are the arguments apt and clever, are the examples telling, has the opponent's case been adroitly impugned, is the language choice and apposite? Yet a case that is clever and plausible will not necessarily convince. Hence they also listened on a second level: namely, does the speaker have a *good* case? Do I myself believe it? The listener recognizes easily the rhetorical cosmetics the speaker is using, since the listener regularly employs them himself. He will be aware of how the speaker has attempted to camouflage the weaker aspects of his case. And because you cannot identify the weaker aspects without being aware of the stronger, the listener will also be alert to the speaker's effectiveness in playing to the real strengths of his case.[65]

---

[63] Cf. Hor. *Ars* 391–407. From *Ann.* 3. 26 it would appear that Tacitus believed that early man lived in a state of happiness and virtue, untouched by evil desires, committing no criminal acts and hence having no need of laws to punish wrongdoers. Heilmann (1989) assumes that Maternus speaks for Tacitus here and that there is no exaggeration or humor in what he says: for Heilmann the speech is a straightforward statement of Tacitus' ethical and political credo.

[64] See R. Martin (1981: 63).

[65] Cf. *Ann.* 4. 31. 2.

The fame of the poet as disputed by Aper and Maternus illustrates
how the reader may size up the underlying strengths and weaknesses
of an argument. Praise for a poet is weak and evanescent, Aper
declares. Yet sitting beside him is proof to the contrary: Maternus,
holding the manuscript of the offending *Cato* in his hands, and with
*Thyestes* in the works. *Cato* has created such a stir that Aper at the
end of his speech admits to anxiety about Maternus' well-being. On
the other side of the political fence is the emperor himself, who has
given 500,000 sesterces to the poet Bassus. Aper's attempt to explain
this away is amusing and clever, but it is weak. A half-million
sesterces is a lot of money, even in Aper's terms.[66]

Look now at Maternus' reply concerning the issue of fame. Would
Aper like, Maternus asks, to measure Homer's renown against that
of Demosthenes? Or that of Euripides and Sophocles against that of
Lysias and Hyperides? On the Roman side, Maternus says he is willing to compare the fame of a single play by Ovid, the lost *Medea*,
against anything by Asinius Pollio or Messala Corvinus. And there
are more detractors of Cicero than there are of Virgil, he notes. Virgil,
in fact, is the capstone of his *exempla*: a poet beloved, he says, by
Augustus and by the people. Proof of the former is found in the extant
correspondence of Augustus, of the latter in the incident in the
theater, when the people rose to their feet when verses of Virgil were
read out; when they realized that the poet himself was present, they
venerated him as if he were Augustus. Maternus then has some
remarks to make on Aper's choice of Eprius Marcellus and Vibius
Crispus as examples of successful orators. A repellent duo, he asserts
(13. 4). What do they have that anyone would want? Because they
fear for themselves, or are feared by others? Because, even though
bound by the shackles of flattery, they seem neither slavish enough
to their masters nor free enough to us? They have no more independence than a freedman, he asserts.[67]

It is clear who has the stronger case on the issue of fame.[68] When
a speaker argues by describing character types rather than real
persons, such as Aper's account of the poet who gets no respect (or

---

[66] But contrast the five million sesterces given to Eprius Marcellus for his prosecution of Thrasea Paetus under Nero (*Ann.* 16. 33. 2).                    [67] *Dial.* 13. 4.

[68] It is surely a mistake to say, as Hass-von Reitzenstein does (1970: 152, 194 n.
388), that Maternus' statement at 4. 2 decides the question of the priority of oratory
over poetry before the first pair of speeches even gets under way. I believe that both
good and poor arguments are advanced on each side.

Maternus' of the mythical poet of yesteryear, for that matter), warning signals will be triggered in the mind of anyone versed in ancient rhetoric (however much he might applaud the cleverness and inventiveness of the speaker). On the other hand, when a speaker cites a series of specific examples, naming names, the listener will still be on his guard, but he will have something solid with which to make a judgment.

### CONCLUSIONS

In one respect Häussler may have come closest to explaining what I believe is going on in the *Dialogus*, although not in the sense he meant nor for the reasons he gives. Häussler, as noted earlier, likens the characters in Tacitus to people swathed in a wrapping that must be removed before the real personalities come into view. But the wrapping has been put not so much around people as around the arguments that Tacitus assigns to them.

In fact, the concentration by scholars on the individuals in the *Dialogus* has created much needless confusion because of the twentieth-century assumption that, in order for each interlocutor to be consistently characterized, the arguments given to him must be consistent also.[69] The characters are indeed 'consistent,' but in ancient, not modern, terms. By training, habit, and volition the speakers aim to present the strongest case they can for a particular point of view. This results in what moderns perceive to be exaggeration and contradictions, but what the ancients would have regarded as a natural and obligatory result for any speaker worth his salt. Thus, when Maternus gives two quite dissimilar pictures of contemporary public life, the differences are due chiefly—probably wholly—to the different rhetorical aims of his two speeches. In the first he describes it as dangerous and bloody (*sanguinans*, 12. 2) because he wants to justify his abandoning public life. In the second he wants to show that great oratory flourishes in times of political upheaval; hence he must describe his own age, in which great oratory no longer thrives, as secure and peaceful. Paradoxically put, Maternus is being consistent in his inconsistency.

---

[69] See the acute comments on characterization in the *Dialogus* by Hass-von Reitzenstein (1970: 94, 113-16).

There is an important additional point to be made, which many recent scholars have emphasized as well: in the *Dialogus* no speaker is satirized, no line of argument is without merit.[70] Tacitus has created the most effective cases he can for the several interlocutors; their speeches are ones that he might have declaimed himself had he agreed to defend the several points of view. It is wrong to claim, for example, that Tacitus' *chief* aim is to attack the views of Quintilian in the speech on education that he gives to Messala,[71] or to make us mistrust Aper by characterizing him as brash, rude, and materialistic.

Despite Messala's one-sided picture of education both in the time of Cicero and in his own day, there is at bottom much truth in what he says: for example, students in earlier days did indeed learn more by observing eminent statesmen speaking about real-life political and civil questions than do their contemporary counterparts, and it is reasonable for the reader to consider this a symptom, if not a cause, of the decline of oratory. Messala's argument here is based on the premise that the political life of each age is a determining factor, and, as such, it complements Maternus' thesis about political conditions in his last speech. Yet there, because Maternus concentrates almost wholly on the contrast between peace and unrest, his account is one-sided and incomplete, and requires views like that of Messala to round it out.[72]

As for Aper, he is neither brash nor rude.[73] For one thing, Tacitus

---

[70] See Häussler (1969: 46–67), Goodyear (1970: 15–16), Williams (1978: 45), Murgia (1980: 111), R. Martin (1981: 65–6), Heldmann (1982: 271), Barnes (1986: 236).

[71] Brink (1989: 488–94) argues that for Messala there was no hope of reviving Ciceronianism and thereby improving modern education and oratory: for Messala it was an aetiology 'of irretrievable decline' (p. 493); hence his speech is a trenchant critique of Quintilian. Williams (1978: 31), on the other hand, says: 'His attitude is . . . optimistic, since all that is needed is educational reform.' But nowhere does Messala argue or imply either alternative. His rhetorical agenda requires him to paint the education of Cicero's day in bright colors and of his own in dark colors. Whether improvement is possible does not come into consideration. It is Maternus in his last speech who argues that great oratory is no longer possible: if anyone in the *Dialogus* is to be regarded as rejecting Quintilian (and this for me is an open question) it would be, in my view, Maternus, not Messala.

[72] Klingner (1932: 153–4 = 1961: 492–3) well emphasizes the fact that Maternus measures political health according to the criteria of peace and quiet alone; other values are not brought into play.

[73] So Williams (1978: 28), speaking of Aper's 'brashness and pragmatism and vulgar sense of values.' Barnes (1986: 237) agrees; cf. Brink (1989: 495–6). The values by and large are those of the twentieth century, not first-century Rome.

would scarcely so characterize his old teacher. For another, the dialogue is carried on in an atmosphere of urbane politeness, in which sensitivity to feelings of the others is paramount. Such behavior is, as Messala declares, 'the rule by which discussions of this sort are conducted.'[74] As for Aper's materialism, his claim that the successful orator will acquire wealth, reputation, and influence was both a fact and a goal of Roman upper-class life. He observes that the display of statues and portrait busts is among the lesser rewards of the successful public man (8. 4); still, they are coveted as much as wealth and property, which, he says, you will find people more often denouncing than disdaining. Maternus in his reply concedes that somehow such busts and statues had gotten into his house 'against my will' ('quae etiam me nolente in domum meam inruperant,' 11. 3). Evidently he is not about to remove them.

If, as I have claimed, Tacitus is not satirizing any of the interlocutors, and if no line of argument is without merit, what are we to make of Aper's defense of modern oratory? Tacitus himself, after all, was convinced of the decline. Yet, although we may reject Aper's main thesis, his ideas on many matters are acute and credible. For example, his view of history and of historical development over the span of nearly a thousand years prompts him to speculate about the relative difference between 'then' and 'now,' and how one can justify styling something as 'old' (*antiquus*). This is not as easy as some assume: one's view of past time can be slippery and deceptive.[75] Nor is it unimportant; what Romans were willing to call *antiquus*, as well as the moral values that they attached to the word, colored much of their thinking.[76] Aper well argues that because something is old that does not mean it is better (a common assumption, but nowhere more common than at Rome).[77] In his remarks on 'taste'

[74] *Dial.* 27. 2: 'cum sciatis hanc esse eius modi sermonum legem, iudicium animi citra damnum adfectus proferre.' Compare also Aper's graceful compliments to his fellow speakers at 23. 5-6.

[75] An example is Messala's confidently classing Asinius Pollio and Messala Corvinus among the ancients, ignoring the fact that both practiced declamation on unreal topics (discussed earlier) and that Pollio gave one of his most famous speeches before the centumviral court (38. 2: Maternus supplies this fact).

[76] Barnes terms it silly and a quibble (1986: 237); Messala claims that it is merely a matter of terminology (25. 1-2). Contrast R. Martin's comment (1981: 62): 'His [Aper's] attempt to see the problem in an historical perspective is an important feature of the dialogue.' Horace addressed the problem in much the same spirit as does Aper: *Ep.* 2. 1. 34-49.

[77] Cf. Tacitus' comments at *Ann.* 2. 88. 3, 3. 55. 4-5. In the second passage (5)

(*iudicium, aures*) he asserts that standards of artistic excellence change over time, because they are the products of historical development. When he maintains that this evolution is one of ever-increasing improvement, we might be disinclined to follow him. Yet his basic point is telling: we all reflect to some extent the sensibilities of our own era, however much we might admire this or that earlier age or writer; this is yet another view that complements the main thesis of Maternus' last speech. Cicero had the same argument with his contemporaries that I am having with you, he says (22. 1), and, for all of Cicero's greatness as a writer, there are many aspects of his style that to us seem oldfashioned, inept, and unsophisticated (22. 3–23. 1). Even the greatest admirers of the ancients, he observes, imitate them selectively.[78]

I have argued that the case Tacitus has created for each speaker is a good case, one that he might have written for himself if asked to defend a given point of view. His intention is not to satirize any of the interlocutors, since each has some important truths to impart, however one-sided their speeches may be. But might he not have 'stacked the deck,' so to speak, by giving here and there an interlocutor weak or specious arguments in order to satirize or undermine a certain person or point of view? I am inclined to think not, or at least to think that, if such was his intention, he did so with a light touch. Take, for example, Aper's selection of Eprius Marcellus and Vibius Crispus as exemplars of the successful orator. We can be sure that Tacitus did not admire these men, both because of the unfavorable opinion he expresses in his historical works of *delatores* as a class and of Marcellus and Crispus as individuals.[79] In the *Dialogus* Maternus echoes these views by excoriating both the *delatores* as a group (12. 2; cf. 13. 5) and Marcellus and Crispus (13. 4). It would thus seem that Tacitus has given to Aper examples that are weak and under-mine his case. But this is true only when judged at the second level of reading that I outlined earlier—at the level of recognizing the real strengths and weaknesses that underlie a case. At the first level of

---

Tacitus says 'Nor was everything better in the past, but our age has produced much for posterity to praise and imitate.' Contemporary literature has achieved much, there-fore, and Syme (1958: 624 n. 3; cf. 339 and 565) with reason sees in the remark a 'veiled and personal claim.' I owe these references to Professor A. J. Woodman.

[78] *Dial.* 23. 6.

[79] See *Ann.* 1. 74. 1–2; 16. 29, 33. 2; *Hist.* 2. 10. 1; 4. 4–8, 41–4. Cf. Winter-bottom (1964).

reading, that of appreciating the rhetorical expertise of a clever speaker, the choice of Marcellus and Crispus is splendid. Aper selects them not only because they were undeniably among the most prominent speakers in Rome circa AD 75, but also because they lent themselves to being presented as what might be called 'worst-case examples.' By this I mean that the most striking example an orator could cite to prove that one activity was superior to another was a person who, despite a whole series of disadvantages, surmounted them by means of that activity alone, and succeeded because of it. Aper is therefore bent on giving as negative a picture of Marcellus and Crispus as he can. They came from 'the outermost parts of the world,' he says ('in extremis partibus terrarum,' 8. 1)—to wit, Capua and Vercellae. The families into which they were born in these remote backwaters were lowly and impoverished. What is more, both are men of bad character ('neuter moribus egregius,' 8. 1), while one of them suffers from a repellent physical deformity. Oratorical talent alone, he argues, has raised them to the pinnacle of success in Roman political life. When viewed from this perspective, Marcellus and Crispus are impressive examples indeed of the power of oratory.[80]

Another element of the *Dialogus* deserves emphasis: its humor. Aper and Maternus are its chief vehicles, Aper's robust and free-wheeling sense of fun contrasting with the subtler wit of Maternus. Aper is in his element when attacking the case of his opponents; he (which is to say, Tacitus) enjoys himself greatly, when, for example, he mocks the harried poet or criticizes the faults of earlier orators, particularly Cicero. Maternus' wit comes most to the fore in the intervals between speeches: his sly comments on Aper's performance are particularly delicious (11. 1, 15. 3, 24. 1-2). He also shows a sense of humor when arguing certain aspects of his own case. After describing the utopian world of the early poet, he says mischievously, 'or if this seems excessively mythological and made up, you will certainly concede the following point, Aper . . .' (uel si haec fabulosa nimis et composita uidentur, illud certe mihi concedes, Aper . . .) (12. 5). This is a partly tongue-in-cheek riposte to Aper's preference,

[80] Tacitus has chosen the two examples 'impartially,' for his readers would know that one of them, Marcellus, was soon to fall from power and commit suicide (Dio 65. 16. 3-4), but that Crispus would continue on, enjoying a long life of delation and honors, dying in old age late in the reign of Domitian.

stated earlier (8. 1), for modern, up-to-date examples. Messala in his earnestness is a foil to Aper and Maternus; the latter at one point even twits him gently for his seriousness (27. 1).

Earlier I argued that the reader appraises an ancient speech, at least in the Roman period, on two levels: as a connoisseur who appreciates rhetorical expertise and ingenuity, and as a critic who is able to size up the underlying strengths and weaknesses of a case. A continuous sorting process goes on in the mind of the reader as he moves through the text, therefore, the sorting being triggered by a complex set of catalysts: cultural, psychological, rhetorical, intellectual. Since the case that each speaker argues is blinkered and one-sided, the reader selects the arguments of the several speakers that convince him and, in effect, creates in his mind a composite case of his own.[81] Let me stress that there is nothing novel or unusual in this double reading or in this sorting process. It is part of the cultural matrix of the age, a mirror of how they spoke and how they thought. It also seems to me to be a mirror of Tacitus himself in his other works: in style, thought, and narrative method.

A striking feature of the *Dialogus*, especially when one compares it with its chief Ciceronian model, the *De oratore*, is the self-effacement of the author.[82] Cicero in that work is ever-present, both in his lengthy addresses to Quintus in the prefaces to each of the three books, and in the open admission that Crassus is his spokesman. But Tacitus in the *Dialogus* is present only in the first two chapters, first to respond to Iustus' question and second to introduce his two teachers, Aper and Secundus. From the moment they enter Maternus' bedroom ('intrauimus . . . deprehendimus' at 3. 1) to the final word, his presence is not felt. The last sentence reads, 'cum adrisissent, discessimus': '*They* laughed. We left.'

Tacitus gives us in his own person only one clue about the nature of the argumentation and how we should view it. This comes at the beginning in a single clause (1. 3), 'cum singuli diuersas quidem sed probabiles causas adferrent'[83] 'They individually advanced differing

---

[81] R. Martin (1981: 64) well observes: 'The reader is left to piece together his own conclusions from the arguments he has heard.'

[82] Well stressed by Hass-von Reitzenstein (1970: 18, 33–4, 96–100), who notes that Cicero's role in the *De natura deorum* is close to that of Tacitus in the *Dialogus*. Cicero at *Att.* 13. 19. 3–5 describes his methods of using interlocutors in his dialogues.

[83] Reading *quidem* of V rather the meaningless *vel easdem* of most of the other manuscripts. See Murgia (1978: 172).

points of view, but ones that are *probabiles*'). *Probabiles* might mean two things: either 'having the appearance of truth,' which would appeal to those reading on the first level, or 'diverse points of view that should cause one to say *probo*— "I approve,"' which answers more to the second level.[84] Or perhaps *probabiles* signifies both. In any case, the modern reader has the same challenging task as did the ancient listener: following along on two levels (enjoying it along the way) and conducting the sorting process. At the end, readers decide for themselves.

REFERENCES

Bardon, H., 'Tacite et le Dialogue des Orateurs', *Latomus*, 12 (1953), 166–87.
Barnes, T. D., 'The Significance of Tacitus' *Dialogus de oratoribus*', *Harvard Studies in Classical Philology*, 90 (1986), 225–44.
Barwick, K., 'Zur Erklärung und Komposition des Rednersdialogs des Tacitus', in *Festschrift W. Judeich* (Weimar, 1929), 81–108.
——*Der Dialogus de oratoribus des Tacitus. Berichte der sächsischen Akademie der Wissenschaft*, 101/4 (1954).
Bringmann, K., 'Aufbau und Absicht des taciteischen Dialogus de oratoribus', *Museum Helveticum*, 27 (1970), 164–78.
Brink, C. O., 'Quintilian's *De causis corruptae eloquentiae* and Tacitus' *Dialogus de oratoribus*', *Classical Quarterly*, 39 (1989), 472–503.
Cameron, A., 'Tacitus and the Date of Curiatius Maternus' Death', *Classical Review*, 17 (1967), 258–61.
Caplan, H., 'The Decay of Eloquence at Rome in the First Century', in *Studies in Speech and Drama* (Ithaca, NY, 1944), 295–325.
Church, A. J., and Brodribb, W. J. (trs.), *Complete Works of Tacitus*, ed. M. Hadas (New York, 1942).
D'Elia, S., 'L'evoluzione della storiografia tacitiana', *Rendiconti della Accademia di Archeologia, Lettere e Belle Arti, Napoli*, 54 (1979), 27–63.
Deuse, W., 'Zur advocatus-diaboli Funktion Apers im *Dialogus* und zur Methode ihrer Deutung', *Grazer Beiträge*, 3 (1975), 51–68.
Fantham, E., 'Imitation and Decline: Rhetorical Theory and Practice in the First Century after Christ', *Classical Philology*, 73 (1978), 102–16.
Goodyear, F. R. D., *Tacitus: Greece and Rome*. (New Surveys in the Classics, 4; 1970).
Goold, G. P., 'A Greek Professorial Circle at Rome', *Transactions of the American Philological Association*, 92 (1961), 168–92.

[84] See Güngerich (1980: 8–9). Hass-von Reitzenstein's discussion (1970: 25–31, 117) is not convincing (among other things, she believes Aper cannot be included among the *singuli*).

Gudeman, A., *Cornelii Taciti Dialogus de Oratoribus*, 2nd edn. (Leipzig, 1914).
Güngerich, R., *Kommentar zum Dialogus des Tacitus*, ed. H. Heubner (Göttingen, 1980).
Hass-von Reitzenstein, U., *Beiträge zur gattungsgeshichtlichen Interpretation des Dialogus 'de oratoribus'* (Diss. Cologne, 1970).
Häussler, R., *Tacitus und das historische Bewusstein* (Heidelberg, 1965).
——'Zum Umfang und Aufbau des *Dialogus de oratoribus*', *Philologus*, 113 (1969), 24-67.
Heilmann, W., ' "Goldene Zeit" und geschichtliche Zeit im Dialogus de oratoribus', *Gymnasium*, 96 (1989), 385-405.
Heldmann, K., *Antike Theorien über Entwicklung und Verfall der Redekunst* (Munich, 1982).
Herrmann, L., 'Quintilien et le Dialogue des Orateurs', *Latomus*, 14 (1955), 349-69.
Janson, T., *Latin Prose Prefaces* (Stockholm, 1964).
Jones, C. P., 'A New Commentary on the Letters of Pliny', *Phoenix*, 22 (1968), 111-42.
Kappelmacher, A., 'Zur Abfassungszeit von Tacitus' *Dialogus de oratoribus*', *Wiener Studien*, 50 (1932), 121-9.
Kennedy, G., *The Art of Rhetoric in the Roman World* (Princeton, 1972).
Keyssner, K., 'Betrachtungen zum Dialogus als Kunstwerk und Bekenntnis', *Würzburger Studien*, 9 (1936), 94-115.
Klingner, F., 'Tacitus', *Die Antike*, 8 (1932), 151-69. Also *Römische Geisteswelt*, 4th edn. (Munich, 1961), 490-513.
Koestermann, E., 'Der taciteische Dialogus und Ciceros Schrift De re publica', *Hermes*, 65 (1930), 396-421.
Köhnken, A., 'Das Problem der Ironie bei Tacitus', *Wiener Studien*, 30 (1973), 32-50.
Leo, F., 'Anzeige von: Taciti Dialogus de oratoribus, ed. A. Gudeman (Boston, 1894)', *Göttingische gelehrte Anzeigen*, 160 (1898), 169-88. Also *Ausgewählte kleine Schriften*, ed. E. Fraenkel (Rome, 1960), ii. 277-98.
Luce, T. J., 'Tacitus' Conception of Historical Change: The Problem of Discovering the Historian's Opinions', in I. S. Moxon, J. D. Smart, and A. J. Woodman (eds.), *Past Perspectives: Studies in Greek and Roman Historical Writing* (Cambridge, 1986), 143-57.
Martin, R. H., *Tacitus* (Berkeley, 1981).
——and Woodman, A. J., *Tacitus: Annals Book IV* (Cambridge, 1989).
Merklin, H., ' "Dialogus"-Probleme in der neueren Forschung: Überlieferungsgeschichte, Echtheitsbeweis und Umfang der Lücke', *Aufstieg und Niedergang der römischen Welt*, II/33/3 (Berlin and New York, 1991), 2255-83.
Michel, A., *Le Dialogue des orateurs de Tacite et la philosophie de Cicéron* (Paris, 1962).
Murgia, C. E., 'Loci Conclamati in the Minor Works of Tacitus', *California Studies in Classical Antiquity*, 11 (1978), 159-78.
——'The Length of the Lacuna in Tacitus' *Dialogus*', *California Studies in*

*Classical Antiquity*, 12 (1979), 221-40.

—— 'The Date of Tacitus' *Dialogus*', *Harvard Studies in Classical Philology*, 84 (1980), 99-125.

—— 'Pliny's Letters and the *Dialogus*', *Harvard Studies in Classical Philology*, 89 (1985), 171-206.

Paratore, E., *Tacito*, 2nd edn. (Rome, 1962).

Reitzenstein, R., 'Bemerkungen zu den kleinen Schriften des Tacitus', *Göttingische gelehrte Anzeige*, 14 (1915), 226-76. Also *Aufsätze zu Tacitus* (Darmstadt, 1967), 70-120.

Russell, D. A., *'Longinus': On the Sublime* (Oxford, 1964).

Shackleton Bailey, D. R., *Cicero Epistulae ad Familiares*, i (Cambridge, 1977).

Sherwin-White, A. N., *The Letters of Pliny* (Oxford, 1966).

Steinmetz, P., 'Secundus im Dialogus de oratoribus des Tacitus', *Rheinisches Museum*, 131 (1988), 342-57.

Syme, R., *Tacitus*, 2 vols. (Oxford, 1958).

Talbert, R. J. A., *The Senate of Imperial Rome* (Princeton, 1984).

Williams, G., *Change and Decline* (Berkeley, 1978).

Winterbottom, M., 'Quintilian and the *Vir Bonus*', *Journal of Roman Studies*, 54 (1964), 90-7.

Woodman, A. J., 'Questions of Date, Genre, and Style in Velleius: Some Literary Answers', *Classical Quarterly*, 25 (1975), 272-306.

# 18

# The Virgil Commentary of Servius

## DON FOWLER

Servius (called Marius or Maurus Servius Honoratus in MSS from the ninth century onwards) was a grammarian of the fourth century AD, the author of a celebrated commentary on Virgil. This is generally held to be based on a commentary (now lost) by an earlier fourth-century AD commentator, Aelius Donatus (the teacher of St Jerome), and exists in two forms: the longer, known as *Servius Auctus*, *Servius Danielis*, *DServius*, or *DS*, was first published in 1600 by Pierre Daniel, and is thought to be a seventh- to eighth-century expansion of the shorter form on the basis of material from Donatus' commentary not used by Servius himself. We know little about Servius' life, but he appears as a young man in Macrobius' dialogue the *Saturnalia* (dramatic date 383–4, but probably composed later in the fifth century) as a respectful follower of the pagan leader Aurelius Symmachus (*Sat.* 1. 2. 15).

Servius' commentary comes at the end of a long period of Virgilian commentary, which had begun in the first century BC.[1] The commentary form itself goes back to Hellenistic and earlier Greek scholarship, above all on Homer, and in a sense Servius' work bears the same relationship to Homeric commentary as the *Aeneid* does to the *Iliad* and *Odyssey*. The format is the familiar one of a lemma (one or more words of the text) followed by comments, in the manner of a modern variorum edition: sometimes scholars are named, but more commonly (especially in the shorter version) we have merely expressions like 'some say . . . others . . .' The text is typically seen as raising a 'problem' (*quaestio*), to which a 'solution' is offered: the methodology goes back to the beginnings of Homeric commentary.[2]

---

[1] Cf. H. Nettleship, 'The Ancient Commentators on Virgil', in his edition with J. Conington, 4th edn. (London, 1881).

[2] Cf. Aristotle, *Poetics*, ch. 25, with the commentary of D. W. Lucas (Oxford, 1968).

From a modern point of view, this means that the tendency is towards the removal of 'difficulties', rather than their incorporation into a more complex reading, but the same objection might be made against many modern commentaries.

The range of interest is also similar to that of modern commentaries (unsurprisingly, since modern commentary has been shaped in part by the Servian model), and includes grammatical points, rhetoric and poetics, and general cultural background. The usage of other writers is often compared, but when we can check the data they are not always correct, and statements about lost works need to be used with care. There is a particular interest in the formulae of traditional Roman law and religion, reflecting the contemporary struggle between Christianity and paganism, and Servius is alert to possible impieties. He is concerned, for instance, when in line 4 of the poem Juno is called *saeva*, 'savage', 'cruel':

**saevae:** cum a iuvando dicta sit Iuno, quaerunt multi, cur eam dixerit saevam, et putant temporale esse epitheton, quasi *saeva circa Troianos*, nescientes quod *saevam* dicebant veteres *magnam*. sic Ennius 'induta fuit saeva stola'. item Vergilius cum ubique pium inducat Aeneam, ait 'maternis saevus in armis Aeneas', id est magnus.

**savage:** since Juno is named from her action of helping (*iuvando*), many ask why he called her 'savage', and they allege that the epithet is a 'temporary' one, meaning as it were 'savage towards the Trojans', unaware that the ancients used to use 'savage' to mean 'great'. So Ennius: 'she was clad in a savage dress' [*Sc. fr. 410*]. Similarly, although Virgil always represents Aeneas as pious, he says 'Aeneas savage in his mother's arms' (12. 107), that is, 'great'.

That calling Juno 'savage' is disturbing to an ancient pagan is a point modern critics may well want to accommodate in their own readings; the 'solution' of the unnamed 'many', that she is not always savage but just at this point towards the Trojans is an obvious one, though it perhaps underplays the theological problem; but the statement that in the 'ancients' (*veteres*) *saevus* 'savage' can mean *magnus* 'great' is much more dubious. For Servius, it is unthinkable that Juno or Aeneas could be *saevus*, and so he tries to give the word another meaning: the 'solution' is again of a type not unfamiliar in modern commentaries.

The Servian commentaries can be studied from various aspects.

They deserve (and are beginning to receive[3]) treatment in their own right, as fourth-century AD writings with an ideology of their own and they are an important document in the history of ancient literary criticism, rhetoric, and education. Most readers of Virgil, however, use them as a heuristic device, a mine of information and views to excavate for use in constructing their own readings of the Virgilian texts. They tend to be used opportunistically: quoted if they support an interpretation, ignored if they do not. There is nothing wrong with this approach, so long as it is clear that Servius' authority in itself does not in any way validate a reading. Particularly useful here is the information about rites and formulae of which we would otherwise be unaware. At *Aen.* 2. 148, for instance, Aeneas describes how Priam accepts the deceiver Sinon with the words *quisquis es, amissos hinc iam obliviscere Graios | (noster eris)*, 'whoever you are, forget now the Greeks you have lost: you will be one of us', and Servius comments:

**quisquis es:** licet hostis sis. et sunt, ut habemus in Livio, imperatoris verba transfugam recipientis in fidem 'quisquis es noster eris'. item 'vigilasne, deum gens' verba sunt, quibus pontifex maximus utitur in pulvinaribus: quia variam scientiam suo inserit carmini.

**whoever you are:** even though you are an enemy. As attested in Livy, these are the words of a general accepting a runaway into trust, 'whoever you are, you shall be one of us'. Again later 'are you awake, race of the gods?' [*Aen.* 10. 228] are the words that the chief priest uses in relation to the ritual couches: because Virgil inserts into his poem a variety of knowledge.

For Servius, these two instances of formulae are part of his view of Virgil as a master of learning who has 'inserted' into the *Aeneid* a mass of arcane matter—similar views were held about Homer— while for a modern critic, they provide possible starting-points for readings of the two passages in question. It is worth noting, however, that the passage of Livy referred to is not extant (it *may* come from a lost book), and a slightly different story is told later about the religious background of the phrase in book 10: the Servian commentary is a text like any other, not an infallible source of incontestable information.

Servius' 'literary' explication of the text consists in part of elemen-

---

[3] Cf. N. Horsfall, 'Review of P. Brugisser, *Romulus-Servianus*', *Classical Review*, 41 (1991): 242–3.

tary explanations of meaning of words and the construction of sentences (often introduced with the phrase *ordo est* . . ., meaning 'take the words in the following order':[4] cf. 1. 109 **saxa vocant Itali mediis quae in fluctibus aras**: *ordo est*, '*quae saxa in mediis fluctibus Itali aras vocant*', 'take the words in the order "which rocks in the middle of the waves the Italians call altars"'). There are also, however, more advanced observations on rhetorical figures of thought and speech and on narrative technique. It is this last element which may be most interesting for modern critics. Servius often comments on what he calls *persona*, and what modern narratologists would see as matters of voice and mood (focalisation, 'point of view'). In 1. 23, for instance, Juno is described as *veteris . . . memor . . . belli*, 'mindful of the old war', referring to Troy: but since the Trojan war was not particularly old at the dramatic date of the *Aeneid*, there is a *problema* awaiting a *lysis* or solution. Modern commentators tend to take *veteris* as focalised by Juno, and meaning something like 'past' rather than 'ancient' (with a hint of bitterness), but Servius adopts a different solution:

**veteris belli**: quantum ad Vergilium pertinet, antiqui; si ad Iunonem referas, diu (DServius id est per decennium) gesti. tunc autem ad personam referendum est, cum ipsa loquitur; quod si nulla persona sit, ad poetam refertur. nunc ergo 'veteris' ex persona poetae intellegendum. sic ipse in alio loco 'mirantur dona Aeneae, mirantur Iulum flagrantesque dei vultus' partem ad se rettulit, partem ad Tyrios, qui deum *eum* esse nesciebant.

**the old war**: pertaining to Virgil, 'ancient'; if you refer it to Juno, 'fought for a long time' (DServius: that is for ten years). One must refer an expression to the point of view of a character only when he or she speaks; if there is no character speaking, it is referred to the poet. Therefore here 'old' is to be taken as coming from the character of the poet. So Virgil himself in another passage says 'they admire the gifts of Aeneas, they admire Iulus and the blazing face of the god' [*Aen.* 1. 709-10], referring in part to himself, in part to the Tyrians, who did not know that he was a god.

Since Virgil speaks in 1. 23, Servius is not prepared to accept an embedded focalisation, even though it is a natural one with a phrase like 'mindful of . . .': he therefore says that *veteris* 'old' must 'pertain to Virgil', i.e. represent his point of view rather than Juno's. The example cited within the note is, however, more complicated. When

---

[4] Cf. H. L. Levy in *TAPhA* 100 (1969), 237.

Cupid, disguised as Iulus, goes to the banquet in Dido's palace, he is much admired: the denomination 'Iulus' represents the point of view of the Tyrians, who do not know that it is really Cupid, while 'the blazing face of the god' is clearly from the point of view of the omniscient narrator, who knows his real nature. Despite his explicit statement that 'who sees?' should coincide with 'who speaks?', therefore, Servius is in fact willing to accept variation in focalisation as a critical tool, and does so elsewhere in his commentary: even where a modern critic might wish to take a different line, the comments are extremely suggestive.

Rhetorical analysis naturally plays an important role throughout. This may consist simply in the labelling of rhetorical figures in the poems, from *aposiopesis* (e.g. 2. 100) to *zeugma* (e.g. 1. 120), but it may be more extensive, especially in the comments on the speeches of characters such as Sinon in book 2 or Drances in book 11. The rhetorical tendency to see all speech as performance directed towards an end rather than revelatory of character has in the past seemed antiquated and unhelpful, but now perhaps attracts more respect. One interesting aspect of this approach to rhetoric is the way Servius reads descriptions of speakers' moods in the introduction to speeches.[5] In 1. 521, for instance, when Ilioneus speaks to Dido, he is described as beginning to speak *placido . . . pectore*, 'with a calm breast', and Servius comments:

**placido sic pectore coepit:** more suo uno sermone habitum futurae orationis expressit. (DServius bene ergo 'placido', ne timore consternatus videretur, quem ideo aetate maximum et patientem ostendit, ut ei auctoritas et de aetate et de moribus crescat. ergo 'placido' ad placandum apto; et definitio est oratoris, qui talem se debet componere, qualem vult iudicem reddere.)

**thus he began with placid breast:** in his usual fashion, Virgil expresses the tone of the coming speech in one phrase. (DServius: 'placid' is well used, so that he does not seem disturbed by fear. He therefore shows himself of full years and patient, so that his authority is increased by his age and character. Therefore 'placid', as suitable for placating; and it is the definition of an orator, who ought to compose himself in the same way as he wants to render the judge.)

It is not so much that Ilioneus really is calm at this point, as that he

---

[5] Cf. C. Lazzarini, 'Elementi di una poetica serviana', *Studi Italiani di Filologia Classica*, 82 (1989), 82–6.

speaks calmly, puts on an air of calm. This approach to these introductory phrases may be useful in cases like 12. 55, where Amata's speech to Turnus is introduced with the words *ardentem generum moritura tenebat*, 'and she, about to die, was holding back her blazing son-in-law'. The violent prolepsis in *moritura*, 'about to die', has disturbed modern critics, notably Housman: Servius does not comment, but we might say that here too *moritura* represents the tone she adopts, rather than being simply an anticipation of her death. She speaks *as* one about to die, takes on that role. This example also reveals, however, some of the dangers of this rhetorical approach: one would not want to remove all sense of a tragic prolepsis from *moritura*, given the way the participle links Amata to tragic female figures in the poem like Dido.

Apart from their own interest as late antique texts, the Servian commentaries are always worth consulting on passages in Virgil's poems: the more interesting observations are by no means always picked up by modern commentators, even those (such as R. G. Austin) who make an especial point of using the Servian material. They are not an infallible, neutral source of information about Roman customs or lost texts, nor do they embody 'what the ancients thought' about Virgil or anything else: even Servius' knowledge of Latin, as a native speaker, is not necessarily to be preferred to that of a modern scholar (he is as far distant in time from Virgil as a modern scholar from Shakespeare). Had the commentaries been written two centuries later, they would have attracted much less attention as containing 'medieval' rather than 'ancient' comment. Even where a critic may wish to disagree, however, the commentaries are always a potentially productive stimulus for criticism.

FURTHER READING

Editions: G. Thilo and H. Hagen (Leipzig, 1881–1902), 'Harvard Servius' (vol. 2 (*Aen.* 1–2) Lancaster, 1946, vol. 3 (*Aen.* 3–5) Oxford, 1965). On the manuscript tradition, see P. K. Marshall in *Texts and Transmission*, ed. L. D. Reynolds (Oxford, 1983), 385–8. For a dissenting view of the relationship of the longer and shorter forms, see D. Daintree, 'The Virgil Commentary of Aelius Donatus—Black Hole or "Éminence Grise"?', *Greece and Rome*, 37 (1990), 65–79.
   Index: J. F. Mountford and J. T. Schultz (1930).

Life: *Real-Encyclopädie der Klassischen Altertumswissenschaft* (Stuttgart, 1894–1980) s.v. (P. Wessner); H. Georgii, 'Zur Bestimmung der Zeit des Servius', *Philologus*, 71 (1912), 518–28; R. Kaster, 'Macrobius and Servius: *Verecundia* and the Grammarian's Function', *Harvard Studies in Classical Philology*, 84 (1980), 219–62, and *Guardians of Language: The Grammarian and Society in Late Antiquity* (Berkeley, 1988), 169–97.

General works: E. Thomas, *Essai sur Servius et son commentaire sur Virgile* (1880); A. F. Stocker, 'Servius Servus Magistrorum', *Vergilius*, 9 (1963), 9–15; R. D. Williams, 'Servius, Commentator and Guide', *Proceedings of the Virgil Society*, 6 (1966–7), 50–6; E. Fraenkel, *Kleine Beiträge* (Rome, 1964), 2. 339–90; M. Mühmelt, *Griechische Grammatik in der Vergilerklärung* (Munich, 1965); G. P. Goold, 'Servius and the Helen Episode', *Harvard Studies in Classical Philology*, 74 (1970), 101–68 (cf. C. E. Murgia, *California Studies in Classical Antiquity*, 7 (1974), 257–77); J. E. G. Zetzel, *Latin Textual Criticism in Antiquity* (Salem, 1981), 81–147.

Hermeneutics: J. W. J. Jones, 'Allegorical Interpretation in Servius', *Classical Journal*, 56 (1960–1), 217–26; G. Rosati, 'Punto di vista narrativo e antichi esegeti di Virgilio', *Annali della Scuola Normale Superione di Pisa, Class. di Lett. e Fil.* (1979), 539–62; C. Lazzarini, 'Historia/fabula: Forme della costruzione poetica virgiliana nel commento di Servio all'Eneide', *Materiali e Discussioni*, 12 (1984) 117–44 (cf. David B. Dietz, 'Historia in the Commentary of Servius', *Transactions of the American Philological Association*, 125 (1995), 61–97), and 'Elementi di una poetica serviana', *Studi Italiani di Filologia Classica*, 82 (1989), 56–109, 240–60.

# 19

# Ancient Literary Genres: A Mirage?

## THOMAS G. ROSENMEYER

D. A. Russell, the author of *Criticism in Antiquity* (London, 1981) writes as follows: 'Historically, "genre theory" is very much more a Renaissance inheritance than an ancient one; when we come to look for it in the critics of antiquity, as of course we must, it appears a much more patchy and incomplete thing than is commonly supposed. Moreover, the gap between theory and practice . . . is uncomfortably wide' (148–9).[1] Russell's 'as of course we must' reflects the classicist's standard conviction that if we look hard enough, we can always find antecedents of modern habits of thought among the ancients, who can be counted on to have been there ahead of us. Ironically, with regard to genre theory, that turns out to be true, in a special way. Anyone familiar with the pertinent discussions of the past twenty or thirty years knows that today genre theory has reached an impasse, or more accurately speaking, a variety of impasses.[2] There is no lack of endeavors to find alternatives to the classical triad endorsed by Schlegel, Goethe, and Vischer. But there is little agreement, not only on the question of how many genres there are or should be, but more crucially on the question of how a genre is to be defined. Is the criterion to be language? meter? structure? length? theme? social appeal? mode of communication?

---

A briefer version of this paper was a contribution to the panel on Literary Genres at the XIth Congress of the International Comparative Literature Association in August 1985 in Paris.

[1] For the vigor and usefulness of genre thinking in the Renaissance, see Lewalski ch. 1.

[2] The treatments that have been most helpful to me include those of Richter, Raible, Brooke-Rose, Ben-Amos, and Fowler. Dubrow has a good first chapter and a serviceable brief bibliography.

What receptorial and epistemological conditions must be satisfied before the concept of genre can be authenticated? How is the sense of genre to be coupled with the reader's (or interpreter's) experience, and with traditional philosophical categories?[3]

It may cause surprise, in the light of the title of this paper, that I am concerned with genre theory, and not just genres; that is, with the ancient conceptualization of genres rather than the modern apprehension of how the literary production of antiquity is to be classified. My excuse is that our modern usage, as applied to the Greek and Roman texts, is hollow unless it is warranted by the ancient. The ancient classification of literature may be said to come close to an awareness of genre distribution if there is a body of thought about the capaciousness and the kinship patterns of the classes and the class terms. Only if the ancient reflections about poetry can be interpreted as attempts to discover and understand the relationships among different kinds of poetry can we truly say that the class terms cover genre concepts.

The confusion of modern and postmodern thinking about genre becomes evident when we look at the attunements of the *rota Vergilii* by Julius Petersen (119–26), Northrop Frye (passim), and Paul Hernadi (166) on the one hand,[4] and the 1980 issue of *Glyph* (vol. 7) on the other. The latter is a collection of essays ostensibly dedicated to the discussion of genre, but the common reader would have to muster his most elaborate technique of allegorization before he could convince himself that that is what the pieces are about. (Note especially the headings 'Genus Universum' and 'The Infinite Text.') Saussurean binarism, the hermeneutic shifting and proliferation of interpretive horizons, and the Derridean demolition of typology have left genre theory in a shambles. T. S. Eliot's old notion of closed orders violently reshaped with the insertion of new, original contributions has not gained a solid foothold (Jameson 314). Nor have recent attempts, such as Elizabeth Bruss's, to revive talk about genres by falling back on speech-act theory. What remains is a consensus that the eighteenth-century triad has so outlived its usefulness that endeavors to revive it must be written off as wasted energy.[5] The epic

---

[3] For an attempt to activate the transcendental analytic and dialectic of Kant, see Rogers.

[4] For John of Garland's *rota Vergilii*, see Lawler 38 ff. and Newman, 250.

[5] For the triad, see Müller-Dyes, an informative primer of issues and terms. Müller-Dyes acknowledges his debt to Hans Robert Jauss.

is not the novel, in spite of ingenious efforts to mesh the two. The lyric today has moved so far beyond the imaginary structure postulated by Emil Staiger that any talk of it along his lines is shadow boxing.

Nevertheless, and despite the reluctance in some quarters to employ the term 'genre,'[6] current criticism and theory remain committed to the view that the intelligent discussion of literature, and indeed any response to literature, require some preliminary sorting out of the materials available, if only for heuristic ends. The force of the hermeneutic circle is inescapable, even at the level of unanalytic, unselfconscious appropriation. It is palliated only with the help of orienting devices such as genre classification. Further, the assumption still prevails that the creators of literature—if they can be separated satisfactorily from the creators of non-literary verbal and mimetic structures—must articulate their intentions by positioning themselves vis-à-vis the traditions in which they have been raised and which define their writing (Guillén 147). Authors, consumers, critics, producers, middlemen, and original geniuses cannot move without acknowledging the conventions within which or against which they wish to work. But though these choices often seem quasi-automatic, cultural determinants and historical processes modulate the definitions so that a general field theory of genre distribution is more unlikely than ever. Practical choices are made in an ad hoc manner, by way of narrow continuance, unaided by a blueprint of divisional standards. The modern schemes developed by Klaus Hempfer and others appear singularly irrelevant to the needs of poets and lovers of poetry as they go about their business.

Now let me validate my observation that the ancients may be said to have been there ahead of us. The claim, often voiced, that the classical triad of epic, lyric, and drama is an ancient classification and is not merely the product of our perception of a historical sequence— first lyric, then epic, then drama—has very little truth in it. Those scholars who have made a study of what is available in the ancient sources, both Greek and Latin, have come away disappointed. They include Irene Behrens, Claudio Guillén, L. E. Rossi, Ernst-Richard Schwinge, Marco Fantuzzi, and, most interestingly, Gérard Genette.

---

[6] Note Colie: 'One is hard put to it to distinguish between genre as metaphor and genre as myth' (121). Hempfer prefers to talk about 'Schreibweisen,' which recalls Goethe's distinction between 'Dichtarten' and 'Dichtweisen.'

In an exemplary article, Genette reviews the development of what came out of Plato and Aristotle and shows how their synchronic anatomies were largely muscled aside in favor of historical cataloguing.[7] Let me summarize some of the points made by these scholars and add to them to highlight a few way-stations in the presumptive career of ancient genre thinking.

Plato is held to have been the first to set up a triad. What he really did was to posit a dyad and then scramble it. At *Republic* 3. 392Cff. he patiently explains the difference between narration (*diegesis* or *apangelia*) and imitation (*mimesis*), and exemplifies the former by rewriting the mission of Chryses in *Iliad* 1, using indirect rather than direct speech. Turning to a consideration of what he calls *poiesis* and *mythologia*, he confirms his distinction between two types of utterance. In *mimesis*, the poet has characters speak in their voices; in *diegesis* (or *apangelia*), the poet speaks in his own voice. We will leave aside, for the time being, the intriguing question whether the dyad of (1) narration and (2) imitation is identical with the dyad of (1) speaking in one's own voice and (2) making others speak in theirs, and also the further question whether (2) making others speak in theirs is neatly separable from the poet's utterance. Plato subsequently allows for a third, mixed mode in which both *mimesis* and *diegesis* are used. However, in the end, Plato can find compelling instantiations of only two of these modes. According to him, the mode employing only characters' voices is instanced by drama, and the mixed mode employing the voices of both the poet and the characters is instanced by the epic.

As for the poet speaking only in his own voice (let us call it the discursive mode), Plato asserts that this is the rule in the dithyramb. But this last choice, though evidently prompted by the need to fill a slot demanded by the original dyad, reflects a counsel of despair. As John Herington has shown in his Sather Lectures, the bulk of archaic and classical Greek 'lyric' (i.e. poetry that is neither epic nor drama) is instinct with dramatic forms and procedures. Martin West and others have gone so far as to propose that when Archilochus levels

---

[7] Genette errs in believing that because Aristotle restricted the notion of poetry to the representation of events ('actions' would be the better term), he looked upon Sappho and Pindar as falling outside the area under study (for a similar error, see Janko's analysis of the tenth-century *Tractatus Coislinianus*). But all in all, Genette's article remains the most accomplished recent survey of the development and decline of classical genre theory.

his vituperations against Lycambes, the poetic 'I' is conceived in the dramatic mode and has little to do with the person and the life of the poet Archilochus (West 27 ff.).[8] Lycambes is, then, a fictive butt of satire, and the poetic engagement is much closer to that of Old Comedy than to what is usually understood by 'lyric.' Whatever one may think of this extreme position, it is clear, especially in the case of choral lyric, that the lyric's rendering of the poet's voice is by no means straight or pure, and that the dancing choruses of Alcman and Stesichorus and Pindar might as well be called actors transmitting the voices of dramatic characters.

It appears that Plato was at a disadvantage as he looked for an instance in which the voice of the author emerges unmediated. Instead of turning to the poetry of love or hatred (and his failure to do so lends support to West's position), he picked the dithyramb. Nietzsche notwithstanding, our information about the dithyramb is confused. We have a number of ancient notices, but they do not add up to an intelligible picture. At one time the dithyramb may have been a hymn intoned on the occasion of a blood sacrifice. In the sixth and fifth centuries it appears to have developed into a quasi-theatrical performance turning on the exploits of heroic ancestors. We have a dithyramb by Bacchylides (no. 17), entitled *Theseus*, which features a sung dialogue between half-choruses and thus moves decisively away from the pure narrative or confessional suggested by Plato's choice. In the course of the later fifth century the term 'dithyramb' came to designate a form of free verse given over to a maximum of excitement and *frisson*. The conclusion of A. W. Pickard-Cambridge still holds: 'We must be content to be ignorant of much we should like to know about all that the term "dithyramb" would have suggested to Plato's generation' (220; see also Froning). Our confusion is deepened by the circumstance that several ancient critics (Cicero, Dionysius of Halicarnassus, and Dio of Prusa) talk about the dithyramb as if it were different from or at most parallel to the rest of the lyric tradition (Färber 24).[9]

I assume we must take Plato's word for it that in his time there was a species of dithyramb in which the scope for the *mimesis* of characters was severely limited, and whose mode could therefore be

---

[8] For a response to this interpretation see Burnett 21, note 14.
[9] See also Harvey for the vagaries of Hellenistic and post-Hellenistic taxonomies of lyric.

termed discursive rather than dramatic. But is not the use of any voice (including one's own) an instrument for *mimesis* and hence dramatic? And conversely, could not other voices also be used in a discursive communication? In fact, when Plato asks what kind of poet should be allowed to practice his craft in the commonwealth, he refers to the poetic craft in general as a *diegesis*, a discourse. In this light all poets, including those in the dramatic branch, are discoursers. The best of them have as little *mimesis* about them as possible; that is, they are not receptive to the tension between actor and character. That would seem to be true of the dithyramb that Plato has in mind. In this context 'discourse' is the superordinate term, and the enactment of other voices is a subspecies of it. On the other hand, as is well known, in *Republic 10 mimesis* receives the broader mission of designating all artistic activity. That enlarged mission is anticipated in the earlier passage *Republic* 398B, where Socrates refers to the acceptable poet as one who 'would imitate the speech of what is respectable,' *ten tou epieikous lexin mimoito*. Plato, then, uses *mimesis* in two senses: in the sense of artistic representation, and in the sense of dramatization. Poets can be thought of either as fashioning their poetry, or as discoursing.

In Aristotle a similar flexibility obtains. In the wake of *Republic* 10, which Plato may have written in response to challenges from his young student (Else, *Structure*), *mimesis* becomes the usual superordinate term, while also remaining more narrowly associated with the mode of drama. In its larger sense, Aristotle reckons with four types of *mimesis* (*Poetics* 1447$^a$13 ff.): via rhythm (the dance); via rhythm and *harmonia* (music); via *logos* (forms of spoken poetry and prose); and via all three (drama). Aristotle dropped Plato's counsel of despair to instance the use of the poet's voice alone in the dithyramb, and by implication in lyric poetry. He took over Plato's dyad of the dramatic and the discursive, but located the latter in the epic. We will return to Aristotle. Meanwhile, some further thoughts about Plato.

What needs to be understood is the frame within which Plato introduces his primary distinction between the dramatic and the discursive. It is, of course, part and parcel of his discussion of education (cf. also *Laws* 2. 655 ff.), and especially of his emphasis on the value of the stable personality dominated by good sense and reason. These qualities are prerequisites for the office of guardian in his commonwealth and, more importantly, the only channel through which an approximation to a knowledge of the ultimate verities can be assured. Within that pedagogic program, the highest value is stability, which is predicated upon two further values, calmness and identity. A stirring up of the soul is counterproductive because it jars the rational firmness on which insight is founded. A superimposition of alien souls upon the soul of the reciter or the listener interferes with the self-identity and the continuity of the thinking soul and makes for disorientation. Hence the mimetic principle—the willingness to tune in to other voices and to have those voices grafted upon one's own—is pernicious. To be a member of an audience listening to characters expressing their sorrows and joys is just as bad as becoming an actor oneself and imperiling one's own identity by adopting an alien role. For the poet-actor to produce such an amalgam is tantamount to surrendering his cultural function.

As I have indicated, Plato was not unsympathetic to Aristotle's extension of the meaning of 'mimetic' to embrace all forms of literary and artistic production. Granted Plato's social and philosophical objectives, all varieties of poetry constitute a danger to the common-wealth. Perhaps it is an index of Plato's undoubted sensitivity to the charms of poetry, and also of his readiness to grant religious institutions their due, that he looked for ways to admit certain kinds of poetry after all. And so he turned to the dithyramb. His choice was influenced by his strong conviction that the only permissible poetry was one in praise of gods and heroes. But a rigorous application of his own stated principles should have ruled out even such poetry as that. After all, however impersonal or communal the performance of a religious hymn might be, its dramatic implications, its inevitable featuring of mythical materials, and its dissipation of the poet's own voice brand it a hazard. The dithyramb's traces of impersonation and appeal to ritual fervor should have been sufficient to make it unwelcome. But Plato, for whatever reasons of compromise or deference, allowed it. And so we are told that Plato is the originator of the triad of epic, lyric, and drama.

He is not. Let us disregard the notorious fact that 'lyric,' in Greek, does not include iambic or elegiac, and further, that the choral lyric of which the dithyramb is an example is very different from monody. Plato is not, in the passage with which we are concerned or any-where else, a literary theorist. He is an educator opposed to the use of poetry in the training of philosophers and citizen leaders. He sets up a disjunctive scheme to distinguish what he considers to be pernicious in poetry from its opposite. As we might have expected, he is hard put to locate an instance in the opposite column, and finally tags a species of ceremonial singing (if that is what it was) which might just as well have been put in the other column. His election of the dithyramb carries nothing like the enthusiasm with which the Romantics turn to the lyric as their master genre. It is an evasive maneuver. There is no balanced survey, historical or dialectical, of the available varieties of literature. There is no reasoned effort to come to grips with the question of how the masses of poetic material might be divided. As A. W. Schlegel observed in 1801: 'beim Plato . . . kein poetischer Einteilungsgrund' (cited by Guillén 413–14). Plato's mature method of *diairesis* would hardly have lent itself to the purpose. Progressive polarization is not the most promising method for ordering the diffuse traditions which together constituted what Plato regarded as the chief rival to his own movement of cultural and social rejuvenation. *Symploke eidon*, on the other hand, the 'weaving of forms,' the alternative organizational pattern evoked in the late dialogues (see *Soph.* 259E), might well have furnished the proper model, *if* Plato had had any interest in covering the questions a genre theorist needs to ask.

If not Plato, then perhaps Aristotle? Some have argued that Aristotle's *Poetics* is at least in part an answer to Plato's moral and aesthetic strictures. It serves notice that a person can go through a literary experience, and even through an experience of drama, and emerge a citizen in good standing. Whether or not Aristotle was less open to the power of poetry than Plato, it does appear that he was less obsessed with its dangers. As a natural scientist interested in collecting and sorting out information, he was more likely than his teacher to map the varieties of literary communication without putting the search at the mercy of a higher purpose.

Early in the *Poetics* (1447ᵃ13 ff.) he lists, in passing, some of the artistic kinds: epic, tragedy, comedy, dithyrambs (a bow to Plato?), flute music, and string music. The list is not meant to be complete, or particularly systematic. *Eidos*, 'species,' does not in the *Poetics* have the firm technical standing it has in Aristotle's logical and biological works. Hence if, at the beginning of the treatise, Aristotle lists several *eide* of poetry, it is with no demonstrable thought of how together they might make up a system of genres.[10] The folding of instrumental music into the vocal kinds and the omission of other kinds that might have been included mark the informal, even scrappy character of the series. As Aristotle continues with his distinctions among the means and the objects of *mimesis*, his procedure becomes more rigorous. But this rigor in the investigation of how various classes of poetry establish their effects does not, in the end, result in a systematic genre classification, let alone the setting up of a triad.

In the *Rhetoric* (3. 1. 1404$^a$) Aristotle recognizes a categorical difference between poetry and prose. In the *Poetics*, on the other hand, he argues that not all verse is poetry (1447$^b$13 ff.)—one of his most fundamental contributions to the theory of literature. This leaves us with three unequal fractions: verse that is also poetry; verse, such as that of the scientist-philosopher Empedocles, which is not poetry; and prose, which is not itself similarly subdivided. It might be possible, applying Aristotle's own criterion that poetry is the verbal art that represents human agency in action, to subdivide prose also into mimetic prose (cf. 1447$^b$9-13) and a non-mimetic prose. Aristotle seems to acknowledge the former as a kind of poetry, just as Dionysius of Halicarnassus later recognizes poetic elements in prose (*De comp. verb.* 1. 7, p. 6. 8 ff. Usener–Radermacher). But neither Aristotle nor his Alexandrian and Pergamene successors bothered much with formal subdivisions of prose literature. At best what we find is a division into historiography and oratory, with philosophy as an occasional third partner. Oratory is itself further split up into three branches, of which one, the epideictic, comes to be accepted as an umbrella rubric covering the most disparate literary texts. The prose romance, presumably the most widely accepted type of literary prose, is rarely referred to. A real interest in the possible varieties of prose sets in with the age of the Greco-Roman *Konzertredner* when high poetry had become an academic concern and genuinely creative impulses had been channeled into prose equivalents. Menander Rhetor and other writers on rhetoric could establish an elaborate inventory of prose mini-genres.[11] As far as Aristotle is concerned, literary prose is, in essence, rhetoric.

In the domain of poetic verse, Aristotle falls in with Plato's dyad of

---

[10] Rossi 82-3 collects evidence for Aristotle's use of *eidos*, *genos*, *idea*, etc.
[11] Russell, *Menander*; see also Russell *Criticism* 156-8, and Cairns.

the dramatic and the discursive. But now the discursive is exemplified not by the shadowy dithyramb, which Aristotle associates with neither of the two basic schemes, but by the epic. Where Plato regards the epic as a kind of communication that allows both the voice of the poet and the voice of the characters to come through, Aristotle, who is less interested in voices and presences and more in modes, labels the epic discursive, or, as we might now translate, 'narrative.' But if Aristotle's approach is a variation and shifting of Plato's, why do its terms generate only two literatures, epic and drama, instead of three? Are we not compelled to ask why the third position, the combination of the discursive and the dramatic, is left empty, and what would have to be entered into it if it were completed?

This is the question asked by Genette. But I am less confident that an unprejudiced reading of the *Poetics* makes us feel the lack of a mixed mode. Aristotle never tells us that his scheme is a tripartite one, or indeed that he has a scheme. The handling of the epic in the *Poetics* might justifiably lead to the conclusion that, in important respects, for Aristotle the epic is as much a subcategory of drama as an independent entity. This is the implication of his reading of the *Iliad*, a reading that, ironically, returns us to Plato's assessment that the epic is dramatic as well as discursive. As for the lyric, Aristotle's references to it in the *Poetics* are always marginal. There were Aristotelian writings in which, one may conjecture, more systematic attention was paid to the lyric. But, except for a few tantalizing fragments, they are lost. If there was a second book of the *Poetics*, the scholarly assumption is that it concerned itself with comedy rather than the lyric. If Aristotle's treatment of tragedy is taken as a model of how he would proceed with comedy, we might expect him to talk of structure, of segments, of the medium, of the world represented, of the social level of representation, of the addressee, of the emotions involved, and much else. We have no assurance that he used this model for the much less tractable body of lyric, iambic, and elegiac poetry. The chances are that he did not. Note, for instance, that in subsequent criticism we look in vain for an emphatic differentiation between choral lyric and monody, in spite of Plato's earlier incidental division of lyric into two groups: solo, which includes instrumental music; and choral (*Laws* 6. 764DE). Dionysius of Halicarnassus (*De comp. verb.* 19. 131 p. 85. 12 ff. Usener–

Radermacher) compares Pindaric periods with Lesbian sequences without any apparent awareness that the two are formally and conceptually at odds.

Aristotle's decision to look at epic as a foil and near-subspecies of drama shows that the plotting of precise relations among the genres is not his primary aim. In the portion of the *Poetics* that has come down to us he makes some very interesting initial distinctions among the media, objects, and methods of literary composition. His thumbnail sketch of how some classes of literary and other creative composition are defined by virtue of those differentiae moves him a considerable distance toward the elements of a genre theory. He further provides a historical explanation—the varying talents that offered themselves—to account for the doubleness of all literary activity: serious and comic, focusing on worthy actions or on scurrilous doings ($1448^a1$ ff., $1448^b24$ ff., $1449^a9$ ff.). Finally, he discriminates between tragedy and epic on a number of fronts ($1449^b9$ ff.). But his various ordering schemes, rapidly executed, are dropped just as soon as they have been broached, and thereafter Aristotle zeroes in on tragedy and its demands and opportunities. His passing observations on epic, comedy, and (an unexpected maneuver) historiography are all made for the sake of elucidating the special characteristics of tragedy. At $1456^a33$ Aristotle says: 'so much for the other categories [*eide*]; now let us talk about language and thought,' and proceeds with a discussion of factors operative in all literary composition. The use of *eide* here is once again informal. The term appears to designate methods, media, and objects rather than classes, but we cannot be sure.

Notwithstanding the extreme sophistication of Aristotle's judgments and his initial moves in the direction of a comprehensive system of classification and predication, his own efforts point towards evaluating the practices of a limited number of arts as they had evolved in the hands of professional poets and musicians. The origins of such terms as *tragoidoi, tragoidia, epe, mele,* are shrouded in early history. Homer gives us such designations as *threnos, paieon, hymenaios,* and *hyporchema* for various kinds of choral action. Other class terms, often of doubtful standing, are to be found in the archaic poets. The critics take them over, without inspecting or questioning them. Throughout Aristotle's discussion, especially in the crucial early portions of the *Poetics*, he seems to be fighting his way through a taxonomic wilderness marked by a superabundance of terminology and a lack of clear separations.

Neither Plato nor Aristotle saw a need to free himself from the automatism of craft terms. The professionals and their citizen associates were responsible for the creation and performance of particular types of poetry governed by traditional rules appropriate to each occasion. The philosophers adopted the terms and the assumptions handed to them, and argued within the limits set by these traditions. The poets of the archaic age were aware of the constraints placed upon them by the conventions of their crafts. Pindar remarks (*Nem.* 4. 33) that the *tethmos*, the statute of his particular engagement, prevents him from doing this or that and encourages him to proceed with his task as he sees it (Rossi 75–7). But this awareness of the desirability of the imposition of boundaries did not produce the kind of questioning about genre we are looking for. The critics did not confront a particular work and ask: does it belong to the domain of genre A or to that of genre B, and what are the implications of either assignment? Perhaps, if we had some intelligence about the motives of those who, late in the sixth century, carved out and institutionalized the compound product of *tragoidia*, tragedy, we might be able to say that they were aware enough of choices and discriminations to be dubbed 'genre thinkers.' But that is unlikely. The example of Ion, as he appears in Plato's dialogue of the same name, tells us that the professionals reflected upon the nature and the sources and effects of their craft, but only of the particular craft in which they were expert (Skiadas). For them, other branches of music or poetry were, it seems, largely objects of condescension or suspicion.[12] Pindar's sallies against other artists corroborate this view.

Aristotle, turning now to this and now to that specific art, and reflecting upon it, moved toward a kind of encyclopedia of the separate arts. As in an encyclopedia, each branch receives a place and a discussion of its own. The fact that Aristotle also came close to offering an overview of a number of arts (an overview disturbed by his prevailing concern with tragedy), with some remarkable insights into their potential overlap or friction, suggests that he was breaking the ground for a theory of genres. But he nevertheless remains primarily a tabulator of distinctions. He does not inquire into the ontological status of his classes, or the difficulties of class member-

---

[12] For a possible exception in Bacchylides, see Pinte.

ship. He does not ask whether the classes are paradigms in the minds of the artists or interpretive schemata for the use of recipients, or both. Much less does he aim to force the phenomena with which he is dealing into the straightjacket of the logical machinery of his *Topics*. The strict terminology of genus and species is, happily, absent from the *Poetics*. His method is descriptive rather than fully analytical or reconstitutive. From the vantage point of our modern disappointments with the search for genres, we may be inclined to regard this as an advantage.

The method is also elastic and expansive. Aristotle includes instrumental music among the species of *poietike* to be considered.[13] His comparisons with painting and sculpture endorse a highly flexible attitude toward class boundaries. It is worth remembering that, as Else has shown (*Aristotle's Poetics* 9), *poietike* is not only the art of poetry but the art of making in general; and that, above all, *poietike* is an activity, 'the shaping purpose as it guides the poet's mind.' The species subsumed under it are therefore also activities, processes. The upshot of this is that in Aristotle's eyes the *eide poietikes*, the forms of the process of making, are the various technical ways in which the process of composing can be worked out. What matters is the art. The various methods of realization are not eternally fixed. They are defined, tentatively and in the wake of artistic practices, via the means of communication, dialect, occasion, and other variable factors that are best studied historically. The fragments of Aristotle's *On Poets* demonstrate, in the example of Empedocles—is he a poet or isn't he?—that Aristotle could be on occasion remarkably inconstant. As in his other studies, Aristotle begins from *ta endoxa*, from popular usage. He accepts the crafts and the lore and the justifications that come with them. But a *rota Aristotelica* is not his business. Hence we judge his handling of literary species an ad hoc enterprise, a descriptive anatomy of whatever forms presented themselves to him. Only in the case of drama does he begin to raise questions that lead beyond stocktaking.

The critics who followed Aristotle, especially those who shared the cataloguing spirit of the librarians of Alexandria,[14] often aimed at a

[13] See also Aristotle's division of music into moral, practical, and sacred, *Politics* 8. 7. 4. 1341$^b$24 ff.

[14] Contrast Steinmetz 456: Wilamowitz notwithstanding, Alexandrian taxonomy derives not from library classifications, but from stylistic judgments.

greater comprehensiveness and at longer and more differentiated inventories. One librarian was given the epithet of the *eidos*-assigner, Apollonius the *eidographos* (*Etym. Magnum* 295. 51). His criteria appear to have been dialect, function,[15] content, and possibly others such as delivery, metrics, and the movements of the speakers or singers. It is unlikely, however, that he or his Hellenistic colleagues went beyond the cataloguing of the special features of the several classes. Cataloguing, coming out of the Sophists and the Academy, was the very heart of their work. Division, comparison, taxonomy, were pursued with so much zeal that the energy spent on the process allowed the conclusion that, once cataloguing had taken place, the argument was complete. That much of this work was archaeological is made evident by Horace's procedure. In his *Ars poetica* he foregrounds literary kinds which were extinct or slighted in his own day. Quintilian and Diomedes are among those who give us longer lists, including items about which they had only vague knowledge (Behrens 19 ff., 23 f., 25 ff.).[16] They subdivide the packages they have taken over from their predecessors into neater and more manageable compartments, and catch in these compartments much that Aristotle had left out.[17] Because the later critics prize a tidiness to which Aristotle did not aspire, they set up firm dyadic or triadic schemes of organization and harden Plato's differentiae of the discursive and the dramatic. Their main objective is to reduce the multiplicity of forms and place them under a few master headings, or genres. But the critics shy away from big questions about the completeness of the system and the systemic force of each genre. The term 'canon' used to describe a selection of texts composing a binding tradition is not ancient but of eighteenth-century origin (Pfeiffer 207).

If the catalogues presented differ slightly from critic to critic, the variances are deceptive. All of them derive from the empirical craft divisions associated with the performing practices of the professionals. For most of the later critics the principal criteria were those of outer form, precisely the criteria that Aristotle had played

---

[15] Horace, *Epistles* 2. 1. 126–38; see also Brink 158, 16 ff; Aristotle, *Politics* 8. 7.

[16] For Diomedes see his 'De poematibus', in book 3 of his *Ars grammatica*, ed. H. Keil, *Grammatici Latini* (Leipzig 1857), vol. 1, pp. 482 ff.). This section of the *Ars* contains matter from Suetonius's lost *De poetis*.

[17] The wealth of classification in the post-Aristotelian critics is best studied in Färber.

down or opposed (Schwinge 142).[18] Another standard of judgment which, under the impact of the rhetorical schools, came to loom especially large in the thinking of the later critics, was the criterion of occasion. Works were distinguished from one another according to the occasion, public or private, for which they were composed: whether the text was to be read in honor of a prince's birthday or to wish a friend good speed on his journey or to celebrate a divinity. This, more than anything else, was a perpetuation of old popular distinctions. Euripides's *Alcestis* and *Helen* are not tragedies in our sense, but they were counted as *tragoidiai* because of the identity of the festival at which they were staged, and of their place in that festival. Such labeling has its uses, but it does not encourage the reflections upon which a bona fide genre theory is based. The criterion of occasion might, under proper conditions, have been elaborated into an appreciation of the influence of societal forces, with perhaps a foreshadowing of the Marxist dimension or of Foucauldian laments. But, except for Aristotle, antiquity evinced little interest in speculations about the ties between art and society.

Finally, there is one factor that I am inclined to think doomed any genre thinking from the start. This is the ancient critical commitment to the operation of *zelos, aemulatio*. I suspect that if one were to ask an ancient dramatist or a writer of epic why he was working in his medium and not in another, and which model he was following, he would cite his allegiance to the *protos heuretes*, the founder of the line in which he was engaged. Let us, with Richter[19] and others, distinguish between the historical approach and the dialectical perspective. The ancients would have to be grouped with the supporters of the former, but only because they associated great names with the poetic branches, and not because they were interested in the order in which the branches developed. Instead of genre criticism, the ancients practiced model criticism. Their allegiances and affiliations connect, not with a mode or a kind, but with a father, a personal guide. If they ally themselves with a work, it is identified as the work of a revered author, the precipitation of a literary act, not a fatherless

---

[18] For Aristotle's polemic against defining all verse as poetry, see *Poetics* 1445[b]; 1451[b]. See also Cicero, *Orator* 67, and Horace, *Satires* I. 4. 40 ff.

[19] Richter's formulation echoes similar distinctions by the Slavic formalists. See also Fantuzzi 439-40, and Hinck ix. But Richter's prediction that most of the battles in the immediate future would be among defenders of classical genre concepts (rather than among the skeptics coming out of Kant) has not been borne out.

text or a textual segment or a generic idea. Like the Pythian priestess inspired by her god, writers and critics are inspired by the effluences, *aporroai*, that stream into their souls from the sacred mouths of great models (Longinus, *On the Sublime* 13. 2). Where genre thinking is scientific, inferred from a sufficient sampling of texts and their properties, model thinking is, as it were, moral, and triggered by predecessors. Quintilian's history of literature (*Instit. orat.* 10. 1) recites, not genres, but practices, and above all, proper names. Nonnus emulates Homer, Seneca Sophocles, Catullus Sappho, Horace Alcaeus, Cicero Plato or Demosthenes.[20] Did Old Comedy die out because Aristophanes could not, in the climate of the times that followed, be admired?

It is precisely because epic and drama had acknowledged fathers that they came to be regarded as definable legacies. On the side of the lyric, obvious paradigms were harder to select. When Callimachus puts an end, for all practical purposes, to the composition of heroic epic, he is not engineering the obsolescence of a genre, but modifying the *Odyssey*, i.e. fighting with Homer, but no more than Stesichorus fought with Homer, or Archilochus. From the very start of recorded literature, authors generally disregarded Quintilian's admonition (10. 2. 21–2) to stay timidly within the perimeters set by the traditions. The Hellenistic manhandling of genres, that is to say, the remodeling of the great ancestors' achievements, carries forward an old Greek pastime.[21] What results is not a *Kreuzung der Gattungen*,[22] a hybridizing of genres, but an exercise in the freedom of *aemulatio*. If Callimachus, defying metrical precedent, has two victory hymns in elegiacs and one in trimeters, and a religious hymn not only in elegiacs but in the Doric dialect, we should recall Alcaeus's monodic hymns, the choral epic of Stesichorus, and other remarkable specimens of brisk modulation. These are not violent reshapings of fixed orders but ready adjustments of family relations, energetic and enterprising rather than iconoclastic or Oedipal. Plato's nostalgic picture of an old world in which there was no challenge to the observance of certain types of music (*Laws* 3. 700 f.)

---

[20] For matching authors rather than kinds, see Guillén 399 ff.

[21] My sense that Hellenistic ways of dealing with earlier texts can be matched in the archaic age goes against the schema of Rossi, who sees successive ages distancing themselves progressively from their generic commitments.

[22] The term is Kroll's, 202 ff. See also Klein, and Bulloch 35–6.

locks into place a commitment to impersonal tradition which existed only on the lower levels of artistic activity. His castigation of the new poets and their rebellious ways is an unrealistic denial of the spirit of *zelos*. The prestige of the father and the rivalries within the family account most satisfactorily for what stability there is in the formal and aesthetic continuities over the years, while also explaining the great variety of creative departures. There is no need for an appeal to a biological model of growth and decline as long as the model of the family quarrel, or rather the playful engagement with the parent, is available.

The availability of the parental model helped to forestall the recognition of any need for an authentic theory of genres. The unreflected adoption of craft terminology, along with the inveterate tradition of imitating, and quarreling with, great masters of the craft, satisfied the classifying instincts of the ancient critics. New terms were invented, and new crafts were acknowledged as they emerged— Quintilian's remark on satire, 'satura quidem tota nostra est' (Satire, for its part, is completely our own, 10. 1. 93), is relevant here. But with the exception of Plato and Aristotle, the ancient critics exhibited no interest in exploring genres. And as we have seen, Plato's and Aristotle's assessments fell short of attaining the systematic character which the eighteenth and nineteenth centuries believed they could trace back to them.

REFERENCES

Behrens, Irene, *Die Lehre von der Einteilung der Dichtkunst* (Zeitschrift für romanische Philologie, 92; Halle/Saale: Niemeyer, 1940).
Ben-Amos, Dan, 'Catégories analytiques et genres populaires', *Poétique*, 19 (1974), 265-93.
Brink, Charles O., *Horace on Poetry. Epistles Book II* (Cambridge: Cambridge UP, 1982).
Brooke-Rose, Christine. 'Historical Genres/Theoretical Genres', *New Literary History*, 8 (1976-7), 145-58.
Bruss, Elizabeth W., *Autobiographical Acts: The Changing Situation of a Literary Genre* (Baltimore: Johns Hopkins UP, 1976).
Bulloch, A. W. (ed., tr., and comm.) *Callimachus: The Fifth Hymn* (Cambridge: Cambridge UP, 1985).
Burnett, Anne P., *Three Archaic Poets* (Cambridge, Mass.: Harvard UP, 1983).

Cairns, Francis, *Generic Composition in Greek and Roman Poetry* (Edinburgh: Edinburgh UP, 1972)

Colie, Rosalie L., *The Resources of Kind: Genre Theory in the Renaissance* (Berkeley and Los Angeles: U of California P, 1973).

Dubrow, Heather, *Genre* (London: Methuen, 1982).

Else, Gerald F., *Aristotle's Poetics: The Argument* (Cambridge, Mass.: Harvard UP, 1957).

——*The Structure and Date of Book 10 of the Republic* (Abhandlungen der Akademie Heidelberg 1972/3; 1972).

Fantuzzi, Marco, 'La contaminazione dei generi letterari nella letteratura greca ellenistica', *Lingua e stile*, 15 (1980), 433-50.

Färber, Hans, *Die Lyrik in der Kunsttheorie der Antike* (Munich: Neuer Filser-Verlag, 1936).

Fowler, Alastair, 'Genre and the Literary Canon', *New Literary History*, 11 (1979-80), 97-119.

Froning, H., *Dithyrambos und Vasenmalerei in Athen* (Beiträge zur Archäologie, 2; Würzburg: Triltsch, 1971).

Frye, Northrop, *Anatomy of Criticism* (Princeton: Princeton UP, 1957).

Genette, Gérard, 'Genres, "types", modes', *Poétique*, 32 (1977), 389-421.

*Glyph 7* (1980) The Strasbourg Colloquium: Genre.

Guillén, Claudio, *Literature as System* (Princeton: Princeton UP, 1971).

Harvey, A. E., 'The Classification of Greek Lyric Poetry', *Classical Quarterly*, 5 (1955), 157-75.

Hempfer, Klaus W., *Gattungstheorie* (Munich: Fink, 1973).

Herington, John, *Poetry into Drama* (Berkeley and Los Angeles: U of California P, 1985).

Hernadi, Paul, *Beyond Genre* (Ithaca: Cornell UP, 1972).

Hinck, Walter (ed.), *Textsortenlehre—Gattungsgeschichte* (Heidelberg: Quelle und Meyer, 1977).

Jameson, Fredric, *Marxism and Form* (Princeton: Princeton UP, 1971).

Janko, Richard, *Aristotle on Comedy: Towards a Reconstruction of Poetics II* (Berkeley and Los Angeles: U of California P, 1984).

Klein, T. M., 'The Role of Callimachus in the Development of the Concept of the Counter-Genre', *Latomus*, 33 (1974), 217-31.

Kroll, Wilhelm, *Studien zum Verständnis der römischen Literatur* (Stuttgart: Metzler, 1924).

Lawler, Traugott (ed.), *The Parisiana Poetria* (Yale Studies in English, 182; New Haven: Yale UP, 1974).

Lewalski, Barbara K., *'Paradise Lost' and the Rhetoric of Literary Forms* (Princeton: Princeton UP, 1985).

Müller-Dyes, Klaus, *Literarische Gattungen: Lyrik, Epik, Dramatik* (Freiburg: Herder, 1978).

Newman, J. K., *The Classical Epic Tradition* (Madison: University of Wisconsin Press, 1986).

Petersen, Julius, 'Zur Lehre von den Dichtungsgattunger', in *Die Wissenschaft von der Dichtung* (Berlin: Junker, 1939), 119-26.

Pfeiffer, Rudolph, *History of Classical Scholarship* (Oxford: Clarendon, 1968).

Pickard-Cambridge, A. W., *Dithyramb, Tragedy and Comedy* (Oxford: Clarendon, 1927).

Pinte, Daniel, 'Un classement des genres poétiques par Bacchylide', *L'Antiquité classique*, 35 (1966), 459-67.

Raible, Wolfgang, 'Was sind Gattungen?', *Poetica*, 12 (1980), 320-49.

Richter, David H., 'Pandora's Box Revisited', *Critical Inquiry*, 1 (1974-5), 453-78.

Rogers, William E., *The Three Genres and the Interpretation of Lyric* (Princeton: Princeton UP, 1983).

Rossi, L. E., 'I generi letterari e le loro leggi scritte e non scritte nelle letterature classiche', *Bulletin of the Institute of Classical Studies*, 18 (London, 1971), 69-94.

Russell, D. A., *Criticism in Antiquity* (Berkeley and Los Angeles: U of California P, 1981).

——and N. G. Wilson (eds., trs., and comms.), *Menander Rhetor* (Oxford: Clarendon, 1981).

Schwinge, Ernst-Richard, 'Griechische Poesie und die Lehre von der Gattungstrinität in der Moderne', *Antike und Abendland*, 27 (1981), 130-62.

Skiadas, Aristoxenos D., 'Über das Wesen des Dichters im platonischen *Ion*', *Symbolae Osloenses*, 46 (1971), 80-9.

Staiger, Emil, *Grundbegriffe der Poetik* (Zurich: Atlantis, 1946).

Steinmetz, Peter, 'Gattungen und Epochen der griechischen Literatur in der Sicht Quintilians', *Hermes*, 92 (1964), 454-66.

West, Martin L., *Studies in Elegy and Iambus* (Berlin: de Gruyter, 1974).

# 20

# *Criticism Ancient and Modern*

## DENIS FEENEY

mihi de antiquis eodem modo non licebit?

(Cic. *Or.* 171)

Classicists have long taken it for granted that an acquaintance
with the literary criticism of the ancients is a useful skill for the
student of their literature to master.[1] This rather general and often
unarticulated assumption, part of a larger professional concern with
unanachronistic historical fidelity, has recently been given a much
sharper focus in the work of Francis Cairns and Malcolm Heath.[2] The
latter scholar in particular has claimed, not merely that ancient
literary criticism is a useful supplement to the critical apparatus of
the modern scholar, but that ancient literary criticism is in effect the
only apparatus which the modern scholar may use for the purpose of
'poetics', an activity defined as 'a historical enquiry into the workings of a particular system of conventions in a given historical and
cultural context'.[3] In the case of fifth-century Attic tragedy, for
example, despite the fact that we have no contemporary critical
testimony to speak of outside Aristophanes, we are assured by Heath
that 'even a fourth-century writer is a priori more likely to be a
reliable guide to tragedy than the unreconstructed prejudices of the
modern reader'.[4]

---

[1] I am putting as much stress on the 'and' in the title as Donald Russell did when I
heard him introducing R. D. Williams's talk at Oxford on 'Virgil and Homer'. I first
tried out some of these ideas on the Bristol English–Latin Seminar in November 1991;
and an audience at Berkeley heard a (suitably disguised) version in April 1994. My
thanks to those present for their comments. I must also thank several people who read
a draft of the chapter: Stephen Hinds, Jacques Lezra, Laura McClure, Terry
McKiernan, Georgia Nugent, Neil Whitehead, and Jeffrey Wills (who suggested my
motto from Cicero). The editors had me think again on various points, and made me
wish I had had the space to develop the case further.

[2] Cairns (1972); Heath (1987, 1989).

[3] Heath (1987: 1 n. 1).     [4] Heath (1987: 3).

In order to set up the competition which I wish to conduct in this essay, let me, to the accompaniment of litotes, bring on to the stage the scholar whom we honour with this volume, a man more versed than most in ancient literary criticism, and a man whom few would convict of possessing more than his share of 'unreconstructed prejudices'. A striking leitmotif of Donald Russell's synthetic judgements on ancient literary criticism is his apprehension that, however much 'we cannot help reasoning that the Greeks and Romans must after all know best, since the language and the culture were their own', nonetheless, 'this ancient rhetorical "criticism" . . . is fundamentally not equal to the task of appraising classical literature'.[5] This is true, by Russell's account, of the ancient critics' principles of style and allegory (6–7, 98, 131), of their study of *imitatio* (113), literary history (117, 168), and genre (149, 152).[6] Both in *Criticism in Antiquity* and in his valedictory lecture, when he stands back to sum up his impressions of pervasive antithetical currents in ancient literature—impressions which could have been formed only by the most broad and searching reading—he concedes that they do not correspond to anything formulated by an ancient critic (indeed, to anything that *could have been* formulated by an ancient critic).[7]

My own rhetoric will probably have indicated which of the agonists wins my vote, and I have already elsewhere indicated that I think the ancient critics are to be used 'as an aid, even a guide, but not as a prescription, or a straitjacket'.[8] But I would like to develop those earlier brief remarks and justify in detail my partiality for Donald Russell's position. Then I would like to suggest why all critics everywhere should expect to find themselves in his predicament. For the issues raised by my comparison rapidly multiply. An examination of the role of ancient criticism in the study of ancient texts soon spins into its corollary—currently very topical—of the examination of the role of modern criticism in the study of ancient texts;[9] and that issue in turn confronts us with the problem of what

---

[5] Russell (1981: 1, 6). Page references in the next sentence of the text are to this book.

[6] For his reservations about the penetration of ancient *imitatio*-studies, see also Russell (1979: esp. 9).

[7] Russell (1981: 6–7; 1989: 21). Cf. G. A. Kennedy (1989a: 493), on the fact that 'the ancient criticism we have seems oblivious of major historical features of the literatures'; and Williams (1968: 31), on ancient reflections on the nature of poetry: 'the answers of theorists lagged quite a lot behind the practice of poets'.

[8] Feeney (1991: 3).      [9] De Jong and Sullivan (1994).

we take to be the explanatory power of criticism anyway. No doubt by the end of the essay I will have taken up positions which Donald Russell would not care to occupy with me, but at least we will have begun in the same camp, and he may be sure that my own forays could not have been undertaken except under his auspices, and with the well-supplied commissariat of his scholarship.

We must begin by delineating the difficulties involved in Heath's claim that ancient testimony is our sole legitimate interpretative key: 'when we are dealing with the evidence of witnesses who are contemporary or near contemporaries, there is at least a presumption of general reliability; certainly, they are more likely to prove reliable guides than the untutored intuition of a modern reader—which is, in practice, the only alternative, and a patently treacherous one'.[10] For all its polemical tone, such a statement captures a basic frame of mind shared by many classicists, and it takes an effort to shake oneself free of its allure.

For a start, we may observe how many ancient aesthetic objects are removed from our critical attention by the strict application of Heath's law. He has concentrated on topics where a good deal of ancient critical evidence is extant (Attic tragedy, the problem of unity), but, even rhetorically, it is worth asking how he would propose we discuss the ancient novel, which was 'drastically under-theorized', as J. R. Morgan puts it, 'even to the extent that there was no word for it in either Greek or Latin'.[11] If modern critics of ancient literature are to confine themselves to the critical horizon of the surviving ancient evidence, then scholars of the ancient novel might as well shut up shop. Or how are we to talk of ancient art according to Heath's model when, for example, there is in the extant corpus of classical literature precisely one reference to vase-painting?[12]

Heath is far more alert to the difficulties of periodization than his precursor Cairns, who, in order to justify his use of a third/fourth-century AD model for interpreting literature back to the archaic period, had to make his now notorious claim that 'in a very real sense antiquity was in comparison with the nineteenth and twentieth

[10] Heath (1987: 3).

[11] Morgan (1993: 176). I can only agree with Morgan: 'The obvious point is that there is a lot which is in excess of ancient theory, but that just means that theory had not caught up with practice' (224).

[12] Ar. *Eccl.* 996; my thanks to Barry Powell for this interesting information.

centuries a time-free zone'.[13] Still, despite Heath's acknowledgement of the possible anachronism of using ancient critics who are not contemporary with their texts,[14] he remains on thin ice in describing Aristotle as a near contemporary witness to Attic drama. Euripides and Sophocles had been dead for anything between forty-five and eighty-five years by the time the *Poetics* were composed, and Aeschylus for anything between ninety-five and one hundred and thirty-five. By this kind of calculation Pope is a near contemporary witness of Shakespeare's aesthetic, and Tennyson a near contemporary witness of Pope's—and this is quite apart from the problem, to which I return shortly, of what *kind* of witness Aristotle is.

The difficulties in historical perspective glimpsed here open up larger problems with the historicist stance represented by Heath and Cairns. One of the main flaws in this kind of approach is that it cannot do justice to the very sense of history which it purports to champion, for critics such as Heath and Cairns exhibit a systematic refusal to come to terms with the fact that their own critical practice is historically sited.[15] The claim that only a given culture's modes of criticism can work for that culture has some kind of initial plausibility, perhaps, but we have to recognize that this claim itself comes from an identifiable modern philological tradition. Heath is always denouncing modern prejudice, but the idea that we can only read ancient literature in terms of ancient criticism is itself a modern prejudice.[16]

And it is one which it is theoretically impossible to control in the way Heath wishes to, for any modern selection of ancient critical techniques and approaches is inherently partial, in every sense of the word. Heath asserts quite rightly that 'we do not inspect "the poem

---

[13] Cairns (1972: 32).

[14] Heath (1987: 2-4; 1989: 10-11, 122).

[15] Heath (1987: 79) recognizes that 'the preoccupations of literary criticism . . . are historical and change in the course of history', but his argument proceeds as if he is exempt from the implications of his insight. My own emphasis on the historical sitedness of the critic is of course ultimately indebted to Gadamer (1960). For classicists' perspectives on the 'hermeneutics of reception', see Martindale (1993a) and Nauta (1994).

[16] Quite unrealizable, at that, as pointed out by D. F. Kennedy (1993: 8): 'If historicism achieved its aim of understanding a culture of the past "in its own terms", the result would be totally unintelligible except to that culture and moment . . . Far from past being made "present", it would be rendered totally foreign and impenetrably alien.'

itself" without presupposition, and our presuppositions dispose us to find plausible or implausible interpretations of one or another kind';[17] but precisely the same is true of our inspection of criticism. At the most basic level, there is simply so much ancient criticism, and it is so multifaceted, that the modern critic must pick and choose: as Andrew Ford well says of the Homeric scholia, in the course of a sympathetic but dissenting review of Heath (1989), 'we are always taking from them what we find congenial and discarding the rest'.[18] Despite acknowledging the problematic nature of the critical material,[19] in his *modus operandi* Heath does not actually treat the corpus of ancient literary criticism as something that requires interpretation on a footing with the literature. But the corpus is itself, if you like, 'literary', not an inert tool. This is immediately obvious in the case of an Aristotle or a Horace, but it is also true of Servius and the largely anonymous company of the scholia. We are not dealing with a problematic body of material ('literature') which can be explained with the aid of a less problematic body of material ('criticism'): we are dealing with numerous, often contesting, strands of problematic material which interact with each other in innumerable categories of time and space.[20]

The critical terrain, in short, is riven and complex, and our modern image of it is an interpretative construct, every bit as open to anachronism and *parti pris* as our construction of the 'literature'. An example of this is to be found in Heath's use of Aristotle's *Poetics* as evidence in reconstructing the 'emotive hedonism' which he sees as the ruling aesthetic of the tragic drama of the previous century. In using Aristotle as *evidence* for poetic practice in this way, he first of all removes Aristotle from a philosophical context, for, as Halliwell says, in the *Poetics* 'the theory is *normative*, and its principles, while partly dependent on exemplification from existing works, are not simply deduced from them. The theorist's insight claims a validity which may well contradict much of the practice of playwrights hitherto.'[21] Further, Heath's reading of what Aristotle has to say about the

---

[17] Heath (1989: 122).
[18] Ford (1991: 147); I must declare my debt here to this finely argued essay. Cf. Martindale (1993*b*: 123) on Heath's approach: 'we all . . . in order to validate our readings, appropriate, *selectively*, pieces of past data. There are reasons for this selectivity, but those reasons are always and never good enough as it were.'
[19] Heath (1987: 2–3).       [20] Ford (1991: 146–7).
[21] Halliwell (1987: 83, his italics; cf. 9–10, and 1986: 3–4).

emotions is very much at odds with other recent interpretations of the *Poetics*, notably that of Halliwell, by whose account Aristotle's concept of aesthetic pleasure is one 'in which cognition and emotion are integrated'; indeed, 'Aristotle's conception of the emotions, pity and fear, itself rests on a cognitive basis'.[22] This kind of approach to Aristotle has been behind some compelling recent studies of tragedy, especially those of Martha Nussbaum[23]—though her ethics-based approach is not without its own risks, especially that of making the play, as Terry McKiernan puts it, 'a piece of moral philosophy worn inside-out, with the example or parable on the outside and the argument that the example illustrates hidden within'.[24]

All this has serious implications for Heath, since it is an important part of his purpose to discredit 'intellectualizing' readings of Attic tragedy. If Heath has to read Aristotle in a reductive way in order to make this possible, he also has to disparage another strand of ancient criticism—just as venerable and authoritative, it may seem to other observers—that is, the didactic one, as exemplified in the only genuinely contemporary substantial evidence we have, Aristophanes' *Frogs*. Heath's distinctive intellectual honesty has him acknowledge the prominence of the didactic bent in the ancient tradition, but he dismisses it as a 'habit', not something interesting or important, and certainly not something which gives 'support for the intellectual interests of modern tragic interpretation'.[25] When an ancient critic makes a remark about a text's emotional impact, Heath will commend him, but not when he makes a remark about its didactic impact; it is difficult to see this preference as one that emerges naturally from the material under inspection. Although I have a good deal of sympathy with many of Heath's objections to the intellectualizing reading of Greek tragedy as it is actually practised, I do not see how he can write it down by elevating one strand of ancient criticism over another.

[22] Halliwell (1986: 76; see his whole discussion of pleasure, 62–81, and, for specific engagements with Heath, Halliwell (1989; 1992: 255). Only after writing this chapter did I see the powerful article of Lada (1993; see esp. 114–18).

[23] Nussbaum (1986: esp. 12–15; 1990: esp. 378–91, on the theoretical issues).

[24] My thanks to him for letting me quote from an unpublished essay on ethics in tragedy. Similar reservations in Harrison (1991: 15–17).

[25] Heath (1987: 47). Heath's main ground for rejecting intellectualizing interpretations as part of 'poetics' is that the poets cannot have intended them (44–5); but, even if we conduct the debate on these terms, I do not see on what evidence he can claim that they did not.

Heath represents a set of assumptions shared by many classicists, even if he pushes them to their extremest limit. There are doubtless many ways of accounting for the appeal of such an approach—a concern with professional rigour; a belief that only an historicizing approach is intellectually respectable; a desire to make criticism as 'objective' as philology, so that this movement in literary criticism in Classics becomes the counterpart of the anxieties of students of modern literatures over what exactly their craft (τέχνη) is (a dilemma that goes back to Socrates' interrogation of Ion). I suspect, however, that the main reason why so many classicists attribute such authority to ancient literary criticism is that it relieves them of the distasteful task of attributing any authority to modern literary criticism. The historicist bent of classical training predisposes many of us to be hostile to the idea that the ancient world can be illuminated by modern schemes which may be quite at odds with the conceptual apparatus of the Romans and Greeks,[26] yet it is an issue which we continually confront, and Charles Segal is quite right to describe it as 'perhaps the central hermeneutic question of our field today'.[27]

It should be clear from my discussion so far that in my opinion we are all (including Malcolm Heath) doing modern literary criticism all the time, and that students of ancient literature have to learn to live with the hermeneutic gap: 'interpretation . . . involves a constantly moving "fusion of horizons" between past and present'.[28] Just as in the case of ancient literary criticism, however, we are of course always engaged (consciously or not) in selecting which currents of modern criticism to value and which to disparage, and it becomes a decided problem to justify or even to isolate the criteria by which we perform this selection.[29] If we grant that there is a necessary gap of incommensurability between our criticism and the ancient text (a protasis which not all my readers will accept), does it follow that all modern modes of analysis are equally valid or rewarding?

---

[26] Martindale (1993a: 5-6) on historicism in the Classics.

[27] Segal (1992: 153).

[28] Martindale (1993a: 7); cf. the points made by D. F. Kennedy (1993), quoted at n. 16 above. The most obvious example of Heath's use of the techniques of modern literary criticism is in his synoptic discussion of individual tragedies in the compass of a few pages; this is not a form of criticism practised in the ancient world, or in the modern world either until John Dryden's 'Examen of *The Silent Woman*' in his 1668 *Essay on Dramatic Poesy* (my thanks to Richard Knowles for this information).

[29] On this problem, see Goldhill (1994: 52).

Attempts have been made to suggest continuities, or at least deep similarities, between certain ancient and modern preoccupations, especially in semiotics and scepticism.[30] The value of such connections will reside in the use to which they are put in practice, and the 'naturalness' of the connections may of course always be challenged on the grounds that we are finding only what we are predisposed to look for: when Simon Goldhill says that the 'fifth century underwent "a linguistic turn" ',[31] it is easy to remark that only the intellectual heir of the twentieth-century's 'linguistic turn' is in a position to talk in these terms. Still, when we are dealing with semiotics and rhetoric we may feel more confidence in finding analogies between our interest in language and theirs if we reflect that analogy is itself, after all, one of *their* words. We have, I think, a different kind of problem—though not of course *per se* a disabling one—when there appear to be clear discrepancies between ancient and modern approaches.

Of the critical techniques currently in play, the most problematic from this point of view is probably psychoanalysis, because its scientistic apparatus lays open the issue of its truth-claims in a particularly overt form. These truth-claims have for some time been under attack on their own terms anyway, and it is clear that in psychiatric and psychological education and practice the psychoanalytic model of the mind has nothing like the authority that it had even twenty years ago.[32] Even if, for the sake of argument, we concede that the model has some kind of validity for late nineteenth-century and twentieth-century European culture, we still need to contend with the fact that anthropologists and historians are practically united in doubting the value of applying it to other cultures.[33]

[30]  G. A. Kennedy (1989*a*, 1989*b*: pp. xi–xii), Sullivan (1994: 14–21).

[31]  Goldhill (1986: 2).

[32]  Grünbaum (1984) and (1993); for an ancient historian's perspective, S. R. F. Price (1990: 360–70); a highly critical overview in Crews (1993), with reaction and discussion in Crews (1994). My thanks to Jude, and to my neighbour, Dr James Gustafson, for their conversations about contemporary psychology and psychoanalysis.

[33]  Price (1990: 370): 'Freudian theory is thus at best extremely problematic, and its imposition on another culture singularly futile'; Dinnage (1993: 66): 'Anthropologists now tend to feel, understandably, that psychoanalytic studies of societies, particularly of non-Western societies, apply unproven theories and a Western bias to cultures with quite different assumptions.' As Neil Whitehead points out to me, such perspectives in anthropology only became possible once the Freudian model had lost a good deal of its authority in its own home culture.

It is bad luck for exponents of psychoanalytic criticism in Classics—whether they acknowledge it as such or not—that they are entering a field dominated by the Foucauldian view of sexuality and the self as variably constructed cultural phenomena, in which the current agenda is to 'define and refine a new, and radical, historical sociology of psychology'.[34] Very few practitioners do in fact make the kind of claim for the transhistorical and transcultural applicability of Freudianism that is advanced by Caldwell, for example,[35] but this only throws into relief the usual evasion of the issue. Repression, unconscious, desire, lack, other: with what stringency are these terms being used?

A major difficulty is brought into focus with a question asked by Segal: 'One of the big problems with applying any kind of psychological criticism is to try to decide what is the object of the analysis. Are you trying to analyze the author; or ... the relationship between the reader and the text ... ; or ... a particular character?'[36] Increasingly the answer to this question is 'the text', or 'the narrative'.[37] Françoise Meltzer puts the case very economically (though remaining faithful to the idea that Freud does have something to teach us about the psyche), in discussing Freud's necessary use of the known in order to describe the unknown (*das Unbewusste*, the original of 'the unconscious'): 'Freud will be "condemned" to describe the unconscious rhetorically, through analogies, metaphors, similes, etymological play, and anecdotes. And the way that future critical theory will choose to read those rhetorical tropes employed by Freud will ultimately . . . tell us as much about the "economy" of rhetorical structures and the inner workings of

[34] Halperin (1990: 40; cf. esp. 41-6 for the 'essentialist/constructionist' debate over 'homosexuality'). Of course our reconstruction of that ancient sexuality and self will always be in dialogue with our own deeply acculturated sense of sexuality and self, of which some kind of Freudianism—however diluted—is inevitably a part; cf. D. F. Kennedy (1993: 40-3).

[35] Caldwell (1990: 344); cf. Segal (1992: 153), justifying his use of psychological and anthropological models with the assertion that 'certain categories of human experience are universal'.

[36] Segal (1992: 171). I must declare my debt here to the highly interesting response of S. Georgia Nugent to the APA Panel on 'Roman poetry and recent developments in psychoanalytic criticism', 28 Dec. 1993.

[37] Brooks (1984) has been particularly influential; his work has stimulated fine work on the *Aeneid* in Quint (1993: 50-96). An interesting parallel to this move is to be found in the emergence of narrative therapy, on which see White and Epston (1990), a reference I owe to Dr James Gustafson.

narration as it will about the psyche.'³⁸ The linguistic turn of Lacan in particular and of post-structuralism in general is presumably largely responsible for this shift of emphasis towards looking at psychoanalysis as a model of figural language; important, too, have been the mounting reservations about the feasibility of analysing literary constructs ('characters', 'authors') as if they were human beings in an interactive setting;³⁹ and there may be a part played also by a tacit loss of faith in the scheme as a model of the mind—particularly in transcultural studies. The use of psychoanalytical models by Brooks and Quint may be regarded by the acolytes, for whom Freud and Lacan remain clinicians, as a domestication.⁴⁰ Still, for most critics the use of psychoanalysis in narratology is doubtless made more acceptable by the fact that the figural nature of the model's claims is so much more obvious than it is when the psyche is the object of analysis. But then one is left wondering what the power of the model really is, and whether any more is being said than that Freud was some kind of narratologist *avant la lettre* (a description which need not be read dismissively, depending on how much value you accord narratology).

Whatever models we employ, we have to acknowledge that there is no use pretending that we are not employing them, and we also have to acknowledge that we will often be employing them unconsciously (they will be 'employing' *us*). As students of long-vanished cultures, we face continually the challenge of respecting our place in history as observers and the place in history of the artefacts we are observing.⁴¹ There is—unfortunately, in the opinion of some—no universally valid way of adjudicating this process, for the criteria by which we perform it are always under negotiation.

These issues are intractable enough, but we need, in conclusion, to uncover a larger presupposition which underpins the approach not only of Heath but of most critics, classicists or not. This is the

³⁸  Meltzer (1990: 149).

³⁹  Bonime and Eckardt (1993).

⁴⁰  Meltzer (1990: 161): 'as with Freud, the unconscious for Lacan represents a clinical problem, a force underlying the behavior of real, living and breathing patients; it is not only an abstract concept to be imagined in differing ways. If the literary critic is ultimately faced with the text, the practicing analyst faces the patient . . . "Unconscious" at the moment of such confrontations begins to mean and to matter in fundamentally separate ways.'

⁴¹  The oscillations involved in being self-conscious about this double commitment are the subject of ch. 1 of D. F. Kennedy (1993).

assumption that criticism somehow explains literature, is adequate to it in some worthwhile sense. Let us begin with the comparatively mundane observation that great works can or even must break the bounds of interpretative possibility, redefining the critical practice needed to read them, addressing an audience which is not (yet) there: in Wordsworth's formulation, 'every author, as far as he is great and at the same time *original*, has had the task of *creating* the taste by which he is to be enjoyed: so has it been, so will it continue to be'.[42] Margaret Hubbard makes this point very cogently of Horace's *Odes*, for example, adducing Cicero's philosophical works as an analogy.[43] From this perspective, Heath's search for the most contemporary witnesses presents us with the apparent paradox that it is precisely the contemporary generation who are often worst placed to respond to original works in ways which later generations will find at all helpful (this will of course be an unacceptable conclusion for those who remain convinced that the goal of classical philology's interpretations is no more than to reconstruct the ideal contemporary response). Heath himself acknowledges the 'obvious danger . . . in arguing from Greek literary theory and criticism to the underlying principles of Greek literary practice—that is, from secondary to primary poetics'; as he puts it, 'it is inevitably uncertain whether any given critic or theorist has correctly grasped the nature even of contemporary literary composition'.[44] We have to face the fact that a seance with an Augustan *grammaticus* on the subject of Horace's *Odes* would almost certainly yield us very little that we would value (except that his very incomprehension might jolt us into realizing just how shocking and novel these now tamely canonical poems were on first appearance).[45]

---

[42] From *Essay Supplementary* to the *Preface* (1815); my thanks to David Hopkins for this quotation.                                    [43] Hubbard (1973: 25).

[44] Heath (1989: 10); cf. the points made by G. A. Kennedy (1991: 116).

[45] This paragraph is not meant to impugn the value of such contemporary critical evidence as we may have for any period; nor is it meant to deny the practical usefulness of reconstructing, as best we can, how a contemporary reader might have reacted to any particular work. The problem is that most critics are very good at getting into a position where they can claim that there is an uncanny overlap between the way they read a text and the way the ideal contemporary reader would have read it too. Further, scholars of this persuasion imply by their practice that something like the *Odes* or the *Aeneid* could somehow be apprehended in one take, 'exhausted', if you will, by their first readership. Finally, the search for the ideal contemporary reader's response makes it practically impossible to entertain the notion of a diverse, contentious initial audience.

It is precisely his distance on the tradition which makes it possible for Donald Russell to make the synthetic critical judgements he does,[46] and acknowledging this fact helps put us in a position to appreciate the pitfalls of confusing the modes of explanation with the modes at work in the phenomenon being explained. The analogy with the use and study of language is perhaps instructive. Alcaeus and Stesichorus had an active knowledge of Greek incomparably superior to that of anyone now alive, yet they knew no formal Greek grammar, and the Regius Professor understands—in some meaningful sense of the word—the workings of the Greek language in ways that they could not, and in ways that for certain purposes we will value more highly than whatever intuitions about language may be gleaned from witnesses of the archaic period. Similarly, the anthropologists have been tussling for a long time with the problems involved in recognizing that the very act of analysis, by constructing a sense-making whole, creates an intelligibility of a kind that is not accessible to the members of the society being analysed.[47] The clearest discussion of this dilemma which I know of is provided by David Trotter, reviewing a book on the semiotics of gesture: 'the cognitive power which the idea of codification generates in the historian's own understanding of language has been projected onto the world he is studying, where it becomes a moral and social power universally available'.[48]

For our purposes, it is not a matter of saying that one of these modes of knowledge or experience is preferable to the other in each case. Rather, we must recognize that the incompatibility which many detect between modern criticism and ancient literature is not something *sui generis*, but an example of a gap which will be found

---

[46] Above, n. 7; cf. Russell (1967: 141–3 = Ch. 11 in this volume, pp. 280–3), where he 'stands back from the detail' of the rhetorical tradition in order to put the large picture within the frame of a modern critical theory, only then being in a position to advance his propositions about how to read Catullus and Propertius.

[47] Even if they would no longer adopt the patronizing perspective of Malinowski—as reported by Macintyre (1970: 113)—'who insisted that the native Trobriander's account of Trobriand society must be inadequate, that the sociologists' account of institutions is a construction not available to the untutored awareness of the native informant'. The language/grammar analogy is itself used in this connection, normally in a recuperative fashion, as if the interpretative scheme of the observer is genuinely valid for the participant, only 'unconsciously': Lawson and McCauley (1990 : 77).

[48] Trotter (1992: 14).

between any critical act and its object of study.[49] There are diverse
ways of dealing with the gap. For myself, I would follow the lead of
Bernard Harrison, who constructs a theory designed to show 'why
since Plato [literature] has been permanently at war with theory,
and why its role is endlessly to exceed and transgress the insights
and outlooks fostered by theory'.[50] Classicists, of all people, should
have the historical perspective to see that any critical act is provisional: in this way we may resist not only the historicists' claim to
objective recovery of contemporary response, but also the whiggish
triumphalism of many of the modern schools. For the gap which
Donald Russell rightly sees between the literature and theory of the
ancients has always been there, and always will be.

### REFERENCES

Bonime, F., and Eckhardt, M. H. (1993) 'On Psychoanalysing Literary
    Characters', in E. Berman (ed.), *Essential Papers on Literature and Psycho-
    analysis* (New York and London), 202-16.
Brooks, P. (1984) *Reading for the Plot: Design and Intention in Narrative*
    (Cambridge, Mass.).
Cairns, F. (1972) *Generic Composition in Greek and Roman Poetry* (Edinburgh).
Caldwell, R. (1990) 'The Psychoanalytic Interpretation of Greek Myth', in L.
    Edmunds (ed.), *Approaches to Greek Myth* (Baltimore), 344-89.
Crews, F. (1993) 'The Unknown Freud', *New York Review of Books* (18 Nov.):
    55-66.
——(1994) 'The Unknown Freud: An Exchange', *New York Review of Books*,
    3 Feb.: 34-43.
De Jong, I. J. F., and Sullivan, J. P. (eds.) (1994) *Modern Literary Theory and
    Classical Literature* (Leiden).
Dinnage, R. (1993) 'Bringing up Raja', *New York Review of Books* (16 Dec.):
    66-8.
Feeney, D. C. (1991) *The Gods in Epic* (Oxford).
Felman, S. (1982) 'Turning the Screw of Interpretation', in S. Felman (ed.),

---

[49] Indeed (as Jacques Lezra suggests to me), if literature is itself in some ways a form
of literary criticism, then literature may be thought of as building this gap into what
is constitutively literary.
[50] Harrison (1991 : 17); cf. Felman (1982 : 207), on 'literality [*sic*] as that which
is essentially impermeable to analysis and to interpretation, that which necessarily
remains unaccounted for, that which, with respect to what interpretation does
account for, constitutes no less than *all the rest*: "All the rest is literature," writes
Verlaine.' I had not realized, until Stephen Hinds pointed it out to me, that my
historical perspective here gives way to a transhistorical essentializing definition of
'the literary'. Well, let it give way.

*Literature and Psychoanalysis: The Question of Reading: Otherwise* (Baltimore), 94–207.

Ford, A. (1991) 'Unity in Greek Criticism and Poetry', *Arion*, 3rd ser. 1: 125–54.

Gadamer, H.-G. (1960) *Warheit und Methode: Grundzüge einer philosophischen Hermeneutik* (Tübingen).

Goldhill, S. (1986) *Reading Greek Tragedy* (Cambridge).

——(1994): 'The Failure of Exemplarity' in de Jong and Sullivan (1994), 51–73.

Grünbaum, A. (1984) *The Foundations of Psychoanalysis: A Philosophical Critique* (Berekeley and Los Angeles).

——(1993) *Validation in the Clinical Theory of Psychoanalysis: A Study in the Philosophy of Psychoanalysis* (Madison, Conn.).

Halliwell, S. (1986) *Aristotle's Poetics* (London and Chapel Hill, NC).

——(1987) *The Poetics of Aristotle: Translation and Commentary* (London).

——(1989) Review of M. Heath, *The Poetics of Greek Tragedy* (1987), *Journal of Hellenic Studies*, 109: 231.

——(1992) 'Pleasure, Understanding, and Emotion in Aristotle's *Poetics*', in A. O. Rorty (ed.), *Essays on Aristotle's Poetics* (Princeton), 24–60.

Halperin, D. M. (1990) *One Hundred Years of Homosexuality, and Other Essays on Greek Love* (New York and London).

Harrison, B. (1991) *Inconvenient Fictions: Literature and Limits of Theory* (New Haven and London).

Heath, M. (1987) *The Poetics of Greek Tragedy* (London).

——(1989) *Unity in Greek Poetics* (Oxford).

Hubbard, M. (1973) 'The Odes', in C. D. N. Costa (ed.) *Horace* (London), 1–28.

Kennedy, D. F. (1993) *The Arts of Love: Five Studies in the Discourse of Roman Love Elegy* (Cambridge).

Kennedy, G. A. (1989a) 'Ancient Antecedents of Modern Literary Theory', *American Journal of Philology*, 110: 492–8.

——(1989b) *The Cambridge History of Literary Criticism*, i. *Classical Criticism* (Cambridge).

——(1991): 'Heath on Unity and Daitz's *Living Voice*', *American Journal of Philology*, 112: 115–18.

Lada, I. (1993) ' "Empathetic Understanding": Emotion and Cognition in Classical Dramatic Audience-Response', *Proceedings of the Cambridge Philological Society*, 39: 94–140.

Lawson, E. T., and McCauley, R. N. (1990) *Rethinking Religion: Connecting Cognition and Culture* (Cambridge).

Macintyre, A. (1970) 'The Idea of a Social Science', in B. R. Wilson (ed.), *Rationality* (Oxford), 112–30.

Martindale, C. (1993a) *Redeeming the Text: Latin Poetry and the Hermeneutics of Reception* (Cambridge).

——(1993b) 'Descent into Hell: Reading Ambiguity, or Virgil and the Critics', *Proceedings of the Virgil Society*, 21: 111–50.

Meltzer, F. (1990) 'Unconscious', in F. Lentricchia and T. McLaughlin (eds.), *Critical Terms for Literary Study* (Chicago), 147–62.

Morgan, J. R. (1993) 'Make-Believe and Make Believe: The Fictionality of the Greek Novels', in C. Gill and T. P. Wiseman (eds.), *Lies and Fiction in the Ancient World* (Exeter), 175–229.

Nauta, R. R. (1994) 'Historicizing Reading: The Aesthetics of Reception and Horace's "Soracte Ode" ', in de Jong and Sullivan (1994), 207–30.

Nussbaum, M. C. (1986) *The Fragility of Goodness: Luck and Ethics in Greek Tragedy and Philosophy* (Cambridge).

Price, S. R. F. (1990) 'The Future of Dreams: From Freud to Artemidorus', in D. M. Halperin, J. J. Winkler, and F. I. Zeitlin (eds.), *Before Sexuality: The Construction of Erotic Experience in the Ancient Greek World* (Princeton), 365–87.

Quint, D. (1993) *Epic and Empire: Politics and Generic Form from Virgil to Milton* (Princeton).

Russell, D. A. (1967) 'Rhetoric and Criticism', *Greece and Rome*, 13: 139–54 (= Chapter 11 in this volume).

——(1979) 'De Imitatione', in D. West and A. J. Woodman (eds.), *Creative Imitation and Latin Literature* (Cambridge), 1–16.

——(1981) *Criticism in Antiquity* (London).

——(1989) *The Place of Poetry in Ancient Literature* (Oxford).

Segal, C. (1992) 'Boundaries, Worlds, and Analogical Thinking, or How Lucretius Learned to Love Atomism and Still Write Poetry', in K. Galinsky (ed.), *The Interpretation of Roman Poetry: Empiricism or Hermeneutics?* (Frankfurt), 137–56, with 'Discussion', 170–5.

Sullivan, J. P. (1994) 'Introduction', in de Jong and Sullivan (1994), 1–26.

Trotter, D. (1992) 'Gesture as Language', *London Review of Books* (30 Jan.): 14–16.

White, M., and Epston, D. (1990) *Narrative Means to Therapeutic Ends* (New York and London).

Williams, G. (1968) *Tradition and Originality in Roman Poetry* (Oxford).

# ACKNOWLEDGEMENTS

Only the pieces by Jennifer Barnes, Jonathan Barnes, and Andrew Laird appear here for the first time. Permission to reprint the following items is gratefully acknowledged.

P. Murray, 'Poetic Inspiration in Early Greece', in *Journal of Hellenic Studies* 101 (1981), 87–100.

N. J. Richardson, 'Homeric Professors in the Age of the Sophists', *Proceedings of the Cambridge Philological Society* 201 (1975), 65–81.

E. Belfiore, 'A Theory of Imitation in Plato's *Republic*' in *Transactions of the American Philological Association* 114 (1984), 121–46.

S. Halliwell, 'Plato and Aristotle on the Denial of Tragedy' *Proceedings of the Cambridge Philological Society* 30 (1984), 49–71.

A. M. Dale, '*Ethos* and *Dianoia*' in *Collected Papers* (Cambridge: Cambridge University Press, 1959), 139–55.

N. J. Richardson, 'Literary Criticism in the Exegetical Scholia to the *Iliad*', *Classical Quarterly*, 30 (1980), 265–87.

A. A. Long, 'Stoic Readings of Homer' in R. Lamberton and J. J. Keaney (eds.), *Homer's Ancient Readers: The Hermeneutics of Greek Epic's Earliest Exegetes* (Princeton: Princeton University Press, 1992), 41–66 (reprinted in A. A. Long, *Stoic Studies* (Cambridge: Cambridge University Press, 1996), 58–84.

E. Asmis, 'Epicurean Poetics', *Proceedings of the Boston Area Colloquium in Ancient Philosophy*, 7 (1991), 63–93. Reprinted in D. Obbink (ed.), *Philodemus and Poetry: Poetic Theory and Practice in Lucretius, Philodemus and Horace* (Oxford: Oxford University Press, 1995), 15–34.

D. A. Russell, 'Rhetoric and Criticism', *Greece and Rome*, 14/2 (1967), 130–45.

D. M. Schenkeveld, 'Theories of Evaluation in the Rhetorical Works of Dionysius of Halicarnassus', in *Museum Philologicum Londiniense* (Amsterdam, 1975), i. 93–107.

D. C. Innes, 'Longinus: Structure and Unity', in J. G. Abbenes, S. R. Slings, and I. Sluiter (eds.), *Greek Literary Theory after Aristotle: A Collection of Papers in Honour of D. M. Schenkeveld* (Amsterdam, 1995), 111–24.

D. M. Schenkeveld, 'The Structure of Plutarch's *De Audiendis Poetis*', *Mnemosyne*, 35 (1982), 60–7.

D. A. Russell, 'Ars Poetica', in C. D. N. Costa (ed.), *Horace* (Cambridge, 1973), 113–34.

B. J. Gibson, 'Ovid on Reading: Reading Ovid. Reception in Ovid *Tristia* II', *Journal of Roman Studies*, 89 (1999), 19–37.

T. J. Luce, 'Reading and Response in the *Dialogus*', in T. J. Luce and A. J. Woodman (eds.), *Tacitus and the Tacitean Tradition* (Princeton, 1993), 11–38.

D. P. Fowler, 'The Virgil Commentary of Servius', in C. Martindale (ed.), *The Cambridge Companion to Virgil* (Cambridge: Cambridge University Press, 1997), 73–8.

T. G. Rosenmeyer, 'Ancient Literary Genres: A Mirage?', *Yearbook of Comparative and General Literature*, 34 (1985), 74–84.

D. C. Feeney, 'Criticism Ancient and Modern', in D. C. Innes, H. Hine, and C. B. R. Pelling (eds.), *Ethics and Rhetoric* (Oxford: Oxford University Press, 1995), 301–10.

# SUGGESTIONS FOR
# FURTHER READING

Items marked with an asterisk (*) are highly recommended.

### I. ANTHOLOGIES OF KEY TEXTS TRANSLATED INTO ENGLISH

DORSCH, T., and MURRAY, P. (2000) *Classical Literary Criticism* (Harmonds-worth: Penguin Classics). This contains Murray's translations of Plato, *Ion, Republic* 2–3, 10; and revisions of Dorsch's translations of Aristotle, *Poetics*, Horace, *Art of Poetry*, and Longinus. The translations are annotated with an introduction by Murray.

HALLIWELL, S., INNES, D. C., RUSSELL, D. A. *et al.* (1995) *Poetics* of Aristotle, ed. and tr. S. Halliwell; Longinus, *On the Sublime*, tr. W. H. Fyfe, rev. D. A. Russell; Demetrius, *On Style*, ed. and tr. D. C. Innes, based on W. Rhys Roberts (Cambridge, Mass.: Loeb Classical Library).

*RUSSELL, D. A., and WINTERBOTTOM, M. (1972) *Ancient Literary Criticism: The Principal Texts in New Translations* (Oxford: Oxford University Press). Recommended as an authoritative collection of a very wide range of ancient sources. There is a useful General Index as well as Indices of Proper Names and Greek and Latin Terms.

RUSSELL, D. A., and WINTERBOTTOM, M. (1989) *Classical Literary Criticism* (Oxford: Oxford University Press), a smaller version of the 1972 collection with a useful introduction.

Some Greek and Latin texts with useful commentaries can be found under the names of individual authors listed under 6 below.

### 2. ANCIENT LITERARY CRITICISM AND POETICS: GENERAL TREATMENTS

*ABBENES, J. G. J., SLINGS, S. R., and SLUITER, I., eds. (1995) *Greek Literary Theory after Aristotle: A Collection of Papers in Honour of D. M. Schenkeveld* (Amsterdam).

AHL, F. (1984) 'The Art of Safe Criticism in Greece and Rome', *American Journal of Philology*, 105: 174–208.

ATKINS, J. W. H. (1934) *Literary Criticism in Antiquity: A Sketch of its Development* (Cambridge).

FEENEY, D. C. (1991) *The Gods in Epic* (Oxford), 5-56.

FORD, A. (2002) *The Origins of Criticism: Literary Culture and Poetic Theory in Classical Greece* (Princeton).

GOLDHILL, S. (1999) 'Literary History without Literature: Reading Practices in the Ancient World', *SubStance (Review of Theory and Literary Criticism)*, 88: 57-89.

*GRUBE, G. M. A. (1965) *The Greek and Roman Critics* (Toronto).

*KENNEDY, G. A. (1989) *Cambridge History of Literary Criticism*, i. *Classical Literary Criticism* (Cambridge).

HEATH, M. (1989) *Unity in Greek Poetics* (Oxford).

MARTINDALE, C. (2001) 'Banishing the Poets' (Review of Y. L. Too, *The Idea of Ancient Literary Criticism*), *Arion*, 8/3: 115-27.

*RUSSELL, D. A. (1981) *Criticism in Antiquity* (London).

—— (1989) 'The Place of Poetry in Ancient Literature' (Valedictory lecture published by Oxford University Press) (Oxford).

—— (1996) 'Literary Criticism in Antiquity', *Oxford Classical Dictionary*, 3rd edn. (*OCD* iii) (Oxford), 869-71.

SANDYS, J. E. (1921) *A History of Classical Scholarship*, i (Cambridge), 1-383.

TOO, Y. L. (1998) *The Idea of Ancient Literary Criticism* (Oxford).

*VERDENIUS, W. J. (1963) 'The Principles of Greek Literary Criticism', *Mnemosyne*, 36, reprinted as a monograph with a bibliography of Verdenius' works (Leiden, 1983), 14-59.

### 3. RHETORIC AND EDUCATION IN ANTIQUITY

See also items listed under Aristotle, Demetrius, Cicero, 'Longinus', etc. under 6 below.

BONNER, S. F. (1949) *Roman Declamation* (Liverpool).

—— (1977) *Education in Ancient Rome* (Berkeley).

CLARKE, M. L. (1953) *Rhetoric at Rome* (London).

GILL, C. (1984) 'The Ethos/Pathos Distinction in Rhetorical and Literary Criticism', *Classical Quarterly*, 34: 149-66.

HARRIS, W. V. (1989) *Ancient Literacy* (Cambridge, Mass.).

INNES, D. C. (1985) 'Theophrastus and the Theory of Style', in W. Fortenbaugh, P. Huby and A. A. Long (eds.), *Theophrastus of Eresos: On his Life and Work* (New Brunswick, NJ), 251-67.

—— Hine, H., and Pelling, C. eds. (1995) *Ethics and Rhetoric* (Oxford).

JAEGER, W. (1944-6) *Paideia* (3 vols. Oxford).

KENNEDY, G. A. (1963) *The Art of Persuasion in Greece* (London).

—— (1972) *The Art of Rhetoric in the Roman World* (Princeton).

—— (1983) *Greek Rhetoric under Christian Emperors* (Princeton).

LAUSBERG, H. (1998) *Handbook of Literary Rhetoric: A Foundation for Literary Study* (Leiden; German orig. 1960).

LEEMAN, A. D. (1963) *Orationis Ratio: The Stylistic Theories and Practice of the Roman Orators, Historians and Philosophers* (Amsterdam).

McCall, M. (1969) *Ancient Rhetorical Theories of Simile and Comparison* (Cambridge, Mass.).

Marrou, H. I. (1977) *History of Education in Antiquity* (New York; French orig. 1948).

Morgan, T. (1998) *Literate Education in the Hellenistic and Roman Worlds* (Cambridge).

North, H. (1952) 'The Use of Poetry in the Training of the Ancient Orator' *Traditio* 8: 1–33.

*Porter, S. E., ed. (1997) *Handbook of Classical Rhetoric in the Hellenistic Period 330 B.C.–A.D. 400* (Leiden and New York).

Russell, D. A. (1973) 'The Scholar and his Books', in *Plutarch* (London: Duckworth), 42–62.

*——(1979) 'De Imitatione', in D. West and A. J. Woodman (eds.), *Creative Imitation and Latin Literature* (Cambridge), 1–16.

*——(1983) *Greek Declamation* (Cambridge).

——(1996) 'Rhetoric, Greek' *Oxford Classical Dictionary*, 3rd edn. (Oxford), 1312–14.

Svenbro, J. (1993) *Phrasikleia: An Anthropology of Reading in Ancient Greece* (Cornell).

Webb, R. (1997) 'Imagination and the Arousal of the Emotions in Greco-Roman Rhetoric', in S. Braund and C. Gill (eds.), *The Passions in Roman Thought and Literature* (Cambridge), 112–27.

Winterbottom, M. (1996) 'Rhetoric, Latin', *Oxford Classical Dictionary*, 3rd edn, 1314.

Woodman, A. J. (1988) *Rhetoric in Classical Historiography* (London and Sydney).

Worthington, I., ed. (1994) *Persuasion: Greek Rhetoric in Action* (London and New York).

*Reception and Later Applications of Ancient Rhetoric*

This is a miscellaneous list to indicate the diversity of domains in which classical rhetoric has been influential. The items have been chosen primarily because they are engaging and thought-provoking.

Baldwin, C. S. (1928) *Medieval Rhetoric and Poetic (to 1400) Interpreted from Representative Works* (New York, repr. 1959).

Barthes, R. (1988) 'The Old Rhetoric: An Aide-Mémoire', in *The Semiotic Challenge* (New York), 11–94.

Baxandall, M. (1971) *Giotto and the Orators* (Oxford).

Bizzell, P., and Herzberg, B., eds. (1990) *The Rhetorical Tradition: Readings from Classical Times to the Present* (Boston).

Booth, W. C. (1983) *The Rhetoric of Fiction* (2nd edn. Chicago).

Fish, S (1995) 'Rhetoric', in F. Lentricchia and T. McLaughlin (eds.), *Critical Terms for Literary Study* (2nd edn. Chicago), 203–23.

Kennedy, G. A. (1999) *Classical Rhetoric and its Christian and Secular Tradition from Ancient to Modern Times* (2nd rev. edn. Chapel Hill, NC).

KENNEDY, G. A. (1998) *Comparative Rhetoric: An Historical and Cross-Cultural Introduction* (Oxford and New York).

LEITH, D., and MYERSON, G. (1989) *The Power of Address: Explorations in Rhetoric* (London).

MACK, P. ed. (1994) *Renaissance Rhetoric* (New York).

—— (1996) 'Humanist Rhetoric and Dialectic', in J. Kraye (ed.), *Cambridge Companion to Renaissance Humanism* (Cambridge).

NIETZSCHE, F. (1989) *Friedrich Nietzsche on Rhetoric and Language*, ed. and tr. S. Gilman, C. Blair, and D. Parent (Oxford and New York).

VICKERS, B. (1970) *Classical Rhetoric in English Poetry* (London).

*—— (1988) *In Defence of Rhetoric* (repr. with corrections 1997; Oxford).

YATES, F. (1966) *The Art of Memory* (London).

## 4. ANCIENT ALLEGORICAL READING, PHILOSOPHY, AND POETRY

See also Homer, Aristophanes and the Sophists, Plato, Aristotle under 6 below.

*BOYS-STONES, G., ed. (2003) *Metaphor, Allegory and the Classical Tradition* (Oxford).

BUFFIÈRE, F. (1956) *Les Mythes d'Homère et la pensée grecque* (Paris).

DELACEY, P. (1939) 'The Epicurean Analysis of Language', *American Journal of Philology*, 60: 85–92.

—— (1948) 'Stoic Views of Poetry', *American Journal of Philology*, 69: 241–71.

FORD, A. (1999) 'Performing Interpretation: Early Allegorical Exegesis of Homer', in M. Beissinger, J. Tylus, and S. Wofford (eds.), *Epic Traditions in the Contemporary World: The Poetics of Community* (Berkeley and Los Angeles), 33–53.

HALLIWELL, S. (1996) 'Philosophers on Poetry', in *Oxford Classical Dictionary*, 3rd edn.

LAMBERTON, R. (1986) *Homer the Theologian: Neoplatonist Allegorical Reading and the Growth of the Epic Tradition* (Berkeley).

MOST, G. (1989) 'Cornutus and Stoic Allegoresis: A Preliminary Report', *Aufstieg und Niedergang der römischen Welt*, ii. 36/3, 2014–65.

RUSSELL, D. A. (1989) 'Greek Criticism of the Empire', in *Cambridge History of Literary Criticism* , i. 297–329.

—— and KONSTAN, D. (2005) *Heraclitus: Homeric Allegories* (Society of Biblical Literature).

SHEPPARD, A. (1980) *Studies on the 5th and 6th Essays of Proclus' Commentary on the Republic* (Göttingen).

—— (1997) 'Phantasia and Inspiration in Neoplatonism', in M. Joyal (ed.), *Studies in Plato and the Platonic Tradition: Essays Presented to John Whittaker* (Aldershot), 201–11.

WHITMAN, J. (1987) *Allegory: The Dynamics of an Ancient and Medieval Technique* (Oxford).

5. ANCIENT SCHOLARSHIP AND COMMENTARY

KASTER, R. A. (1988) *Guardians of Language: The Grammarian and Society in Late Antiquity* (Berkeley).

——(1995) C. *Suetonius Tranquillus De grammaticis et rhetoribus*, edited with a Translation, Introduction, and Commentary (Oxford).

LAZZARINI, C. (1984): 'Historia/Fabula: Forma della Costruzione poetica Virgiliana nel commento di Servio all'Eneide', *Materiali e discussione*, 12: 117-44.

MEIJERING, R. (1987) *Literary and Rhetorical Theories in Greek Scholia* (Groningen).

*PFEIFFER, R. (1968) *History of Classical Scholarship: From the Beginnings to the End of the Hellenistic Age* (Oxford).

*REEVE, M. D. (1996) 'Scholia', in *Oxford Classical Dictionary*, 3rd edn., 1368.

*RICHARDSON, N. (1985) 'Pindar and Later Literary Criticism in Antiquity', *Proceedings of the Liverpool Latin Seminar*, 5: 383-401.

SCHENKEVELD, D. M. (1970) 'Aristarchus and Homêros philotekhnos', *Mnemosyne*, 23: 162-78.

SCHLUNK, R. (1974) *The Homeric Scholia and the Aeneid: A Study of the Influence of Ancient Homeric Literary Criticism on Vergil* (Ann Arbor).


6. PROMINENT ANCIENT CRITICS

*Homer, Aristophanes, and the Sophists*

Texts and commentaries

DOVER, K. J. (1993) *Aristophanes, Frogs* (Oxford).

LANATA, G. (1963) *Poetica Pre-Platonica* (Florence).

RADERMACHER, L. (1951) *Artium Scriptores* (Vienna). A collection of pre-Aristotelian texts.

SOMMERSTEIN, A. (1996) *Aristophanes, Frogs* (Warminster).

Books and articles

DE ROMILLY, J. 'Gorgias et le pouvoir de la poésie', *Journal of Hellenic Studies*, 93: 155-62.

*——(1975) *Magic and Rhetoric in Ancient Greece* (Cambridge, Mass.).

DOVER, K. J. (1972) *Aristophanic Comedy* (London), 183-9.

*HARRIOTT, R. (1969) *Poetry and Criticism before Plato* (London).

KERFERD, G. (1981) *The Sophistic Movement* (Cambridge and New York).

LADA, I. (1993) ' "Empathetic Understanding": Emotion and Cognition in Classical Dramatic Audience-Response', *Proceedings of the Cambridge Philological Society*, 39: 94-140.

——(1996) 'Emotion and Meaning in Tragic Performance', in M. S. Silk (ed.), *Tragedy and the Tragic* (Oxford), 397-413.

LADA-RICHARDS, I. (1999) *Initiating Dionysus: Ritual and Theatre in Aristophanes' Frogs* (Oxford).

*MACLEOD, C. (1983) 'Homer on Poetry and the Poetry of Homer', in Macleod, *Collected Essays* (Oxford), 1–15.

*SEGAL, C. (1962) 'Gorgias and the Psychology of the Logos', *Harvard Studies in Classical Philology*, 66: 99–155

——(1992) 'Bard and Audience in Homer', in R. Lamberton and J. Keaney (eds.), *Homer's Ancient Readers: The Hermeneutics of Greek Epic's Earliest Exegetes* (Princeton), 3–30.

SILK, M. S. (2000) *Aristophanes and the Definition of Comedy* (Oxford).

SOLMSEN, F. (1975) *Intellectual Experiments of the Greek Enlightenment* (Princeton).

## Plato

### Some Greek texts with commentary

DE VRIES, G. J. (1969) *A Commentary on the Phaedrus of Plato* (Amsterdam).

DODDS, E. R. (1959) *Plato Gorgias* (Oxford).

DOVER, K. J. (1980) *Plato Symposium* (Cambridge).

*HALLIWELL, S. (1988) *Republic 10* (Warminster).

*MURRAY, P. (1996) *Plato on Poetry* (Cambridge), this volume includes *Ion*, and *Republic 376–98, 595–608*.

### Studies

ANNAS, J. (1981) *An Introduction to Plato's Republic* (Oxford), 305–34.

ASMIS, E. (1992) 'Plato on Poetic Creativity', in R. Kraut (ed.), *The Cambridge Companion to Plato* (Cambridge), 338–64.

BALDWIN, A., and HUTTON, S,. eds. (1994) *Platonism and the English Imagination* (Cambridge).

BROCK, R. (1990) 'Plato and Comedy', in E. M. Craik (ed.), *Owls to Athens: Essays on Classical Subjects Presented to Sir Kenneth Dover* (Oxford), 39–49.

BURNYEAT, M. (1999) 'Culture and Society in Plato's *Republic*', *The Tanner Lectures on Human Values*, 20 (Salt Lake City).

CLAY, D. (1983) 'The Tragic and Comic Poet of the *Symposium*', in J. Anton and A. Preus (eds.), *Essays in Ancient Greek Philosophy* (Albany), 186–202.

ELSE, G. F. (1986), *Plato and Aristotle on Poetry*, ed. P. Burian (Chapel Hill, NC).

*FERRARI, G. R. F. (1989) 'Plato and Poetry', *Cambridge History of Literary Criticism* i. 92–148.

GILL, C. (1993) 'Plato on Falsehood—Not Fiction', in Gill and T. P. Wiseman (eds.), *Lies and Fiction in the Ancient World* (Exeter and Austin, Tex.), 38–87.

GRISWOLD, C. (1981) 'The Ideas and Criticism of Poetry in Plato's *Republic*, Book 10', *Journal of the History of Philosophy*, 19/2: 135–50.

HANKINS, J. (1990) *Plato in the Italian Renaissance*, 2 vols. (Leiden).

HOWLAND, R. L. (1937) 'The Attack on Isocrates in the *Phaedrus*', *Classical Quarterly*, 31: 151–9.

JANAWAY, C. (1995) *Images of Excellence: Plato's Critique of the Arts* (Oxford).

LAIRD, A. (1999) 'Platonic Formalism: Socrates and the Narratologists', ch. 2 in *Powers of Expression, Expressions of Power* (Oxford), 44–78.

*MORAVCSIK, J., and TEMKO, P., eds. (1982) *Plato on Beauty, Wisdom and the Arts* (Totowa, NJ).

MURDOCH, I. (1977) *The Fire and the Sun: Why Plato Banished the Artists* (Oxford).

NEHAMAS, A. (1988) 'Plato and the Mass Media', *The Monist*, 71: 214–34 (repr. in A. Nehamas, *Virtues of Authenticity: Essays on Plato and Socrates* (Princeton, 1999), 279–99).

NIGHTINGALE, A. W. (1995) *Genres in Dialogue: Plato and the Construct of Philosophy* (Cambridge).

RUTHERFORD, R. B. (1995) *The Art of Plato: Ten Essays in Platonic Interpretation* (London and Cambridge, Mass.).

TIGERSTEDT, E. (1969) *Plato's Idea of Poetical Inspiration* (Helsinki).

VICAIRE, P. (1960) *Platon: Critique littéraire* (Paris).

*Aristotle*

Texts with notes or commentary

COPE, E. M. (1877) *The Rhetoric of Aristotle with a Commentary*, 3 vols. Cambridge).

HALLIWELL, S. (1995) *Aristotle, Poetics* (Loeb Classical Library; Cambridge, Mass.).

*LUCAS, D. W. (1968) *Aristotle Poetics* (Oxford).

Translations with notes and commentary

*HALLIWELL, S. (1987) *The Poetics of Aristotle* (London).

HEATH, M. (1996) *Aristotle, Poetics* (London).

*JANKO, R. (1987) *Aristotle, Poetics* (Indianapolis).

*KENNEDY, G. A. (1991) *Aristotle On Rhetoric: A Theory of Civic Discourse* (Oxford).

Studies

The *edited collections* of essays listed here contain some very important material.

ANDERSEN, Ø., and HAARBERG, J., eds. (2001) *Making Sense of Aristotle: Essays in Poetics* (London).

BARNES, J., SCHOFIELD, M., and SORABJI, R., eds. (1979) *Articles on Aristotle*, iv. *Psychology and Aesthetics* (London).

BELFIORE, E. (1992) *Tragic Pleasures: Aristotle on Plot and Emotion* (Princeton).

COPE, E. M. (1867) *An Introduction to Aristotle's Rhetoric* (London and Cambridge).

FORD, A. (2004) 'Catharsis: The Power of Music in Aristotle's *Politics*', in P. Murray and P. Wilson (eds.), *Music and the Muses: The Culture of Mousike in the Classical Athenian City* (Oxford), 309–36.

HALL, E. (1996) 'Is there a Polis in Aristotle's *Poetics?*', in M. S. Silk (ed.), *Tragedy and the Tragic: Greek Theatre and Beyond* (Oxford), 295–309.

*HALLIWELL, S. (1986) *Aristotle's Poetics* (London).

HEATH, M. (1989) 'Aristotelian Comedy', *Classical Quarterly*, 39: 344–54.

——(1991) 'The Universality of Poetry in Aristotle's *Poetics*', *Classical Quarterly*, 41: 389–402 (repr. in L. Gerson (ed.), *Aristotle: Critical Essays* (London, 1999), iv. 356–73).

HOUSE, H. (1956) *Aristotle's Poetics* (London).

JANKO, R. (1984) *Aristotle on Comedy: Towards a Reconstruction of Poetics ii* (Berkeley).

JONES, J. (1962) *On Aristotle and Greek Tragedy* (London).

NUTTALL, A. D. (1996) *Why does Tragedy Give Pleasure?* (Oxford).

OLSON, E., ed. (1965) *Aristotle's Poetics and English Literature: A Collection of Critical Essays* (Chicago). This contains criticism by Thomas Twining, Thomas Taylor, Quiller-Couch, and other interpreters from the 18th–20th centuries.

*RORTY, A. O., ed. (1992) *Essays on Aristotle's Poetics* (Princeton).

——ed. (1996) *Essays on Aristotle's Rhetoric* (Berkeley: University of California Press).

ROSTAGNI, A. (1926–7) 'Il dialogo aristotelico ΠΕΡΙ ΠΟΙΗΤΩΝ', *Rivista di Filologia e di Instruzione Classica*, 54: 433–70; 55: 145–73.

SCHRIER, O. (1998) *The Poetics of Aristotle and the Tractatus Coislinianus: A Bibliography from about 900 till 1996* (Leiden).

SEGAL, C. (1996) 'Catharsis, Audience, and Closure in Greek Tragedy', in M. S. Silk (ed.), *Tragedy and the Tragic: Greek Theatre and Beyond* (Oxford), 149–72.

SIDWELL, K. (2000) 'From Old to Middle to New? Aristotle's *Poetics* and the History of Athenian Comedy', in D. Harvey and J. Wilkins (eds.), *The Rivals of Aristophanes: Studies in Athenian Old Comedy* (London), 247–58.

*SOLMSEN, F. (1941) 'The Aristotelian Tradition in Ancient Rhetoric', *American Journal of Philology*, 62: 35–50, 169–90.

*STINTON, T. C. W. (1975) 'Hamartia in Aristotle and Greek Tragedy', *Classical Quarterly*, 25: 221–54 (repr. in Stinton, *Collected Papers on Greek Tragedy* (Oxford, 1990)).

WAGNER, C. (1984) 'Katharsis in der aristotelischen Tragoediendefinition', *Gräzer Beiträge*, 11: 67–87.

*Callimachus and 'Alexandrian' Poetics*

CAMERON, A. (1995) *Callimachus and his Critics* (Princeton).

FRAZER, P. M. (1972) *Ptolemaic Alexandria* (Oxford).

*HUTCHINSON, G. (1988) *Hellenistic Poetry* (Oxford).

INNES, D. C. (1989) 'Tradition, Originality and the Callimachean Legacy in Latin Poetry', *Cambridge History of Literary Criticism*, i. 246–54.

KENNEDY, G. A. (1989) 'Hellenistic Literary and Philosophical Scholarship', *Cambridge History of Literary Criticism*, i. 200–5.

NELIS, D. P. (1996) 'Hellenistic Poetry at Rome', in *Oxford Classical Dictionary*, 3rd edn.

NEWMAN, J. K. (1967) *Augustus and the New Poetry* (Brussels).

PARSONS, P. (1996) 'Callimachus of Cyrene', in *Oxford Classical Dictionary*, 3rd edn.

PFEIFFER, R. (1968) *History of Classical Scholarship: From the Beginnings to the End of the Hellenistic Age* (Oxford).

RENGAKOS, A. (2001) 'Apollonius Rhodius as a Homeric Scholar', in T. Papanghelis (ed.), *A Companion to Apollonius Rhodius* (Leiden).

ZANKER, G (1987) *Realism in Alexandrian Poetry: A Literature and its Audience* (London).

*Demetrius*

Greek texts with notes and introductions

*INNES, D. C. (1995) *Demetrius, On Style* (Loeb Classical Library; Cambridge, Mass.; see 1. Anthologies of Key Texts Translated into English above.

ROBERTS, W. R. (1902) *Demetrius, On Style* (Cambridge).

Translation with introduction

GRUBE, G. M. A. (1961) *A Greek Critic: Demetrius on Style* (Toronto).

Studies

INNES, D. C. (1989) 'Demetrius, On Style', *Cambridge History of Literary Criticism*, i. 196–8.

SCHENKEVELD, D. M. (1964) *Studies in Demetrius, On Style* (Amsterdam).

SOLMSEN, F. (1931) 'Demetrios *ΠΕΡΙ ΕΡΜΗΝΕΙΑΣ* und sein peripatetisches Quellenmaterial', *Hermes*, 66: 241–67.

*Philodemus*

ASMIS, E. (1991) 'Philodemus' Poetic Theory and *On the Good King according to Homer*', *Classical Antiquity*, 10: 1–45.

——(1992) 'Neoptolemus and the Classification of Poetry', *Classical Philology*, 87: 206–31.

GREENBERG, N. (1961) 'The use of *poiema* and *poiesis*', *Harvard Studies in Classical Philology*, 65: 263–89.

INNES, D. C. (1989) 'Philodemus', *Cambridge History of Literary Criticism*, i. 215–19.

JANKO, R. (2000) *Philodemus on Poems, Book 1* (Oxford).

OBBINK, D. (ed.) (1995) *Philodemus and Poetry: Poetic Theory and Practice in Lucretius, Philodemus and Horace* (Oxford).

PORTER, J. I. (1994) 'Stoic Morals and Poetics in Philodemus', *Cronache Ercolanesi*, 24: 63–88.

See also Brink (1963) under Horace below.

### Cicero

Texts and commentaries

*CAPLAN, H. (1954) *Ad Herennium* (Loeb Classical Library; Cambridge, Mass.). An important text attributed to Cicero; this edn. functions as a good introduction to technical rhetoric.

DOUGLAS, A. E. (1966) *Brutus* (Oxford).

HENDRICKSON, G. L. (1939) *Brutus, Orator* (London).

HUBBELL, H. M. (1949) *De inventione, De optimo genere oratorum, Topica* (Loeb Classical Library; London).

LEEMAN, A. D., PINKSTER, H. (*et al.*) eds. (1981–96) *M. Tullius Cicero De oratore* (vols. i–iv in German) (Heidelberg).

SANDYS, J. E. (1885) *Orator* (Cambridge).

WILKINS, A. S. (1902) *Rhetorica*, 2 vols. (Oxford).

——(1965) *De oratore* (Hildesheim), 3 vols. with commentary; orig. Oxford 1888–92.

WISSE, J., WINTERBOTTOM, M., and FANTHAM, E., eds. (2004) *M. Tullius Cicero De oratore libri III* (5th vol. on 3. 96–230 in English) (Heidelberg).

Studies

CLARKE, M. L. (1964) '*Non Hominis Nomen, Sed Eloquentiae*', in T. A. Dorey (ed.), *Cicero* (London), 81–107.

DOUGLAS, A. E. (1973) 'The Intellectual Background of Cicero's Rhetorica: A Study in Method', *ANRW* i/3. 95–138.

FANTHAM, E. (1978) 'Imitation and Evolution: The Discussion of Rhetorical Imitation in Cicero, *De oratore* II, 87–97, and Some Related Problems of Ciceronian Theory', *Classical Philology*, 73: 1–16.

——(1989) 'The Growth of Literature and Criticism at Rome', *Cambridge History of Literary Criticism*, i. 227–44.

MAY, J., ed. (2002) *Brill's Companion to Cicero: Oratory and Rhetoric* (Leiden and Boston). This volume contains an excellent bibliography and a bibliographical essay by C. Craig.

PORTER, J. I. (2001) 'Cicéron, les 'κριτικοί' et la tradition du sublime dans la critique littéraire', in C. Auvray-Assayas and D. Delattre (eds.), *Cicéron et Philodème: La Polémique en philosophie* (Paris), 315–41.

WILKINSON, L. P. (1982) 'Cicero and the Relationship of Oratory to Literature', in E. J. Kenney (ed.), *The Cambridge History of Classical Literature*, ii. *Latin Literature* (Cambridge), 230–67.

*Dionysius of Halicarnassus*

Text and translation

USENER, S. (1974–85) 2 vols. (Loeb Classical Library; Cambridge, Mass.).

Translations

PRITCHETT, W. K. (1975) *Dionysius of Halicarnassus, On Thucydides* (Berkeley).
ROBERTS, W. R. (1901) *Three Literary Letters* (Cambridge).
——(1910) *On Literary Composition* (Cambridge).

Studies

BONNER, S. F. (1939) *The Literary Treatises of Dionysius: A Study in the Development of Critical Method* (Cambridge).
BOWERSOCK, G. (1985) 'Dionysius of Halicarnassus', in P. Easterling and B. Knox (eds.), *Cambridge History of Classical Literature*, i (Cambridge), 643–6.
HEATH, M. (1989) 'Dionysius of Halicarnassus *On Imitation*', *Hermes*, 117: 370–3.
HURST, A. (1982) *Aufstieg und Niedergang der römischen Welt*, 2/30/1: 839–65.
INNES, D. C. (1989) 'Dionysius of Halicarnassus', *Cambridge History of Literary Criticism*, i. 267–72.
NOÈ, E (1979) 'Ricerche su Dionigi d'Alicarnasso', *Ricerche di storiographia antica*, 1 (Pisa) 21-116.


*Horace*

Some Latin editions with commentary

*BRINK, C. O. (1971) *Horace on Poetry ii: Ars Poetica* (Cambridge).
*——(1982) *Horace on Poetry iii: Epistles ii* (Cambridge).
BROWN, P. M. (1993) *Horace, Satires i* (Warminster).
LEJAY, P. (1911) *Œuvres d'Horace: Satires* (Paris).
RUDD, N. (1989) *Epistles Book ii and Epistle to the Pisones (Ars Poetica)* (Cambridge).

Translations with notes and introduction

KILPATRICK, R. S. (1986) *The Poetry of Friendship: Horace, Epistles I* (Edmonton, Alberta).
——(1990) *The Poetry of Criticism: Horace Epistles ii and Ars Poetica* (Edmonton, Alberta).

Books and articles

BARCHIESI. A. (2001) 'Horace and Iambos: The Poet as Literary Historian', in A. Cavarzere, A. Aloni and A. Barchiesi (eds.), *Iambic Ideas: Essays on a*

*Poetic Tradition from Archaic Greece to the Late Roman Empire* (Lanham, Md.), 141–64.

BECKER, C. (1963) *Das Spätwerk des Horaz* (Göttingen).

*BRINK, C. O. (1963) *Horace on Poetry: Prolegomena to the Literary Epistles* (Cambridge).

EDWARDS, M. J. (1992) 'Horace, Homer and Rome: *Epistles* i. 2', *Mnemosyne* 45/1: 83–8.

FISCHER, B. (1991) *Shifting Paradigms: New Approaches to Horace's Ars Poetica* (Atlanta, Ga.).

FRAENKEL, E. (1957) *Horace* (Oxford), 76–153, 383–99.

FREUDENBERG, K. (1993) *The Walking Muse: Horace on the Theory of Satire* (Princeton).

HERRICK, M. (1946) *The Fusion of Horatian and Aristotelian Criticism 1531–1555* (Urbana, Ill.).

INNES, D. (1989) 'Augustan Critics', *Cambridge History of Literary Criticism*, i. 254–67.

JOCELYN, H. D. (1995) 'Horace and the Reputation of Plautus in the Late First Century BC' in S. J. Harrison (ed.), *Homage to Horace* (Oxford), 228–47.

LAIRD, A. (forthcoming) 'The *Ars Poetica*', in S. J. Harrison (ed.), *The Cambridge Companion to Horace* (Cambridge).

RUDD, N. (1982) *The Satires of Horace* (Bristol).

RUTHERFORD, R. B. (forthcoming) 'The Literary Epistles', in S. J. Harrison (ed.), *The Cambridge Companion to Horace* (Cambridge).

SYME, R. (1960) 'Piso Frugi et Cassius Frugi', *Journal of Roman Studies*, 50: 2–20.

TATE, J. (1928) 'Horace and the Moral Function of Poetry', *Classical Quarterly*, 22: 65–72.

WHITE, P. (1977) 'Horace, *A.P.* 128–30: The Intent of the Wording', *Classical Quarterly*, 27: 191–201.

WISEMAN, T. P. (1988) 'Satyrs in Rome? The Background to Horace's *Ars Poetica*', *Journal of Roman Studies*, 79: 29–37.

See also reading listed under Philodemus above.

*Ovid*

TARRANT, R. (2002) 'Ovid and Ancient Literary History', in P. Hardie (ed.), *The Cambridge Companion to Ovid* (Cambridge), 13–33.

*Plutarch*

KONSTAN, D. (2004) 'The Birth of the Reader: Plutarch as a Literary Critic', *Scholia*, 13: 3–27.

TAGLIASACCHI, A. M. (1961) 'Le teorie estetiche e la critica letteraria in Plutarco', *Acme*, 14: 71–117.

*Tacitus*

Latin texts of *Dialogus* with commentary

*MAYER, R. (2001) *Tacitus: Dialogus de Oratoribus* (Cambridge).

PETERSON, W. (1893) *Cornelii Taciti Dialogus de Oratoribus* (A revised text, with introductory essays and critical and explanatory notes) (Oxford).

Studies of *Dialogus*

BARNES, T. D. (1986) 'The significance of Tacitus' Dialogus de Oratoribus', *Harvard Studies in Classical Philology*, 90: 225–44.

*BARTSCH, S. (1994) *Actors in the Audience: Theatricality and Doublespeak from Nero to Hadrian* (Cambridge, Mass.), 98–125.

BRINK, C. O. (1989) 'Quintilian's *de causis corruptelae eloquentiae* and Tacitus' *Dialogus de Oratoribus*', *Classical Quarterly*, 39: 472–503.

HASS-VON REITZENSTEIN, U. (1970) *Beiträge zur gattungsgeschichtlichen Interpretation des Dialogus 'de oratoribus'* (Diss. Cologne).

*LEVENE, D. S. (2004) 'Tacitus' Dialogus as Literary History', *Transactions of the American Philological Association*, 134/1: 157–200.

SYME, R. (1958) *Tacitus* (Oxford).

WILLIAMS, G. (1978) *Change and Decline: Roman Literature in the Early Empire* (Berkeley), 26–51.

WINTERBOTTOM, M. (2001) 'Returning to Tacitus' *Dialogus*', in C. Wooten (ed.), *The Orator in Action and Theory in Greece and Rome* (Leiden and Boston).

See also Winterbottom (1964) under Quintilian below.


*Quintilian*

Texts with notes or commentary

*AUSTIN, R. G. (1965) *Quintiliani Institutionis Oratoriae Liber XII* (Oxford).

PETERSON, W. (1891) *Quintiliani Institutionis Oratoriae liber X* (a revised text edited for the use of colleges and schools; Oxford).

*RUSSELL, D. A. (2001) *Quintilian: The Orator's Education*, 5 vols. (Loeb Classical Library; Cambridge, Mass., and London).

Studies

The Introduction to Russell (2001) above is useful.

ALBALADEJO, T., DEL RÍO, E., and CABALLERO, J., eds. (1998) *Quintiliano: Historia y actualidad de la retórica* (Calahorra, Spain).

CLARKE, M. L. (1975) 'Quintilian on Education', in T. A. Dorey (ed.), *Silver Latin II* (London), 98–118.

FANTHAM, E. (1989) 'Latin Criticism of the Early Empire', *Cambridge History of Literary Criticism*, i. 286–91.

GOODYEAR, F. R. D. (1982) 'Rhetoric and Scholarship', in E. J. Kenney (ed.),

*The Cambridge History of Classical Literature*, ii. *Latin Literature* (Cambridge), 674–6.

KENNEDY, G. A. (1962) 'An Estimate of Quintilian', *American Journal of Philology*, 83: 130–46.

——(1969) *Quintilian* (New York).

——(1994) 'Peripatetic Rhetoric as it Appears (and Disappears) in Quintilian', in W. Fortenbaugh and D. C. Mirhady (eds.), *Peripatetic Rhetoric after Aristotle* (New Brunswick, NJ), 174–82.

*WINTERBOTTOM, M. (1964) 'Quintilian and the *Vir Bonus*', *Journal of Roman Studies*, 54: 90–7.

——(1975) 'Quintilian and Rhetoric', in T. A. Dorey (ed.), *Empire and Aftermath: Silver Latin II* (London), 79–97.

As well as Bonner (1949), Clarke (1953) etc. listed above under 3. Rhetoric and Education, see also Brink (1989) under Tacitus above.

### 'Longinus'

#### Text and translation

RUSSELL, D. A. (1995) *Longinus: On the Sublime* (Loeb Classical Library; Cambridge, Mass.). See 1. Anthologies of Key Texts Translated into English above).

#### Text and commentary

RUSSELL, D. A. (1964) *Longinus: On the Sublime* (Oxford).

#### Articles and short discussions

BOMPAIRE, J. (1973) 'Le *Pathos* dans le traité du Sublime', *Revue des Études Grecques*, 86: 323–43.

INNES, D. C. (1995) 'Longinus, Sublimity and Low Emotions', in D. C. Innes, H. Hine, and C. Pelling (eds.), *Ethics and Rhetoric* (Oxford), 323–33.

——(2002) 'Longinus and Caecilius: Models of the Sublime', *Mnemosyne*, 55/3: 259–84.

MARTANO, G. (1984) 'Il saggio sul Sublime', *Aufstieg und Niedergang der römischen Welt*, ii/32/1. 364–403.

*RUSSELL, D. A. (1981) 'Longinus Revisited', *Mnemosyne*, 34: 72–86.

*SEGAL, C. P. (1959) 'ΎΨΟΣ and the Problem of Cultural Decline', *Harvard Studies in Classical Philology*, 64: 121–46.

——(1987) 'Writer as Hero: The Heroic Ethos in Longinus, On the Sublime', in J. Servais (ed.), *Stemmata: Mélanges de philologie, d'histoire et d'archéologie grecques offerts à Jules Labarbe* (Liège and Louvain-la-Neuve), 207–17.

#### 'Longinus' and sublimity in later criticism and theory

BRODY, J. (1958) *Boileau and Longinus* (Geneva).

HENN, T. R. (1934) *Longinus and English Criticism* (Cambridge).

LAMB, J. (1997) 'The Sublime', in H. B. Nisbet and C. Rawson (eds.), *The Cambridge History of Literary Criticsm, iv. The Eighteenth Century* (Cambridge).

LOMBARDO, G. and FINOCCHIARO, F. (1993) *Sublime antico e moderno: Una bibliografia* (Palermo).

MONK, S. H. (1960) *The Sublime* (2nd edn. Ann Arbor).

## 7. POST-CLASSICAL TRADITIONS OF THEORY AND CRITICISM

*ABRAMS, M. H. (1953) *The Mirror and the Lamp: Romantic Theory and the Critical Tradition* (Oxford and New York).

BEHLER, E. (1993) *German Romantic Literary Theory* (Cambridge).

BOLGAR, R. R. (1954) *The Classical Heritage and its Beneficiaries* (Cambridge).

BROWER, R. A. (1959) *Alexander Pope: The Poetry of Allusion* (Oxford).

CAVE, T. (1988) *Recognitions: A Study in Poetics* (Oxford).

*CURTIUS, E. R. (1953) *European Literature and the Latin Middle Ages*, tr. W. R. Trask (London and New York; German orig. 1948).

FARAL, E. (1924) *Les Arts poétiques du XIIe et du XIIIe siècle: Recherches et documents sur la technique littéraire du moyen âge* (Paris).

GALLO, E. (1971) *The Poetria Nova and its Sources in Early Rhetorical Doctrine* (The Hague).

GRAFTON, A., and JARDINE, L. (1986) *From Humanism to the Humanities: Education and the Liberal Arts in Fifteenth and Sixteenth Century Europe* (London).

GIBSON, R., and KRAUS, C., eds. (2002) *The Classical Commentary* (Leiden).

HARDISON, O. B., ed. (1974) *Medieval Literary Criticism: Translations and Interpretations* (New York).

HATHAWAY, B. (1962) *The Age of Criticism: The Late Renaissance in Italy* (Ithaca, NY).

——(1968) *Marvels and Commonplaces: Renaissance Literary Criticism* (New York).

KALLENDORF, C. (1989) *In Praise of Aeneas: Virgil and Epideictic Rhetoric in the Early Italian Remaissance* (Hanover and London).

McLAUGHLIN, M. L. (1995) *Literary Imitation in the Italian Renaissance* (Oxford).

NISBET, H. B., and RAWSON, C., eds. (1997) *Cambridge History of Literary Criticism, iv. The Eighteenth Century* (Cambridge).

POCOCK, G. (1980) *Boileau and the Nature of Neo-Classicism* (Cambridge).

ROBERTS, M. (1985) *Biblical Epic and Rhetorical Paraphrase in Late Antiquity* (Liverpool).

——(1989) *The Jeweled Style: Poetry and Poetics in Late Antiquity* (Ithaca, NY).

SILK, M. S., and STERNE, J. P. (1981) *Nietzsche on Tragedy* (Cambridge).

STOCK, B. (1996) *Augustine the Reader: Meditation, Self-Knowledge and the Ethics of Interpretation* (Ithaca, NY).

WEINBERG, B. (1961) *A History of Literary Criticism in the Italian Renaissance*, 2 vols. (Chicago).
ZARATE RUIZ, A. (1996) *Gracián, Wit, and the Baroque Age* (Renaissance and Baroque Studies and Texts, 17; New York).

## 8. AESTHETICS

### Introductions

*BEARDSLEY, M. (1966) *Aesthetics from Classical Greece to the Present: A Short History* (New York).
GAUT, B., and MCIVER LOPES, D., eds. (2001) *The Routledge Companion to Aesthetics* (London and New York).
PREZIOSI, D. (1998) *The Art of Art History: A Critical Anthology* (Oxford).
SCHAPER, E. (1968) *Prelude to Aesthetics* (London).
*SHEPPARD, A. (1987) *Aesthetics: An Introduction to the Philosophy of Art* (Oxford).

### Specific Readings

BOSANQUET, B. (1892) *A History of Aesthetic* (London).
BOURDIEU, P. (1984) *Distinction: A Social Critique of the Judgement of Taste* (Cambridge, Mass.).
COLLINGWOOD, R. G. (1925) *Outlines of a Philosophy of Art* (Oxford).
EAGLETON, T. (1990) *The Ideology of the Aesthetic* (Oxford).
GADAMER, H. G. (1986) 'The Relevance of the Beautiful', in *The Relevance of the Beautiful and Other Essays* (Cambridge and New York).
KANT, I. (1987) *The Critique of Judgment*, tr. W. Pluhar (Indianapolis).
MARTINDALE, C. (2005) *Latin Poetry and the Judgement of Taste: An Essay in Aesthetics* (Oxford).
ZANGWILL, N. (2001) *The Metaphysics of Beauty* (Ithaca, NY).

### 9. MODERN THEORIES OF LITERATURE

The items below, which exemplify or treat criticism after 1900, have been listed separately from those under 7 above, for convenient reference.

BAKHTIN, M. (1981) *The Dialogic Imagination* (Austin).
CALVINO, I. (1987) 'Why read the Classics?', in *The Literature Machine*, tr. P. Creagh (London), 125-34.
DAY, G. (1996) *Re-Reading Leavis: Culture and Literary Criticism* (New York).
*EAGLETON, T. (1996) *Literary Theory: An Introduction* (Oxford and Minnesota; 1st edn. 1983)
ELIOT, T. S. (1920) *The Sacred Wood* (London).
——(1933) *The Use of Poetry and the Use of Criticism* (London).

*FOWLER, D. P., and FOWLER, P. G. (1996) 'Literary Theory and Classical Studies', *Oxford Classical Dictionary*, 3rd edn. (Oxford), 871–5. There is an important response to this by M. S. Silk, 'Pindar Meets Plato: Theory, Language, Value and the Classics', in S. J. Harrison (ed.), *Texts, Ideas and the Classics: Scholarship and Theory in Classical Literature* (Oxford, 2001), 26–45.

GENETTE, G. (1982) *Figures of Literary Discourse* (Oxford).

*JEFFERSON, A., and ROBEY, D., eds. (1986) *Modern Literary Theory* (2nd edn. London).

LENTRICCHIA, F., and MCLAUGHLIN, T., eds. (1995) *Critical Terms for Literary Study* (2nd edn. Chicago).

MACHEREY, P. (1978) *A Theory of Literary Production*, tr. G. Wall (London and New York).

MATEJKA, L., and POMORSKA, K. (eds.) (1978) *Readings in Russian Poetics* (Ann Arbor).

*PREMINGER, A., and BROGAN, T., eds. (1993) *The New Princeton Encyclopedia of Poetry and Poetics* (Princeton).

RIFFATERRE, M. (1983) *Text Production* (New York).

SELL, R. D., ed. (1991) *Literary Pragmatics* (London).

SHKLOVSKY, V. (1990) *Theory of Prose*, tr. B. Sher (Elmwood Park, Ill.; Russian orig. 1925).

STEINER, G. (1963) *The Death of Tragedy* (New York).

——(1996) 'Tragedy, Pure and Simple', in M. S. Silk (ed.), *Tragedy and the Tragic* (Oxford), 534–47

TODOROV, T. ed. (1981) *Introduction to Poetics*, tr. R. Howard (Brighton).

WELLEK, R. (1965) 'The Concept of Classicism and the Classic in Literary Scholarship', *Proceedings of the 4th Congress, International Comparative Literature Association* (Eugene, Or.).

*——and WARREN, A. (1949) *A Theory of Literature* (London).

10. MODERN CRITICAL CATEGORIES AND ANCIENT THEORY

The bibliography in the subsections below is intended to prompt reflection on connections, parallels, and also contrasts between ancient and modern ideas. The list of headings is by no means complete or comprehensive, and divisions between the subsections are somewhat arbitrary.

*Author, Authority, and Inspiration*

CHERNISS, H. (1977) 'The Biographical Fashion in Literary Criticism', in *Selected Papers* (Leiden), 1–13.

FOUCAULT, M. (1998) 'What is an Author?', in D. Preziosi (ed.), *The Art of Art History: A Critical Anthology* (Oxford), 299–314.

GOLDHILL, S. (1993) 'The Sirens' Song: Authorship, Authority and Citation', in M. Biriotti and N. Miller (eds.), *What is an Author?* (Manchester and New York), 137–54.

GRAZIOSI, B. (2002) *Inventing Homer: The Early Reception of Epic* (Cambridge and New York).

LEFKOWITZ, M. (1981) *Lives of the Greek Poets* (Baltimore).

MAYER, R. G. (2003) 'Persona⟨l⟩ Problems: The Literary Persona in Antiquity Revisited', *Materiali e Discussione*, 50: 55–80.

MURRAY, P., ed. (1989) *Genius: The History of an Idea* (Oxford).

NAGY, G. (1989) 'Early Greek Views of Poets and Poetry', *Cambridge History of Literary Criticism*, i (Cambridge), 1–77.

PEASE, D. A. (1995) 'Author', in F. Lentricchia and T. McLaughlin (eds.), *Critical Terms for Literary Study*, (2nd edn. Chicago), 105–20.

RUSSELL, D. A. (1981) 'The Poet and his Inspiration' and 'The Poet as Teacher', in *Criticism in Antiquity* (London), 69–98.

SPENTZOU, E., and FOWLER, D. P. (2002) *Cultivating the Muse* (Oxford).

WOODMAN, A. J., and POWELL, J., eds. (1992) *Author and Audience in Latin Literature* (Cambridge).

*Genre*

For some additional reading on genre, see the references at the end of Chapter 19 in this volume.

Accounts of classical conceptions

*BARCHIESI, A. (2001) 'The Crossing', in S. J. Harrison (ed.), *Texts, Ideas, and the Classics: Scholarship, Theory, and Classical Literature* (Oxford), 142–63.

CAIRNS, F. (1972) *Generic Composition in Greek and Roman Poetry* (Edinburgh).

CONTE, G. B. (1994) *Genres and Readers* (Baltimore and London).

DEPEW, M., and OBBINK, D. (2000) *Matrices of Genre: Authors, Canons, and Society* (Cambridge, Mass.).

FARRELL, J. (2003) 'Classical Genre in Theory and Practice', *New Literary History*, 34/3: 383–408.

KROLL, W. (1924) 'Die Kreuzung der Gattungen', in *Studien zum Verständnis der römischen Literatur* (Stuttgart), 202–24.

NAGY, G. (1999) 'Epic as Genre', in M. Beissinger, J. Tylus, and S. Wofford (eds.), *Epic Traditions in the Contemporary World: The Poetics of Community* (Berkeley), 21–32.

RUSSELL, D. (1981) 'Classification of Literature', in *Criticism in Antiquity* (London), 148–58.

*TAPLIN, O. (1986) 'Tragedy and Comedy: A *synkrisis?*', *Journal of Hellenic Studies*, 106: 163–74.

——(1996) 'Comedy and the Tragic', in M. S. Silk (ed.), *Tragedy and the Tragic: Greek Theatre and Beyond* (Oxford), 188–202.

Twentieth-century theories and discussions

BAKHTIN, M. (1986) 'The Problem of Speech Genres' in *Speech Genres and Other Late Essays* (Austin, Tex.) and in D. Duff (ed.), *Modern Genre Theory* (Harlow and New York, 2000), 82–97.

DERRIDA, J. (1981) 'The Law of Genre', in W. Mitchell (ed.), *On Narrative* (Chicago), 58–77, and in D. Duff, ed., *Modern Genre Theory* (Harlow and New York, 2000), 232–49.
DUBROW, H. (1982) *Genre* (London).
FOWLER, A. (1982) *Kinds of Literature* (Oxford).
FRYE, N. (1957) *Anatomy of Criticism* (Princeton).
GENETTE, G. (1992) *The Architext: An Introduction* (Berkeley and Oxford).
RIFFATERRE, M. (1972) 'Système d'un genre descriptif', *Poétique*, 9: 15–30.
TODOROV, T. (1990) *Genres in Discourse* (Cambridge).

*Representation and* Mimesis

Accounts of ancient conceptions

*HALLIWELL, S. (2002) *The Aesthetics of Mimesis: Ancient Texts and Modern Problems* (Princeton).
MCKEON, R. (1952) 'Literary Criticism and the Concept of Imitation in Antiquity', in R. Crane (ed.), *Critics and Criticism: Ancient and Modern* (Chicago), 147–75.
RICOEUR, P. (1991) 'Mimesis and Representation', in M. Valdes (ed.), *A Ricoeur Reader: Reflection and Imagination* (New York and London).
*RUSSELL, D. (1981) 'Mimesis', in *Criticism in Antiquity* (London), 99–113.
VERDENIUS, W. J. (1949) *Mimesis: Plato's Doctrine of Artistic Imitation and its Meaning to Us* (Leiden).

Various modern notions of represention and 'realism'

AUERBACH, E. (1957) *Mimesis: The Representation of Reality in Western Literature* (Princeton).
BARTHES, R. (1982) 'The Reality Effect', in T. Todorov (ed.), *French Literary Theory Today* (Cambridge), 11–17.
BOYLE, N., and SWAYLES, M. (1986) *Realism in European Literature: Essays in Honour of J. P. Stern* (Cambridge).
MITCHELL, W. J. T. (1995) 'Representation' in F. Lentricchia and T. McLaughlin (eds.), *Critical Terms for Literary Study* (2nd edn. Chicago), 1–10.
*STERN, J. P. (1973) *On Realism* (London).

See also Ancient Literary Criticism and Poetics, Plato, Aristotle and Aesthetics above.

*Narrative, Plot, and Character*

*DE JONG, I. J. F. (1987) *Narrators and Focalizers: The Presentation of the Story in the Iliad* (Amsterdam), 1–7.
FANTUZZI, M. (1988) *Ricerche su Apollonio Rodio: Diacronie della dizione epica* (Rome).

FUSILLO, M. (1986) ' "Mythos" aristotelico e "récit" narratologico', *Strumenti critici*, 52/1/3: 381–92.

GENETTE, G. (1980) *Narrative Discourse* (Oxford).

GILL, C., ed. (1990) *The Person and the Human Mind: Essays in Ancient and Modern Philosophy* (Oxford).

HORNBLOWER, S. (1994) 'Narratology and Narrative Techniques in Thucydides', in S. Hornblower and A. Spawforth (eds.), *Greek Historiography* (Oxford), 131–66.

LAIRD, A. (1997) 'Approaching Characterisation in Virgil', in C. Martindale (ed.), *The Cambridge Companion to Virgil* (Cambridge), 282–93.

LAZZARINI, C. (1989) 'Elementi di una poetica serviana: Osservazioni sulla costruzione del racconto nell'Eneide', *Studi italiani di filologia classica*, 8: 56–109, 241–60.

LOWE, N. J. (2000) *The Classical Plot and the Invention of Western Narrative* (Cambridge).

MITCHELL, W. J. T., ed., (1981) *On Narrative* (Chicago).

MOMIGLIANO, A. (1985) 'Marcel Mauss and the Quest for the Person in Greek Biography and Autobiography', in M. Carrithers, S. Collins, and S. Lukes (eds.), *The Category of the Person: Anthropology, Philosophy, History* (Cambridge), 83–92.

*PELLING, C. B. R., ed. (1990) *Characterization and Individuality in Greek Literature* (Oxford).

RIMMON-KENAN, S. (1983) *Narrative Fiction: Contemporary Poetics* (London).

WINKLER, J. J. (1985): *Auctor and Actor: A Narratological Reading of The Golden Ass* (Los Angeles).

See also Aristotle above.

*Fiction*

Classical conceptions:

EDEN, K. (1986) *Poetic and Legal Fiction in the Aristotelian Tradition* (Princeton).

*FEENEY, D. C. (1991) *The Gods in Epic* (Oxford), 5–56.

FINKELBERG, M. (1998) *The Birth of Literary Fiction in Ancient Greece* (Oxford).

*GILL, C., and WISEMAN, T. P. eds. (1993) *Lies and Fiction in the Ancient World* (Exeter and Austin, Tex.).

LAIRD, A. (forthcoming) 'Fiction, Philosophy, and Logical Closure', in S. J. Heyworth (ed.), *Classical Constructions: Papers in Memory of Don Fowler* (Oxford).

LOWE, N. (2000) 'Comic Plots and the Invention of Fiction', in D. Harvey and J. Wilkins (eds.), *The Rivals of Aristophanes: Studies in Athenian Old Comedy* (London), 259–72.

NELSON, W. (1973) *Fact and Fiction: The Dilemma of the Renaissance Story-Teller* (Cambridge, Mass.).

PRATT, L. (1993) *Lying and Poetry from Homer to Pindar* (Ann Arbor).

REARDON, B. (1991) *The Form of Greek Romance* (Princeton).

RESCHER, N. (1991) 'Thought Experimentation in Pre-Socratic Philosophy', in T. Horowitz and G. Massey (eds.), *Thought Experiments in Science and Philosophy* (Savage, Md.).

ROHDE, E. (1914) *Der griechische Roman und seine Vorläufer* (Leipzig).

RÖSLER, W. 'Die Endeckung der Fiktionalität in der Antike', *Poetica*, 12: 283-319.

*TRIMPI, W. (1971) 'The Ancient Hypothesis of Fiction: An Essay on the Origins of Literary Theory', *Traditio*, 27: 1-78.

——(1974) 'The Quality of Fiction: The Rhetorical Transmission of Literary Theory', *Traditio*, 30: 1-118.

Some modern theories of literary fiction

COHN, D. (1998) *The Distinction of Fiction* (Baltimore).

KERMODE, F. (1966) *The Sense of an Ending: Studies in the Theory of Fiction* (Oxford).

LAMARQUE, P., and OLSEN, S. (1994) *Truth, Fiction and Literature* (Oxford).

MACHEREY, P. (1978) *A Theory of Literary Production* (London; French orig. 1966).

RIFFATERRE, M. (1990) *Fictional Truth* (Baltimore).

*Poetic Diction and Imagery*

BARFIELD, O. (1928) *Poetic Diction: A Study in Meaning* (London).

BOYS-STONES, G., ed. (2003) *Metaphor, Allegory, and the Classical Tradition* (Oxford).

JAKOBSON, R. (1960) 'Closing Statement: Linguistics and Poetics', in T. Sebeok (ed.), *Style in Language* (Cambridge, Mass.), 350-77.

*McCALL, M. (1969) *Ancient Rhetorical Theories of Simile and Comparison* (Cambridge, Mass.).

NAGY, G. (1996) *Poetry as Performance* (Cambridge and New York).

NOWOTTNY, W. (1962) *The Language Poets Use* (London).

RICOEUR, P. (1977) *The Rule of Metaphor: Multi-disciplinary Studies of the Creation of Meaning in Language* (Toronto).

SILK, M. S. (1974) *Interaction in Poetic Imagery* (London).

*Intertextuality*

Intertextuality is now frequently invoked in discussions of classical literature; although it is a modern category, some of the readings below (*) present possible analogues in ancient theory as well as examples in literary practice.

BARCHIESI, A. (1984) *La traccia del modello: Effetti omerici nella narrazione virgiliana* (Pisa).

*CONTE, G. B. (1986) *The Rhetoric of Imitation* (Cornell).

*D'IPPOLITO, G. (2000) 'Il concetto di intertestualità nel pensiero degli antichi', in V. Bécares Botas, P. Pordomingo, and R. Cortés-Tovar (eds.), *Intertextualidad en las literaturas griega y latina* (Classica Salmanticensia, 2; Madrid), 13-32.

FOWLER, D. P. (1997) 'On the Shoulders of Giants: Intertextuality and Classical Studies', *Materiali e discussione*, 39: 13-34 (repr. in *Roman Constructions: Readings in Postmodern Latin* (Oxford, 2000), 115-37).

HINDS, S. (1998) *Allusion and Intertext: Dynamics of Appropriation in Roman Poetry* (Cambridge).

KRISTEVA, J. (1974) *La Révolution du langage poétique* (Paris). Kristeva's original discussion of intertextuality here is developed in Kristeva's *Desire in Language: A Semiotic Approach to Literature and Art* (Oxford, 1981).

LAIRD, A. (1999) 'Speech and Symbolic Power: Discourse, Ideology and Intertextuality', ch. 1 in *Powers of Expression, Expressions of Power* (Oxford), 25-43.

VAN ERP TAALMAN KIP, A. (1994) 'Intertextuality and Theocritus 13', in I. De Jong and J. P. Sullivan (eds.), *Modern Critical Theory and Classical Literature* (Leiden), 153-69.

WILLIAMS, G. (1983) 'Roman Poets as Literary Historians: Some Aspects of Imitatio', *BICS* 8: 211-37.

*Ekphrasis*

Ekphrasis was a rhetorical term which has acquired a new momentum and meaning in recent criticism.

BARCHIESI, A. (1997) 'Ekphrasis', in C. Martindale (ed.), *The Cambridge Companion to Virgil* (Cambridge), 271-81.

ELSNER, J., ed. (1996) *Art and Text in Roman Culture* (Cambridge).

FRIEDLÄNDER, P. (1912) *Johannes von Gaza und Paulus Silentiarius: Kunstbeschreibungen Justinianischer Zeit* (Leipzig).

FOWLER, D. (1991) 'Narrate and Describe: The Problem of Ekphrasis', *Journal of Roman Studies*, 81: 25-35 (repr. in *Roman Constructions* (Oxford, 2000), 64-85).

GOLDHILL, S., and OSBORNE, R., eds. (1994) *Art and Text in Ancient Greek Culture* (Cambridge).

HEFFERNAN, J. (1993) *The Museum of Words: The Poetics of Ekphrasis from Homer to Ashbery* (Chicago).

LESSING, G. E. (1984) *Laocoön: An Essay on the Limits of Painting and Poetry*, tr. E. McCormick (Baltimore; orig. 1762).

MITCHELL, W. J. T. (1986) *Iconology: Image, Text, Ideology* (Chicago).

WEBB, R. (2000) 'Picturing the Past: Uses of Ekphrasis in the *Deipnosophistae* and Other Works of the Second Sophistic', in D. Braund and J. Wilkins (eds.), *Athenaeus and his World: Reading Greek Culture in the Roman Empire* (Exeter), 218-26.

# INDEX OF PRINCIPAL
# PASSAGES CITED

(This Index contains references to some literary texts as well as ancient
critical sources)

# GENERAL INDEX

References to the Suggestions for Further Reading are given in italic figures.

Lightning Source UK Ltd.
Milton Keynes UK
UKHW012327210223
417431UK00001B/8